Charlie Chaplin
and the Nazis

Charlie Chaplin and the Nazis

The Long German Campaign Against the Artist

Norbert Aping

Foreword by Kevin Brownlow

McFarland & Company, Inc., Publishers
Jefferson, North Carolina

A previous version of this book was published in German as *Liberty Shtunk! Die Freiheit wird abgeschafft. Charlie Chaplin und die Nationalsozialisten* (Marburg: Schüren, 2011).

Documents from the Chaplin archives are copyright © Roy Export Co. Ltd. Digitization of the Chaplin Archives by Cineteca di Bologna; www.charliechaplinarchive.org.

Unless otherwise noted, photographs are from the author's collection.

LIBRARY OF CONGRESS CATALOGUING-IN-PUBLICATION DATA

Names: Aping, Norbert, 1952– author, translator. | Brownlow, Kevin, writer of foreword.
Title: Charlie Chaplin and the Nazis : the long German campaign against the artist /
Norbert Aping ; foreword by Kevin Brownlow.
Other titles: Liberty Shtunk! English
Description: Jefferson, North Carolina : McFarland & Company, Inc., Publishers, 2024. |
Includes bibliographical references and index.
Identifiers: LCCN 2023038304 | ISBN 9781476687407 (paperback : acid free paper) ∞
ISBN 9781476649405 (ebook)
Subjects: LCSH: Chaplin, Charlie, 1889-1977—Appreciation—Germany. | National socialism
and motion pictures. | National socialism in motion pictures.
Classification: LCC PN2287.C5 A6513 2023 | DDC 791.43/65843086—dc23/eng/20230920
LC record available at https://lccn.loc.gov/2023038304

BRITISH LIBRARY CATALOGUING DATA ARE AVAILABLE

ISBN (print) 978-1-4766-8740-7
ISBN (ebook) 978-1-4766-4940-5

On the cover: *inset*: Adolf Hitler, 1930 (Heinrich Hoffmann photograph, National Archives); cover photograph of Charles Chaplin as the Tramp: from the archives of Roy Export Co. Ltd.

Printed in the United States of America

*McFarland & Company, Inc., Publishers
Box 611, Jefferson, North Carolina 28640
www.mcfarlandpub.com*

To Wilhelm Staudinger,
with affection, admiration and gratitude

Table of Contents

Acknowledgments

In 2004, during the final phase of my work on Laurel and Hardy's history of German reception, I visited Wilhelm Staudinger's Chaplin archive, which he had been collecting from all over the world since the 1950s. The wonderful archive rooms with their rich, wide-ranging collection of films, books, magazines, advertising materials and merchandising items were a world of their own, guarded by a connoisseur with an extraordinary knowledge and the ability always to reflectively "think outside the box." Wilhelm Staudinger's enthusiasm was so infectious that I also wanted to explore the history of Chaplin's reception in Germany. From then on, Wilhelm Staudinger generously supported my research and has accompanied *Charlie Chaplin and the Nazis: The Long German Campaign Against the Artist* with commitment until today. Therefore, the present book is dedicated to him, and my heartfelt thanks go to him in all friendship.

Likewise, my heartfelt thanks go to Kate Guyonvarch, director of the Chaplin Association, Bubbles, Inc., and Roy Export S.A.S. in Paris. She has generously supported my research right from the start and has, among other things, granted me access to Chaplin's newspaper clipping albums in Montreux and his documents in Bologna. Evelyne Lüthi-Graf and her staff, as well as Cecilia Cenciarelli, head of the progetto Chaplin, lent me their wonderful support at the Archives de Montreux in Clarens and at the Cineteca di Bologna, respectively. I thank them warmly as well.

Kevin Brownlow needs no introduction. When I approached him in spring 2010 about his documentary *The Tramp and the Dictator*, he spontaneously helped by sending me some remarkable material. We have exchanged ideas ever since. He not only wrote the forewords to both editions of my book but also read the final manuscript of the English version and offered valuable suggestions. My heartfelt thanks therefore go especially to him—and for being such a great conversationalist. The same applies to Glenn Mitchell, whom I am privileged to have known for about 15 years. He also read the final manuscript, as he did with my 2008 book *The Final Film of Laurel and Hardy*. Thus, Kevin Brownlow and Glenn Mitchell saved me from mistakes.

My classmate Professor Dr. Christhard Hoffmann, University of Bergen (Norway), has accompanied me with his critical expertise as a historian with a focus on anti–Semitism research in both editions of this book. For this, I thank him dearly.

Further, I thank Robert Dickson (Los Angeles), who provided me with U.S. film censorship records from the Margaret Herrick Library, Academy of Motion Picture

Arts and Sciences (Beverly Hills). I also thank Juan B. Heinink (Bilbao), Werner Mohr (Berlin) and Valdo Kneubühler of the Bibliothéque du Film in Paris for helpful reference materials.

For further discussions, I would like to thank Wolfgang Klaue, head of the former Staatliches Filmarchiv der DDR, Eberhard Spiess, former deputy director of the Deutsches Institut für Filmkunde (now DFF—Deutsches Filminstitut & Filmmuseum, Frankfurt am Main), Dr. Wolfgang Gersch and Andreas-Michael Velten. I have also been supported by Rolf Aurich, Herbert Birett, Rainer Dick, Gero Gandert, Wolfgang Jacobsen, Dan Kamin, Alain Kerzoncuf, Klaus Oberdieck, Dr. Ulrich Rüdel, Lisa Stein Haven and John Wedemeyer, to whom I extend my gratitude.

The helpfulness in archives and libraries was admirable. For this, I thank Thomas Ballhausen (Filmarchiv Austria, Wien), Hans-Michael Bock and Erika Wottrich (CineGraph, Hamburg), Cordula Döhrer and Lisa Roth (library and document archive of the Deutsche Kinemathek—Museum für Film und Fernsehen, Berlin), Renate Göthe (head of Press Dokumentation Library, Filmuniversität Babelsberg KONRAD WOLF), Detlef Kasten (Stadtbibliothek Hannover), Ute Klawitter and Julika Kuschke (Bundesarchiv—Filmarchiv, Berlin-Lichterfelde), Dr. Klaus A. Lankheit (Institut für Zeitgeschichte, Munich), Hans-Peter Reichmann and Christof Schöbel (DFF—Deutsches Filminstitut & Filmmuseum, Frankfurt am Main), Eckard Vorwerk (library of the Oberlandesgericht Celle), and Henning Zühlsdorff (Leuphana Universität Lüneburg) as well as the staffs of the Politisches Archiv des Auswärtigen Amts (Berlin), the Bayerische Staatsbibliothek (Munich), the Deutsche Nationalbibliothek (Frankfurt am Main and Leipzig), the Bundesarchivs (Koblenz), the Forschungsstelle für Zeitgeschichte (Hamburg), the Landesarchiv Berlin, the libraries of the Helmut Schmidt Universität (Hamburg) and the Institut für Germanistik II (University of Hamburg), the Staatsarchiv Stade, the Staatsbibliothek zu Berlin—Stiftung Preußischer Kulturbesitz, the Stadtarchiv Buxtehude, and the Technische Informationsbibliothek (Religionswissenschaft) of the Leibniz Universität (Hannover).

My special thanks go to Geoff Webber, who reviewed my English translation and helped to avoid many an error.

I thank Dr. Annette Schüren for publishing the German edition of this book. I thank McFarland for publishing the English edition. And finally, I especially thank my partner in life, Marlies Paske, who patiently accompanied me during the work on the English edition.

Foreword
by Kevin Brownlow

Here is an unusually important book. Chaplin's comedy of 1940, *The Great Dictator*, represents one of the few occasions in which film history becomes entwined with political history. Norbert Aping's research has been so thorough and so successful, I wish his book had been available when Michael Kloft and I made our television documentary on the subject.

Our film, *The Tramp and the Dictator* (2002), came about when Victoria and Christopher Chaplin discovered rolls of 16mm Kodachrome, shot during production by Charlie's brother Sydney, in a trunk in a cellar at their father's Manoir de Ban in Switzerland. I was shown this footage at the Chaplin office in Paris and could not see how to make a film out of it, since it repeated what was in *The Great Dictator*, rather than enlarging upon it. But Michael Kloft, television producer from Spiegel TV, also saw the footage and suggested a twin portrait of Chaplin and Hitler.

That made sense, since both men were born in the same week of the same month of the same year, one becoming the best-loved man in the world, the other the most hated. We worked together on the film in reasonable harmony, but I was dismayed by the television habit of "re-versioning"; the German version was radically different from mine, and an Italian version was a cinematically hopeless mishmash.

It was not the first attempt at the subject. In Berlin, in 1986, Andreas-Michael Velten produced a documentary to accompany his master's thesis, having contacted a number of NSDAP veterans including Dr. Fritz Hippler, Reichsfilmintendant and director of *The Eternal Jew*, Richard Schulze-Kossens, Hitler's SS adjutant, and Walter Frentz, Hitler's personal cinematographer, none of whom would be interviewed about Chaplin, Hippler being particularly vitriolic. And no television company seemed interested in turning it into a mainstream production, despite the box office lure of the main characters.

So I welcome this book as a fine example of careful and tenacious research. And because my German is not good enough to read the original book straight through, I am delighted it is now being published in English.

For those to whom Chaplin is as distant a name as Dan Leno, it cannot be emphasized firmly enough that he was for a long time the best-loved man in the world. His rise from uneducated Lambeth boy to stage success to icon of American cinema was incredibly fast. Exhibitors merely had to put a life-size cutout of Charlie outside their cinema, with the words "HE'S HERE!," and they could guarantee a full

1

house. Bertolt Brecht said in 1926, "There are only two directors in the world. The other is Charlie Chaplin." Lenin said, "The only man I want to meet." In Walter Ruttmann's German film *Berlin—Symphony of a City* (1927), Chaplin is summed up by a pair of boots in snow—conveying in one simple shot *The Gold Rush* (1925), a film which everyone in the audience would already have seen at least once. But in 1935, as Norbert Aping reveals, the Nazis withdrew the screening approval for *The Gold Rush*. No wonder Chaplin felt personally challenged by this lunatic regime.

The poet W.H. Auden wrote, "When we really hate someone we cannot find him comic; there are no genuinely funny stories about Hitler." This was one of the stumbling blocks for Chaplin. He admitted after the war that had he known the truth about the concentration camps, he would never have made the picture. Some still wish he had not. When he first announced it, his fellow producers, most of whom were Jewish, pleaded with him not to proceed as it would make the situation for the Jews in Germany worse than it was already. Thus his sense of responsibility was weighed down to an agonizing degree. Fortunately, he was financing the film himself and could not be stopped by the usual methods.

His film became "an unparalleled phenomenon, an epic incident in the history of mankind," as Chaplin's biographer David Robinson put it. "The greatest clown and best-loved personality of his age directly challenged the man who had instigated more evil and human misery than any other in modern history."

The morality of the film will be argued long into the future. When we did *The Tramp and the Dictator,* no one had tried to make a comedy about Josef Stalin; there is now Armando Ianucci's movie satire *The Death of Stalin* (2017). The comparison between Chaplin and Hitler was too strong to be ignored, particularly when newsreels were silent. Our film featured an interview in which a veteran American director recalled thinking, when Hitler first appeared on screen, how absurd he looked—and how like Chaplin.

The talkies were the most precious gift the Jews could inadvertently have presented to Hitler. Of course, he was dependent on the newly developed public address system, not to mention the wireless, but how could he have succeeded in transmitting his message without the benefit of talking pictures? (In his case, roaring pictures.) And the marketing of sound was triumphantly achieved by the Jewish Warner Bros. (their smash hit *The Jazz Singer* was even a Jewish story) and the equally Jewish William Fox.

Hitler, during World War I, had worn a lugubrious walrus moustache. After the war, the fashion among ex–NCOs was a clipped toothbrush moustache, a style which would never have gained such popularity in Germany had Chaplin films been shown there as widely as in the rest of the world. But Charlie's comedies were made in America, and American films were difficult to see in Central Europe, even before the United States entered the war.

I heard from someone who had interviewed Mussolini's chauffeur that Hitler adopted Charlie's moustache because he wanted to be loved. That seems to me a ridiculous notion. Hitler thought Chaplin was a Jew and his Propaganda Ministry described him as "a disgusting Jewish comedian." So the real puzzle is why Hitler retained his Chaplinesque moustache when two-thirds of the world associated it with hysterical laughter.

As early as 1926 and 1927, in Bulgaria, Denmark, France and even the United States, German diplomats tried to fight a reissue of *Shoulder Arms* (1918), the comedy about World War I in which Charlie captured the Kaiser. One might have thought that to push Chaplin off the screen would be deeply unpopular in any country.

Unity Mitford, the English aristocrat who fell in love with Hitler, assured her sisters and anyone else who would listen that Hitler had a sense of humor. She said that he did an amusing imitation of Neville Chamberlain, but that his best routine was himself. Again, I find this hard to believe. Yet Albert Speer, Hitler's architect and protégé, who was perhaps closer to the führer than any other man, recalled a routine even closer to the film: "Hitler was a very good mimic ... in his small circle [he] gave a clowning imitation of Mussolini's mock heroics. The Fuehrer, in his best grand-opera, strutting style, stuck his chin way out, spread his arms akimbo, raised his right hand in the Fascist salute and spluttered a short speech in Italian gibberish; something like 'macaroni, giovanezza, basta, ciao, Italia, andante, arriverderci, cosi fan tutte, bambino.'"

In reading this harmless anecdote, one is struck by its supreme irrelevance. This politician was responsible for mass slaughter on a terrifying scale and whether or not he had a sense of humor is surely insignificant. Chaplin supporters didn't think so. As Ray Bradbury said to us, "When you are faced by a totalitarian regime and the madness they inflicted on the world, courage isn't enough. You have to be able to laugh in their face, throw back your head and say, 'You don't count, I discount you this way, I give you the laugh of all time, the great laugh of acceptance which melts you down,' and Chaplin was able to do that. He did exactly the right thing and Hitler and the others hated him for it."

Foreign films for German audiences are still dubbed into German. There was no chance of *The Great Dictator* being dubbed until it was shown after the war, when Chaplin's final speech would have been heard in German. So if Hitler saw it, he would presumably have seen it in English. What would Charlie's inventive gibberish have meant to him? (There is a rumor that he saw it twice and was so upset he had a fit!)

When a Fox executive suggested making a new version of a Dickens novel, William Fox explained to his executive Sol Wurtzel, "The reason we don't want to make *Oliver Twist* is because of [Henry] Ford's attitude." However, when Fox released *Just Imagine* (1930), a picture set 50 years in the future, people were shown to have cheap little planes, just as they currently had cheap little cars. The planes were called Tannenbaums and Goldfarbs and a character says, "I guess they finally got even with Henry Ford."

Henry Ford, despite being a pacifist, and supporting the Peace Ship, the *Oscar II*, in 1915 in the hope of ending the Great War, was an enthusiast for the Nazis. He insisted that the Jews were polluting young minds with jazz and in particular "its abandoned sensuousness of sliding notes" (!). As early as 1921, he initiated a series of anti–Semitic articles in his *Dearborn Independent*, which included "The Jews in Hollywood" and which he supplied at his own expense, ready printed in smart brown covers, to the Brown House in Munich. Ford supported Hitler from an early date. Heinrich Hoffmann's daughter told me that there was only one photograph on the wall of Hitler's office, and that was of Henry Ford. However, despite having said, "We look to Heinrich Ford as the leader of the growing Fascisti movement in America," Hitler tended to add, "No money yet." (But then he would say that, wouldn't he?)

In 1938, Hitler awarded Ford the NSDAP's highest civilian honor it could give to any foreigner. In World War II, neither the Blitzkrieg nor Operation Barbarossa could have happened without Ford trucks. After D-Day, American troops found it most convenient that German trucks had the same spares as their own. Ironically, Ford was also supplying the Soviet Union with trucks and tractors....

And this is the vital element missing from *The Great Dictator*. Since Hitler was also backed by chemical, steel and electrical industry cartels in the late '20s and '30s, the absence of big business is a strange oversight. We managed to squeeze Henry Ford into our documentary, thanks to the appearance of an obvious lookalike playing the Factory Boss in *Modern Times*. But for some reason, Chaplin avoided all references in his Hitler film. His research must have told him about the photograph in Hitler's office and the extracts of Ford's newspaper series appearing verbatim in *Mein Kampf*. Hitler had dictated that book in jail after the failure of the Munich putsch. Ford merged his German assets with those of IG Farben in 1928 and opened factories in Germany. And as noted, in 1938, for his 75th birthday, the great industrialist received the Grand Cross of the German Eagle, the highest decoration Hitler could award a foreigner.

Ironically, Chaplin supported the other dictator, Josef Stalin, who would massacre four times as many people as Hitler—although we didn't know for many years that we had been allied with a greater barbarian. *The Great Dictator* was never shown in Soviet Russia, Stalin having signed a pact with Hitler at the time of its release. Chaplin was very businesslike where his films were concerned, and the Russians were accustomed to illegally duping American pictures. Yet they paid Henry Ford in hard currency. "My films must be worth several tractors," said Chaplin.

It sounds absurd, but I wish television documentaries could have footnotes. Despite lengthy credits, very few sources are listed and where people have struggled for accuracy, there ought to be space for uncertainty. One footnote I would like to have provided would state that Chaplin came under scrutiny from a committee headed by Senator Gerald Nye which was investigating "premature anti–Fascism" in Hollywood. Chaplin was a leading offender, having embarked on his *Great Dictator* script in 1938. And what was wrong with being a "premature anti–Fascist"? It implied one was sympathetic to Communism. Hence so many of Chaplin's political problems in the United States.

Nowadays, we might wonder why so few in Hollywood responded to the Nazi terror before the two nations were involved in open warfare. Chaplin, who based his film not only on his abortive "Napoleon" project, but also on a Syd Chaplin film about a monarch and his barber-double (1921's *King, Queen, Joker*), was fascinated by Hitler because "he was a bad imitation of me." (He threatened to sue for plagiarism of moustache!) He studied newsreels and then tried out his mimicry at parties. The screenwriter Ouida Bergère, Mrs. Basil Rathbone, remembered his performing the entire globe-as-balloon routine at her house.

I feel a sense of relief with the publication of this book, even though it finds the testimony from one of its witnesses, Nicola Radošević, unreliable. It contains far more information than any television documentary—and because of Norbert Aping's position in the legal profession, he was able to reach documentation the rest of us might never have known about. His book conveys a reassuring impression of completeness.

Albert Speer wrote in 1977 that he regarded Chaplin as one of the most important figures in film history, and because of his ability to prove that misery could be endured with dignity and humor, also in our general history. "I am convinced that Chaplin's contribution to *The Great Dictator* has been the best 'documentary' about the Hitler period. And it will in all probability remain so."

Imagine if he had said that in 1940…

Kevin Brownlow is the pioneer of film archaeology, having restored numerous silent films. His 1968 standard work The Parade's Gone By *was followed by other books and numerous film documentaries. In 2010, he received an Academy Honorary Award for his lifetime achievement.*

Preface

Charlie Chapin and the Nazis covers a topic which has been frequently addressed in the international Chaplin literature. Until the German edition of my 2011 book *Liberty Shtunk! Die Freiheit wird abgeschafft. Charlie Chaplin und die Nationalsozialisten*, however, it had never been comprehensively examined. For the English-language edition, I have revised, updated and restructured the German version.

International Chaplin literature has mostly been limited to reflections on Chaplin's *The Great Dictator* and its making. Beyond that, only a few other single aspects have been covered. This has led to numerous inconsistencies and unfounded conclusions. For example, Chaplin is said to have become the projection figure of "the Jew" only after Hitler's takeover, being hushed up by the German press after March 1933 until attacking him because of *The Great Dictator*. *Charlie Chaplin and the Nazis*, however, is much more complex. In their introduction to *Chaplin: The Dictator and the Tramp* (2004), Frank Scheide and Hooman Mehran referred to Chaplin scholars Timothy J. Lyons and Graham Petrie and expressed a desire for basic research in many areas of Chaplin literature, which would help to develop fresh approaches and critical perspectives.

This book attempts to critically trace a comprehensive picture of the relationship between Chaplin and the Nazis. It includes the German nationalist attacks against Chaplin, which from 1921 reacted one-dimensionally and exaggeratedly to Chaplin's *Shoulder Arms*, a pacifist war comedy that treats the German soldiers like Keystone Cops. This was one of the cornerstones of later Nazi agitation against Chaplin. Contrary to previous claims, Nazi attacks were not limited to Chaplin's visit to Berlin in March 1931, the revocation of the approval of *The Gold Rush* in early 1935 (incidentally, the only official ban that was targeted specifically against Chaplin and his films during the Weimar Republic and the Third Reich), the exhibition "Der ewige Jude" and the diatribe *Film-"Kunst," Film-Kohn, Film-Korruption*, both in late 1937, or the issue of *The Great Dictator*. Neither did they begin as late as 1933, after Hitler's takeover. Nor did Chaplin's name disappear from the Nazi press landscape after 1933 until the agitation against him over *The Great Dictator*. Right up until 1936, there were even a few benevolent articles about Chaplin and frequent reports about the production progress of *Modern Times* and its European distribution. Then a new wave of agitation against Chaplin started, triggered by the so-called Tobis trial.

In fact, the Nazi attacks on Chaplin as well as the reactions to him covered the period from March 1926, when the Nazis did not yet have any significant constituencies in the Weimar Republic, to April 1944, when the "total war" proclaimed by Propaganda Minister Goebbels had long since been lost and slogans such as "Wir haben uns in die Heimaterde festgekrallt!" (We have Clung to our Home Soil!) were subsequently issued.

Chaplin was the foreign film artist against whom the Nazis agitated the most by far. They observed him as a supposed Jew, arranged for the Hauptarchiv der NSDAP (NSDAP Main Archive) in the Third Reich to create its own Chaplin file, and subjected reports about him to their press control, which the Nazi state employed to direct its information policy. Thus, the "Chaplin case" exemplifies the Nazis' understanding of art and propaganda and their fight against inconvenient artists. In 1927, the *Jüdisches Lexikon* published the claim that Chaplin's name was actually "Thonstein." This was temporarily adopted by the Nazis in the Third Reich and, in 1950, also by an anti–Semitic, anti–Communist organization in its fight against "the destruction of Christian culture." This organization assigned Chaplin the first name "Israel," and as of 1952, he was also called "Israel Thonstein" in his FBI files.

The Nazi attacks against Chaplin were wide-ranging but limited in argumentation and content. To reveal the paranoia of the Nazi agitation, the allegations of the Nazi press about Chaplin were examined for their factual content and juxtaposed with both the sources provided and the circumstances emerging from the context. In the final phase of the Third Reich, the contradictory nature of Nazi cultural policy became evident with the example of two German feature films, in which it did not shy away from making use of Chaplin's Tramp and the famous dance of the roll from *The Gold Rush*. Against this background, *Charlie Chapin and the Nazis* is a time travel through art, narrow-minded politics, enemy images, deceptions, distortions, slander and surprising twists with Chaplin admirers from the Weimar Republic who fought him in the Third Reich. In retrospect, none of this affected Chaplin's films and his outstanding importance in cultural history.

The research included, among other thing, Nazi printed matter (Kampfblätter [propaganda journals] and other diatribes), all German film trade journals, widely distributed film magazines, newspapers and magazines, and German newspapers in exile and foreign publications, as well as surviving records of the Weimar Republic and Third Reich film censorship and also the evidence of the Nazi press control. Furthermore, it included film libraries and the following archives: Bundesarchiv (Berlin and Koblenz), DFF—Deutsches Filminstitut und Filmmuseum (Frankfurt am Main), Filmuniversität Babelsberg KONRAD WOLF, Landesarchiv Berlin, Margaret Herrick Library—Academy of Motion Picture Arts and Sciences (Beverly Hills), Politisches Archiv des Auswärtigen Amts (Berlin), Staatsbibliothek zu Berlin—Stiftung Preußischer Kulturbesitz, Stiftung Deutsche Kinemathek (Berlin), Wilhelm Staudinger's private Chaplin Archive which in 2010 he passed on to the Adolf and Luisa Haeuser-Stiftung für Kunst und Kulturpflege and has since been housed on permanent loan at the DFF—Deutsches Filminstitut & Filmmuseum in Frankfurt am Main, Chaplin's huge collection of newspaper clippings at the Archives de Montreux, and his inexhaustible document archive at the Cineteca di Bologna.

This book provides synopses and sometimes scene descriptions of Chaplin films which opposed the Nazis. However, to detail every single scene in its careful construction would have gone beyond the scope and shifted the focus of this book. Since Chaplin's work is characterized by an abundance of carefully composed scenes, it will hardly be possible to reliably describe a Chaplin film in detail after watching it for the first time. It is necessary to virtually dissect each scene in order to recognize all the subtleties and not get lost by overlooking a nuance that Chaplin has conceived. This is probably why film critics in the Weimar Republic professed themselves unable to retell Chaplin films. Indeed, some contemporary reviews describe content that does not appear in the films in question. But back then, no one had the technical possibilities that DVD, Blu-ray and streaming offer today with pausing, frame-by-frame switching, rewinding and repeating.

Chaplin's ingenious construction may be illustrated by the example of the opening scenes during the first minute of his film *The Pilgrim*, which the *Völkischer Beobachter. Kampfblatt der nationalsozialistischen Bewegung Großdeutschlands* (Ethnic Observer. Propaganda Journal of the National Socialist Movement of Greater Germany) attacked in late 1929. In it, Chaplin gives the viewer the whole backstory. You see a gate. Does it perhaps belong to a factory? The viewer's curiosity is aroused. A man in uniform appears, so it is maybe a prison gate. The assumption is confirmed by the fact that he sticks up a wanted poster, which shows Charlie. The uniformed man also playfully sweeps his broad brush across Charlie's nose. So Charlie is a recently escaped convict who must have a long record. A $1000 reward for his capture was a lot of money in the early 1920s, when one could eat well for a dollar. In the second shot, you see a man in a bathing suit rushing out of the water to a bush to retrieve his clothes. Why a bush? Of course, he would not have changed without the privacy of a bush. Dumbfounded, he lifts the clothes he finds in place of his own: a convict suit. Of course, Charlie has switched the clothes! The third shot begins with Charlie dressed as a priest—and now in retrospect everything falls into place. Those who are still not convinced will see in the following scenes how Charlie feels uncomfortable in his new clothes, avoids the police, and also does not immediately discover the pockets in the strange coat.

Introduction

Charlie Chapin and the Nazis has mostly been confined in Chaplin literature to the development and making of as well as reflection on *The Great Dictator*. This applies to the Chaplin biographies of Gerith von Ulm (*Charlie Chaplin, King of Tragedy*, 1940), Theodore Huff (*Charlie Chaplin*, 1952), Robert Payne (*The Great Charlie*, 1952), Georges Sadoul (*Vie de Charlot*, 1953), John McCabe (*Charlie Chaplin*, 1978), Wes D. Gehring (*Charlie Chaplin: A Bio-Bibliography*, 1983), David Robinson (*Chaplin: His Life and Art*, 1985; the most thoroughly researched Chaplin biography to date), Joyce Milton (*Tramp: The Life of Charlie Chaplin*, 1996), Kenneth S. Lynn (*Charlie Chaplin and His Times*, 1997), Jeffrey Vance (*Chaplin: Genius of the Cinema*, 2003), Simon Louvish (*Chaplin: The Tramp's Odyssey*, 2009) and Sid Fleischman (*Sir Charlie Chaplin, the Funniest Man in the World*, 2010). Louvish also claims that the Nazis' agitation against Chaplin started in 1935 with the revocation of *The Gold Rush*'s approval, while Lynn and Vance assume it began with the announcement of Chaplin's plan to make a satire about Hitler, which had been triggered by the diatribe *Juden sehen Dich an* that Chaplin received in the 1930s. Milton, on the other hand, essentially addresses the idea for *The Great Dictator*, which she claims did not stem from Chaplin. Stephen Weissman's psychoanalytic biography *Chaplin: A Life* (2009) only briefly touches on the film.

Charles J. Maland's multifaceted study *Chaplin and American Culture: The Evolution of a Star Image* (1989) has explored, among other things, the background of *The Great Dictator* in the United States, while several other international books have been thematically focused essentially on this film: *The Great Dictator—Il grande dittatore di Charlie Chaplin* (2003), edited by Anna Fiaccarini, Cecilia Cenciarelli and Michela Zenga, *Chaplin: The Dictator and the Tramp* (2004), edited by Frank Scheide and Hooman Mehran, Christian Delage's *Chaplin Facing History* (2005) and *Chaplin and War* (The Chaplin Society of Japan, 2007) with contributions by David Robinson, Cecilia Cenciarelli and Ono Hiroyuki. According to Hiroyuki's *Chaplin and Hitler*, published in Japan in 2015, all Chaplin postcards were supposedly banned by the Third Reich in the fall of 1933 and all books and magazines about Chaplin in 1935. However, such official bans cannot be substantiated.

Three German publications have taken a somewhat broader look at Charlie Chaplin and the Nazis beyond *The Great Dictator*. Michael Hanisch's book *Charlie Chaplin, über ihn lach(t)en Millionen*, published in 1974 in the GDR, contains a rough sketch of the German Chaplin reception up to the Third Reich. However, he

offers little insight into Charlie Chaplin and the Nazis. He confines himself to a few
partial aspects and draws far-reaching conclusions from a few sources, whose context he has not investigated, and which do not stand up to scrutiny. According to
Hanisch, the Nazis first fought Chaplin in the Third Reich and after 1933 banned his
name from the German press until his plan for *The Great Dictator* became known.
Thus, neither the anti–Semitic exhibition "The Eternal Jew" nor the notorious smear
book *Film-"Kunst," Film-Kohn, Film-Korruption* appear in Hanisch's book although,
in 1937, Chaplin had been attacked directly by both of them. With minor modifica-
tions, Hanisch repeated this in his contributions to the Chaplin anthology *Zeitmontage* (1989) and to *Charlie Chaplin: His Reflection in Modern Times* (1991), adding
another discrepancy about Chaplin's alleged Jewish name Thonstein.

Wolfgang Gersch's 1988 miniature *Chaplin in Berlin*, also published in the GDR,
focuses on the Berlin visit of March 1931. His press review of Berlin daily newspapers essentially covers the period from March 8 to March 16, 1931, but excludes the
Berlin edition of the *Völkischer Beobachter*, which contained several smear articles
against Chaplin during that period. Gersch's brief excursus on German Chaplin references from 1932 to 1940 includes "The Eternal Jew" and *Film-"Kunst," Film-Kohn,
Film-Korruption*. In this context, without checking, he reproduces the 1947 memoirs
of a film merchant, according to which Nazis disrupted screenings of Chaplin's *City
Lights* in 1932 and caused the bankruptcy of its German distributor. Chapters 5 and
6 of this book examine the validity of this claim.

Andreas-Michael Velten's contribution to the companion volume to the 1989
"Chaplin and Hitler" exhibition at the Munich Stadtmuseum explored partial
aspects of Charlie Chaplin and the Nazis more thoroughly than Hanisch and, following Gersch, took into account "The Eternal Jew" as well as *Film-"Kunst," Film-Kohn,
Film-Korruption*. From Gersch he has adopted, also unchecked, the referred assertion of Nazi disruptions of *City Lights*. Velten's belief that Chaplin became the Nazi
projection figure "the Jew" only after Hitler's takeover cannot be maintained, since
the Nazis had repeatedly attacked Chaplin already since 1926. However, he drew
attention to the *Film-Kurier*'s Chaplin attack "A Dog Barking at the Moon/Un petit
chien hurle à la lune" of early September 1933. Yet Velten did not explore the concrete causes and consequences of this or the continuation of attacks on Chaplin in
the Nazi press until 1938.

The essays "Chaplin Reception in Weimar Germany" by Sabine Hake (1990) and
"Satire und Aufruf. Zu Chaplins Antifaschismus" by Jost Hermand in *Charlie Chaplin—Schlussrede aus dem Film Der Große Diktator 1940* (1993) have contributed little
to the topic considered here. For her sketch of the Nazi press landscape of the Weimar Republic, Hake limited herself to the *Völkischer Beobachter* and *Der Angriff*
references of March 1931 cited by Gersch. Like Gersch and Velten, Hake and Hermand also assumed the claim about Nazi disruptions of *City Lights* as fact without
checking it. Moreover, Hermand claims, without citing a source, that Goebbels was
behind these actions—which cannot be verified.

Other German-language publications, such as Karl Schnog's *Charlie Chaplin.
Filmgenie und Menschenfreund* (1960), Joe Hembus' foray *Charlie Chaplin und seine
Filme* (1972) in feuilleton style, and Wolfram Tichy's *Chaplin* (1974) only touch on

Charlie Chaplin and the Nazis in passing. Curt Riess' "personal biography" *Chaplin* (1989) confines itself to the debatable assertion that Chaplin was able to shoot *The Great Dictator* "for all the Jews of the world" only because he unexpectedly learned of his Jewish origin during the Third Reich. Markus Spieker's *Hollywood unterm Hakenkreuz* (1999) covers the import of U.S. films into the Third Reich, and Charlie Chaplin and the Nazis play only a marginal role. On the other hand, Florian Odenwald's 2006 *Der nazistische Kampf gegen das "Undeutsche" in Theater und Film 1920–1945* provides a handful of examples of Nazi agitation against Chaplin in 1920s propaganda journals, quotes from some known articles on the Berlin visit of March 1931, and then returns to Chaplin one last time with the revocation of *The Gold Rush*'s approval. Liliane Weissberg's *Hannah Arendt, Charlie Chaplin und die verborgene Tradition* (2009) refers to it only to the 1937 exhibition catalogue *The Eternal Jew*, but confuses it with *Juden sehen Dich an* from 1933.

Richard Attenborough's 1992 feature film *Chaplin* also focuses on *The Great Dictator* in some scenes. For example, Chaplin studies Hitler in his studio from Leni Riefenstahl's *Triumph des Willens* (1935) and answers a Nazi at a Hollywood party that he does not have the honor of being a Jew. Kevin Brownlow and Michael Kloft's documentary *The Tramp and the Dictator* (2002) takes a closer look at the backgrounds of *The Great Dictator*. Serge Toubiana's shorter 2003 TV feature *Chaplin Today* about *The Great Dictator* follows a similar approach, while Richard Schickel's *Charlie: The Life and Art of Charlie Chaplin* from the same year only touches on the subject.

Under these circumstances, primary research was necessary. It needed to be systematically explored what the breeding ground was from which the Nazi attacks on Chaplin commenced, how they developed during the Weimar Republic, how Chaplin became the most despised foreign artist in the Third Reich according to official accounts, and until when the Nazi agitation against him continued. Nazi propaganda journals were searched, for one thing. Since approximately a hundred such organs appeared in the late 1920s on a regular basis, most of them regional, a selection was necessary. *Der Angriff, Der Führer, National-Zeitung* (Essen), *Der Stürmer, Völkischer Beobachter, Der Weltkampf* and *Westdeutscher Beobachter* were checked, as well as a number of other Nazi smear publications.

The image of Chaplin in the Weimar Republic and in the Third Reich was represented by the most important film magazines for the general public, *Die Filmwoche* and *Filmwelt*, but above all by the German film trade journals that appeared regularly, in some cases daily. Therefore, they were also given a comprehensive analysis. After Hitler's takeover, the number of trade journals declined. Ten of them remained on the market for some time. The best-known and most influential trade journals of the Weimar Republic and the Third Reich were *Film-Kurier* and *Lichtbildbühne*. On July 1, 1940, *Lichtbildbühne* was merged with *Film-Kurier*, which was the last trade journal to appear until the end of September 1944, after which it was replaced by *Film-Nachrichten* until the end of March 1945. Like seismographs, the trade journals reported on all kinds of film-related topics that could be of importance to their readership. Readers were cinema operators, distributors, producers and members of the film-technical supply industry. So far, only the *Film-Kurier* has been indexed by yearly registers, which, however, have established focal subjects. Therefore, the registers do not include the English- and French-language articles of the "English Section Française," which appeared regularly at times from April 1933 onward, nor the countless short news items in various sections, in which a great deal of individual information can be found.

Toward the end of the 1920s, about a thousand German daily newspapers featured a periodic film section. Their number remained very high during the Third Reich, until it declined during World War II due to paper shortages. In Berlin alone, about 60 different daily newspapers were published during the Weimar Republic, many of them twice a day, some even three times. Chaplin's multi-layered image as a film artist, private person, free spirit and political-humanitarian figure of contemporary history resulted in his coverage not only in the film pages of the newspapers but other pages as well. Therefore, a selection was also necessary when sifting through the German newspapers. In addition, individual articles in provincial newspapers could be found in the newspaper clipping collections of the DFF—Deutsches Filminstitut und Filmmuseum in Frankfurt am Main, the Filmuniversität Babelsberg KONRAD WOLF and the Berlin Stiftung Deutsche Kinemathek. As much as possible, German newspapers in exile, which the Nazi state tried to eye closely, were also included, as well as publications in foreign film journals, daily newspapers, magazines and cultural journals. In addition, literature by and about Chaplin, the film industry, German anti–Semitism, Nazism and other topics were added, as well as various reference works and Chaplin's FBI files.

The film censorship records of the Weimar Republic and the Third Reich were an indispensable source because they provide information about interventions in films and their marketing and reveal political motivations. However, about 30,000 of the approximately 70,000 German censorship records are believed to be lost. In addition, the administrative files on German film censorship were completely destroyed in 1944 during one of the many Allied bombing raids on Berlin. These administrative files concerned the individual censorship processes of the Film-Prüfstelle (Board of Film Censors) and the Kontingentstelle (Quota Authority), which were housed in one office building. The Kontingentstelle, which had been established in the Third Reich, subjected films to a preliminary examination and determined whether they could be submitted to the board of film censors at all. Occasionally, protocols of the Berlin Film-Prüfstelle and documents from the censorship proceedings have survived as annexes in the collection of judgments of the Film-Oberprüfstelle (Appeal Board of Film Censors) at the DFF—Deutsches Filminstitut und Fernsehmuseum in Frankfurt am Main.

Also included were, among other items, the files of the Berlin Polizeipräsidium (Police Headquarters) on the deployment on Chaplin's Berlin visit in March 1931, trade law documents on the development of the distributing company that brought City Lights to German cinemas, the Chaplin file of the Hauptarchiv der NSDAP, materials of the Nazi press control, Goebbels' extensive diaries, catalogue and documents of the Reichsfilmarchiv, censorship documents from Great Britain and from the United States, and last but not least, Chaplin's FBI files.

Added to this was a selection of international film literature, newspapers and magazines. If the international literature on Chaplin is already difficult to survey, it will probably never be possible to even approximate the countless publications in international press products of all kinds. Chaplin's large-format albums with press reactions to him and his films alone, which are housed in the Archives de Montreux, contain a rough estimate of several hundred thousand newspaper and magazine clippings from 1915 through the early 1970s. Except for an album of clippings in Hebrew, the vast collection is essentially limited to English-language press products. In other European languages, too, an infinite abundance of Chaplin articles may have been published. In any case, enormous quantities of German- and French-language articles can also be traced. Sad to say, most of the satirical Chaplin cartoons and photographs found therein could not be reproduced due to copyright reasons.

Deep insights were also provided by the collection of Chaplin documents archived at the Cineteca di Bologna. Topical cross-references also led to other archives to trace activities of German diplomats against *Shoulder Arms* and *The Great Dictator*, an imprisonment and a criminal trial from 1942, and other references to the Third Reich.

This allowed a review of how the agitators manipulated information as well as how and to what extent Chaplin as a person and an artist was exposed to inhuman Nazi agitation. Hitler's takeover initiated a radical cultural upheaval in Germany. Within a few months, the German film press, among other groups, was brought into Nazi line. Authors who had admired Chaplin during the Weimar Republic turned into agitators against him. The Nazis agitated against everything that was "un–German" from their point of view with deliberate fake news employing repulsive language, which Victor Klemperer called Lingua Tertii Imperii (LTI). The contrast with Chaplin's incomparable humanitarian art could not have been sharper.

To help readers get started with the complex events and background, each chapter has been preceded by a brief overview of the content.

1

Charlie Chaplin—a Jew?

The Nazis not only fought Chaplin because of his film *The Great Dictator*; he also embodied the enemy image "Jew" for them. But was Chaplin a Jew? The question was put to him on various occasions. It was also raised again and again in the press and in literature about him, and often Chaplin was considered a Jew. He himself was not always completely uninvolved in this. He was also attributed various Jewish birth names. Among them, Thonstein is the most prominent and the most momentous. Therefore, its manifestations are looked at. And did Jewish characters play a significant role in Chaplin's films at all? Since these topics are of fundamental relevance to the Nazis' relationship to Chaplin, the survey will open with them.

Chaplin's Ancestry

Chaplin himself apparently never particularly cared whether he was considered a Jew, and occasionally only flirted with the idea of being one—perhaps also because he himself was not exactly sure of it. Being a Jew was defined differently according to religion, ancestry or culture. The overt religious explanation was based on the following: mother Jewish, acceptance into the Jewish religious community through the act of Brith, bar mitzvah, etc., and membership in a religious congregation. Anti-Semites and Nazis, on the other hand, declared persons of Jewish origin who belonged to another religion or were without religion to be "Jews" even if they had a certain amount of "Jewish blood," i.e., their parents or grandparents had belonged to a Jewish community. This was the basis for terms such as "Halbjude" oder "Vierteljude" (Half-Jew or Quarter-Jew). The issue of "race" was thus decided on the basis of religious affiliation. In the worldview of the anti–Semites, however, all kinds of other people were also called "Jews" if they fitted into the ideological image of the enemy. In Chaplin's case, his type of humor, which allegedly stemmed from the ghetto, certainly played a role.

Chaplin was quite contradictory on the subject. As stated by his biographer David Robinson, probably the earliest statement dates back to 1915, when Chaplin answered a reporter on whether he was a Jew, that he had no such luck.[1] In his 1922 travelogue *My Trip Abroad*, Chaplin reproduced a conversation with a Jewish girl who asked him if he was also Jewish. His answer: "No, I am not a Jew, […] but I am sure there must be [Jewish blood] somewhere in me. I do hope so."[2] In 1940, Chaplin told the U.S. magazine *Collier's*: "I am not a Jew and I do not have a drop of Jewish blood in me. If they said I was a Jew, I never objected. For I would be proud to be one."[3] This again coincides with Gerith von Ulm's assertion in her controversial 1940 biography of Chaplin, *Charlie Chaplin—King of Tragedy*: "There is no evidence for the widespread assumption that Chaplin was a Jew."[4] Conforming to Marcel Martin, Chaplin had commented on the subject in 1946: "They say about me: Chaplin is a Jew. That is true, and I have never denied it."[5] In 1952, Chaplin biographer Theodore Huff suggested Chaplin's father came from a British naturalized family of French-Jewish origin.[6] In 1965, on the other hand, Alvah Bessie reported in his book *Inquisition in Eden* on a 1949 conversation with Chaplin about, among other things, Edward Dmytryk's U.S. film *Crossfire*, which Chaplin considered anti–Semitic: "Bessie: 'Funny, [...] I am a Jew too, and I don't know why I was not aware of this.' Chaplin: 'I'm not a Jew.' Bessie: 'I always thought you were.' Chaplin: 'Many people do, [...] and I've never bothered to deny. But I'm not.'"[7] In 1993, Jost Hermand claimed without citing a source that Chaplin had even "affirmed" not being Jewish.[8] Did he mean either the statement attributed to Chaplin during his March 1931 visit to Berlin (see below) or his response to a Nazi's question after the U.S. premiere of *The Great Dictator* (see Chapter 12)? On the contrary, Chaplin's friend Ivor Montagu, in his 1968 book *With Eisenstein in Hollywood,* wrote that Chaplin rigorously refused to publicly deny being Jewish in order not to play into the hands of anti–Semites.[9]

Internationally, Chaplin was widely regarded as a Jew.[10] One of the first to be convinced that Chaplin was Jewish was the Yiddish-speaking author Sholem Aleichem in 1915.[11] In Germany, Chaplin was thought to be a Jew from the first half of the 1920s onward. In late 1923, the German journalist-poet Kurt Tucholsky, who was Jewish himself, wrote about Chaplin in the radical democratic, bourgeois-left weekly *Die Weltbühne*: "By the way: what a joke that the world laughs at a Jew!"[12]

Chapter 2 will take a closer look at the fact that Chaplin was believed to be a Jew in the German press in 1925 and 1926; this marked the beginning of the Nazi agitation against him. It also claimed that he was born in London's East End. Most likely, however, he was born in the London borough of Walworth, part of Southwark.[13] In 1927, the *Jüdisches Lexikon* published in Germany even explicitly determined Chaplin's Jewish origin. This will be discussed separately below.

In *Hallo Europa!*, the German edition of Chaplin's travelogue *My Trip Abroad*, German translators Charlotte and Heinz Pol in their 1928 introduction assumed Chaplin's Jewishness as a matter of fact, contrary to Chaplin's own account in this book of his conversation with the little girl:

> He is English and at least of Jewish origin, as he himself tells a little girl in the last chapter of his book. [... Both will] be recognized instantly from his works anyway. For his humor, his knockaboutism is typically English. And what lies dormant behind things, this moving, vast sea of his comedy, the strange colorfulness of his gestures and feelings that seem to ironize themselves, above all the not-so-important melancholy of his eyes, all this is Jewish. [...] His art is a straight line made up of all sorts of tiny zigzags.[14]

The same year, Erich Gottgetreu, editor of the leftist journal *Die Volksbühne*, traveled to London to visit the National Library of the British Museum to "get all the literature on Chaplin, most of it long out of print, that appeared in England when he became famous there." In September 1928, he wrote the following in his article "Chaplin Catches the German Kaiser": "Presumably Chaplin emerged from Whitechapel, the distinctly Jewish quarter. This is all the more significant, since Chaplin's whole manner is originally Jewish and touchingly ghetto–Jewish [...]. Chaplin himself always answers the psychologically essential question about his Jewishness elusively."[15]

Chaplin's supposed Jewish origins in London's East End were repeatedly emphasized in the Nazi press from 1926 onward and persisted elsewhere until at least the mid–1930s. In 1935, the U.S. newspaper *The Southern Israelite* claimed that Chaplin was a grandson of Chaim Kaplan, a Jewish tailor from High Street in Whitechapel, who had changed his Jewish name to the more "aristocratic" sounding name Chaplin. This was apparently contradicted in May of that year by the Canadian *Jewish Post*: "Chaplin not a Jew. But will not Publish a Denial." The denial came promptly in the same month from Alf Reeves, Chaplin's confidant and general manager of the Chaplin Film Corporation.[16] Even after that, at the end of May, Heinz Pol maintained in *Die neue Weltbühne* that Chaplin was Jewish.[17]

In his 1931 essay "Chaplin's Shoes," Hermann Ulrich also assumed Chaplin's Jewish origins. Yet, he did not consider the centuries-old Ahasuerus myth of "the eternal Jew" appropriate for the artist: "[...I do not want to claim...] that Chaplin is the 'eternal Jew.' I do not deny that he is a 'rascal' and a 'tramp' or you name it. [... He] is all that only because and inasmuch as he is an 'eternal Jew,' and [...] he is as much the 'eternal Jew' as he is Jewish, and as every Jew is."[18]

In 1941, Gottgetreu once again addressed Chaplin's origins in the New York German-language exile newspaper *Aufbau*,

Charlie Chaplin, *Hallo Europa!*, book cover, 1928.

referring to an essay by the British-Jewish writer Israel Zangwill, who claimed to have discovered Eastern Jewish elements in Chaplin's art and to have discussed them with Chaplin: "Again Charlie tried to dodge and deny his Jewishness. Zangwill got angry. He called him characterless and a liar. Which Chaplin left it like that. He kept quiet." In addition, Gottgetreu quoted an unnamed Viennese journalist to whom Chaplin was supposed to have related his Jewish origins during his March 1931 trip to Europe and to have said the following about his parents: "I inherited my talent, my art and my sadness from them. And it is just their legacy that I passionately want to fight for equal rights of all people, races and creeds."[19]

Among those fascinated by Chaplin's art was the well-known German-Jewish philosopher Hannah Arendt. For her interpretation of the Jew as a pariah, Chaplin played an important role.[20] In 1948, when she wrote several essays on "the hidden Jewish tradition," she devoted a lengthy section to Chaplin: "The Jewish people [...] have spawned an astonishingly beautiful and unique achievement in modern times: the films of Charlie Chaplin."[21] In her Franz Kafka section, she wrote: "Even Chaplin's obscure personality character was clearly linked to Jewish origin."[22]

According to his 1954 book, Mack Sennett, Chaplin's first film producer in 1914 at the Keystone Film Company, apparently knew little about his star's origins and more or less echoed Huff's 1952 version that Chaplin was of French-Jewish descent.[23]

David Robinson's seminal biography *Chaplin: His Life and Art* was published in 1985. After Chaplin's death, Robinson obtained access to the Chaplin family's private files and did not discover any reference to Jewish ancestors in them, tracing the lineage back to 1786.[24] This coincides with Harold Manning's and Reginald R. Chaplin's 1983 and 1985 research that goes back as far as 1670.[25] Glenn Mitchell's well-researched 1997 *The Chaplin Encyclopedia* did not reveal any evidence of Chaplin's Jewish ancestry either.[26] In the lineage compiled by Robinson, an ancestor with the first name Shadrach appeared in Chaplin's paternal line in 1786. In the Old Testament (third chapter of the Book of Daniel), this was the name of one of the three Jews whom King Nebuchadnezzar threw into the fiery furnace because they refused to worship a golden idol he had erected; they survived by virtue of their faith in Jehovah. However, English Puritans, i.e., Christians, maintained a tradition of Old Testament first names for a long time.

As late as 1989, writer Curt Riess, who claimed to have been friends with Chaplin, considered him a Jew in his "personal" *Charlie Chaplin—Biographie*, which should be taken with a grain of salt. His version, how Chaplin managed the balance as an actor between the roles as a Jewish barber and as Hynkel in *The Great Dictator*, sounded bizarre: "But how could he play [the] dictator Hitler, whom [despite his] much finer traits [he] somehow resembled [...]—and still be a tramp? [...] Perhaps this was made possible for him by the fact that he had unexpectedly learned he was Jewish."[27] Riess did not tell readers who had informed Chaplin.

According to Hellmuth Karasek's 1992 book *Billy Wilder—Eine Nahaufnahme*, Wilder had learned the following from Chaplin's son Sidney about the latter's visit to the London cemetery where Chaplin family ancestors were buried: "[There] I found the name Kaplan. Kaplan! And [my father] has so often claimed that he is not a Jew."[28] It remained unclear whose tombstone it was. Did Sidney Chaplin possibly rehash the version of the Jewish U.S. newspaper *The Southern Israelite*, denied by Alf Reeves for Chaplin, according to which Chaplin was Chaim Kaplan's grandson? If it should have been Chaim Kaplan's tombstone: then why did not it say "Chaplin," which Kaplan was supposed to have adopted as a more aristocratic-sounding name? Or had Sidney merely inferred a Jewish origin from the name Kaplan without really establishing it? In any case, none of this is consistent with the documented family trees of Chaplin's family.

"Thonstein"

The Chaplin entry in the *Jüdisches Lexikon*, written by Dr. Ludwig Davidsohn under the editorial supervision of Dr. Felix A. Theilhaber, is of particular significance. This encyclopedia, published in Germany in 1927, had been in preparation since 1919 and emphasized scholarly reliability. Consequently, Davidsohn had also assumed "full scholarly responsibility" for his Chaplin entry. According to this and based on two sources, Chaplin was the son of an Eastern Jewish family named Thonstein that had immigrated to England in the mid–19th century.[29] The first source is the German translation of Jim Tully's series of articles in the *Prager Tagblatt* of April and May 1927, but it does not bear any reference to Thonstein.[30] Tully's original four-part series "Charlie Chaplin: His Real Life Story" had been published in the U.S. magazine *Pictorial Review* from January to April 1927.[31] Chaplin had filed suit against this publication in January 1927, but it had been dismissed in March.[32] Tully's Chaplin biography "Charlie Chaplin: His Life Story," announced for May and then November 1927 by the Albert and Charles Boni Publishing Company in New York,[33] never came out.

As his second source, Davidsohn named Arnold Ulitz's poem "An Chaplin" from the "*Berliner Tageblatt* of November 1926," but it is not to be found in any of the 58 issues of that month's newspaper, nor under that title elsewhere in Ulitz's oeuvre.[34] On February 17, 1927, however, Ulitz's poem "Meute" appeared in the *Berliner Tageblatt*, and in it he defended Chaplin against the moralizers' smear campaign on him for his divorce from Lita Grey. This poem did not address Chaplin's origin.[35]

In fact, Davidsohn's claim about Chaplin's Jewish origin has never been verified. The name Thonstein is not to be found in Chaplin's family tree. The name of Chaplin's father was Charles Chaplin and his mother's name before her marriage was Hannah Harriet Pedlingham Hill.[36] Had Davidsohn written his entry to "incorporate" the supposed Jew Chaplin, who was widely regarded as such and did not emphatically deny it, with an invented mini-family tree, so to speak, in order to be able to welcome another famous personality into the Jewish community? In any case, Davidsohn did not change his entry when the second volume of the encyclopedia was published in 1928 and included corrections to the first volume.[37] Yet, at that time it could not be proven conclusively

Chaplin was not of Jewish origin either. Incidentally, the ten-volume *Encyclopaedia Judaica—Das Judentum in Geschichte und Gegenwart*, published in Berlin from 1918 to 1934, did not mention Chaplin.[38]

On October 19, 1928, the Viennese Jewish weekly *Die neue Welt* provided a new twist to the Thonstein rumor: "Recently [Chaplin's mother] died, as a Jewess. It turned out that she came from an East Jewish family who had immigrated to London, and her real name was Thonstein. So Charlie is not a great hero. But this does not hinder enjoying his masterpieces to the full."[39] This contradicted the *Southern Israelite*'s claim about Chaplin's alleged Jewish grandfather Chaim Kaplan from Whitechapel. But *Die neue Welt* also failed to give a source for the new finding. Nor did the journal *Hammer—Blätter für deutschen Sinn*, which Theodor Fritsch (see below), co-founder of the Deutsche Antisemitische Vereinigung (German Anti-Semitic Association) in 1886, had been publishing since 1902. On November 15, 1928, he commented on *Die*

CHAPLIN, CHARLES SPENCER, einer der berühmtesten Filmschauspieler der Gegenwart, geb. 1889 in London als Sohn einer Mitte des 19. Jhdts. in England eingewanderten Ostjuden-familie, die urspr. den Namen Thonstein führte, wanderte neunzehnjährig nach Amerika aus und wurde Mitglied einer zweitrangigen Varieté-Truppe. Durch den Filmunternehmer Mac Sennet in Los-Angeles kam er zum Film und wurde bald der Liebling des amerikanischen Publikums und in der Folge weltbekannt. Ch. ist Verfasser, Regisseur und Hauptdarsteller der meisten seiner Filme (,,Goldrausch", ,,Hundeleben", ,,Pariser Frauen"). Seine Stärke liegt — von seiner hervorragenden Mimik und geschickten Spiegelung der spezifisch amerikanischen Komik, die aus dem ständigen Kampfe mit der Tücke des Objekts fließt, abgesehen — in der Fähigkeit, plötzlich mitten im vermeintlichen Scherz durch Darstellung hoffnungsloser Schwermut, zeitloser, jüdisch anmutender Tragik und stummer Verzweiflung bis ins Innerste zu erschüttern. Ch. zeichnet sich durch große Wohltätigkeit und Förderung anderer Talente aus; so entdeckte er u. a. die Filmtalente Jackie Coogan und Adolphe Menjou.

Lit.: Jim Tully, ,,Charlie Chaplin" (Prager Tagblatt 24., 28. IV.; 6., 11. V. 1927); Arnold Ulitz' Gedicht ,,An Chaplin" (Berl. Tageblatt im Nov. 1926).

T.   L. D.

Jüdisches Lexikon Volume 1, Chaplin entry "Thonstein" by Ludwig Davidsohn, 1927.

Neue Welt's report under "Entlarvt!" (Unmasked) as follows: "On the occasion of a polemic that appeared in America about his Jewish origin, movie star Charlie Chaplin directly denied that he descended from Jewish parents. [...] Why he denies his Jewish origin, the mentioned Jewish papers do not know or pretend not to know."[40]

On March 13, 1931, in the aftermath of Chaplin's recent visit to London, the Swiss *Jüdische Presszentrale Zürich* provided a new twist to his ancestry. Now he was supposed to have been born "in the slums of London [...] as the son of a poor Jewish immigrant whose original name was Thonstein." No word of explanation why his mother should no longer be *née* Thonstein. The magazine also commented on why Chaplin's art should be considered Jewish: "Chaplin is an essentially Jewish character, he is an eminently Jewish humorist. His strength lies once in his outstanding mimicry and the unique comedy that flows from the constant struggle with the perfidy of the object. Above all, however, this becomes apparent in his unparalleled ability to suddenly embody in the midst of supposedly funny situations the hopeless gloom of time-less, Jewish-like tragedy and mute despair. Thus, he shakes his audience to their very core."[41]

The Viennese Jew-ish newspaper *Die Stimme* took up the assertion of the *Jüdische Presszentrale Zürich* a few days later on the occasion of Chaplin's visit to Vienna, but refrained from determining Chaplin's origin. It saw "the essence of the problem of Chaplin" in "Is his art Jewish?" and answered the question in the affirmative on the basis of circumstantial evidence: "Charlie's film character is ghetto. Charlie's tragicom-edy is golus [note: fate of Jews in the Diaspora]. Char-lie's main characteristic is a feeling of inferiority. Char-lie's problematic—Jewish. [...] A comic Jew, a ghetto character, makes us laugh and cry. He, the genius Chaplin, the dollar million-aire Chaplin, the most cele-

Hammer. Blätter für deutschen Sinn, magazine cover, November 1928.

brated man in the world, probably does not know it, but it is unmistakable [...]." But *Die Stimme* also pointed out: "It is completely far from our thoughts to claim every great creative person, every genius for Judaism. It is a fact that a relatively large num-ber of outstanding people are Jews. But we are not ready to take part in the taste-lessness of transforming genuine Aryans into Jews simply because they are great people."[42]

Unlike *Die Stimme*, the Vienna- and Bratislava-based *Jüdische Presse* followed the Swiss report shortly thereafter, shifting the origin of Chaplin's father Thonstein to "the East" from which he had immigrated to England "in the middle of the last century," as the Viennese *Die neue Welt* had done in 1928.[43] However, according to *Die Neue Welt*, Chaplin is supposed to have stated during his Berlin visit: "I do not have the slightest connection with Judaism. My parents were not Jews. If the Jews nevertheless consider me one of them, there is nothing I can do." This newspaper commented:

In Vienna, [Chaplin] is said to have conceded his Jewish origins "to 50 percent" [...]. In Berlin [...] he had to accept it, as he resignedly remarked [...]. There is just nothing you can do about it, he regretted with a shrug, with a slight bow to the swastikas who are already raising Cain [...]. [In the past,] he did not want to fall out with the Anglo-Saxon world, today he does not want to fall out with the Germanic world.[44]

In any case, in the 1926 and 1928 first and second edition, respectively, of the U.S. *Who's Who in American Jewry*, Chaplin is not mentioned.[45] This was logical, since Chaplin was neither a U.S. citizen nor a Jew. But in 1935, Chaplin was included in the *Biographical Encyclopedia of American Jews* with his parents Charles and Hanna Thonstein, who had come from Eastern Europe to London in 1850 and had performed there as a vaudeville comedian and singer, respectively, under the stage names Charles Chaplin and Lilly Harley.[46] The source of this information remained undisclosed, and Chaplin's British nationality did not matter any more. Reproducing the essence of Chaplin's entry in the *Jüdisches Lexikon*, the 1938 third edition of *Who's Who in American Jewry 1938–39* added that Chaplin was an "Episcopalian."[47] The editor claimed to have requested all persons represented with biographical data to proofread the entry intended for them before publication.[48] Had Chaplin reacted to this, and if so, had he expressly approved his entry or merely not contradicted it? This could not be clarified. In any case, the entry meant that Chaplin was a member of the Christian Episcopal Church and, as the anti–Semitic *Hammer* had already written, was baptized. In 1931, the Jerusalem newspaper *The Palestine Bulletin* had reported that Chaplin was not Jewish, but descended from a Christian London family.[49] Now, in late October 1940, the Jewish Chicago newspaper *The Sentinel* asked "When Is a Jew not a Jew?" and questioned Chaplin's inclusion in *Who's Who in American Jewry 1938–39.*[50]

In his 2002 essay "è della stirpe dei giudei"/"And He Is of the Seed of the Jews," written in Italian and English for the journal *Griffithiana*, Joseph Halachmi pointed out the following: In 1937, the Hebrew *Encyclopedia Klallit Izre'el* had claimed Chaplin's Jewish origin and given his mother's first name as Haya (Khaya). In addition, in the 1940s, Chaplin was featured in the Pictures of Famous Jewish Personalities series of the Oriental cigarette brand Kedem (card 114).[51] As the name Thonstein can be understood as "made of clay," Halachmi speculated that Thonstein could mean "golem" in Yiddish, composed of the word elements "zany" and "clodhopper." "Golem" is the Hebrew term for a formless mass or lump, and in Jewish mysticism stands for an artificially created human being. Inspired by this myth, Paul Wegener and Henrik Galeen made the famous silent film *The Golem* in 1915 with Wegener in the title role. Halachmi stretched his speculation further: Thonstein may have been Chaplin's Yiddish nickname, possibly given to him by a Jewish audience during his British Music Hall days.[52] Even if Yiddish was spoken in London's East End, Halachmi's speculation at least does not explain that Thonstein was the birth name of Chaplin's father, which Chaplin would have borne as his legitimate child.

"Thonstein" was also represented in 1941 with Libby Benedict's Chaplin entry in the third volume of the ten-volume *The Universal Jewish Encyclopedia*, published in New York from 1939 to 1943. The work tied in with the *Jüdisches Lexikon*, and rights to it had also been acquired.[53] Benedict referred to an unspecified Hungarian-Jewish newspaper from March 1931, according to which Chaplin was said to have descended from the Eastern European Jewish family of Thonstein. Because of this newspaper report, Chaplin had been attacked as a Jew by an anti–Semitic Hungarian newspaper and had therefore cancelled his planned visit to Budapest (following Vienna?). Unlike the *Jüdisches Lexikon*, however, Benedict made clear that Thonstein is nowhere documented as Chaplin's mother's birth name either. In the context of *The Great Dictator*, Benedict also emphasized that Chaplin had denied being Jewish. She was probably addressing Chaplin's statement after the film's premiere (see Chapter 12). On Chaplin's Jewish appearance, Benedict quoted from Gilbert Frankau's undated U.S. article in the *New York Herald Tribune* that Chaplin's eyes are "at once the merriest, the saddest, and the most intelligent eyes ever seen in a Hebrew countenance."[54] What makes the entry special is that it "has been checked as much as we were able by the office of the United Artists Corporation, November 4, 1940, during Charles Chaplin's sojourn in New York."[55] Chaplin's inclusion in the encyclopedia was criticized as superfluous shortly after the publication of the third volume because he himself had repeatedly denied his Jewish origin.[56]

Chaplin's Jewish origin had indeed been reported in March 1931 by two Jewish Budapest newspapers. On March 14, 1931, *Egyenlöség* had written "how difficult it was to describe certain fields of interest or professions as typically Jewish." About the origin of the "brilliant Jew" Chaplin as one of the most important representatives of Jewry, the newspaper reported that "his father had emigrated from Eastern Europe to England in the middle of the last century" and that the "family name had originally been Thonstein."[57] A week later, *Egyenlöség* related that Chaplin had said in Vienna that his "father was a Jewish actor who sang jargon songs on the small stages of the London ghetto."[58] On March 17, 1931, *Uj Kelet* quoted Chaplin as saying that his father had educated him "traditionally Jewish." Other newspapers had claimed about Chaplin that he "was [born] in one of the poorest quarters of London to very poor Jewish parents who had emigrated to London from Russia to escape persecution, and whose original name was Thonstein."[59] Whether the quotes attributed to Chaplin are authentic is not certain.

"Karl Tonstein"

In any case, Chaplin's alleged Jewish origins and his "true" name Thonstein were thus cemented for a considerable time. For Nazi propaganda, the Chaplin entry in the *Jüdisches Lexikon*, as well as German, Austrian and Swiss articles from 1928 and 1931, were probably downright proof of Chaplin's Jewish origin. At the end of 1937, the name "Thonstein" appeared in Hans Diebow's smear brochure "Der ewige Jude" (see Chapter 9) and developed its own momentum. In mid–October 1938, the *Film-Kurier* reprinted William Dudley Pelley's extensive list "Who's Who in Hollywood—Find the Gentile" from the U.S. Nazi-oriented gazette *Liberation—The Silvershirt Weekly* of August 14, 1938.[60]

Liberation was the organ of the Christian-fascist Silver Shirt Legion of America, Silver Shirts for short. Its Fuehrer was the anti–Semite Pelley, who, among other things, had written the screenplays for the U.S. films *The Light in the Dark* (Clarence Brown, 1922) and *The Shock* (Lambert Hillyer, 1923), both starring Lon Chaney. Pelley presented a fascist radio program similar to the infamous Father Charles Coughlin, founded the Silver Shirts on the day of Hitler's takeover with the mission to "curb back the influence of the Jews in America" and dressed like an SA man. In 1936, he launched the anti–Jewish Christian Party. The Silver Shirts, in turn, frequently joined forces with the German-American Bundists (see below). In

Screen shot from *The Tramp and the Dictator*, 2002: U.S. meeting of the German-American Bund (© Photoplay Productions Ltd. & Spiegel TV).

1942, after the U.S. entry into World War II, Pelley was sentenced to 15 years imprisonment in the U.S. for his fascist activities considered as high treason, but was released as early as 1950.[61]

Ninety of the 250 leading U.S. actors listed by Pelley were supposed to be Jews, Chaplin among them. The list also "disclosed" several "true Jewish names" of actors who had adopted English-sounding stage names. The *Film-Kurier* added Chaplin's "true Jewish name Tonstein" to that list,[62] presumably based on Diebow. At the end of November 1938, film officer Curt Belling "completed" the name even further in *Der Angriff*. He translated Chaplin's first name "Charles" into German as "Karl" and turned Chaplin into "Karl Tonstein" (see Chapter 10). Belling was followed up by *Der Angriff* in mid–January 1939 with the article "Who's Who in Hollywood. All Jews!" and added "not Thonstein?" to Pelley's list for Chaplin and his Jewish wife Paulette Goddard.[63] After April 1939, however, "Tonstein" had had its day in the Nazi press, for henceforth Chaplin was again Charlie Chaplin. Therefore, Michael Hanisch's repeated assertions that Chaplin had already been given the first name "Karl" in Germany in October 1938 and that from the end of November 1938 "the German press only of 'the Jew Karl Tonstein' […] was spoken of" are unfounded.[64]

"Israel Thonstein"

Yet, "Thonstein" lived on in the U.S. There, Chaplin was attributed the first name "Israel" instead of "Karl." Was this because in Nazi Germany male Jews had to bear "Israel" as an additional first name since the beginning of 1939?[65]

In 2010, Holly A. Pearse made a sweeping claim in the British *The Jewish Quarterly*, without specifying time data, that the German-American Bund had spread the word in the U.S. that Chaplin's birth name was "Israel Thonstein."[66] The German-American Bund or Amerikadeutsche Bund was an association of Germans living in the U.S. and had emerged at the end of March 1936 under the leadership of Fritz Kuhn from the Freunde der Hitlerbewegung (Friends of the Hitler Movement), which had been founded in 1932 and had ties with the Ku Klux Klan. In early December 1935, Kuhn was elected as head of the Freunde der Hitlerbewegung. Nevertheless, the relationship of the Nazi-oriented German-American Bund (see also Chapter 10) to the Third Reich was ambivalent. After Kuhn was found guilty of embezzlement by a U.S. court in early December 1939 and eventually served a lengthy prison term, the association became increasingly less important and, in the aftermath of Pearl Harbor, was at times considered a German ring of spies.[67]

Pearse's claim implies that "Israel Thonstein" would have been circulated between March 1936 and about the end of 1939. However, she does not provide any sources, and evidence for this has not been found. Pearse has also claimed that "Israel Thonstein" was given as Chaplin's name "in a 1948 Jewish encyclopedia."[68] Which encyclopedia did she mean? In any case, Benedict did not add a first name to "Thonstein" in her 1941 Chaplin entry in *The Universal Jewish Encyclopedia*, reprinted unaltered in 1948 and 1969.[69]

Most likely, however, the origin of the name tampering is the undated tract *Jew Stars Over Hollywood*, published by the anti–Semitic, anti–Communist Patriotic Tract Society of St. Louis. The Patriotic Tract Society distributed it to protect "against the destruction of Christian culture" and against its "replacement by anti–Christian Judaism" and fought the "typical Jewish [Hollywood] Sodom and Gomorrah" of "Communist propaganda" and "disgusting immorality." *Jew Stars Over Hollywood* put on the front page: "The motion picture industry has become a Jewish industry, run by and for Jews." To this end, it pilloried some 50 filmmakers in the categories of writers, actors and producers, Chaplin among them. His entry read: "Charles Chaplin. Jew name: ISRAEL THONSTEIN. Actor and producer. Born in London, England, on April 16, 1889. Family emigrated from Eastern Europe and settled in England in 1850. First appeared on stage at the age of seven."[70] The Patriotic Tract Society also published the pamphlet *Red Stars in Hollywood*, which included Chaplin as a Communist, but without a "Thonstein" reference. It was published after April 12, 1948, because it quoted from a speech of that date.[71]

In 1993, Hermand dated *Jew Stars Over Hollywood* to 1940 without providing any further details.[72] But from the only known tract's version so far follows that it was not available until the end of June 1950 at the earliest. Indeed, it lists four names of the so-called "Hollywood Ten": Alvah Bessie, John Howard Lawson, Albert Maltz and Dalton Trumbo.[73] The "Hollywood Ten" were ten Hollywood screenwriters, actors and directors who had refused to testify before the House Un-American Activities Committee (HUAC) of the United States House of Representatives in October 1947 about the membership of filmmakers in the Communist Party. Regarding Bessie, Lawson, Maltz and Trumbo, *Jew Stars Over Hollywood* states, respectively, "is now under sentence to prison for contempt of the United States

20, 1896. Son of Louis Birnbaum and Hadassah Bluth. Married Gracie Allen.

SUE CAROL
Jew Name: EVELYN LEDERER
Actress. Born in Chicago, Illinois, on October 30, 1908. Daughter of Samuel Lederer.

CHARLES CHAPLIN
Jew Name: ISRAEL THONSTEIN
Actor and producer. Born in London, England, on April 16, 1889. Family immigrated from Eastern Europe and settled in England in 1850. First appeared on stage at age of seven.

SAM COSLOW
Songwriter. Born in New York City on December 27, 1902. Son of Harry Coslow and Rebecca Hirsch. Married Esther Muir.

GEORGE CUKOR
Motion picture director. Born in New York City on July 7, 1899. Son of Victor Cukor and Helen Gross.

BETTE DAVIS
Actress. Born in Lowell, Massachusetts, on April 5, 1908. Daughter of Harlow Davis and Ruth Favor.

MELVYN DOUGLAS
Jew Name: HESSELBERG
Actor. Born in Macon, Georgia, on April 5, 1901. Son of Edward Hesselberg and Lena Shackleford. Married Helen Gahagan.

— 5 —

Jew Stars Over Hollywood, tract cover, ca. late spring or summer 1950.

Jew Stars Over Hollywood, Chaplin entry "Israel Thonstein," ca. late spring or summer 1950.

Congress for refusing to deny membership in the Communist Party." The four had indeed been sentenced to one year in prison and fined $1000 each for this, Lawson and Trumbo as early as April and May 1948, respectively, but Bessie and Maltz not until late June 1950.[74] Consequently, *Jew Stars Over Hollywood* could not have been issued until all four sentences had been determined.

"Israel Thonstein" outlived *Jew Stars Over Hollywood*. Chaplin had already been under observation since August 1922 by the U.S. Federal Bureau of Investigation (FBI) because of alleged Communist activities. It continued its dossiers even after Chaplin's death with reports on the theft of his body in March 1978. Focusing on Communist activities, dossiers of more than 400 pages were produced, with poor content and little factual basis.[75] In the header of the March 1947 dossier, Chaplin's "real" name, "Thonstein," still appeared without a first name.[76] The FBI had picked up "Thonstein" along with Chaplin's allegedly Jewish *curriculum vitae* from *Who's Who in American Jewry 1938–39* and also consulted Gerith von Ulm's 1940 biography *Charlie Chaplin—King of Tragedy*, according to which Chaplin was not Jewish. On top of that, he allegedly spoke with a Jewish accent.[77] "Israel Thonstein" first appeared in two dossiers from the fall of 1952.[78] Presumably *Jew Stars Over Hollywood* was the source, but it is not known when the FBI learned about it.

A side note: After his relocation to Switzerland in 1953, Chaplin was kept under surveillance by the Swiss Federal Police.[79] Chaplin, who had been observed by the FBI, the Nazis and the Schweizer Bundespolizei for decades, had obviously been considered a "highly suspicious and dangerous subject!"

Later Perspective on Chaplin's Origin

When Chaplin's *My Autobiography* was published in 1964, many Jewish readers were disappointed to learn that he was not Jewish nor was his name Thonstein.[80] Therefore, it astonishes that according to Manfred Rüsel's entry in the 1992 *Neues Lexikon des Judentums*, Chaplin was still the son of an Eastern Jewish family that had immigrated to Great Britain. Only the name Thonstein was no longer mentioned.[81] At that time, Robinson's Chaplin biography had already been published in 1985 (original English version) and in 1989 (German version), respectively, from which it emerged that Chaplin was not Jewish. John McCabe also found no evidence of Chaplin's Jewish origins for his 1992 Chaplin biography, but emphasized that in his films, Chaplin had "almost always acted in part like a Jew" and "would like to be part Jewish. Who is to deny him?"[82] Chaplin's verified non–Jewish lineage had apparently not been considered in the preparation of the *Neues Lexikon des Judentums*, and even in its 2000 reissue, the Chaplin entry was not revised.[83]

It was not until the exhibition *Pioniere in Celluloid—Juden in der frühen Filmwelt* (Pioneers in Celluloid. Jews in the Early World of Film) took place that something changed. Now Chaplin was a non–Jew, who was "always considered to be Jewish by admirers and critics, Jews and non–Jews."[84] This is the state of Chaplin research today. In 2010, Pearse considered Chaplin's non–Jewish birth less significant. The key was that he "looked, acted, and 'felt' like a Jew" and, to Jewish eyes, "told Jewish stories."[85] In 2014, James Jordan called Chaplin "a non–Jew who can be read as Jewish" in the U.S. magazine *European Judaism*.[86] And in the same year, Peggy Shinner pointed out in a *Chicago Tribune* interview that Hannah Arendt had also known that Chaplin was not Jewish.[87]

Jewish Characters in Chaplin Films

Chaplin himself identified with the outsider, the underdog. The many contradictory assertions mostly interpreted that Chaplin was Jewish. Many recognized in his Tramp Charlie the embodiment of the "eternal Jew," who roams the world homeless and underprivileged, is without any possessions and never loses the courage to live despite all defeats. The supporters of this probably also based their approach more on a specific form of Eastern Jewish humor, the ghetto comedy, which resulted from the age-long Jewish experience of oppression and poverty.

Apart from interpretations, Chaplin's oeuvre was not dominated by Jewish characters and Jewish life. In his films, Jews were not particularly positive individuals. Nor did Chaplin idealize or even heroize them. Rather, Jewish characters in his films are everyday people with their shortcomings. Religion does not even seem to play a significant role. For thematic reasons, *The Great Dictator* is Chaplin's only film that focuses on Jews, but again they are human beings with all their faults, as they can be found everywhere. This, in turn, is just typical of "Jewish humor" and Eastern Jewish ghetto stories.

Only in *The Vagabond* (1916) does Chaplin caricature a Jew and the Jewish dietary laws (pork ban). At the beginning of the two-reeler, an old Jew is greedily downing some ham at a small buffet in the tavern, where these special meat dishes are signposted. Charlie, a street musician, comes into the inn to collect money from the guests for his violin playing, and the Jew feels caught out by Charlie. The Jew turns away abruptly from the buffet, as if nothing had happened at all. Charlie smoothes the way for him: He exchanges the signs so that the pork ham is now labeled as roast beef, and with a mischievous gesture invites the Jew to confidently continue helping himself to it. Indignantly, the Jew turns his back on Charlie and the pork ham, but then looks longingly back at it in an unobserved moment.

In another 1916 two-reeler, *The Pawnshop*, the pawnshop owner is a Jew with headgear and full beard. Yet, the film is not concerned with any stereotypical Jewish idiosyncrasies of the store owner and his daughter. Nor is there anything special in the fact that the pawnshop is run by a Jew, which was customary at that time. So Chaplin used a cliché which would have been understood in that period: The pawnbroker also has a good heart. When he wants to fire the scrappy good-for-nothing Charlie, who also makes eyes at his daughter, Charlie whines to him in pantomime that he has a whole flock of children to feed. The pawnbroker then relents and gives Charlie another chance. The way the pawnbroker presents diamonds to a confident and well-dressed customer—who turns out to be a crook—is in the manner of a good businessman and by no means a caricature.

It is no different with the 1919 short subject fragment *The Professor*, in which Chaplin, as Professor Bosco, tugs at the beard of the Jewish cashier of the lodging house. A special reason why in *Sunnyside* (1919) the farmer is portrayed as a Jew wearing a house cap, reading a presumably Yiddish newspaper in Hebrew characters, and chewing on a straw is not even discernible. The fact that he dislikes Charlie obviously has no relation to Jewish life either. Charlie is in love with the daughter of the Jewish gentleman. She returns Charlie's love. It is only when Charlie sings a song that is not exactly acceptable while they are making music together, and the daughter looks slightly piqued, that her father appears and orders Charlie out of the house.

In *The Pilgrim* (1923), the deacon in an obvious Christian setting does not accept the money for the mortgage because "one should not do business on the Sabbath." Among English-American Puritans, "Sabbath" was an absolutely common designation of the Christian Sunday. This was observed as strictly as the Jewish Sabbath and included the prohibition of business activity. The fact that the deacon, precisely by rejecting the money, inadvertently causes Charlie's former cellmate to stay in the house and steal the cash can be plausibly explained even without a religious background.

Moreover, stereotypical gags referring to Jews were not uncommon in U.S. slapstick comedies. In the 1925 two-reeler *The Caretaker's Daughter*, Charley Chase consigns his decrepit car to a Jewish used-car dealer and, through furtive gestures, manages to persuade a customer to purchase his vehicle in order to make a fast buck. But as the dealer collects a hefty fee for this, Charley turns the shrewd guy's profile to the camera, presenting his hooked nose. Charley nods knowingly with a puckered mouth as if to say: "Sure, I should've known that Jew would rip me off." In Laurel and Hardy's *Blotto* (1930), Stan looks for a way to escape his strict wife in the evening to visit a nightclub with his friend Ollie. Initially, Stan pretends to his wife that he wants to read something. He picks up a Yiddish newspaper in Hebrew characters that he cannot read, crumples it up and throws it away. Above all, Roach's comedian Max Davidson of German-Jewish origin, who sympathetically caricatured the Jewish way of life in his comedies, should not be forgotten.

Nazis Against Jews

Hostility toward Jews has existed in Christian Europe since the Middle Ages. Modern anti–Semitism was a political-social movement that emerged in Germany toward the end of the 1870s and was directed against the legal equality of Jews that had been enforced in the 19th century.

On February 24, 1920, at the Munich Hofbräuhaus, the former Deutsche Arbeiterpartei (German Workers' Party) was renamed the Nationalsozialistische Deutsche Arbeiterpartei (NSDAP), which henceforth pursued anti–Semitism more fanatically and aggressively than ever. At this event, Adolf Hitler, then an Austrian citizen, proclaimed its 25-point party program. Among other things, the program was published in July 1922 on page 1 of the *Völkischer Beobachter* under the headline "Deutsche Volksgenossen! Antisemiten! Nationalsozialisten!" (Ethnic-Germans! Anti-Semites! National Socialists!) and took up only the space of two newspaper columns. It lacked nothing in clarity. No. 4 of the program read: "Only those who are national comrades can be citizens. Only those of German blood can be a national comrade, without regard to confession. Therefore, no Jew can be a national comrade."

It continues: "In order to create a German press, we demand that […] all editors and employees of newspapers published in the German language must be ethnic comrades. […] We demand the legal battle against an art and literary trend that exerts a corrosive influence on our national life, and the closure of events that violate the above demands."[88] The complete NSDAP program can be found in Appendix 1.

The party program of the NSDAP thus challenged the legal status of German citizens of Jewish faith, who had been granted German citizenship constitutionally for the first time by the German Empire in April 1871.[89] This had not led to the automatic acceptance of Jewish fellow citizens. In 1883 and 1887, for example, Wilhelm Berg's Berlin *Antisemiten-Brevier* (Anti-Semite Breviary) and Thomas Frey's (alias Theodor Fritsch) *Antisemiten-Katechismus* (Anti-Semite Catechism) were published.[90]

Frey was the pseudonym of the anti–Semitic *Hammer* editor Theodor Fritsch,

Masthead: *Völkischer Beobachter*, editor Adolf Hitler, 1922.

one of the "trailblazers and spearheads of the New Germany" recognized by the Nazis.[91]

Fritsch did not use his real name until the tenth edition of the book, which was published in 45 editions until 1939.[92] For their racial ideology, the authors of the NSDAP party program had been able to draw on the book *Kampf gegen das Judenthum* (Fight Against Judaism) by the physician Dr. Gustav Stille, published in 1891. By 1912, it had gone through eight editions with increasingly radical content and served as the source of Philipp Stauff's *Semi-Kürschner* of 1913. Stauff publicly pilloried "writers, poets, bankers, financiers, doctors, actors, artists, musicians, officers, lawyers, revolutionaries, suffragettes, social democrats, etc., of Jewish race and affiliation, who were active or known in Germany from 1813 to

Theodor Fritsch, 1933.

1913." For his part, Stille railed, among other things, against the "Judenherrschaft" (Jewish Rule) of the "nomadic parasites" with the consequences of German-Jewish "mixed marriages [… as] a sad sign of the waning of all racial feeling" and thus of "racial defilement"—a term Stille introduced in the last edition of his book. Jews would have to be removed from all spheres of public life, and he blatantly called for a "struggle against Jewish power until its complete extermination." Here are the roots of the paranoia that Jews all over the world are to blame for all sorts of grievances, e.g., the lost world war, and are masterminds of an internationally organized world conspiracy.[93] Even before the publication of *Mein Kampf* (two volumes, 1925 and 1926),[94] Hitler, in his May 1923 speech at the Munich Krone Circus, called the Jews "Völkervampyr" (Vampire of Nations), adding religiously dressed-up: "The Jew is […] not man [, but] the devil's double."[95] In its advertising section, the *Völkischer Beobachter* urged its readership not to buy from Jews and not to purchase their products.

2

Chaplin Targeted

Shoulder Arms *and* The Gold Rush, *1921–26*

At the end of 1921, in Germany, began the first politically motivated attacks on Chaplin, whose films were not released in the cinemas of the Weimar Republic until late August 1920. This emanated from German nationalist circles, which regarded Chaplin's alleged Germanophobia just as the Nazis would later do. Therefore, the present chapter will also examine this development up to the first Nazi attacks directed against Chaplin.

This chapter covers:

- the delayed German release of Chaplin films
- Chaplin's conquest of German cinemas
- German nationalist politics
- German nationalist attacks against *Shoulder Arms* and Chaplin as "Deutschenfresser" (German-Eater)
- the lawsuit against Chaplin over *Shoulder Arms*
- the start of Chaplin films in Munich, home of the *Völkischer Beobachter*'s editorial office
- the reasons for the *Völkischer Beobachter*'s initial lack of reaction to Chaplin films
- *The Gold Rush*'s problems with the German censorship
- Walter Hasenclever's review of *The Gold Rush* as trigger for Nazi agitation against Chaplin
- the language of Nazi agitation and its scope
- *The Gold Rush*'s German business success

Chaplin Comes to Germany

When Chaplin became famous in the U.S. with his Keystone films in 1914, they were rapidly shown in European cinemas, for example in France, Great Britain and Sweden, but not in Germany. Chaplin films were first imported to Germany after the end of World War I.

After the start of World War I, film imports dropped sharply, and then regulations caused by the war came into play. Even before the U.S. declared war on the

German Empire on April 6, 1917, the "Verordnung über das Verbot der Einfuhr entbehrlicher Gegenstände" (Decree Prohibiting the Import of non-essential Goods)
had come into force on February 25, 1916,[1] responding to the economic situation in
Germany created by World War I. "Non-essential Goods" included films. According
to this, the "Bekanntmachung über die Regelung der Einfuhr" (Official Announcement on the Regulation of Imports) of January 16, 1917, had stipulated that all products from abroad could only be imported into the territory of the Reich with the
approval of the "competent authority," which remained unchanged until the end of
World War I. This "competent authority" was the Reichskommissar für Aus- und
Einfuhrbewilligung (Reich Commissioner for Export and Import Licensing) in Berlin.[2] In the U.S., the "Trading with the Enemy Act" established the American War
Trade Board on October 17, 1917. The U.S. law prohibited U.S. citizens from trading with enemy states, so U.S. films could not be exported to Germany. Chaplin's
film *Shoulder Arms*, made for First National, had its U.S. premiere on October 20,
1918, while the war was still on. After the end of the war, Germany remained enemy
territory for the U.S. until the signing of the "Versailles Peace Treaty" on April 17,
1919. Nevertheless, the treaty did not immediately end the export ban on U.S. films
to Germany, because Germany and Austria-Hungary remained expressly excluded
from the lifting of trade restrictions for the time being. This did not change until the
American War Trade Board was incorporated into the U.S. State Department beginning in July 1919 and the latter released film exports to Germany on July 14, 1919.

German import restrictions from the Empire were also not lifted until the Weimar Republic's "Übergangsgesetz" (Provisional Law) of March 4, 1919.[3] As a result, in
mid–1919, plans were made to establish an Außenhandelsstelle für die Ein- und Aus-
fuhr belichteter Filme (Foreign Trade Office for the Import and Export of Exposed
Films), to which the Reichskommissar für Aus- und Einfuhrbewilligung transferred
his powers.[4] The establishment of the Außenhandelsstelle dragged on until it finally
began operations in December 1920. To protect the German film industry, import
quotas were regularly determined starting in 1921. After negotiations with representatives of the German film industry about the quota for the first year, its distribution
among German distribution companies was fixed at the beginning of March 1921.

So was Chaplin an unknown in Germany? When he visited Berlin in March
1931, German distributor Fritz Knevels told *Film-Kurier* that he (Knevels) had distributed the first, unnamed Chaplin film in Germany in 1915. The report stated:
"[This film] was a flop at the time. No one recognized Charlie Chaplin's high art, so
Knevels had the film shown in more than 100 front-line cinemas in a row. He had
a photograph sent to him of every major screening to prove to his German friends
that the soldiers were shaken by sidesplitting laughter when the Chaplin film was
shown."[5] So far, this could not be confirmed,[6] and the following also contradicts it:
British front-line soldiers had brought life-size Chaplin advertising displays with the
slogan "He's here!" and placed them over their trenches to make the German soldiers
laugh—in vain, because they did not know Chaplin. Later, it was no different with
Chaplin figurines, which U.S. volunteers of German origin brought over to brighten
their dugouts.[7] And German soldiers who were U.S. POWs apparently still did not
know Chaplin films (see below).

Nevertheless, by then there had been numerous German reports about Chaplin since late 1915, so at least people knew his name. By 1919, possibly via illegal import, animated cartoons featuring Chaplin's Tramp reached Germany. The following year, German artists and intellectuals called for Chaplin's own films, some of which they had watched in neighboring European countries after the end of World War I. Chaplin's movies were thus eagerly awaited. *Chaplin läuft Rollschuh* (*The Rink*, 1916) was his first film to be released to the cinemas of the Weimar Republic. Its premiere took place on August 30, 1921, in Berlin's glamorous Ufa-Palast am Zoo as a supporting program to an Asta Nielsen feature film.[8] This was quickly followed by other short Chaplin come-

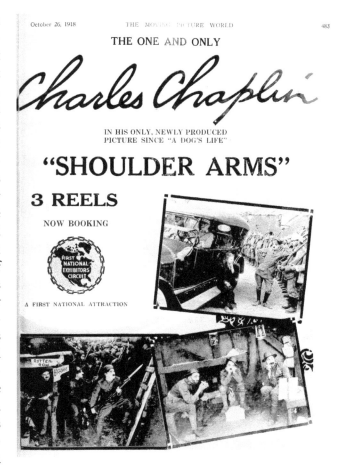

First National ad for *Shoulder Arms, Moving Picture World*, October 26, 1918.

dies, which triggered a wave of enthusiasm and took German audiences by storm. Chaplin's name was also a trademark, and therefore the German distribution titles always contained "Chaplin" until 1925. Throughout the German press, Chaplin's art became the subject of countless publications, the scope and content of which is unparalleled to this day. In its wake, merchandising articles such as Chaplin figurines and collectible pictures came onto the market. In a short time, Chaplin films had become a lucrative economic factor in Germany. After Ernst Matray had first appeared in Chaplin-like guise in a German short film in the summer of 1920, German short films with downright Chaplin impersonators such as Arcadi Boytler, Ferry Frank, Ernst Wanner and Ernst Bosser appeared on the German film market starting at the end of 1921.

Already in July 1922, Tucholsky called Chaplin the "most famous man in the world":

No parliamentarian is the most famous man in the world and no politician, neither Wilson nor Poincaré—no inventor is, no tenor, no airplane pilot. The most famous man is undoubtedly Mr. Charlie Chaplin, at whom everybody has laughed at least once: the Parisians and the

Londoners, all the Americans and the Australian sailors, the visitors to the Chinese cinemas and recently also the Germans, the old continent and the new one—and that the Martians have not laughed at him yet is only due to the poor connection to this cinema-less planet.[9]

This complex development has been traced in detail in this author's 2014 book *Charlie Chaplin in Deutschland 1915–1924—Der Tramp kommt ins Kino* (Charlie Chaplin in Germany 1915–1924—The Tramp Comes to the Movies).[10]

Chaplin Movies and Völkischer Beobachter in Southern Germany

As the southern German film market had already been important since the Kaiser Empire, the reintroduction of film censorship in the Weimar Republic in the late spring of 1920 resulted in the establishment of Film-Prüfstellen (Boards of Films Censors) in Berlin and Munich.[11] Film trade journals published in Berlin, such as the *Film-Kurier* and the *Lichtbildbühne*, only sporadically included southern German film news. To keep up to date, journalists and those interested in film could, however, obtain information about the southern German film market from regional trade journals. From 1919 until the fall of 1922, the *Deutsche Lichtspiel-Zeitung* was published in Munich. In early 1919, *Der deutsche Film in Wort und Bild* had also been launched as a "journal for the entire cinema industry" with Josef Aubinger as editor-in-chief, whose "Münchener Brief" had been a column of the *Lichtbildbühne*. In April 1922, this southern German had to cease publication, but from November of that year it was continued, again with Aubinger as editor-in-chief, by the *Süddeutsche Filmzeitung*, which was renamed *Deutsche Filmzeitung* at the beginning of 1928 and remained on the market until the end of 1941.

The first Chaplin films in southern Germany were screened on November 3, 1921, in Munich's Sendlingertor-Lichtspiele at the Hansa-Film-Verleih G.m.b.H. trade show for cinema operators. The distributor presented the 1916/17 Mutual two-reelers *Chaplin läuft Rollschuh, Chaplin als Sträfling* (*The Adventurer*) and *Die Chaplin-Quelle* (*The Cure*),[12] which had already proved to be crowd-pleasers elsewhere in Germany. They made Chaplin famous in southern Germany as well. Subsequently, in mid–January 1922, *Chaplin bei der Feuerwehr* (*The Fireman*), another 1916 Mutual production, had a press screening in the Sendlingertor-Lichtspiele.[13] Southern German audiences, however, probably first became acquainted with Chaplin in early December 1922 through his 1916 Mutual two-reeler *Chaplin auf der Walze* (*The Vagabond*). It was the first Chaplin film mentioned by the *Süddeutsche Filmzeitung*.[14]

By then, the Berlin Film-Prüfstelle had already approved no fewer than 22 Chaplin short subjects (one- and two-reelers) for public screening in Germany. By the end of May 1923, the number had increased to 31. Meanwhile, the *Süddeutsche Filmzeitung* had reported on 15 Chaplin films.[15] Shortly before Christmas 1923, the Chaplin classic *The Kid* (1921), which had already been praised by the German press as the "greatest commercial film in the world"[16] and touted as "the World Film,"[17] was screened in Munich's Sendlingertor- and Rathaus-Lichtspiele.[18]

The *Münchener Beobachter* newspaper had been published in Munich since early August 1919. In 1920, it was acquired by the Nationalsozialistischer Deutscher Arbeiterverein (National Socialist German Workers' Association), renamed the *Völkischer Beobachter*, and published by Adolf Hitler as the "Kampfblatt der national-sozialistischen Bewegung Großdeutschlands" (Propaganda journal of the National Socialist Movement in Greater Germany). Its editors were called "Schriftleiter," but this was a common term in the press of the Weimar Republic. After Hitler's takeover, the term was given a Nazi connotation by the "Schriftleitergesetz" (Editors Act). From the beginning, the *Völkischer Beobachter* was the mouthpiece of massive anti–Semitic smear attacks. Like German-ethnic circles, the journal did not make any distinction between Jews and Bolshevism, which was equally fraught. At the beginning of October 1920, this slogan appeared: "Judentum und Bolschewismus sind eins" (Judaism and Bolshevism are one).[19] This combination was to recur constantly in the arguments of the Nazis. In *Mein Kampf*, Hitler wrote: "In Russian Bolshevism we have seen the 20th century attempt of Judaism to seize world domination."[20] This was common to ultra-right and ethnical-racial circles as well. Also in October, the *Völkischer Beobachter* ran the headline "Auf dem Weg zum jüdischen Filmmonopol" (On the Way to a Jewish Film Monopoly).[21] "Filmjuden" (Film-Jews) were attacked.[22] In the Weimar Republic, the headlines of the Nazi propaganda journal included "Ufa und jüdisches Finanzkapital" (Ufa and Jewish Finance Capital),[23] "Die Film-Verjudung" (Film Judaization),[24] "Jüdische Finanzdiktatur beim Film" (Jewish Financial Dictatorship in Film)[25] and "Jüdische Filmdiktatur in Amerika und England" (Jewish Film Dictatorship in America and England).[26] The "verjudete" (Judaized) film was to be replaced by the ethnic-German film and represent the German essence, which was not to be further corroded by foreign, "Jewish-Bolshevik" influences. For this reason, the Nazis, during the so-called "Systemzeit" (System Period), as they contemptuously referred to the period of the Weimar Republic, also fought German films that did not take action against the "Weltdiffamierung des Deutschen Volkes" (International Defamation of the German People).[27]

For the time being, the *Völkischer Beobachter* only sporadically covered movies. The reason was banal: The journal could not afford cinema tickets. Film screenings were therefore only attended if the editorial staff received free tickets. At the beginning of the 1920s, this apparently happened rarely.[28] The *Völkischer Beobachter* also lacked the funds to regularly subscribe to other southern German newspapers and film trade journals. Moreover, by October 14, 1921, the *Völkischer Beobachter* had just completed five periods of police bans from publication. This was followed, from May 24, 1923, by three further, shorter periods of 21 days of ban in total. As a result of the Hitler Putsch, both the *Völkischer Beobachter* and the NSDAP were banned altogether on November 10, 1923. Subsequently, the Nazi propaganda journal ceased publication. After the re-establishment of the NSDAP on February 27, 1925, Hitler's party organ also returned to the market on April 3, 1925, after 510 days of absence.[29] In the period from October 15, 1921, to May 23, 1923, the *Völkischer Beobachter* could have reported on films in southern Germany. The political turmoil surrounding the existence of the *Völkischer Beobachter*, however, probably relegated the importance of film news to the background to a large extent, apart from actions against politically particularly disliked films such as *Nathan der Weise* in March

1923 (see Chapter 5). The *Völkischer Beobachter*'s regular coverage of films did not begin until after its re-launch in April 1925, when temporarily no new Chaplin films were released. But in the first quarter of 1926, after the German premiere of the next Chaplin film, the *Völkischer Beobachter* attacked Chaplin (see below).

German Nationalist Prelude: Shoulder Arms

The *Völkischer Beobachter* had apparently also missed the Chaplin lecture with which the film journalist Heinz Udo Brachvogel had opened the trade show of November 3, 1921. Brachvogel, who was successively press director of several German film companies[30] and is said to have known Chaplin personally, openly addressed rumors that circulated about Chaplin's alleged Germanophobia. Chaplin as a Germanophobe—that would have been exactly after the *Völkischer Beobachter*'s fancy even at that time. Yet, nothing could be gleaned about the exact content of such rumors from the coverage of the trade show by the trade journal *Der deutsche Film in Wort und Bild*. In any case, Brachvogel explained to those present that it was a pure invention.[31]

It seems also possible that the reference to an unnamed and undescribed film did not provide a sufficient target for the *Völkischer Beobachter*. The Munich-based right-wing *München-Ausburger Abendzeitung*, which is likely to have followed the coverage in *Deutsche Lichtspiel-Zeitung*, may have taken a similar stance. When this trade journal announced in August 1921 that the leading actor of a U.S. film considered Germanophobe was planning to visit Germany, the *München-Ausburger Abendzeitung* immediately reacted allergically (see Chapter 5). On the other hand, neither the *Deutsche Lichtspiel-Zeitung* nor *Der deutsche Film in Wort und Bild* dropped a line about the allegedly Germanophobe Chaplin film. Probably for this reason, the *München-Ausburger Abendzeitung* did not respond to it and did not address the issue a little later when Bremen and Berlin newspapers scolded Chaplin for this film (see below).[32] The newspaper also wrote nothing about the first two Chaplin films, *Die Chaplinquelle* and *Chaplin läuft Rollschuh*, which were shown in Augsburg in December 1921 as a

Heinz Udo Brachvogel, 1929.

supporting program to the 1921 feature films *Im Rausche der Macht* (*I Hatets Bojor*, August Blom) and *Sappho* (Dimitri Buchowetzki), made in Denmark and Germany, respectively.[33]

Most likely, Brachvogel had referred to Chaplin's anti-war film *Shoulder Arms*. It had been released to U.S. cinemas on October 20, 1918, a few weeks before the Compiègne Armistice Agreement on November 11, 1918, which ended the combat operations of World War I. on October 28, 1918, daytime strip "Benny Is Quite an Elaborate Dreamer" of the short-lived screwball newspaper comic strip Balmy Benny by Gene Ahern appeared, in which Private Benny dreams that he helps Tramp Charlie capture the German Kaiser and the Crown Prince during the war.[34] U.S. reviews of the film at the time were excellent and did not indulge patriotism, despite the imminent victory in World War I. The trade journal *Variety* stated: "Chaplin has done his best with *Shoulder Arms*. More than his other films, this one will silence the critics. Charlie Chaplin in uniform, without hat or sticks, reveals what a great comedian he is." *Variety* also suggested Chaplin's film would have arguably had an even greater impact had it been released after World War I.[35] When *Shoulder Arms* was re-released in July 1922, *The New York Times* called it one of the "few war films to outlast the war."[36] The prediction had hit the mark.

Chaplin's film provoked nervous reactions in the Weimar Republic from anti-republican circles loyal to the Kaiser, who never recovered from the collapse of the German Empire. They felt their political home to be in the national conservative Deutschnationale Volkspartei (German National People's Party), DNVP for short, founded on November 24, 1918, as a successor to the Deutschkonservative Partei (German Conservative Party). This party was extremely nationalist, national liberalist, anti–Semitic, ethnic and monarchist-restorative. The term "deutschnational" stood for "völkisch" (ethnic) and "vaterländisch" (nationalistic).[37] For the Nazis, the attitudes of German nationalist circles were fertile ground.

In 1928, the media entrepreneur and industrialist Alfred Hugenberg became chairman of the DNVP. Among other things, he ruled over an extensive newspaper empire, including Scherl-Verlag since 1916, as well as the Ufa since 1927. In 1891, Hugenberg had co-founded the Alldeutscher Verband (All-German Association) in the German Empire, which was particularly effective in promoting ethnic agitation. Its program was militaristic, nationalistic, racist and anti–Semitic, seeking the

Balmy Benny newspaper strip, October 28, 1918: "Benny Is Quite an Elaborate Dreamer," by Gene Ahern.

greatest possible unification of ethnic–Germans in a state that would
expand its territory and needed new
areas of settlement for this purpose.
For the Reichstag election on July
31, 1932, the DNVP competed with
the NSDAP for the right-wing elec-
torate. Hugenberg was one of the
trailblazers of Nazism and, for a
few months, was a member of Hitler's first cabinet as Reichsminister für Wirtschaft, Ernährung
und Landwirtschaft (Reich Minister of Economics, Alimenta-
tion and Agriculture). He later
sold Ufa to the Nazi state.[38] In June
1933, the DNVP, which until then
had been represented by deputies
in the Reichstag, dissolved itself.
These deputies then switched to the
NSDAP parliamentary group.

Since the German nationalist offensive on Chaplin's *Shoulder Arms* coincided in content with
the Nazis' attacks on the film that
started in the spring of 1927, its
beginning and development is of
importance here.

Milwaukee Journal, **November 17, 1918: "Charlie Chaplin in *Shoulder Arms* Who Made the Kaiser Quit," last panel, cartoon by unknown artist
(Archives de Montreux, PP-75 Fonds Charles
Chaplin, Roy Export Co. Ltd.).**

Outrage in Bremen and Berlin

Brachvogel's precautionary warning not to misjudge *Shoulder Arms* was all
too justified. On November 18, 1921, a few days after the Munich trade show, *Chaplin läuft Rollschuh* was released in Bremen cinemas, including the Kaiser Theater.
An instant hit, Chaplin's two-reeler was prolonged until early December "by popular demand": "The famous American comedian […] intends to continue to make us
laugh for some time."[39]

But German nationalist columnist Fritz von Holz did not feel like laughing at
all when he learned that *Shoulder Arms* was being shown in London at the same
time. Was Fritz von Holz possibly the slightly different name of the German nationalist, anti–Semitic writer Friedrich Carl Holtz who had called for support for the
Kapp Putsch in 1920? This could not be established, but the following seems remarkable. From December 1918 to December 1922, Holtz had published the weekly *Hamburger Warte*, which was close to the paramilitary front fighters' association Der

Stahlhelm (the Steel Helmet) and had been banned due to an incendiary article on the murder of Walther Rathenau. In March 1931, Holtz claimed in the fascist weekly *Fridericus*, which he subsequently published, to have commented on Chaplin's September 1921 visit to Berlin that there was no reason to take "special notice" of the "little windbag" Chaplin (see Chapter 3).[40] However, nothing has been found about this in the *Hamburger Warte*.[41]

Von Holz called for a boycott of Chaplin films by the "entire population" as an "imperative of national self-evidence" in his bilious article "Nationale Würde auch im Film!" (National Dignity in Film too!) in the Bremer Nachrichten of December 9, 1921:

> Chaplin has been one of the most active men in wartime propaganda against Germany, and even now he is active in agitation against Germany. [… *Shoulder Arms*] is one of the most hateful smear films of the war period. The German army, the Kaiser, the Crown Prince and Hindenburg are ridiculed in it. German officers and soldiers act as they had been portrayed by our enemies' atrocity propaganda during the war: brutal abuse of prisoners, attempted rape of French women, after their capture by the enemy, German officers are mistreated by their own subordinates. At the end, Chaplin kicks the captured Kaiser. All German-conscious men and women refuse energetically to see a film in which this "Subjekt" [Creature] Chaplin appears. Cinema operators who find out about it should have so much sense of decency and purity that they refuse to show such a film from the outset. […] Never again Chaplin films![42]

There seemed to have been no Bremen boycott of Chaplin films. From mid–March 1922, *Chaplin als Sträfling* was shown in several Bremen cinemas and was also prolonged "because of the roaring laughter" until it was replaced at the end of the month by *Chaplin schiebt Klaviere* (*His Musical Career*, 1914).[43]

Friedrich Carl Holtz (1921). Is he Fritz von Holz?

But von Holz's article was grist to the mill of the German nationalist Berliner *Börsen-Zeitung*. In mid–December 1921, it welcomed the fact that Chaplin had shown "his true colors" as a Germanophobe agitator. Without calling for a boycott, it joined the protest "wholeheartedly and without further comment."[44] That year, Walther Funk had become editor-in-chief of the *Berliner Börsen-Zeitung*, which he headed until 1930. In 1931, he joined the NSDAP, became Hitler's personal economic advisor the following year, was the first Reichspressechef (Reich Press Chief) in the Third Reich and, from 1939 on, Reichsbankpräsident (President of the Reichsbank)—one of the main war criminals sentenced to life imprisonment for crimes against humanity at the Nuremberg trial.[45]

In early June 1926, the newspaper called for "the coalition of the right-wing movement" in a shift away from parliamentarism.[46] In 1930, the *Berliner Börsen-Zeitung* celebrated its 75th anniversary. In its lavish Festschrift, Dr. Richard Jügler, head of the newspaper's political section, lamented the collapse of the Kaiserreich and pointed out that "the criminal lie of German war guilt[47] was fought through the pens of our most competent colleagues." He demanded the revision of the "disgraceful Versailles verdict" with its "dishonest madness," the rescission of territorial changes, and Germany's return to power with own colonies and with an "intact" Wehrmacht.[48]

Most of the German nationalists, who were fighting Chaplin and *Shoulder Arms*, knew the film only from reports and hearsay. If they had viewed the film somewhere, they would have realized that the attacks on it were completely unfounded. The film is in no way spitefully directed against Germany. Chaplin rather puts the emphasis of the plot on depicting the hardships of the soldiers in the waterlogged shelters and their dreams of a comfortable home. In his case, merely a few German soldiers are dimwitted bearded hunks, only two of them chunky and only one with a big bushy beard. The majority, however, look as normal as they act. The young soldier, who prefers to lie down and has had enough of the war when the hut of the French girl collapses, seems downright human. Only their leaders are vicious, like the somewhat undersized officer who bullies his subordinates. Therefore, Charlie feels solidarity with the German soldiers he has captured. He hands out cigarettes, and only the diminutive German officer contemptuously accepts them and throws them to the ground. A "grave offense" given the short supply of cigarettes during the war! Charlie then spanks the officer, and the soldiers thank him, shaking hands. Chaplin also does not portray the German Kaiser Wilhelm II as a bloodthirsty monster. Only when the Kaiser treats Charlie arrogantly, does Charlie kick him. Rather than Chaplin's caricatured portrayal of the Crown Prince, the lifestyle of the aristocrat, who drinks champagne and smokes from a long cigarette holder in the middle of the war, could have raised a fuss. *Shoulder Arms* also does not intend to be a realistic factual account, let alone nationalistic propaganda. The film is

Walther Funk, editor-in-chief of *Berliner Börsen-Zeitung,* **1933.**

just a dream: At the end, Charlie, who just a moment ago seemed to be a celebrated war hero, is seen sleeping in a tent on a cot, shaken out of sleep by his comrades.

On the other hand, there was occasionally objective reporting in Germany in connection with *Shoulder Arms*. This was the case in November 1921 when the *Lichtbildbühne* reported on a lawsuit against Chaplin based on a news item in the

Screen shot from *Shoulder Arms*: German soldiers express their gratefulness to Charlie (*Shoulder Arms* © Roy Export S.A.S.).

Screen shot from *Shoulder Arms*: Charlie has captured the Kaiser, the Crown Prince and Hindenburg (*Shoulder Arms* © Roy Export S.A.S.).

U.S. trade journal *Variety*.⁴⁹ In the U.S., screenwriter Leo Loeb had sued him to pay $50,000 because he allegedly had used Loeb's script "The Rookie" for *Shoulder Arms*.⁵⁰ Loeb's action was dismissed in late December 1921 because he was not allowed to sue Chaplin, a British citizen, in the U.S.⁵¹ This did not prevent Loeb from reopening the case, on which the *Lichtbildbühne* reported in June 1924.⁵² In his deposition for the District Court, Southern District of New York, Syd Chaplin had testified in May of that year that his brother had not learned of Loeb's "The Rookie" until long after the filming of *Shoulder Arms* had ended. Chaplin had developed the story of the film during production without any script. This corresponded to Chaplin's account in the lawsuit,⁵³ in which Loeb finally failed in 1927.

Eydtkuhner Grenzzeitung *and "German-Eater"*
in a U.S. POW Camp Screening

On April 5, 1922, the East Prussian local newspaper *Eydtkuhner Grenzzeitung* turned *Shoulder Arms* completely fact-free into a Germanophobe tendency film with the curious article "Die Rache des Verschmähten" (Revenge of the Spurned). In the same month, the German-Jewish film journalist Egon Jacobsohn quoted in his remarkable and ad-free magazine *Film-Hölle* (Movie Hell) from this newspaper under the headline "Auch Charlie Chaplin hetzt gegen Deutschland? Herstellung eines Filmes gegen Germany" (Does Charlie Chaplin also agitate against Germany? Production of a Film Directed against Germany).⁵⁴ According to the *Eydtkuhner Grenzzeitung*, of which no archival holdings seem to exist,⁵⁵ Chaplin was a barber by profession. Because he was treated like a stranger during his 1921 Berlin visit, he had wanted to take revenge on Germany. The article continued: "At the moment, Chaplin is having a film produced in South America called *Gewehr über*. In it, the old German army, the Kaiser, the Crown Prince, and Hindenburg are dragged through the mud. Even the old rubbish stories about officers and soldiers offending French women are dug out again. The film Figaro has stated that this is only the first installment in a large-scale, French-funded smear campaign against Germany."

Nothing of this article, reproduced in full in Appendix 2, is true. Chaplin was not a barber, *Shoulder Arms* had already premiered in October 1918, the filming had not taken place in South America, and the film had not, after all, been a French-funded "first installment of a large-scale propaganda campaign." The author of the *Eydtkuhner Grenzzeitung* could have read in the July 1921 *Lichtbildbühne* that *Shoulder Arms* had long since been screened in theaters and had grossed $880,000 in North America.⁵⁶ Chaplin's visit to Berlin had also not been without any press attention either.⁵⁷ Jacobsohn therefore did not hide that he considered the report of the *Eydtkuhner Grenzzeitung* to be cheap propaganda: "The claim of the local rag [...] is certainly one of the slanders with which numerous film stars who have become annoying have been showered recently."

But what would Jacobsohn have said if only two days later, on April 7, 1922, he had read in the trade journal *Westdeutsche Film-Zeitung* the even more hostile article "Charlie Chaplin als Deutschenfresser" (Charlie Chaplin as "German-Eater").

According to the trade journal, Chaplin's "Germanophobe trash and smear film of French origin, now running in South America under the title 'Arma al hombro' (Gewehr über!)," supposedly did "not lack outrages by German officers, rapes of French women, etc., etc.": "The Kaiser, the Crown Prince, and Hindenburg are dragged through all the excremental puddles of French cinematic imagination, captured at the end by Charlie Chaplin and paraded for the special amusement of the American troops."[58]

Neither the *Eydtkuhner Grenzzeitung* nor the *Westdeutsche Film-Zeitung* reported that the film told of a dream. With a few exceptions, the content of *Shoulder Arms* was never properly presented in Germany until the end of the Third Reich. On the contrary, in 1925, screenwriter and later Ufa press chief Waldemar Lydor[59] again dismissed *Shoulder Arms* as "Hun propaganda." In his *Film-Kurier* article "My First Chaplin Film," he recalled being a U.S. POW in France. One evening, he and his fellow German prisoners were invited to a Red Cross movie show at the camp by their U.S. guards, who treated them with great camaraderie. A drama and *Shoulder Arms* were screened. At that time, Chaplin was unknown to Lydor, so he asked who Chaplin was. He was told, "ecstatically and reproachfully at the same time": "Oh, you don't know Chaplin? He's funny! He's the best comedian in the States. Even in England, every child knows him!"

In *Shoulder Arms*, Lydor disliked that clumsy Charlie rescues a Belgian girl "from the rough fists of crude Boches" (i.e., "pig," then a common French swearword for Germans), that a small German lieutenant "dines at a lusciously decorated table […] with accompanying champagne," the German soldiers with their "long beards and fat bellies" were portrayed as "vile scoundrels" and Charlie finally captured "Kaiser, Crown Prince and Hindenburg," "who were met with kicks by their enemies." Lydor concluded: "Chaplin's art is certainly exceptional, but this 'funny' parody of a nation was still too strange for us. Therefore, we distinctly told our American guards our opinion about this 'Hun propaganda'! Nevertheless, they were honestly dismayed by this, because they took the story only from the humorous side and did not want to offend us, especially since they did not know the content of the Chaplin film before the screening."[60]

Lydor, on the other hand, apparently regarded the comedy seriously. Therefore, he also succumbed to the temptation to exaggerate the actions of German soldiers and officers and to distort *Shoulder Arms* as a smear film. Lydor also could not recall some details quite accurately. The diminutive German lieutenant toasted the current day in the pouring rain in the German trenches, but did not dine there with relish. Chaplin did also not portray the "Boches" with long beards and big bellies "as low-down scoundrels." Apart from the attempted rape by a German officer, prevented by Charlie, there is no evidence of any perfidy on the part of the German soldiers. They do capture Charlie's comrade, who is then to be summarily shot. This was hardly humiliating treatment in war. An enemy soldier on the other side's territory was pretty much considered a spy, facing the death penalty.

Initially, France, Great Britain and Switzerland were the only European countries to which the screening rights of *Shoulder Arms* were sold in October and December 1918. Starting on April 20, 1919, *Shoulder Arms* was shown at the Paris

Gaumont Palace as well as in ten other cinemas in the city.[61] This made the film quite accessible to Germans, too. Probably the greatest influence from 1919 onwards in French journals came from Louis Delluc, who published his book *Charlot* in 1921.[62] Although Chaplin films boomed in Germany beginning in late summer 1921, no German distributor acquired German screening rights for *Shoulder Arms*—probably because of the well-known animosities toward the film. Licenses for *Shoulder Arms* were also not sold to Austria and Hungary as successors to the Danube monarchy, which had also lost World War I. As of December 1931, Finland, Poland,

(Dates furnished by Vogel Productions, Inc. to Dec. 1931
Picture: SHOULDER ARMS (F.N. means distributed by Associated First Nat'l Pic. Inc.)

TERRITORY	RELEASE DATE	DUE	DELIVERY DATE	NOTE
United States	Dec. 16, 1918	Dec. 16, 1923	Dec. 16, 1923	
Canada	" " "	" " "	" " "	
1 Great Britian	Dec. 2, 1918	Dec. 2,1923		
2 France	Oct. 11,.1918	Oct. 11,1923		
3 Belgium	Nov. 21,1919 Feb.13 '20	Nov. 21,1924, Feb.13, 1925		
4 Switzerland	Oct. 11, 1918	Oct. 11,1923		
5 Holland	Censored			
6 Norway	Feb. 9, 1920	Feb. 9,1925		
7 Sweden	Nov. 30,1920	Nov. 30,1925		
8 Denmark	Jan. 31, 1920	Jan. 31,1925		
9 Finland	....	....		
10 Spain	Mar. 9,1919	Mat 9,1924		
11 Portugal		"		
12 Germany	....	....		
13 Russia	....	....		
14 Italy	Feb. 16,1927	Feb. 16,1932		
15 Balkans	....	....		
16 Egypt	Feb. 19,1919	Feb. 19,1924		
17 Jugo Slavia	....	....		
18 Austria Hungary	....	....		
19 Poland	....	....		
20 Czecho Slavakia	Sep. 5, 1924	Set. 5, 1929		
21 Japan	Dec. 19,1918	Dec. 19,1923		
22 China	Feb. 8,1919	Feb. 8,1924		
23 Philippines	Jan. 24,1919	Jan. 24, 1924		
24 India	Apr. 17,1919	Apr. 19,1924		
25 Burma	"	"		
26 Ceylon	"	"		
27 Dutch East Indies	Mar. 13, 1919	Mar. 13, 1924		
28 Straits Settlements				
29 Fed.Malay States	"	"		
30 French Indo China	"	"		
31 Siam	"	"		
32 Australia	Oct. 29,1918	Oct. 29, 1923		
33 New Zealand	"	"		
34 South Africa	Feb. 12,1923	Feb. 12, 1928		
35 West Indies	Oct. 28,1918	Oct. 28, 1923		
36 Columbia	"	"		
37 Venzuela	"	"		
38 Central America	"	"		
39 Mexico	Apr. 2,1919	Apr. 2,1924		
40 Brazil	July 22,1919	July 22.1924		
41 Argentina	Oct. 31,1918	Oct. 31,1923		
42 Paraguay	"	"		
43 Uruguay				
44 Chile	Nov. 1,1918	Nov. 1,1923		
45 Peru	....	....		
46 Bolivia	....	....		
47 Ecuador	....	....		

Red underline indicates delivery dates, therefore release date is about 2 or 3 months later, advancing the due date accordingly.

Worldwide sales of *Shoulder Arms* as of December 1931 (Charlie Chaplin Archive, digitized by Cineteca di Bologna, www.charliechaplinarchive.org).

Yugoslavia and other Balkan states had also not acquired any screening rights. The Soviet Union did not purchase Chaplin rights at all for many years.[63]

Therefore, it is not true that *Shoulder Arms* was banned in Germany, as Gerith von Ulm, Sabine Hake and Simon Louvish claimed in 1940, 1990 and 2009, respectively, without providing any sources. Von Ulm even wrote of an immediate ban on the film after a one-time German screening.[64] Because the film was not imported, it was never reviewed by the Berlin and Munich Film-Prüfstelle[65]—nor, for that matter, was Chaplin's 1918 *The Bond*, in which Charlie knocks down the Kaiser with a giant mallet. German moviegoers had to wait for *Shoulder Arms* until well after the end of World War II. In the fall of 1957, a heavily abridged version, intermixed with several other films, was shown in Federal German cinemas as part of the unauthorized Chaplin compilation *Das waren noch Zeiten*.[66] GDR Chaplin fans had to wait much longer. *Shoulder Arms* was not shown there until March 7, 1981, on the TV program of DDR2.[67]

The Gold Rush

With *The Kid*, Chaplin had succeeded in blending the apparent contrasts of tragedy and comedy that would henceforth characterize his films. But with *The Gold Rush,* which premiered in the U.S. on June 26, 1925, he achieved an extraordinary artistic unity. Chaplin had once again been ahead of his time and had set new standards in film comedy. His masterpiece spans a gold-digging adventure to a love story rife with hurt, confusion and misunderstanding, and still results in a happy ending. The emphasis on emotion also found its way into the films of such famous U.S. comedians as Harold Lloyd, Buster Keaton, Larry Semon and Harry Langdon.[68] U.S. critic Walter Kerr called *The Gold Rush* and Buster Keaton's 1926 feature film *The General*, co-directed with Clyde Bruckman, the only two comedy epics that silent film had created.[69]

The Gold Rush is set at the end of the 19th century, at the time of the gold rush in Alaska. Charlie is woefully under-equipped to fight snow and ice. But he is all the more confident for it. On a mountain pass, he gets caught in a snowstorm and is able to save himself in a mountain cabin. Still, this dwelling is ruled by the criminal Black Larsen, who is wanted by the police. The situation comes to a head when the gold prospector Big Jim McKay joins Larsen and Charlie. Big Jim is on his way to the rich gold mine he had discovered. At the cabin, the three fated companions are united by unbridled hunger. Since they have absolutely nothing to eat in the wasteland, they draw lots to see which of them will find food. Larsen's is drawn; he must go out into the hostile environment. Left behind hungrily in the cabin, Charlie cooks one of his shoes, trying to calm the terribly growling stomachs. By virtue of his imagination, Charlie enjoys his shoe piece by piece, like a gourmet. Big Jim, on the other hand, goes crazy with hunger and soon deliriously thinks Charlie is a giant chicken that he wants to slaughter and consume immediately. Then a bear bursts into the cabin and becomes Charlie's savior, because Big Jim now lets go of him. Charlie is able to shoot the bear, and they finally get a real meal. After that, they go their separate ways.

Big Jim meets Larsen, who has already killed two policemen, at his gold mine. Now, he also gives Big Jim short shrift and hits him over his head with a shovel. Big Jim loses his memory and no longer knows the location of his gold mine. But Larsen's success is only fleeting: The gold mine lies near an abyss that crumbles away, and Larsen plummets to his death.

Charlie, meanwhile, has had a more peaceful time. He has come to the nearest gold settlement and has fallen in love with the beautiful Georgia in the jerkwater town's saloon. She even dances with him, but only to make her beau Jack Cameron jealous. Later, while frolicking in the snow with her friends, she comes upon the cabin of engineer Hank Curtis. Charlie is looking after Hank's cabin while Hank is on an expedition. On a whim, Georgia accepts Charlie's invitation to spend New Year's Eve with her friends at his place. So he shovels snow in the village to earn some money for the upcoming purchases, and enthusiastically decorates the cabin. But the ladies have long forgotten the invitation and are celebrating in the saloon instead. In a dream, Charlie sees them coming and performs the dance of the rolls for them. But the sad reality soon catches up with him. Dejected, he makes his way back to the saloon. In the meantime, Georgia has remembered the invitation. Full of high spirits, the group of girls sets off with Jack to the cabin to tease Charlie. At the cabin, Georgia realizes how much she must have hurt Charlie. Jack wants to steal a kiss from her, but she, still feeling her remorse, rebuffs Jack with a slap in the face.

The desperate Big Jim comes to the settlement. He hopes to find Charlie, because only he can show him the way to his gold mine. Meanwhile, in line with the plot of the silent version of the film, Georgia writes an apology letter to Jack in the saloon, assuring him that she loves him. She hands the letter to a waiter, who delivers it to Jack. Jack reacts with scorn and tells the waiter to pass it to Charlie, who has just entered the saloon. Charlie, of course, thinks that Georgia's letter is meant for him and, overjoyed and impetuous, confesses his love to Georgia, who reacts with consternation. Big Jim has already discovered Charlie and drags the him away to then set off for the gold mine. In Chaplin's 1942 sound version, this sequence of events has been considerably shortened to show that Georgia's letter is actually intended for Charlie. Georgia's reaction to Charlie's confession of love therefore seems incomprehensible. In general, the sound version contains a few more cuts, and the intertitles have been removed because the commentary spoken by Chaplin himself in the original American version of the reissue made them superfluous.

Big Jim and Charlie reach Black Larsen's abandoned cabin. During the night, a mighty storm comes up and sweeps them toward a chasm. At the last second, they can save themselves, and Big Jim recognizes his gold mine: The storm had blown them there. Now, Big Jim and Charlie are millionaires who can afford to sail to Europe in the luxury cabin of a passenger ship. On board are reporters who ask Charlie to pose for the camera once again in his tattered gold-mining clothes for their coverage. Through a mishap, he falls onto steerage, right at the feet of Georgia, who, full of disappointment, also wants to go to Europe. She thinks Charlie, whose wealth she does not yet know about, is the stowaway they are searching the ship for. Since she does not want him to be locked up, she even offers to pay for his passage. Both realize their true feelings for each other. The misunderstanding about the supposed stowaway Charlie soon clears up. Charlie introduces Georgia to the stunned reporters as his fiancée, and with a kiss, the film fades into the closing title—in the silent version, because in the sound version, the film ends before the kiss.

On Its Way to German Cinemas

In the German film trade press, *The Gold Rush* was preceded by a lot of news: Had the film been completed, would it be about Chaplin's career "from poor boy to multimillionaire," had Chaplin been offered $35,000 for the Chicago screening alone, and would he travel to European premieres of the film, probably including Berlin?[70] After the U.S. premiere in late August 1925, *Lichtbildbühne* reported extensively that *The Gold Rush* was "a smash hit" blessed with "an overabundance of amusing detail."[71] Around the time of preparations for the German release, U.S. distributor United Artists was just finishing setting up its own branch in Germany.[72] In August 1925, it was decided to invest in a newly founded German distributor, the Ifa-Film-Verleih GmbH.[73]

Meanwhile, *The Gold Rush* had already been released in France. The German-Jewish expressionist writer Walter Hasenclever[74] was living in the French capital in 1925 and regularly contributed to the Berlin *8 Uhr-Abendblatt—Nationalzeitung*. In early October 1925, he attended a Paris screening of Chaplin's film. His report "Charlies Geheimnis" (Charlie's Secret), reproduced in full in Appendix 2, appeared in the Berlin newspaper on October 9, 1925. In it, he characterized Chaplin as a Jew as early as the fall of 1925, before the *Jüdisches Lexikon* officially incorporated him as such in 1927. Hasenclever stated among other things:

> [Chaplin] is one of those fairy-tale characters beloved by children and animals. He has already become a mystique, a Homeric hero of the 20th century who inhabits the deified heaven. [...] As he trolls shadowy across the screen, he seems to be a poet's invention. Cervantes and Shakespeare gave birth to him. [...] Yes, who knows, if Jesus and Mohammed visited this oh so peaceful earth once again, they would perhaps appear in Charlie's guise at the pacifist congress. Bludgeoned down by all the diplomats, whom we imagine as the fat, big gentlemen from his films, they would proclaim to the sporting crowd: "Love your enemies!" [...] Every real fame has a deep justification. Chaplin comes from the ghetto. Nowhere does he deny this origin. He carries the symbols with him. He is the eternal Jew. Hence, his immense popularity. He embodies a character that we all know, because there is something of him in all of us. The oppressed world traveler and adventurer [...]. David before King Saul. [...] Thus, in his roles as the last upstart of the scattered people cursed to eternal restlessness, he continues his triumphal procession across the earth. He has conquered the new world and won back the old. [...] The tragic lives in the small things, in the heroic banality. Dramatists of all countries, learn from him![75]

Ifa-Film-Verleih GmbH's hopes of releasing the highly acclaimed film to the German market were dashed: *Goldrausch* ran into difficulties with the Berlin Film-Prüfstelle. These can only be partially traced, because its administrative files no longer exist and the censorship records for *Goldrausch* have also not been preserved. It is certain that *Goldrausch* was initially approved by the Berlin Film-Prüfstelle on October

20, 1925.[76] Very likely, the distributor had submitted the film in its original version with English intertitles—the usual procedure to save the cost of German adaptation if a film was already banned in its original version. Subsequently, German author Karl Vollmoeller wrote the German intertitles commissioned by the distributor, and thus *Goldrausch* had to be resubmitted to the Berlin Film-Prüfstelle. As reported by the *Film-Kurier*, Vollmoeller's editing had caused problems.[77] Vollmoeller is said to have met Chaplin personally during his stay in the USA in the mid-1920s and to have consorted with him.[78] For now, on October 30, 1925, the film was only approved in a version shortened by 80 meters.[79] It is no longer possible to determine which scenes had to be removed. Very likely, the distributor had Vollmoeller rework the German intertitles to avoid this cut. In any case, Ifa-Film-Verleih GmbH failed with this.

In the third round, the Berlin Film-Prüfstelle banned *Goldrausch* on December 22, 1925, because of five scenes with "subjectively brutalizing effect." This did not include the scene where Big Jim puts a knife to Charlie's throat, which elsewhere had caused concerns, but it did the scene where Black Larsen shoots the policemen and leaves them lying in the snow![80] Probably the Film-Prüfstelle also considered the thrilling moments in which Charlie and Big Jim hover over the abyss in the cabin to be a matter of concern, because it ruled that the film was so exciting overall that it could harm the health of young moviegoers. Both aspects could be a reason for banning the film under the "Lichtspielgesetz" (Film Act).[81] In the appeal proceedings, for which Vollmoeller edited the German intertitles a third time as a precaution,[82] the Film-Oberprüfstelle ordered a cut of the scene with Black Larsen and the policemen for its brutalizing effect and then, on January 9, 1926, finally approved Chaplin's film for juveniles as well. The Film-Oberprüfstelle pointed out that even young moviegoers could clearly recognize that *Goldrausch*, as a comedy, did not describe real life and that young audiences would therefore not take the exciting scenes at face value.[83]

Arrival and Attack

Heralded by the distributor as "The Film of Laughter in Tears,"[84] Chaplin's *Goldrausch* finally received its German premiere at Berlin's Capitol cinema on February 18, 1926, in the presence of numerous celebrities.[85] Almost everywhere, sometimes elegiac, rave reviews effusively praised the film. Among other things, it was said, "[t]he gold we mean is in the hearts of the people, [and] unfortunately we are absolutely not able to create anything remotely similar in Germany."[86] In *Die Weltbühne*, Chaplin admirer Hans Siemsen[87] believed *Goldrausch* to be such a complex movie that, in his opinion, an entire book could be written about it.[88]

In its film review of February 20, 1926, the Social Democratic *Vorwärts* regarded Chaplin's Tramp Charlie as a Jewish character. Had this newspaper followed Hasenclver's view without explicitly referring to him? The high praise that the *Vorwärts* paid to Chaplin and his film, comprised, among other things:

> At last, once again Charlie Chaplin and right away in his best works, whose inventor, director and actor he is in one person. Chaplin is an international superpower, the most famous film

actor in the world. But that would not say everything. He is not merely a grotesque comedian, like others, but he has created a new type, the poor Jew, pursued by misfortune, who, having been displaced to the gold country, must take up the fight with all the powers, a schlemiel who just barely escapes the threatening catastrophes or who, by his cleverness and agility, can cope even with the more robust and those physically far superior to him. He is basically the old joker who has appeared over and over again in every folk art since antiquity, but he has given it a new form and the social content that only modern capitalism could develop.[89]

The Communist *Rote Fahne*, central organ of the German Communist Party, KPD (section of the Communist International), on February 21, 1926, admired Chaplin as "friend of the working class," from which he came and considered *Goldrausch* his best film to date. It praised him as an exceptional artist whose film

GOLDRAUSCH
Uraufführung ab Freitag
Täglich 5.00, 7.00 und 9.15

Vorverkauf 12—2   Telephonische Bestellungen: Nollendorf 7098—99

Jugendliche haben Zutritt!

Ad for the German premiere of *Goldrausch* (*The Gold Rush*), February 18, 1926.

work, with the character Charlie as the "serious, tormented, set-back and oppressed man," was in its "deeper content [...] a piece of history of the oppressed class" and "whom Lenin, should he ever travel to the USA, wanted to meet in person."[90]

The German release of *Goldrausch* was accompanied by an issue of the popular program guide series *Illustrierter Film-Kurier*. In it, in addition to the usual description and cast information, Hasenclever's article "Charlies Geheimnis" and two statements from November 1925 by German-Jewish celebrities about Chaplin were reprinted.[91] Politician and publicist Maximilian Harden, who had converted from the Jewish faith to Christianity at the age of 16, was enthusiastic about Chaplin's "deep humanity" and called him a "master of genius." Harden wrote in the *Film-Kurier*, "Chaplin is for me the height of acting creative power and human impulsiveness."[92] Theater director Max Reinhardt was of Jewish origin, but very much assimilated into his Christian habitat. He sent Chaplin the following telegram in the fall of 1925 after attending a *Gold Rush* screening in the U.S.; the *Reichsfilmblatt* reproduced it: "I consider your art among the highest art of all. I love you."[93]

In November 1925, Scott Sidney's U.S. feature film *Charleys Tante* (*Charley's Aunt*) from the same year with Chaplin's half-brother Syd in the leading role had been screened in the Munich Sendlingertor-Lichtspiele. The *Völkischer Beobachter* warmly recommended this movie on November 14, 1925. Without a teasing remark, the propaganda journal had also drawn attention to the fact that the leading actor was "the brother of the famous Charlie Chaplin."[94] Not a word had been said about the brothers' alleged or actual Jewish ancestry.

That all changed when the *Völkischer Beobachter* took notice of *Goldrausch* in the spring of 1926 and for the first time reacted to a Charlie Chaplin film and targeted Chaplin. Its "Hauptschriftleiter" (editor-in-chief) was Hitler's chief ideologue Alfred Rosenberg. He was author of the 1930 anti–Christian book *Der Mythus des 20. Jahrhunderts—Eine Wertung der seelisch-geistigen Gestaltenkämpfe unserer Zeit* (The Myth of the 20th Century—An Evaluation of the Mental-Spiritual Gestalt Struggles of Our Time), about a Nazi race-based religion and one of the major war criminals who was sentenced to death for crimes against humanity by the Nuremberg War Crimes Tribunal on October 1, 1946, and executed.[95] Since 1923, the journalist and later film screenwriter Josef Stolzing-Czerny, who supported Hitler's *Mein Kampf*, had been a member of the NSDAP and was editor of the *Völkischer Beobachter*.[96] Stolzing-Czerny had apparently read the *Illustrierter Film-Kurier* issue of *Goldrausch* before the movie's Munich premiere in August 1926.[97] There it was written in black and white by a Jewish author: Chaplin played the "eternal Jew" and came from the ghetto—therefore he had to be a Jew! On top of that, according to Hasenclever, Chaplin was a pacifist, and the Nazis hated pacifists.

The homeless, underprivileged and property-less Tramp Charlie, who despite all defeats never loses the courage to live and also resists the loss of individuality, was absolutely incompatible with Nazi ideology. It revolved around the Aryan master race, which always asserts itself against others with slavish obedience, appears in mass marches and strives to limit the personal freedom of the individual, especially when it came to Jewry, whom the Nazis accused of planning world domination. Probably Hasenclever had also touched on the Nazi attitude toward vagrants, who were officially regarded as "incapable of community" in the Third Reich: "A person who is able to work, but who is work-shy, prone to delinquency or crime, or whose other behavior selfishly disturbs the peace of the community, is incapable of community."[98] In 1935, Heinz Pol suggested in *Die neue Weltbühne* that the Nazis had fought Chaplin not so much as a Jew but because of the social content of his films, in which he "takes sides with the underdog and against the official powers."[99] But there is no evidence to support such an assumption, and Nazi writers did not confirm this either.

Whether Stolzing-Czerny knew *Goldrausch* seems doubtful. His article "Der mystisch gewordene Charlie Chaplin" (Chaplin Gone mystical), which is reproduced in full in Appendix 2, is not a review of the film, but an attack on the "hymn […] of the Jewish press" by Wilhelm [*sic*] Hasenclever and on Chaplin as a Jew. Chaplin's unique artistic achievement, the attractiveness of his films, and the fact that Tramp Charlie was a fictitious or fairy-tale movie character, as Hasenclever had called him, were of just as little concern to Stolzing-Czerny. He probably had not read the *Rote Fahne*'s *Goldrausch* review, which regarded Chaplin as a Communist sympathizer. Otherwise, he probably would have attacked Chaplin as a Bolshevist as well. Among others, Stolzing-Czerny wrote:

Whew! Such adulation takes your breath away, and you cannot help but wonder: either it was paid for heavily, or the film magic has gone to the author's head to such an extent that he can only view the world from the perspective of the flickering screen. Charlie Chaplin may have a special ability to act just for the film, which does not surprise us with a Jew, because they are used to waving around with head and limbs so excitedly when they speak, that actually the spoken word seems superfluous to us, because we can already understand them by their gestures. And film, as we know, requires vivid facial expressions. But we have enough film actors who perform at least as well as Chaplin, who came from the ghetto. And they do not have to be hyped as fairy tale characters, mythical personalities and Homeric heroes. Not even if they are Jews. [...] Juda needs heroes for the glorification of its world domination, even if it is only such from the flickering box! Whereas the World War has not given us a single Jewish hero.[100]

Stolzing-Czerny also pulled Hasenclever to pieces: "[He ...] has made a name for himself by the fact that all the plays he has written so far have been a flop. The man has missed his profession: he is a born 'Reklamechef' [Advertising Boss]!"

Compared to subsequent Nazi attacks against Chaplin, Stolzing-Czerny's contribution still seemed somewhat moderate. But it contains all the elements of agitation: unobjective and denigrating statements for the purpose of provoking hatred against persons or groups, stirring up fears of them, defaming them or even demonizing them, for which purpose information is occasionally omitted so that actual contexts are distorted. For example, the use of the term "Reklamechef" in his article is a common anti–Semitic stereotype for the allegation that Jews can only "advertise" and "make much ado about anything," i.e., have nothing substantial to say and are therefore not to be taken seriously.

Rosenberg's Weltkampf *and Streicher's* Stürmer

Rosenberg had also been the publisher of the Munich monthly *Der Weltkampf* (The World Struggle) since 1924. It dealt with "world politics, völkisch culture and [the] Jewish issue of all countries." In May 1926, with the article "Charlie Chaplins Geheimnis," this Nazi magazine responded to Chaplin, *Goldrausch*, the success of which could not be overlooked in Germany, and one of the many jubilant reviews. The writer of the article was Rudolf Jordan, the future SA-Obergruppenführer (S.A. major general) and NSDAP-Gauleiter of Halle-Merseburg and Magdeburg-Anhalt.[101] Initially, he mocked the elaborate advertising for *Goldrausch* and some reviews of the film: "Of course, this cleverly devised trick did not fail to have its effect, and the entire clan of our Jewish and Jew-friendly theater directors burst into full enthusiasm over their great racial comrade's latest Chaplinade. And the 'factories of our public opinion,' the entire Jewish and pro–Jewish press, echoed in word and image the art of the great man with the cutaway and the little black hat."[102] Jordan felt particularly offended by how Hasenclever had aptly sketched Chaplin's profoundly peaceful, universal comedy, from which the "dramatists of all countries" should learn. He dismissed Hasenclever's appreciation as "drivel from a 'playwright' still respected in some circles today" and "strong meat for any decent person." Stolzing-Czerny had not attacked Harden and Reinhardt's tributes to Chaplin from the *Illustrierter Film-Kurier*. Jordan vehemently caught up with this. He also went on to hurl crude accusations at several other people who had made favorable comments about Chaplin. His main target, however, was Hans Siemsen, who had astutely analyzed Chaplin's work in his 1920 and 1922 essays for *Die Weltbühne*, which he had collected in his 1924 booklet Charlie Chaplin.[103] Since Siemsen had characterized Chaplin as a revolutionary whom God may bless,[104] Jordan called him the "last romantic of our century" and accused the non–Jewish author of "Jewish extravagance."

Jordan's language was more aggressive than Stolzing-Czerny's, and other Nazi agitators would intensify this to the point of a martial tone. Nazi agitation was determined by creating a black-and-white picture: Its target was systematically belittled, while its own political agenda was uncritically portrayed as invariably being good. The variation in content and expression of this and future Chaplin-baiting, however, remained remarkably limited. Mostly only new slurs were invented. Thus, the Nazi agitation against Chaplin also reflected what Karl Kraus, in his 1933 *Die Dritte Walpurgisnacht*,[105] and, above all, Victor Klemperer, in his analysis of the Lingua Tertii Imperii (LTI), the ubiquitous language of the Third Reich, had elaborated on Nazi jargon. It was militaristically and warlike influenced, was unobjective, sounded loudmouthed and haughty, and sometimes used a Christian Biblical idiom, which Klemperer called "Prostitution der Evangeliensprache" (Prostitution of Gospel Language). Despite constantly exaggerating superlatives, however, the LTI was monotonous and indulged in repetition. The frequent falseness of the content could only be inadequately concealed linguistically. In this incarnation, the LTI had usurped the spoken word and all records and was virtually official language in the Third Reich. Klemperer summarized the linguistic poverty of the LTI as follows:

I have once studied the *Mythus des 20. Jahrhunderts* and then a paperback for the retail salesman, now browsed a legal and now a pharmaceutical journal, I have read novels and poems that

Der Weltkampf, magazine cover, 1926.

were allowed to be published in these years, I have heard the workers sweeping the streets and speak in the machine shop: it was always, printed and spoken, among the educated and the uneducated, the same cliché and the same tone. And even among [the] most harshly persecuted victim[s] [...] LTI reigned everywhere. The LTI was both all-powerful and wretched—and so all-powerful precisely because of its linguistic wretchedness.[106]

After that, another Nazi newspaper took Chaplin and his film for a ride. In 1923, the controversial teacher Julius Streicher had founded the Nuremberg weekly *Der Stürmer* (The Storm Trooper), which he dedicated to the "struggle for truth." It was nowhere near the truth! Streicher reached his mostly simple-minded readers with simple, exceptionally aggressive language. In this way, he influenced them non-stop with coarse, slanderous articles about alleged scandals and with constantly recurring clichés. The undifferentiated anti–Semitic target was right there in the footer on page 1: "The Jews are our Disaster!" Readers were also advised to avoid Jewish doctors and lawyers.[107] Visually, main illustrator Philipp Rupprecht implemented this under the pseudonym Fips from 1925 until the *Stürmer* was discontinued in 1945. Rupprecht's cover images and other drawings stereotypically depicted mostly male Jews in an extremely repulsive and devious manner. The bodies were often obese. Eyes protruded from unshaven, bloated faces with conspicuously large, curved noses and bulging lips that signaled sexual greed. *Der Stürmer* was arguably the worst Nazi smear gazette. In 1937, the exile newspaper *Jüdische Revue*, published in the Ukraine, described it as the "prototype of ultimate wickedness that humans can achieve."[108]

The extent to which its propaganda caught on was represented by the appalling examples of letters to the editor of *Der Stürmer*, which not infrequently revealed sadism.[109] Streicher was later Gauleiter of Franken and, because of his extreme anti–Semitic agitation, was also sentenced to death as a major war criminal by the Nuremberg War Crimes Tribunal on October 1, 1946, for crimes against humanity and subsequently executed.[110] In his Entnazifizierungsverfahren (Denazification Proceedings), Rupprecht merely received a sentence of ten years in a labor camp and was released from it as early as 1950.[111]

When *Goldrausch* was shown in Nuremberg in October 1926, Streicher, too, was unconcerned with art, and he mobbed Chaplin under the headline "Charlie Chaplin der Musterjude" (Charlie Chaplin the Model Jew):

Charlie Chaplin is Jewish. He is a born tomfool. As a result of his terrible flat feet, he can hardly walk. His actions are those of a dawdler who always gets into trouble with the law. The easier-thinking viewer laughs at this character on the screen, the more knowledgeable one will be disgusted by it. Charlie Chaplin can thrill no one but the Jews, and they were also mostly the audience of this film. A man who is abnormally shaped, always swindling his way through life gypsy-like and stealing, is for the German something abysmally repulsive, something abominable.[112]

After crude, disparaging blows against Hasenclever, among others, Streicher turned on Chaplin's origins from the "London district of criminals" where he "was trained [...] to become what he is today," and on Jews:

Now surely everyone understands why here the whole Jewish population recognizes itself and why it trembles at this. The Jewish race is confronted with its career. In times immemorial, it emerged from the criminal quarters of all countries. To this day, this Spottgeburt (Spawn) of filth and fire has been the Auswurf (Throat Scum) of all peoples. Wherever the Jew appeared, he got into conflict with the laws. He was expelled and partly exterminated, where people still recognized him in time. Thus, like the gypsies, the eternally wandering Jew prowled the world. Now his own life is presented to him in the cinema so that he shivers. When Germans see the pictures of the history of their nation, they do not shiver. The German is fascinated by the power and greatness of his past. He draws from it the strength to start his march into the future with unshakable faith in his heart. But for the Jew [...] fear creeps into his chest and madness into his brain. The Jew has horror in his mind about his future.

Chaplin's alleged origins in a "London district of criminals" may well have sprung from the Nazi stereotype that "the Jew is the bearer of crookedness through the ages." This was spread, for example, by the ardent anti–Semite Hermann Esser, NSDAP member No. 2, propaganda leader of his party and editor of the *Völkischer Beobachter*, in his heresy book published in 1927 with the telling title *Die jüdische Weltpest* (The International Jewish Plague). In the Third Reich, he was, among other things, Bavarian Wirtschaftsminister (Minister of Economics) and then Staatssekretär (State Secretary) in the Reichsministerium für Volksaufklärung und Propaganda (Reich Ministry of Public Enlightenment and Propaganda). Until 1941, his book went through several considerably expanded editions.[113] Other common anti–Semitic stereotypes in Streicher's attack included the description of Tramp Charlie's physiognomy as having "appalling flat feet," an "abnormal figure," and allegedly "typical Jewish deformities," as well as the characterization of the "eternally wandering Jew roaming through the world" who is "confronted with his own life in the cinema."[114]

In the same month, the *Völkischer Beobachter* followed up with the short article "Der Idealist" (The Idealist). The unnamed author made Chaplin out to be a "great and shrewd

Hermann Esser, *Die jüdische Weltpest*, book cover, 1927.

profiteer" as well as a tax evader who, despite his earnings of four million reichsmark from *The Gold Rush*, had paid only 1200 reichsmark in annual income tax. The résumé: "He is an idealist, after all! What?! And he is going to make a film on Christ next. He himself plays the Savior!"[115] The *Völkischer Beobachter* did not name its sources, but the film project apparently traced back to a *Film-Kurier* report from the end of July.[116] However, the account of the alleged tax evasion is likely to be distorted. According to Robinson's research, it was not until the end of 1926 that the U.S. Treasury approached Chaplin with a tax claim of $1,113,000 for several years in the past. Shortly before, Chaplin's second wife Lita Grey had separated from him, and Chaplin announced a few days later that his studio business would be suspended indefinitely.[117] At the end of January 1927, it could be read in Germany that Chaplin was not allowed to leave the U.S. because of open tax claims and that he was ready to pay a million dollars in additional taxes.[118] Chaplin reached a final agreement with the tax authorities at the end of April 1927.[119] This means: In October 1926, there were most likely neither tax demands nor an accusation of tax evasion against Chaplin in the U.S. Therefore, the assertion of the *Völkischer Beobachter* was probably a piece of agitation.

Goldrausch—*Success in Germany*

In 1926, the NSDAP was still a faction, and its propaganda journals therefore still exercised little influence with their foul methods. The overwhelming part of the German cinema audiences loved Chaplin as before, and thus *Goldrausch* also became a box-office success right from the start. During the German premiere on February 18, 1926, the movie triggered "recurring bursts of applause" at Berlin's Capitol, so that the theater's owner had the film stopped and rewound after the famous dance of the rolls in order to immediately re-screen this scene for the unleashed audience! This is said to have been the first rerun of a film scene during a regular screening, which even met with approval in the U.S.![120] A month later, Ifa-Film-Verleih GmbH reported that 100,000 visitors had seen the Chaplin film so far and that another million would probably see it now, since *Goldrausch* was now being shown in at least 46 movie theaters in Greater Berlin alone.[121]

From the end of April 1926, *Goldrausch* was by far the biggest seller of tickets in several Hamburg cinemas. The *Film-Journal* called it the film that "really everyone must have seen" and that makes people want to attend it more than once.[122] Thus, the film was replaced only in mid–June—by Chaplin's 1918 *Ein Hundeleben* (*A Dog's Life*).[123]

In August 1926, following *Goldrausch*'s Munich premiere at the Deutsches Theater, René Prevôt's review was published in the *Süddeutsche Filmzeitung*:

It is always daring to herald an art event as the "very greatest" of its kind. This type of trumpeting arouses great expectations in us, and at the same time makes us skeptical. We prefer to feel the quiet subtlety that lies in the shattering comedy of the new Chaplin film, to feel its unique blend of tragic grotesquerie as an elemental event in the domain of film. [...] *Goldrausch* has no unusual plot, is not a novelty in technical terms, and does not stand out for virtuoso direction or craftsmanship. It is rich in original ideas and poignant in its basic human traits. [...] Here the film [...] fulfilled a spiritual dream of its creator. [...] The experience of this film gently wraps itself around the audience, like a unifying bond of humanity.[124]

Goldrausch was also a success in Western Germany.[125] In 1927, Irmalotte Guttmann, an employee of the *Lichtbildbühne*, examined the 1926 German cinema market with the Cologne box office revenues of *Goldrausch* as an example. In this city, Chaplin films were generally in great demand Audiences flocked to the large downtown premiere theaters, with their seating capacity of up to 1800, making *Goldrausch* an instant "smash hit," so that its schedule was prolonged after two weeks.[126] Whatever the political attitudes, the situation was similar in the city's working-class neighborhoods, with smaller movie theaters around 200 to 400 seats, where cinema visits were among the few pleasures available to low-income residents.[127] To cross-check her Cologne research results, Guttmann compared them with the

Ifa ad about *Goldrausch*'s success, late February 1926.

box-office revenues of *Goldrausch* in the Free City of Danzig, which at that time, with its predominantly German-speaking population, was under the control of the Völkerbund (League of Nations).[128] In Danzig, *Goldrausch* was also the most successful movie.[129]

In August and September 1926, on the Northern America route of the German shipping line Norddeutscher Lloyd, *Goldrausch* also entertained passengers every evening in the on-board cinema of the liner *Columbus*.[130] And since the German success continued, Arthur W. Kelly, vice-president of United Artists' German branch, announced in early October 1926 that Chaplin wanted to visit Germany, among other places. He loved the country, and *Goldrausch* had enjoyed particular success there.[131] In the meantime, the newly founded United Artists Filmverleih G.m.b.H. had assumed distribution of the film from Ifa-Film-Verleih GmbH. In late spring of that year, United Artists Filmverleih G.m.b.H. had the pleasure of reporting that the Berliner Zentralinstitut für Erziehung und Unterricht (Berlin Central Institute for Education and Instruction), the so-called Lampe Committee,[132] had recognized *Goldrausch* as "künstlerisch hochstehend" (artistically outstanding).[133] The Lampe Committee's decision had two effects: Cinema operators had to pay less Vergnügungssteuer (Entertainment Tax) for the screening of the film, and the film was included in media educational concepts of state-run schools. Surprisingly, in 1928 the Social Democratic Party of Germany (SPD) in the Hessian state parliament yielded the following parliamentary inquiry on this subject: "Is the government aware of the fact that the [Berliner Zentralinstitut] für Erziehung und Unterricht strangely calls films of *Goldrausch*'s ilk [...] 'artistic'?"[134] The contrast to the aforementioned enthusiastic *Goldrausch* review in the SPD party newspaper *Vorwärts* (February 1926) could not have been more striking, and the *Film-Kurier* quipped to the parliamentary inquiry: "Commentary superfluous. Narrow-mindedness speaks for itself."[135]

According to *Film-Kurier*, Chaplin's *The Gold Rush* had grossed nearly $1.7 million in 1926.[136] When the film was re-released in Germany in the summer of 1927, the box office was again expected to be excellent.[137] At the start, *Film-Journal* wrote in June of that year: "Nothing more needs to be said about Chaplin's *Goldrausch*. Every child has heard about this film. Every theater owner knows what business can be done with it. It is and remains one of the greatest works in the history of cinematography. You can see this film twice or twenty times without tiring of its touching comedy, its tragedy, its great and pure art."[138] The *Film-Journal* was right. In Hamburg alone, *Goldrausch* was re-released several times from 1927 to 1929.[139] In August 1931, the film was shown in the Berlin Kamera and in March 1932 it was part of the Easter festival program of the Berlin Marmorhaus, where it was accompanied by the "ravishingly playing" Lewis Ruth Band. The *Film-Journal* noted that the film's highlights "will be just as relevant 20 years from now" and will still thrill audiences as they did at the time of *Goldrausch*'s premiere.[140] As the Easter festival program was also successful, Terra Filmverleih GmbH announced its interest in re-releasing *Goldrausch* throughout Germany.[141] This ultimately went up in smoke. But even without the involvement of this distributor, *Goldrausch* was re-released after Hitler's takeover in the spring of 1933 (see Chapter 7).[142]

3

Who Needs Facts?

Divorce, Shoulder Arms *and Creativity—1927–31*

At this time, the Nazi propaganda press' first Chaplin attacks were limited to defaming him as a person and artist. His films were no more than a sporadic external cause for agitation. Only the *Völkischer Beobachter*'s early April 1931 attack on *Lichter der Großstadt* contained rudiments of yet another distorted description of the film (see Chapter 4). Films highly celebrated by audiences and critics, such as *Ein Hundeleben* (*A Dog's Life*) and *Die Nächte einer schönen Frau* (*A Woman of Paris*) from 1918 and 1923, respectively, which were released in the Weimar Republic in 1926 after *Goldrausch*,[1] remained without any Nazi reaction, which often focused on events outside of Chaplin's filmmaking. In 1927, this was the case with Chaplin's divorce from Lita Grey. The ultra-right agitators were not interested in factual reports. Rather, they sought to influence their readership in a clichéd anti–Semitic manner. To this end, facts were taken out of context, abbreviated, distorted and twisted, and this was done with a remarkably low scope. Hans Steinhoff's 1941 anti–British propaganda film *Ohm Krüger*, starring Emil Jannings in the title role, stated the following about the handling of truth and facts: "The world is quick to forget, and if you tell a lie over and over again, eventually it will be believed." The statement is said to have stemmed from the Nazi Reichsminister für Volksaufklärung und Propaganda, Dr. Joseph Goebbels, and might also describe the agitation against Chaplin.

This chapter deals with:

- Chaplin's divorce from Lita Grey in the light of the German press and the Nazi agitation
- the political turncoats Curt Belling and Hans-Walther Betz
- Chaplin's latest feature film, *The Circus*
- *Shoulder Arms* in the German nationalist, Nazi and leftist press
- another lawsuit about *Shoulder Arms* over plagiarism allegations
- German diplomats fighting *Shoulder Arms* abroad
- Dr. Hans Buchner's general attack against Chaplin
- Nazi agitation against Chaplin's *The Pilgrim*
- Max Jungnickel and Alfred Rosenberg attacking Chaplin as "Thief of Intellectual Property" and as "neo–German Ideal of Beauty, the jerk," respectively

A Nasty Divorce

In April 1925, it was rumored that Chaplin and his second wife Lita Grey were separating, and that he thought about remarrying his first wife Mildred Harris.[2] The couple separated at the end of 1926, and Grey filed her divorce action in early January 1927. In it, on the advice of her lawyers, she morally disparaged Chaplin as a human being, and did not spare intimate details of their marital life. The divorce action was leaked to the public and could be purchased as a book, first in the U.S. and soon in other countries. Grey had Chaplin's real estate assets confiscated during the divorce proceedings, along with his film studio,[3] and the U.S. Treasury subsequently froze his accounts. Chaplin had to suspend the shooting for his film *The Circus*.[4] The gruel-

Ohm Krüger ad, 1941.

ing confrontation with Grey and accidents during filming, including a fire in the circus tent that destroyed footage of difficult acrobatic scenes,[5] caused Chaplin to suffer a nervous breakdown.[6] United Artists hurried to announce that work on *The Circus* would be resumed soon, and the German branch reported that the film would be released in Germany in the fall of 1927.[7] This proved impossible to accomplish.

U.S. film comedian Roscoe "Fatty" Arbuckle, once also enormously popular in Germany, was the prime example of how a scandal could shatter a career from one day to the next. In 1921, he had been accused of raping and murdering starlet Virginia Rappe during a party. Even before the trial, the press had reported incessantly about the case from the "immoral" Hollywood milieu. Arbuckle's production company Paramount had very quickly dropped him.[8] After three criminal trials he was finally acquitted, but remained an outcast in the film business with a broken marriage and an addiction to drugs and alcohol; he could only work as a director under a pseudonym. Only shortly before his untimely death in 1933 did he appear in front of the camera again.[9]

In 1927, when the international press reported extensively on Chaplin's divorce proceedings, and in the U.S. women's morality societies demanded that the "sex fiend's" films be banned from theaters,[10] his career was at stake. U.S. movie theater owners, meanwhile, were undeterred and passed a resolution against boycotting Chaplin films in early February 1927.[11] The numerous German newspaper accounts of the divorce also largely stood by Chaplin. The magazine *Die deutsche Republik* called his divorce proceedings "a smear campaign [...] that a Strindberg could not have devised more appallingly"[12]—referring to the Swedish writer August Strindberg, who had written the oppressive marriage drama *Totentanz* (*Dödsdansen*) in 1900. It was hoped that the running of the gauntlet would come to an end and that he would be able to overcome the terrible stress to which he had been subjected by the marital strife.[13] The *Reichsfilmblatt* suggested that Europe had every reason to protect Chaplin, "for what is at stake is the most valuable treasure that cinematic art has to offer."[14] The *Film-Journal* saw him as a victim of moral bigotry, calling the attacks on him in the U.S. "disgusting": "For us, Chaplin will always remain the great artist. For his private life, which certainly moved in better forms than his wife's shrewd legal representative would like to have the public believe, is in any case the concern of the Chaplin couple alone."[15] Should Chaplin want to turn his back on Hollywood, he would be welcomed with open arms in Berlin and be able to live there. When Lita Grey's divorce action was published in Austria in German translation in 1927, the publisher of the volume *Charlie Chaplin, der Beklagte…Der Mensch und der Künstler* (Charlie Chaplin, the Defendant… The Man and the Artist) did not participate in the witch hunt. In his eyes, this publication was directed against Grey as a "gold-digger," i.e., a woman who knew how to hook wealthy men and then fleece them.[16]

In February 1927, *Film-Kurier* reprinted Rollin Kirby's cartoon from the *New York World*. There the Tramp with the inscription "Chaplin the Artist" on his jacket stands, showered with garbage. This affected him as a private person, but not as an artist. The *Film-Kurier*'s caption of the caricature reads: "Chaplin's Art remains untouched."[17] Even the speculative journalism of the yellow press did not strive to discredit Chaplin. In July 1927, the *Berliner Illustrierte Zeitung* published the article "'D-5228,'

Chaplins Kunst bleibt unberührt.

Film-Kurier, February 19, 1927: "Chaplins Kunst bleibt unberührt" [Chaplin's Art Will Remain Untouched], cartoon by Rollin Kirby.

Charlie Chaplin's Most Tragic Film—The Marriage Drama of the World Famous Film Comedian," about how the divorce proceedings threatened to "crush" Chaplin. Although the magazine satisfied the sensationalism of its readers with Grey's accusations against Chaplin, it at least labeled them with the easily readable note "What His Wife's Action Alleges About Him."[18]

Nazi Propaganda

The editors of the Nazi journals *Völkischer Beobachter, Der Weltkampf* and *Der Stürmer* forged the marital strife of the alleged Jew Chaplin into a moral spearhead against him. From the beginning of 1927, the *Völkischer Beobachter* expanded its distribution and was published in both a Bavarian and a Reich edition. In the February 15, 1927, Bavarian edition, Chaplin was attacked as "der gestürzte König" (the overthrown king) before whom "America had been on its knees in adoration for more than a decade" with the article "Der Eheskandal Charlie Chaplins" (Charlie Chaplin's Marriage Scandal). In keeping with the propaganda journal, after two years of marriage, the 18-year-old "Delilah of this Kino [Cinema]-Simson" (allusion to the Biblical story of Samson and Delilah) had had enough of Chaplin's "cruel and inhuman treatment, [...and] great and severe mental suffering and afflictions." His sexual deviancy made the divorce suit "a phenomenally dirty piece of reading." The *Völkischer Beobachter* compared the divorce suit to the affair of the wealthy Nuremberg Jew Schloß, from which it now could be roughly seen "what Lita Grey had to endure in her marriage." To the journal's chagrin, no one except the ethnic press had really wanted to take up the Nuremberg moral scandal, because "people cannot get over fear of the Jews [...] that even the most primitive chivalrous feeling cannot rise against it. [...] America behaves differently in a similar case, and that, mind you, concerns one of its movie darlings, not a mediocre Jew [...] People over there apparently still have a sense of decency and honor." The journal also came to Lita Grey's defense insofar as parts of the German press wrongly treated her as an "ingrate" and a "profiteer" because of the fight over money in the divorce case.[19]

About a month later, the *Völkischer Beobachter* railed against the "facade-like" business ethics of the U.S. film industry with "On Charlie Chaplin's Marriage Scandal." Leading "moralistic" Jewish film greats such as Carl Laemmle (Universal), William Fox (Fox Film Corporation) and Adolph Zukor (Paramount) had, as a result of the divorce proceedings, "risen up to write a kind of pastoral letter to their stars so that their business would not be screwed up by immoral behavior." In the same breath, the Nazi newspaper "disclosed" about the authors of the "pastoral letter": "This [...] justification is indeed classic! If, on top of that, you know that most of the [...] film lords come from [...] pornographic film and have a dubious career behind them, you have only resounding laughter to spare for [their] morality edict!"[20]

In March, Alfred Rosenberg sharpened his pen for "Kostproben aus der Giftküche weltzersetzender Mächte" (Samples from the Devil's Workshop of World-destroying Powers) in the permanent column "Der gedeckte Tisch" of *Der*

Weltkampf. He thus attacked Chaplin and "international Jewry" with his article "Goldgräbereien" (Gold-digging):

> Charlie Chaplin has his second marriage scandal. In the U.S., his wife publishes revealing details about the "jüdischer Wüstling" [Jewish libertine] who had demanded outrageous things from her in marriage. And since the woman is setting the tone in America, so the formerly "verhimmelter nigger-groteskhafter Galizier" [Glorified nigger-grotesque Galician] is now boycotted. This is most welcome. The entire Jewish press, of course, stands up for its greatest hero [and against his "gold-digger wife"]. [...] So the splendid cause has its two sides: first, the Hebrew libertine, and second, a crazy American women's legislation which enables the 'gold-diggers' to do their 'work.' Both are rotten.[21]

However, there had not been a broad Chaplin boycott in the U.S.

On May 11, 1927, the *Prager Tagblatt* printed the last part of Jim Tully's series of articles on Chaplin, which was concerned with the "private man" and had Chaplin metaphorically walking through the New Testament Garden of Gethsemane.[22] In June 1927, as a sequel to "Goldgräbereien," Rosenberg continued his campaign with "Chaplin in Gethsemane" against the artist, riddled by his broken marriage, as a narrator of cheap, tasteless and vulgar stories. He implied that Chaplin had taken a "vivid interest in everything pathological" such as a murder case in the U.S. in which two "Jewish millionaires" got off with penitentiary sentences because the electric chair was "only for Aryans." This referred to a spectacular murder case on which Alfred Hitchcock's famous 1948 film *Rope* was based: In 1924, homosexual lovers Nathan Leopold and Richard Loeb killed young Bobby Franks and were sentenced to life in prison instead of being executed. Rosenberg went on to state:

> Charlie Chaplin [is recommended to us] by the cockalorums of Israel [as] the "Homeric hero of the 20th century." We also know from the same illustrious mouth that the whole "world" is Germanophobe because, unlike the "great Western democrats," it has not chosen the "Galizier" [Galician] Chaplin as an ideal. Now a Prague Jewish paper feels compelled to present Chaplin to us once again with his somewhat estranged marriage. [...] Tully [...] had the "prachtvoller junger Zyniker" [Splendid young cynic] walk alone through his Garden of Gethsemane. The Zotenerzähler [Teller of Obscene Jokes] in—Gethsemane. This mockery demonstrates how much the mindset [of the set table] also resides among "advanced liberal" Jews.[23]

In 1930, Rosenberg included this article in his diatribe *Der Sumpf* (The Swamp), his "profile of the 'intellectual' life of the November Democracy," with which he branded cultural life in the Weimar Republic as "intellectual Bolshevism," among other things.[24]

In January 1928, Rosenberg apparently continued his line in *Der Weltkampf* with the spiteful article "Chaplin, der liebe Jesus" (Chaplin, the dear Jesus) as a "galizisches Heldenideal von heute (Galician ideal of today's hero)." In the fall of 1927, he had picked up a Chaplin-friendly article in the *Hannoverscher Kurier*, a newspaper close to the national-liberal Deutschen Volkspartei (German People's Party), which in turn fought the Nazis. The author, Kurt Liepmann, saw in Chaplin the "little guy in a major key, tattered by fate and unarmed, long since abandoned to the twist of fate" and praised him as follows: "O holy Chaplin, you are the dear Jesus of our time, since we are all so utterly lonely. And you are suffering for us all." Rosenberg vehemently disagreed: "Of course, it is understood that Herr Liepmann has not been prosecuted for blasphemy. That only happens when there is something to find fault with Jehovah and his fabulous laws."[25]

Streicher outdid Rosenberg in his *Stürmer* in July 1927 with the article "Charlie Chaplin—Der jüdische Schweinehund" (Charlie Chaplin—The Jewish Bastard), packed with stereotypical anti–Semitic agitation. His version of Chaplin's *curriculum vitae* again started with his birth in a "criminal quarter," and apparently stirred in facts in the divorce context, and condemned Chaplin as absolutely morally depraved:

> Now [the "Filmjude" (Film-Jew) Charlie Chaplin] stands there, stripped to the bone, in front of the whole world [whom his racial comrades …] praised […] greater than Christ. He is recognized, the "genius," the Jewish one. Recognized as "großes Riesenschwein" [Great filthy swine]. He was born in the London criminal quarter. Has a real Jewish career. In America, he emerged as a "film actor." Believed, in line with Talmud laws, to be able to play fast and loose with non–Jewish girls. Until he had "entrasst" [abducted from her race] the wrong one, but who could not be thrown away. Her relatives forced the Jew to marry the Gentile. As stated by the laws of the Talmud, however, the marriage of a Jew with a Gentile woman has no validity. […] The Jew, after all, regards the Gentile woman merely as cattle. […] Chaplin did not treat his non–Jewish wife like a husband, but like a pig. He compelled her with brute force to unnatural, shameless acts. He spent the nights among whores and pimps. The tormented woman filed for divorce. […] The nimbus that "Alljuda" [World Jewry] had spread around him threatened to go to hell. That is when Chaplin came up with a better solution. He "reconciled" for the sake of himself and his people. "So that the name of God may not be desecrated," i.e., the people of Israel may not be exposed. Charlie Chaplin did not divorce his wife. He will have compensated the Gentile with money and induced her to be silent. And now he fakes the Jewish "genius" again. He gropes around on the screen with his giant flat feet for the amusement of the "Masses and Man," who do not think that behind […] his shenanigans hides the mockery of the Jew on Gentile mankind.[26]

Alfred Rosenberg, *Der Sumpf*, book cover, 1930.

Streicher's far-fetched firebrand speech had nothing in common with the facts. There could be no question of a cover-up with a hush money payment. Chaplin was divorced on August 25, 1927. The previous (August 22) hearing had been unspectacular. In terms of content, however, it had a lot to offer: The couple had agreed to a record settlement of a combined $825,000 for Lita Grey and their two joint sons, the highest settlement ever in a U.S. divorce case to date. Even though Grey's lawyers collected half of it for themselves, she was satisfied and had withdrawn almost all the allegations—except for the accusation of mental cruelty by Chaplin.[27]

If Streicher had applied just the faintest grain of journalistic care to find out the amount of Grey's settlement, he would probably only have had to look in any German newspaper outside the radical right-wing spectrum. In August 1927, it was not only the impending divorce hearing that was reported, but even more so its course and outcome: Chaplin had "bought his way out" with $850,000 in settlement for the wife plus another $100,000 per child[28]—$225,000 more than had been agreed in the settlement. Because of this financial bloodletting, Chaplin, according to the *Film-Kurier*, wanted to produce his films much faster in the future in order to generate new income more quickly[29]—and would have failed to keep his assumed intention with any of his further films. Not a syllable of all this was to be found in the three Nazi journals.

Curt Belling, the Chaplin Admirer

If Streicher and his comrades in arms had only cared a little about objectivity, they would only have had to look at what was probably the first Nazi film magazine. From June 1927 on, "Kinocurt" Curt Belling published the *Berliner Tribüne—Illustrierte Filmwochenschrift*, which had a low circulation. He changed the title several times until the magazine was finally discontinued in early 1930. Belling's linguistic style was moderate, and he reported favorably on Jewish artists. Siegfried Arno, who was later persecuted by the Nazis, even wrote a dedication for the magazine in 1929, when it was called *Neue Film Hölle* (The New Film Hell).[30]

In particular, Belling championed Chaplin as "the world's best artist."[31] Regarding the latter's divorce proceedings, Belling published his sympathetic articles "Film-Reklame" and "Chaplin's Counterclaim" in July and August 1927 about the battered artist's effort to defend himself against dirt that was being thrown at him. "Film-Reklame" stated:

> Every day devastating reports make the headlines of all continents, telling about Charlie Chaplin's "perverse" and strange doings. For my part, I believe that these reports do not have the effect expected by Chaplin's wife, on the contrary! More than ever, Charlie Chaplin enjoys the sympathy of the public, even though some over-moralized housewives' clubs are trying to boycott his films. As a demonstration of sympathy for Chaplin as the best comedian in the world, one of the largest New York movie theaters scheduled a week of Chaplin films in his honor. A Berlin Ufa theater also recently had re-released *Goldrausch*. Let's wait for *Zirkus*— this film will be a huge success, supported by Lita's involuntary publicity![32]

Even more sympathetic was "Chaplin's Counterclaim" in the *Deutsche Film-Tribüne*, which stemmed from an August 4, 1927, New York news story about Chaplin's accusations against Grey: "Charlie Chaplin, who had a knack to win over the world with his humanly tragicomic comedy films and whose divorce affair was the sensation of all continents for months, now struck back. [...] This should clear up the whole, more than disgraceful affair."[33]

In the Third Reich, Belling turned out to be the prototype of the contemporary who hangs his coat to the wind. After Hitler's takeover, he became press officer of the film department in Joseph Goebbels' Reich Ministry for Popular Enlightenment and Propaganda,[34] then Presseleiter der Reichspropagandaleitung der NSDAP und Hauptstellenleiter der NSDAP, Amtsleitung Film (Head of NSDAP Reich Propaganda Department's Press Office and Head of the NSDAP's Central Office, Main Office Film).[35] The author or co-author of several Nazi books on film[36] now agitated against the film–Jew Chaplin in the style of the Lingua Tertii Imperii Victor Klemperer had studied. The climax was the infamous 1937 smear book *Film–"Kunst," Film-Kohn, Film-Korruption*,[37] co-authored by Hans-Walther Betz and Carl Neumann.

Zirkus

The divorce battle did not "crush" Chaplin. He continued his work on *The Circus*, and he could count on the loyalty of his audience.

In *The Circus*, Charlie is watching a fairground attraction. Next to him, a pickpocket steals a wallet and a pocket watch with chain from a spectator. The pickpocket's victim suspects something, but finds nothing on the thief, because he has nimbly slipped the loot into Charlie's back trouser pocket. But the thief does not give up his loot yet. A little later, he tries to grab it out of Charlie's pockets, but is caught by the police, who return his supposed property to the astonished Charlie. Charlie immediately helps himself to it, in order finally to be able to eat his fill. Now the victim of the theft comes by, realizes it is his property and accuses Charlie of stealing. Charlie flees and gets caught in a circus in a running performance by boring clowns. Charlie's appearance with the police hot on his heels is perceived by the audience as an original comic act, which they eagerly applaud. With his involuntary comedy, Charlie soon advances to become the circus' main attraction, which the director does not allow him to realize. He leaves Charlie believing that he is the least important assistant and treats him as such.

The circus director's stepdaughter Merna, a trick rider, does not have an easy time either. At the slightest mistake, her stepfather beats her and deprives her of food. So Charlie and Merna, fellow sufferers, develop feelings for each other. She enlightens Charlie about how unfairly he is being treated. When her stepfather wants to beat her for it, Charlie takes heart and threatens to leave the circus if he hits Merna again. And a decent fee is what Charlie wants. He is happy, and he succeeds—until he has to realize that Merna does not love him, but the elegant, handsome tightrope artist Rex. From then on, Charlie is no longer in form. He does not even get a single laugh during his performance in the ring. The director already wants to fire him. But then Charlie offers to stand in for Rex, who did not show up for the performance. Charlie had already practiced secretly on the tightrope because he thought he could win back Merna's heart. But the performance turns into a fiasco. The director beats his stepdaughter again. Charlie, who now does not care about anything, lunges out at him, knocks him down and gives him a black eye. The director fires him.

Merna wants to leave the circus and her stepfather with Charlie, but Charlie has to face the fact that Merna's true love is Rex. Charlie brings the couple together, and reluctantly the director gives his blessing to the marriage. He even allows Charlie to join the circus as it moves on. But Charlie realizes that three is a crowd that will only disrupt the young couple's togetherness. So he stays behind as the circus moves on. Sitting where the ring was set up just a short time ago, he pensively paws with his little cane at the torn paper from the ring through which Merna had jumped during her performance. Slowly, Charlie gets up, and sadly leaves the former circus ring. The further away he gets, the more cheerful his movements become, until he disappears into the fade-out of the film, apparently full of hope.

Following the film's U.S. premiere, box office records came in from abroad in early February 1928.[38] In Germany, Nazi agitation had not affected Chaplin or his film. United Artists' German branch was reported an "unprecedented success" with 125,000 visitors during a 45-day run in the Berlin premiere theater, surpassing the

EIN BEISPIELLOSER ERFOLG!

125 000 Berliner sahen

CHARLIE CHAPLIN

in

„ZIRKUS"

in den **45** Tagen
der URAUFFÜHRUNG im „CAPITOL" am Zoo
35
der bedeutendsten Lichtspieltheater Groß-
Berlins mit zusammen 40 000 Sitzplätzen
bringen den Film ab 23. März in der ersten
Spielwoche als Erstaufführung. Mehr als
100
weitere Berliner Lichtspieltheater zeigen
danach in den folgenden drei Wochen

CHARLIE CHAPLIN in „ZIRKUS"

Germania-Palast, Frankfurter Allee
Alhambra, Koppenstraße
Concordia-Palast-
Schwarzer Adler
Viktoria-Lichtspiele
Simplon-Lichtspiele
Markgrafendamm-Lichtspiele
Apollo-Lichtspiele, Lichtenberg
Kosmos-Lichtspiele, Lichtenberg
Istina-Lichtspiele
Frankfurter Lichtspiele
Litauer Lichtspiele
Elysium
Flora-Lichtspiele
Frankenburg
Merkur-Palast
Filmstern
Film und Brettl
Greifswalder Filmbühne
Mila-Lichtspiele
Prater-Lichtspiele
Metropol-Lichtspiele
Ufa-Theater, Weinbergsweg
Ufa-Theater, Alexanderplatz
Ufa-Theater, Weißensee
Filmpalast Schönhauser Tor
City-Lichtspiele
Bio, Alexanderplatz
Casino-Lichtspiele, Brunnenstraße
Gala-Lichtspiele, Usedomstraße
Kristall-Palast, Gesundbrunnen
Humboldt-Theater
Ballschmieder
Prinzen-Palast
Marienbad-Palast
Metro-Palast, Chausseestraße
Weidenhof-Lichtspiele
Mercedes-Palast Utrechter Straße
Theater des Weddings
Fortuna-Lichtspiele, Müllerstraße
Elektra-Palast
Schiller-Lichtspiele
Filmeck, Skalitzer Straße
Deutsch-Amerikanisches Theater
Skala-Palast, Oranienstraße

Roland-Lichtspiele
Oppeiner Lichtspiele
Universum-Lichtspiele, Reichenberger Straße
Phoebus-Palast, Anhalter Bahnhof
Rivoli, Bergmannstraße
Palladium
Süd-West-Lichtspiele
Helios-Lichtspiele
Mercedes-Palast, Neukölln
Passage-Theater
Kuckuck-Lichtspiele
Eden-Lichtspiele
U. T., Hasenheide
Rollkrug
Wien-Berlin-Lichtspiele
Knoschebeck-Palast
Apollo-Lichtspiele, Bergstraße
B. T. L., Potsdamer Straße
Odeon-Lichtspiele
Concordia-Lichtspiele, Bülowstraße
Astoria-Lichtspiele, Potsdamer Straße
B. T. L. Turmstraße
Gesellschaftshaus
Orion-Lichtspiele
Stern-Lichtspiele
Kant-Lichtspiele
Atlantie-Lichtspiele
Piccadilly
Theater am Wilhelmplatz
Olivaer-Lichtspiele
Lichtspiele des Westens
Roland-Lichtspiele

Minerva-Lichtspiele
Regina-Lichtspiele
Reichs-Lichtspiele
Kurfürsten-Theater
Wittenberg-Kino
Neues Lichtspielhaus, Augsburger Straße
Rivoli, Halensee
Turms-Palast, Schöneberg
Flora-Palast, Schöneberg
Kammer-Lichtspiele, Goltzstraße
Luna-Lichtspiele
Wittelsbach-Palast
Amor-Lichtspiele
Deutsche Lichtspiele, Spichernstraße
Corso-Lichtspiele, Uhlandstraße
Lichtspiele Kaiserplatz
Thalia-Lichtspiele
Hohenzollern-Lichtspiele, Friedenau
Albrechtshof, Steglitz
Schloßpark Film- und Bühnenschau
Filmburg
Flora-Lichtspiele
Union-Lichtspiele, Lichterfelde
Hindenburg-Lichtspiele
Zehlendorfer Lichtspiele
Kurfürst, Tempelhof
Tivoli, Tempelhof
Globus-Lichtspiele, Südende
Lichtspielhaus, Baumschulenweg
W. B. T.-Lichtspiele, Oberschöneweide
Filmpalast, Tegel
Bürgergarten-Lichtspiele, Reinickendorf
Eichhorn-Lichtspiele
Tivoli, Pankow
Filmpalast, Niederschönhausen
Universum-Lichtspiele, Weißensee
Corso-Lichtspiele, Prenzlauer Promenade
Concordia-Lichtspiele, Spandau
Walhalla-Lichtspiele, Spandau
Residenz-Lichtspiele, Potsdam
Obelisk-Lichtspiele, Potsdam
Union-Theater, Nowawes
Union-Theater, Friedrichshagen
Union-Theater, Cöpenick
Filmstern, Cöpenick u. s. m.

United Artists ad about *Zirkus'* success, late March 1928.

Berlin premiere success of *Goldrausch*. From the end of March 1928, the success was to continue in 140 Berlin cinemas, and in February and early June 1929, *Zirkus* was re-released in the Berlin cinemas Kamera and Universum.[39] The Lampe Committee also recognized *Zirkus* as having artistic merit,[40] so that only a reduced amusement tax was charged for its screenings. Financially, *Zirkus* outdid its predecessor *Goldrausch*. The box office was excellent throughout Germany, for example in Hamburg, Hanover, Stuttgart and Munich, as well as in the self-governing Freie Stadt Danzig. Chaplin's "individual, highly original artistic film" was considered "the record-breaking business of the season"; "the biggest business—even bigger than the *Ben-Hur* success."[41]

According to international surveys, the film was particularly successful. Four thousand German cinema owners ranked *Zirkus* seventh among the top films of the 1927-28 season.[42] According to the *Manchester Guardian*, it was counted among the "six enduring films" of special value in Great Britain, as reported by the *Film-Kurier*.[43] In the U.S., *The Circus* ranked among the top ten movies of 1928. In the end, Chaplin's film grossed $3.8 million,[44] and in 1929, the first year of the Academy Awards, the Academy of Motion Picture Arts and Sciences awarded Chaplin an honorary Oscar for "his versatility and genius as writer, performer, director and producer" of *The Circus*.

Hans-Walther Betz, the Chaplin Devotee

Like Belling, Hans-Walther Betz, co-author of *Film–"Kunst," Film-Kohn, Film-Korruption*, also underwent a metamorphosis into the Nazi extreme during the Third Reich. In September 1926, Betz had become the editor-in-chief of the liberal trade journal *Der Film* and was responsible for the "Reviews of the Week."[45] That same month, he attended the German premiere of Chaplin's program *Charlie haut sich durchs Leben* (Charlie fights his way through life) with the 1915 Essanay two-act plays *The Champion* and *A Night in the Show* at the Berlin Primus-Palast. Betz had been very much taken with it in his review. Nothing had suggested that 11 years later, he would spread nastiness about the artist and use the LTI (Lingua Tertii Imperii):

> This farce lived up to all the expectations that were set in a Chaplin film. Pace and strong comedy, bigotedly denying its tragic character, as well as keen and jaunty acting are the essential features of this film. [...] The audience laughs, tosses and turns, bounces in its seats. [...] The print was bad. Refurbish it, and you will have a new film that will make hundreds of thousands of people laugh.[46]

Betz was also a guest at the festive gala celebrating the German premiere of Chaplin's *Zirkus* at Berlin's Capitol on February 7, 1928. His extensive, effusive review identified him as a connoisseur of Chaplin's art:

> A convincing symphony of everyday life. Lament and nonsense in a brotherly round dance. Strength and weakness in clownish juxtaposition. Result: the suppressed genius triumphs, sets out for triumphant jubilation, but—now the most painful and delicious wisdom remains. Final morality: smiling surrender. Happy end. But painful, heartbreakingly painful. [...] Here the highest value reveals itself: the Chaplinades are made for everyone, for poor and rich

of the wallet, for poor and rich of the heart. They resonate because they find kindred spirits, inspire because they address each and every one. [...] This is Charlie Chaplin and his work. This is also his fame. This is sheer life and philosophy. [...] Chaplin [...] the Pierrot of his time. Deep and superficial, straight and blurred. Unhappy, happy, staggering, recognizing. Glorious, glorious. [...] A stirring, stormy textbook. A joke book full of crushing wisdom. A reading book, exciting and terrific, written with heart and soul, deeply gripping, for young and old. The reading book of this much-loved and best-hated present age. And finally: the great, wonderful cultural history of everyday life.[47]

Re-release of the "Smear Film" Shoulder Arms

During Chaplin's divorce battle, *Shoulder Arms* was re-released on Broadway at New York's prestigious Strand Cinema on February 26, 1927, went into U.S. distribution, and did better at the box office than many new films.[48] This was reflected in both the German nationalist press and the *Völkischer Beobachter*. Because both political positions coincided, the resurgence of the issue is significant.

It all started on March 24, 1927, with a radio-telegram report by the New York correspondent of Alfred Hugenberg's *Berliner Nachtausgabe*, the only newspaper in the Hugenberg press to address the issue.[49] In thick letters, it read: "Chaplin als Deutschenfeind!" (Chaplin as Germanophobe!). And the question was asked whether the re-release of the "smear film" was only meant to distract from Chaplin's divorce scandal: "It is a typical Chaplin film of those years, with all those later reused grotesque antics that alone would hardly [...] explain the interest of the audience. But the Germanophobe tendency never appeared so brazenly as here, where [he] works with the crudest of clown jokes. [...] The [film's] disgusting scenes are loudly applauded by the Broadway mob."[50]

On March 25, 1927, the *B.Z.* (*Berliner Zeitung*) *am Mittag* defended Chaplin and *Shoulder Arms* against the *Berliner Nachtausgabe*:

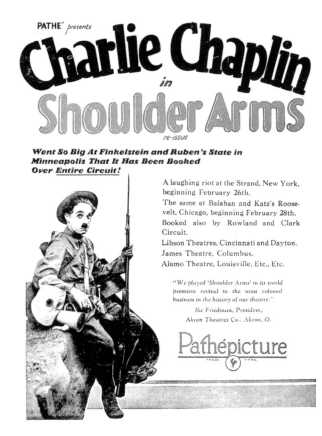

Pathépicture ad for the U.S. reissue of *Shoulder Arms* starting on February 26, 1926.

Chaplin als Deutschenfeind!

Wieder ein Hetzfilm in Amerika. — Ablenkung von seinem Eheskandal?

Zuspruch unseres Korrespondenten.

ha. **New York,** 24. März. Die großen Erfolge der antideutschen Filme, die in der letzten Spielzeit mehrere große Broadway-Theater New-Yorks beherrschten, haben bereits mehrmals zur Auffrischung alter aus den Kriegsjahren stammenden Filme geführt, in denen gegen Deutschland und die Deutschen in wüster Weise gehetzt wird. Diese Konjunktur wird jetzt von einer Verleihfirma ausgenutzt, die im „Cameo-Theater", einem eleganten Broadwaykino, den 1918 hergestellten Chaplinfilm „Shoulder Arms" neu und leider mit vielem Erfolg herausbringt. Es ist ein typischer Chaplinfilm dieser Jahre mit all jenen später wieder benutzten grotesken Mätzchen, die allein kaum ausreichen würden, um das Interesse des Publikums zu erklären. Aber die antideutsche Tendenz trat noch niemals so unverschämt zutage wie hier, wo ein Grotestschauspieler mit größten Clownspäßen arbeitet.

Vom Inhalt des Filmes sei folgendes verraten: Chaplin, mit Stock und Hütchen, kommt an einen deutschen Schützengraben gewackelt, wo er einen winzigen, monokeltragenden Leutnant, der von einem Schulbuben dargestellt wird, und einen baumlangen Soldaten trifft. Der Leutnant hält seinem Untergebenen eine Flasche Bier vor die Nase, trinkt aber stets selbst, sobald dieser zugreift. Schließlich ist der Offizier total betrunken und bearbeitet den Soldaten mit Fußtritten. Chaplin tritt nun in Aktion. Er nimmt den Leutnant gefangen, und dieser hebt angstvoll die Hände empor. Chaplin bietet ihm eine Zigarette an, die der Leutnant zertritt. Dafür wird er von Chaplin über das Knie gelegt und verprügelt. Deutsche Soldaten, die hinzutreten, klatschen Beifall.

In diesem Stil geht es weiter. Schließlich erscheinen der Kaiser und der Kronprinz, die auf die gleiche Weise „chaplinisch" abgefertigt werden. Diese ekelhaften Szenen finden lauten Beifall beim Broadway-Pöbel.

Chaplin hat diesen Film im Auftrag einer Firma hergestellt, gegen die er heute keinen Einspruch auf Zurückziehung erheben kann. Allerdings meinen unterrichtete Kreise, daß die Auffrischung der „Shoulder Arms" dazu dienen soll, Chaplin wieder restlos populär zu machen, wie er es vor seinem Eheskandal war.

Berliner Nachtausgabe, March 27, 1927: "Chaplin als Deutschenfeind!"

To call [*Shoulder Arms*] Germanophobe is an almost incomprehensible, completely humorless misunderstanding on behalf of the correspondent. [...] The true tendency of this film is not against Germany, but against war, or rather against the war depictions that were commonplace in America. At that time in America, only depictions were tolerated that showed the bloody war as a splendid heroic epic with waving flags and plumed helmets. [...] Chaplin dared to parody and ridicule these ridiculous depictions of war with astonishing courage and with ravishingly funny satire. He dared to be the first to show the filth of war, plagued by vermin, he hangs a grater in the dugout and scratches his back comfortably. He dared to show the suffering of the soldiers. [...] And he parodies the "heroic stories" by capturing larger parts of the German army, including the Kaiser alone, armed only with a little cane. Does the correspondent believe that this Munchausenism, which is truly piled on thick enough, was taken by anyone as mockery of Germany, and not as a mockery of the war-glorifying swaggering? Each rightly-minded reader will recognize this immediately.[51]

This was followed on March 29, 1927, by *Die Weltbühne*:

Now that the old Chaplin film *Shoulder Arms* is being shown again in New York, you are overflowing with shrieks and rage. Well, it is really a mistake that this splendid film, in which Charlie captures the Kaiser and once stands in front of a German company, his left arm resting daintily on the chest of a Landwehrmann, [...] is running [only] in New York. [...] Chaplin's [film] belongs only to Germany. The others already know. Germany does not know yet.[52]

Similarly, the *Hamburger Echo* shook its head at the "almost incomprehensible, completely humorless misunderstanding" of the *Berliner Nachtausgabe*: "Only Hugenberg correspondents fail to grasp these precious Munchausenisms, the mockery of Germany. German audiences will not fall for these obvious publicity bluffs to decry good cinematic art that has not been created in their own studios."[53]

Already on March 26, 1927, the German nationalist *Berliner Börsen-Zeitung* with its editor-in-chief Walther Funk had partially reproduced the news of the *Berliner Nachtausgabe* and reported that "official German authorities" had achieved only partial success in their attempt to prevent the Chaplin film from being re-released: "The [film] company declared that the film had already been sold and could not be withdrawn. Nevertheless, in the end, the deletion of the nastiest parts was enforced. In them, Chaplin captures the former Kaiser and Hindenburg, tears the Kaiser's medals off his uniform to decorate soldiers with them, and kicks him after his capture."[54]

Now, on March 26, 1927, the *Völkischer Beobachter* entered the scene and reprinted in full the news item of the *Berliner Nachtausgabe* under the headline "Another smear Film in America," adding that diplomatic action has been a "weak German protest."[55] Thus, common German nationalist and Nazi attitudes had become evident. Both journals received support from Waldemar Lydor in the *Reichsfilmblatt*. At the beginning of April 1927, he intensified his rejection of Chaplin's "wartime smear film," which was known from his *Film-Kurier* article of April 1925: "The German is portrayed only as a culture-murdering 'Boche' and 'Hun,' namely with a big belly, long full beard and prehistoric spiked helmet," who "naturally stalks the innocent maidens" to rape them. This time the diminutive lieutenant was even supposed to have enjoyed caviar in the dugout, and Charlie, to have rescued several girls at once "from the clutches of the violent Huns."[56]

The *Lichtbildbühne* joined in a few days later. Under its German-Jewish editor-in-chief Dr. Hans Wollenberg, the trade journal had hitherto thought highly of Chaplin. Now it reproduced word for word the derogatory description of *Shoulder Arms* from the *Berliner Nachtausgabe,* complaining about a series of unending Germanophobe smear films, among which Chaplin's film was, on top of it all, particularly successful. This change of mind was admittedly surprising: As late as the beginning of 1926, the *Lichtbildbühne* had called *Shoulder Arms* one of Chaplin's "four immortal masterpieces."[57]

Shoulder Arms *in Bulgaria*

Diplomatic interventions against *Shoulder Arms* in Europe had already begun in late summer 1926 and continued until at least 1928. Chaplin's anti-war film is thus an early model for the struggle of German diplomats against *The Great Dictator* (see Chapter 12).

On September 15, 1926, an official of the German legation in the Bulgarian capital of Sofia attended the screening of *Shoulder Arms*, which had premiered the previous day under the German-translated Bulgarian distribution title *Chaplin hinter der Front* (Chaplin Behind the Front). Afterwards, he informed the Gesandtschaftsrat (Legation Counselor) Willy Noebel, who was German Gesandter (envoy) to South America in the early 1940s when the Third Reich fought Chaplin's *The Great Dictator* there. Noebel immediately approached the Bulgarian government and succeeded in having *Chaplin hinter der Front* cancelled the very next day. In his September 15, 1926, report to the Berlin Auswärtiges Amt (Foreign Office), he stated that he still wanted to investigate how it had been possible that "this sorry effort of the worst kind," which "offends German sensibilities," passed the Bulgarian board of film censors at all.[58] Just three days later, Noebel reported that the mishap had been fully resolved:

> The Germanophobe film *Chaplin hinter der Front* only passed the local board of film censors because the chairman of the Bulgarian Ministry of Education's Supervisory Committee for film screenings was on vacation and his deputy did not pay any special attention to the matter. This [quite pro–German] gentleman [...] has [... meanwhile] apologized for his negligence. The same day, the film [...] was confiscated by the Supervisory Committee via telegraph and its [...] further screening [...] barred.[59]

Noebel saw this as a "satisfactory settlement," and it possibly bore further fruit from the German point of view. *Shoulder Arms* was not officially shown in the Balkans, at least until 1932.[60]

Denmark

By 1926, *Shoulder Arms* had also been released in Belgium, Denmark, France, Great Britain, Italy, Norway, Portugal, Sweden, Switzerland, Spain and Czechoslovakia.[61] In at least some of these countries, German diplomats attempted either to prevent the film from being screened or to ensure that it was cut.

In early April 1926, the *Lichtbildbühne* complained about the Copenhagen release of the "decidedly Germanophobe smear film": "It should be reasonable to expect from a country as culturally advanced as Denmark that such stupid taunts of a neighboring state will not be released to the public."[62] In June 1927, Tucholsky went to a cinema in the Danish capital to see Chaplin's film, which had already been "defused" by "humorless German officials." He reported where the censorship scissors had been employed: "And then a car appears, and the two chauffeurs have wide bands of caps with eagles on them, but whatever you expect, does not happen. No Crown Prince is captured here, no Kaiser is captured here, no Hindenburg is captured here. Just 'an' officer...."[63] Further details of this Copenhagen edit of *Shoulder Arms* are not known. In October 1927, German-Jewish writer Hans Sochaczewer saw the film twice in Copenhagen, in versions that differed from one another. One is said to have been more complete than the version screened in July of that year, the other shortened. Around the time of Sochaczewer's visits to the cinema, Ulrich von Hassell, the German ambassador in Copenhagen, demanded that the Danish authorities remove several *Shoulder Arms* scenes, especially anything concerning Kaiser Wilhelm II and Field Marshal Hindenburg. The Danish press mocked von Hassell's request, but he scored a success.

Sochaczewer vented his displeasure at the Danish censorship action in the cultural magazine *Literarische Welt* and saw no reason to keep Chaplin's film out of Germany.[64] Tucholsky demanded that *Shoulder Arms* at last be shown in Germany: "The film should be played in a place where it has never been played before, and to where it belongs. [...] This shining film belongs in the darkest Germany. Over the Rhine, Chaplin, over the Rhine." At the same time, Tucholsky complained that

German diplomacy, almost ten years after the end of World War I, remained predominantly monarchist in spirit. Hardly any German embassy openly and honestly endorsed the Weimar Republic, he said. German diplomats also preferred the former imperial banner in black-white-red to the state flag of the Weimar Republic with the German colors black-red-gold, which they disparagingly referred to as "herring salad." Tucholsky's attitude received unspoken applause from the leftist journal *Sozialistische Bildung*, which rated Chaplin's films as "truly great art": "Maybe there will be a change of mind to show Chaplin's anti-war film. Or are [the authorities] afraid that we might be poisoned by the movie's pacifist idea?"[65]

France

In October 1927, *Shoulder Arms* was shown as *Charlot Soldat* in Alsace-Lorraine, France, bordering Germany.[66] The French authorities had previously reached an agreement with Leopold von Hoesch, the German ambassador in Paris, that German sensitivities should not be offended. Therefore, the scene was removed in which Charlie captures the Kaiser and his entourage. For the *Lichtbildbühne*, this was the third Chaplin exciter of the year, as the film "was originally loyally banned in France because its original version was a mockery of the German army." The agreed cut had been performed "not entirely appropriately," so that even this version, from the German point of view, was "still suitable for reviving old hatred." At least, however, the impact of *Charlot Soldat* had been softened during the "box office storm" at the Parisian Max Linder Cinema in the same month by a Verdun war film in the supporting program that "endeavored to present the events of the war objectively."[67] *Charlot Soldat* was re-released in the abridged version in Parisian cinemas in June 1931 on the occasion of Chaplin's European trip. The Communist journal *Arbeiterbühne und Film* deplored that the "genuine American film farce" had been manipulated and was therefore of "pure curiosity value."[68]

Switzerland and Great Britain

In 1927, *Shoulder Arms* was initially released to Swiss cinemas, but was then banned. Whether the German Envoy Frederic von Rosenberg had worked towards this is unknown. Following Lydor's article of April 1927, in January 1928, the *Reichsfilmblatt* was piqued that Chaplin's "Germanophobe smear film" with its "strong mockeries of German personalities" had been approved to be shown in Switzerland at all. It felt all the more relieved by the ban, because "any cause for conflict is fortunately disposed of once and for all."[69]

Analyzing *Shoulder Arms* remained purely the concern of left-wing German circles. Chaplin admirer Erich Gottgetreu saw the film in London in September 1928. Whether *Shoulder Arms* was screened there uncut or altered is unclear. In any case, Gottgetreu was one of the first to recognize that recruit Charlie had dreamt his experiences. He wrote about this in *Die Volksbühne*:

It is the most beautiful dream that has ever been dreamt, and one of the few co-products of the great struggle of nations. It is a dream equal in meaning to "Svejk" of whose spirit translated into ghetto Jewish and unintentionally anti-war tendency it breathes much. The dream of a man with a messianic longing for peace and happiness and with the strongest will to assimilate, which can be attributed to the instinct of self-preservation, who wants to cope with the torn and tearing present, because he has to come to terms with it. The dream of a man who is eternally on the way, nevertheless on the right way. The dream of an unconscious revolutionary. And the deed of a Shakespeare in the age of cinema.[70]

Loeb Once Again

After Loeb had unsuccessfully demanded compensation from Chaplin in 1921 because of the unauthorized adaptation of his screenplay "The Rookie" for *Shoulder Arms*, he sued the production company First National instead.[71] In this trial, Chaplin was heard as a witness in the spring of 1927. According to the report of a German daily newspaper, he supposedly designed his testimony like a grotesque reel with gestures from his films, so that the judge laughed heartily at the performance.[72] Possibly, however, the account belongs to the countless anecdotes that have been told about Chaplin over the decades. For it is doubtful that the court would have tolerated not being taken seriously by the witness Chaplin.

German coverage of the trial was somewhat muddled, probably because a clear distinction had not been made between First National as the current defendant and Chaplin as the former defendant and current witness. In November 1927, the *Lichtbildbühne* claimed in its news story "Chaplin Wins Plagiarism Trial" that the suit "directed against Chaplin" had been dismissed that month.[73] But it had actually been dismissed in 1921. So it could only be Loeb's lawsuit against First National. Loeb was also unsuccessful with this suit after two rounds in May and November 1927. As in 1921, he was unable to prove that Chaplin had "stolen" his idea.[74] Loeb is said to have appealed against the latest judgement in the lawsuit against First National.[75] Whether he had any success with it is unknown, but seems unlikely. Neither in the German film trade journals nor elsewhere has anything been found to suggest that a court had ordered First National to make payments to Loeb after all. The Nazi agitators, who later exploited allegations of plagiarism against Chaplin for propaganda purposes and even invented such (see below and Chapter 9), also remained silent. Chaplin's lawyer Nathan Burkan hailed the dismissal of Loeb's suit against First National as a victory for artistic freedom.[76]

Buchner's Chaplin Defamation

The Nazis' film-baiting was significantly expanded in 1927 with the book *Im Banne des Films—Die Weltherrschaft des Kinos* (Under the Spell of Film—The international Domination of Cinema) by Dr. Hans Buchner, editor of the *Völkischer Beobachter*. Published by the same media company as Rosenberg's *Der Weltkampf*, it was the first Nazi book on film. Initially, Buchner seemed to promise a solid factual analysis of the young mass medium. But after a few pages, it becomes obvious that he, too, only pursued the Nazi goal of excluding "the non–German spirit and the non–German culture." He demanded that "an end must be put to support party-politically determined influences and endeavors alien to the people, to the legally established so-called [Film-]Prüfstellen, which are nothing more than part of the corrosive system that etches at the core of the nations like a devouring leach." To this end, he asked the rhetorical question: "Where will it all end? What is going on here, barely perceptible, creeping, slowly and steadily corroding?"[77]

Buchner addressed Chaplin as one of the few foreign artists with longer comments. He did not focus on Chaplin's artistic significance in international film, for example, as the left-leaning cultural magazine *Die Neue Bücherschau* was to do in April 1928 in its essays "Before Charlie Chaplin" and "From Charlie Chaplin to Vsevold Illarionovich Pudovkin."[78]

Buchner, like other Nazi agitators, blended artistic creation and private life. He denied originality to Chaplin the artist. While he did not explicitly refer to Chaplin as a Jew, he pilloried him both as an enemy of the German people, as a Bolshevik, and as an anti-religious enemy of all the nations of the world. In this context, Buchner quoted extensively from Siemsen's 1924 *Charlie Chaplin*, whose pacifist stance and assessment of Chaplin as one of the most important artists he fought in the same breath. The Siemsen quote concluded as follows: "[Chaplin] teaches that nothing should be taken seriously, nothing but the very simplest human things. [...] He teaches the perfect, the radical disrespect. God bless him. He is a revolutionary." Buchner commented as follows: "In reality, of course, [Chaplin] is not a revolutionary, but a Bolshevik. And Chaplin is not the only one! This is where the state, religion and culture must beware! Here is where their tasks must begin!"[79]

Buchner also tried to distract attention from the biases that could not warm

Hans Buchner, *Im Banne des Films*, book cover, 1927.

to the "vaterländische films" (Nationalistic Films): "One wonders why the large audience remained dull, apathetic, and preferred to watch Charlie Chaplin."[80] He went on that Chaplin's objectionable behavior had become known from the divorce proceedings and had led to the "morality clause" in the U.S. film industry, which, conforming to the will of U.S. film producers, should in the future contractually obligate all actors to a "decent and honorable" lifestyle.[81] Buchner further quoted from a list of the annual incomes of U.S. film actors. Chaplin was ranked third with 3.12 million Reichsmark after top-of-the-list Harold Lloyd with 4.16 million Reichsmark, not counting his share from the box-office takings of his movies. In addition, Buchner accused Chaplin of having pursued a publicity strategy with his divorce: "The extent of these profits can be gauged from the fact that Chaplin, in addition to his fixed income, earned several million dollars in a single year alone from his *The Gold Rush*. [...] Film stars occasionally lapse into all-too-human humanity, which is by no means detrimental to their reputation, but only becomes the subject of an all the more profitable advertisement."[82] He concluded two things from the list of incomes: rich Chaplin had behaved financially shamefully toward Lita Grey, and German actors earned only "starvation wages" compared to their U.S. colleagues.

Buchner now merged several slanderous accusations and constructed from them the stereotypical Nazi anti–Semitic Chaplin smear pattern as a parasitic "raffinierter Geschäftemacher" (Clever wheeler-dealer), helping himself unabashedly to ideas of non–Jews. In this regard, Buchner stated that Chaplin's trademark was "psychopathischer Kretinismus" (psychopathic Cretinism). He did not even create this himself, but had "copied it from a brilliant Italian" and turned this serious money for his own benefit.[83] According to Buchner, this "ingenious Italian" was Billie Ritchie:

> What a cult was made out of Charlie Chaplin! With what participation the whole world followed the fate of Chaplin, the "revolutionary per se," the "last romantic," the genius, the original, whose film character, whose mask is everything, with which he stands and falls, hobbles and prances, cries and laughs. Without which he would not be; which constitutes all his originality. But there lived some time ago an Italian comedian named Billie Rietschie [*sic*]. He anglicized his name from Ricci. This one played long before the war in a Chaplin-like guise, when Chaplin was still performing in a London ensemble as a shoeshine boy! In 1908, a little comedy film with Billie Ritchie was shot in this makeup. The film will probably no longer exist, since the film company no longer exists. The similarity between the two characters is striking. That "kökschen" [Charlie's bowler hat] on the frizzy hair, that toothbrush moustache, sloppy tie, slouchy shoulders, jacket closed at one button, laps pulled back, both hands buried in pants pockets, concertina pants, well-worn giant slippers, a coquettish cane—that is Billie Ritchie, 15 years later that is Charlie Chaplin. Did Chaplin know him? Of course, he knew him and "commandeered" Ritchie's guise as suitable for himself. Thus, from the "beloved fairy-tale figure" remains a "Kopist" [Thief of intellectual property] who has copied the mask from an original and is making millions with it.[84]

In fact, Ritchie did not create Chaplin's Tramp Charlie, nor did, according to a rumor, the English "Tingeltangel-Schmierist" (Honky-tonk Entertainment gook artist) Billy Hurrydale, reported by Billy Wilder in the *Berliner Börsen-Courier* in 1927.[85] Nothing is known about Hurrydale. Did Wilder maybe mean Ritchie? Even the assumption that Chaplin's fictional character can be reduced to the Tramp costume already falls short. It is Chaplin's revolutionary cinematic innovations, his abilities as a film creator and actor, that set him apart in film history. Buchner completely ignored this. Moreover, Ritchie's and Chaplin's film costumes are not identical. The two actors also did not employ them to the same effect. Finally, Buchner also failed to explain what the artistic similarities between their films were supposed to be. In fact, Ritchie and Chaplin resemble each other artistically only to a very small extent, as Steve Massa has pointed out.[86]

Billy Ritchie, ca. mid–1910s.

By early January 1915, Ritchie had already claimed in a letter from his lawyer to have developed the Tramp costume and Chaplin's kind of comedy as early as 1887. Here, the three different years of birth attributed to Ritchie become significant: 1874, 1877 and 1879.[87] If he had developed the costume and the character of the Tramp Charlie in 1887, he would have been 13, ten or even only eight years old at the time. His very young age alone would give reason to doubt his account. The creation of such a complex film character would have required both life and professional experience, which Ritchie could hardly have possessed even as a 13-year-old at best. Reports that Ritchie was a premature innovative stage performer are unknown. Ritchie was also said to have anticipated the look and mannerisms of Chaplin's Tramp in a 1908 film. According to Massa's research, however, Ritchie's first film was *Love and Surgery*, released to U.S. theaters on October 25, 1914.[88] Chaplin's second Keystone film, *Kid's Auto Race at Venice*, in which he is seen for the first time in Tramp costume, was released eight and a half months before, on February 7, 1914. His third Keystone film, *Mabel's Strange Predicament*, in which he began to develop the Charlie character, followed two days later. This is precisely why Ritchie is considered a Chaplin impersonator![89] It was not until 1915, when the Swedish board of film censors banned Chaplin's Keystone film *The Rounders*, that Chaplin was mistaken for Billie Ritchie as an actor.[90] After all, Ritchie was not Italian either. He was born William Hill in 1874 in Glasgow, Scotland.[91] His stage name "Billie" is the nickname form of "William." No part of William Hill reveals Italian traces.

The *Lichtbildbühne* reviewed Buchner's *Im Banne des Films* under the headline

"Im Banne des Vorurteils" (Under the Spell of Prejudice). Commenting on Chaplin, the reviewer wrote, "We do not want to slam [Buchner's] definition of Chaplinesque art over him," and went on: "For all that, it is vital to pay attention and to recognize the enemy, i.e., not to overlook Buchner's peculiar 'Film-Bann' (Movie Spell)."[92] *Filmtechnik* and *Film-Journal* also disapproved *Im Banne des Films*.[93] *Filmtechnik* highlighted that Buchner, on the one hand, railed against the immorality of the film industry, while on the other hand, the cover of his book was graced by a drawing of a naked woman.

Selective Nazi Reaction

In 1928, Nazi propaganda journals kept silent about Chaplin's *Zirkus*, even when it started in Munich in February.[94] On March 13, 1928, Goebbels and the notorious anti–Semitic graphic artist Hans Herbert Schweitzer, alias Mjölnir, and known as "the Illustrator of National Socialism,"[95] saw it in a Berlin cinema. In his diary, Goebbels noted: "Tonight, with Schweitzer, saw the Chaplin film *Circus*. Sometimes killingly funny. Full of the most hilarious antics. Yet, the last thing is missing. The Jew is not creative."[96] Goebbels had obviously gotten his money's worth. What he missed as "the last thing" he did not put down in his diary. After that, the Nazi press did not attack *Zirkus* until it was re-released in late summer 1931 (see Chapter 4). Goebbels' ambivalent attitude toward the film was not expressed.

Chaplin again made the headlines of the *Völkischer Beobachter* in September 1928 because of his September 1921 visit to Berlin. A few months earlier, the French translation of his book *My Trip Abroad* had appeared. In it, he told about his invitation to the home of German-Jewish lawyer Justizrat (Counsel) Dr. Johannes Werthauer, where he dined royally and was entertained by a Russian band. He suddenly associated this with the mysterious Russian monk Rasputin, which made him ponder how a perfect murder could be fictitiously committed in Werthauer's house.[97] Werthauer was a pivotal hate personality of the Nazis. He was among the first 33 persons to be expatriated by them on August 23, 1933, because they were said to have violated "by their conduct the duty of loyalty to the Reich and the people." Chaplin's reminder of a barely meaningful association was obviously no more than a marginal note. Nevertheless, in "Chaplin über Werthauer" (Chaplin on Werthauer), the *Völkischer Beobachter* inflated it to a political issue of the "infamous" Chaplin and linked it with a report on the involvement of the Russian poet Maxim Gorky in the conflict between the Kremlin and Ukrainian separatists.[98]

Just like *Zirkus*, the Nazi propaganda press passed *Carmen*, the unauthorized extended version of Chaplin's 1915 two-reeler *A Burlesque on Carmen*.[99] It had its German premiere at Berlin's Titania-Palast on January 20, 1929, and was released in Munich in June.[100] In mid–June and mid–July 1929, *Carmen* and *Abenteuer*, a program of Chaplin short subjects, with telegram-style ads in the "Münchener Beobachter," the regional section of the *Völkischer Beobachter*. This kind of local cinema ads had appeared in the propaganda journal for some time.[101]

Chaplin had parodied Cecil B. DeMille's 1915 feature film *Carmen*, based on

Prosper Mérimée's 1847 novella, for the Essanay Film Manufacturing Company. He had dubbed his Don José Darn Hosiery and had played that role. After his departure from Essanay, the production company did not release Chaplin's two-reel version *A Burlesque on Carmen*, but on April 22, 1916, the version *Carmen*, which had been blown up to twice its length. In this version, Essanay had inserted scenes from the cutting room floor that Chaplin had discarded, and a few scenes shot without his participation in order to cash in on a much longer film and the name of the superstar Chaplin. Suddenly in the film was Ben Turpin, with whom Chaplin had not collaborated for *A Burlesque on Carmen*. Essanay's hybrid version obviously had disregarded Chaplin's creative process. Chaplin had insisted that only his two-reel version be shown in theaters and had filed an action against Essanay which had been dismissed in May 1916.[102]

During the Berlin premiere, the weaknesses of the extended *Carmen* version did not escape the atten-

Warum wurde

CHARLIE CHAPLIN

in

„Carmen"

zum ersten Male in Deutschland

U r a u f f ü h r u n g
Sonntag, den 20. Januar
12 Uhr mittags
Titania-Palast, Steglitz

von allen führenden Theaterbesitzern
gemietet?

Weil der erfahrene Theaterbesitzer sagt:
„Ich muß meinem Publikum mal wieder
etwas Besonderes bieten, um ein volles
Haus zu bekommen, und darum miete ich
Charlie Chaplin als Don José in Carmen
von

Fritz Knevels-Film-Verleih (FilmTraCo)
Zimmerstr. 15   B E R L I N S W 68   Zentrum 3933

Fritz Knevels-Film-Verleih ad for the German premiere of
***Carmen*, January 20, 1929.**

tion of film critic and future Chaplin hatemonger Betz. In his review, he pointed out that this version did not yet show Chaplin at the height of his skills, but recognized in it Chaplin's "surprising wealth of mimic expressive possibilities." He continued, "[Chaplin] played himself up [, …] poetized himself and [recognized] the meaning of the film comedy … as a Mephistophelian negation of the awareness of value." Betz thanked the Berlin distributor Express-Filmverleih GmbH for bringing *Carmen* to

Germany and predicted that the four-reeler would attract "the keenest interest of the audience for Chaplin's sake alone."[103]

The Pilgrim

In April 1929, United Artists' German branch merged with Terra Filmver-leih GmbH—probably against Chaplin's wishes. Chaplin feared that the merger of United Artists with Warner Brothers, which he had opposed, could materialize in this way.[104]

In the fall of that year, distributor Terra–United Artists acquired the German screening rights for Chaplin's *The Pilgrim* (1923)[105] and *Feine Leute* (*The Idle Class*, 1921) and applied for their approval to the Berlin Film-Prüfstelle, which passed the films without objections.[106] Sabine Hake has claimed, without providing any facts, that *The Pilgrim* was supposedly made as early as 1917 and, due to difficulties with German film censorship, was not released in Germany until years after its U.S. premiere.[107] This is incorrect. *The Pilgrim* had first been submitted to the Berlin Film-Prüfstelle in the fall of 1929. According to *Film-Kurier*, years earlier, the U.S. distribution company at the time, very likely Vogel Productions, was said to have demanded "absurd amounts" for the German screening rights of the film.[108] This may not have changed too much: In early December 1929, Terra–United Artists announced its "Christmas present [...] to the German theater owners" with five of Chaplin's First National films, which were to be released in two programs shortly before Christmas 1929 and at the end of February 1930. The distributor added that the rights to them had been acquired "at great sacrifice"[109]—possibly spurred in particular by the great business success of Chaplin's *Zirkus* over the previous year.

On December 19, 1929, the German premiere of the first program with *The Pilgrim* and *Feine Leute* took place at Berlin's Universum am Lehniner Platz.[110] In his masterpiece *The Pilgrim*, Chaplin had succeeded in an almost unbelievable condensation of the narrative structure down to all its nuances. On his escape, convict Charlie snatches the clothes of a bathing priest. But Charlie does not feel at all comfortable in the cassock and fears that he will be discovered quickly. Therefore, he buys a train ticket to Texas at the station. The train ride becomes a nail-biting event, because Charlie feels recognized by fellow passengers. In panic, he leaves the train at the next station, a small town, and almost falls into the arms of a sheriff who, to his amazement, greets him amicably. The sheriff is a member of a delegation of the local parish who want to welcome the new priest and believes Charlie to be the man. Charlie quickly adapts to his new role, especially since a pretty young lady arouses his interest.

It is just time for the service, so the group proceeds straight to the church. Before the liturgy, the churchwarden asks Charlie to read him a telegram because he has forgotten his glasses. It says that the arrival of the real priest will be delayed by a week, so Charlie invents a trivial message that causes the churchwarden to throw the telegram away. In the church, Charlie is uncomfortable but there is no way out, so he resigns himself to his fate. Everything seems to be quite harmless,

Picture: "THE PILGRIM" (Dates furnished by Vogel Production, Inc. N.Y., to Dec. 1931)
(F.N. means distributed by Associated First Nat'l Pict. Inc.)

	TERRITORY	RELEASE DATE	DUE	DELIVARY DATE	NOTE
	United States (F.N.)	Feb. 23, 1923	Feb. 16, 1928		
	Canada (F.N.)	Feb. 23, 1923	Feb. 16, 1928		
1	Great Britian	Aug. 27, 1923	Aug. 27, 1928		
2	France	Feb. 20, 1925	Feb. 20, 1930		
3	Belgium	Oct. 23, 1923	Oct. 23, 1928		
4	Switzerland	Aug. 1, 1924	Aug. 1, 1929		
5	Holland	Mar. 24, 1925	Mar. 24, 1929		
6	Norway	Sold but not delivered			
7	Sweden	Dec. 26, 1927	Dec. 26, 1932		
8	Denmark	Sold but not delivered			
9	Finland	....	....		
10	Spain	Dec. 11, 1925	Dec. 11, 1930		
11	Portugal	Dec. 11, 1925	Dec. 11, 1930		
12	Germany	Dec. 19, 1929	Dec. 19, 1934		
13	Russia	....			
14	Italy	Feb. 24, 1927	Feb. 24, 1932		
15	Balkans	Dec. 12, 1924	Dec. 12, 1929		
16	Egypt	June 16, 1923	June 16, 1928		
17	Jugo-Slavia	....	....		
18	Austria-Hungary (Aust)	June 30, 1928 (Aust)	June 30, 1933		
19	Poland	....			
20	Czecho-Slavakia	Dec. 26, 1924	Decc. 26, 1929		
21	Japan	March 19, 1923	March 19, 1928		
22	China	April 4, 1923	April 4, 1928		
23	Philippines	March 3, 1924	March 3, 1929		
24	India	June 19, 1923	June 19, 1928		
25	Burma	"	"		
26	Ceylon	"	"		
27	Dutch East Indies	July 28, 1924	July 28, 1929		
28	Straits Settlement	"	"		
29	Fed. Malay States	"	"		
30	French Indo China	"	"		
31	Siam	"	"		
32	Australia	May 14, 1923	May 14, 1928		
33	New Zealand				
34	South Africa	June 19, 1928	June 19, 1933		
35	West Indies May 16	April 26, 1923	April 26, 1928	May 16.	
36	Columbia	....	....		
37	Venzuela	April 26, 1923	April 26, 1928		
38	Central America	....	....		
39	Mexico	June 12, 1923	June 12, 1928		
40	Brazil Oct. 29	March 14, 1923	March 12, 1928	Oct. 29.	
41	Argentina Oct. 1	May 28, 1923	May 28, 1928	Oct. 1.	
42	Paraguay	"	"		
43	Uruguay	Oct. 10, 1923	Oct. 10, 1928		
44	Chile	Apr. 7, 1923	Apr. 7, 1928		
45	Peru	"	"		
46	Bolivia	"	"		
47	Equador				

Red underline indicates delivery dates, therefore release date is about 2 or
3 months later, advancing the due date accordingly.

Worldwide sales of *The Pilgrim* as of December 1931 (Charlie Chaplin Archive, digitized by Cineteca di Bologna, www.charliechaplinarchive.org).

until the churchwarden discreetly informs Charlie that his sermon is now expected. Charlie goes to the lectern and opens the holy book just at the point where the story of David and Goliath is told. He now interprets this story in his own pantomime, alternating between David and Goliath, not without checking the Bible from time to time to see what happens next. The parishioners are embarrassed—they have never experienced anything like this before! Only one little boy, who did not know what to do during the singing due to boredom, applauds enthusiastically, happily accepted by Charlie.

Charlie will stay in the house of a lady and her daughter, whom he had already seen with pleasure at the station. On the way there, he meets his former cellmate, who has just separated a pub goer from his cash. Charlie wants to get rid of him, but the crook smells a good set-up. In his new

Terra-United Artists ad for *The Pilgrim* with poster design, December 19, 1929.

accommodation, Charlie has only eyes for the daughter of the landlady. She receives a visit from an unsympathetic fellow along with his constantly arguing wife and their brat, who keeps on pestering Charlie. So he prefers to help the daughter with the preparation for the afternoon coffee. Distracted by the rascal, he accidentally decorates a bowler hat with cream instead of a black hemispherical plum pudding. Charlie, of course, fails to cut this cake at the coffee table. But at least the unsympathetic family leaves in a piqued mood.

In the evening, Charlie and the daughter chat by the garden fence. Charlie's cellmate reappears and has himself invited into the house, claiming to be Charlie's old school friend. Twice the villain steals the churchwarden's money, but both times Charlie is able to recover the loot. Then the crook steals the homeowner's money, which is meant for the mortgage. Charlie gets in his way, but he knocks him out and flees. Charlie also succeeds in taking back this money from the thief as well. But now Charlie finds himself in a precarious situation and is arrested by the sheriff, who, however, has realized that there is a good core in Charlie after all. Instead of locking him up, the good-natured man takes him to the Mexican border to give him the opportunity to escape. But the simple-minded Charlie does not understand this and bravely returns to him again and again, even when he is supposed to pick flowers for him across the border. Then the sheriff kicks Charlie into Mexico and quickly rides off. Now Charlie realizes that he is free and wistfully bids America farewell and looks forward to a happy future in Mexico. But then a gunfight starts between bandits. Where is Charlie to go now? Into the hail of bullets that may cost him his life, or back to America, where prison awaits him? Homeless, he will wander along the border, with one foot in Mexico and the other in America—and with that, the film fades out.

The Pilgrim and Feine Leute were welcomed with open arms. The Lichtbild-bühne considered The Pilgrim a "treasure" and ranked it with The Kid, Goldrausch and Zirkus:

> The whole film is a great furioso of wit, comedy, ravishing ideas [...]. It is an unthinkable undertaking to try to reproduce a Chaplin film with words, and therefore only hints can be given here. [... It] is one of the most beautiful [films] in the world. [... Chaplin, the actor] is one of the very few who have grasped the deep meaning of cinematic dramatics. [... Watch The Pilgrim], once, twice, three times, you will forget your day-to-day worries and be newly inspired by a deep love for him, the only one, for Charlie.[111]

The audience followed the advice. The Pilgrim and Feine Leute set box-office records not only in Berlin, even during the Great Depression following Black Friday on October 24, 1929 (which was a Thursday). The Christmas business of 1929 was "extraordinary" for the two movies in all districts of the capital with overcrowded cinemas.

Record box-office revenues for several weeks followed in the cinemas that replayed the two films. Among them were 19 Berlin premiere theaters, 17 of which prolonged the program.[112] The schedule was also extended in Frankfurt am Main, Stuttgart, Mannheim and Hamburg. In Hamburg, where The Pilgrim and Feine Leute were shown in eight cinemas in February and March 1930, over 43,000 paying moviegoers flocked to them during the first three days alone.[113] Why a Bavarian ministry (Ministry of Culture?) vetoed The Pilgrim, as reported by the Film-Kurier in July 1930,[114] and what the consequences were, are unknown.

At the end of 1929, the Völkischer Beobachter reacted to a Chaplin film for the first time since Goldrausch. In its usual polemicizing style, it tried to suggest that readers needed to be protected from The Pilgrim's "cunningly devised comedy":

> This little, knocked-about Charlie Chaplin, with the Jewishly clever child's eyes, who is kicked and tormented by everyone, but who at the right moment squeezes his tormentor's throat and easily dances over his enemies and their morals, is none other than the eternally unchanging Mauschel [Yiddish-speaking Cheater], who roams the world, pleasing, poisoning and enjoying it. He is never evil [...]. In the end, he is even kind, but not to the last consequence. In all this lies Chaplin's essence. There is the veiled abyss, his hidden slyness. In his passivity, he can be even more wicked. He is the incarnation of his race [... and he dances] on the Christian rite.[115]

This, of course, does not do justice to the content of *The Pilgrim*, and certainly Chaplin does not "dance on the Christian rite." Did the *Völkischer Beobachter* use anti–Jewish stereotypes from the Christian tradition? This was not at all uncommon in Nazi propaganda, even if the Nazis were no red-hot advocates of the Christian church. Yet, it can only be assumed as to why the propaganda journal attacked Chaplin so fiercely precisely because of this film. Was it intolerable that the supposed Jew Chaplin caricatured a Christian service? Religious circles may have disliked Charlie's vivid, easily understandable sermon. But it certainly does not mock the Christian religion. Rather, Chaplin has carefully observed and accurately portrayed the conduct of church services. Just as appropriate is his portrayal of parish life, which is not determined by constant piety, as is exhibited in church on Sundays. Finally, even the escaped convict Charlie stands out for his honesty and sincerity. He demonstrates civil courage when he uses a trick to wrest the stolen cash from his former buddy and returns it to the parish.

The *Völkischer Beobachter* did not address the short subject *Feine Leute*. In a double role, Chaplin plays Tramp Charlie, who indulges in the rich-people sport of golf with his modest means, and the son-in-law of a rich family whose vice is alcohol. The characters look identical. Charlie accidentally, and with some impudence, gets into a fancy-dress ball. And there, both the other guests and the alcoholic's wife confuse them. She is even happy that for once her husband is not drunk and her ultimatum "The alcohol or me!" has worked. But he has to watch her caressing a supposed rival. The story does not end well for Charlie, because the alcoholic's father-in-law turns out to be the man Charlie had been nasty to on the golf course. With a kick in the backside, Charlie is thrown out of the house.

Does the "Idiot" Chaplin Buy Gags from an Old Clown?

On New Year's Day 1931, only the Berlin edition of the *Völkischer Beobachter* ran the smear article "Chaplin Buys Himself Ideas and Fame" by Nazi writer Max Jungnickel, author of the 1933 biography *Goebbels*. The Berlin edition was published from March 1, 1930, and was temporarily discontinued on April 1, 1931. It contributed to the *Völkischer Beobachter*'s increased daily circulation of about 120,000 copies at the time.[116] Jungnickel may have further spun out Buchner's 1927 claims about Billie Ritchie as the alleged creator of Chaplin's Tramp. Jungnickel presumably wanted to portray Chaplin as an uninspired filmmaker in order to harm business with his new film *City Lights*, which was about to be given its world premiere and subsequent German premiere:

> Now the Jewish press lackeys have praised their Jewish darling to the seventh movie heaven. They have written books about him, and in towel-length essays they have touted him as a genius and a philosopher. A completely ecstatic journalistic choirboy fell on his knees and warbled about the "divine Chaplin"! [...] No one came close to him. [...] With Chaplin, everything is masterful and unique. He is a poet, a director, one of the most ingenious men and the most gifted film actor. [...] That is how all Jewish press offices made it up. And now it is revealed that Chaplin is just an ordinary "Hanswurst" [Tomfool] who obtains his ideas, his movie direction, his jokes for good dollars from an old, worn-out clown. Bad luck for Judah! This is what the "Divine" looks like. [...] Chaplin would be a downright goose egg without

the old clown he has hired. An awesome exposure of the divine Chaplin: [...] a "raffinierter Schwindler" [Shrewd Crook]. Strange how the Jewish darlings are screwed by these facts. Since they do not have any ideas, they just buy [... for] good money [...] fame and honor, legends and genius. [...] It really cannot get any lower than that. And it has been known for long that this Chaplin is the "gehässigster Deutschenfeind" [Most spiteful Germanophobe], [who] has produced the most savage smear films against Germany. Now that he has been exposed as a phony, hopefully the German will not be lured again by Jewish mermaid tunes into a boob cinema where this Chaplin shows up with his bogus ideas. Being a nothing and agitating and then still taking the "Hungergroschen der Bespieenen" [pittance of those he spits at], no, no! We must not put up with this anymore.[117]

In the *Berliner Börsen-Courier*, influential film critic Herbert Ihering promptly exposed Jungnickel's piece of "factual" fiction, which did not provide sources or the name of the "old, worn-out clown," as a clumsy attempt to discredit Chaplin's extraordinary cultural achievement. Ihering unmasked the second-rate writer Jungnickel as the mouthpiece of the NSDAP's cultural-political calculations. At the same time, Ihering succinctly put Chaplin's significance for the movies into perspective:

> There was hardly any dispute about two achievements: not about the fact that the only art that has verifiably achieved something lasting after World War I is architecture. [...] Secondly, not about the fact that Chaplin films created the term "film" in the first place. Now someone is discovering that Chaplin was a fraud. Who? The lyrical hack writer Max Jungnickel. Where? In the *Völkischer Beobachter*. Now there is nothing more irrelevant than Mr. Jungnickel's opinion. The only interesting thing is whether the *Völkischer Beobachter* adopts the view of this powerless "Sprachtändler" [Linguistic Bungler]. [... Is it therefore] Mr. Jungnickel's own opinion? Or is it the official cultural policy of the *Völkischer Beobachter*, i.e., the NSDAP? If this diatribe is meant in terms of cultural policy, if a new film scandal, a new terror is already slowly to be announced here—then the case is simple. Modern architecture, the expulsion of [German sculptor and graphic artist Ernst] Barlach from the Weimar Museum, the offensive against Chaplin—the cultural policy of the *Völkischer Beobachter* is then not the expression of a people's movement, but the struggle against talent and achievement, against art, against spirit. It is a simple case. You would know.[118]

The Nazis did not only mobilize against Chaplin in their propaganda journals. NSDAP ideologue Alfred Rosenberg had founded the Kampfbund für Deutsche Kultur (Combat League for German Culture) in 1928[119] and toured the country with his rabble-rousing speeches, either alone and or with others.[120] "From Danzig to Lindau our Speakers are Banging the Drum" was the *Völkischer Beobachter*'s headline in January 1931.[121] Whipping mottos of such events, which by now had become very popular, were for example: "Blut und Ehre" (Blood and Honor), "Um die Wiederverlebendigung des Ehrgefühls" (Resurrecting the Sense of Honor)[122] and "Was nicht Rasse ist, ist Spreu" (What Is Not Race Is Chaff).[123]

In mid–February 1931, "drum-banging" orator Rosenberg appeared before an audience of 2000 at an event organized by the Nationalsozialistischer Deutscher Studentenbund (National Socialist German Student League) at the Königsberg Stadthalle. In his "masterful" lecture "Über den Schicksalskampf der deutschen Kultur" (The Struggle for the Destiny of German Culture), Rosenberg directly attacked Chaplin as the embodiment of the "neudeutsches Schönheitsideal" (Neo-German Ideal of Beauty), the "Idiot." This had to be countered by the resurgence of the "Mythos der Nation" (Myth of the Nation), and this could only be done by "Errichtung des ersten deutschen Nationalstaates im Geiste Hitlers" (Establishing the First German National State in Hitler's Spirit). The Nazi *Preußische Zeitung*, founded at the beginning of 1931 under the slogan "Freiheit und Brot!" (Freedom and Bread!) by the subsequent East Prussian Gauleiter Erich Koch, who in 1959 was sentenced to death in Poland for war crimes,[124] reported that Rosenberg was met with "minute-long storms of applause" for this and other statements.[125] Following the Königsberg event, in Danzig, Rosenberg addressed "a select audience with his lecture 'Kampf um die deutschen Charakterwerte' (Struggle for German Character Values) to the same profound success."[126]

In March 1931, the *Leipziger Volkszeitung*, "Organ für die Interessen des gesamten werktätigen Volkes" (Organ for the Interests of the Entire Working Class), retorted Rosenberg's Chaplin slur with Tramp Charlie's fictitious appearance at the Königsberg event of the Nationalsozialistischer Deutscher Studentenbund, for which he had sewn a swastika onto his costume. The audience waited for what the English "jerk" would have to say. Instead, he asked the house to explain to him what was understood by "undeutsch" (un–German). Then he juggled all sorts of things like mad and disappeared.[127]

4

Chaplin in Berlin,
City Lights—1931

Apart from Nazi attacks, interest in Germany focused on Chaplin's *City Lights*. In New York on February 7, 1931, he had declared that he wanted to attend his film's national premieres in the European capitals and to leave for London, Paris and Berlin in the next few days.[1] On February 13, he embarked from New York on the liner *Mauretania* for London to attend the February 27 British premiere of his film at the Dominion Theatre.[2] In Britain, Chaplin was welcomed by dramatist and critic George Bernard Shaw, and the film's festive London premiere became an event "on an unprecedented scale" that "made its mark on the cosmopolitan city."[3]

His visit to England began triumphantly,[4] but the mood turned against him: He had snubbed the Royal Family by not accepting their invitation to a charity event. In any case, he left for Berlin earlier than planned, accompanied by his secretary Carlyle T. Robinson and his valet Kono. In Berlin, the British Embassy is said to have refused to receive him publicly through Ambassador Sir Horace Rumbold,[5] but he invited Chaplin to dinner on March 10.[6] Curtis Melnitz,[7] former general manager of United Artists' German branch, established a Chaplin headquarters in Berlin. Karl Vollmoeller is said to have "detached" his mistress Ruth Landsberg for Chaplin,[8] who, among other things, acted as his interpreter and translator during his stay.[9] For the time being, the headquarters provided excellent organization of the visit and made it an impressive demonstration of Chaplin's popularity in Germany. He was at the center of Berlin media coverage and received a great deal of attention in the German press as well.[10] German nationalist newspapers such as the widely circulated *Rheinisch-Westfälische Zeitung*, which belonged to the Hugenberg Group and reported dismissively on the London premiere of *City Lights*,[11] published articles against Chaplin or remained silent about the media event. The Nazi agitation against him, however, gained momentum. Then Chaplin was caught between the millstones of political strife, and his visit ended abruptly, even before the German premiere of *City Lights*. The wave of Nazi agitation rolled on.

This chapter examines:

- waiting for *City Lights* and Chaplin
- the acquisition of the German distribution rights for *City Lights*
- Joseph Goebbels and his Berlin propaganda journal *Der Angriff*
- Chaplin's arrival in Berlin

- his sojourn between Nazi, other radical right-wing agitation and Communist propaganda
- the continuing Nazi agitation after Chaplin's departure
- the German premiere of *City Lights* and right-wing reactions
- Nazi agitation against *City Lights* and re-released Chaplin films

A New Chaplin Film

Since June 1928, there had been reports in Germany that Chaplin's next film would have sound effects. It was to be called *City Lights* and would probably be distributed in Germany under the title "Streiflichter" (Highlights),[12] but was later renamed *Lichter der Großstadt.* Filming with *Circus* leading lady Merna Kennedy was already to have begun but she was replaced by Virginia Cherrill.

According to news reports in August 1928, production was to be completed in October of that year and the film was to be released "in Germany no later than December."[13] It was also said that Chaplin would attend the German premiere in Berlin.[14] Erich Burger's book *Charlie Chaplin. Bericht seines Lebens* was to be published at the same time,[15] but it was postponed until 1929. But would *City Lights* perhaps be a talking film after all? There were contradictory reports about this from February 1929 to July 1930. Allegedly, Chaplin wanted to screen *City Lights* together with a sound movie, in which he would not be acting. Then again, it was said that he would add a score to the film, for which he would play the violin himself. In addition, he would coax sounds from a small whistle. It was also rumored that he was planning a spoken prologue and epilogue for *City Lights*.[16] But in March 1930, it was said that Chaplin wanted to establish an anti-talkie association and refuse European distribution of his film in order to prevent it from becoming a vanguard of the talkies.[17]

From August 1930 to February 1931, there was also back and forth about premiere locations. According to *Film-Journal*, *City Lights'* world premiere was scheduled for the end of August 1930 in London and the German premiere for October 15, 1930, at the reopening of Berlin's Tauentzien-Palast. From another source, however, the trade journal had learned that Chaplin wanted to arrange personally the world premieres in Hollywood and in New York.[18] Finally, on February 2, 1931, *City Lights'* world premiere took place at the Los Angeles Theatre and earned Chaplin a new record attendance.[19] He enjoyed an "unprecedented storm of crowds [... and] ovations." *City Lights* caused traffic jams and "turned out a success beyond the wildest dreams."[20]

At the end of February 1931, the *Lichtbildbühne* devoted almost a full page to "Chaplin's World Premiere." Heinrich Fraenkel, editor of the trade journal's foreign section, had attended the world premiere and wrote in his enthusiastic "Erinnerungen eines beinahe zu Tode Getrampelten" (Recollections of Somebody Trampled Almost to Death): "It is hopeless to try to describe a Chaplin film. You will have to watch it for yourself."[21] Soon it was announced that Chaplin, "like no other film artist," would also "make [German] audiences laugh and cry again."[22] When the film was in general U.S. distribution, for example, it received the following heartfelt praise: "Every third year the world is allowed to step away from the melancholy of its depression and rejoice in the marvel of a new Charlie Chaplin comedy."[23] Overall, *City Lights* was internationally acclaimed.

German Distribution of City Lights

In mid–January 1931, the German press reported that, based on deals made so far with U.S. theater owners and foreign license holders, Chaplin expected *City Lights* to generate $8,000,000, or the equivalent of 32 million reichsmark in revenue, with $6 million from U.S. and $2 million from foreign distribution.[24] He also arranged the European premiere of *City Lights*. London's cinemas had competed for it. The Dominion was awarded the contract for a 20-week run and had to pay Chaplin £40,000.[25] In London, Chaplin also negotiated the sale of screening rights to other European countries and reportedly generated "fancy prices," including a guaranteed sum of three million francs for the screening rights at the Paris Théatre Marigny.[26]

City Lights was "eagerly awaited"[27] in Germany as "undoubtedly the most interesting sound film creation [*sic*] of recent years."[28] In May 1929, the Berlin-based Terra Filmverleih GmbH had brought itself into play as the German distributor of *City Lights*. Chaplin was said to have protested against this and considered having the film distributed elsewhere, perhaps by his own organization, which had yet to be established.[29] Terra Filmverleih GmbH's plan did not come to fruition. In late 1929 and early 1930, this company had been involved in the distribution of the successful Chaplin programs *The Pilgrim* and *Feine Leute* and *Lohntag* (*Pay Day*), *Vergnügte Stunden* (*A Day's Pleasure*) and *Auf dem Lande* (*Sunnyside*). At the beginning of 1931, however, it was in financial straits and therefore had not negotiated with Chaplin at all. Since 1926, it had been backed 100 percent by Terra Film AG,[30] whose stock had belonged almost exclusively to the Industriegewerkschaft (Industrial Union) Farbenindustrie since 1928.[31] As early as the beginning of May 1930, it had been assumed that Terra Film AG would be liquidated, and in fact a loss of almost 600,000 reichsmark had been publicized in June,[32] which could also not be compensated by expected income because it was not yet due.[33] At the time, Melnitz had been an Executive Board member of Terra Film AG. A group around him had acquired the Industriegewerkschaft Farbenindustrie's stock portfolio in Terra Film AG, but soon passed it on.[34] By the end of 1930, Terra Film AG's losses had mounted to such an extent that judicial settlement proceedings were opened at the end of August 1931, with the result that the company could be reorganized as early as the fall of that year.[35] Nevertheless, Terra Filmverleih GmbH is said to have offered Chaplin $190,000, the equivalent of 800,000 reichsmark, for the German screening rights to *City Lights* in February 1931. The deal failed to materialize because Chaplin demanded 1,000,000 reichsmark, or $237,500.[36] In 1932, the distributor was also unable to realize its intention to re-release *Goldrausch* throughout Germany in 1932 (see Chapter 2).

Südfilm AG won the race. At Chaplin's invitation, its director Isidor Gold-schmid traveled to London at the end of February 1931 to negotiate the contract.[37] Chaplin sold Südfilm AG the German screening rights to *City Lights* for $210,000 or even $220,000, then the equivalent of around 850,000 or 890,000 reichsmark, and was said to have commanded a cash down payment of 500,000 reichsmark upon signing the contract.[38] This price was criticized as "incompatible with the economic situation in Germany."[39] Chapter 6 will take a look at the funding.

Chaplin's Arrival

On March 7, 1931, it had been vaguely suggested that Chaplin would also find time to come to Berlin,[40] but on the evening of March 8, he suddenly departed from London by train from Liverpool Street Station for Berlin, a move that was called "hasty."[41] The idea was entertained that Chaplin would attend the German premiere of *City Lights*.[42] The Communist newspaper *Die Welt am Abend*, on the other hand, reported that he would leave Berlin after a few days and return for the German premiere in April.[43] In fact, it got scheduled for the end of March 1931 at Berlin's Ufa-Palast am Zoo.[44]

In Harwich, Chaplin boarded the canal ferry *Prague* and spent the crossing to Hoek van Holland with German star conductor Wilhelm Furtwängler,[45] who was on his way back to Germany with the Berlin Philharmonic Orchestra after a concert in the British capital.[46] Chaplin continued his journey by express train, during which he told the correspondent of the non-partisan German daily newspaper *B.Z.* (Berliner Zeitung) *am Mittag*: "I am happy to visit Germany and to see it again. I have thousands of friends in Germany who write to me, but I know only a few people there personally. I hope to see more of Germany during my upcoming visit than last time and learn more about it." The express stopped in the Lower Saxony, the capital of Hanover, at about 2:00 p.m. on March 9, 1931.[47] As the stopover had not been announced on a grand scale, only a few journalists, press photographers and admirers had gathered there. Reporters boarded the train to interview Chaplin during the continuation of his journey and to be close to the action upon his arrival in Berlin. Among them was Ufa's Auslandspressedienst-Chef (Head of Foreign Press Service) Albert A. Sander,[48] who will be discussed further in Chapter 7. Sander was to arrange to film Chaplin's arrival in Berlin for the newsreel *Ufa-Tonwoche*.[49] Since Chaplin wanted to relax, his secretary Robinson did not let anyone in to him except Sander.

Around this time, 147 daily newspapers were published in Berlin. Ninety-three of them were sold six times a week or even more often—a world record. In the politically highly split spectrum of the imperial capital, these newspapers included 45 morning, 14 evening, two noon and several Monday newspapers, at least 17 of them belonging to the right-wing or radical right camp.[50] On March 8, 1931, Berlin newspapers announced Chaplin's arrival at a Berlin train station the next day in a big way. For example, the *Vorwärts* enthusiastically wrote in its late edition *Der Abend*: "The ingenious creator of the kicked underdog beneath the mask of grotesque humor […]

comes to Berlin today. [A great man] who affects people emotionally, carries them away and makes them laugh. That is more important than a representative royal appearance with Reichswehr escorts and Grand Tattoo."[51] Heaven's tribute to Chaplin in the liberal democratic newspaper *Tempo* included the following: "If ever it did honor to humanity to celebrate a man who provided it with cheerful hours, this was it. [...] By making people laugh, [Chaplin] touched their hearts and evoked one of the best qualities of the heart: the ability to empathize and to be compassionate. At the same time, he strengthened the spirit [...] not to let it get us down."[52] Heinz Pol wrote in the *Vossische Zeitung*:

> We all are a bit of this little, cheeky, clumsy vagabond with his great desire. Like him, we are all a little afraid of the serious side of life, and once in a while we all like to play a trick on the good guy [...]. We all fall for someone else's tricks and tricks once in a while, and we all crawl our way back out of the hole we have fallen into. [Chaplin's ...] greatest merit remains that he discovered [Tramp Charlie] for film, and that he thereby raised film in general to a high artistic and human level [... and] so often brought us relieving laughter. We have almost forgotten this laughter in the last few years, but when we sneaked into the cinema, tired, angry and depressed, and watched a Chaplin comedy, we left with a different spirit. [...] And therefore we salute Charlie Chaplin.[53]

A series of poems appeared in greeting. Prominent writer and poet Erich Kästner dedicated his *An Charlie Chaplin* in the *B.Z. am Mittag* to the event with the

B.Z. am Mittag, March 9, 1931: "Charlie, unsere Herzen fliegen dir zu" [Charlie, Our Hearts Just Come to You], cartoon by unknown artist.

addition "Charlie, unsere Herzen fliegen dir zu" (Charlie, Our Hearts Just Come to You).[54] Victor Wittner published *Chaplin* in the *Vossische Zeitung*,[55] *Tempo* reproduced *Lieschen liebt Charlie aus der Ferne* (Jane Doe Loves Charlie from Afar) by Lieschen Laßdas (Lieschen Let t Be),[56] and *Die Weltbühne* Kurt Tucholsky's *Schepplin*, written in Berlin jargon.[57]

The press of March 8 had also alerted the Berlin police. Since "enthusiastic receptions are to be expected in Berlin" and "wide circles of the Berlin public will not miss the opportunity to extend a warm welcome to their darling of the silver screen," the police asked about the planned setting. Chaplin was to arrive at the Friedrichstrasse train station at about 5:30 p.m. the next day and check into the famous Hotel Adlon on the boulevard Unter den Linden, where he had reserved a suite by telegraph. For this, the government district had to be passed through. With "Special Order No. 23," the Berlin Police Headquarters ordered on March 9 that the station building, the forecourt, the way to the hotel and its courtyard, the Pariser Platz, be safeguarded. At the request of the Polizeipräsident (police chief) Albert Gzresinski, however, the applicable no-protest zone regulations in the government district should not be strictly observed. Further measures were to be taken after Chaplin's arrival at the hotel.[58]

In the afternoon of the same day, a substantial police contingent arrived in good time at the Friedrichstrasse train station and thoroughly cordoned off the area.[59] The press announcements of Chaplin's arrival had met with an extraordinary response. At 4:50 p.m., newsreel cameramen had set up at the station. About 800 people had already gathered on the platform, so that the sale of platform tickets was stopped. Also present were Südfilm AG director Goldschmid for the German film industry, film actors Marlene Dietrich and Fritz Kampers, and "film kid" Ben Jack, costumed like Jackie Coogan from *The Kid*. When the express train arrived on schedule, Chaplin was received in the station by about 2000 cheering people. *Tempo* ran the headline "Ordnungsdienst für Chaplins Einzug" (Security Force for Chaplin's Arrival).[60] The *8 Uhr-Abendblatt* documented this as follows: "In a flash, all regulatory measures are nixed. Everybody runs, rushes, pushes forward. Roaring cheers, wild waving of hats and arms: Charlie, the darling of the world, has been recognized standing at the window of one of the front rail cars."[61] After he disembarked, the police had to cut his way down to the exit stairs. Goldschmid and Kampers' planned welcome addresses were cancelled, and Dietrich could only fleetingly shake Chaplin's hand.[62] Not until March 14 did Chaplin attend a performance of Ferenc Molnar's stage play *Liliom*, starring Hans Albers, at the Berlin Volksbühne, accompanied by Goldschmid.[63] Flowers that were to be presented to Chaplin were taken by his interpreter Landsberg, but she did not get to see him at the station either.[64] In front of the station, another 1300 or so people were waiting for him and received him with a storm of cheers, so that he could not speak into a newsreel microphone. The Berlin press later reported that the station and forecourt were "black with people." As well, "all the windows of the houses and hotels opposite the station […] were filled with people shoulder to shoulder shouting, waving, cheering."[65] Finally, Chaplin, lifted on shoulders, was seen disappearing "in one wild tangle of people."[66]

Crowds also lined the route from the train station to the hotel. The central

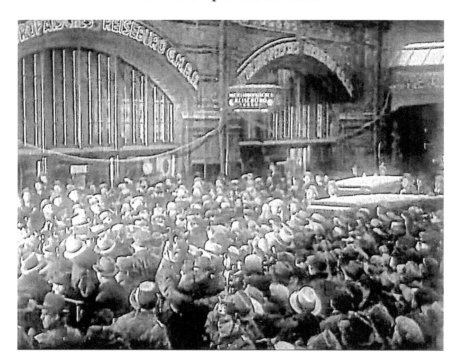

Screen shot from *Ufa-Tonwoche* No. 27, 1931: Chaplin's welcome at Berlin station Friedrich-straße, March 9, 1931 (Friedrich-Wilhelm-Murnau-Stiftung).

promenade of the Berlin boulevard and the plaza in front of the hotel were packed.[67] The Viennese press reported tens of thousands of onlookers.[68] The convoy of cars with Chaplin on board could only slowly proceed in the direction of the hotel. The *Film-Kurier* wrote: "The Chaplin car needs twice the time of an ambling pedestrian."[69]

Not just Chaplin friends had gathered on the central promenade. There were "political rallies […] of radical elements," which prompted the "police officer on duty to have the central promenade of the Linden cleared [by mounted police]," as Police Chief Gzresinski informed the Berlin evening press.[70] The *B.Z. am Mittag* later voiced concerns about the police operation: "The police [not for the first time] confused harmless curiosity and exuberant pleasure of the public with political demonstrations or similar dangerous situations […] and [proceeded] consequently with extreme strictness and unnecessary rigor." Under the headline "Schupo [Uniformed Police], please be kinder," the newspaper recommended that the police follow the example of Chaplin's "friendly yet energetic constable" in *Chaplin als Hüter der öffentlichen Ordnung* (*Easy Street*).[71] According to *Die Welt am Abend*, "the marauding police soldiery […] raged on senselessly."[72] Probably, however, this newspaper had exaggerated in its ideological rejection of the democratic German state, its police and its social democratic police chief. On March 20, Gzresinski responded to a law student's written criticism of the police's actions: "There were also vigorous 'Nieder' [Down!] shouts and, judging by the circumstances, it may have been of right-wing radicals. The *Tönende Wochenschau* also proves that counter-demonstrations took place."[73]

At the Adlon, Chaplin received flowers and love letters, as well as film proposals

Charlie Chaplin befucht Berlin.
Eine riefige Menfchenmenge umlagert ben Bahnhof bei ber Ankunft bes Filmkomikers.

Stuttgarter Illustrierte, **March 22, 1931: Chaplin's welcome at Berlin station Friedrichstraße, March 9, 1931.**

and entire film manuscripts. Chaplin impersonators had also crept in, but were quickly turned out. A vast crowd gathered in Paris Square, cheering Chaplin frenetically and wanting to shake his hand. After he drove up, the police had to struggle to pave a narrow lane for him to reach the hotel entrance.[74] Hotelier Louis Adlon's wife Hedda recalled the scene: "So Chaplin pushed his way through the crowd, shaking hands, signing autographs, nodding his head, and returning greetings." Before he reached his suite in the celebrity wing with rooms 101–114, he noticed that his trousers were slipping—onlookers had cut off the buttons of his clothes.[75] When he showed up on the balcony of his suite on the second floor of the hotel and waved to the crowd, the excitement flared up again.[76] To the first questions from reporters, such as what he was looking for in Berlin, he replied "peace and quiet."[77] But that was precisely what was not available.

The next day, the hotel was again mobbed by crowds waiting to see Chaplin.[78] According to the Jerusalem newspaper *The Palestine Bulletin,* Nazis insulted him in front of the Adlon with "You Jew Chaplin," although he descended from a Christian London family. One rowdy allegedly compared the Jewish ideal embodied by Chaplin with the German ideal of Siegfried, the hero of the Nibelungen. The police eventually dispersed the Nazis, according to the report.[79] However, neither the police files nor the Berlin press contain any references to this incident, and *The Palestine Bulletin* did not cite any sources. Had the newspaper confused the turmoil on Unter

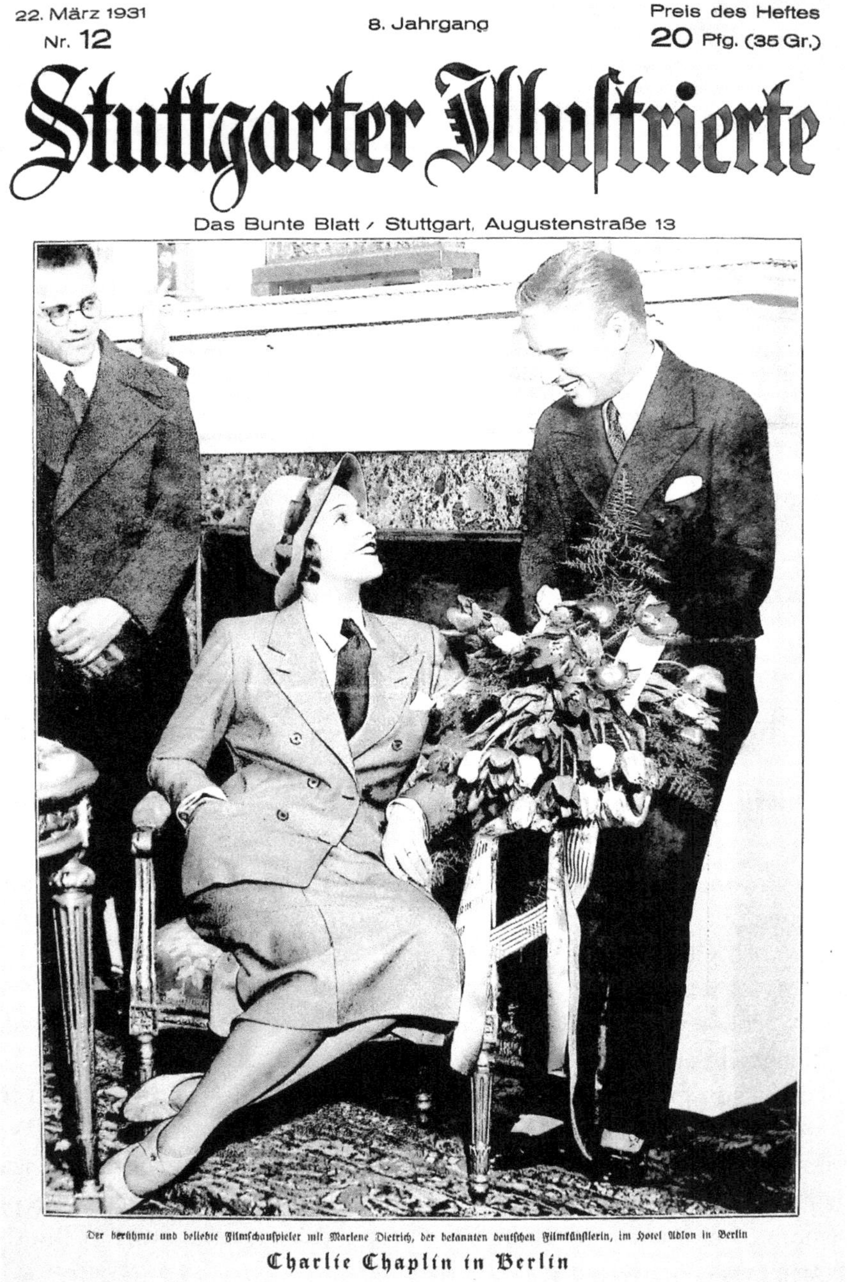

22. März 1931
Nr. 12

8. Jahrgang

Preis des Heftes
20 Pfg. (35 Gr.)

Stuttgarter Illustrierte

Das Bunte Blatt ⁄ Stuttgart, Augustenstraße 13

Der berühmte und beliebte Filmschauspieler mit Marlene Dietrich, der bekannten deutschen Filmkünstlerin, im Hotel Adlon in Berlin

Charlie Chaplin in Berlin

Stuttgarter Illustrierte, **March 22, 1931: Chaplin meets Marlene Dietrich, Berlin, March 9, 1931.**

den Linden with the throng in front of the Hotel Adlon and concluded that the "politically radical elements" were Nazis? In Berlin, Chaplin is said to have explicitly denied being Jewish, as the Viennese Jewish *Neue Welt* reported on April 1, 1931 (see Chapter 1).[80] Already on March 19, the Viennese Jewish newspaper *Die Stimme* had stated about the issue of Chaplin's Jewish ancestry and Nazi reactions in front of the

Adlon: "Only the swastika people have a fine instinct. They found out that Chaplin was Jewish, and for this reason they demonstrated in front of his Berlin hotel. Wotan does not get along with Charlie [...]."[81]

The Berlin press wrote of a "stormy reception" that "thousands" had given him, so that the police had to "protect him from bursts of enthusiasm." The last time there had been such a crowd as that, was at the end of February 1928 during the Berlin visit of the Afghan King Amanullah Khan. Chaplin was stunned by his "staggering" welcome.[82] On March 10, 1931, Ufa ran the following advertisement for its newsreel: "Starting today, the *Ufa-Tonwoche*'s special report on Charlie Chaplin's welcome in Berlin will be shown in all Ufa cinemas."[83] The other newsreels *Deulig-Woche*, *Emelka-Tonwoche* and *Fox tönende Wochenschau* reported Chaplin's triumphant welcome as well, but also disruptive actions by his adversaries.[84] None of these four newsreels seem to have survived, except for an excerpt that was repurposed for the 1940 "documentary" *Der ewige Jude* against Chaplin (see Chapter 12).

For the Christian nationalist *Tägliche Rundschau*, all this definitely went too far. The newspaper felt hit above all by the fact that in 1926 there had been talk that Chaplin wanted to make a film about Christ.[85] In "Chaplin-Rausch" (Chaplin Craze), it stated:

> Chaplin's artistic value shall not be up for discussion here, although it must also be allowed to doubt an ultimate seriousness of his attitude—after all, his press bureau announced a tragi-comic film about Christ (!) a few years ago. All the more firmly, however, a stand must be taken against the almost pathological Chaplin hype, which in many respects recalls the mass psychosis of boxing match rages.[86]

The Catholic *Märkische Volks-Zeitung* took the same line. Considering Chaplin to be "one of the greatest actors," it attacked the "nasty advertising" that exploited his visit with "pages of turgid reports" in the "most submissive tone." They resembled "court reports of imperial times" and "turned the crowds into zombies [who] let the blood freeze in their bodies in the cold, yelling and roaring to hear a word from [Chaplin's] mouth."[87]

In the fall of 1933, Chaplin described his reception in his travelogue "A Comedian Sees the World" for the U.S. magazine *Woman's Home Companion*:

> I had been told that in Germany I had become a favorite and that I must expect quite a reception. I can assure you I'm not disappointed. Thousands cover the station and throngs are outside, I hear in English such phrases as "*Gold Rush* Charlie! ... *Circus* Charlie!" Everybody is excited. Pressmen und officials are all mixed up and swept aside by the multitudes. Throngs along the roads. That, I think, was the most exciting reception of all—even greater than London. At the Hotel Adlon we are met by more crowds, so I am shot up in the elevator and into my room, where I immediately go out onto the balcony and wave them below. There is a "Hoorah!" in response and I leave the window.[88]

Some 30 years later, Chaplin's account in his autobiography was briefer: "I shall not describe the wild enthusiasm of the multitudinous crowds that attended my second arrival in Berlin—although the temptation is almost irresistible. [...] I must confess I have not been overly modest in describing my own welcoming crowds [when Mary Pickford and Douglas Fairbanks showed me films from their trips abroad after returning to the U.S.]."[89]

Der Angriff

At the beginning of the 1920s, the future Reichsminister für Volksaufklärung und Propaganda Goebbels was not yet a high-profile enemy of Jews. Despite his excellent linguistic skills, the newly graduated academic was initially unable to establish himself professionally. In 1924, he was introduced to NSDAP circles and became a member; his membership No. 8,762 was later retroactively changed to No. 22. Goebbels now mutated from a fine-minded German philologist to an ardent anti–Semite, abandoning earlier personal attitudes as needed. He became the prototype of the anti–Semite and demagogue who would stoop to anything to gain power. In Mönchengladbach, he founded the local group of the NSDAP and in September 1924 became editor-in-chief of the Westphalian ethnic–German newspaper *Völkische Freiheit*.[90] In 1925, he attacked in it child star Jackie Coogan of *The Kid* fame. Coogan had become a favorite of moviegoers in Germany from the fall of 1923, especially with his own feature films such as Albert Austin and Victor Heerman's *My Boy* of 1921.[91] A German book about him had been published in 1924.[92] In the fall of that year, he had also visited Berlin during his European trip with his father and manager.[93] Goebbels wrote in *Völkische Freiheit*: "'Judenjüngelchen' [Jew-boy] Jackie Coogan, alias Jakob Cohn, has now been received in audience by the Pope. As the newspapers report, the little Mosesbengel [Mosaic Rascal] was very impressed by the Vatican. Well, now the Pope has also seen the little Cohn!"[94] Coogan, however, came from an Irish Catholic family and had been raised Catholic.[95] The Jewish name Goebbels had attached to him used the disparaging pun on the joke figure of the "little Cohn," which had been familiar in Germany since at least the early 20th century. He is the anti–Semitic stereotype of the half-pint, bow-legged Jewish weed who is of course unfit for military service.[96]

When Hitler appointed Goebbels as NSDAP Gauleiter of Berlin in 1927, the party had only 500 members there. From May 1928, he was a Reichstag deputy and from summer 1929 Reichspropagandaleiter (Reich Propaganda Leader) of the NSDAP. To elude official bans from speech and appearance and to continue the party's propaganda methods with the means of a newspaper, in July 1927, he founded the

Masthead: *Der Angriff*, editor Joseph Goebbels, 1931.

Berlin diatribe *Der Angriff* "für die Unterdrückten" (for the oppressed) und "gegen die Ausbeuter" (against the exploiters), which used coarsening, blatant anti–Semitic propaganda slogans. In his book *Kampf um Berlin*, Goebbels wrote about the origins, aims and design of the propaganda journal:

> [We did not want] to create a newspaper for information purposes. [...] The organ [was to be] like a whip, waking up the tardy sleepers from their slumber and hurrying them forward to restless action. [...] The whole thinking and feeling of the reader should be drawn into [the National Socialist] direction. [...] The masses think simply and primitively. They love to generalize complicated facts and to draw their clear and uncompromising conclusions from them. [Political agitation ...] that works [with the] complexity of things, [...] will always overtax the understanding of the guy of Main Street.[97]

Those who read *Der Angriff* were hardly interested in factual information, but probably feasted on polemics. At first, it appeared only weekly. When it caught on and was available on newsstands six times a week, in the summer of 1929, the propaganda journal attacked U.S. film magnates of Jewish origin in the article "The Jews in the Movies." In connection with United Artists, Chaplin's name was mentioned in passing without a sideswipe.[98] With Chaplin's visit to Berlin, this changed fundamentally. At the time, the Nazis had received a boost from German film censorship, not only in the case of *Im Westen nichts Neues* (see Chapter 5). The 386-meter-long Social Democrat political promotional *Ins Dritte Reich* (Into the Third Reich) was directed against the Nazis. On January 29, 1931, the Film-Oberprüfstelle banned the film because in the present political situation, it would upset the Nazis and thus affect public safety and order. On March 13, 1931, in the second round of censorship, *Ins Dritte Reich* was only approved after the removal of four scenes with a total length of 34 meters, which boldly portrayed Nazism.[99]

Against the "Jewish Film Clown"

In 1988, Wolfgang Gersch claimed in his book *Chaplin in Berlin—Illustrierte Miniatur nach Berliner Zeitungen von 1931*: "Goebbels [...] had set his fascist rowdies on Chaplin."[100] It may be reasonable to assume that the "Down!" shouters on the central promenade Unter den Linden were "fascist rowdies" and that Goebbels had "set them on Chaplin." Nazis had been railing against him for years, and now would have been able to express their contempt directly on the street. But Chaplin was also attacked by other right-wing or radical right-wing circles, so the "Nieder!" shouters may have come from within their ranks as well.

Gersch's assertion is an assumption, and it cannot be confirmed. On March 15, 1931, the *Berliner Herold* reported the following on "Our Chaplin Page" about Chaplin's ride from the train station to the hotel: "The continuation of the ride had to be interrupted for a moment. A Schupo squad took action against a procession of protesters. 'The gangland of Berlin?' asked Chaplin. 'On the contrary ... they call them Nazis here.'"[101] Responding to this, *Der Angriff* on March 17 demanded retaliation: "The clean Mr. [Otto] Dubro [publisher of the *Berliner Herold*] makes his living only from the advertisements of the many nationally minded landlords. Since they always claim that they only stick by us, we advise them to rub Dubro's nose in his meanness."[102] This was neither an admission nor a denial. In his richly detailed diaries, Goebbels recorded nothing about Nazi disruptive actions upon Chaplin's arrival in Berlin. In fact, he commented on Chaplin in his diaries only once in 1928 (see below). According to his entries of March 8 and 9, 1931, Goebbels had returned to Berlin from Frankfurt and was confined to bed due to flu and exhaustion. With symptoms of cough, colds and abdominal pain, he was "completely hoarse, full of reluctance and anger," and "slept a lot" during the day while Chaplin was being chauffeured to the Adlon. So Goebbels concluded: "I must slow down the pace a bit."[103] This rather suggests that he was not involved in organizing an anti–Chaplin action. In his book *Kampf um Berlin*, he described the early days of the NSDAP in Berlin in 1926 and 1927. For March 1931, therefore, it is unproductive. Written documents about the organization of the Nazi street fight, which was to the fore at that time, have not been handed down. Presumably, it was organized verbally as a rule, which would explain the lack of written records. Finally, in his letter of March 21, 1931, Polizeipräsident Grzesinski also merely assumed that "right-wing extremists" were the "Down!" shouters.

Beyond conceivable actions in the streets, the Nazi propaganda journals did indeed attack Chaplin on a massive scale. Contrary to Gersch's assumption, the *Völkischer Beobachter* joined in, but only in its Berlin Edition, which Gersch did not include in his book.[104] On March 10, *Der Angriff* broke the first ground when numerous articles about Chaplin's arrival appeared in the Berlin daily press. In "Press and Business. Hooray, He's Here!," *Der Angriff* denied serious journalistic quality to reporting other than its own and scornfully referred to editors as "Journaillisten" (Yellow Press Hacks). It insinuated that the Chaplin-friendly newspapers had "cheap business interests" and claimed that the film bosses were giving Chaplin, who was no longer a drawing card, a hand according to the motto "one hand washes the other." Thus, they created artificial enthusiasm for him. If Jungnickel had degraded Chaplin to an unimaginative "Hanswurst" (Tomfool) at the beginning of 1931, *Der Angriff* called him a "jüdischer Filmaugust" ("Jewish Film Clown"). *Der Angriff* wrote:

> The "Journaillisten" went completely delirious. [...] He is there! And everything else is forgotten, [...] even the evil Nazis. Who is there? Amanullah again? [...] Or some other Negro chief? [...] Another, a greater one has deigned to visit us in worn-out Germany. The Jewish film comedian Chaplin has arrived in Berlin. [...] Mr. Chaplin's business has been dull lately. It had become embarrassingly quiet around the Jewish film clown, who was systematically praised as an "artist" by the Jewish press of the whole world. And this silence caused a low ebb in the cash registers of the American film Jews. So they sent Chaplin [to] the Old World, which is still the best market for American kitsch films. [...] The headlines blared, the newsmen went berserk, the hype got off to a good start.[105]

Here lay the beginning of regularly repeated false claims of Nazi agitation about Chaplin's supposedly waning star and economic failures of his films. For all the hostility, however, even *Der Angriff* could not completely hush up the many exuberant reactions of the public as well as of the Berlin and nationwide newspapers. Therefore, on March 11, it converted this fact into "The Disgusting Hype About the 'Kriegshetzer' (War-monger) Chaplin." Combined with the familiar rebuke that

Das unnachahmliche Goebbels-Lächeln.

Chaplin imponiert uns Berlinern nicht. — Wir sind ganz andere Grotesk-Komiker gewöhnt!

Vorwärts, March 10, 1931: "Das unnachahmliche Goebbels-Lächeln" [The Inimitable Goebbels Smile], cartoon by unknown artist.

Jews constantly mocked non–Jews, *Der Angriff* marked the first attack by a Nazi propaganda journal against *Shoulder Arms*—allegedly the start of Chaplin's film career, but in fact his 65th film:

> One […] wonders if there can really still be Germans who do not puke of such scribblings. […] The advanced intoxication of the world by the Jewish press and literature could not be shown more clearly than by this Chaplin hullabaloo. It represents the most outrageous thing that a nation has ever accomplished in terms of national loss of dignity. These […] people crawled on their bellies before a "hergelaufener Jude" [Jewish bum]. They licked the boots of a Jew, who started his career in America with a wild Germanophobe smear film. This film insulted and besmirched the German soldiers in the vilest and most vicious manner, and has been spread all over the world. In this film, titled *Shoulder Arms* (*Gewehr über*), German soldiers appeared throughout as idiots and sadists. The Kaiser and the Crown Prince were portrayed as stupefied beasts whom the Jew Chaplin captures. No country in the world would have even permitted Chaplin to enter the country after such a film.[106]

With *Shoulder Arms*, *Der Angriff* was able to stir up the hornet's nest of German sensitivities at will, without bothering about facts. That same month, the Nazi film magazine *Thüringer Film-Zeitung* joined in, also attacking Chaplin and the press that cheered him, and incidentally transferring his Berlin visit from September 1921 to 1928.[107] It seems doubtful that even a single member of the editorial staffs of these two journals knew *Shoulder Arms*, or at least Hans Sochaczewer's October 1927 article in *Literarische Welt*, "Chaplin's War Film," which included a very detailed overview of the film's content (see Chapter 3). By the way, Goebbels claimed to have always followed the press intensively.[108]

Der Angriff's characterization of *Shoulder Arms* can be refuted by just watching the film. In May 1931, Stefan Großmann exposed the inflammatory intent of the propaganda journal with the article "Chaplin's War Film" in the cultural weekly *Das Tagebuch*. Großmann had watched *Shoulder Arms* in a tiny Parisian cinema with piano and violin accompaniment when the film was re-released in France on the occasion of Chaplin's European trip. He did not discover anything Germanophobe in it. Among the French audience, neither was there any triumph when Charlie protected a young French woman from a German officer. Großmann concluded: "If we were not outraged subjects, but grown-up people capable of joviality, we could occasionally on a Sunday morning calmly enjoy Charlie's war puppet-theater film. World history has already dumped it to the old celluloid. But we are Germans, we even preserve our anger that has turned gray."[109] Paul Ruhstrat, editor of the *Deutsche Republik*, had also seen the film in France and, like Großmann, was surprised that *Shoulder Arms* could be considered Germanophobe: "Does anyone feel offended by this film? Probably only those who do not know it. Otherwise, all the policemen and all the fat men in the world would feel offended by some of Chaplin's other films. For these characters from his early one-reelers are portrayed like the 'enemies' in *Shoulder Arms*."[110] According to the June report of *Die Welt am Abend*, *Shoulder Arms* ran in France without the scene "in which Chaplin drags Wilhelm, Hindenburg and the Crown Prince behind him as prisoners on a rope through the trench."[111] This scene was not missing; it did not exist.

How right Grossmann and Ruhstrat were being revealed the Chaplin entry of the renowned Catholic encyclopedia *Der Große Herder*. With the nonreflective remark that the "genius of the grotesque film" had made the film *Napoleon* during World War I and had "railed against Germany,"[112] Chaplin appeared there, too, as an enemy of the Germans. *Der Große Herder* probably confused Chaplin's never realized Napoleon project with *Shoulder Arms*.

Right-wingers Among Themselves

Other right-wing newspapers also wrote about the "Chaplin-Rummel" (Chaplin-Hype) and were disgusted by the attention Chaplin received. The ethnic–German weekly *Deutsche Nachrichten* (Berlin) summarized this in a three-line news item: "The Jewish film actor Chaplin [Jacob Cohn] delights Berlin. His racial comrades and the obtuse hacks fall over themselves with jubilation over this 'great one.'"[113] This resembled Goebbels' Jackie Coogan–bashing in the *Völkische Freiheit* of late 1924. The reason given by the right-wing conservative daily *Der Jungdeutsche* was just as flimsy: "Herr Chaplin is a Jew, and Germany must prove that it is not anti–Semitic."[114]

Major retd. Adolf Stein also belonged to the right-wing German nationalist camp. As "perhaps the strongest journalistic force in Germany,"[115] a DNVP member since 1919, the pro-monarchist became one of the "most influential German journalists of the twentieth century."[116] From 1920, Stein was head of the Deutscher Pressedienst's Maternservice (Matrix Service) in Alfred Hugenberg's German national media group, which distributed pre-written articles to more than 350 German regional and local newspapers.[117] Under the pseudonym Rumpelstilzchen (Rumpelstiltskin), based on the Grimm's fairy tale character, Stein was "Hugenbergs Landsknecht" (Hugenberg's Mercenary),[118] who regularly wrote mostly polemic commentaries that he himself called "Plauderbriefe" (Chatting Letters). They were distributed throughout the country as "Berliner Allerlei" (Berlin Potpourri) on feature sections of some 35 to 40 German provincial newspapers.[119] The skillfully written commentaries of the "Plauderers der Rechtsradikalen" (Chatterbox of the Right-Wing Radicals)[120] appeared linguistically moderate, but in content they followed right-wing or radical right-wing diction. In December 1932, Erich Kästner described Stein's "unspeakable stuff" in the *Vossische Zeitung* as a "salad of the dullest social gossip [...] garnished at regular intervals with a slander—all of it poured over, kneaded through, and infused with the most insipid sauce of attitude [...], chattered down week after week as if it came from a non-stop parrot [...], clumsy [and] vulgar." About Rumpelstilzchen's readership, Kästner said: "What a stomach people must have to enjoy this year in and year out!"[121] Until the mid–1930s, Stein's commentaries were compiled in a total of 15 annual anthologies, which, from 1931, were published by Willi Bischoff and could also be obtained from the NSDAP's central publishing house Franz Eher Nachfolger.[122] Stein as a "political fighter with his pen" and Bischoff were regarded by the Nazis as "trailblazers and spearheads for the new Germany."[123] In his March 12, 1931, commentary "Charlie Chaplin ist da" (Charlie Chaplin Is Here), Rumpelstilzchen was "generous" with facts. Like *Der Angriff*, he imputed purely business calculations to Chaplin for his visit, but considered *Shoulder Arms*, in which Chaplin "unspeakably made fun of the German army and threw mud at it," less objectionable because the film had not decided the world war. After all, Chaplin was neither important nor politically dangerous.[124] But then Rumpelstilzchen came out with a "piece of news," for which he did not present any sources. The crowds by which Chaplin was welcomed had not been enthusiastic devotees, gathering of their own free will, but jobless persons who had been hired as claqueurs for a fee specifically for this occasion:

> There are enough jobless persons at the moment who want to see something that does not cost anything. But—I really have to reveal confidential information—the "masses" were ordered. Whether by Charlie Chaplin or his company itself, I have not been able to ascertain. In any case, hundreds of extras had their bread for that day, as they had to mime at the train station and in front of the Hotel Adlon as if they were playing at [Max] Reinhardt's Oresteia. Sometimes they stood too close so that the cinematographers were hindered. This was genuine cinematic promo.[125]

The newspaper *Fridericus* of the front-line soldiers' association was closely tied with the Nazis "as a community of those who want to help build the Third Reich,"[126] as was openly confessed at the 12th Frontsoldatentag (Front Soldiers' Convention) of May 1931 in Breslau. *Fridericus* took the same line.[127] It was indicative that Stahlhelm founder Franz Seldte became Hitler's Reichsarbeitsminister (Reich Secretary of Labor) and that the jacket illustration of Rumpelstilzchen's volume *Mang uns mang...* with 1932 and 1933 commentaries featured three uniformed members of the SA, SS and the Stahlhelm arm in arm.[128] After the banning of his *Hamburg Warte*,

Friedrich Carl Holtz (see Chapter 2), another "trailblazer and spearhead for the new Germany,"[129] had continued the journal under the title *Fridericus* in Munich. After it was banned there too, he moved with it to Berlin in 1923.[130] In his hostile article "Viel Lärm um nichts" (Much Ado About Nothing) from the second half of March 1931, Holtz settled accounts with the allegedly former "little barber" Chaplin. Once again, the reason was the "Germanophobe smear film" *Shoulder Arms*, which Holtz described even more curiously than usual. As early as Chaplin's visit to Berlin in September 1921, Holtz had seen no reason to pay "special attention" to the "kleiner Schaumschläger" (Little Windbag) Chaplin, who at that time had also been invited "glorified" to Justizrat Werthauer's "Tafelei" (Feast). About the present, from his point of view completely inappropriate reception in Berlin, Holtz wrote vilely and unattributed:

> [Chaplin] is Jewish. Therefore his visit is, of course, pumped up as a sensation by the Berlin street press of his race. And all Berlin film-extras have to show up at the Friedrichstraße train station, to mime "popular enthusiasm," and to 'spontaneously' break through Schupo cordons as they have been drilled beforehand.—And the whole, well-placed theater will be sound filmed, of course.

At least Holtz limited the presence of claqueurs to the area of the station."[131]

In any case, Rumpelstilzchen's source remained the great unknown. This did certainly not bother the unnamed Berlin correspondent of the Nazi *Thüringer Film-Zeitung*. He perfidiously expanded Rumpelstilzchen's story about hired claqueurs in its second March 1931 issue and also did not substantiate anything. Now, only a smaller group of them was supposed to have triggered the huge crowd. Chaplin was supposed to have been behind this and to have duped the unknown principals for their part: "The German film industry is not at all to blame for the splendid parade of 400 'Steifleinenen'" [Stiff-linen-wearing People, i.e., men in suits] from the "Filmnachweis" [Labor

Rumpelstilzchen, *Mang uns mang…*, 1933, book cover by unknown artist: uniformed members of the S.A., S.S. and the Stahlhelm arm in arm.

Exchange's Job Center for Filmmakers] at Friedrichstrasse station. They apparently caused the increase of further crowds to there in the first place. It is a Chaplinade of the best order that these 400 now have to sue for their fees in the Arbeitsgericht (Labor Court). "Good old Charlie seems to have deceived their principals as much as the rest of Berlin."[132]

The three versions must be judged by the consistent reports of the tremendous crowds from the train station along the boulevard Unter den Linden, including its central promenade, to the Pariser Platz in front of the Hotel Adlon, which for example outside of Berlin had also been reported by the *Hannoverscher Anzeiger*.[133] These were thousands of onlookers, and not just "hundreds of extras" that Rumpelstilzchen spoke of. Was he seriously suggesting that they had all been hired? Not very different was the version of *Fridericus*, according to which "all Berlin film-extras" filled the area in front of the station, which according to other reports was "black with people." The story in the *Thüringer Film-Zeitung* about 400 paid "Steifleinenen" at the station sounds more realistic at first glance. But could they have mobilized thousands of people for the whole area out of thin air?

Despite the far smaller number of claqueurs, the report of the *Thüringer Film-Zeitung* is even more questionable. Its information is so vague that it renders verification virtually impossible, especially since documents from the Berlin Arbeitsamt (Job Center) and Arbeitsgericht for March 1931 have not been preserved.[134] The 400 unemployed "Steifleinene" were not remotely identified. It remained unknown who had hired them at what conditions via the Arbeitsamt. What exactly was Chaplin's role in this, and which "Steifleinene" (all or only some of them?) had sued whom at the Arbeitsgericht? No one else reported on such a lawsuit, not even the Nazi propaganda journals. Yet its subject would have been spectacular, considering the enormous reception Chaplin had enjoyed. Furthermore, the assertion of the *Thüringer Film-Zeitung* is inherently inconsistent. If the claqueurs had been ordered for March 9, and the magazine claimed to have already known about a lawsuit in the second half of the month, the hired extras would have immediately approached the court instead of first trying to find an out-of-court solution. This contradicts the daily routine of legal practice. Certainly, urgent situations are conceivable, which force an immediate appeal to the court. However, the *Thüringer Film-Zeitung* did not even hint at this. Therefore, it very likely fabricated the story and thereby made Rumpelstilzchen's "report" appear even more outrageous. This would comply with the *Thüringer Film-Zeitung*'s claim in its first issue of March 1931 that the Berlin press had been punished immediately by the rest of the German press because of its "submissive" Chaplin coverage,[135] about which, however, just as little is known. Certainly, it is quite astonishing that the *Thüringer Film-Zeitung* in the same issue seemed to have appreciated Chaplin as an artist after all:

> Of course, none of this has anything to do with the fact that we also admire "Charlie" as a film artist and at the same time cherish the hope that one day a similarly great comedian will emerge from our cinematic newcomers. Our good German money should be kept in our country. The overly powerful American competition must be forced to buy our films, instead of a poor country like ours being constantly deprived of vast sums for production in America.

In the Nazi camp, on the other hand, no one except the *Thüringer Film-Zeitung* claimed that claqueurs had been hired. On the contrary, Nazi journals assumed the obvious fact that Chaplin had been received by his followers and by onlookers. This had already been reluctantly expressed by *Der Angriff* on March 11. In mid–March, Streicher wrote in his *Stürmer*: "The dimwitted masses, unable to form their own opinions, were reeling with excitement at Chaplin's arrival in Berlin. Women scuffled for autographs. Pale youths had their patent leather shoes trampled. Women threw themselves to the ground in front of Chaplin."[136] In July of that year, it labeled as fools those who had "licked Chaplin's greasy hand" in Berlin because they thought he was the "greatest comedian of all time." Moreover, they would inexplicably revere Albert Einstein as an "immortal scholar" and the Austrian-Jewish tenor Richard Tauber as a "god-blessed singer and artist."[137] Nor did the *Westdeutscher Beobachter*, founded in May 1925 as the NSDAP propaganda journal of the Reichsgau Köln-Aachen, claim the employment of paid claqueurs. The editor of the propaganda journal, which initially appeared only on Sundays and from September 1930 as a daily newspaper, was the future Reichsorganisationsleiter (Chief of Reich Organization) of the NSDAP and head of the Deutsche Arbeitsfront (German Labor Front), DAF, Dr. Robert Ley.[138] In late April and mid–May 1931, the *Westdeutscher Beobachter* reported on Chaplin's Berlin visit, stating that Chaplin was "in the midst of his madcap followers" and that "even high-order civil servants" had "complimented the American film Jew."[139] Before Chaplin, "Germany in 1931 was in the dust before a clown." The *Westdeutscher Beobachter* commented: "Ugh! Disgusting!"[140]

Finally, the Osnabrück hotelier Eduard Petersilie, another comrade-in-arms from the pro-fascist camp, joined forces with *Fridericus*. In the newspaper *Der Stahlhelm* of March 15, Petersilie, under his pseudonym Peter Silie, published as the only commentary of this journal on Chaplin's welcome in Berlin the poem "Chaplin." At first glance it seems harmless. In fact, however, it is anti–Semitic. The "kleene Flimmerjüd" (Little Flickering Jew) Chaplin presented himself "graciously to his delighted people," among them "women shrieking hysterically 'Hoch und Kikriki' Hurrah and cock-a-doodle-doo."[141] Incidentally, on April 10, 1931, the *Stahlhelm* was banned from publication until July 9, 1931, because of a politically subversive July 5 article.[142]

Nazis Against Chaplin Cult and Chaplin Films

Surprisingly, *Der Angriff* was silent about details of Chaplin's activities in Berlin, such as visits to the operetta, cabaret, vaudeville and theaters, meetings with personalities from the art scene such as Max Reinhardt in Karl Vollmoeller's Palais Unter den Linden[143] and from politics, his walk through Old Berlin, his visit of the Berlin Polizeigefängnis (Police Prison)—and the March 11, 1931, visit to the official residence of Police Commissioner Grzesinski at Alexanderplatz, where he also met the latter's deputy, Dr. Bernhard Weiß.[144] Both were arch-enemies of Hitler and Goebbels and were distortedly represented in Goebbels' 1933 photomontage monograph *Das erwachende Berlin*. Weiß was even at the center of the smear volumes *Das*

Buch Isidor—Ein Zeitbild voll Lachen und Hass and *Knorke! Ein neues Buch Isidor für Zeitgenossen,* which Goebbels had published in 1928 and 1929, respectively.[145]

On March 11, a broadcast political newspaper review accused *Der Angriff* of "reactionary Byzantinism" and "Nazi court reporting," which *Der Angriff* countered the next day with the "'Byzantinism' of others," because Chaplin's career start with *Shoulder Arms* had been deliberately suppressed. Furthermore, the sycophantic subservience of journalists of the "Jewish press" to Chaplin, who had constantly dulled his admirers' minds, had been ignored. Now, however, these reporters realized that they themselves had been duped by him. Therefore, *Der Angriff* predicted Chaplin's *Lichter der Großstadt*: "[The film] is likely [...] to be a failure, despite all the hype"[146] (the film's business development will be examined in Chapter 6). On the same day, the *Völkischer Beobachter* commented for the first time on Chaplin's Berlin visit, both in the Bavarian Edition and in the Berlin Edition. In its column "Streiflichter," the propaganda journal attacked on the front page the overflowing "enthusiasm" of the "asphalt press" for a "jüdischer Spaßmacher" (Jewish jester), who had come to Berlin only for the profits: "Now democracy has finally been able to embrace its darling and its 'hero' ideal—'St. Francis of Broadway,' as his Jewish biographer calls Chaplin. And why the trip? To secure the expected $6 million for his new film by 'personally presenting' it. Jewish propaganda and bourgeois stupidity will already make this happen."[147]

In this heated atmosphere, an anonymous letter was received at the Hotel Adlon on March 13, demanding "that Chaplin move out immediately" or else "something would happen." The letter was handed over to the Schutzpolizei (Uniformed Police), who forwarded it to the Kriminalpolizei (Detective Squad).[148] Was the unrealized threat a continuation of the "Nieder!" shouts of March 9? Nothing has become known about this, and the police files no longer exist.[149] In any case, on the day the letter was received, Heinz Henkel slandered Chaplin in *Der Angriff* as an inhuman and anti–Christian "object of enthusiastic ovations by the asphalt mob."[150] Henkel had watched the Chaplin program *Pay Day, Sunnyside* and *A Day's Pleasure,* which had been re-released in the Berlin Universum at the beginning of March 1931, after it had had its German premiere there on March 28, 1930. In *Der Film,* Hans-Walther Betz wrote at that time:

> Three Chaplin films, three times the most delicious pleasure. In one evening, the Kurfürstendamm audience laughed more than usually in an entire quarter of a year. [...] The highlight of dramaturgical achievement. [...] The director [Chaplin] drew the gags from his own genius. [...] Three characters between the agony of life and sweet idleness. [...] Three great, good people. [...] Chaplin has the love of understanding, and he forgives everyday life its banality.[151]

No wonder this program was another "huge success" even in troubled times.[152] Henkel, by contrast, presented the following distorted view, as the *Völkischer Beobachter* had done in early 1930 with *The Pilgrim*:

> Chaplin mocks everything that is earnest and sacred to all people: their work, their family, their faith. [... The three films ...] reveal to us the spiritual and ethical attitude of the "greatest comedian in the world" with all clarity. He vilely feasts on the mistreatment of a manservant, on the hunger and on the harassment of a construction worker. Clumsily and hatefully mindless, he mocks the Christian church by comparing [...] the crowd of rural churchgoers to a herd of cattle. This is no longer satire, this is brutally cynical slander! Christianity is

insulted just as clearly and deliberately as in [Chaplin's] celebrated *The Pilgrim*, so celebrated by the world press, only a little more cautiously in form.[153]

It takes a dose of malice to characterize the three films as Jewish "brutally cynical denigration of Christianity." In *Pay Day*, Christians are not attacked. Once again, others make life difficult for Charlie and constantly bully him. Charlie earns a living for himself and his wife on the construction site. There, a beefy foreman calls the shots, and Charlie does not have an easy time with him. In real life, things are often not much different. During the lunch break, which is respected for workers, Charlie has nothing to eat. Apparently, his quarrelsome wife provides for him poorly. For the time being, he has to be content with the few breadcrumbs that fall down to him from the foreman's meal on the scaffolding—Charlie sits one floor

Lohntag (Pay Day), poster art 1930 (DFF—Deutsches Filminstitut & Filmmuseum: in the holdings of the DFF—Deutsches Filminstitut & Filmmuseum, Frankfurt am Main/Chaplin-Archiv, Dauerleihgabe der Adolf und Luisa Haeuser-Stiftung für Kunst und Kulturpflege)

below him. But still he does not starve. Sporadically, the elevator, which constantly goes up and down, brings a frankfurter sandwich or a banana that a well-supplied workmate has carelessly put there. To consider this mockery of work as a livelihood seems far-fetched. Neither marriage nor family are vilified. Chaplin, of course, exaggerates Charlie's Xanthippe. But the film is, after all, a comedy. The type of the nagging wife can certainly be found in reality. Everything else offers insights that describe an unsatisfying married life as a prison: Passing his wife, who wants to take his hard-earned wages on payday, Charlie manages to lop off something for himself. After boozing and singing with friends, he returns to his not particularly cozy home and has to do without supper, because a pack of cats has snatched it away from him. To catch up on some sleep, he lies down in the bathtub, which is filled with laundry, but also with water. And then his scolding wife appears before him like an avenging angel. Chaplin certainly did not invent such things. Unsatisfying marriages have pervaded theater and literature since time immemorial. This popular theme was gladly spread in films again and again. So Chaplin merely caricatured everyday life, which is all too familiar to many people.

In *Sunnyside*, too, there is nothing to suggest that Christians and Jews are antagonists. Charlie's grumpy employer kicks him in the backside once in a while. On the other hand, the employer is an avid churchgoer and hangs pious slogans on his wall. Such hypocritically sanctimonious contemporaries are not a "brutally cynical" invention of Chaplin. They can be encountered everywhere.

Charlie is no choirboy either. He does not lose confidence over his humiliations, and so he makes advances to a village beauty. When Charlie drives cattle, he is absorbed in reading so that he does not notice that the small herd has moved into some buildings. In search of the cows, Chaplin by no means taunts the appalled churchgoers when he goes to retrieve an animal from the church. Since they block Charlie's entrance, he gets into the place by poking some villagers in the rear end with his shepherd's crook. The next moment, he leaves the church, riding on the ox, to the angry protest of the people, who immediately take up his pursuit. By rounding up a lost drove, Chaplin is just as little mocking Christianity. He only shows the consequences of carelessness at work, which are irreversible. Chaplin portrays all this neither crudely nor spitefully. The only obvious reference to Jewish life is that the father of Charlie's beloved reads a newspaper printed in Hebrew letters. Presumably he is Jewish.

Finally, in *A Day's Pleasure*, Chaplin does not vilify the family, which many people consider sacred. Charlie's Sunday trip with his wife and child begins with his stubborn car. When he turns the starter crank, the engine starts; as soon as Charlie sits behind the wheel, the engine dies. After several attempts, the family finally reaches their destination, an excursion steamer. Many things happen there that can spoil such a day. For example, trying to set up a folding deck chair proves to be an almost impossible task, nasty passengers take Charlie's seat away, there is even a fight, and seasickness does the rest. On his way home, Charlie causes chaos with his car at a junction where a policeman is regulating the traffic. People maneuver back and forth, and the car gets bumped in the process. When tar spills onto the road, Charlie and the traffic policeman get stuck in it. Charlie finally frees himself from the sticky mass by simply stepping out of his shoes. After such an eventful day, he hurriedly makes his way home in socks. *A Day's Pleasure* caricatures the longed-for relaxing family getaway that turns out completely differently. The refreshing comedy results from the consecutive misadventures. For all the grotesque exaggeration, this is not pulled out of thin air. Viewers have experienced similar things themselves at times, so they can empathize. And like Charlie, they will try their best again next Sunday to finally have a nice day after all.

In addition to Henkel's "film review," *Der Angriff* attacked Chaplin personally with "Chaplinkult statt Proletkult" in the same issue. He allegedly was an extravagant multimillionaire who lived according to the motto "preach water and drink wine": He lodged in a "suite of the most expensive hotel of Berlin." At home, he played "the violin in [a] marble bathtub of his magnificent villa" and "destroys [his] precious instrument with the steam." The propaganda journal "unmasked" Chaplin, among other things, as follows:

> The Communist editorial Jews have once again shown what kind of people they are. With bombastic headlines and bold prints they have welcomed and celebrated [...] the American film comedian Chaplin. [...They] will know why they create the Chaplin hype, only they do not tell their workers. And rightly so. Even the most stupid will have noticed by now that Chaplin is neither a proletarian nor a fighter for the cause of the proletariat. But because he is Jewish, they throw all caution to the wind and forget their hatred of millionaires. Instead of the cult of the proletariat, they turn to the cult of the comedian.[154]

This went decidedly too far for the *Film-Kurier*. It noted that the Berlin press had done too little to counter Goebbels' *Angriff* around Chaplin's reception, having sent only "sixth-rate" reporters instead of Chaplin connoisseurs like Heinz Pol, Arnold Höllriegel (in May 1928, he interviewed Chaplin in the U.S.), Hans Siemsen and Erich Burger: "And Goebbels can laugh, because his commentaries are written by his best."[155]

The left-liberal *Die Welt am Montag* found nothing objectionable in the fact that an acknowledged artist was also advertising his latest film, regarded his *Shoulder Arms* as a long-completed episode, and made the Nazi press take note of the following:

> Well, if we are going to make a big fuss about a prominent guest—then [...] better about such a fine fellow as Chaplin [...]. [He] is a living concept for the people who cheer for him. [... They] have laughed at least once about the divine schlemiel [...] that their bellies jittered. For this, after all, we can be grateful. [...] To compete with the personality of the celebrated man himself is reserved for our dear swastikas. [... Chaplin] is at any rate more selfless than the "Heil" cries of the Natioten [note: Nazi Idiots] who cheer their political tomfools because they hope to do good business in the Third Reich—and possibly already in the Republic.[156]

In mid–March 1931, *Der Stürmer*, with its "Chaplin Rummel," echoed in essence the previous agitation of *Der Angriff* claiming, among other things, that Chaplin had become the idol of the German people because the princes of the past had disappeared. "Das Filmjüdlein" (The Little Film Jew) only played the proletarian to this. Privately, he was living in luxury. While a German unemployed person had to get by with only 15 reichsmark per week, Chaplin lodged in the Adlon for 250 reichsmark per day—then a fortune. Nevertheless, the "Jewish press" made common cause with him and led "the proletarians by the nose" and thus did not deserve to be cheered by them. Some samples from Streicher's extensive attack:

> Today, the heart and the cheers of the people have been won by [...] simple men from the people. They went to the people and from district to district preached the truth, the new doctrine of Nazism. [...] The peasant, the city dweller, the worker, young and old cheer them and stretch out their arms in salute. This enthusiasm is not a trained pretense, no, it comes from the heart, voluntarily and impetuously. And again the visage of the Jew is distorted with rage and fury. [...] There came from America a [wispy] little film Jew to Berlin, with pitch-black frizzy hair, with thin crooked legs, a greasy stiff little hat, a little black moustache on his face: Charlie Chaplin. The Jewish papers praised this clown as the "greatest comedian" of all time, babbled about his "secret tragedy" and "spiritual depth" and about the "ethical side" of his "classical humor." [...] The German sucker bought it in the end. It is common courtesy and

Der Stürmer, **March 1931, front page: "Chaplin Rummel" [Chaplin Hype], drawing by Fips [Philipp Rupprecht].**

a token of education to worship and admire this Jewish clown. With this, these people prove that they are not capable of forming their own opinion about this film-Jew.[157]

About a month later, the trade journal *Mitteldeutscher Lichtspieltheaterbesitzer* set the record straight on such absurd accusations:

Now Chaplin [...] was understandably celebrated in a big way, more than a politician, statesman or any other artist. A certain press flew into a terrible fury about this. Along with certain party bigwigs, it is upset that there is something else besides party politics that will get the masses going. [...] Chaplin enjoys greater popularity in Germany than a Mr. Hitler or any party bigwig. This creates a feeling of unease and displeasure among those who want to subject the German people to a narrow-minded party-political dictatorship. [...] Chaplin's reception in Berlin benefits the film [...]. So film enthusiasm has not yet died off. Today it is needed more than ever.[158]

Caught Between the Stools

The Nazi press was then fueled by news about an interview Chaplin allegedly granted to the Communist Junge Garde (Young Guard) for the KPD party newspaper *Die Rote Fahne*.

In contrast to the Nazi propaganda press, the central organ of the KPD had reported on March 10, 1931, that "many workers enthusiastically cheered 'their Chaplin' [as] friend of the working class."[159] He was "the greatest film artist of the present age," the first to portray "the little man who has been trampled, maltreated and humiliated by capitalism [...] in a cinematically extraordinarily enthralling way."[160] However, Chaplin had an interview request from the Young Guard turned down through his secretary Carlyle T. Robinson, also known as "Cerberus" among journalists, saying he was "much too tired and weary." This was also conceded somewhat subdued in the padded article of *Die Rote Fahne* on March 11, 1931.[161] *Die Welt am Abend* also reported that Robinson had not let anyone meet Chaplin, but had prophesied that he might visit the Soviet Union.[162] The next day's issue additionally devoted an entire page to Chaplin on various topics: "Charlie! The Film-Proletarians Dedicate This Page to You!"[163] At that point, there was no mention of an interview. Then, on March 13, it was claimed, not on the journal's front page but in the review section, that the Junge Garde had managed to talk to Chaplin on the phone. On this occasion, Chaplin had declared: "My greetings and all my sympathy for the Communist Youth of Germany."[164]

The right-wing press, including *Deutsche Zeitung*, reacted allergically, most notably the *Berliner Börsen-Zeitung* on its March 14 front page. Walther Funke had recently resigned as editor-in-chief, but the newspaper's political line had not changed: The direction of the political section remained in the hands of Richard Jügler. Based on its own article on *Shoulder Arms* from December 1921 (see Chapter 2), the *Berliner Börsen-Zeitung* attacked the leadership of the Junge Garde. The latter had openly declared that the purpose of its activity "was the preparation of the armed revolt against the bourgeois state and the bourgeoisie." The newspaper threatened: "Should

Die Rote Fahne, March 12, 1931: "Chaplin page."

Mr. Chaplin have to admit that he made this statement, he will have to be told that it was extremely inappropriate of him to speak in this way about German domestic political conditions. [...] Incidentally, we reserve the right to take a closer look at the whole Chaplinade in more detail as soon as the guest will have left Berlin."[165] This "closer look" was probably aimed at influencing the upcoming premiere of *Lichter der Großstadt* and was therefore to be taken seriously from an economic point of view.

Chaplin and his Berlin staff issued a denial on the same day, which was printed in full in the *Vorwärts'* Morning Edition of March 15. In it, Chaplin disclaimed having granted a telephone interview or wanting to do so. The idea of such an interview would be "simply ridiculous," since he knew as little about the political conditions in Germany as he did about those in America, England and France. Moreover, he knew nothing about politics. Then, however, Chaplin referred to having received a four-person delegation of unemployed Berlin film actors and musicians, which *Die Rote Fahne* itself had not claimed before, but reported about it first on March 15. He had told them that he sympathized with them, but at the same time made it clear that conditions in America were almost worse.[166]

The Junge Garde reacted to Chaplin's denial in *Die Rote Fahne* on March 15. In the article "Chaplin and Us," it confirmed having spoken with Chaplin on the phone and added: "Chaplin is the son of a poor unknown actor from the London slums. We know, however, that he is not a Communist, of course. [... Nevertheless,] some film-makers and a representative of the *Rote Fahne* were the only voices of the people that reached Chaplin [during his Berlin sojourn]."[167] The same issue of *Die Rote Fahne* also published a second article with the headline "*Die Rote Fahne* with Charlie Chaplin." Placed in the feuilleton of the journal, it was now also claimed that a delegation of the Junge Garde, under the leadership of the editorial staff of *Die Rote Fahne*, had "broken through the secretary's blockade" and had even been "received with great joy" by Chaplin. "The revolutionary film proletarians" had handed over to "the great artist workers' letters of *Die Rote Fahne* dedicated to him," and a copy of the newspaper, because he had "shaped the social plight of a class like no other," he was "one of ours," and his films had contributed "a certain part to the final struggle of the working class." Despite the strenuous past few days, Chaplin had had "a lengthy personal conversation" with them, in the course of which he had made "significant statements." He had called capitalism an enemy and expressed "all his deepest sympathy for the unemployed": "Pass on to the struggling workers and unemployed my most friendly and profound greetings."[168]

It is true that Chaplin did not comment any more on the allegations of *Die Rote Fahne* of March 15. But his denial of the telephone interview might even more have included a personal interview, which was also only claimed afterwards. Moreover, *Die Rote Fahne*'s coverage was obviously amplified and, in accordance with its own political concerns, focused on the proletarian class struggle. Chaplin's alleged "significant statements" were reported only briefly by *Die Rote Fahne*. Or had they confined themselves to the short remarks and greetings attributed to him, which do not seem particularly "significant"? It is also noticeable that the news about a personal interview with Chaplin after the prelude with the telephone interview would have been sensational and a case for a big lead on page 1. Instead, it was placed in a supplement of *Die Rote Fahne*'s feuilleton. Thus, *Die Rote Fahne*'s claims remain questionable and are not substantiated elsewhere. On March 16, even *Die Welt am Abend* made clear that no reporter had succeeded in conducting an interview with Chaplin and that he had only "granted a conversation to representatives of the film extras"—without mentioning the alleged accompanying member of *Die Rote Fahne*'s editorial staff![169]

In the *Berliner Börsen-Zeitung* on March 15, 1931, the pro–Chaplin film critic Dr. Fritz Olimsky followed up with the "Chaplinade" announced the day before, in which he sympathized with him "as an unfortunate product of his managers" during the Berlin hustle and bustle. Olimsky also looked forward to *Lichter der Großstadt*: "We will have to wait and see how the new work will appeal to us. It is said that Chaplin is not suited for the talkies; he himself seems to be of this opinion. Perhaps this present exaggerated Chaplin hype is the last flare-up of a flash in the pan with which his artistic fame will expire."[170]

Below it was the following unsigned short note: "The British Gaumont Pictures Corporation has decided not to acquire the screening rights for the new Chaplin film *City Lights* for its 320 cinemas. Chaplin had demanded fifty percent of the net receipts."[171] Was this a warning directed at Chaplin or at Südfilm AG, which had paid such a high price for the German screening rights of *City Lights*? Olimsky's "Chaplinade" does not seem to have been a threat, as Gersch interpreted the article.[172] This is also supported by the *Berliner Börsen-Zeitung*'s summary of March 17, written by an unidentified journalist with a reference to Chaplin's alleged interview with the Junge Garde. In it, *Shoulder Arms* came up again; the newspaper had been upset by it in December 1921 and had not forgiven Chaplin. Nevertheless, the author felt sympathetic to the fact that Chaplin had taken advantage of the contemporary historical opportunity to shoot this film. This time Chaplin was supposed to have "kicked the Crown Prince and the Kaiser" and even "put half a dozen German general staff officers over his knee." Probably this writer had not seen the film either. The *Berliner Börsen-Zeitung* wanted to let Chaplin leave in peace, but it did not want to let the press, which had hailed him in Berlin, get off scot-free:

> A flash in the pan has burned out. As long as Chaplin was a guest on German soil, we have refrained, in accordance with the commandments of politeness, from a discussion of this visit and its circumstances. We are also far from casting stones at the departing man, but we consider it necessary to emphasize, especially to foreign countries, that the authors of this unrestrained Chaplin propaganda, which Berlin has had to endure, have done their hero a disservice. [...] In the end, it should not matter to us whether Chaplin has assured the Communist youth of his sympathies or not. How many will he have made happy here with his sympathy! [...] Let him end this episode as he is used to from his films: the lonely wanderer disappears into the horizon. [...]. [...T]hose who dragged him out of his milieu, who crowded around him wagging their tails and filled the columns of German newspapers with Byzantine hymns of praise, these are the ones who should be pilloried![173]

No matter how this is to be understood: Neither Olimsky nor other editors of the *Berliner Börsen-Zeitung* reviewed *Lichter der Großstadt* after its German premiere in the Saturday column "Die Filmwoche." After its world premiere on February 8, 1931, the *Berliner Börsen-Zeitung* called Chaplin's new work a "triumph of the silent film," which had "brilliantly succeeded in driving the 100% sound film competitors out of the field."[174]

The newspaper *Der Jungdeutsche* also drew its own unkind balance of the Chaplin visit on March 17, as a letter to a "hick" about the "sooo great artist" who earns millions in financially weak Germany, but returns only one percent of it to the German tourist industry. Always in the same mask, he would always embody the same old tramp as a "normal hero" for the whole world. Vagrants were fashionable anyway, "and a bit of crime spices things up, especially if it only stems from stupidity." The journal apparently did not sympathize with the Nazis and mentioned that they had presented the Germans with "real heroes" who liked to make a racket and beat up dissidents. Now and then, also one of their leaders would break his word of honor.[175]

Departure and Continuing Attacks

This political reporting had turned the mood against Chaplin. To find peace and quiet from the London hustle and bustle, he had left prematurely for Berlin. But here, too, he was passed around everywhere.[176] On March 13, it had been rumored that he now wanted to escape the Berlin rejoicings and embraces as well.[177] In fact, on March 15, Chaplin abruptly broke off his visit even before the German premiere of *Lichter der Großstadt*, which he had wanted to attend. Accompanied by Melnitz and Robinson and without much public attention, he quietly left Berlin for Vienna via Prague. He seemed to be on the run. Nevertheless, the next day, the *Film-Kurier* wrote that Chaplin would be back in Berlin for his film's premiere.[178] This remained an unconfirmed assumption, and Chaplin never returned.

In Vienna, as in Berlin, Chaplin was welcomed triumphantly by thousands of admirers.[179] And there too he stayed only briefly.[180] After numerous stops, Chaplin's further European trip finally took him to St. Moritz in Switzerland and to Rome, whence he left on March 7, 1932, for Japan, which he reached on May 14, 1932, via Cairo to Singapore after many stops in between. He returned to Los Angeles on June 16. Starting in September 1933, his five-part travelogue appeared in the U.S. magazine *Woman's Home Companion* under the title "A Comedian Sees the World." In it, Chaplin was silent about the reasons for his hasty departure for Vienna, just as he had been in his 1964 autobiography. In the latter, he briefly discussed the Nazi influences during his Berlin stay: It was 1931, soon after the Nazis had emerged as a power in the Reichstag, and I was not aware that half of the press was against me, objecting, that I was a foreigner and that the Germans were making themselves ridiculous by such a fanatical demonstration. Of course that was the Nazi press, and I was innocently oblivious of all this, and had a wonderful time.[181]

Die Rote Fahne's reports and Chaplin's denial furnished an opportunity for the Nazi press, which continued its agitation around Chaplin's Berlin visit until mid–May 1931. On March 17, 1931, *Der Angriff*, while not claiming that Chaplin was a Communist, commented on his departure:

> The Communists also made pure fools of themselves with their Chaplin hype. [...] Now the comedian, who has meanwhile escaped to Vienna, has delivered a kick to them from there.

He did not remotely think of being a Communist, he declared, and the Communist interviews were a pack of lies. Now "their Charlie" will hardly think of setting up a bank account
for Mr. Münzenberg's young people.[182]

The *Thüringer Film-Zeitung*, on the other hand, saw Chaplin's "fraternization
with the Berlin Communists" as a "disgraceful finale" to his Berlin visit:

Good old Charlie [has] cozied up to Berlin celebrities of all levels [...] when he had himself
dragged to the Reichsinnenminister [Reich Minister of the Interior], to Herr Severing and to
the two Berlin Police Chiefs, in order to later disburden himself about his Bolshevist attitude
to *Die Rote Fahne*, after he had shortly before collected two million [reichsmark] for his new
film from the stupid Germans. You see: God's zoo is big, but Berlin's is still the biggest![183]

In his commentary of March 12, 1931, Stein-Rumpelstilzchen also singled out
Chaplin's description from *Hallo Europa!* of his September 1921 visit to Justizrat
Werthauer's "palazzo" and wrote with undisguised anticipation of the Third Reich:
"But that is just the social class of those who today alone are still solvent, on whose
will—until the landslide comes, and it will come soon—for the time being politics
and on whose taste art still depends."[184] Probably *Der Angriff* had picked this up
and constructed from it on March 19, 1931 in "Werthauer und Chaplin: When will
these profiteers finally be put out of business?" In it, the journal shifted this visit
by two years to the time when the German hyperinflation had reached its zenith
and the German economy had collapsed: "1923! Inflationary misery and hardship
in the German Reich. Every day, the betrayed and deceived commit suicide. But at
Jew Dr. Werthauer's Russian and American musicians play while attendants serve
abundant meals. How does it say in 'the Sages of Zion'? Israel will ride to feast on
your backs!"[185] Thus, *Der Angriff* had portrayed Chaplin and Werthauer as parasitic
Jewish contemporaries who unscrupulously feasted while desperate people without
income suffered hardships. By "the Sage of Zion," the paper alluded to the anti–
Semitic pamphlet *The Protocols of the Elders of Zion*, about the alleged Jewish world
conspiracy, which dates from the beginning of the 20th century and has since been
debunked as a forgery.[186] In addition, *Der Angriff* dealt in its own way with a traffic
accident in which Werthauer's son had been involved and had therefore been sentenced to pay compensation to the accident victim. Father and son Werthauer had
then filed various criminal charges, among others, against public officials. The propaganda journal maintained that this was done solely with the intention of systematically plundering the treasury, and demanded that Werthauer should bear the costs
incurred. In its issue of March 19-20, 1931, the *Völkischer Beobachter* joined in with
the smear article "Genossen unter sich" (Consorters Among Themselves).[187] This was
not new either, because already in September 1928 the propaganda journal had targeted the banquet in the Werthauer's home.[188]

In the April 1931 issue of the Communist journal *Die Linkskurve*, Otto Biha
defended Chaplin against the disparaging attacks of the Nazi press, which saw in
him the "whiner" who does not resist anything:

This [...] unoriginal characterization of Chaplin roughly matches the infantile mindset of the
fascists who see in Einstein the "relativity Jew" and in every human being who is not exactly
imbecile a cultural Bolshevik agent of the 70 Elders of Zion. Charlie Chaplin is anything
but such an agent. He is the greatest mimic performer of the little man's sorrow and joy in

capitalist society, and exposes the inner principles of life. Under the mask of morality, justice and truth he shows the ridiculous dummies of social masquerade.[189]

However, it also became apparent that the Chaplin image of the Communist press was certainly not only positive. For Biha attacked the hymns of praise of the non–Nazi "reactionary press" on the wealthy Chaplin, who was "in his private life a shrewd tomfool at the courts of world finance."

While Chaplin's Berlin visit was over for *Der Angriff* as an issue, the *Völkischer Beobachter* agitated against it until the end of March 1931. On March 21, 1931, in its Berlin issue, the propaganda journal dealt side blows against the despised "asphalt press" and Chaplin's "racial comrade" Albert Einstein, pacifist and 1921 Nobel Prize winner for physics whom Chaplin had visited in his Berlin apartment on March 15, 1931. Above all, the article "Chaplinade" went into excess with new Chaplin slurs, such as "sich anschmierender, unsagbar widerlich und lächerlich anmutender Hanswurst" (Ragged, Brown-nosing, unspeakably disgusting and ridiculous Tomfool) and "obszöner Judäer Charlie" (Obscene Judean Charlie) whom no one would forgive for his Germanophobe *Shoulder Arms.* Like a mantra it was repeatedly emphasized that the "darling of the world," celebrated by the "Jewish press," was only interested in collecting many millions of dollars with *City Lights,* which he had conceded "as quick as a shot." The *Völkischer Beobachter* blatantly threatened violence against the wealthy Chaplin, who allegedly mocked the working class:

> With respect, gentlemen of the "Journaille," [...] we do not [love] your racial comrade [Chaplin]. He delighted the world with his botch *Shoulder Arms,* in which he [...] threw mud at German soldiers in the vilest manner. [...] He has never improved since then. [...] He is not an advocate of the poor. [...] But we are honest enough that [...] this "kleine, krummbeinige, plattfussbehaftete Filmfritze" [Little, bow-legged, flat-footed Film Chap] Chaplin [also] forced laughter from us by [...] his racially conditioned peculiarity. [...] Mr. Chaplin, [...] we advise you not to extend your stay here until the advent of the Third Reich! For well-intentioned reasons, Mr. Chaplin![190]

The fact that Chaplin had long since departed from Berlin seemed to have slipped the attention of the *Völkischer Beobachter.*

In April 1931, the Communist magazine *Arbeiterbühne und Film* contrasted the "factual and sympathetic statement of *Die Rote Fahne*" on Chaplin's alleged Junge Garde interview with the "disgusting" article of the *Völkischer Beobachter* of March 21, 1931, and raised the question: "What do the not-yet-completely-dumbed-down 'followers' of the 'national idea,' who surely love Charlie Chaplin as much as many class-conscious proletarians rightly do, have to say about this blossom of ethnic 'art criticism'?"[191] Communist objections certainly did not impress the Nazi press.

At the end of April 1931, the *Westdeutscher Beobachter* called Chaplin a "shrewd Jew" who had come to Berlin only for the sake of business and had "taken a few lousy million from Germany with him across the pond."[192] The propaganda journal found another reason to get excited in Chaplin's farewell in the London train station from enthusiastic crowds. These, however, would have taken no notice of the conductor Furtwängler, who was traveling on the same train. Therefore, the *Westdeutscher Beobachter* complained on May 13, 1931, under the headline "Disgusting. How the Clown Scores Off the Artist" that "the clown Chaplin had triumphed over

the artist Furtwängler." Moreover, the New York *Musical Courier* had made fun a little later about how Chaplin had also been adulated in Berlin.

The *Westdeutscher Beobachter* wrote that "Germany in 1931 lay in the dust at the
feet of a clown" and commented: "Faugh!"[193] Even more crude than the *Völkischer
Beobachter* of March 21, 1931, however, was Streicher's approach in July of that
year. With almost sadistic glee, he wrote in *Der Stürmer*: "One fine day, it will be
delightful to see the pale and shocked faces of the Jews in Germany when National
Socialism takes the reins of power. Then, of course, the 'waving of the cane,' the
'simple-minded smiles' and the 'waddling with the feet' will no longer be of much
use [for Chaplin]. The reckoning will follow by legal means."[194]

Undoubtedly, however, the criticism of *Arbeiterbühne und Film* would have
fallen on deaf ears with the *Völkischer Beobachter*. Immediately after its "Chaplinade" of March 21, 1931, the propaganda journal continued to agitate against Chaplin in its Berlin Edition. On March 22-23, 1931, it referred, among other things, to the
Jüdische Presszentrale Zürich's enthusiastic lead on Chaplin and his London triumph
on the 13th of that month: "Business came to a standstill, the deputies just stared at
the gallery. Prime Minister MacDonald furloughed his cares for a weekend and dedicated it to this brilliant film artist."[195] The *Völkischer Beobachter* commented on
the verbatim quote: "That even business is faltering must apparently be the absolute
maximum, which in Jewish eyes is proof of admiration."[196]

On March 22-23, 1931, it referred, among other things, to the enthusiastic article
on Chaplin by the Jewish Press Headquarters in Zurich. "Theo Welcomes Chaplin"
in the Berlin edition of the *Völkischer Beobachter* of March 24, 1931, was decidedly
more vicious.[197] Ernst Schwartz described two pub conversations between himself as
Ernesto and his presumably fictitious unemployed friend Theo from March 9, 1931,
before and after Chaplin's arrival in Berlin. At first glance, they seemed like harmless anecdotes, but they contained low blows. In the first conversation, Theo wanted
to persuade Ernesto to welcome the "world genius" Chaplin with him at the train
station.

Ernesto pretended not to know Chaplin, and stuck to it, even when Theo showed
him a "little picture" of Chaplin and Albert Einstein as private citizens. Allegedly,
Ernesto did not know Einstein either. So who in the "little picture" was Chaplin and
who was Einstein? "Here this one," Theo triumphed, "this one is Scharlin!" Ernesto
asked, "Scharlin? Scharlin? Scharlin who?" Now Theo echoed angrily: "Well Scharlin, the only one! Scharlin, the great one! Scharlin Schäpplien!" Ernesto replied: "Do
you mean the Clown from the movies, with the big flat feet and the saggy pants?"
Now Theo swooned about Charlie "with his redeeming love" and drew attention to
the "other great, very great loner" in the picture next to Chaplin. Ernesto followed
up with a snide remark about Einstein: "Is the old one, with the empty eyes under
the astonished eyebrows, who smiles so fabulously stupidly, also a movie clown?"
Theo blurted out his fascination with the two personalities: "Come off it! [...] That's
the other world genius! [...] Albert Einstein! A German and an Englishman! And
yet spiritually equally ingenious. Do they not already resemble each other out-
wardly, as if from one root? Teuton Einstein and Anglo-Saxon Schäpplin! So what:
they are Jews, if that's the way you want it." Ernesto took just this as an opportunity

to enlighten Theo that one Jew resembled the other anyway, and that it was therefore absurd to assign Chaplin and Einstein to nationalities. In any case, Ernesto did not want to accompany Theo and preferred to drink a beer in comfort. Theo was annoyed by Ernesto's "old racial obsession" and set off alone for the train station. Later that day, Theo returned, frozen to the bone, complaining that he had waited in vain for Chaplin on the street. When Chaplin rode past in a car, the view of him was spoiled by the rear end of a police horse, Theo said. He moaned in frustration: "I hope I do not have to lie in bed tomorrow, because I have to be on the dole in the morning."

Chaplin's Berlin visit finally served the *Völkischer Beobachter*'s Bavarian Edition as a spur for a whole page on "the Jewish problem" at the end of March 1931. There were articles such as "The Jew in the Opinion of Thinking Germans. Everyone Agrees: A Harmful Foreign Body," "The Robber Dynasty of Jakob Moses," "The Eternal Jew," "Luther's Fight Against the Jews," "Jewish Leaders of the American Criminal World" and "A Typical Business of the Jews—White Slavery."[198]

Lichter der Großstadt *Starts Up*

For the German premiere of *Lichter der Großstadt* on March 26, 1931, the Verein Berliner Presse (Berlin Press Club) had arranged two festive screenings at the Ufa-Palast am Zoo.[199] Chaplin is said to have demanded a guarantee sum of 150,000 reichsmark from the movie theater.[200] "Stacks of preorders" had been received, and when advance sales began on March 17, tickets were sold out the same day.[201] On March 26, "a police squad had to be employed in front of the Ufa-Palast am Zoo in order to regulate the car traffic on the jammed Hardenbergstrasse and the pedestrian traffic on the sidewalks in a makeshift manner."[202]

It was still rumored that Chaplin might make a last-minute appearance.[203] Instead, he sent a message of greeting via telegram, which was read out at the beginning of the first event and applauded by the prominent premiere audience from the press, film industry and society.[204] This included the acting Prussian Kultusminister (Minister of Culture) Dr. Adolf Grimme, Reichsinnenminister (Reich Minister of the Interior) Dr. Joseph Wirth, Nobel Prize winner for literature Thomas Mann and the head of the Film Oberprüfstelle, Ministerialrat (Undersecretary) Dr. Ernst Seeger. The Berlin Funkorchester (Radio Orchestra) then opened with Richard Strauss' "Till Eulenspiegels lustige Streiche" (Till Eulenspiegel's Merry Pranks).[205] In front of the venue, an actually blind young flower vendor stationed herself with her sales stand, and the premiere guests literally pried the flowers out of her hands after the screening.[206] The "magnificent premiere"[207] was also reported on the radio.[208] The Nazi *Thüringer Film-Zeitung*, of course, griped about the event that the Berlin press had damaged the local cinemas with it, which "in any case have their difficulties to turn the corner in these dreary times."[209]

With *Lichter der Großstadt*, Chaplin continued the course he had begun with *The Gold Rush*. Admittedly, the new film did not achieve *The Gold Rush*'s balance between touching pathos and comical, fast-paced scenes. But Chaplin had blended a captivating plot full of finely articulated gag-laden comedy and pathos to such a degree, making the film another highlight of his oeuvre.

A young blind flower vendor is sitting on a street corner. She hears a car door slam, footsteps approaching her, and assumes it is a wealthy man. So she offers him a flower. But it is Charlie who—touched by her reaction—buys the flower from her with the last of his small change. Charlie is fascinated by her and begins to watch her secretly. The car owner returns, slams the door and drives off. The flower girl thinks it is her customer, and Charlie, believing this, quietly slips away. During the night, Charlie sees an obviously rich man trying to take his own life, because his wife had walked out on him. He is about to jump into the water with a rope around his neck

Südfilm A.G. ad for the German premiere of *Lichter der Großstadt* (*City Lights*), March 26, 1931.

and a heavy rock. Charlie convinces him not to, and the grateful man takes him to his mansion. After a night of partying together, Charlie sees the flower vendor walking past the mansion. With money from his new rich friend, he buys all the flowers and drives her to her home. But the rich man is his friend only when drunk. Once he is sober, he has him thrown out of his villa. Charlie cannot count on further support, because his patron is traveling to Europe. Charlie has fallen madly in love with the flower vendor and wants to help her, even wants to pay for a new method of eye surgery he read about in the newspaper. But how? He tries his luck as a garbageman but is soon fired. Then it seems that he is able to save the day: He is tempted to take part in a boxing match to win the prize money. But the lanky Charlie loses to the strong professional. Charlie is devastated, but that's when his rich friend returns from Europe. Drunk again, he recognizes Charlie and gives him $1000 for the eye surgery.

Burglars break into the villa and beat up his friend. Charlie is accused of theft, but manages to escape and slip the money to his beloved before he is arrested and sent to prison for nine months. The operation has been successful, and Charlie's great love has even been able to start a fancy flower store. She longs for her benefactor. In every young handsome customer she hopes to recognize him. There stands Charlie, pitiful, ragged, and mocked by newsboys, in front of her store. At first, she is amused by the tramp, but then she goes to him compassionately and slips a coin into his hand. She has never been able to see her benefactor before, but she recognizes him from the touch of his hand. A tragic recognition, but Charlie's face reflects hope, happiness and joy for having found her again.

Surprisingly, immediately after the German premiere of *Lichter der Großstadt*, the leftist magazine *Sozialistische Bildung* claimed that the end of the film was missing: "The German Südfilm-Gesellschaft […] believed it owed its audience a 'happy ending' and suppressed Chaplin's end of the film in which the blind girl gives her benefactor the kiss-off and marries a rich young man. People celebrate Chaplin like crazy when he shows up in person in Berlin, but two weeks later, nobody is ashamed to mutilate his opus. That is German 'film culture.'"[210] But the *Sozialistische Bildung* was mistaken. *City Lights* was screened worldwide, including Germany, with the end of Chaplin's own theatrical cut.[211]

Lichter der Großstadt also earned overwhelmingly enthusiastic reviews in Germany. Manfred Georg wrote in *Tempo* that Tramp Charlie's boxing match "is among the funniest slapstick that has been displayed in Chaplin films. […] Once again, an endless number of people will go home happier than when they entered the cinema."[212] In the *8 Uhr-Abendblatt*, Kurt Pinthus called the film a "splendid event" that, with its humanity and comedy, "makes the audience scream with delight."[213] In *Der Film*, Betz raved in his long review, which is representative of many others:

> [It] was a film event of the greatest style. […] The poet Chaplin is far more of a novelist than a dramatist. [… His] lavish power of imagination gave the work its inner momentum, the inexhaustible possession of creative will, its intellectual depth. […] Absolute perfection was shown by Chaplin the performer. No one is greater than he. None more sensitive and inventive. None more overwhelming. Chaplin shows with every movement man in his misery and in his delight. He shows a life, a destiny, a world. The child and the philosopher. The downtrodden and the victor. Parsifal and Erdgeist [Gnome]. No one is more delightful than Chaplin. […] We have experienced one of the most beautiful and richest cinema evenings. The audience roared with pleasure and left the theater fulfilled. Everyone knew that this evening was an unforgettable experience for them. There was heavy applause after the end.[214]

Die Rote Fahne mingled its praise of "the artistic and satirical peak performance of the actor Chaplin" with well-known class-struggle clichés. With his "magnificent film," he had openly as never before "revealed his true social nature with such perfection of dramatics." From the beginning, he expressed "his deepest sympathies" with the "disenfranchised, the unemployed, and the homeless" and demonstrated that "a living tramp is more precious than all the empty bourgeoisie unveilings of memorials."[215] *Die Welt am Abend*, which at times discovered a parody of the talkies in *Lichter der Großstadt*, roughly joined in.[216] The *Düsseldorfer Nachrichten* thought highly of *Lichter der Großstadt*, but called for a "stop with Chaplin for now" when it learned that *Shoulder Arms* was being shown in Paris.[217] The German nationalist *Deutsche Zeitung*, like other right-wing newspapers, was not among the avowed Chaplin admirers and ran the headline "Chaplin's burnt-out lights" because "Chaplin has reached the end of the line" and could "hardly get anything new" from the character he had created.[218] According to *Der Jungdeutsche*, "Chaplin has lost his way." *Lichter der Großstadt* was like a joke that could be told in five minutes, but was "rolled out to two hours [including supporting program] by an inconceivably tedious presentation." Chaplin's film character had "plunged into crisis," so that his trip to Berlin had been "imperative propaganda" and "smoothing things over" for his film.[219] Hugenberg's *Rheinisch-Westfälische Zeitung* also claimed to have waited in vain for the film's alleged merits and instead reported the rumor that Chaplin's "*City Lights* Banquet" had cost him 100,000 reichsmark; where this had taken place remained an open question.[220]

Der Angriff and the *Völkischer Beobachter* remained silent about the Berlin premiere, the *Völkischer Beobachter* probably because its Berlin edition was discontinued on April 1, 1931. But *Der Angriff*, similar to the Bavarian edition of the *Völkischer Beobachter* years before, printed ad-like notes where *Lichter der Großstadt* was being screened in Berlin cinemas.[221]

"Filmfratz" Chaplin

When the *Film-Kurier* reported one day before the German premiere of *Lichter der Großstadt* that Chaplin was to be awarded the Cross of the Legion of Honor in Paris,[222] *Der Angriff* reacted on March 28, 1931, with its biting note "Klamauk um

Outdoor advertising for *Lichter der Großstadt* (*City Lights*), unknown German cinema, ca. 1931/32 (DFF—Deutsches Filminstitut & Filmmuseum, Frankfurt am Main/Chaplin-Archiv, Dauerleihgabe der Adolf und Luisa Haeuser-Stiftung für Kunst und Kulturpflege).

Charlie" (Hullabaloo for Charlie): "Filmfratz [Film Rascal] Chaplin was awarded the Cross of the Legion of Honor in Paris. Maybe he will now also become President of the Council of the League of Nations!"[223] This in turn prompted Kurt Reinhold in early April to write his commentary "Entlarvt" (Unmasked) in the magazine *Tagebuch*. Tongue-in-cheek, he attested that the propaganda journal, "in an incomprehensible fit of diffidence [...] it had missed the most beautiful opportunity" to "have a racial enlightening effect." For it bordered on treason not to have discussed *Lichter der Großstadt.*

Reinhold just as vividly demonstrated the redundant scenario of Nazi agitation. He advised *Der Angriff* to call Chaplin by his "good Galician name Chaim Schapiro." In that case, he could only be "a genuine Film Jew." Reinhold went on to say that it would be most effective if Goebbels exposed Chaplin as a "greasy moocher [... in] a pitiful mask" who ripped off "the rich Michel" well and properly. *Lichter der Großstadt*, of course, has a "typical Jewish plot" in which Charlie, as an "ugly, horny little mouse, exploits the blind flower girl" to approach her with obvious intent. Of course, Charlie was as cowardly as all Jews. To help *Der Angriff*'s apparently weak agitation machinery along, Reinhold suggested that Goebbels also have his "terror troops" protest the film. Finally, Reinhold sighed, "So that was not to be read [in *Der Angriff*]. In our country, you even have to step in for your enemies."[224]

Reinhold had aptly exposed the pattern of Nazi polemics, which puts a slant on everything and lies about it until it fits its own purpose. This was involuntarily revealed when *Lichter der Großstadt* was shown in Munich in April 1931. The "film review" of the Bavarian edition of the *Völkischer Beobachter*, which for once touched on the content, deliberately aimed with its distortions to put the film in a bad light. One might have thought that the review was about a completely different film: The propaganda journal seriously insinuated that the core of *Lichter der Großstadt* was underlying criminality, depravity, venal love and a lack of fairness. Moreover, the film suffered from "clumsy craftsmanship" and "years of endless self-repetition" of the creatively burned-out Chaplin, which in turn corresponded to the German nationalist version of the *Deutsche Zeitung* of "Chaplin's burned-out lights." The journal's gush, which in addition misrepresented the spectators' reactions, read:

The "great" Charlie even risked a European trip for his latest film. In addition, the Jewish advertising campaign had not missed its effect, so that the Jewish community flocked in large numbers to the public premiere [...]. But the over-loud outbursts of merriment soon died down, and in the end there was only chastened applause. The film shows the dreary story of the homeless vagabond, kicked out everywhere. Since he has given her a thousand dollars, the blind flower vendor thinks he is a rich man. But the always drunk millionaire bestowed it on him. The money, however, has been snatched from him by the policeman, from whom Charlie stole it again, so that the flower vendor can buy back her eyesight in the eye clinic. But Charlie does not give her the thousand dollars right away. He pockets part of it and pays her with it when she emotionally kisses him. This characteristic Jewish trait is constantly repeated in Chaplin's oeuvre, and reappears in the antics that have been so familiar for 20 years. Chaplin passes off this disgustingly painted comedy as real humor. His star, however, is fading. He cannot dream up anything more. Everything reappears in the antics with which he has been caricaturing, ridiculing and dragging everything into the mud for 20 years. Chaplin passes off this disgustingly made-up comedy as real humor. The sentimentality still tolerably scattered in *Goldrausch* is here thrown into the audience with shovels full of frantic mawkishness. It is truly witless and unfunny […] to win a boxing match by unfair tricks [and] to perform a plethora of pranks for which little children would be beaten. The film's music, as sentimental as it is lowbrow, was also composed by Chaplin. It proves even more how old Chaplin has become […]. In later years, […] no one will be able to understand how this "Bajazzo eines minderwertigen Volkes" [Buffoon of an inferior people] could dominate film for decades."[225]

Major Stein-Rumpelstilzchen simply trivialized the film on April 1, 1931, and saw Chaplin's end coming:

[T]he whole of Berlin attends Chaplin's *Lichter der Großstadt* and is—disappointed. Certainly, one laughs at the grotesque puppet, and many a young girl may even dash away a tear because of the usual sentimentalities. Apart from a few variations, it is all the same. We know enough about this figure of the flat-footed guy who, by far the most in the whole world, is floored, gets in trouble and looks crestfallen. No, then better off outdoors.[226]

In the second half of April 1931, the Stahlhelm newspaper *Fridericus* expressed satisfaction that the Monégasque press had reacted appropriately to Chaplin's visit to the Princedom of Monaco. It had published "not a line about *City Lights*" and had not commented on "[the revealing of] his pretty uninteresting 'plans.'" Once again, the newspaper put the boot in for *Shoulder Arms*, complaining about the attention Chaplin had received in Berlin, where "the press mob [were] breaking windows to get to their darling Chaplin. The little Monaco puts them to shame, but—wanna bet?—they do not even notice!"[227]

At the end of April 1931, *Lichter der Großstadt* was shown at the cinema Modernes Theater in Bonn. Just like the *Völkischer Beobachter*, the *Westdeutscher Beobachter* dismissed the film as a bland work that left the viewer emotionally untouched and deserved absolutely no applause:

Plenty of sentimentality. It is a piece of rubbish that really is not worth the hubbub. To retell the story of the Tramp and the blind flower vendor is absolutely unnecessary by any stretch of imagination. Well-known, gradually boring jokes are interspersed in the irrelevant plot. One leaves the film temple with a feeling of inner emptiness […]. We Germans can boast of having created better films, which possess more wit, inventiveness, and greater artistic maturity, and are not remotely as vapid as the sorry effort of this American film Jew, gloriously blared out by Jewish advertising.[228]

The *Westdeutscher Beobachter*, of course, failed to prove that any German filmmaker could seriously match Chaplin's genius, ingenuity and art—there were none. Objectivity and faithfulness to the facts were simply alien to the politically biased propaganda journal. It is remarkable that Italian fascists, unlike German Nazis, still appreciated Chaplin and had bestowed upon him a "black shirt of honor" during his visit to Rome in March 1931.[229]

Whether the Nazi agitation against *Lichter der Großstadt* was limited to disparaging articles will be examined in Chapter 5.

The "Filmjüdlein," His Brother and More Films

Nazi agitators were usually on the scene when there was a chance to badmouth Chaplin. The May 1931 rumor that Chaplin wanted to marry Maria Martin alias Mizzi

Müller from Marienbad, whom he had met on the Riviera,[230] was not picked up, for example, to rehash his divorce from Lita Grey. But the *Nürnberger Zeitung*'s article "Sid [*sic*] Chaplin flieht aus Portugal" (Syd Chaplin Flees Portugal) from June 19, 1931, appeared to be fit to fuel agitation against Chaplin. According to this, Chaplin's half-brother Syd had traveled to Portugal, which at that time was said to have been shaken by "revolutions, bombs and assassinations." On the evening of Syd's arrival in Lisbon, the following is said to have happened during "his nice moonlight stroll": "All of a sudden I heard gunshots. I got caught in a flock of flustered people and was kicked to the ground." Two days later, he saw "a mass of people" standing in front of a house where apparently a meeting was taking place: "Suddenly someone raises his arm and throws a black thing into the window … a small bomb. Terrible bang … screams … rattling windows […] Full of fear, I am running for shelter into the first house that comes along. In no time, a bunch of dangerous-looking characters surrounded me. 'British citizen,' I protest in English. But they do not understand me." Syd then showed his passport and pointed out his last name, which made no impression because his brother had been known in Portugal only as "Karlchen" (Carlitos). Therefore, Syd shouted, "Brother of Karlchen!," waved his cane like Tramp Charlie, laughed "foolishly" and waddled his feet. "Finally, one of the revolutioners begins to understand. He whispers to the others, they burst out laughing and lead me back to my hotel in triumph."[231]

From this anecdotal and somewhat adventurous-sounding, exotic yet harmless story, Streicher brewed for the Nuremberg *Stürmer* his smear article "Chaplin's Brother" directed against Charlie and Syd Chaplin. He made "Bolshevik hordes of criminals" out of the participants of the political meeting. Instead of courting the millionaire Syd Chaplin, "another splendid specimen of a Jew," they should have shot him on the spot. After all, in Russia, Jews would usually be put against the wall. Streicher commented as follows: "The World Jewry elevates every fool to genius, every bungler to artist, and every simpleton to a sage of world fame, if he is a racial comrade." He then attacked Charlie Chaplin for his marriages and films, among other things, with a side blow at *Lichter der Großstadt*:

> A small, lanky film Jew with a stupid, featureless face, with staring, soulless eyes, in which hidden and veiled lurks the beast, the Jewish beast. He plays in movies and tries to make the clown, the August, the tomfool. He wants to force laughter, wants to feign humor and appears like a "holzgeschnitzte Puppe ohne Seele" [carved wooden doll lacking soul]. When he is not bungling in movies, he is on the prowl for non–Jewish women. He has married and then divorced probably half a dozen times. He takes beautiful, blind film actresses home and discards them after half a year. The international Jewish press then reports with pleasure about the latest, racially defiling offense of a "jüdisches Schwein" [Jewish Pig] in long articles."

In August 1931, Streicher's comrades-in-arms took on Chaplin to task two more times. The *Westdeutscher Beobachter* "disclosed" the stage names of Jewish film stars. Chaplin, who had "not yet revealed his incognito," was given the birth name "Cahn," and his *Kid* was also included: "So the little Jewish boy Jakob Cohn quickly becomes Jackie Coogan."[232]

When, at the end of the month, the Berlin cinema Kamera had *The Pilgrim* and *Zirkus* on its schedule, Chaplin was also targeted by *Der Angriff*, which had not previously commented on *Zirkus*. In its far-fetched article, it denied the cinema good taste for screening the two "photographed atrocities" of a comedian whose career had already expired:

Charly [*sic*] Chaplin thinks he is grotesque; he thinks he is the film comedian of the world. [...] At a time when film itself was still in its infancy, these bulky boots with the guy stuck in them might have seemed funny in a certain way. [The] divine one [...] came to Neuyork [*sic*], stepped on a block of wet concrete with his [...] shoes and thus created a monument for himself. [...] The only comforting thing [with *The Pilgrim* and *Zirkus*] was that Charly [*sic*] was responsible for pretty much everything in these films.[233]

5

Nazi Disruptions
of *City Lights*?—1931–32

After the Nazis' vehement verbal attacks concerning Chaplin's Berlin visit and *Der Angriff*'s propagandistic prediction that *Lichter der Großstadt* would be a flop in Germany, street-fighting methods against the film seemed to be only one step further in the heated German political situation. "Fascist rowdies" formed on the central promenade of the boulevard Unter den Linden on March 9, 1931, shouting "Down!" as Chaplin made his way to the Hotel Adlon. In front of the hotel, Nazis are said to have shouted "Du Jude Chaplin."

This chapter examines:

- how the Nazis in the Weimar Republic agitated against films they rejected and disrupted their screenings
- whether the Nazis also disrupted screenings of Chaplin's *Lichter der Großstadt* and other Chaplin films
- whether the Nazis caused the insolvency of the German distributor of *Lichter der Großstadt*

Max Krakauer's Report

German-Jewish film businessman Max Krakauer had been managing director of Südfilm AG's Leipzig branch in the distribution district of East Germany.[1] He reported the following about Nazi attacks on Chaplin's *Lichter der Großstadt*: Südfilm AG had acquired the German screening rights of Chaplin's film in 1932 for $250,000, the equivalent of about one million reichsmark, hoping for an exceptionally lucrative business deal. At first, the box office results of *Lichter der Großstadt* had been excellent. Then the Nazis discovered that Chaplin was a Jew and a multimillionaire who behaved like a Communist. After they had failed to defame him and his film in public by means of agitation, they had mounted SA guards in front of the cinemas that played the film. They had tried to "enlighten" the moviegoers in their own way about Chaplin and his film by harassing them and preventing them from attending the screening. When that did not work, the SA people scared off the moviegoers during the screenings with stink bombs, releasing white mice and similar actions. Under Nazi pressure and not least that of Hugenberg's Ufa, which had been

125

infiltrated by the Nazis, cinema owners increasingly had refused to accept the copies of *Lichter der Großstadt* that they had ordered. This had caused Südfilm AG such economic difficulties that it eventually went bankrupt.[2]

At first glance, Krakauer's account seems plausible, even if he has transferred the purchase of the German screening rights of *Lichter der Großstadt* from 1931 to 1932, and keeping in mind that the Nazis only may have decided that Chaplin was Jewish. The scenario he describes fits the tools of the Nazis, who were primed for violence. As early as the beginning of the 1920s, Adolf Hitler had organized armed goon squads attempting to suppress political opponents with sheer violence for different reasons and, as it would turn out, did not hesitate to kill for it.[3] Film merchants therefore took the NSDAP and the threats of its functionaries seriously. It is not plausible, on the other hand, that they would have subjected the film to disruptive actions simply because they had discovered after its German premiere that Chaplin was a Jew and a multimillionaire who had allegedly joined forces with the Communists. In fact, the Nazis had been targeting him as a Jew and a rich wheeler-dealer since 1926 (see Chapter 2). Therefore, the question arises why Nazis had not disrupted screenings of Chaplin's films earlier. There would have been plenty of opportunities. Including *Goldrausch* and *Lichter der Großstadt*, the Film-Prüfstelle Berlin had since approved some 60 Chaplin films for public screening. Doubts about Krakauer's report begin primarily with Jost Hermand's 1993 claim that Goebbels "ordered [that] the screening of *Lichter der Großstadt* be clamped down on with stink bombs and white mice in 1932."[4] Hermand fails to provide a source, and Goebbels' extensive diaries do not substantiate his claim. As noted in Chapter 3, Goebbels commented on Chaplin and his films only once: on March 13, 1928, before and after a visit to Chaplin's *Zirkus* in a Berlin cinema.[5] The German-Jewish philologist, writer and chronicler Victor Klemperer

Max Krakauer (1950), author of *Lichter im Dunkel*, 1947.

had kept a diary since 1918 and was an attentive observer of the Nazis and their activities. In his diary, nothing can be found about the incidents alleged by Krakauer.[6] He had seen *Lichter der Großstadt* as early as April 6, 1931, at the U.T.-Lichtspiele in Dresden.[7] But at least the Saxon capital was located within the area of operating of Südfilm AG's branch, which was headed by Krakauer.

However, Krakauer lacks details such as box-office takings and the location, time and frequency of Nazi disruptions of *Lichter der Großstadt*. It is therefore difficult to verify the validity of his assertions. Maybe for this reason, the authors Wolfgang Gersch, Sabine Hake, Jost Hermand and Andreas-Michael Velten have taken Krakauer's version, vague in every respect, unexamined as fact and thus have not presented any further findings.[8]

Scope of the Examination

In the following, therefore, an attempt is made to create an objective picture of how *Lichter der Großstadt* fared in the Weimar Republic. To this end, the German film trade journals and Nazi propaganda journals have been analyzed for the period of the Weimar Republic, as well as random samples of newspapers from March 1931 onward, with a focus on Berlin, and magazines. First and foremost, the film trade journals highlighted all possible developments that could be of significance for the smooth business processes of their readership. For this reason, reports on interferences of all kinds were of particular interest from the beginning of the Weimar Republic, and the film trade journals served this need for information extensively with regional and national reports that also investigated the motives for such actions and their prosecution.

Chaplin had been one of the biggest movie stars of the Weimar Republic, popular with audiences and critics alike. As a result, he was generally the focus of informational interest across the entire spectrum of German print media, even when not necessarily favorable to him. Therefore, it would have been anything but a side note if Nazis had tried to ban *Lichter der Großstadt*. Most likely, the press would have reported such a development.

Since 1919, a number of films had provoked the ire of Nazi agitators because they contradicted their ideology. On the basis of these cases, the present chapter will attempt to find an answer to the following question: Are the alleged disruptive actions against *Lichter der Großstadt* plausible with this background, and what differences are there possibly in disruptions between Chaplin's film and other films?

The reasons for film disruptions could be completely different. Flops were booed as in much the same way as in the theater, and sometimes the trade press agreed. At times, claqueurs were hired to start a film off by loudly applauding it, which was criticized in reviews as dishonest applause lacking any spontaneity.[9] Another bad habit in the silent era was that spectators read the intertitles aloud to the annoyance of other visitors. In the sound film era, it was replaced by humming along to the film melodies. As an antidote, the *Film-Kurier* recommended "copious amounts of insect powder."[10] Probably almost all cinema owners also knew visitors who disturbed film screenings with bad behavior or sometimes even damaged the furnishings.[11] Then again, cinemas were the stage for lovesickness, scenes of jealousy or excesses of envy.[12] Moreover, movie theaters suffered from the so-called "Kinohetze" (Cinema Baiting) until well into the 1920s. Disputes were also fought over issues of morality and sexuality. Certain circles fought against the medium of film, regardless of political attitudes: they considered it to be culturally harmful, not least for educational reasons.[13] In addition, it became the trigger of a conflict when cinemas hosted political events or moviegoers tried to get discounted or free tickets at the height of the economic crisis in the early 1930s.

The press first and foremost reported on politically motivated film disturbances of all kinds. Sometimes it was clear that Nazis were responsible, or their involvement was assumed, or it turned out that they had not been involved. Since German nationalist circles also attacked films, their actions could not always be clearly differentiated from those of the Nazis. Then again, politically motivated reactions failed to materialize when they were most expected. In any case, the trade press complained that hardly a day went by without major cinemas reporting attempts at disruption.[14]

Due to the subject, the focus is on Nazi actions. Therefore, the account of the results of the general research in the German film trade journals has been limited to those films that were actually, or at least probably, disrupted by Nazis. In detail, these are:

- *Anders als die andern—§ 175. Sozialhygienisches Filmwerk* (Richard Oswald, 1919)
- *Nathan der Weise* (Manfred Noa, 1922)
- *Panzerkreuzer Potemkin* (*Bronenossez Potjomkin*, Sergei Eisenstein, 1925)
- the alleged "Germanophobe smear films" *Die vier apokalyptischen Reiter* (*The Four Horsemen of the Apocalypse*, Rex Ingram, 1921), *Die große Parade* (*The Big Parade*, King Vidor, 1925) and *Mare Nostrum* (Rex Ingram, 1926)
- *Der Jazzsänger* (*The Jazz Singer*, Alan Crosland, 1927)
- *Im Westen nichts Neues* (*All Quiet on the Western Front*, Lewis Milestone, 1930)
- *O Alte Burschenherrlichkeit* (Rolf Randolf, 1930)
- *Die Dreigroschenoper* (Georg Wilhelm Pabst, 1930)
- *Cyankali* (Hans Tintner, 1930)

First Disruptions with Political Background

Soon after the end of World War I, the press reported on anti–Semitic agitation with flyers and riots, for example in downtown Berlin. This did not always apply to film.[15]

The first at least partially anti–Semitic film disturbances concerned the feature film *Anders als die andern—§ 175. Sozialhygienisches Filmwerk* with Conrad Veidt as a violin virtuoso who falls in love with a male student. German-Jewish director Richard Oswald made the film in 1919 in collaboration with the German-Jewish sexologist Magnus Hirschfeld, who had founded the world's first Institut für Sexualwissenschaft (Institute for Sexology) in 1918 in Berlin. For the first time in film history, a film openly took a stand against the culpability of homosexual acts between men. At the time, Professor Karl Brunner fought against so-called sex education and sex films. He believed them responsible for "the fact that pornography [...] is the order of the day in the cinema." He sermonized about this in the Berlin area,[16] which he combined with anti–Semitic propaganda.[17] At the end of May 1919, he attended the preview of Oswald's film at the Berlin Apollo Theater, jumped up while the film was playing, and loudly called it a "mess." Oswald stopped the screening and shouted back, "If anyone calls this film a mess, he is a bastard himself, Prof. Brunner!" After lengthy applause for Oswald, Brunner left the cinema, loudly cursing, and the film continued without any further disruptions.[18] There were also "noisy rallies" against

Anders als die andern in several other theaters.[19] They probably emanated from sympathizers of the anti–Semitic Alldeutscher Verband (see Chapter 1), who on July 10, 1919, in Berlin Biophon-Theater-Lichtspiele, dubbed Veidt's pupil a "true specimen of the Jewish race" after his first appearance. There were jeers, whistles and shouts of "Shame!" to the dance of young men in women's clothes. This was accompanied by comments such as "Are we Germans supposed to let ourselves be contaminated by the Jews?," "How can we be offered such a thing?" and "Where is the science in this?" After the interruption of the screening, part of the audience left the cinema. The German nationalist newspaper *Deutsche Zeitung* used this incident as an opportunity to protest against Jews, perversion and the decay of morals, and to demand the reintroduction of film censorship, which had been abolished with the proclamation of the Weimar Republic.

Since the police had refused to intervene against *Anders als die andern*, the newspaper became even more explicit: "Should not the people take the law into their own hands? We welcome the event as a sign of the Germans' reawakened sense of self-esteem. In addition, we hope for the growing resistance against the un–German spirit that is spreading so widely. In Germany, the German must prevail!"[20] In response to the incidents, Oswald invited representatives from the scientific community and writers to an informational matinée at the Berlin Prinzess Theater on July 17, 1919. Among those present were "Wahrer der Sittlichkeit" (Preserver of Morality) who used the screening to launch anti–Semitic attacks.

The press defended Oswald's "discreet and tactful fight against article 175" against the "artificial scenes of turmoil [...] from the same filthy cesspool from which the smear campaign against Jews and socialists emanate." However, this did not prevent similarly motivated actions against *Anders als die andern* in August and September 1919 in Hamburg and Kiel.[21]

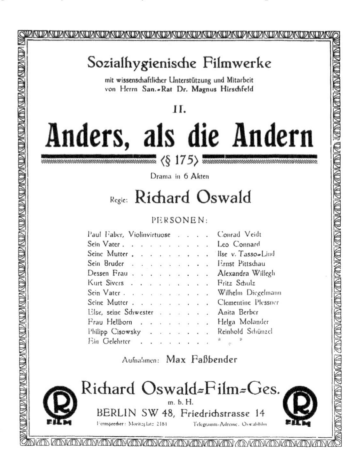

Richard Oswald Film-Ges. ad for *Anders, als die Andern* (§ 175), 1919.

At the end of July 1919, Jaap Speyer's German drama of morality *Die Tochter der Prostituierten* from the same year triggered riots at the Berlin Passage Theater. Because it allegedly stemmed from the "Jewish-Socialist cesspool," "several well-dressed men and women" protested against the "shamelessness" with "deafening anti–Semitic shouts" in the movie theater. Some men also entered the projectionist's room, demolished equipment and stole some films. The screening of *Die Tochter der Prostituierten* was finally cancelled, and the cinema owner was forced to refund the admission fee.[22]

In August 1919, "Catholic circles in West Germany" railed against Nils Olaf Chrisander's 1919 German film *Das Gelübde der Keuschheit* (The Vow of Chastity), about monks' sexual problems caused by celibacy. In Düsseldorf, a priest, his sexton and a "bunch of young people" not only disrupted a screening of the film but also tore up the cinema screen. Police were able to prevent the outraged moviegoers from beating up the disruptors. Instead of bringing the disruptors to account, however, the police ordered the closure of the cinema for that day. In Cologne, preceding protests even resulted in the film not being shown at all.[23]

Communists also disrupted films that contradicted their ideology. In August 1922, William Karfiol's German film *Der Todesreigen—Ein Zeitbild aus Rußland* (A Document of Present-Day Russia) broke all records in Hamburg, so that its theatrical run was prolonged until the end of February 1923.[24] Since it did not portray conditions in the Soviet Union in a favorable light, Hamburg Communists organized "terror" against it. But they also became active regionally and directed attacks of their comrades in Braunschweig. There, the police could not get the "terror" under control, so that the cinema owner had to cancel the screening.[25]

Nazis vs. Nathan der Weise

German-Jewish director Manfred Noa had made this film in 1922 for the Munich Emelka company, based on Gotthold Ephraim Lessing's 1779 dramatic poem inspired by humanism. In it, Nathan the Jew, portrayed by Werner Krauß, who played several Jewish roles in Veit Harlan's infamous 1940 anti–Semitic smear film *Jud Süß*, has renounced Orthodox Judaism and lives out religious tolerance toward Christians, Jews and Muslims. The film became the earliest example of Nazi film campaigning that exerted coercion on the schedule of movie theaters.[26]

In February 1923, Munich "swastikas" threatened the owner of the Regina-Lichtspiele in the Bavarian capital that they would "smash up the place" if he did not withdraw the film from the schedule.

For the time being, the cinema owner gave in to the pressure, and the Emelka boss offered Hitler the chance to convince himself in a special screening that *Nathan der Weise* provided no cause for Nazi attacks.[27] Hitler sent as his representative Hermann Esser, future author of the anti–Semitic smear book *Die jüdische Weltpest* (see Chapter 3). Next to Hitler, he was considered the only demagogic talent of the early NSDAP, "a noise-maker who is almost better at this business than Hitler [...], a demon of speech, albeit from a lower hell."[28] After the internal screening, Esser wrote

Bayerische Filmgesellschaft m.b.H. ad for the premiere of *Nathan der Weise*, January 12, 1923.

in the *Völkischer Beobachter* that *Nathan der Weise* was an evil Jewish tendency film that "dripped with mendacious and hypocritical humanity." At the same time, Esser threatened violence if the film should be shown again: "We […] have grave concerns about large-scale riots […]. The consequences of which would be the sole responsibility of the organizers of this provocative film propaganda. It is essential for them to know that in the anti–Semitic-national-Christian Munich there is no longer any room left for Jewish hubris and arrogance."[29] The director of the Regina-Lichtspiele now finally cancelled *Nathan der Weise*, whereupon the Emelka hurriedly scheduled another special screening of the film for the entire Munich daily and specialized press on February 21, 1923, in its screening room. Representatives of the *Völkischer Beobachter* did not attend.[30] Nazi disruptions of screenings of the film have not been reported.

Panzerkreuzer Potemkin, *the Successor*

Russian director Sergei Eisenstein's classic 1925 film *Panzerkreuzer Potemkin*, about the roots of the Russian October Revolution, was particularly controversial in all political camps of the Weimar Republic. It had been through a censorship ordeal of bans and cuts.[31] In the *Berliner Börsen-Zeitung*, the head of the political section Jügler attacked the film as a "germ bomb smuggled into Germany" and an "apotheosis of human meanness." The *Film-Kurier* vigorously defended *Panzerkreuzer Potemkin*.[32] It also was the second film to become a target of the Nazis.[33] If they had limited themselves to threats against *Nathan der Weise*, for the first time they resorted to violence against Eisenstein's film.

At the end of April 1926, the German premiere of *Panzerkreuzer Potemkin* took place in a considerably edited version at Berlin's Apollo Theater, which was not one of the designated premiere theaters. Renowned film critic Willy Haas called it "a crying shame" that the film had not been released in a proper premiere theater.[34] Even for the *Berliner Börsen-Zeitung*, the film was the "strongest film experience in months" and Eisenstein a "genius."[35] The *Völkischer Beobachter* thought it was "uninhibited Bolshevik May propaganda through film" and a "deliberate instruction to murder."[36] When tentative attempts were made to show the film in Munich in June, the propaganda journal ran "alarm messages" and threats.[37] The much louder *Der Stürmer* called *Panzerkreuzer Potemkin* a "Jewish criminal film," an "incitement to class struggle [and] for a Bolshevik blood frenzy in Germany" and the "most ingenious of all the Communists' propaganda tools to date." According to Streicher, Jews were the masterminds behind this "blunt invitation to the German Communists to unleash the revolution."[38]

This left its mark. Despite the film's approval, the police banned its screening at the Stuttgart Palast-Lichtspiele, even in a subsequently edited "kids" version, because "the most radical right-wing minds" had taken umbrage at it and political rallies were expected.[39] The German nationalist–oriented Reichswehr did not accept *Panzerkreuzer Potemkin* either: In November 1926, a cavalry regiment in Neustadt, Upper Silesia, prohibited its soldiers from going to the cinema.[40] The Reichsmarine (German Navy) did the same with its sailors in early 1927 in Swinemünde.[41]

After much back and forth, in August 1926, the German distributor presented

Panzerkreuzer Potemkin

Das größte Monumentalwerk
der russischen Filmkunst
ist reichszensiert.

URAUFFÜHRUNG DEMNÄCHST

Sichern Sie sich noch heute Termine!

Albert Angermann ad for the upcoming German premiere of *Panzerkreuzer Potemkim* (*Bronenossez Potjomkin*), 1926.

Panzerkreuzer Potemkin to Munich press representatives in another, post-censored version.[42] Even this did not reassure the *Völkischer Beobachter* "after the most objective assessment." Therefore, the propaganda journal signaled its readiness to fight to put "an end to the *Potemkin* ballyhoo."[43] At the meeting of the Bavarian parliament's Constitutional Committee on April 1, 1927, the Bavarian NSDAP deputy Dr. Rudolf demanded that the Bavarian government take action against this "shameless [...] smear film of the worst kind." Instead of providing living quarters, he said, the "entire Jew-infested German film system [...] reopens almost every week these [cinematic] pestilences for the people." The Committee rejected Rudolf's request.[44] When *Panzerkreuzer Potemkin* was shown in the Munich cinemas Lichtspielhaus and Filmpalast on April 3, 1927, Nazis organized "noisy protest rallies" in front of and inside the two cinemas in the afternoon. In the Lichtspielhaus, "young [...] members of the swastika [...] brandished sticks" after they had drunk "new courage with malt liquor." Surprisingly, this time Nazis and Communists did not bandy blows as usual, but "as partners of the Hitler people," Communists joined them in beating the moviegoers.[45]

Meanwhile, "Hitler's raiding patrol leader" Lieutenant (ret.) Edmund Heines, Breslau police chief during the Third Reich, captained his thugs in the Filmpalast. They threw a stink bomb during the screening and created a row that turned into a fistfight. Several visitors felt nauseated, "panic broke out," and most of the audience left the theater frightened. After their arrival, the alarmed police removed a couple of troublemakers.[46]

In the evening, however, Nazis flocked together again in the Filmpalast, and Communists stood in formation in front of the cinema. After hours of rowdiness and throwing of stink bombs, the police cleared the cinema. In the street, Communists sang the Internationale, while the Nazis left shouting "Down with *Potemkin*" and "Heil Hitler." Neither the cinema operators nor the Bavarian Ministry of the Interior were swayed by this scandal, so that *Panzerkreuzer Potemkin* remained on the Munich schedule.[47] In October 1927, 15 Nazis had to stand trial for their acts of violence in the two cinemas.[48]

Although *Panzerkreuzer Potemkin* had been approved in the meantime in an uncut version, at the end of June 1928 the Reichswehr Ministry prohibited soldiers throughout the country from attending. To enforce this order, plainclothes soldiers were stationed in front of Berlin's Titania Palace without informing the management, sending away Reichswehr members.[49] In October of that year, "young rowdies" complained about the film's "Communist propaganda" before the start of an afternoon screening at the Stuttgart Union Theater. An anonymous telephone threat to assault the projection room to destroy the film print turned out to be a false alarm.[50] After these riots, it was remarkable that the re-release of Eisenstein's film in a sound version in the fall of 1930 seemed to have passed off without a hitch.

Nazis and "Germanophobe Smear Films"

Erich von Stroheim's 1919 U.S. film *Du sollst nicht begehren* (*Blind Husbands*) was a rare example of a film being preceded by a Germanophobe reputation that was then not confirmed in Germany.[51] No German distributor, on the other hand, would have seriously considered importing the French film *Weshalb wir das Ruhrgebiet besetzt halten!*, shown in Paris in 1923,[52] because Germany probably did not come off unscathed in it. Other feature films with allegedly Germanophobe content, however, were a perennial issue in the Weimar Republic, especially if they dealt with World War I.[53] Then cinema owners also called for boycotts against producers of such movies.[54] Despite the *Panzerkreuzer Potemkin* experience, *Der Angriff*, *Der Stürmer* and *Völkischer Beobachter* limited themselves to articles against a very few "Germanophobe smear films" from October 1926 to October 1927.

Two U.S. anti-war films by director Rex Ingram, based on stories by Spaniard Vicente Blasco Ibáñez, caused considerable uproar in Germany and were not publicly screened. *The Four Horsemen of the Apocalypse*, produced in 1921 by MGM predecessor Metro and starring Rudolph Valentino, contained violent scenes in which German soldiers commit atrocities, while the 1926 MGM production *Mare Nostrum* starring Antonio Moreno was about a naval officer who falls in love with an Austrian spy and whose son is killed when a U-boat torpedoes a passenger liner.

When *The Four Horsemen of the Apocalypse* was released in some European countries in 1922, German diplomats intervened.[55] After Valentino's death in August 1926, MGM had the scenes with the atrocities removed from the film for all markets—possibly due to the international Locarno Treaties, which were signed on December 1, 1925, and resulted in Germany becoming a member of the League of Nations in September 1926. In early October 1926, however, the *Süddeutsche Filmzeitung* emphasized that this did not put an end to its reservations about the film. At the end of the month, the *Völkischer Beobachter* polemicized against *The Four Horsemen of the Apocalypse* for the first and only time as "the Jewish Metro-Goldwyn-Mayer corporation's snub to the German public," against which "a particularly strong stand has to be taken."[56] A few days later, the new MGM version was shown to representatives of the Reichsverband Deutscher Lichtspieltheater-Besitzer e.V. (Reich Association of German Cinema Theater Owners) at a closed event at Berlin's U.T. on Kurfürstendamm. They still dismissed it as "anti–German and inflammatory."[57] This remained the final decision.

After the New York premiere of *Mare Nostrum*, the *Lichtbildbühne* immediately conveyed its disapproving review of March 1926 to the German Consulate General in the United States. In June, the *Film-Kurier* claimed: "It was Rex Ingram who injected the spiteful Germanophobe bias into the film."[58] Later, the German film industry received support from France.[59] From there, pressure was exerted on MGM to remove from the market all films produced by the latter that were perceived as smear films.[60] After lengthy negotiations, on January 2, 1928, MGM recalled all promotional material for *Mare Nostrum* in the U.S. and from all over Europe in order to destroy it.[61] This time, no Nazi propaganda journal had raised its hand.

In the fall of 1926, King Vidor's 1925 anti-war film *Die große Parade* (*The Big Parade*), probably one of the first to take a stand against the senselessness of the so-called heroic death, ran into trouble with the German board of film censors.[62] As a consequence, the German distributor Ufa had it re-edited and, as a precaution, screened this version to 200 representatives of German and American daily newspapers and film trade journals. The majority of them voted to release this version to German cinemas.[63] In June 1927, the *Völkischer Beobachter* attacked *Die große Parade*'s supporters as people who were "for the most part already physically not German." They would be responsible that "this smear film [would soon] be shown in Berlin if the audience does not take care of its rapid removal from the schedule."[64] *Die große Parade* was approved on October 20, 1927,[65] and its German premiere took place two days later at Berlin's U.T. am Kurfürstendamm,[66] which Hans-Walter Betz reported full of praise in *Der Film*.[67] Goebbels noted in his diary on October 24, 1927: "Tonight with Schweitzer in the film *Die große Parade*. Pacifist. The Jews are applauding when German soldiers enter the trenches against Germans. Otherwise, fabulously done. Such films for and not against Germany."[68] On October 28, 1927, *Der Angriff* described the film as "pacifist favorite food for the ghetto of Kurfürstendamm" and as "unerring [, slick] propaganda," which, unfortunately, had not been prevented by force: "We only register that such a film can be screened in Germany without German-conscious men protesting against it with fists."[69]

In 1929, the NSDAP Reichstag deputy Hermann Göring organized "Deutsche Morgenstunden" (German Morning Hours) with films that the Nazis rejected. In *Der Angriff*, he attacked the Reich government, which did not take any action against such films and the alleged "Kriegsschuldlüge" (War-Guilt Lie):

> The war and smear films, which were made years ago in America and are still partly running now, have and had no other purpose than to constantly show the world that Germany was to blame for the war, that Germany was the beast that had hurled itself over enemy territory. But how did the German government make use of [the medium of film as] a propaganda tool to convince the world of the contrary and to show it the true face of the German? Nothing happened in this direction. Never did we hear of German films which, for their part, contributed to the enlightenment of our innocence.[70]

Der Angriff *Threatens Ufa*

In 1929, the Nazis felt politically strong enough to threaten Hugenberg's Ufa. The thorn in their side was the sound film version of Alan Crosland's 1927 U.S. feature film *The Jazz Singer*, which had been screened previously in a silent version. At the end of November 1929, the sound film version was shown in Berlin's Gloria-Palast, which belonged to the chain of Ufa theaters. Because of Yiddish being spoken and sung in it in a synagogue, *Der Angriff* immediately demanded that Ufa remove this "all–Jewish tendency film, which deeply offends the sensibilities of all German-conscious circles" from the schedule within three days: "Otherwise all National Socialist in the Reich will be advised to shun Ufa's theaters in the future."[71] The trade press was appalled by Goebbels' ultimatum, but Ufa reacted opportunistically. It referred to the silent version of the film, about which no one had complained, and cited Jewish sources which in turn criticized certain sequences in *Der Jazzsänger*.[72] A few days later, *Der Angriff* had nothing more to offer than didactic and malicious advice.[73] Ufa immediately folded and signaled that it would negotiate with Goebbels to prevent a Nazi boycott. In the end, *Der Jazzsänger* remained on the schedule. But Goebbels had scored an increase in prestige: In the future, Ufa would coordinate its schedule with him.[74]

The rapprochement between Ufa and the Nazis was illustrated in early April 1930 by *Der Angriff*'s reaction on Josef von Sternberg's 1930 Ufa production *Der blaue Engel*, based on Heinrich Mann's novel and starring Marlene Dietrich. The film, today considered a masterpiece, was controversial at the time. According to *Lichtbildbühne*, it was sometimes criticized as "inferior depraved kitsch" and an "ugly youth-debauching botch" that "dragged teachers […] through the muck."[75] *Der Angriff* predicted that Mann's time was up. But it conceded to Ufa that it, too, needed time to recognize political developments and act appropriately.[76]

National-Film ad for the German premiere of the sound version of *Der Jazzsänger* (*The Jazz Singer*), November 26, 1929.

The Extraordinary Case of Im Westen nichts Neues

The film most intensively fought by the Nazis was the U.S. antiwar film *Im Westen nichts Neues* (*All Quiet on the Western Front*), which premiered in Germany in early December 1930. This marked the beginning of a new dimension of street-fighting agitation by the Nazis some four months before the German release of *Lichter der Großstadt*. The Nazis staged threatening disruptive actions until mid–January 1933 and even bomb attacks followed.[77] Therefore, this particular case offers a glimpse of how they might have fought Chaplin's film.

Lewis Milestone had shot the film in 1930 for Carl Laemmle's Universal

Pictures, based on Erich Maria Remarque's 1929 novel. Starting in November 1928, the *Vossische Zeitung* had pre-published the novel. The book edition, published at the end of January 1929, was so successful that the novel was translated into 26 languages that same year. With translations in over 50 languages by now, Remarque's book reached circulations in the two-digit millions.

From the very beginning, German right-wing circles regarded the novel as a "Germanophobe sorry effort." It is about high school students who, at the beginning of World War I, enthusiastically obey their teacher's inciting call to enlist in military service. But already during their military basic training they are inhumanly drilled by a sadistic sergeant, who in civilian life was a mailman who had always treated the students submissively. Much too late, they realize only at the front the horror of war and the senselessness of dying a hero's death. During a furlough, one of the students, Paul Bäumer, enlightens younger students of his former school and warns them not to follow the patriotic call as blindly as he did. Climactically, Paul falls in battle shortly before the end of the war. In mid–February 1929, the *Völkischer Beobachter*, in its Supplement "Der deutsche Frontsoldat," published two lengthy articles attacking the liberalism and anti–Prussian, pacifist stance of Remarque's novel as an assault on the "holiest" of the front-line soldiers, who had risked health and life for the Fatherland as a matter of course.[78] The Nazis despised the work so much that they banned the film immediately after Hitler's takeover and publicly burned the novel in Berlin's Opernplatz in May 1933.

A native of Laupheim in Baden-Württemberg, German-Jewish Laemmle had emigrated to the U.S. in 1893. As the head of Universal, he became wealthy and generously endowed his hometown with charitable donations, whereupon on September 20, 1919, Laupheim bestowed honorary citizenship on him as a "Wohltäter der Gemeinde" (Benefactor of the Municipality).[79] In Germany, however, Laemmle was heavily controversial on account of the 1918 Universal films *The Kaiser, the Beast of Berlin* (Rupert Julian), *The Heart of Humanity* (Allen Holubar) with Erich von Stroheim playing the lecherous Prussian Lt. von Eberhard who terrorizes a Red Cross nurse (Dorothy Phillips) and throws a baby out of a window, as well as *Yellow Dog* (Colin Campbell), because they featured atrocities committed by German soldiers. When it was announced in August 1921 that von Stroheim would visit Germany, Egon Jacobsohn called for a boycott of *The Heart of Humanity* in his *Film-Hölle*.[80] This was followed by Ludwig Seel's "open letter to Mr. Carl Laemmle" in the trade journal *Deutsche Lichtspiel-Zeitung* on August 20, 1921, attacking Laemmle for his "Schmutzfilme" (Smut Films) which were "allerschlimmste Deutschenhetze" (Ultimate Germanophobia).[81] The next day, this letter found its way into the right-wing *München-Augsburger Abendzeitung*, which added its own aggressive comments under the headline "An den Pranger!" (Put Him in the Stocks!).[82] In September 1921, the trade journal *Allgemeine Kino-Börse* also printed Seel's open letter,[83] and Jacobsohn, in his *Film-Hölle* article "Der Höllenbraten" (Bastard from Hell) against the "Vaterlandsleugner" (Traitor to the Fatherland) Laemmle, who had bought Laupheim's honorary citizenship.[84] Still in January 1922, *Der deutsche Film in Wort und Bild* complained about Germanophobe Universal films, which were sometimes met with German "Würdelosigkeit" (Lack of Dignity).[85] Others considered Laemmle to be the nationally minded former German "Uncle Carl" who still loved his old homeland.[86] In September 1927, German film trade journals reported that on the occasion of his sixtieth birthday he had offered $5000 for film ideas.[87] The *Völkischer Beobachter* countered in November with "Help Laemmle to an idea!" and threatened with violence: "So come on, dear readers, help the dear man to a good idea, he needs it! Of course, it would be best to do something like this verbally and with the necessary physical force, we would already have the idea!"[88] When Laemmle's plan to film Remarque's novel on a grand scale became known in the fall of 1929,[89] the *Völkischer Beobachter* ran the following headline against this "film scandal"[90] at the beginning of April 1930: "Remarque's War Novel as a Germanophobe smear Film. Jew Laemmle Turns Remarque's *Im Westen nichts Neues* into a mean smear Film against the German Army."[91] In 1937, the Nazi smear book *Film-"Kunst," Film-Kohn, Film-Korruption* presented him as a "Jewish German agitator" who had "most shamelessly ridiculed the German people, the German Wehrmacht and the German name and dragged it into the mud, thus whipping up the hatred of the Americans against everything German."[92]

Im Westen nichts Neues was widely considered a masterpiece. In August 1930, it was rumored that producer Laemmle had been nominated for the 1930 Nobel Peace Prize.[93] In November, the original version was awarded two Oscars, for Best Picture and Best Director. However, the persisting German reservations prompted Universal to prepare a cut version especially for Germany, shortened by about 50 minutes and running about only 85 minutes. Missing from it, among other things, was how the recruits beat up the sergeant who takes pleasure in grinding them, as well as the scene in which the Kaiser is blamed for the war. After the German consul in Los Angeles had previewed this version at Universal's invitation,[94] the German Auswärtiges Amt no longer objected to *Im Westen nichts Neues* being shown

Deutsche Universal ad for the German premiere of *Im Westen nichts Neues* (*All Quiet on the Western Front*), December 4, 1930.

in Germany.[95] Finally, the Berlin Film-Prüfstelle approved it in November 1930 with a further cut of 12 meters.[96] In this version, the movie became one of the first foreign-language sound films to be dubbed into German, but in the process it was "toned down" even further from a German perspective. This still divided critics. German nationalist and right-wing radical circles reacted with restraint to vehement disapproval against the German premiere, while others were full of praise, including Hans-Walter Betz in *Der Film*.[97] Unlike in 1928, the Reichswehr Ministry did not prevent its soldiers from attending *Im Westen nichts Neues*.[98]

Im Westen nichts Neues *in December 1930*

The festive German premiere of the dubbed version of *Im Westen nichts Neues* took place undisturbed on December 4, 1930, in Berlin's cinema Mozartsaal on Nollendorfplatz (today's Metropol Theater) before an audience representing politics, justice, administration, the arts and the press. The numerous prominent guests included several Prussian ministers; former Reich Chancellor Philipp Scheidemann; the entire personnel of the American Consulate General; the head of the Film-Oberprüfstelle Dr. Ernst Seeger; the writers Alfred Döblin, Carl Zuckmayer, Alfred Polgar, Else Lasker-Schüler and Dr. Lion Feuchtwanger; General Music Director Otto Klemperer; film directors Gerhard Lamprecht, Georg Wilhelm Pabst and Lupu Pick; as well as the journalists Theodor Wolff (*Berliner Tageblatt*), Egon Erwin Kisch and Dr. Kurt Pinthus.[99] The very next day, about 300 Nazis "decorated with swastikas" (*Der Film*) or only 40 to 60 troublemakers (police reports) provoked a well-prepared riot in the Mozartsaal under Goebbels' leadership. He directed the operation and issued commands with "forceful language."[100] The Social Democratic *Vorwärts* described the events in its Morning Edition of December 6, 1930, under the headline "Goebbels Directs Theater Row. Stink Bombs and Mice Against the Film *Im Westen nichts Neues*." Apart from a certain party-political tone, this vivid account matched reports in the film press:

> Yesterday, Nazis had bought up a large number [about 200] of tickets at the Theater on Nollendorfplatz [… which] were handed out to SA people and members of the Nazis' "cultural department" at three staging areas in front of the theater before the beginning of the screening. […The] first disruptions started [after the film had been running for less than ten minutes]. Nazis yelled: "Jews out!" and "Hitler at the gates." Theatergoers were mobbed, and speeches were made from the theater's tiers. Goebbels attended in person to determine whether his people were also roaring and raving according to his orders. The infamous former pastor [Ludwig] Münchmeyer ["Reichsredner" of the NSDAP][101] gave [one of his] speeches from the tier. […] The Nazis [… threw] dancing mice and white rats from the tier into the parquet […], while others added stink bombs. The screening finally had to be interrupted, and the police appeared in the auditorium. The troublemakers were removed from the cinema. After the theater was cleared, whole boxes full of stink bombs, which the rowdies could no longer make use of, were found in the tiers. In front of the theater, Nazis continued to cause a riot. [… The] rowdies were demanding their admission fees back. They threatened the cashiers and broke a pane of the box office window. The theater management had [previously] secured the money. The gathering was then quickly disbanded by the vigorously intervening police on the forecourt of the cinema.[102]

If stink bombs could have been brought into the cinema by the crates, past entrance controls and ushers, the Nazi disrupters probably had sympathizers among the Mozartsaal employees. The film trade journals *Der Film*, *Film-Kurier* and *Licht-bildbühne* took a stand against the Nazis with the headlines "Stink Bombs Against Remarque," "Goebbels in the Box," "The Fight Over the Remarque Film" and "Censorship Through Terror?"[103] The *Rheinisch-Westfälische Filmzeitung* called it a climax of the "scandal plague,"[104] while *Der Film* concluded: "Where intellect and substance are not sufficient for an intellectual discussion, the mob takes the floor."[105] The trade journal *Kinematograph*, published by August Scherl GmbH and thus belonging to the right-wing Hugenberg Group, mentioned the turmoil only in passing days later and accused Laemmle of a lack of understanding for German sensitivities.[106]

In contrast, the portrayal of events in the Nazi propaganda press read decidedly different. This followed the standard strategy of distorting the actual events in such a way that peaceful Nazis happened to witness tense situations or even to be attacked by political opponents and finally had to defend themselves when all their efforts at appeasing tempers had failed.[107] On its front page of December 6, 1930, *Der Angriff* insinuated that the "healthy-sensing part of the Berlin population [...] had taken the law into their own hands" against the portrayal of "German World War soldiers as ever-devouring, half-brutish monsters." Some NSDAP party members had attended the first screening on December 5, 1930, only by chance. Without their involvement, "[an] elementary storm of indignation" had spontaneously broken out over "gray-haired men, German mothers, German lasses, youths, whose sport training is visible on every muscle of their face, [and] former front-line soldiers in thin coats and heavy overcoats." This would have been felt by "the pale and blue painted perfumed Jewish women with their bald, obese companions," who "with insolent mouths under the protection of the rubber truncheons of the police [...] still [dared] to threaten with fists decked with diamonds." For "robust workers' fists write quick response." And in the thick of it, a cool-headed Goebbels, who only wanted to inform himself:

The dirt on the screen rolls on. Dr. Goebbels stands with two of his stalwarts at the red parapet of the tier. Nobody else around him. It should be emphasized to the Jewish sensationalist reports that Dr. Goebbels did not think in the least of organizing this storm of outrage. Coincidentally, some Reichstag deputies of the NSDAP were also in the parquet. These gentlemen appeared in the cinema without an appointment, merely for the sake of information. As we have heard, Dr. Goebbels intends to watch the end of the film on Sunday evening [December 7, 1930] for informational purposes.

Der Angriff also peculiarly described the use of stink bombs and rodents:

A pestilential stench surges up. A scream! And into the icy silence a sonorous male bass booms from the stalls: "Here a Jew has sh[...] himself!" Roars of laughter. Judah's children squat in red upholstered chairs, but suddenly jump up, because a piping voice is ringing out: "Mice in the hall! Mice in the hall!" And now they jump up, the otherwise brave Jews, Zion's roses of Jericho. Slowly, with a good measure of persuasion [...] policemen cleared the Walstatt [Battlefield].[108]

For the second screening of *Im Westen nichts Neues*, Goebbels appeared again, accompanied by several NSDAP Reichstag deputies. During the film's second act, he gave the signal for the riot to begin. As a result, the screening was stopped and the third screening of the day was cancelled.[109] The *Völkischer Beobachter*, however, blamed the riots on the "Marxists among the audience," claiming that they had attacked the peaceful Nazis who happened to be present and who had only defended themselves. In the midst of the resulting melee, Goebbels had tried to exert a moderating influence and to prevent worse. For his pains, he was "brazenly" treated by the police as a "ringleader" and "guarded in his seat" by two policemen.[110] A week later, the report in *Der Führer* was similarly distort-

Muß sich ein Volk von Selbstachtung das gefallen lassen??

Vier Jahre lang hielt Deutschland der Welt stand —

Der Angriff, December 6, 1930: "Muß sich ein Volk von Selbstachtung das gefallen lassen?" [Must a Nation of Self-respect Put Up with This?], cartoon by unknown artist.

ing.[111] The editor-in-chief of the *Kampfblatt für nationalsozialistische Politik und Kultur und Hauptorgans der NSDAP im Gau Baden* (Propaganda Journal for National Socialist Politics and Culture and Main Organ of the NSDAP in the Gau Baden), which was launched in November 1927 as "Wake-up Calls of National Socialist Faith and Will," was Robert Wagner, *né* Backfisch, who as Gauleiter of Baden was one of the central Nazi minds in the Third Reich.[112]

After the disruptive actions of December 5, 1930, *Der Angriff* called for demonstrations as a "mass protest."[113] Polizeipräsident Grzesinski then imposed a ban on demonstrations and had the Mozartsaal cordoned off. The *Völkischer Beobachter* raged against the ban in its Berlin Edition: "Commune and Grzesinski-Schupos as worthy protection for Remarque's smear Film" and "Grzesinski Protects Jewish smear Film. The Decent Germans are not even Allowed to Protest anymore!"[114] The *Westdeutscher Beobachter* joined in with tirades against the "soiled screen."[115] In *Der Stürmer*, Albert Forster covered the "outrageous provocation of an American film-Jews" with familiar Nazi set pieces and accused the Reich government of protecting the "crime against the people." The German people would be allowing themselves to be "spat upon" by the "disgraceful work" of "Jew L[ae]mmle," who, as a "goddamned creature," would carry a "mixture of Negro and Mongolian blood" within himself and would have organized natural resources for the U.S. to fight against Germany during World War I.[116] On the side of the Nazis, *Der Stahlhelm* printed an ugly, disfiguring drawing of film character Kat Katczinsky (Louis Wolheim) with this comment: "The film [...] presents this gangster face to the world as a prime example of German front-line soldiering."[117] *Der Stahlhelm* probably alluded to Wolheim's role in Lewis Milestone's 1928 *The Racket* as the lead gangster, whose model was Al Capone.

The actions directed by Goebbels did not miss their effect. Several German states appealed the approval of *Im Westen nichts Neues*. When it became known that the Film-Oberprüfstelle would decide on the matter on December 11, 1930, *Der Angriff* ordered a "pause in fighting," not without at the same time issuing a "well-intentioned warning" in case that the film should remain approved. For the masses would gather and, considering the ban on demonstrations, would be "leaderless" and could go into "violent riots."[118] The *Völkischer Beobachter* announced a march of 60,000 people for this purpose,[119] a figure that was lowered in 1937 in the smear book *Film-"Kunst," Film-Kohn, Film-Korruption* to 40,000 persons.[120] Both figures are unconfirmed.

Diese Verbrechervisage wird in dem Film „Im Westen nichts Neues" der Welt als Musterbeispiel deutschen Frontsoldatentums gezeigt.

Der Stahlhelm, December 14, 1930: Kat Katczinsky (Louis Wolheim), drawing by unknown artist. Caption: "Diese Verbrechervisage wird in dem Film *Im Westen nichts Neues* der Welt als Musterbeispiel des deutschen Frontsoldatentums gezeigt." [The film *Im Westen nichts Neues* presents this gangster face to the world as a prime example of German front-line soldiering.].

On December 11, 1930, the Film-Oberprüfstelle Berlin revoked the approval of *Im Westen nichts Neues*—and a few days later approved the right-wing extremist film *Der Stahlhelm am Rhein*.[121] The *Im Westen nichts Neues* screening would affect Germany's reputation, because, among other things, the German Wehrmacht would be biasedly portrayed by the sadistic Himmelstoß and by "Hun-faced" Katczinski as "German barbarian[s]."[122] Laemmle then withdrew the film from the German market.[123] Grzesinski's ban on demonstrations had thus also become irrelevant. *Der Angriff* hailed this as "our victory," and this time Goebbels triumphantly took up his pen in person with "Forced to His Knees."[124] The *Westdeutscher Beobachter* ran an even more dramatic headline, "Der Schandfilm zur Strecke gebracht!" (The disgraceful Film Hunted down!). The journal also claimed that now a "joyful excitement" was going through the "national Germany" and, aware of the Nazi power, added: "So Goebbels was right when he said: 'The film will be banned, or else we will ban it!'"[125]

The Reichsbanner, a political military association for the protection of the democratic republic, which the Weimar coalition of the SPD, the Catholic Zentrum (Center Party), and the Deutsche Demokratische Partei (German Democratic Party) had founded, protested against the ban in several rallies.[126] The Communist journal *Sozialistische Bildung* was convinced that Goebbels had "employed adolescent

Ufa ad for *Das Flötenkonzert von Sanssouci*, December 1930.

Hitler hordes […] for a showdown" and that state German authorities had "sacrificed their beliefs and dignity to the Nazi mob for the higher honor of Doctor Goebbels."[127] Because the Nazi actions alone had disrupted public safety and order, the *Film Journal* concernedly asked: Would such deliberate provocations also encourage other factions to adopt similar measures against films that would be against their principles?[128] In the case of Georg Wilhelm Pabst's *Die Dreigroschenoper* and Gustav Ucicky's *Das Flötenkonzert von Sanssouci*, the trade journal was proven right.

Goebbels' diary entries from December 5 to 14, 1930, prove that the actions against *Im Westen nichts Neues* had been planned from the outset and that the Nazi propaganda journals had spread fake news.[129] In the nine entries, he wrote, among other things:

- Consultation with deputies and then it's off to the movie in the evening. After just 10 minutes, the cinema is like a madhouse. The police are powerless. The enraged crowd is physically attacking the Jews. […] The police sympathize with us. […] Outside, the box office is assaulted. Window panes rattle. Thousands of people enjoy this spectacle with pleasure. The screening is cancelled, the next one too. We have won. […] This morning. The newspapers are full of our protest. But even the *B.T.* [*Berliner Tageblatt*] does not dare to rail against us. The nation is on our side. So: victory! (December 6)
- The talk of the day is our Mozartsaal blast. […] I have once again had a good nose for it. (December 7)
- It is going on again tonight. We will not let up. (December 8)

- At 4 o'clock the film ban is announced. [...] What a triumph. (December 12)
- Great excitement in the world press. We are once again in the focus of public interest. (December 13)
- The Republic is furious about our film victory. [...] In the public's eyes, we are the powerful men. (December 14)

After the first hot phase of the Nazi campaign against *Im Westen nichts Neues*, the German film *Das Flötenkonzert von Sanssouci*, starring Otto Gebühr as Frederick the Great, premiered at the Berlin Ufa-Palast am Zoo on December 19, 1930. What happened there had the character of an intermezzo. This time, left-wing visitors disrupted the screening with hisses, whistles, heckling, stomping and the throwing of stink bombs, which did not match the Nazis' intensity defending the movie.[130] *Der Angriff* accused the "Lausejungs [rascals] of the Reichsbanner" of "copycatting."[131] Similar disruptions by left-wing circles against *Das Flötenkonzert von Sanssouci* followed in other German cinemas until March 1931, and on one occasion eggs filled with black liquid were hurled against the screen.[132]

Im Westen nichts Neues: *January 1931 until January 1933*

The film continued to generate a plethora of press articles in the months to come. In January 1931, Albert Einstein warned at a rally of the League for Human Rights: "The banning of this film in Germany means a diplomatic defeat for our government throughout the world. This ban unveils such perilous weakness on the part of the government, which has bowed to the clamor of the street. It is imperative, that it redeems itself before the world."[133] At the beginning of February 1931, Heinrich Mann and Carl Zuckmayer demanded at another League meeting, which was held under the motto "Never Again War," that *Im Westen nichts Neues* should be reapproved, and read out Einstein's statement.[134]

In neighboring countries, *Im Westen nichts Neues* was shown in versions that differed significantly from Laemmle's German cut. The Film-Oberprüfstelle's ban resulted in German moviegoers in border areas traveling in droves on chartered trains to Belgium, France and the Netherlands to see the film.[135] Mannheim Social Democrats, together with the Reichsbanner, organized trips every Sunday to Strasbourg's Palast cinema, where the French version was screened minus the love scene between German soldiers and French women. The Strasbourg "pilgrimages" were the subject of a complaint in January 1931 in the Essen Nazi *National-Zeitung*, edited by Josef Terboven, Oberpräsident der Rheinprovinz (Governor of the Rhine Province) in the Third Reich, Reichsverteidigungs-Kommissar des Wehrkreises VI (Reich Defense Commissioner of Military District VI) from the beginning of World War II, and from 1940 to 1945 Reichskommissar (Reich Commissioner) in occupied Norway.[136] Regarding the cut love scene, which degraded "the honor and reputation of French women," the journal addressed the German organizers of the Strasbourg cinema visits: "At least these gentlemen will be taught a lesson in political decency by the French government."[137] According to the *National-Zeitung*'s triumphant report of mid–February, the Saxon state parliament had, at the request of the Nazi deputies, ordered Remarque's novel to be removed from all schools in the state.[138]

To the displeasure of *Der Stahlhelm*, thousands of visitors from West Germany and Westphalia flocked for weeks to the Alhambra cinema in Enschede, the Netherlands.[139] The *Westdeutscher Beobachter* considered the "well-planned" screenings to be an open disrespect for the German state and called the German moviegoers in question "characterless."[140] Moreover, some German Nazis broke into the Enschede cinema and burned the copy of *Im Westen nichts Neues*, as the *National-Zeitung* gleefully reported.[141] Therefore, the Nazis may have considered the plan of the Abrüstungskonferenz (Disarmament Conference) convened in Geneva in early March 1931 to screen the film to the delegates from 14 countries as a setback. However, the Conference's statutes did not permit official film screenings. The Abrüstungskonferenz regretfully reported this to Universal while expressing its appreciation for *Im Westen nichts Neues*.[142]

The Film-Oberprüfstelle's dubious ban of December 11, 1930, was deemed to be so dissatisfactory that the Reich government amended the "Lichtspielgesetz" on March 31, 1931. Now films that would have to be banned as such could be approved "for screening to certain groups of people or under restrictive conditions."[143] The amendment, which became known as the "lex Remarque," was vague, however, and was itself rejected as a special law,[144] but for Deutsche Universal, this was an opportunity to re-release *Im Westen nichts Neues* in Germany. It submitted a new, even more abridged version to the Berlin Film-Prüfstelle, which was approved in June 1931[145] and recognized by the Lampe Committee as being artistically valuable.[146] In September, Deutsche Universal re-cut the film for a third time and applied for its unrestricted approval. After U.S. Universal had committed itself to showing only this version abroad in the future, the Berlin Film-Prüfstelle approved it for all German cinemas.[147]

Immediately thereafter, new Nazi disruptive actions were expected.[148] At first, however, the new version could be shown undisturbed "in many cities of the Reich with unprecedented success."[149] But it was the calm before a new storm. For shortly after the re-approval, the *Völkischer Beobachter* demanded that no more films be shown in German cinemas "which for any reason run contrary to the National Socialist ideology and cultural concept." And anyway: "Foreign films begone!"[150] Local Nazi groups were called upon to promote "well-intentioned" cinema owners and to either change the minds of others through boycott measures or else to ruin them.[151]

Then Nazis again resorted to violence. For July 4, 1931, a private screening of *Im Westen nichts Neues* had been announced at the Kiel Capitol. To prevent this, the night before, SA and SS arranged to disrupt the screening. A Nazi captain recruited volunteers who mingled with moviegoers and threw a tear gas bomb during the screening.[152] A riot squad appeared to ensure that the screening continued without disruption. When the audience left the Capitol afterwards, Nazis harassed, threatened and mistreated them. Nazis also gathered for similar actions after the night screening. The police were eventually able to disperse the disruptors, and, on July 7, 1931, several Nazis were arrested for throwing the tear gas bomb. The police were eventually able to disperse the disruptors.[153]

Shortly thereafter, *Im Westen nichts Neues* was to be launched in three Cologne movie theaters, including the Volksbühne. Immediately after the announcement, the front of the Lichtspieltheater was smudged with paint, presumably by Nazis. The *Westdeutscher Beobachter* tried to camouflage this as "spontaneous protests by the outraged population."[154] The journal followed up with a diatribe against the Cologne police, who protected closed events for "Israelite-looking people" and for "Marxists identified by a membership book": "That is what they call a closed event! This is how Jewish greed for profit and Marxist insolence know how to evade legal restrictions!"[155] In addition, the *Westdeutscher Beobachter* spread the rumor that the Cologne audience showed no interest in the film and that the organizers therefore "openly peddled tickets."[156] On the other hand, the film had been playing "for a week [...] to thousands in Düsseldorf, Cologne, Herne, Recklinghausen, Gelsenkirchen and Bielefeld [...] without any disturbances," as the *Rheinisch-Westfälische Filmzeitung* reported.[157] In fact, according to the local press, Nazis had been "given a short shrift" at the Düsseldorf Capitol: "On Saturday evening at about 8:30 p.m., a horde of about 50 Nazi youths tried to storm the theater and disrupt the performance. The police raiding squad made no bones about it and cleared the street."[158]

Parallel to these screenings in Western Germany, Nazis provoked several cinema riots in Baden-Würtemberg's Stuttgart on July 11 and 12, 1931. After the two showings of *Im Westen nichts Neues* on the first day of this schedule, they rallied noisily in front of the Palast-Lichtspiele, singing the German national anthem and chanting battle songs. It needed "strong detachments of the Schutzpolizei with the rubber truncheons" to break up this riotous assembly.[159] The next day, several hundred police officers had to be called in, because Nazi disruptors partially paralyzed traffic with "wild scenes of noise and scuffles."[160] At the same time, the Stuttgart student body demanded that the operator of the Palast-Lichtspiele cancel *Im Westen nichts Neues*. The students emphasized their clamor with actions similar to those their fellow Nazi Erlangen students had employed a few months earlier against the backdrop of another film (see below).[161] Presumably, the Nationalsozialistischer Deutscher Studentenbund was behind this in Stuttgart as well.

Shortly before, *Im Westen nichts Neues* was shown in the cinemas Capitol, Margulies Theater and Roxy-Palast in the Hessian city of Frankfurt am Main. Nazis committed explosive attacks on two of these theaters. With this, Nazi violence against this film most likely peaked. Neither the local press nor the *Lichtbildbühne* failed to notice. On July 10, 1931, the following had happened: SA people threw a pipe bomb from an adjoining building into the Margulies Theater towards the end of the afternoon screening. The explosion caused minor property damage but no one was injured.[162] The next day, the screening for the Allgemeiner Deutscher Gewerkschaftsbund (General Federation of German Trade Unions) at the Roxy-Palast was filled to capacity, down to the last of the 1000 seats. Towards the end of the screening, an egg hand grenade was thrown into the foyer; the explosion caused considerable property damage. Again, no one was injured.[163] In mid–April 1932, four Nazis were arrested for the assault on the Roxy-Palast. The main perpetrator, former head of Frankfurt's largest SA barracks, had turned himself in and come clean because he felt abused and abandoned by his SA leadership.[164] It came to light that Hessian SA cadre members had provided the explosives for both cinemas.

The main trial against the attackers took place on October 24, 1932, before the Schwurgericht (Jury Court) of the Frankfurt Landgericht (Regional Court). Public attention was immense, so much so that audience tickets had to be issued; they ran out before the main trial. The perpetrators were sentenced to severe penitentiary terms.[165] In 1941, bomber Adalbert Gimbel boasted in the book *So kämpften wir!* about the Frankfurt "Hussarenstückchen" (*coup de main*) in the Margulies Theater. He regretted that the planned effect of the assault had been thwarted by treachery from within his own ranks, and that "upright fighters" had been sentenced to "serious prison terms." Smugly, he added: "But Judas also met his just punishment in the winter of 1933/34. One day, he was found dead in a Taunus ditch with his neck broken. If I remember correctly, the man had been very careless while sledding [...]."[166] In other words, vengeful Nazis had killed their party comrade.

The Frankfurt bombings did not mark the end of violence and other disruptive actions against *Im Westen nichts Neues.* On July 28, 1931, Nazis and Reichsbanner members had a battle with injuries during the screening at the Kammerlichtspiele in Cuxhaven, Lower Saxony.[167] At the end of July-beginning of August, Nazis disrupted a screening at the Krefeld Atrium and were dispersed by the police.[168] When the film was re-released in Munich in October, stink bombs were thrown—whether by Nazis or not has not been established.[169]

Nazi attacks against *Im Westen nichts* continued until a few days before Hitler's takeover. In mid–January, it was screened in Lower Saxony Fallersleben near Braunschweig. Nazis protested this. The mayor did not bow to them. But Nazis and members of the Stahlhelm then gathered in front of the town hall and loudly chanted their slogans. Then they moved on to the cinema and tore up the screen. Since the situation threatened to end in bloodshed, the mayor, under pressure, banned the further screening

Adalbert Gimbel/Karl Hepp, *So kämpften wir,* book cover, 1941.

after all. At about the same time, the cinema Lichtspielhaus in Saxonian Limbach near Chemnitz got off somewhat more lightly. Unidentified disruptors, presumably Nazis, threw stink bombs into the auditorium. After a thorough airing, the screening could be continued.[170]

O alte Burschenherrlichkeit

The following three Nazi film disturbances from December 1930 to April 1931 can be understood in the light of the Berlin riots that *Im Westen nichts Neues* had triggered. The success of these riots encouraged the Nazis to launch public actions elsewhere as well, which made it possible to put pressure on government agencies without too much risk.

In December 1930, the Dresden student body demanded that Karl Hartl's operetta-like 1930 German film *Ein Burschenlied aus Heidelberg* be banned because it allegedly denigrated the "honor and reputation of the German student body." The harmless film admittedly showed nothing more than a glorified Heidelberg of students with "Paukboden [Duelling Chamber] and Bierkomment [Student Rule of Behavior in Pubs]" as "small backgrounds for its joyfully singing romanticism." Stormy riots broke out during the screening. Whether Nazi students were its initiators remained uncertain.[171]

On December 15, 1930, Rolf Randolf's German film *O alte Burschenherrlichkeit* was on the schedule of the Glocken-Lichtspiele in the university town of Erlangen. The film is about student life, and there are romantic entanglements as well.

Hegewald-Film ad for the German premiere of *O alte Burschenherrlichkeit*, September 24, 1930.

After the German premiere at the end of September 1930,[172] Dr. Georg C. Klaren, author of the film, declared that the film contained, among other things, "a few sharp words against the 'Mensur [Duelling] nonsense.'"[173] Movie star Betty Amann played the female lead, talking "gibberish German-American." Allegedly, students spontaneously demanded, even before the first screening, that *O alte Burschenherrlichkeit* be dropped immediately from the program. In fact, local members of the Nationalsozialistischer Deutscher Studentenbund had united from the outset with comrades-in-arms who had arrived from Nuremberg especially for this screening, and arranged to disrupt it. They were also joined by members of student fraternities. Immediately after the beginning of the feature film, when unbiased viewers could hardly have caught anything of the content, a catcall of disruptors commenced.[174] Nazi students demanded that the "Jewish" film be removed from the program, since the "American whore [Betty Amann] should not be allowed to defile the good old German student customs."[175]

The screening was interrupted until the arrival of the police, whom the cinema owner had alerted. On site, the officers were met with a "wild storm of protest." Hundreds of students and other Erlangen residents who had gathered in front of the cinema then moved to the city center singing German nationalist student songs and bawling battle and Heil shouts. The situation evolved so menacingly that the cinema owner did not screen *O alte Burschenherrlichkeit* that day any more. The disruptors celebrated their triumph with the patriotic student song "Burschen heraus." Afterwards, the *Lichtbildbühne* wrote about "battle zone Erlangen"[176] answering its question "Who exercises film censorship in Germany?" with: "In Erlangen: students."[177] The next day, numerous students gathered again in front of the cinema, this time accompanied by the rector of the university. They repeated their clamor for the film to be cancelled and wanted a resolution they had prepared against the film to be submitted to the Bavarian Ministry of the Interior. This was Streicher's cup of tea: He reprinted it in *Der Stürmer*. It applauded the student protest against the "trash film" and the "rector who has the courage to be German."[178] The *Völkischer Beobachter* even twice went into detail about the students' fight "against filth and trash in the movies," who did not accept that "American film–Jews" mocked and kitsched-up student customs.[179]

The riots launched by the Nationalsozialistischer Deutscher Studentenbund were not spontaneous. Baldur von Schirach had led the Bund since 1928. In 1929, he had launched the "attack on the universities." The brutal appearance of the Bund, in which there was "no room for cowards," was marked by numerous brawls. It boasted: "We confess aloud that we are ruthless."[180]

Pabst's Dreigroschenoper

In 1930, director Georg Wilhelm Pabst had filmed Bertolt Brecht's *Die Dreigroschenoper* for the Berlin-based Tonbild Syndikat AG (Tobis). Brecht's works were also publicly burned after Hitler's takeover. After a long legal dispute over copyright issues between Brecht and the production company, the film's premiere took place smoothly in February 1931 in Berlin's Atrium.[181] But in Nuremberg's Phoebus-Palast, it triggered a "well-prepared [...] Nazi" riot that demonstrated the fighting strength of the NSDAP to its own clientele. During the film's wedding scene, Nazi rowdies shouted, probably sang the Horst Wessel song, scattered sneezing powder, threw stink bombs and rotten eggs, set off firecrackers, attacked the audience physically, and generally tried to disrupt the performance "in every way."[182] *Der Film* commented as follows: "Our dear friends, the specialists in cinema dins, called Nazis, have disrupted the Nuremberg screening of *Die Dreigroschenoper*. [...] After the arrival of the raiding squad, the screening continued in a brightly lit auditorium."[183] Nazi propaganda journals praised the cinematic terror as a defense against "the Jewish cinematic mess." In *Der Stürmer*, Streicher called *Die Dreigroschenoper* a "sorry effort of the worst kind" from the "deepest underworld" that mocked Christianity with a clergyman "as a positive dolt" and showed "sub-humanity in all its depravity." For "the Talmud code requires the Jew to degrade everything that is sacred to Christian sensibilities." According to a letter to the editor of *Der Stürmer*, the

intervening policemen were "rabid" members of a "bludgeoning action."[184] A shaken Swabia cinema owner gave vent to his anger about such a Nazi "conspiracy," which had "nothing to do with film business itself anymore" and had also been prepared long in advance: "After all, you do not just carry stink bombs and white mice loosely in your jacket pocket."[185] The *Lichtbildbühne* also complained about the spiral of violence, hoping "that the police authorities everywhere would be willing and able to put a swift end to these shameful events surrounding the film industry."[186] Of course, this did not have the desired effect on the *Völkischer Beobachter*, which used its well-known enemy images and prejudices against Bolshevists and Jews for the Munich screening of *Die Dreigroschenoper*.[187]

Since late January 1930,

Tobis-Warner ad for the German premiere of *Die Dreigroschenoper*, February 19, 1931.

Dr. Wilhelm Frick had been Staatsminister für Inneres und Volksbildung (Minister of State for the Interior and National Education) in the state of Thuringia. He was one of the leading Nazis who established Hitler's dictatorship, served as Reichsminister des Inneren (Reich Minister of the Interior) from 1933 to 1943, and was sentenced to death by the Nuremberg War Crimes Tribunal on October 1, 1946, for crimes against humanity as a major war criminal.[188] In his Thuringian position, Frick was the supreme authority of the state police and misused *Die Dreigroschenoper* for political manipulation. In early March 1931, he applied to the Film-Oberprüfstelle Berlin to ban the movie. He not only justified his move as Streicher had, but also brazenly cited the previous actions against the film as proof that public safety and tranquility had been disturbed by it, withholding the fact that Nazis had provoked it. On March 4, the *Film-Kurier* called it "Frick terror" and the Nuremberg "protest" an "ordered work."[189] In the state of Baden, Nazis had also harshly protested the film, which *Der Führer* highlighted on its March 18 front page.[190] The state of Baden also applied to ban the film. The Film-Oberprüfstelle dismissed both applications. Thereupon, *Der Führer* asked with equal measures of self-confidence and indignation, "Who actually governs Germany now?"[191]

Tintner's Cyankali

Hans Tintner's 1930 film *Cyankali*, starring Grete Mosheim and based on the novel by German-Jewish physician Friedrich Wolf, held other political fuel for conflict: pregnancies in social hot spots and the prosecution of abortion. After three censorship reviews by the Berlin Film-Prüfstelle from early April to mid–May 1930,[192] *Cyankali* premiered at Berlin's Babylon on May 23, 1930,[193] but was banned by the Film-Oberprüfstelle at the end of August that year before re-approving it in a slightly modified version in mid–December.[194] This provoked vehement criticism in the German film industry and was the catalyst for a hot-blooded debate about the culpability of abortion under § 218 of the Reichsstrafgesetzbuch (Criminal Code of the German Reich),[195] which resulted in mass protests, spreading from Stuttgart to Berlin,[196] and took up much space in the Communist press, which called for legalizing abortion.[197] Dr. Wolf was in investigative custody for a few days in February 1931 on charges of participation in an abortion.[198]

In the Free City of Danzig, the temporary ban of the Film-Oberprüfstelle did not apply. There, however, the film was just as controversial. During an August 1930 screening, stink bombs were thrown. As a result, German nationalists, members of the Catholic Deutsche Zentrumspartei, the SPD and local actors got the film cancelled in the cinema concerned. In addition, they called for a boycott of all theaters that wanted to include it in their schedules.[199] In the spring of 1931, *Cyankali* was to be shown, among other places, at the Vereinigte Lichtspiele in Pforzheim, Baden-Württemberg. *Der Führer* demanded actions to be taken against the "tendency film" that would burden the state with the responsibility for children born out of wedlock instead of leaving it with the "whipped-up, decadent, [...] unrestrained sex life of Bolshevist metropolitans" who had "arrived in the Bolshevist paradise of rampant free love at the state's expense."[200] Since the operator of the cinema did not bow to the protest of the Pforzheim NSDAP local group, on March 28, 1931, several hundred members surrounded the cinema. The rowdies chanted: "Bread instead of *Cyankali*! Down with the Jewish film! Germany awake!"[201] The police had their work cut out until the siege of the Lichtspieltheater was broken upon the arrest of 17 Nazis.[202] *Der Führer* downplayed the party action as a defense of the Christian religion and German customs by a few "upright" people, and complained that the police had intervened against such justified concerns.[203] This had the desired effect in that the police department banned *Cyankali* for religious reasons because of "the upcoming Holy Week."[204] *Der Führer* was triumphant over the "insight of the Pforzheim police headquarters."[205]

This feeling of elation was short-lived, because the ban was lifted after a prompt appeal.[206] To prevent the Nazis from further disruptions, the owner of the Vereinigte Lichtspiele scheduled night shows of *Cyankali* as a precaution. At the same time, he advertised a special service to enable the moviegoers' late-night return home comfortably. For that he had reached an agreement with the Pforzheim magistrate for streetcars to run at night. But the city council immediately withdrew the magistrate's promise, so the cinema owner chartered buses as a replacement transport.[207] Accompanying this, a special screening of *Cyankali* was held for about 300 members of the state and municipal authorities, the medical profession, lawyers, teachers, clergymen and the press.[208] *Der Führer* proclaimed the decision of the municipal authorities not to permit late-night streetcar traffic as

Achtung! Es kommt der Film auf den die Massen warten!

Der Atlantis-Sprechfilm der Defa

CYANKALI

Nach Dr. Friedrich Wolfs berühmtem gleichnamigen Bühnenstück

REGIE: HANS TINTNER

Photographie: Günther Krampf

MIT GRETE MOSHEIM

Nico Touroff, Louis Ralph, Margarethe Kupfer, Herma Ford, Paul Henckels, Hermann Vallentin, Josefine Dora, Blandine Ebinger

MUSIK: SCHMIDT-GENTNER auf Triergon

·URAUFFÜHRUNG:

AB FREITAG, DEN 23. MAI

BABYLON

Am Bülowplatz gegenüber der Volksbühne

Fox ad for the German premiere of *Cyankali*, May 23, 1931.

the local NSDAP's victory, which had implemented the party program in an "ideal way" against the "Jewish film without paying the slightest homage to an exaggerated prudery." The fact that *Cyankali* was no longer objected to or even disturbed after the special screening was swept under the rug by the journal.[209] The disruptions of March 28 had consequences for "some right-wing radical rowdies": They were sentenced by the Pforzheim Amtsgericht (Local Court). The *Film-Kurier* hoped that this sentence would "act as a deterrent for the future."[210] Nazis, however, were hardly impressed by the criminal justice.

No Nazi Disruptions of Chaplin Films

The Nazi film disruptions show that the NSDAP had become more radical during the economic crisis beginning in 1930. The party's increase in political influence caused a transition from verbal assaults to public campaigns. Far from an objective exchange of opinions, this had become the standard means of the Nazis in their cultural struggle. Its functionaries boasted about it, even if disruptions were repeatedly camouflaged as alleged storms of general popular anger. In 1931 and 1932, the *Völkischer Beobachter* was banned seven more times for a total of 51 days.[211] But this did not diminish its influence on its readership. In June 1931, the journal called for boycotting or even ruining cinema owners who showed unwelcome films.[212]

In 1932, the Nazis' consciousness of power continued to grow. The Government of the Reich under Reich Chancellor Heinrich Brüning had succeeded in April in curbing Nazi street terror by banning the SA and SS But shortly thereafter, this Reich government was unseated, and the new Reichskanzler (Reich Chancellor) Franz von Papen, in office since June 1, 1932, lifted the ban as early as mid–June in order to pander to Hitler. As a result, some 500,000 members of the party army took to the streets again, spreading fear and terror.

Following the pattern of the Nazi actions against *Im Westen nichts Neues* of December 1930, SA men moved out in the Third Reich to disrupt the German premiere of the 1934 British film *Katharina die Große* (*The Rise of Catherine the Great*) at the Berlin Capitol am Zoo on March 8, 1934, which the Berlin Film-Prüfstelle had approved in late February 1934.[213] The reason for the planned SA disruptions was that the once-popular German-Jewish actress Elisabeth Bergner played the lead and her German-Jewish husband Paul Czinner, with whom in 1933 she had fled from the Nazis to Great Britain, had directed the film. After their escape, the couple had also made anti–Nazi statements. In front of the Capitol, the SA men mingled with other protesters, shouted anti–Semitic slogans with them in front of the cinema, such as "We don't want Jewish films," and harassed moviegoers, pelting them with eggs and rotten tomatoes, among other things. An official of the Reichsministerium für Volksaufklärung und Propaganda is said to have eyewitnessed the SA march and to have been so dismayed that he tried to inform Goebbels. When he failed to contact him, he is said to have decided to call Hitler personally. The latter is said to have ordered the police to put an end to the riot.[214] In any case, a massive police force managed to prevent the rioters from getting further than the foyer of the cinema, where they still threw eggs at the movie posters.[215] In hindsight, the trade press presented the disruptions as "sharp protests from the audience," whose taste had become so "healthy" by this time that in Germany, films by and with Jewish artists would only provoke indignation.[216] After two days, *Katharina die Große* was cancelled and was no longer screened during the Third Reich.[217] The *New York Times* reported on March 11 that the day before, in the *Völkischer Beobachter*, Nazi "Kultur Dictator" Rosenberg had defended the cancellation of the film as a necessary measure: "The attempt to present in Berlin émigré Jews, especially the warped Elisabeth Bergner, and to make money for them in Germany represents an inartistic attempt against which we turn especially because it is not an isolated case."[218] In the aftermath, on March 21, an unidentified person threw a bomb at the car in which the Austrian-Jewish owner of the Capitol was riding in the vicinity of the Berlin Ministry of the Interior. While he had a narrow escape, the driver was severely injured.[219] To what extent Goebbels had directed the SA disruptions in pursuit of his political goals has not yet been clearly proven.[220]

This climate of violence against films was thus prepared, and the methods of such Nazi actions were known when Chaplin visited Berlin in March 1931 and Lichter der Großstadt was first shown in Germany at the end of the month. This would thus most likely have determined physical attacks against *Lichter der Großstadt* and Südfilm AG—if there had been any. If *Lichter der Großstadt* had been plagued with Nazi disruptions, similar actions might well have been expected against the short Chaplin subjects that distributor Fritz Knevels had re-released with 100 new prints on the occasion of Chaplin's visit to Berlin.[221] Disruptions of screenings of *Lichter der Großstadt*, moreover, would almost certainly have found a triumphant echo in the Nazi press. Since Chaplin was revered as one of the world's most famous artists by the German bourgeois and left-liberal press, as well as largely by the film trade journals, for the sake of his films, it is highly probable that well-known editors and writers would have publicly defended him against such excesses—as they had strongly defended him against moralistic accusations in 1927.

An example from the left-leaning press of the Unabhängige Sozialdemokratische Partei Deutschlands (Independent Social Democratic Party of Germany), USPD, which stood in the tradition of the revolutionary workers' movement, may illustrate this. In its column "Nazi-Beobachter" (Nazi Observer), the *Leipziger Volkszeitung* regularly took a close look at crimes and other atrocities committed by the Nazis and their followers.[222] Nazi disruptions of *Lichter der Großstadt* and attempts to influence moviegoers would all have been reason for a report in the "Nazi-Beobachter." The Leipzig *Mitteldeutsche Lichtspieltheaterbesitzer* would probably have joined in. Right on Krakauer's professional doorstep, the trade journal had reported on local attacks against *Im Westen nichts Neues*.[223] Above all, the foreign press would also have put Nazi disruptions of *Lichter der Großstadt* in its front page headlines.

Nevertheless, there is no evidence for the public Nazi disruptive actions and Ufa's influence against *Lichter der Großstadt* and Südfilm AG or against other Chaplin films. Despite the boycott day of April 1, 1933, even the re-release of *Lichter der Großstadt* in the early days after Hitler's takeover apparently came off without any disruptions (see Chapter 7). Therefore, Krakauer's account that Nazis kept moviegoers from attending *Lichter der Großstadt* and thus forced Südfilm AG into insolvency cannot be substantiated. The reasons for the distributor's insolvency will be examined in the following chapter.

6

Südfilm AG and *City Lights*, 1931–32

Since Nazi disruptions of the screenings of *Lichter der Großstadt* were not the reason for Südfilm AG's insolvency, this chapter examines Südfilm AG's development and business practices. It will focus on the influence that the acquisition of the German screening rights of *Lichter der Großstadt* had on the film's exploitation success in 1931 and 1932 and on the distributor's liquidity.

A Distributor with a Major Program

In 1915, the Süddeutsche Filmhaus GmbH was founded as a film distributor, and in March 1922 it was transformed into a stock corporation with headquarters in Frankfurt am Main under the name Südfilm AG.[1] The company maintained branches in all German distribution districts (Berlin, Breslau, Düsseldorf, Hamburg, Königsberg, Leipzig and Munich) as well as in Saarbrücken, which was autonomous at that time. At the same time, Südfilm AG started a joint venture with Emelka AG. Both companies held shares in each other. With its Director Emil Fieg at the helm, starting in 1922, Südfilm AG brought to Germany numerous short comedies and several feature films by the successful U.S. comedian Harold Lloyd, such as the 1923 box-office hit *Ausgerechnet Wolkenkratzer* (*Safety Last*), directed by Fred Newmeyer and Sam Taylor.[2] The Lloyd films were followed by many short U.S. slapstick comedies produced by William Fox and Al Christie. In 1923, the distributor also paved the way to Germany for the Danish comedy team Pat and Patachon with Lau Lauritzen's 1922 feature film *Er, sie und Hamlet* (*Han, Hun og Hamlet*). This was the beginning of an extraordinary success story in the cinema of the Weimar Republic, to which Südfilm AG and other distributors contributed to some extent. From 1926 to 1932, comedies by the two Danes earned the company notable box-office receipts. Particularly popular were Walt Disney's *Mickey Mouse* and *Silly Symphonies* cartoons, which were distributed from 1930 onward, and the undying U.S. Westerns, which also drew audiences to the theaters. Furthermore, Südfilm AG had the advantage of exploiting its films in its own chain of cinemas and, like other distributors, it also produced new films.

Goldschmid Becomes Südfilm's Director

The severe economic hardship that German inflation caused the population in the early 1920s helped the German film industry to keep production costs low and to thrive.[3] However, the tide turned in the mid–1920s with the end of inflation. Südfilm AG ran into economic difficulties, so that for the time being it was only able to pay its shareholders a dividend of six percent for the 1926-27 financial year.[4] In the meantime, Emelka AG had gradually acquired a majority of shares in Südfilm AG, aiming to take over the company completely. Because Emelka AG failed to finance this project, it limited itself to acquiring Südfilm AG's pool of cinemas.[5] The remaining branches of distribution and film production were transferred to the London-based British International Pictures. Its president John Maxwell became the new chairman of Südfilm AG's Supervisory Board, and Aristid Hubrich, director of the British company, a board member. Südfilm AG's registered seat was relocated from Berlin to Frankfurt/Main.[6]

Isidor Goldschmid was hired as a Südfilm AG Director and also joined the executive board in early February 1928.[7] Previously, Goldschmid had been director and member of Viennese Apollo-Film A.G.'s managing board as well as liquidator of the Austrian Filmwerke A.G. In addition, he had also maintained his own film and distribution company in Vienna. His employment with the Viennese film distributor Viktor Micheluzzi had resulted in London contacts with British International which had engaged him as its general representative for continental Europe.[8]

Südfilm A.G. ad for Harold Lloyd's *Ausgerechnet Wolkenkratzer* (*Safety Last*), 1924.

Südfilm A.G. ad for the Pat and Patachon film *Er, sie und Hamlet* (*Han, Hun og Hamlet*), 1923.

An mein Volk!

Heil sei dem Tag, an dem ich euch erschienen! Es war ein Sieg auf der ganzen Linie! Vernehmet mit Staunen, was die Großmacht Presse über mich verkündet:

Was Micky in zehn Minuten erlebt, wäre ausreichend, um einige Lustspieldichter in diesem Lande für Jahre mit Einfällen zu versorgen.
Berliner Tageblatt

Erschütternd komisch, übertrifft alle bisherigen Leistungen der Tonfilmkunst an Akkuratesse, an wundervoll sich anschmiegender humoristischer Musik. Man kam aus dem Lachen nicht heraus.
8 Uhr Abendblatt

Ein so witziges, köstlich übermütiges Schwelgen in lauterster Kindlichkeit hat man selten gesehen. Das Publikum lachte entzückt und wollte überhaupt nicht weggehen.
Berliner Volkszeitung

Größte Kunst triumphiert im engsten Rahmen — glänzende Groteske. Ein unerhörter optischer Rhythmus macht diese Filme beispiellos. Der einzige bisher vollkommene Tonfilm auf der Welt. Eine unerhörte Harmonie.
Der Deutsche

Diese herrlichen Zeichentrickfilme finden ein begeistertes Publikum.
Tempo

Tonfilmwunder, die den Siegeszug durch alle deutschen Kinos antreten.
B. Z. am Mittag

Filme, die in Erinnerung bleiben, die beglückend sind. Manchen Siebenakter für einen solchen.
Reichsfilmblatt

Überwältigend komisch — bringt uns das große Kinderlachen wieder — wahre Meisterwerke — Micky ist eine Klassikerin des Humors.
Der Tag

Kabinettstücke grotesken Humors, erfüllt von tausend Schnurren und verrückten Einfällen — Märchenwelt, in rhythmisch gebundener Bewegung lebendig geworden.
Deutsche Allgemeine Zeitung

Ein Wirbelwind aus Spaß, Laune und Komik. Ein tolles Getümmel der Stimmen und Einfälle. Diese Kurzfilme sind von bezwingendem Humor, man möchte sie bald im Programm unserer großen Kinos sehen. — Gipfel tonfilmischen Witzes!
Berliner Börsen-Kurier

Eine Stunde bester Unterhaltung — köstlich der Humor — eine Unzahl wirklich ausgezeichneter Einfälle. Kunstwerk für Feinschmecker.
Der Film

Dieser Nachmittag im Marmorhaus zählte zu den kurzweiligsten Veranstaltungen dieser Spielzeit. Denn es liefen die schönsten, süßesten Zeichentrickfilme der Welt. Es ist ein Märchen der Jetzt- und der Jazz-Zeit. Prachtvoll. Micky und die Silly-Tiere, ihr seid die herrlichsten Schauspieler unserer Tage.
Licht-Bild-Bühne

Vorzüglich gelungen. *Deutsche Zeitung*

Eine der verwegensten Möglichkeiten und der gelungensten Verwirklichung filmischer Phantasie — ein

Ausrasen der losgelassenen Tollheit bis zur Wiederherstellung des Naturzustandes.
Vossische Zeitung

Ein Tonfilm-Wunder — mit so unerschöpflichem Humor, daß man aus dem Staunen gar nicht herauskommt. Es ist zwerchfellerschütternd!
Morgenpost

Ein erschütternd komisches Spiel. Eine ganze Schlagerserie! *Berliner Morgenzeitung*

Ganz erstaunlich — eine Höchstleistung.
Berliner Börsenzeitung

Micky, der Star aller Stars, das verrückteste Wesen, das die Leinwand je gesehen hat. Hellstes Entzücken. Unerhört komisch. Es war ein Nachmittag, wie man ihn netter, amüsanter und kurzweiliger gar nicht denken kann. Möge Micky bald, sehr bald dem großen Publikum zugänglich gemacht werden.
Neue Berliner 12 Uhr

Wunder . . . das Erlebnis bleibt phantastisch. Walter Disney gehört zu den wenigen Menschen, die es verstehen, die andern zum Lachen zu bringen, zu einem großen befreienden Lachen.
Vorwärts

Es ist bezeichnend, daß eine Reihe von Theaterbesitzern diese Filme gleich serienweise in besonderen Vorstellungen für Erwachsene und Kinder zeigen wollen.
Kinematograph

Es lacht das Publikum, die Wände hallen wider. Kurzfilme, einer immer schöner, zwerchfellerschütternder als die andere. In der Tat ein Tonfilm — Wunder — Vollendung. Welch ein Geschenk für die Massen der Arbeitenden. Vergessen des Alltags, eine Stunde Freude und Unbeschwertheit. Höchste Künstlerschaft im Primitiven.
Film-Kurier

Orgien der Ausgelassenheit und Genialität. Man hat so etwas noch nicht gesehen oder gehört. Aller — allererste Klasse.
Film-Journal

Ich bin jugendfrei und künstlerisch wertvoll und wirke daher steuerermässigend!

Ich bin der grosse Schlager der Saison!

Jeder Tonfilm-Theaterbesitzer setze sich umgehend mit der Südfilm A.-G. in Verbindung.

Südfilm A.G. ad for *Mickey Mouse* cartoons, February 1930.

Although economic difficulties had led to all Südfilm AG businesses being taken over by other companies, Goldschmid wanted to push through a six percent dividend for shareholders at the annual general meeting in early April 1928. He predicted a "happy and profitable future" for the distributor's domestic and foreign business and announced a promising program for the 1928-29 season as an "Easter surprise." Although the general meeting declined to approve a dividend, Goldschmid's forecast seemed to come true. According to reports on the front pages of the *Film-Kurier,* business for the new distribution season had been "excellent."[9] At the end of September 1928, directors Fieg and Goldschmid reported at the supervisory board meeting of Südfilm AG "that the company's sales had achieved record figures." This result was approved by the supervisory board.[10] The situation was marred about two weeks later in the *Berliner Tageblatt*, according to which Südfilm AG was facing production restrictions. The distributor immediately denied this,[11] but at a general meeting held a week later, Goldschmid's dividend plans were rejected again.[12] Nor would they have been justifiable. Südfilm AG's net profit of 80,000 reichsmark from the previous year's distribution business had dwindled to 35,000 reichsmark according to the current balance sheet. Immediately after the general neeting, the assembly of Südfilm AG's general managers of the German distribution districts discussed how to improve the meager result. Max Krakauer took part on behalf of the Leipzig branch.[13]

Südfilm Expands

In mid–January 1929, after a meeting with Maxwell in London, Goldschmid presented "the plans and capacity of Südfilm under the most favorable prospects" and surprisingly even announced an interim dividend of 7.5 percent.[14] Fieg then resigned from the executive board to go freelance and was replaced by Ernst Haller, who had been the long-time proxy. In addition to this personnel matter, the agenda of the supervisory board meeting in February 1929 also included the increase in the company's capital that Goldschmid was seeking. It was not approved because Maxwell was prevented from attending.[15] In April of that year, Goldschmid presented the schedule for the 1929-30 season, which included major projects. This was not too much to hope for, because Südfilm AG, in close cooperation with British International, was involved in the still fledgling but high-potential talkies.[16] The new distribution schedule included two German-language versions: *Atlantic*, based on Ewald André Dupont's 1929 British film of the same name, and Alfred Hitchcock's *Mary*, based on his 1930 British film *Murder!* They were joined by Hitchcock's silent version of his 1929 feature *Erpressung* (*Blackmail*)[17] and three 1930 sound films: two German productions, Richard Oswald's *Der Fall Dreyfus* and Richard Eichberg's *Der Greifer*, the German version of his British International movie *Night Birds*, as well as René Clair's French film *Unter den Dächern von Paris* (*Sous les toits de Paris*).

Immediately before Fieg quit, Goldschmid had claimed after a conversation with Maxwell in London that British International had granted Südfilm AG an increase in share capital of one million reichsmark. This was a false report that got the shareholders of Südfilm AG into a flap, because the supervisory board had not passed a resolution about it in February 1929. They wanted to investigate whether and to what extent Goldschmid had fulfilled his duties. *Film-Journal* asked, "Where is Südfilm's increase in share capital?" and received evasive answers from the executive board.[18] Doubts about Goldschmid's conduct of business were quickly dispelled, however, by headlines such as "Favorable Days for Südfilm," "New Südfilm Success in the Atrium," and "From Success to Success"[19] as well as positive reports in the trade press about the distributor's current schedule.[20] In October 1929, Goldschmid even succeeded, together with German investors, in repurchasing British International's share majority in Südfilm AG. The composition of its supervisory board did not change as a result, and chairman Maxwell supported Südfilm AG's positive public image with frequent visits to its Berlin headquarters.[21]

Reaching Out *for* Lichter der Großstadt?

After *Zirkus* surpassed *Goldrausch*'s success in 1928, the prospects for future lucrative business with *City Lights* also seemed favorable. The forthcoming film was increasingly reported on from 1929, and details of its content became known at the end of November that year.[22] As a result, the January 12, 1930, edition of the *Berliner Tageblatt* ran a remarkable advertisement that obviously concerned the film:

> Who wants to invest 20–30,000 [reichsmark] in the exploitation of the German monopoly screening rights of a new mega Chaplin motion picture? Distribution will be done on a commission basis by a long-established film [stock company]. A huge, sure deal! Hedged by screening contracts in the amount of several 100,000 [reichsmark]. Weekly refund of the investment plus profit to account. Off[ers] u[nder] I.R. 1.250 bes. Rudolf Mosse, Berlin SW 10.[23]

Was Südfilm AG, which had its headquarters at Friedrichstr. 207 in Berlin SW 68, the "long-established film stock company"?[24] Terra Filmverleih GmbH, which at the end of 1929 had released the Chaplin program *The Pilgrim* and *Feine Leute* under the aegis of Terra-United Artists, was, as a limited liability company, in contrast to Südfilm AG, not a stock company. The *Reichsfilmblatt* spotted the ad and reproduced it in its article "Geld zum Vertrieb von Chaplin-Filmen gesucht" (Investor Wanted for the Distribution of Chaplin Films), published a week later. In the trade journal's opinion, it reflected the situation of the German film market in early 1930. In general, the economic conditions were very troubled. Therefore, distributing "films of taste and standard" did not imply good business from the outset.[25] If a "long-established film stock company" had to pre-finance the German screening rights of the "Chaplin mega film" with the help of third-party investments, this suggested that it could not pay them in full out of its own pocket.[26]

Wer beteiligt sich

mit 20–50 000 M. an der Exploitierung der deutschen Monopolaufführungsrechte eines neuen

Chaplin - Grossfilms?

Vertrieb erfolgt kommissionsweise durch altangesehene Film-Akt.-Ges.

Ganz grosses sicheres Geschäft! Sicherstellung durch Aufführungsverträge im Betrage von mehreren 100 000 M. Rückzahlung der Einlage nebst Gewinn in wöchentl. Abrechnung. Off. u. J. R. 1250 bef. Rudolf Mosse, Berlin SW. 100.

Berliner Tageblatt, **January 12, 1930: "Who wants to invest 20–30,000 [Reichsmark] in the exploitation of the German monopoly screening rights of a new mega Chaplin motion picture?"**

Even More Dividends

At the end of January 1930, however, a satisfied Supervisory Board looked back on Südfilm AG's 15 years of business. At this time, the plans to distribute *City Lights* probably did not play a role and therefore were not discussed.[27] Soon after, Terra Filmverleih GmbH was involved in Terra–United Artists' distribution of its second Chaplin program *Lohntag, Auf dem Lande* and *Vergnügte Stunden*, which started at the end of February 1930 and turned into another huge success. Shortly before its release, Goldschmid reported at the general meeting of Südfilm AG that Dupont's *Atlantic* had achieved "unprecedented record sales." Goldschmid predicted a similar business success for Richard Eichberg's and Jean Kemm's 1930 German film *Hai Tang*. Likewise, *Der Fall Dreyfus* and *Der Greifer* would be a "very big hit and unusual success."[28] In addition, Goldschmid raised hope among shareholders: "Assuming normal development of the planned sound film business, a substantial dividend [can be] expected for next year."[29] At the Supervisory Board meeting at the end of August 1930, there was only talk of "satisfactory business development."

But now Goldschmid presented his latest project: Südfilm AG wanted to take over the financially faltering Emelka AG. This plan foundered, and at the end of December 1932, Emelka AG had to apply for a court settlement.[30] Meanwhile, Goldschmid had participated in debates about "justice for distributors and producers," and in October 1930, he had pompously proclaimed that every distributor must release each of his films, whether major productions or cheap films, "with commitment" for the "unpredictable" audience.[31] At the following general meeting of shareholders on November 14, 1930, a proud 15 percent dividend was approved on Goldschmid's proposal submitted on behalf of the Supervisory Board. Those present had allowed themselves to be convinced by Goldschmid's presentation that films from the current distribution schedule "such as [*Der Fall*] *Dreyfus*, *Der Greifer* and *Unter den Dächern von Paris* will spearhead the box office of this season." In general, it was agreed that Südfilm AG had "developed impressively under I. Goldschmid's resourceful management." At the same time, Goldschmid announced new production plans for Südfilm AG,[32] which triggered "Südfilm's production optimism."[33] The program included Phil Jutzi's *Berlin Alexanderplatz*, based on Alfred Döblin's novel, and Martin Fric and Carl Lamac's adaptation of the Edgar Wallace crime novel *Der Zinker*, both of which are still well-known today. Other subjects by Roda Roda and Louis Verneuil rounded out the program. There were also plans to film Jakob Wassermann's famous novel *Der Fall Maurizius*, directed by Karl Boese, Richard Eichberg or Friedrich Zelnik.

At the end of 1930, the *Lichtbildbühne* wrote about "the successful Südfilm": "The outstanding role played by Südfilm under I. Goldschmid's management in the German sound film business deserves special attention. [...] It is certainly not just a coincidence when such a visible series of successes attaches itself to a particular company brand."[34] With the new program, the trade journal saw "Südfilm in further ascent":

> [Südfilm] was able to come onto the market one after the other with programs that, in addition to an unusual reputation for professional vision, and a reputation for artistic and

intellectual pioneering work, have above all earned it the rank of a stock company operating with outstanding commercial success. We may also mention [...] I. Goldschmid [...] and a number of first-class distributors in Berlin and in the Reich. [...] Intellectually as well as commercially, [the new] program [...] also means an imposing achievement, which will take a special place in the range of German films in every respect.[35]

So things were looking promising. In 1930-31, Südfilm AG ranked third among the 40 film distributors in the Weimar Republic, after Parufamet and Ufa as the biggest.[36]

Südfilm Buys City Lights

During this period of Südfilm AG prosperity, the *Film-Kurier* reported in December 1930 of Chaplin asking 600,000 reichsmark for the German distribution rights to *City Lights*, having already turned down two lower bids.[37] The film's extraordinary commercial success in the U.S. had caused Chaplin's prices for national screening rights to skyrocket. At the end of January 1933, he still wanted to generate $6 million.[38] After the New York premiere in February 1931, at which the cheapest seat would have cost $10, Chaplin had reportedly decided to "make a $10 million profit" from *City Lights*.[39] In fact, United Artists' British agency had negotiated around $100,000 just for the booking at London's Dominion, where the British premiere of *City Lights* had taken place. The entire British screening rights are said to have cost approximately 60,000 pounds sterling, which was equivalent to about 660,000 reichsmark.[40] On February 21, 1931, the *Lichtbildbühne* warned against similarly high license prices for Germany because they were "incompatible with the German economic situation."[41] However, during the height of the German inflation of 1923, Ufa paid an enormous amount for the screening rights to *The Kid* and still struck gold.[42]

At Chaplin's invitation, Goldschmid traveled to London for the film's British premiere in late February 1931.[43] On the express to Ostend, from where he embarked for Great Britain, he met the Austrian-Jewish journalist and travel writer Dr. Richard A. Bermann, who wrote under the *nom de plume* Arnold Höllriegel for the *Berliner Tageblatt*, the *Prager Tagblatt* and the *Wiener Tag*. He had also penned several highly successful books.[44] When Höllriegel interviewed Chaplin in Hollywood in May 1928, the actor presented and performed for him his idea for the then–vaguely plotted *City Lights*. Now Chaplin had invited Höllriegel to *City Lights*' London premiere. During the train ride, Höllriegel told Goldschmid about his acquaintance with Chaplin, whereupon Goldschmid suggested that Höllriegel write a brochure about the new film at short notice. This was to be sold at the box offices in Germany and Austria. Höllriegel agreed on the condition that Goldschmid would buy a "considerable part of the edition" of this brochure.[45] It was published in time for *City Lights*' German and Austrian premieres on March 26 (see Chapter 4 and below) and April 4, 1931, respectively.[46]

Following the successful London screening of *City Lights*, Goldschmid and Höllriegel independently attended Chaplin's banquet at the Carlton Hotel. Then, by all accounts, a veritable race for the German screening rights took place. Gold-schmid won it for Südfilm AG.[47] After Chaplin had demanded $220,000,[48] Gold-schmid reached a deal with him for $210,000, or the equivalent of between 837,000 and 850,000 reichsmark.[49] This was still below the price of $250,000, or the equivalent of a good million reichsmark, claimed by Krakauer (see Chapter 5).

A few months later, Chaplin's sales methods came under fire. His high rates were supposed to have made *City Lights* largely a money-losing business in the U.K., for example.[50] At a conference of cinema operators in Rome, German representatives wanted to propose a sharply worded resolution against Chaplin and his pricing.[51] According to a report in the *B.Z. am Mittag* of March 27, 1931, however, Chaplin was said to have charged for *City Lights* approximately the amount that *The Gold Rush* had grossed in Germany.[52]

Despite all premature praise for the film, 850,000 reichsmark was also a severe burden for Südfilm AG. The distributor was only able to raise the amount with the help of various backers,[53] which included Ufa.[54] Maxwell's British International is also said to have helped out substantially.[55] To guarantee the backers' loan, Goldschmid assigned Südfilm AG's revenues from the distribution of *Lichter der Großstadt* to them, up to the amount of the respective loan. However, even Chaplin's appealing name could not hide the fact that it was difficult to cover the costs of such a substantial investment and generate a profit. No documents have survived on the distribution fees for *Lichter der Großstadt* that Südfilm AG charged cinema owners. A price premium might have risked the exploitation. The cinema owners had to factor into their entrance fees the considerable costs of converting to sound film equipment and the entertainment tax. There was talk that sound movies were ruining the film business.[56]

On the other hand, since *Lichter der Großstadt* had a soundtrack with music and sound effects, there was no need to pay a cinema orchestra.[57]

Chaplin's *The Circus* had grossed about $3.8 million worldwide, or approximately 15.4 million reichsmark. Terra Filmverleih GmbH's two Chaplin programs, which had been released at the turn of the year 1929-30 and at the end of March 1930, respectively, had also yielded good profits for this distributor. Record box offices for Chaplin films in Germany[58] had, however, been realized under economic conditions decidedly better than those at the time of the purchase of the German screening rights for *Lichter der Großstadt*. Now, Germany was shaken by the world economic crisis. Compared with 1928, German national income had dropped by 23.30 percent in 1931, and in 1932 it had plummeted by as much as 41 percent.[59] The unemployment rate had even almost tripled between 1928 and 1931.[60] Droves of moviegoers therefore had to be

Südfilm A.G. director Isidor Gold-schmid, May 1930.

content with tickets in the cheapest seat categories, if they could still afford a visit to the movies at all. As a result, compared to 1928, the gross receipts of movie theaters had dwindled by 28 percent in 1931 and by 36 percent in 1932. This corresponded with a 23 percent decrease in movie theater attendance from 1928 to 1931, so that the average rate of movie theater attendance per year and per 10,000 inhabitants had dropped from 5.7 to 5.1.[61] Thus, the average price of a movie

Einer der vielen Millionen Chaplins

Berlin am Morgen, **March 10, 1931: "Einer von vielen Millionen Chaplins" [One of the Many Millions of Chaplins].**

ticket had also declined to 0.72 reichsmark in 1931. In 1932, at 0.68 reichsmark, they had even slipped below the 1926 level (0.69 reichsmark).[62] With an unemployment rate of almost 16 percent, a headline like "3.5 million unemployed. Film attendance and gainful employment" a few months before *Lichter der Großstadt's* German premiere cast a gloomy light on the situation in the German cinema business.[63] In addition, unemployment figures continued to climb dramatically.[64] When Chaplin visited Berlin in March 1931, the left-leaning newspaper *Berlin am Morgen* printed a cartoon about the economic hardship within the German population. Under the headline "Einer der vielen Millionen Chaplins" (One of the Many Millions of Chaplins), well-off people walk carelessly past an unemployed beggar who looks like Tramp Charlie.[65]

The Audience Is Coming

Having acquired the German screening rights, Südfilm AG published a 20-page *Südfilm-Magazin* in March 1931 especially for *Lichter der Großstadt* along with advertising for its further distribution range.[66] The *Rheinisch-Westfälische Filmzeitung* reported that never before had "a film been awaited with greater excitement."[67] Shortly after the German release, Südfilm AG was beating the big drum for the "1931 Film Sensation," which enjoyed "a huge success everywhere."[68] By their very nature, such advertisements do not provide reliable information about the profitability of a film. Südfilm AG's bookkeeping, balance sheets and profitability calculations, which would have revealed the exact economic result of *Lichter der Großstadt* in Germany, have not survived. Only the reporting of the film trade journals offers an insight into the development of the business with the film. The film, which was approved G-rated,[69] was recognized by the Lampe Committee as "artistically valuable" so that less entertainment tax was levied on it.[70] But with talkies now dominating the market, the *Film-Kurier* dampened hopes of record box office only a few days after the German premiere of *Lichter der Großstadt*: "Chaplin has misjudged the talkies with *City Lights* and cost the Germans too much money."[71] Despite this prophecy of doom, *Lichter der Großstadt* was excellently received at first, as Krakauer has also reported. The further Berlin festive screenings that followed on March 26, 1931, were sold out within days, at high ticket prices ranging from three to 15 reichsmark.[72] Until the end of May, *Lichter der Großstadt* ran for 69 days in the Ufa-Palast am Zoo and another Berlin premiere cinema.[73] From the end of August, the film simultaneously switched to 15 other Berlin cinemas.[74] It thus took ninth place among the 244 Berlin premieres of German and foreign films in 1931, and fifth place among the 102 foreign films released in Germany during the same period.[75]

In other German cities, *Lichter der Großstadt* was also considered a box office hit. There was talk of an unusual success, in the Rhineland even of a "Chaplin triumph." In early April 1931, the film was "shown with the greatest success" in Essen. Elsewhere, too, this "sensation" was expected to be a success only comparable to that of the "unforgotten *Goldrausch*."[76] Moreover, at the time, "the best news" arrived from more than 32 other cities. The Ufa-owned Düsseldorf Residenz-Theater showed *Lichter der Großstadt* from April 4 to 16, 1931, in four and then three performances per day—at non-increased admission prices, although the costs for the exclusive screening rights of the local premiere were said to have been "enormous"[77]; from June 2 to 8, 1931, the film was then also shown in the smaller Asta Nielsen Theater.[78] Over Easter 1931, 19,000 paying moviegoers attended the Dresden Ufa-Palast, which had also been sold out after the local premiere on April 5, 1931; Victor Klemperer saw the film there the next day. In Leipzig, there were a notable 17,500 visitors at the same time.

The Palast-Lichtspiele in Stuttgart reported no less than 17,000 tickets sold for the first three days of screening. The

Südfilm Magazin for *Lichter der Großstadt*, front cover, March 1931.

Lichtbildbühne resumed on April 9, 1931: "The best news is also coming from the thirty-two other cities in which the Chaplin film is playing, so that those optimists are indeed right who expected *City Lights* to give a strong boost to the movie theater business."[79] In Hamburg, *Lichter der Großstadt* made it big simultaneously in four premiere cinemas on April 10, 1931, as the "undisputed event of the week" and "dominated [...] the scene." According to the reports, attendance was tremendous after the first week of screenings, so the term was prolonged. The *Film-Journal* summarized: "The popularity of this splendid picture cannot be exhausted at all." After an extensive screening, the movie left the Hamburg schedule in May 1931.[80] In Breslau, now the Polish city of Wrocław, it enjoyed a six-week run.[81] Why the police barred *Lichter der Großstadt* from being shown to schoolchildren in Ludwigshafen, Bavaria, despite its G-rated approval,[82] while it was shown to orphans as part of a special event in Mannheim, Baden-Württemberg, remains a mystery. Was the decision as narrow-minded as that of the authorities in the Slovakian city of Bratislava, who classified Lichter der Großstadt as "not educational" and as "unsuitable for young people"?[83] In any case, the *Film-Kurier* criticized the Ludwigshafen police measure, which was certainly only a marginal note, as a "ridiculous excess of Kleinstaaterei [regionalism]."[84]

After these success stories, however, it was surprising that Südfilm AG discontinued showing *Lichter der Großstadt* "over the summer period of 1931"[85] and, after this break, only re-released it simultaneously in 15 Berlin cinemas at the end of August 1931, calling this the "proper start of the season."[86] Südfilm AG did not disclose the reasons for the interruption, nor have they become known otherwise. Had the distributor possibly deemed the box office results to date unsatisfactory considering the high-cost price and hoped for better chances with a re-release? Or were these tactical considerations to prevent the film from "dying" in the so-called "silly season" with its usually moderate attendance? If the demand had been held awake and additionally stoked, this could have attracted a larger audience. If Südfilm AG Director Goldschmid is to be believed, he was skilled at this type of advertising. On the other hand, the break would have opened up a financial risk if *Lichter der Großstadt* had actually broken box office records everywhere by then. In this case, Südfilm AG would have compromised the existing favorable revenue climate without the certainty of being able to seamlessly continue this after the end of the break.

In any case, *Lichter der Großstadt* had attracted the audience and in this respect was not the failure that *Der Angriff* had predicted in March 1931. Admittedly, this was not a factual prognosis either, but self-fulfilling prophecy in the service of agitation, which would remain a common Nazi method in the future.

The Financial Sky Is Clouding

By the end of June 1931, Südfilm AG's financial situation had darkened. Although *Der Film* and *Film-Kurier* reported distribution revenues of nine million reichsmark during the fiscal year from July 1, 1930, to June 30, 1931, Südfilm AG had suffered a net loss of 150,000 reichsmark. This resulted from "deficiencies on unfulfilled theater contracts," current own liabilities of 5.1 million reichsmark, cash advance payments of 886,000 reichsmark for the coming production season, and advance bookings of nearly one million reichsmark for the 1931-32 season. When the economy had been more favorable, Südfilm AG had already financed too much of its liabilities through credit. Moreover, the funds spent, which the Supervisory Board had granted at Goldschmid's request, were a burden on the budgetary planning because the costs associated with them were "out of proportion to the actual returns."[87] This could well be the case for *Lichter der Großstadt*, but at least included the accusation of having estimated the situation in general too optimistically. Thus, Südfilm AG's management kept a low profile about further dividends.

Maxwell was concerned and traveled to Berlin with Hubrich to gain an overall perspective of Südfilm AG's financial status. They did not meet Goldschmid. He was out of town and could not be reached. Without contacting him, the two learned that Südfilm AG was financing its current liabilities with bills of exchange. For this reason, they were convinced that Südfilm AG urgently needed to be recapitalized. Accusations were raised that Goldschmid had temporarily gone into hiding.[88]

Maxwell's plans for recapitalization were not made public at first, but he did not seem to have had radical measures in mind. In any case, he was able to convince Tobis to provide Südfilm AG with substantial financial backing for its future filming projects. This in turn was seen as an economic risk.[89] For Tobis not only aggressively marketed its sound film patents, but also wanted to expand in film production itself. In fact, by mid–1933, it had become the leading German film production company alongside Ufa.[90] Cooperation with the Berlin-based Deutsches Lichtspielsyndikat AG, whose shareholder was Tobis, was also discussed. Maxwell left Hubrich behind in Berlin intending to check himself "a few weeks" later if everything was straight.[91]

In July 1931, Südfilm AG and Deutsche Lichtspielsyndikat AG established a syndicate. According to a joint press communiqué, the aim was "rationalization through concentration" in order to reduce the cost price of film production and to make the utilization of the distribution organization more streamlined.[92] For the time being, Südfilm AG was to supply films to the numerous cinemas of Deutsche Lichtspielsyndikat AG at the most reasonable discounts possible.[93]

Thus, Südfilm AG was initially out of negative headlines. At the beginning of 1932, Deutsche Lichtspielsyndikat AG's book value per July 31, 1931, was published, showing a narrow profit of 18,000 reichsmark. Later, it ran into economic troubles and had to face court arrangement proceedings, which ended in February 1933.[94] In January 1932, after *Unter den Dächern von Paris* and *Die Million* (*Le million*, 1931), René Clair's latest film *Es lebe die Freiheit* (*À nous la liberté*, 1931) was also successfully distributed by Südfilm AG.[95] Goldschmid therefore traveled to London to negotiate with Maxwell about Südfilm AG's finances, and reportedly returned satisfied with the result.[96] In early February 1932, Südfilm AG's Supervisory Board approved, among other things, the production of seven films by the fall of that year, including the Edgar Wallace film *Der Hexer* (Carl Lamac and Martin Fric). The current distribution program also included the two 1931 Lau Lauritzen films *Knall und Fall* (*Krudt med knald*) and *Schritt und Tritt* (*I kantonnement*), featuring the popular Pat and Patachon. In May 1932, a third Pat and Patachon film, Carl Boese's *Lumpenkavaliere*, was added.[97] This was considered "strong activity."[98] On May 12, the Supervisory Board met again, convening the next general meeting for early June to present the latest balance sheet.[99]

Goldschmid, the "Great Tightrope Walker"

As early as 1929, the *Film-Journal* had questioned Goldschmid's cover-up handling of Südfilm AG's allegedly guaranteed capital increase. Now, at the end of May 1932, editor-in-chief Albert Schneider dropped a bombshell with "Der Fall Goldschmid" (The Goldschmid Case).[100] He attacked Goldschmid as a "great tightrope walker" and fraudulent "financial juggler" who had fooled everyone at Südfilm AG except those who had tried to limit the damages. Schneider focused on four complexes to demonstrate Goldschmid's business practices as an "abenteuerliche Filmexistenz" (Hazardous Film Business Character) and Südfilm AG's resulting economic troubles.

At the top was *Lichter der Großstadt.* Before its world premiere, the German screening rights had been available for 200,000 reichsmark. Goldschmid had let this opportunity pass. Later he acquired them from Chaplin on his own authority, without the consent of the Supervisory Board and contrary to the statutes of Südfilm AG, for 837,000 reichsmark and immediately paid for them in cash. He had raised the funds for this transaction from various sources and had assigned to each of the backers, including Ufa, the entire future revenues from the distribution of *Lichter der Großstadt* as security. Another planned assignment to one of the backers had failed due to the veto of a member of Südfilm AG's Executive Board. Schneider thus accused Goldschmid of criminal embezzlement against Südfilm AG. Since a claim can only be assigned once and multiple assignments of one and the same claim only mean to rob Peter to pay Paul, this also implied fraud to the disfavor of

Film-Journal, May 29, 1932, headline "The Goldschmid Case. A Hazardous Film Business Character Down the Road."

the transferees. Schneider also pointed to Südfilm AG's agreement with Goldschmid in his employment contract, according to which he received commissions on business deals. Therefore, he himself had been interested in a "juicy commission deal" with *Lichter der Großstadt*. His commission on the 837,000 reichsmark license fees paid was over four times as high as if he had purchased it for 200,000 reichsmark. According to Schneider, Goldschmid had approved that the revenues would never cover such costs. To conceal the disadvantageous business deal for Südfilm AG, Goldschmid had sold the U.S. license for the film *Der Fall Dreyfus* to the U.S. distributor Columbia, also for 837,000 reichsmark. But he had only received an "abnormally low" guarantee of 200,000 reichsmark from the latter, which Goldschmid had then immediately assigned to British International.

The situation had been similar in other commercial complexes. Sometimes bribes were also employed. Against the objections of Südfilm AG ranks, Goldschmid had purchased a package of *Mickey Mouse cartoons* at exorbitant prices per reel out of selfish interest in commissions. Beyond that, the "hazardous risk-taker" had arranged for himself to be paid "abnormally high additional monthly fees" on top of his contractually guaranteed income. Schneider's article concluded with the hope that it might be sufficient "to make Mr. Goldschmid disappear as quickly as possible."

Schneider's information came from an unnamed member of Südfilm AG's Executive Board, which at the time included Gustav Berloger, Ernst Haller and Johan Wertheim. Goldschmid immediately called Schneider's information in *Lichtbildbühne* a lie.[101] As a consequence of *Film-Journal*'s negative headline, an extraordinary meeting of Südfilm AG's Supervisory Board was immediately scheduled for June 1, 1932. Even before that, its suppliers and business colleagues issued a formal apology on Goldschmid's behalf.[102] After examination at the two-day meeting, the allegations against Goldschmid were declared unfounded. The Supervisory Board acknowledged that he had fulfilled his duties correctly in all respects.[103] Schneider gave in, and after a hastily arranged meeting with Goldschmid, "the hatchet was buried." Both published a joint statement in the *Film Journal*. Schneider regretted having accused Goldschmid, and Goldschmid stated that Schneider had acted in the best of faith. His retort in the *Lichtbildbühne* had only been intended to hit Schneider's unnamed informant.[104]

Südfilm Tumbling

The "buried hatchet" did not restore quiet conditions for Goldschmid and Südfilm AG. As early as June 1932, Goldschmid had to ask British International for a further injection of capital to finance the company's upcoming program. In return, the British company's shareholding in Südfilm AG, which had been dissolved in the fall of 1929, was revived with a share capital of 510,000 reichsmark. However, British International's support was insufficient, so Goldschmid had to raise additional funds from other sources. One of these was Tobis' expansion of its involvement in Südfilm AG. Nevertheless, for the time being, Goldschmid succeeded in keeping Südfilm AG's business free from the influence of the new creditors.[105]

The general meeting of Südfilm AG's shareholders on June 16, 1932, marked the moment of truth. Goldschmid admitted that Südfilm AG had lost 600,000 reichsmark as of June 30, 1931, and that the situation had not improved since then. His recipe for getting out of the red was nothing more than the Principle of Hope. He was counting on "further [reduction in costs] of film production, which hardly and only slowly adapts to the reduced general purchasing power in Germany," and on the improvement of the generally poor German economic situation. In the summer of that year, however, the economic crisis in the German film industry had not even reached its peak. This was imminent in the 1932-33 season.[106] For the upcoming programming, the general meeting nevertheless granted him the funds.[107] Thereupon, at the end of June 1932, Goldschmid discussed the next distribution schedule with his staff at a two-day meeting in Berlin. The result was to be fine-tuned at the subsequent Branch Managers' conference.[108]

Immediately after the general meeting, the difficulties in the exploitation of Chaplin's *Lichter der Großstadt* also became apparent. On June 20, 1932, the *Film-Kurier* ran the headline on page 1: "Chaplins schwacher Publikumserfolg" (Chaplin's Weak Success with the Public).[109] The trade journal once again called Chaplin's decision not to have shot a talkie an economic mistake, so that *Lichter der Großstadt* had proved to be a "financial fiasco" during Südfilm AG's decline. This was the result of a survey conducted by *Film-Kurier* among German cinema operators, none of whom considered the film a bargain.[110] Three months later, the Communist newspaper *Die Welt am Abend* also stated that *Lichter der Großstadt* did "no business in Germany," because Südfilm AG had acquired the German screening rights "on very harsh conditions" and had suffered "only losses" with the film.[111] These two news items were from the period after *Lichter der Großstadt*'s summer break of the previous year. The break had therefore had no resounding positive effect on box office takings from August 1931 onward, something Goldschmid must have known.

For Chaplin, however, *City Lights* was anything but an economic mistake. In early 1931, *Lichtbildbühne* reported that, because of deals already made with U.S. theater owners and completed sales of screening rights abroad, he expected to earn $6 million in the U.S. and another $2 million from international business—equivalent to about 32 million reichsmark.[112] According to a poll by the U.S. trade journal *Variety*, *City Lights* did not rank among the biggest U.S. film successes of 1931, and Chaplin was not listed among the top six U.S. directors of the year.[113] However, Carlyle T. Robinson, Chaplin's press officer from 1917 to 1932, claimed that Chaplin's film grossed about $4 million worldwide, or the equivalent of about 17 million reichsmark. Thus, *City Lights* had been more successful than *The Gold Rush* and *The Circus*.[114] For example, Paris premiere cinema Marigny took in six million francs in several months with *City Lights*, which, according to a November 1931 *Film-Kurier* report, was "an unprecedented record-breaking achievement by French standards."[115] In early July 1932, the *Lichtbildbühne* put Chaplin's receipts from *City Lights* at $3 million, or about 12.15 million reichsmark, which was still an excellent deal. This coincided with Chaplin's own account in his 1964 autobiography, in which he called the film a "huge success [… that] had made more money than any sound film of the time." Upon his return from his trip around the world in June 1932, his

studio had reported net income from *City Lights* of $3 million to date. In the time
following, it had continued to bring in an additional $100,000 per month.[116]

Of course, this tells nothing about Südfilm AG's business with *City Lights*. Marketing the film in Germany was the distributor's matter. Yet, apart from the special
case of *The Kid*, the screening rights for Chaplin films distributed in Germany since
August 1921 had been considerably more favorable.

Lichter der Großstadt: *the Beginning of Südfilm's End*

To coordinate the outlined 1932/33 Südfilm AG schedule, Goldschmid convened
the Branch Managers' conference for August 14, 1932. Krakauer attended. The new
program included 14 films with such resounding names as Carl Lamac, Max Ophüls,
Richard Oswald, Pat and Patachon and Edgar Wallace, plus twelve Walt Disney cartoons from the popular *Mickey Mouse* and *Silly Symphonies* series. An eight-page
advertisement promised "Success with Südfilm."[117] However, the beauty was only
skin deep. For as early as September 26, 1932, the front page of the *Film-Kurier* carried the bombshell: "Südfilm stellt Zahlungen ein" (Südfilm Suspends Payments).[118]
Südfilm AG's annual reports, communiqués and Supervisory Board minutes
have not survived, but the reasons for its insolvency can also be traced from trade
journals.

The bankrupt company invited creditors to a September 29, 1932, meeting at
the Berlin Prinz Albrecht Hotel and issued a communiqué which stated: "The general economic situation and the disastrous heat wave this summer have hurt the
cinema business to such an extent that the administration of Südfilm AG is forced
to suspend payments as of today."[119] Südfilm AG's main creditors at that time were
Tobis,[120] British International, Südfilm AG co-director Gustav Berloger and Kodak
AG. To further safeguard its interests, Tobis intended to establish the new company
Europa Filmverleih; it wanted "to avoid a further market disturbance of the German film industry [...] and to guarantee German theater owners a smooth supply of
the films they had acquired from Südfilm."[121] The trade journals had also called on
unsecured creditors to attend the meeting, which was filled to capacity. Südfilm AG
Supervisory Board member Dr. Kurt Lachmann appeared on behalf of Tobis. There
was general dismay about Südfilm AG's five million reichsmark debt. The unsecured
creditors were afraid of being "fobbed off with a marginal quota."[122]

At the outset, Goldschmid reported on the company's economic situation. He
conceded that British International had been "badly misled about Südfilm AG's distribution branch" when it acquired a majority of shares in the company in 1928. Its
activities were strained by a constant lack of capital, so that British International
"had to permanently plough money." At the end of the silent era, Südfilm AG had
been on the verge of collapse and had only been able to recover slightly thanks to
the emerging talkies. Chaplin's film played a key role in this: "The purchase of *City
Lights* marked the beginning of the catastrophe."[123] There was no mention in Goldschmid's report that Nazi disruptive actions had ruined Südfilm AG.

He further stated that the Executive Board of Südfilm AG had tried for some time to keep the company afloat and to persuade the main creditors to grant further loans or to enter into standstill agreements. In the middle of 1931, this had only temporarily bought some time, because revenues were constantly on the decrease. The inevitable catastrophe could only have been countered by irresponsible measures such as taking out further loans or concluding adhesion contracts. With an order backlog as per the end of September 1932 of only 4.2 million reichsmark, Südfilm AG's liabilities amounted to over 5.6 million reichsmark, of which 3.9 million reichsmark were owed to the major creditors. Goldschmid presented the prospect of an out-of-court settlement proposal in the near future.[124] Those present were stunned: how did Goldschmid deceive British International in 1928 about Südfilm AG's then supposedly "guaranteed" enterprise value, which shortly afterwards turned out to be "illusory"? Creditors therefore complained: "Who at that time facilitated the Maxwell transaction, checked it and let himself be fooled with [...] illusions?"

Recent transactions, which were also legally dubious, caused additional unrest: Less than two weeks before the Creditors' Meeting, Goldschmid had assigned Südfilm AG's theatrical revenues from Richard Oswald's 1932 feature film *Unheimliche Geschichten* to Tobis.[125] The representative of a major German bank considered this kind of hedging to be illegal and reviewable.[126] In the eyes of the assembled creditors, Goldschmid's claim that one of the reasons for Südfilm AG's collapse had been the heat wave was also nothing more than a flimsy excuse. In the late spring and summer of 1932, Germany had indeed experienced unusually high temperatures that did not necessarily invite cinema attendance. Nevertheless, Karl Hartl's Austrian feature film *Der Prinz von Arkadien*, which had also been distributed by Südfilm AG, had enjoyed a "great opening night" in May at the Berlin premiere cinema Atrium, despite the premature summer weather.[127] Moreover, the trade journals had not reported on noticeable revenue losses for distributors and cinemas in general caused by heat waves during the period from May to September 1932. In the course of the turbulent debate about Goldschmid's business practices, one creditor put the latter's version of weather influences straight: "As recently as August, the company announced a schedule of 19 films [...] and then it goes bankrupt because the sun has been shining six weeks longer than usual."[128]

After the Creditors' Meeting, Schneider could not help making the following comment in *Film-Journal*: "We have already said everything that needs to be said today often enough [...]. Unfortunately, [...] no one listened to us when there was still a lot that could have been saved. Now that it is too late, the letters are piling up, lamenting: 'If only we had....'"[129]

Südfilm Liquidated

First, Henry F. Gunderloch, an expert from the film industry, was appointed as trustee to safeguard Südfilm AG's assets.[130] To the creditors' displeasure, it took longer than expected to establish the company's exact financial status. They were even more upset when Südfilm AG in October 1932, without any explanation, offered them a settlement quota of 30 percent to pay off its debts. They spoke of "scandalous procrastination"[131] and applied for court insolvency proceedings. After the financial situation of Südfilm AG had finally been clarified, the proceedings were concluded at the end of January 1933 with a liquidation settlement—for the quota that had been offered. This meant that Südfilm AG's prospects had been even bleaker than Goldschmid had presented them at the September 29 Creditors' Meeting. According to the latest profit and loss statement, Südfilm AG's loss amounted to more than 2.4 million reichsmark,[132] i.e., one million reichsmark more than Goldschmid had asserted. Even the liquidation settlement could only be concluded because the main creditors British International, Kodak AG and Tobis dropped their claims to an extent that allowed the unsecured creditors to benefit from the settlement quota. By March 1935, even this had only been settled in the amount of one-third, with no prospect of ever receiving the remainder.[133]

In October 1932, As announced, Tobis founded Europa Filmverleih AG which was to exploit Südfilm AG's film stock.[134] The new distributor continued to employ the majority of its staff, including Krakauer.[135] By all accounts, Europa Filmverleih AG's launch was successful.[136] In April 1934, the Creditors' Meeting resolved to liquidate Südfilm AG, which was removed from the Commercial Register in 1937.[137] After the bankruptcy, Goldschmid joined the renowned Chronos-Film G.m.b.H. of film merchant Lothar Stark, but soon after the liquidation settlement had been concluded, he and his family moved to London.[138] In 1937, the Nazi smear book *Film-"Kunst," Film-Kohn, Film-Korruption* portrayed Goldschmid as the "systematically acting Jewish bankrupt" par excellence.[139] However, it did not comment on Chaplin's *Lichter der Großstadt* as one of the reasons for Südfilm AG's collapse, nor did the Nazi propaganda press.

Max Krakauer: An Unreliable Source

Only Krakauer's assertion that Chaplin's *Lichter der Großstadt* contributed to Südfilm AG's insolvency stands up to scrutiny.

Krakauer put his memories of the events surrounding *Lichter der Großstadt* on paper 15 years later and after his persecution as a Jew in the Third Reich, which certainly had been hard to endure. Obviously, this movie had not become an irrelevant matter for him. For Krakauer's narrative of Nazi disruption as the reason for Südfilm AG's bankruptcy revolves around *Lichter der Großstadt*. As its Leipzig branch manager, however, he had attended meetings of various company panels, the most recent being the branch manager's Conference of August 14, 1932. At this stage, at the latest, everyone present knew why Südfilm AG had gone bankrupt. Branch managers like Krakauer most likely had insider information and insight into the economic situation of Südfilm AG and its consequences. In October 1932, Krakauer was employed by the rescue company Europa Filmverleih AG. The trade press, which reported on the company's bankruptcy, must also have been compulsory reading for him as a film merchant. Therefore, he was most likely also informed from this source about "Chaplin's weak audience success" since June 20, 1931. Furthermore, Ufa had even co-funded the acquisition of the film's German screening rights and had organized the successful German premieres of *Lichter der Großstadt* in Berlin and other major German cities. Hence, Ufa would inevitably have harmed itself if, as Krakauer has claimed, it had put pressure on cinema owners to remove Chaplin's film from their schedules.

Under these circumstances, evidence suggests that Krakauer presented the reasons for Südfilm AG's bankruptcy against his better judgment.

7

A Year of Change, 1933

Nazi agitation had not damaged Chaplin's popularity and appreciation of him in Germany. In 1942, the U.S. newspaper *The Kellogg News* even claimed that Chaplin had run for German Reichspräsident (President of the Reich) in 1932 and received several dozen votes.[1] The newspaper did not cite a source, and Chaplin does not appear as a candidate in the official election result.[2]

After Hitler's takeover, the Nazis possessed the political power to legally subjugate the German cultural sector to their ideology and expel Jews from it. Taken all together, Hanisch and Velten claimed that in March 1933, only some Chaplin short films had been shown in German cinemas. No later than the beginning of September of that year, Chaplin's name had disappeared from the press of the Third Reich and had been banned. This changed in 1938, when it became known that he intended to produce a satire about Hitler.[3] However, the opposite is true: Chaplin continued to be reported on in the Nazi-controlled press landscape after September 1933. Also, in March 1933, not only were some Chaplin shorts shown, but also in the spring of that year a series of feature films and an accompanying short film. All this will be retraced in Chapters 7 to 9.

This chapter examines:

- Nazi "cleaning up"
- the early diatribe *Juden sehen Dich an*
- the beginning of the Nazi subjugation of the German film industry
- the "Gleichschaltung" of the German film press
- the beginning and simultaneous denial of the exclusion of German Jews
- Chaplin films in German cinemas after Hitler's takeover
- the continuing interest in Chaplin and his film projects
- the beginning, the trigger and sources of the first major Nazi attack on Chaplin in the German film press and its aftermath

"Cleaning Up"

The Nazis began the "Entjudung" (De-Judaization) of the German people immediately upon Hitler's takeover. From February 17, 1933, to February 16, 1945, the Nazi regime issued no fewer than 2000 anti–Jewish laws, decrees, orders and guidelines.[4]

Hitler immediately appointed Hermann Göring as Reichsminister ohne Geschäftsbereich (Reich Minister without Portfolio), Reichskommissar für den Luftverkehr (Reich Commissioner for Aviation) and Reichskommissar für das preußische Innenministerium (Reich Commissioner for the Prussian Ministry of the Interior). Göring immediately "cleaned up" the State Administration. As early as February 14, 1933, the *Völkischer Beobachter* reported: "three Regierungspräsidenten [District Presidents], three Regierungsvizepräsidenten [District Vice-Presidents] and twelve Polizeipräsidenten [Police Presidents] degraded."[5] Three days later, Göring issued for Prussia his infamous Circular Decree "zur Förderung der nationalen Bewegung" (for the Promotion of the National Movement), better known as the "Schießerlass" (Shooting Order). In this, he demanded the "rücksichtslosen Schusswaffengebrauch" (Unrelenting Use of Firearms).[6] On February 22, 1933, Göring also called up the violent "vaterländische Verbände" (Patriotic Units) SA, SS and Stahlhelm as armed "Hilfspolizei" (Auxiliary Police) under the leadership of the state police in order to "relieve it" and to support it "in the event of riots or other police emergency." These combat units, which are said to have included between 1500 and 2000 "Hilfspolizisten" (Auxiliary Policemen) of the Berlin SA alone, thus formally fought the "enemies of the state."[7] German-Jewish civil servants and also "Aryans" were replaced by Nazis in the public administration wherever they were needed to secure the new machinery of power. The German civil service willingly supported the deprivation of rights of German Jews and political dissidents before Hitler's regime made the public administration its tool.[8] Like the vast majority of civil servants, many other Germans enthusiastically allowed themselves to be cleaned up. The Nazis had nurtured the belief of large parts of the German people that Hitler would help them achieve a new sense of self-esteem, heal national wounds and return the country to its former political greatness. Hitler had outlined the manipulative preparation of this belief in 1926 in *Mein Kampf*: "Propaganda tries to force a doctrine on the whole people, the organization seizes within its scope only those who will not for psychological reasons interfere with the further spread of the idea. [...] Once propaganda has infused a whole people with an idea, the Organization will be able to take appropriate action with a handful of persons."[9]

As early as January 1931, *Der Angriff* had announced its intention to "clean up" the German film industry "properly" and to bring it "into [National Socialist] line."[10] By the summer of 1932, the Nazis had already been able to impose their "Guidelines on the Employment of Film Staffs" on Prussian theaters so that only Reich German artists or artists of German descent were allowed to perform there.[11] From the beginning of March 1933 at the latest, Rainer Schlösser, since August 1933 Reichsdramaturg (Reich Dramaturg) of theater propaganda, single-mindedly ensured that "14 years of cultural Bolshevism, Judaization, and profiteering in 'German' film" would be eliminated as quickly as possible as a "devouring plague," "decomposition from within," and "art that has nothing to do with German blood."[12]

In mid–February 1933, the first banning actions against unwelcome films began. After the Reichstag elections of March 5, 1933, Goebbels' Reichsministerium für Volksaufklärung und Propaganda was established with him at its head on March 13.[13] Its tasks were not defined until the end of June 1933. With the Reichsfilmkammer

(Film Chamber of the Reich), Goebbels brought the German film industry under state control. On the very day his ministry was founded, the head of the Landesfilm-stelle Süd presented the Bavarian Ministry of the Interior with a list of 48 films that were to be banned. It included 30 films with Communist tendencies, among them *Panzerkreuzer Potemkin*, five films with pacifist tendencies, such as the particularly hated film *Im Westen nichts Neues*, and 18 films with sexual tendencies, among them *Cyankali* and *Die Dreigroschenoper*.[14] Chaplin's films were not included in the list. The confiscation of copies of the listed films was immediately initiated throughout Germany. A month later, for example, *Im Westen nichts Neues* was completely withdrawn from circulation. Remarque's novels "deemed damaging for the German reputation" were publicly burned on Berlin's Opernplatz on May 10, 1933.[15] Among the four films mentioned above, in the course of 1933 only the approval of *Die Dreigroschenoper* was formally revoked in accordance with the "Lichtspielgesetz"—because it would glorify criminality.[16]

The most drastic act, however, was the "Verordnung des Reichspräsidenten zum Schutz von Volk und Staat vom 28. Februar 1933" (Decree of the Reich President for the Protection of the People and the State, February 28, 1933), signed by Reichspräsident Hindenburg, Hitler, Reichsminister des Inneren (Reich Minister of the Interior) Frick and Reichsminister der Justiz (Reich Minister of Justice) Dr. Franz Gürtner.[17] It was the Nazis' response to the burning of the Reichstag in Berlin on the night of February 27, 1933, which they blamed on Communists. For this reason, the Emergency Decree, known as the "Reichstagsbrandverordnung" (Reichstag Fire Decree), was declared as "Abwehr kommunistischer staatsgefährdender Akte" (Defense Against Communist Subversive Acts). This suspended the fundamental rights guaranteed in the Weimarer Reichsverfassung (Weimar Reich Constitution), laid the foundation for Hitler's dictatorship, and granted it unlimited power under the guise of a state of martial law. Ernst Fraenkel called the Emergency Decree the "Constitutional Charter of the Third Reich,"[18] since the proclaimed martial law was never declared to have ended during the Third Reich, despite the Nazis' boastfully assuring that under their leadership, Germany, in the midst of a world corrupt with inner strife, was an "island of peace." According to today's knowledge, most likely Nazis had been the arsonists,[19] and thus had fraudulently promoted the alleged state of martial law in order to abolish the Reich Constitution. From then on, they abused the martial law and terrorized not only Communists, but also anti–Nazis of all political color, beyond the legal order as they saw fit. Thus, the totalitarian German "Dual State" was established, which Fraenkel examined in his 1941 U.S. book of the same title: The fascist Nazi state presented itself as a "Normenstaat" (Normative State), but only pretended to be a constitutional state, because it acted unrestrained by legal guarantees as a "Maßnahmenstaat" (Prerogative State) with unlimited arbitrariness.[20]

Juden sehen Dich an

Dr. Johann von Leers' crudely aggressive diatribe *Juden sehen Dich an* (Jews Look at You) was an early publicized evidence of the Nazis' intention to "de–Jew"

Germany in the Third Reich. This obviously struck a chord with the political mood in the country. In the course of 1933, four editions of this shoddy piece of work were published, followed by more in the years to come. Von Leers was the Bundesschulungsleiter (Training Manager) of the Nationalsozialistischer Deutscher Studentenbund and editor-in-chief of the Nazi magazine *Wille und Weg* (Will and Way). He survived the collapse of the Third Reich and continued to write anti–Semitic tracts.[21] According to his preface, von Leers wanted "to show the German people once again vividly who had dominated them [until now] politically, spiritually and economically." Like *Stürmer* editor Julius Streicher, he used the vilest simplifications, which place the work in a series of other notorious anti–Semitic Nazi diatribes. Consequently, von Leers dedicated *Juden sehen Dich an* to Streicher, who contributed an introduction.

In keeping with the repulsive cover drawing of the face of a stout Jew smoking a big cigar, von Leers presented "ugly Jews" in the categories of "Blut-, Lügen-, Hetz-, Zersetzungs-, Kunst- and Geld-Juden" (Blood-, Lying-, Smear-, Subversive-, Art- and Money-Jews). In the chapter "Kunstjuden," he denigrated Chaplin, who was depicted in a tramp costume, as the only foreign film artist alongside hated German-Jewish film actors such as Siegfried Arno and Kurt Gerron. In addition, the thematically narrow-minded introduction read: "To erode the German people from within, Judaism has almost completely subjugated art, theater, criticism and film. [...] Film is completely Judaized. For years, it deliberately cultivated criminality, praised an "ebenso hässliche wie alberne Possenfigur" (Ugly as well as silly buffoon), the Jew Charlie Chaplin, to the skies, and unleashed a hype with Jewish stars, such as Elisabeth Bergner, Gitta Alpar, and similar Judenkallen [Jewish Whores], which ruined German cinematic art."[22] Von Leers provided Chaplin's picture with the following caption:

> This "ebenso langweiliger wie widerwärtiger Zappeljude" [Boring and disgusting fidgeting Jew], has been glorified by the *Israelitisches Familienblatt* in the following way: "Charlie Chaplin, who depicts the eternal war of the spirit against violence, and who constantly visualizes upsettingly the right of the poor (!) to all (?) the people of the world, has become the myth of our time." This time is over.[23]

Among the "Blutjuden," von Leers listed three arch-enemies of the Nazi propaganda press: Jusitizrat Dr.

Johann von Leers, *Juden sehen Dich an*, front cover, 1933.

Werthauer, whom Chaplin had visited in his Berlin villa in the fall of 1921, as well as former Berlin Polizeipräsident Albert Grzesinski and his deputy Dr. Bernhard Weiß. Grzesinski and Weiß had been removed from office by Hitler's predecessor Franz von Papen on July 20, 1932, on the occasion of the so-called Preußenschlag (Prussian Coup), after he had dissolved the Social Democratic Preußische Landesregierung (Prussian State Government) and made himself Reichskommissar for that state. Von Leers also railed against the "Lügenjuden" Albert Einstein and Theodor Wolff, editor-in-chief of the influential *Berliner Tageblatt*. Heading the "Zersetzungsjuden" was the sexologist Magnus Hirschfeld, who in 1919 had collaborated with Richard Oswald on the latter's controversial silent film *Anders als die andern*.[24] On May 6, 1933, Nazis raided and looted Hirschfeld's Berlin Institut für Sexualwissenschaft.[25]

Chaplin photograph from *Juden sehen Dich an*, 1933.

Like Chaplin, others "unmasked" were not Jews. According to von Leers, Polizeipräsident Grzesinski had been born "in the house of the Jew Cohn" as "Grzesinsky."[26] In fact, Grzesinski had been born illegitimately as Albert Ehlert and had received his later surname from his mother's husband. The former Catholic mayor of Cologne and future first Kanzler of the Federal Republic of Germany Konrad Adenauer became a "Blutjude." In the first four editions of *Juden sehen Dich an*, the "shrewd organizer of decomposing theater plays" Erwin Piscator appeared as a "Bolshevik Kunstjude" who had "gone bankrupt at the end."[27] As of 1936, von Leers' infamous "clarification" read: "Dr. Erwin Piskator [sic], mentioned here in earlier editions of this book, is indeed a Communist, but, as credibly proven to me, not a Jew[. He] was therefore to be excluded here."[28]

Gleichschaltung—Enforced Political Conformity

Goebbels' ministry also immediately started to bring the media under its control, to Nazify them and to control the shaping of public opinion. Among other things, the German press was brought into line. During the Weimar Republic, it had mostly written about Chaplin with admiration and high regard, and thus had considerable significance for the marketing of his films. This was even more true for the film trade journals and the film magazines for the public, which were published in high print runs. Initially, the German film trade journals and the German film industry, which was struggling with economic difficulties, considered Goebbels a beacon of hope. As late as the end of February 1933, the trade journal *Kinematograph* assumed that the minister would promote German film according to purely factual needs.[29] It turned out to be a bitter misjudgment. In March 1933, film merchant Adolf Engl, who had been an official advisor to the Munich NSDAP-Filmbeschaffungsstelle (NSDAP Film Sourcing Office) since February 1932, instantly installed himself as the Chairman of the Reichsverband Deutscher Lichtspieltheater e.V. (Reich Association of German Cinema Theaters). Goebbels' mouthpiece, Engl proclaimed the "restoration of orderly economic conditions in the German film industry under strictest conformity to the cultural-political goals of the state leadership."[30]

The NSDAP commissioned Dr. Luitpold Nusser with the "strictest Gleichschaltung of the German film trade press." Nusser had been a dramaturge in Catholic film work and, from mid–1927 to early 1931, editor-in-chief of the *Süddeutsche Filmzeitung*, which had been founded in 1922 and renamed *Deutsche Filmzeitung* in 1928.[31] After that, he had been active as NSDAP party hack. He headed the Unterabteilung Filmpresse (Subdepartment Film Press) in the NSDAP-Hauptabteilung Film (Main Department Film)[32] and in 1932 created the full-length party election film *Hitler über Deutschland*.[33] Immediately after Hitler's takeover, he wrote the anti–Semitic–infused essay "Gedanken über den deutschen Film" (Thoughts on German Film) for the *Nationalsozialistische Parteikorrespondenz* (National Socialist Party Correspondence). When Nusser died in 1935, obituaries stated that he had been a "pioneer of Nazi film policy and … 'one of the movement's oldest and most proactive fighters.'"[34] As such, Nusser swiftly implemented the Gleichschaltung of the film press. Publishers and editorial offices were "entjudet." Nusser ensured that henceforth Nazi politics had a firm place in it, true to the party line. However, in addition to Nazi speeches and instructions on film were accompanied by contributions to Hitler's and Goebbels' birthday, personal honors bestowed upon them (for example, honorary doctorates for Hitler in early May 1933[35]) and reports on NSDAP events. These were alien elements that proliferated over time and, on top of that, were combined with adulation of the party's leading personalities. As a result, the German film press became increasingly boring.

Nusser did not even need to bring the *Deutsche Filmzeitung* into line. Neither the publisher nor the editors were German-Jewish. In late March 1933, Nusser's successor, Dr. Hans Spielhofer, who had hitherto been moderate, already struck a pithy Nazi tone with "Gesinnung und Können," and soon thereafter made an openly anti–Semitic demand for "Reinlichkeit!"[36] Another managing editor was Dr. Robert Volz, who in 1933 established the *Sonderdienst Der Deutsche Film* (Special Service of *Der Deutsche Film*) of the *Nationalsozialistische Pressekorrespondenz*.[37] As a result, the *Deutsche Filmzeitung* became the official organ of the Hauptabteilung der Reichspropagandaleitung der NSDAP, Hauptabteilung IV-Film (Main Department of the NSDAP Reich Propaganda Leadership, Main Department IV-Film) at an early stage in the Third Reich, and thus the Nazis' mouthpiece on film policy.[38]

The most important film trade journal was the *Film-Kurier*, launched at the end of April 1919 by the Hungarian-Jewish publisher Alfred Weiner, which was accompanied by the popular film program series *Illustrierter Film-Kurier*. From the end of October 1928, the *Film-Kurier* was the official organ of the Reichsverbandes Deutscher Lichtspieltheater e.V. At its March 1, 1933, board meeting, Weiner attacked Engl and others, but very quickly lost out to Nusser's Gleichschaltung. Considering the importance of the *Film-Kurier*, Nusser himself took over as editor-in-chief on April 6, 1933.[39] From April 8 to June 10, the trade journal was also the official press organ of the NS Kommission–SPIO—the new Spitzenorganisation der Filmwirtschaft (Confederation of the Film Industry), which was merged into the Reichskultur-kammer (Reich Chamber of Culture).[40] Already in the course of April 1933, a couple of former persons in charge of the *Film-Kurier* had fled from the Nazis to Paris: the German-Jewish editor Lotte H. Eisner, the future curator of the Cinémathèque Française, and publisher Weiner with his French wife. In June of that year, the German-Jewish editor Willy Haas emigrated to Prague.[41] The previous editor-in-chief, Georg Herzberg, was dismissed on May 1, 1933, but returned in May 1934. He was editor-in-chief again from April 1942,[42] but was drafted into the Wehrmacht in April 1943 and was substituted by Felix Henseleit until the paper ceased publication at the end of September 1944.[43] Weiner sold his multi-million dollar publishing house under pressure to Nazis for only 200,000 reichsmark.[44] The future publisher was Paul Franke, who after World War II published, among other things, the popular film program series *Illustrierte Film-Bühne*, effectively the successor to the *Illustrierter Film-Kurier*.

In April, Georges Epstein commented on the news of the *Film-Kurier*'s Gleichschaltung in the *Elsass-lothringische Filmzeitung* with his article "In the Land of 'Gleichschaltung.'" He predicted that recent Nazi films such as Hans Steinhoff's *Hitlerjunge Quex* and Franz Seitz' *SA-Mann Brandt* will be "nothing to write home about" abroad. Regarding the persecution of Jews in Germany, he remarked: "Let us leave the Germans to their swastika cult and lament the victims of their hatred: the refugees from over there can count on our hospitality!"[45]

Bayerische Filmgesellschaft ad for the German premiere of *SA-Mann Brand*, June 14, 1933.

Immediately, the new editors of *Film-Kurier* replied bitingly: "If Mr. Esptein cannot be convinced by words, he will be disabused by the new German films. [...] If Mr. Epstein offers his hospitality to these people, it will be fine with us. In a few weeks, he will have realized whose cause he has supported."[46]

Under Nusser's leadership, the staffs of other German film trade journals were also replaced:

- The *Film-Kurier* and the *Lichtbildbühne*, which had been published since the beginning of 1908, had competed fiercely for importance. Its German-Jewish publisher Karl Wolffsohn also had to sell the journal to Franke for far less than it was worth. After the Gleichschaltung, the *Lichtbildbühne* praised Franke at the beginning of May 1933 as one of the personalities "whose influence completely ensures the ideological Gleichschaltung with the national Government of Reichskanzler and Fuehrer Adolf Hitler."[47] In addition, on April 1, 1933, the longtime German-Jewish editor-in-chief Hans Wollenberg, who was also at the helm of the *Filmspiegel*, which was discontinued in July 1933,[48] was replaced by Hubert Kühl,[49] who was succeeded by Albert Schneider as of November 1, 1935.[50] On July 1, 1940, *Lichtbildbühne* was merged into *Film-Kurier*.[51]

- The oldest German film trade journal was *Kinematograph*, founded in 1907, which continued to be published by the German nationalist Scherl-Verlag during the Third Reich. The German-Jewish editor-in-chief Alfred Rosenthal, better known by his acronym Aros, was forced to leave at the end of March 1933 in the course of the "purge from outside"[52] and fled with his family to France. His successor was Dr. Robert Neumann until the journal was discontinued at the end of March 1935.[53]

- The film weekly *Der Film* had been on the market since late 1916. In 1927, the German-Jewish publisher Max Mattisson took it over, appointed Chaplin admirer Hans-Walther Betz as editor-in-chief and published the free customer magazine *Der neue Film*. Mattisson, too, had to sell his publishing house below value to Nazis. For reasons unknown, Betz was replaced as early as February 1933 by Dr. Kurt London,[54] who was very quickly followed by Willy Klann.[55] In mid–April 1933 came this announcement: "*Der Film* gleichgeschaltet: New publisher ensures new direction."[56] Heinz Udo Brachvogel, who had defended Chaplin's *Shoulder Arms* against German nationalist accusations in November 1921, hailed the change in *Der Film* in the second half of May that year. Completely in line with Nazism, he welcomed Goebbels' film plans with a deep sigh in his article "Germany Burns Its Terrible, Subversive, Disturbing Spirit" and applauded the recent public book burnings.[57] In July 1938, for Betz the bell tolled again; by the end of 1937, he had handed in his Nazi business card as co-author of the smear book *Film-"Kunst," Film-Kohn, Film-Korruption*. He returned as the editor-in-chief, giving *Der Film* and *Der neue Film* a radical Nazi orientation,[58] and coordinated the integration of the Wiener *Kino-Journal* into *Der Film* after the "Anschluss" (Annexation) of Austria.[59] *Der neue Film* was discontinued at the end of August 1939, and *Der Film* was merged with *Film-Kurier* in April 1943.[60] This marked the end of Betz's work as editor-in-chief.

- The German-Jewish publisher Dr. Hans Salomonski published the *Film-Journal*,[61] which had moved its headquarters from Hamburg to Berlin in September 1926,[62] with Albert Schneider as editor-in-chief. Salomonski had to give way in the spring of 1933, and the *Film-Journal* was henceforth published by Film-Journal-Verlag. By the beginning of May 1933 at the latest, the trade journal had been brought into line when Schneider demanded: "Everyone has the Duty to Create Work!"[63] Boastful, he defended the new rulers against criticism: "We refrain from giving advice and vigorously forbid intervention and interference," since the new guidelines were "given by authorities who are far above you."[64] On November 1, 1935, the *Film-Journal* was merged into the *Lichtbildbühne*.[65]

- Eugen Gronemann was editor-in-chief and publisher of the *Rheinisch-Westfälische Filmzeitung*, founded at the end of October 1929. He was presumably German-Jewish and had to step aside in March 1933. He was succeeded as editor-in-chief by Josef Bender, who was soon replaced by Carl Heinz Schneider.[66] More serious, however, was that in June 1933, Tino Schmidt became publisher of the *Rheinisch-Westfälische Filmzeitung*. In January 1932, at the meeting of the Rheinisch-Westfälischen Verbandes Deutscher Lichtspieltheater-Besitzer (Rhenish-Westphalian Association of German Cinema Theater Owners), he had attracted attention through "aggressive [...], unobjective, overly hot-tempered and wrongly presented [attempts]."[67] Since Hitler's takeover, Schmidt had been chairman of the NS-Verbandszelle deutscher Lichtspieltheater-Besitzer (NS Sub-organization of German Cinema Owners), Zelle Rheinland und Westfalen (Rhenish-Westphalian Sub-branch) and later Filmwart (Local Film Leader) of the Gau Düsseldorf with an office in the NSDAP-Gauleitung.[68] He rigorously campaigned for the "Entjudung" of the German film industry.[69] For reasons unknown, the *Rheinisch-Westfälische Filmzeitung* was banned in early May 1938.[70]

The other five German film trade journals were noiselessly brought into line. The *Reichsfilmblatt* had been established in 1923 as the Offizielles Organ des Reichsverbandes Deutscher Lichtspieltheaterbesitzer (Official Organ of the German Cinema Owners' Reich Association). Henseleit was editor-in-chief from 1928 until the journal was merged with *Der Film* at the turn of the year 1935-36.[71] Unlike others, Henseleit did not attract attention with agitating articles after the Gleichschaltung. The editor-in-chief of *Mitteldeutscher Lichtspieltheaterbesitzer,* which had been in existence since 1926, was Walter Steinbauer. In March 1931, when the Nazis were agitating against Chaplin, he had called them "party bigwigs" who "want to subject the German people to a narrow-minded, blinkered party-political dictatorship."[72] After Hitler's takeover, Steinbauer remained editor-in-chief and also implemented the political change of course.

However, the *Mitteldeutscher Lichtspieltheaterbesitzer* was discontinued in

January 1934 after only a few more issues.[73] The trade journals *Film-Atelier*, *Filmtechnik* and *Die Kinotechnik* offered hardly any political points of contact, because they dealt mainly with the technical aspects of film production.

The situation was different for the two leading German public movie magazines, *Die Filmwoche* and the *Filmwelt*, which agitated against Chaplin from 1939 on. Paul Ickes had been editor-in-chief of *Die Filmwoche* since the beginning of 1926 and was still in charge years after Hitler's takeover.[74] In June 1933, he stated bluntly about the film business of the Weimar Republic: "The responsible ministry has slapped the cheeky hands of these ruthless philistines. [...] Healthy German culture must demand healthy film."[75] News "aus der nationalen Filmbewegung" (from the National

NS-Verbandszelle deutscher Lichtspieltheater-Besitzer ad "Denke Deutsch! Handle Deutsch!" [Think German! Act German!], June 1933.

Film Movement) followed sporadically. The editor-in-chief of *Filmwelt*, published by Scherl-Verlag, was also Rosenthal until the end of March 1933, when he was replaced by Arthur Schetter.[76] For a transitional period, *Filmwelt* seemed to have remained apolitical. But then, it too was infused with Nazi topics.

To permanently secure the Gleichschaltung, Goebbels subjected the German press landscape to Nazi press control from May 1933; Chaplin got trapped between these millstones in February 1936. Goebbels did not receive the legal authority for this until about six weeks later.[77] Democratic dimensions had thus been left behind, as Goebbels candidly declared repeatedly: "We National Socialists have never claimed that we represented a democratic point of view, but we have openly declared that we would use democratic means only to gain power, and that after gaining power we would ruthlessly deny our adversaries all the means that had been granted us while in opposition."[78]

Pushing and Denying the Deprivation of Rights of German Jews

The Nazis initially tried to conceal the process of "Entjudung" and were even supported in it by the Christian churches in Germany.[79] In March 1933, during Dr. Nathaniel Wolff's stay in Berlin, German police officers took the American-Jewish cinema owner from his hotel to the police station, then abducted him into a forest, mistreated and finally abandoned him. Hitler fobbed off the complaint of Berlin's U.S. ambassador about this assault by claiming that the perpetrators were "Communists disguised as Hitlerites."[80] In its March 23, 1933, session, the Nazi Reichstag officially fought against such "Gräuelhetze" (Atrocities Propaganda) by the foreign press.[81] Max Friedland, German-Jewish head of Universal's German branch, sent the following telegram to Universal's European branches: "I urgently request that all Germanophobe propaganda be vigorously countered, especially all lies concerning oppression of the Jews. Here peace and order prevail." The catch of Friedland's telegram was that Nazis had forced him to send it.[82]

Hitler's regime quickly belied itself with the so-called Germany-wide Boycott Day of April 1, 1933, against Jewish businesses, which was downplayed as a "warning."[83] For example, SA hordes forced "the largest German film distribution companies" to "[insightfully] recall immediately all Jewish film distributors, branch managers, and representatives."[84] The Nazis' mendacity also became openly apparent a few days later when, by law and with the active support of professional groups,[85] active "non–Aryan" civil servants were removed, and Jewish lawyers were effectively barred from practicing law.[86]

On April 11, 1933, Göring was appointed Premierminister von Preußen (Prime Minister of Prussia). In the functions concentrated on him, he rigorously enforced the Gleichschaltung. Through his Decree against "Miesmacher" (Defeatists) of late June 1933, he suppressed criticism of the Nazi regime[87] throughout the country and brutally persecuted political dissidents. About a year later, critics were called "unteachable representatives of the liberalist–Marxist epoch, pathological loners, whippersnappers, blowflies and enemies of the state," whose "criticizing and crazy fantasising [had] no practical value" and who were denied the right to "spoil the joy of reconstruction for forward-looking ethnic comrades."[88] However, clear-sighted warnings by German artists and intellectuals in exile against the spirit of Nazism and its dangers could not be silenced.[89] For example, Thomas Mann's daughter Erika, who had fled to Switzerland, sang her chanson *Der Prinz vom Lügenland* (The Prince of Storyteller's Country) in Zurich on October 1, 1933, in "a shining uniform, equipped with a silver helmet and riding whip." In his empire "all liars are upstaged," "no one is allowed to tell the truth anymore," and the country is wrapped by a "colorful web of threads of lies."[90]

The ousting of German-Jewish filmmakers began quickly after Hitler's takeover. For example, Max Krakauer left distributor Europa "on the basis of friendly agreement."[91] At the beginning of June 1933, the ousting was laid down by law.[92] A film was only "German" if, among other things, all the filmmakers involved in it, down to the extras, were German.[93] With this so-called "Aryan paragraph," German-Jewish citizens were no longer legally regarded as Germans and were thus excluded.[94] From the end of July of that year, German filmmakers and cinema operators had to become members of the Reichsfilmkammer if they wanted to carry on their professions.[95] Major Stein, alias Rumpelstilzchen, who declared even before Hitler's takeover that "We do not need parties once we are one nation," praised the transition of power in his commentary of February 2, 1933: "Oh, we were all so happy!"[96] Consequently, he commented with satisfaction in his commentary of September 14, 1933: "[T]he Ufa [has] cancelled any contract even with the last Jewish employee or supplier […]. Therefore, the road is cleared for German filmmakers."[97] In the German film press, the tone of anti–Jewish articles became increasingly aggressive,[98] and with the "Schriftleitergesetz" (Editors Act) at the beginning of October 1933, German-Jewish editors were finally prevented from working as journalists.[99] When it was reported in the same month that the "first Jewish sound film in Hebrew" was being produced in Palestine, the *Film-Kurier* wished that in the future, Jewish films in all countries should be made only in Hebrew to direct "Jewish participation in filmmaking […] into the appropriate channels."[100]

February to May: Chaplin in Print Media and in the Movies

The cover of O.F. Heinrich's children's novel *Chaplin auf der Verbrecherjagd*, designed by Emmerich Huber, showed a boy in Tramp Charlie's costume with a little moustache. Despite the rapid upheavals, it was still available in regular bookstores in the early days of the Third Reich. The book had been published by Union Deutsche Verlagsgesellschaft in 1932 and had at least three editions. At the beginning of March 1933, the only Chaplin-related film to be approved by the Film-Prüfstelle Berlin during the Third Reich was *Bei Charlie Chaplin in Hollywood* at a length of 28 meters.[101] This was IG Farbenindustrie Agfa's 1931 newsreel-style 16mm film featuring Arnold Höllriegel's conversation with Chaplin about *City Lights* after its February 2, 1931, world premiere. Therefore, *Bei Charlie Chaplin in Hollywood* had already been approved at the end of April 1931, after the German premiere of *Lichter der Großstadt*. At that time, Höllriegel's film had still been 47 meters long[102] and had been approved alongside *Filmpremiere in Hollywood*.[103] This was a 35-meter excerpt from Max Goldschmidt and Höllriegel's feature-length 1928 Hollywood documentary *Die Filmstadt Hollywood*,[104] in which Chaplin talked about *The Circus*. What has been cut from *Bei Charlie Chaplin in Hollywood* in 1933, and whether the film was shown at all in the Third Reich, cannot be established.

From February to May 1933, however, several Chaplin films were publicly re-screened in Berlin—without Nazi disruptions. On February 14, 1933, a completely sold-out "Chaplin cycle" started at Berlin's Marmorhaus with *Feine Leute* and *The Pilgrim*, which was scheduled for four consecutive Sundays. This had been arranged by the Deutsche Gesellschaft für Ton und Film (Degeto), founded in 1928, in cooperation with the Berlin Lessing University. According to *Film-Kurier*, film expert Dr. Johannes Eckardt, who advocated the "autonomy of film,"[105] introduced the cycle and "spoke about the cinematic creative power of this master of cinematic art and emphasized

Chaplin's mimic expressiveness and the typification of his roles." The trade journal wrote that *The Pilgrim* "with its abundance of fresh ideas [did not] seem [at all] outdated and was met with great applause."[106] The *Lichtbildbühne* reported "quite an extraordinary success" for the decade-old film.[107] Until March 6, 1933, *Goldrausch*, *Zirkus* and *Lichter der Großstadt* were shown in succession. *Goldrausch* proved to be particularly successful, triggering "storms of applause and laughter" which "matched those of the first screening many years before." The *Lichtbildbühne* summarized: "*Goldrausch*—a classic film. Charlie Chaplin—its poet."[108] *Zirkus* ran to "cheering applause," and *Lichter der Großstadt* was "enthusiastically laughed at and applauded by young and old alike."[109]

     The cycle enjoyed "extraordinary success," so Degeto scheduled two more special screenings during weekdays. On March 19, 1933, *Goldrausch* was shown again. In its epilogue, the *Lichtbildbühne* paid tribute to Chaplin's genius, which was to remain a major exception in the Third Reich:

> Degeto's merit is invaluable. To our knowledge, [this is] the first attempt [...] to present the "collected works" of a creative film artist who is poet, director and actor in one person. This attempt has been splendidly successful and is an extremely valuable confirmation for anyone who believes in the art of film. If there were a public library of films, "Chaplin's collected works" would be first and foremost among them. A plate would have to draw special attention to them. But aren't they outdated and obsolete? Do they stand up to comparison with the new and the accomplished? These are the wrong questions. Chaplin's silent films are perfect in their kind. There cannot be anything new [...]. And this is particularly true of *Goldrausch*.[110]

O.F. Heinrich, *Chaplin auf Verbrecherjagd*, book cover, 1932.

Johannes Eckardt, 1950.

Although another Degeto event on April 9, 1933, at Berlin's Capitol was already in the mood of Germany's "national rebirth," and the symphonic poem "Ein Volk erwacht" [A Nation Awakens] introduced the event,[111] *Lichter der Großstadt* could also be screened for the last time on May 16, 1933, at Berlin's Mozartsaal. It was again warmly received. In *Film-Journal*, Albert Schneider emphasized its "unusual appeal." It had "stood the test of time and [would] still find its audience in much later years."[112]

After that, no more public screenings of Chaplin films in the Third Reich could be traced. The Reichsministerium für Volksaufklärung und Propaganda also reached out for the Degeto. In mid–1934, Eckardt became head of the newly established "Film and Film Studies" Department at Lessing University and, from July 1934, worked for the Reichs-Rundfunk-Gesellschaft (Reich Broadcasting Society), a trade association within the Reichsfilmkammer.[113]

In mid–May 1933, it was finally still possible that the remarkable brochure *Film. Kitsch. Art. Propaganda* by Hermann Ulrich and Walter Timmling, a collection of essays from 1931, was published. Ulrich and Timmling saw themselves as "Wertkonservative" (Social Conservatives). With their texts directed against Nazism, they emphasized Chaplin's extraordinary artistic standing. In the essay "Film Propaganda–Film Art," Ulrich contradicted the thesis that art is propaganda: "It is a matter of art or propaganda, basically of: God or Devil."[114] Ulrich had also written a lengthy note about Chaplin, stating: "If I had to designate a film artist, I would have to say first that I could not unreservedly label one as such. Nevertheless, I could without a second thought immediately mention two names as direction and path: Chaplin and [Fedor] Ozep."[115] Finally, in the brochure's epilogue, he expressed his belief that the results of the essays would retain their validity even after the Nazi takeover. A sharper contrast to von Leers' frontal assault could hardly be imagined. No wonder *Film. Kitsch. Art. Propaganda* quickly disappeared from the market.[116]

Der Damm. Oldenburger Schriften. 1

Herausgegeben von Werner Meinhof

Hermann Ulrich,
Walter Timmling

Film

Kitsch. Kunst.
Propaganda.

Oldenburg i. O. 1933

Schulzesche Verlagsbuchhandlung R. Schwartz

Film. Kitsch. Kunst. Propaganda, front cover, May 1933.

Reports Without Attacks on Chaplin

Before the German film press had been brought into line, almost everything still went on as usual. People were interested in Chaplin's next film, which had been speculated about soon after the German premiere of *Lichter der Großstadt*. Chaplin reportedly had no fewer than nine film projects at the time, including a *City Lights* sequel.[117] Would it be a comedy with or a drama without Tramp Charlie, and again a silent film, or a sound film, and how far had the project progressed? In early March 1933, according to *Lichtbildbühne*, Chaplin had taken a "lively" interest in the Gösta Ekmann film *Vielleicht ein Dichter* (*Kanske en diktare*), whose model may have been Tramp Charlie.[118] The German trade journal also reproduced a message from *Variety*, according to which Chaplin wanted to go into the studio with his current comedy subject in May, and then shoot Napoleon's life and star in it himself.[119] Both were rumors. The "current comedy subject" remained unknown; Chaplin had long since abandoned plans for Napoleon, having repeatedly had himself photographed in the costume of the Corsican. In the summer of 1926, Chaplin had reportedly engaged the Spanish actress Raquel Meller for the role of Josephine,[120] but nothing materialized.

In mid–May, according to the *Film-Kurier*, Chaplin was supposed to have arranged a "wave of publicity" for his upcoming sound film in which he would be seen as a deaf-mute. Presumably, this merely revived the May 1932 rumor about Chaplin's planned film "The Jester," starring himself as a deaf-mute clown.[121] As usual, there were contradictory reports about production progress and an upcoming premiere. As early as August 1932, the *Lichtbildbühne* had reported that the completion of the new Chaplin film was not to be expected before 1934.[122] The *Film-Kurier* then speculated in February 1933 that the film would be released in September,[123] whereas the *Lichtbildbühne* reported in March that Chaplin had just hired the first personnel to start shooting in April.[124]

After the Gleichschaltung of the German film press, the quantity of Chaplin news gradually decreased and was mostly limited to brief notes. From May to December 1933, they dealt with the status of work on his upcoming film and international resonance, and again they were teeming with contradictions. According to an August report in *Film-Kurier*, Chaplin, a "declared enemy of the talkies," had allegedly agreed to transfer to RKO the right to add a soundtrack to five of his films made in the early 1920s[125]; whether these were First National or possibly 1916-17 Mutual productions was not made clear. The new film, however, would probably be a silent and set "in the industrial quarter of a big city" (*Lichtbildbühne*).[126] Then again, it was to be the 1923 talkie remake of his 1923 film *A Woman of Paris* (*Film-Kurier*)[127] which, according to a 1934 report, would be Chaplin's film after next.[128] In May 1933, *Filmwelt* claimed to know that Chaplin was planning to start a sound film in September, set in Europe and using "as yet unused ideas and tricks."[129] A month later, the *Film-Kurier* reported that, alongside Chaplin as the deaf-mute, New Yorker Paulette Goddard, supposedly only 19 years old, had been signed to play the female lead.[130] By August, Chaplin would have reopened his studio to complete the film by Christmas.[131] Shooting was supposed to have begun in September, and the film would not be ready for release until March 1934,[132] but this was unlikely to materialize, since

Chaplin had probably only hired Carter DeHaven as assistant director in November.[133] The German film market, however, seemed to remain untouched for the time being. At the end of September 1933, Arthur W. Kelly, representative of United Artists' French branch, had declared during his Berlin stay that his company would not export any films to Germany in the foreseeable future, including Chaplin films.[134] In the Third Reich, United Artists no longer maintained a branch office of its own. From March 1934, however, Bavaria AG took over the German distribution of its feature films[135] and submitted applications for approval for six of them by mid–1935. Of these, the Film-Prüfstelle Berlin only approved two. The final United Artists feature film shown in the Third Reich was Rowland V. Lee's *Der Graf von Monte Christo* (*The Count of Monte Cristo*) from 1934 with Robert Donat in the title role. Its German premiere took place on June 21, 1935, at the Berlin cinemas Mozartsaal and Primus-Palast.[136]

Moreover, Chaplin himself was sometimes reported on in a distant or even dismissive manner. At the end of July, the *Lichtbildbühne*'s report with the speculative headline "Mordmärchen um Charlie Chaplin" (Charlie Chaplin Murder Fairy Tale) probably added a negative undertone. The trade journal did not seem to trust the Berlin *8 Uhr-Abendblatt*"'s factual news item "Mordplan an Chaplin als Kriegsgrund!" (Murder Plot on Chaplin as Reason for War).[137] According to this, Japanese naval cadets had assassinated Japanese Prime Minister Inukai Tsuyoshi on May 15, 1932, and were now on trial in Tokyo. They would also have intended to kill Chaplin during his planned but cancelled visit to Inukai's private home to provoke a war between Japan and the U.S.[138] Indeed, numerous British, Irish and U.S. newspaper articles had reported on the planned attack and the Tokyo criminal trial, in which the prosecutor demanded the capital punishment for three of the accused.[139] In any case, Chaplin had been in Japan from May 14 to June 2, 1932, had had an appointment with Inukai, and had twice met with Inukai's son Ken.[140]

In September 1933, the *Film-Kurier* reported Chaplin's quarrel with his former press manager Carlyle T. Robinson, whose contractual relationship had been terminated in 1932. Chaplin had been annoyed that Robinson's biography about him cost less in bookstores than his autobiography. It was rumored that Robinson would henceforth be shunned in Hollywood just like U.S. writer Jim Tully, whose series of articles "Charlie Chaplin: His Real Life Story" Chaplin had unsuccessfully tried to prevent in court in January 1927 (see Chapter 1).[141] Book titles were not mentioned, but probably they were Robinson's *La Vérité sur Charlie Chaplin*, published in 1933 in France, and Chaplin's *My Trip Abroad* from 1922. Chaplin's series of articles, "A Comedian Sees the World," did not begin until September 1933 in the U.S. magazine *Woman's Home Companion* and was not published as a book at that time.

In early November, the *Film-Kurier* added that the German-Jewish writer Emil Ludwig Cohn was also working on a Chaplin biography in Hollywood.[142] Little was true about that statement. The writer's father had already had his Jewish surname Cohn officially changed to Ludwig in 1883, and Emil Ludwig, whom Goebbels called an "Asphalt-Literat" (Asphalt Writer), had converted to Christianity in 1902.[143] Any Jewish ancestry was, however, enough to identify someone as Jewish to the Nazis. Ludwig never published a Chaplin biography.

Finally, in early November and mid–December, the *Film-Kurier* reproduced two U.S. news items on Chaplin without sideswipes against him. In the first case, U.S. President Franklin Delano Roosevelt planned to limit the enormous salaries of movie stars like Chaplin and Harold Lloyd, who had earned about $1 million each as producers and leads of their latest films, *City Lights* and *Movie Crazy*, respectively.[144] The *Film-Kurier* left open the question how the U.S. president intended to limit the profits of self-employed independent producers such as Chaplin and Lloyd. According to society news, Chaplin had also been appointed Colonel of the Kentucky State National Guard.[145]

Positive Odds and Ends

In addition, there were still occasional favorable German articles about Chaplin. In his May 1933 review of Buster Keaton's 1931 *Buster hat nichts zu lachen* (*Sidewalks of New York*, Zion Myers and Jules White), Fritz Olimsky acknowledged Chaplin one last time as an outstanding film artist in the *Berliner Börsen-Zeitung* before he became Auslandspressechef (Chief International Press Officer) of the Reichsfilmkammer in the fall of 1936: "A deeper meaning can be gleaned from Chaplin's grotesque comedy. All his imitators, by contrast, do not go beyond mere superficiality."[146] In August, *Film-Journal*'s article "The Universal Humor of Charlie Chaplin" presented in detail the comments of a London film critic at the Internationale Lehrfilmschau (International Educational Film Exhibition) in Rome on international film humor. The latter had, after all, expressed that "the Germans had not contributed much to the humor in the film." Moreover, his view of Chaplin was decidedly different from that of the Nazis: He took a look at Chaplin's future approach to the talkies:

> Chaplin is one of the greatest funsters in the world. [...] Unlike his great predecessors, he succeeded in breaking down national barriers. In Germany, England, France, even in China and among the colored races, his kind of humor has become popular. [...] Like Shakespeare, he is able to take turns between the serious and the cheerful, and we have to smile with watery eyes. [...] It would not be a misfortune if the little Tramp should feel compelled to utter a few words. We can have faith in Chaplin's voice and Chaplin's intellect.[147]

In September, *Filmwelt* still included Chaplin's *Goldrausch* in a list of "The Greatest Global Successes," commenting approvingly: "They were, without exception, top-notch works that thrilled audiences in every country, a fact that cannot be emphasized strongly enough. [...] Fortunately, the secret of making a universally successful film has not yet been explored. Nor will we ever succeed in solving this riddle, because the tastes of the world are subject to constant change."[148] Bizarrely, the cover boasted Heini Völker, the youthful protagonist of the recent Nazi propaganda film *Hitlerjunge Quex*. This was not a masterpiece which the Nazis claimed with self-fulfilling prophecy, and certainly not a worldwide success.

Henceforth, *Filmwelt* and *Die Filmwoche* no longer kept their readers up to date on Chaplin's film projects. In July 1933, however, *Die Filmwoche* still distributed the two Austrian film books *Charlie Chaplin, der Beklagte* from 1927 and *Charlie Chaplin, der*

Vagabund der Welt (Charlie Chaplin, the Tramp of the World) from 1931.[149] During the first months of the Third Reich, this was apparently not yet an exception. As before, film lovers asked for their favorites like Gitta Alpar and Szöke Szakall and it did not make any difference whether they were of Jewish origin or not. *The Film-woche* continued to offer the 1933 *Reichsfilmblatt-Almanach* with articles on Jewish artists, and a biography of the Austrian-Jewish tenor Richard Tauber.[150] The film magazines also distributed the popular Ross film postcards. Their fall 1933 collection included one final new Chaplin motif, featuring him on skis in St. Moritz, Switzerland, in February 1932.[151] That the Third Reich subsequently banned the production and the distribution of Chaplin postcards[152] cannot be verified. In any case, for the year 1933, no official ban directed against Chaplin or a report about it could be located.

Ufa ad for the German premiere of *Hitlerjunge Quex*, September 11, 1933.

Until the summer of 1935, Chaplin remained present through two 1929 books which the *Filmwoche* publishing house still had in stock: *Wir vom Film* (We of the Film) by Stefan Lorant, who later founded the British magazine *Picture Post*, with a Chaplin sketch on the cover and a section on Chaplin,[153] as well as *Film-Photos wie noch nie* (Film Stills Like Never Before).[154] The latter included images from the banned films *Die Dreigroschenoper, Im Westen nichts Neues* und *Panzerkreuzer Potemkin*. Chaplin's name was also on the cover, and inside the book, using *The Kid, Goldrausch* and *Zirkus* as examples, he was called the "genius Chaplin" with whom "every film book must be introduced and concluded."

Both film magazines ran letter sections in which readers could address questions to the editors. These sections bore the titles "Fragen, die uns erreichten" (Questions That Reached Us) and "Die Fiwo-Tante antwortet" (Aunt *Filmwoche* Answers), respectively, and proved that the Nazi propaganda apparently did not succeed in removing Chaplin from the perception and appreciation of the audience.

The questions were not printed, but the answers allowed conclusions to be drawn about them. In the spring of 1933, among other things, Chaplin's autograph address could be obtained in this way. At the end of 1935, *Filmwelt* replied that his film *Modern Times* had "recently been released in France [under the French title *Les*] *temps modernes*"[155]—at that time, the world premiere of the film was still to come. When a reader inquired about Chaplin's date of birth, the "FiWo-Tante" made it clear in November 1935 that questions about Chaplin would no longer be answered: "Unfortunately, I can only tell you a little, but for the exact fixing of the requested data I would need too long to dig in all kinds of archives."[156] The claim that all books and magazines about Chaplin were banned in the Third Reich in 1935[157] also cannot be substantiated.

The last Chaplin Ross card during the Third Reich, fall 1933.

Chaplin's and Hitler's Moustaches

Comparing the two moustaches stretched back to late September 1923. While in Munich, U.S. author Clare Sheridan had listened to a speech Hitler gave for several hours in front of 10,000 people. In October, in her *New York World* article "Bavarian Facisti," she described him as a "very small Mussolini lacking personality" who looked "like a barber with a Charlie Chaplin moustache"[158]—an almost clairvoyant outlook on *The Great Dictator*.

In January 1932, in his satirical *Berliner Tageblatt* article "Chaplin als Erzieher" (Chaplin as Educator), critic Rudolf Arnheim had identified Hitler as the plagiarist of Charlie's moustache with an analytical comparison:

> [It] cannot be denied that Hitler's upper lip is decorated in the most fitting way that can be devised for him at all. The black beauty spot is not an insignia. It is a badge of humility. [...] No longer the superman but the average individual is supposed to rule. Anyone who deviates from the norm, even via higher quality, will attract embarrassing attention. And so the

human stencil belongs on the throne. […] Anyone who looks Hitler in the face must think of Charlie Chaplin. A Semitic reminiscence, certainly, but can the viewer be blamed? Is there not a certain tragedy in it that the ruler's moustache is unsuitable for standard blond Teutons? […] The stick-on toothbrush moustache is only imaginable as a contrasting stain of paint. A welcome mockery of Hell and embarrassing even to the good Lord. But let us switch to Charlie Chaplin. Like the swastika from the Orientals, the moustache style of the Third Reich originated from Chaplin. He did not inherit it, but he sticks it on his lip when he wants to portray a little man who seems funny because he wears his ragged poverty like a well-fitting tailcoat […] The little moustache […] wants to pretend greatness by minor means. As an insufficient miniature symbol […] [it] comes across as snobbish in the most literal sense of the word. Reduced to the extreme, like wages and salaries, a crisis product, it represents the noblesse of the 50-penny bazaar: 'Small but excellent!' […] Hitler's moustache, a product of disarmament, is terse and "snappy" like the SA's orders of the day. […] It is the unobjective disproportion between small funds and big lip. Chaplinish. […] The gay prop of a grotesque comedian, as black-haired as he is foreign, becomes a serious insignia.[159]

Kurt Tucholsky had summarized the comparison in one concise sentence in March 1932: "Chaplin has asked Hitler to lend him his moustache. Negotiations are continuing."[160] Two months later, he had developed the satirical potential of the topic into the fictitious school essay "Hitler and Goethe" composing in the role of a naïve schoolboy—full of stylistic blunders, with revealing comparisons, penned in corrosive ink:

> And suddenly the Fuehrer has come. He has a moustache like Chaplin, but nowhere near as funny. […] We have seen […] that a comparison between Hitler and Goethe is very much to the disadvantage of the latter, who cannot claim a party of millions. Therefore, we do not join in Goethe. […] Whether Schiller or Goethe was greater, only Hitler will decide, and the German people can be glad that they do not have two such guys!

Tucholsky finally had this essay marked by a fictitious German-ethnic teacher who was waiting for the Third Reich: "Deutschlanderwachejudaverrecke, hitlerwirdreichspräsident, dasbestimmen wir! Sehr gut! [Germany arise, Juda perish, Hitler becomes Reich President, we decide! Very good A!]."[161]

Such comparisons did not cause a stir as long as the Nazis were not in power and the Fuehrer cult could not unfold. However, if the state-supportive Fuehrer cult was even scratched during the Third Reich, any kind of foreign criticism and satire was intolerable in terms of power strategy—as is the case with today's dictators and autocrats. The Nazis equated this with Germanophobe agitation and reacted allergically. Goebbels' staging of Nazism provides insight into the Fuehrer cult; for example, his stylization and adulation of the ruthless and inhuman dictator Hitler as a superhuman with attributes such as "Wunder unserer Zeit" (Wonder of Our Time), "des Herrgotts Meldegänger zum deutschen Herzen" (The Lord God's Messenger to the German Heart), a "Kinderfreund" (Friend of Children), a "herzensguter Onkel" (Kind-hearted Uncle), and later "der größte Feldherr aller Zeiten" (The Greatest General of All Time).[162] With his illustrated books such as *Jugend um Hitler* (Youth Around Hitler) and *Hitler abseits vom Alltag* (Hitler Outside Everyday Life), in which the dictator was presented as a friend of the youth and a jovial person, Hitler photographer Heinrich Hoffmann assisted in these deceptions.[163]

In 1936, sand was also strewn into the eyes with a book under the cynical title

Deutschland ist schöner geworden (Germany Has Become More Beautiful), a collection of speeches by the Deutsche-Arbeitsfront-Chef (Head of the German Labor Front) Robert Ley.[164] With all this, the ugly side of the dictatorship was covered up and created fascination in large parts of the population. This was reflected by the so-called "Bevölkerungspost" (Letters from the Population) personally addressed to Hitler. Especially in the years 1935 to 1938, the offices of Hitler's private bureau, the Seat of Government, and the NSDAP received an annual "stream of admiration" of up to 12,000 pieces of mail.[165]

However, the Nazis had probably not noticed three satirical foreign contributions from the first half of 1933 about the two moustaches. In March, the British magazine *The Bystander* published "Idols in Wood. No. 2: The Man and the Moustache" by woodcarver S.D. Banks: Hitler with a small vertical moustache and his right arm raised steeply upwards to the "German salute," while Tramp Charlie, with a slightly offset horizontal moustache, politely lifts his bowler hat.[166] In May, the U.S. newspaper *Montes Register* featured moustaches of German Reichspräsident Hindenburg, Hitler and Tramp Charlie under the title "Mustaches You Should Know." In the same month, the writer of a letter to the editor of the U.S. *Baltimore Evening Sun* made no bones about his opinion on comparing the moustaches: "It shows very bad taste to compare such a weak comedian as Hitler with such an important artist as Chaplin [...]."[167]

Against this background, the Nazi attacks on Chaplin gained momentum through the French newspaper *Paris-Midi* on August 22, 1933. This contained the provocative article "Charlie Chaplin jouera dans son prochain film sans sa légendaire petite moustache.... Pour ne pas ressembler à Hitler" (Chaplin Will Appear in His Next Film Without His Legendary Little Moustache to Avoid Being Mistaken for Hitler) by journalist Gaston Thierry, who was also well known in Berlin. Referring to Germany's current political situation, Thierry reported having learned through "an indiscretion" that Chaplin was currently shooting a film "under utmost secrecy in Hollywood," for which he was even prepared to accept financial losses:

> [Chaplin] wants to silently protest against Hitler's persecution of the German Jews [...]. [Charlie] enters a barbershop with his legendary moustache [...] and looks at [...] photographic portraits of famous personalities hung on the walls. He stops in front of Hitler's picture, feels his own moustache, then suddenly grabs a razor in a rage, shaves off his moustache with a single cut without being noticed by the barbers, and leaves. Chaplin plays the scene so powerfully that [his] gesture cannot be misunderstood. It is foreseeable that this film will be banned in Germany [...], but [Chaplin] does not want to abandon the scene at any price.[168]

Film-Kurier *Outraged*

When the *Prager Montagsblatt* reported on July 24, 1933,[169] that the American-Jewish actor Sam Jaffe was planning to produce an anti–Hitler film for RKO, the *Film-Kurier* did not get excited in the news at the beginning of August 1933. RKO had already denied the plan to the German trade journal,[170] which the *Film-Atelier* also communicated to its readers in mid–September.[171] Thierry's article, however, referred to a film project that seemed very concrete, and the *Film-Kurier* reacted to it in its extensive Saturday issue of September 2. This contained, as a cinematic foreign matter, a full page of Hitler's latest proclamation, broken down with sub-headings such as "Nationalsozialistische Bewegung—Deutsches Reich" (National Socialist Movement—German Reich), "Das Judentum, Vernichtung oder Unter-werfung" (Jewry, Extermination or Subjugation), "Gegen jede auf Zerrüttung gerichtete nörgelnde Kritik" (Against All Querulous Destructive Criticism), "Aus-lese des fähigsten Menschenmaterials" (Selection of the Most Apt Human Material) and "In eine unsterbliche Zukunft" (Into an Immortal Future). In the "English Sec-tion Française" appeared the bilingual, absolutely humorless Chaplin attack "A Dog Barking at the Moon" or "Un petit chien hurle à la lune." It filled almost a whole page in the style of *Der Angriff*'s 1931 anti–Chaplin tirades.[172] The text of the English ver-sion is reproduced in full in Appendix 2.

The "English Section Française" had been established at the end of April 1933 for the international readership and pursued Nazi propaganda. It appeared regularly in the *Film-Kurier*'s Saturday issues until the beginning of January 1934, then only sporadically. Its editor in charge was Albert A. Sander. When the U.S. trade jour-nal *Variety* in early April 1933 took a critical look at the changes in the German film industry as a result of the Nazi takeover, Sander accused it of lying in the first install-ment of the "English Section Française" of April 29, 1933.[173] He had already writ-ten articles on film policy for the *Film-Kurier* in the 1920s and had been Leiter der Presse- und Propaganda-Abteilung (Head of the Press and Propaganda Department) of the Deutsches Lichtspiel-Syndikat as well as Ufa's Auslandspressedienst-Chef.

After Hitler's takeover, he was Leiter der Auslandspresseabteilung (Head of the Foreign Press Department) of the Reichsfilmkammer until the fall of 1936, and from early summer 1935 both Chairman of the German section of Fipresci (Fédération Internationale de la Presse Cinématographique—International Federation of Film Crit-ics), founded in 1930, and its second vice-president.[174] Sander penned his mostly boastful, aggressive articles for the "English Section Française" him-self in sometimes German-sounding English and French language.

In his peculiar film-historical introduction to "A Dog Barking at the Moon," Sander claimed that Chaplin, around 1908, first walked through the scene in Tramp costume during a car race for a short newsreel-like film for $5 a day. Such films would have served

Albert A. Sander, 1936.

as interludes and had nothing to do with art: "At that timme [*sic*], Charley's [*sic*] humor was still very crude and primitive. His chief trick was to chew a piece of pie and to spit the contents of his mouth into the face of his partner. And this at a time when Fatty Arbuckle, a decidedly finer actor and better comedian, had given Charley [*sic*] an example of cultivated taste and artistic acting." Chaplin never made interlude films, and his film career did not begin until six years later at Mack Sennett's Keystone. Sander's remarks most likely referred to Chaplin's Keystone split-reel *Kid's Auto Race at Venice*, his second film ever.

Sander also got worked up about Chaplin's avoiding military service during World War I. Instead, as a shrewd money raker, he had lined his pockets with the "silly persiflage" *Choulder* [*sic*] *Arms*, in which he captures "hordes of 'Huns'" all by himself. And now this "slacker 'of all people'" had the colossal impudence" of presenting himself as a critic of Hitler, "who fought on the German front as a common soldier from the beginning of the war to the very end and whose moral, intellectual and spiritual qualities make a man of Chaplin's type look like a dwarf." Sander then praised Hitler to the skies and humiliated Chaplin in the way Nazis treated "critics and detractors": "We have not the least objection against Chaplin's spitting chewed cake in other peoples [*sic*] faces. The creator and leader of the new Germany, the war veteran and staunch friend of the new German film stands much too high to even hear the barking of a dog from London's ghetto."

"A Dog Barking at the Moon" also contained Nazi propaganda, which had been known since 1926. Sander mixed in his own ingredients. He claimed Chaplin's birth and growing up in the disreputable London suburb of Whitechapel had negatively influenced him. His agents had sent him on a European trip, prepared with great publicity hype, to live down his shirking during World War I. In London he had been received "like a prince." But by his impossible and arrogant behavior, Chaplin had lost the sympathy of the British Royal Family. He had also had an invitation from British Prime Minister Ramsay MacDonald to a dinner arranged in his honor at the House of Commons cancelled at short notice, instead of picking up the phone himself. Chaplin had committed other escapades in Germany and in France, so that he would not repeat his "travel experiment." Sander did not specify the time, but probably referred to Chaplin's visits to the three countries in 1931. In March 1931, Chaplin had indeed snubbed the Royal Family in London and had an invitation from the British prime minister cancelled.[175] Sander may have considered Chaplin's alleged interview with the Communist Junge Garde in Berlin "impossible behavior" in Germany (see Chapter 4). In France, the issue for Sander may have been that Chaplin was awarded the medal of L'ordre national de la Légion d'honneur (French Legion of Honor) on April 27, 1931, and had traveled on to the Côte d'Azur without responding to the invitation from the Société des Artistes Français to attend its annual charity gala, as *Comoedia Illustré* had reported on May 23, 1931.[176] Sander failed to mention, however, that the *Film-Kurier* had reported in May 1931 on Chaplin's interview with a British journalist in Paris, in which he complained of not having been understood in Europe, as well as of having been unsettled and discouraged. He had felt like an expelled court jester.[177]

In general, Sander tried to put Chaplin in a bad light. About Chaplin's train journey to Berlin and his "deadly fear of the microphone," he wrote:

When he announced his arrival in Berlin, the writer of this article went to Hanover to meet him and to arrange a short interview for a German newsreel. Chaplin's answer was: "You can photograph me as much as you want, but as soon as I see a microphone, I shall run away, and you will not see me again": "Having heard your voice, I can completely understand your attitude," was the response of the writer.

Indeed, Sander had met Chaplin in Hanover as Ufa's Auslandspressedienst-Chef at the time. The express from Hoek van Holland to Berlin had stopped at the Hanover station. Journalists boarded for the continuation of the journey to Berlin in the hope of being able to interview Chaplin. Among them was Sander, because he accompanied Chaplin to film his arrival in Berlin for *Ufa-Tonwoche* (see Chapter 4). He remained the only one whom Carlyle T. Robinson let in to see Chaplin.[178] So Sander had helped Chaplin's arrival in Berlin to be shown everywhere in the German cinemas. Was he a political turncoat like Curt Belling and Hans-Walther-Betz? In any case, Sander's description of Chaplin's voice did not match the facts. Admittedly, *Die Filmwoche* had claimed in March 1931 that Chaplin did not want to shoot a talkie because he "spoke a vulgar English slang, the jargon of the Cockneys [...]."[179] During his Berlin visit, however, German journalists attested to Chaplin's "very good English." This was also confirmed by available 1931 sound news footage. When Chaplin delivered an address over the airwaves on October 24, 1933, at the request of U.S. President Theodore Roosevelt as part of the New Deal to support the U.S. economy through the National Recovery Administration, U.S. newspapers praised his "pleasant" and "elegant" voice that would be nice to hear more often.[180] Years later, moviegoers were able to hear for themselves in *The Great Dictator*.

International Dispute

How Thierry learned of Chaplin's film plan and the consequences of Sander's *Film-Kurier* article have not been explored in the Chaplin literature because it has been limited to Sander's article of September 2, 1933.[181]

Sander's diatribe against Chaplin was received with a shake of the head in the English- and French-language press, and Thierry named his source. On September 7, 1933, the British trade journal *Kinematograph Weekly* regarded Chaplin's "vicious" critique of Hitler as a successful joke, against which the *Film-Kurier* had lashed out with a "savage tirade." Sander's caption, "A Dog Barking at the Moon," had involuntarily confirmed that the German term "Mondsucht" and the English "lunacy" are related.[182]

That same day, a cartoon by Rollin Kirby appeared in the *New York World-Telegram*, captioned in German-English fashion: "Schrecklichkeit in Hollywood" (Frightfulness in Hollywood). In the bathroom, Tramp Charlie is about to shave off his moustache and is lathering it up when Hitler stomps in with a grim face. Kirby's caption read: "News Item Report. Chaplin will Discontinue His Famous Moustache, Because It Looks Like Hitler's. Arouses Anger in Germany."[183] Another cartoon, undated and signed "fekete" by an unknown artist, may have satirized

Sander's portrayal of Chaplin as a pooch yapping at Hitler. An indignant Hitler in tight-laced spats leans on a large swastika with a clenched fist, while in the background, goose-stepping SA men stretch their right arms to the sky for the "German salute." In front of the dictator stands a little dog with Tramp Charlie's head, complete with bowler hat, cheekily sticking out its tongue at the "Fuehrer."[184] On September 16, 1933, the U.S. trade journal *Motion Picture Herald* believed that the *Film-Kurier* had bitten its lips bloody over a trifle. Chaplin's popular appeal was beyond question, even if the contrast between the actor and the alleged "intellectual" Hitler was glaringly applied.[185] At the end of October 1933, the U.S. newspaper *Minneapolis Tribune* stated prosaically: "The affair is no longer a laughing matter at all, unless one laughs at Hitler."[186]

Only a day after the *Kinematograph Weekly*, Thierry also reacted in *Paris-Midi*. In his article "La moustache de Charlot!," he quoted at length from Sander's hasty and exaggerated attack. He made both the *Film-Kurier* as the "official Nazi film organ" as well as the Nazis, who had masterminded the persecution of the Jews, take the following to heart: Due to their ruthless treatment of the Jews in Germany, the whole world will show solidarity with them, which will also lead to other follow-up reactions. Since Chaplin's "Moustache Prank" was still the mildest satire on the present German reality, Sander's tirade proved that Chaplin had hit the mark![187] The next day, *Paris-Midi* reported that Chaplin would stick to shaving off Charlie's moustache in his next film.[188]

Meanwhile, Sander had received mail from Paris' United Artists representative Kelly in which he stated that he had told Thierry nothing about Tramp Charlie's planned shave. Since Chaplin did not have a Paris press officer at the time, Kelly ruled him out as a tipster, adding that to his knowledge, Chaplin was not Jewish either. Rather, Thierry may have been making fun of Germany and

New York World-Telegram, September 7, 1933: "Schrecklichkeit in Hollywood," cartoon by Rollin Kirby (Charlie Chaplin Archive, digitized by Cineteca di Bologna, www.charliechaplinarchive.org).

Chaplin. Sander was not satisfied with that. In the "English Section Française" of September 16, 1933, he responded with "A Chaplin Denial/Un dementi de Chaplin," vociferously defending the new Reich government's measures to reorganize the German film industry and denying the persecution of the Jews in Germany: "Those Jewish film men, who used to work in the German film industry and who are now living abroad, left Germany of their own free will." Thierry should go to Germany and convince himself that reports about the persecution of Jews are Germanophobe atrocity agitation. Sander considered Kelly's denial of Chaplin's Jewish background tragicomic and concluded his attack as follows: "We have no objections against M. Thierry's continuing to consider himself a humorist. For us, it is sufficient that Charley [*sic*] Chaplin refuses to be identified with his 'jokes.' [...] We are, therefore, glad to learn that the odorous 'joke' of *Paris-Midi* cannot be attributed to Chaplin. It really wouldn't [*sic*] have been to his credit."[189] Thierry, who obviously did not believe Sander's "sensational" declarations, reacted a second and explicitly last time on September 22 in *Paris-Midi*'s "Polemics" column. He clarified that he had learned about Chaplin's film plan from an "English-language magazine."[190]

Thierry's Source

This "English-language magazine" was the British broadsheet *Daily Express*. On June 14, 1933, its Paris correspondent had reported on Chaplin's film plan in the article "Chaplin to Appear Minus His Moustache. Because It Makes Him like Hitler," but maintained a low profile about the nebulous source: "Great secrecy is being observed in the making of the film, on which [Chaplin] is now working in Hollywood. Details concerning the movie have been given to me by an intimate friend of Chaplin, a prominent Hollywood casting director who is now on holiday in Paris."[191] The "well-known casting director from Hollywood" remained the great unknown. Therefore, it cannot be ruled out that the *Daily Express* started a satirical rumor about Hitler's regime. A month earlier, after all, the newspaper had printed this Sidney Strube cartoon: In resignation, Tramp Charlie is sitting in the midst of backdrops, with the script of the film "Napoleon" next to him. In the background, Hitler with swastika emblem on his Napoleon hat stands alongside German officers looking at the book pyre of the Berlin book burning. He offers the "German salute" to the SA men who set it on fire, while Charlie sighs: "And they all told me it was impossible to play a serious part with a moustache like mine."[192]

Whether Thierry was aware of the *Daily Express* report of June 14, 1933, is not certain. Otherwise, he would probably have placed the news in *Paris-Midi* shortly thereafter. Only the *Daily Express*' further "Tail-Piece" report of August 15, in which the British newspaper once again returned to Chaplin's anti–Hitler film,[193] may therefore have prompted Thierry's August 22 article. Other British newspapers agreed with him that such a Chaplin film would hardly have a chance of being shown in Germany: "Hitler is just the type of person who will take this fun seriously and probably forbid all beardless film actors to appear."[194]

Aftermath

The dispute with Thierry was over, but not the topic. On October 3, 1933, the *Film-Kurier*'s front page read in bold print: "Chaplin Denies Anti-Hitler Gesture."[195] Sander's French and English versions of this news item were published on October 7 and 14, respectively: "From America we have learned that Charlie Chaplin has followed the example of his European manager and now denies the rumors about his 'moustache plans' himself."[196] Chaplin had actually spread such a statement in the English-language press at the end of September and had also communicated it to Kelly in a telegram. But he had by no means given in: "I wish to absolutely deny I had any connection with or knowledge of press reports in Paris newspapers or elsewhere regarding removal of my screen character's moustache. Such rumors are absolutely without foundation and must have originated from some source over which I have no control. Kindly express my deepest regrets to those concerned."[197]

Nevertheless, Chaplin was once again at the center of attention when the *Film-Kurier* reported in October that the French playwright Jean Guitton had begun work on a stage play with Chaplin and Hitler as antagonists, while Jaffe's plan of July of that year had now finally failed miserably.[198] Presumably these were also just rumors. Among them was probably the *Lichtbildbühne*'s news item from late October, according to which film producer Al Rosen's lawyer had filed a lawsuit for damages against the president of the Motion Picture Producers and Distributors of America (MPPDA) because he had been barred from producing an anti–Hitler film.[199] Details about these three issues did not come to light.

The moustache topic lived on long beyond that. In the second half of October 1933, the U.S. newspaper *Rockford Register Star*, in its article "Two Trick Mustaches," advised Hitler to shave off his moustache because Chaplin had the elder rights: "If anybody has a right to complain, it would appear to be Mr. Chaplin. We do not know just where Hitler got the idea for his whiskers, but if Charlie wants to cry 'Copy cat!' at Germany's would-be Mussolini, it's all right with us. [...] When we want humor, we would prefer one Chaplin to a thousand Hitlers."[200] An answer to a tongue-in-cheek question "Who is imitating whom?" would admittedly be futile. At that time, trimmed moustaches like those of Tramp Charlie and Hitler were rare neither in Germany nor in other countries nor in comedies. (Another famous comedian to wear one was Oliver Hardy, who narrowed his from a wider smudge in 1927.) Therefore, it does not even matter whether Hitler wore his moustache already on August 2, 1914, on the crowded Munich Odeonsplatz, one day after the declaration of the state of war between the German Empire and Russia. Unlike Chaplin, who had already become a movie star, Hitler was still unknown in his native Austria as well as in Germany,[201] and each would have known nothing about the other. However, it is doubtful whether the young Hitler, who can be seen in a photo from the front with a walrus moustache, sported any kind of a moustache at all as early as August 1914. Most likely, Hitler's personal photographer Hoffmann had retouched a picture of the young Hitler with a moustache into a picture he had taken of the Munich mass meeting of August 2, 1914.[202] He used this, together with an enlargement of a detail, in his 1932 glorifying photobook *Hitler wie ihn keiner kennt* (Hitler as Nobody Knows Him).[203]

In 1935 and 1936, the moustache issue resurfaced in the context of whether Chaplin's next film would be approved for German release (see Chapter 8). When Chaplin was already working on *The Great Dictator*, in April 1939, Hans Siemsen's article "Fifty Years of Chaplin" appeared in the Parisian exile newspaper *Die Zukunft* on Chaplin's 50th birthday. Siemsen, who had escaped arrest by a hair's breadth after Hitler's takeover and had lived in France since 1934, compared the moustaches of the two contrasting personalities:

> [The moustache and the age are] the only similarities between [Chaplin and Hitler]. [...] In all other respects, they are complete opposites. Already with the moustaches nothing matches: Chaplin wears his just for fun when he is acting. He invented it to emphasize the comedy of the shy little man he so often played to the delight of all of us. [... Hitler] has no idea of comedy. He has taken the funny little moustache that Chaplin invented for fun absolutely seriously. No kidding, he imitated it and wears it day and night. What will he look like [...] when it is taken off him one day?![204]

In 1960, Karl Schnog, in his booklet *Charlie Chaplin*, claimed about Chaplin's alleged first, non-realized version of *The Great Dictator*: "[W]e learned about it in the mid-thirties from friends in Hollywood[: initially,] he planned a scene in which Charlie, sitting in front of the shaving mirror, comes across with the portrait of the 'Braunau Caesar' in a magazine. He looks, hesitates, compares and—shaves off his little moustache once and for all."[205] The scene resembles the one described by Thierry, and of course the "Braunau Caesar" meant Hitler. Schnog's claim, however, is just as unsubstantiated as it is obscure which unnamed "friends from Hollywood" had provided him with his knowledge. Was Sander his source after all? If so, Kelly's letter and Chaplin's denial would not have left their mark on Schnog.

8

Modern Times Nazi Style, 1934–36

The period from 1934 was marked by drastic film policy measures of the Third Reich. From the end of November 1935, they had made it impossible to screen all Chaplin films that had once been approved in Germany. Nevertheless, the German film trade journals frequently reported on Chaplin, especially on his follow-up to *City Lights*. Nazi film legislation, however, made it unlikely that this one would be released in Germany. German press control also preempted this, but, of course, could not manipulate the international attention Chaplin's new film received and which left its mark on the German press. However, the *Film-Kurier* and the *Lichtbildbühne* were able to distract its readers from the film's international success or downplay it.

This chapter therefore examines:

- the ongoing expansion of Nazi film power and the ban of Chaplin's films
- the revocation of the *Goldrausch* approval
- German coverage of the production of *Modern Times*, Chaplin's film projects and his persona
- German coverage after the British premiere of *Modern Times*
- the creation of the Chaplin file in the NSDAP Main Archives
- whether *Modern Times* had been released in the Third Reich
- whether the film was a flop in Europe
- *Modern Times* in the Berlin Reichsfilmarchiv

Expansion of Nazi Power in the Film Industry

The *Film-Kurier*'s lead for the new year with "Sieg Heil 1934!" was completely in line with the Nazi mindset.[1] Since the establishment of the Reich Chamber of Film in July 1933, German cinema operators had felt the effects of this. They also had to become its members if they wanted to continue their business. Because not all of them had followed suit so far, official pressure was exerted on them at the beginning of 1934.[2] Securing their existence left them no choice but to comply. In the meantime, the head of the Film-Oberprüfstelle, Dr. Ernst Seeger, had tailored the Weimar Republic "Lichtspielgesetz" to Nazi film policy. With a few momentous changes, he thus secured Nazi power over the German film industry from March 1934; this was immediately announced in the trade press. In the course of the year, the "Lichtspielgesetz" was adapted to this even further, equipped with implementing regulations.[3]

The "Lichtspielgesetz" implemented the position of the Reichsfilmdramaturg (Reich Film Dramaturg). His task was to subject proposed German film productions to preliminary censorship to "keep films running contrary to the spirit of the times off the screen" and thus to eliminate anything repugnant to the state. Furthermore, the Kontingentstelle (Quota Authority), previously part of the Reichsinnenministerium (Reich Ministry of the Inte-

Ernst Seeger, head of the Film-Oberprüfstelle Berlin, late 1932, drawing by unknown artist.

rior), was affiliated to the Reichsministerium für Volksaufklärung und Propaganda. It decided whether foreign films were "unobjectionable" and could be imported into Germany. From then on, distributors could only submit imported films to the Berlin Film-Prüfstelle with the Kontingentstelle's approval. The Munich Film-Prüfstelle as well as the Berlin and Munich Bildstellen were closed down and their tasks concentrated on the Film-Prüfstelle Berlin, which also ruled whether films were "volksbildend" (Instructive to the People), i.e., "staatspolitisch wertvoll" (Politically Valuable). Films that "offend National Socialist moral or endanger respect for Germany abroad or its relations with foreign countries" had to be banned. The Nazi amendments to the "Lichtspielgesetz" were immediately reported abroad.[4]

This established aesthetic censorship, which had previously been prohibited by law, as a part of state policy. Minister Goebbels now had the authority to order a revision of all film censorship decisions by the Film-Oberprüfstelle and to prohibit the screening of films that had already been approved until a new decision was reached. The revocation of previous film approvals in revision proceedings was also facilitated by the fact that the Film-Oberprüfstelle could impose a deadline on the distributor concerned, within which the film in question had to be presented. If the film was not presented by the deadline, that alone was grounds for revoking the approval. Previously, children under the age of six had been generally excluded from attending the cinema. Now they were allowed to attend film screenings "if the conditions determined by the Reichsminister für Volksaufklärung und Propaganda are met." This provided the Nazi regime with another opportunity to indoctrinate young people as early as possible, also by means of film.

With these amendments, absolute power in terms of film policy was concentrated in Goebbels' ministry. Only the dictator Adolf Hitler, who could decide as he saw fit without any legally established procedure, was enthroned above it. Thus, a fivefold system of film censorship now existed in the Third Reich: the preliminary examination of German film scripts by the Reichsfilmdramaturg, the certificate that the Kontingentstelle had no concerns about the import of foreign films, the approval of films by the Film-Prüfstelle, Goebbels' right to veto approved films, and Hitler as super-censor, who could render all other decisions void simply with a stroke of his pen. The German film system was thus an example of how the totalitarian German "double state" worked (see Chapter 7). Fittingly, in June 1934, Goebbels appointed the *Völkischer Beobachter* the official publication organ of the Reichskulturkammer and its individual chambers.[5] Henceforth, their orders were published there, much like in a law gazette.

Revocation of the Goldrausch *Approval*

Towards the end of 1934, Goebbels ordered a revision of the 1926 approval of Chaplin's *Goldrausch*. The administrative files for this procedure have not been preserved. Therefore, it is unknown how Goebbels justified his order and which distributor the Film-Oberprüfstelle then addressed to submit the film and within what deadline. In 1926, Ifa Film-Verleih GmbH had distributed *Goldrausch*. By 1934, however, this distributor no longer existed. In the Third Reich, United Artists did not have its own distribution branch. Possibly the Film-Oberprüfstelle had called on the Berlin-based Terra Filmkunst GmbH as the successor to Terra Filmverleih GmbH, which had merged with the German branch of United Artists during the Weimar Republic (see Chapter 4),[6] to submit *Goldrausch*. In any case, the film had not been submitted on time, so the Film-Oberprüfstelle revoked the approval for *Goldrausch* on January 3, 1935, without a substantive examination for purely formal reasons. Its head Seeger communicated this to all German state governments and arranged for the revocation to be published in official gazettes.[7] Beyond that, it was probably not mentioned in the remaining German press.

A clue to the reasoning behind Goebbels' order is provided by the reaction of the *New York Times* of January 9, 1935, to the revocation of *Goldrausch*'s approval. According to this, the Reichsministerium für Volksaufklärung und Propaganda had succinctly communicated its censorship measure by stating that *Goldrausch* was not in line with the Nazi worldview.[8] On the other hand, in the first half of January 1935, it was said in Great Britain and the U.S. that Chaplin was amused by the order of revision. The reason for this was probably that he was considered a Jew. Yet others suspected that Tramp Charlie's moustache had provoked the revocation because, from the Nazi point of view, it embarrassed Hitler.[9]

In part, such considerations coincide in content with judgments of the Film-Oberprüfstelle on other orders of revision. According to this, Goebbels may have seen *Goldrausch* as an attack on Nazi "Rassenehre" (Racial Honor): Charlie, a supposedly Jewish Tramp, falls in love with Georgia, a non–Jew, and she eventually returns his love.

At the end of March 1934, the Film-Prüfstelle Berlin banned W.S. Van Dyke's 1933 U.S. film *Männer um eine Frau* (*The Prizefighter and the Lady*), starring

Der Leiter der Filmoberprüfstelle.   Berlin,den 7. Januar 1935.

    Nr.7578.

An

      die Landesregierungen.

     Auf Grund der von dem Herrn Reichsminister für Volksaufklä-
rung und Propaganda angeordneten Nachprüfung hat die Filmoberprüfstelle gemäß § 12 des Lichtspielgesetzes vom 16. Februar
1934 am 3. Januar 1935 die Zulassung des Films:

              " Goldrausch "

Antragsteller:"Ifa" Film-Verleih G.m.b.H.Berlin,(zugelassen von
der Filmprüfstelle Berlin am 9. Januar 1926 unter Prüfnr. 12030)
widerrufen. Demgemäß habe ich durch Bekanntmachung im Deutschen
Reichs-und Preußischen Staatsanzeiger Nr.5 und im Deutschen Kriminalpolizeiblatt Nr 2047 vom 7.Januar 1935 die Zulassung des Films
außer Kraft gesetzt und die von der Filmprüfstelle Berlin unter
dem 9. Januar 1926 ausgestellten Zulassungskarten Nr.12030 für
ungültig erklärt.

     Ich bitte, die Polizeiverwaltungen des dortigen Bereichs ent-
sprechend zu verständigen.

[signature: Seeger]

Film-Oberprüfstelle Berlin, note of the revocation of the *Goldrausch* approval, January 7, 1935 (DFF—Deutsches Filminstitut & Filmmuseum, Frankfurt am Main).

American-Jewish boxer-turned-actor Max Baer. In the appeal proceedings, the Film-Oberprüfstelle, chaired by Seeger, confirmed the ban in a landmark judgment on April 21, 1934: The film violated Nazi sentiment and was therefore likely to endanger public order. The judgment stated:

Film censorship […] has to apply a particularly strict standard to films with Jewish actors. [The] Film-Prüfstelle based its ban essentially on the fact that it is unacceptable to National

Socialist sensibilities if a Jew is portrayed and glorified as a sporting hero and moral victor with all the external characteristics of the Negro. [...The] entire film glorifies Max Baer and focuses on his life and career, so that he receives all the sympathy of the audience. [...] The supremacy of the Jew Baer offends National Socialist sensibilities, especially through his relationship with non–Jewish women. [...] The German people are particularly sensitive in all matters touching on racial honor [...].[10]

By the same standards, in July 1934, the Film-Oberprüfstelle, in another review procedure chaired by Arnold Raether as Seeger's deputy, also revoked the approval of the 1933 Austrian film *Frühlingsstimmen* by Paul Fejos: "[The] film [features] actors in leading roles who had previously worked in Germany [... and] who are rejected by the [Nazi] Movement. In addition, one of the non–Aryan actors is shown in a cozy paternal role as the head of a German family. His distinctly non–Aryan appearance offends the German viewer."[11]

In late 1934, the *New York Times* was only too right in summing up the political situation in Germany: "The [typical Nazi's] mental and moral isolation from the Western world is greater than his country's economic isolation."[12]

No More Chaplin Films

According to Heinz Pol's article from the end of May 1935 in the exile magazine *Die neue Weltbühne*, the Prague Jewish newspaper *Selbstwehr* reported that a "Berlin Nazi paper" had printed a facsimile of Chaplin's open letter. In it, Chaplin is said to have denied his Jewish origin and to have declared that he would visit Berlin again quite soon in order not to lose the German market altogether after the revocation of the *Goldrausch* approval.[13] Chaplin may have thought like this. But neither his open letter nor the report of the *Selbstwehr* have been verified so far.[14] The search in *Der Angriff* and in the *Völkischer Beobachter* (Berlin Edition) as well as in the German film press and for another "Berlin Nazi paper" not specified by Pol has also remained without success up to now.

Offensive themes such as non-marital motherhood (*The Kid*) and extramarital relations between an alleged Jew and non–Jewish women (*The Kid*, *Die Nächte einer schönen Frau*, *Ein Hundeleben*, *Zirkus*, *Carmen* and *Lichter der Großstadt*) could probably have been found effortlessly by the narrow-minded new standards. The Nazis had also fought *The Pilgrim* and the Chaplin program with the short subjects *Lohntag* (*Pay Day*), *Auf dem Lande* (*Sunnyside*) and *Vergnügte Stunden* (*A Day's Pleasure*). But Goebbels did not order further approvals of Chaplin films to be revised. At the end of June 1935, another amendment to the "Lichtspielgesetz" provided for a much simpler way that made such a procedure unnecessary. This granted Goebbels the authority to independently ban films already approved by the Film-Prüfstelle without a procedure of revision if he deemed such action "necessary for urgent reasons of public welfare."[15] In early July 1935, Goebbels then completed a radical final step with the "Sechste Verordnung zur Durchführung des Lichtspielgesetzes" (Sixth Decree for the Implementation of the Film Act). It declared all film approvals from the hated Weimar Republic to be void, without any procedure of revision:

- for all silent films with immediate effect and
- for all sound films with effects from July 31 to December 10, 1935, in close succession.

At the same time, high hurdles were set up for the procedure concerning new approvals of all these films. Applications for them could only be submitted until July 31, 1935, and silent films could only be re-approved "in particularly justified exceptional cases." Sound films were not allowed to be altered for this new procedure.[16] Later, further legal restrictions followed for foreign films, which were already irrelevant for Chaplin's *Modern Times*.[17]

The Nazi state had thus gotten rid of all silent film approvals from the despised "System Era." Even though silent films had largely been made obsolete by the talkies and therefore virtually ceased to be produced, in 1932, for example, "silent films were still in great demand."[18] They were screened mainly in small cinemas, most of which could not afford to upgrade to sound film equipment. This did not apply to the Kamera cinema on Berlin's boulevard Unter den Linden, which had been founded by a German-Jewish film merchant. Without eco-

nomic constraint, it had remained a venue for silent films, was appreciated by moviegoers beyond Berlin's borders as a "theater of good film" and was an attraction for tourists from the U.S. In February 1934, the *Film-Kurier* and the *Lichtbildbühne* reported that it had been converted to a sound film theater and would screen only one last program of silent films. The background was that the Reichsfilmkammer had forbidden, without any legal authority, to play "outmoded" films such as silent movies.

After protests from Kamera visitors, the cinema operators postponed the conversion to sound film screenings and continued to show silents. As a result, the Reichsfilmkammer had the Kamera closed in April 1934. "Repeated warnings had not been effective, so that the president of the Reichsfilmkammer was forced to take this step," the trade journals succinctly stated.[19]

Franz Eher Nachfolger Verlag ad for Goebbels' book *Der Angriff*, 1935. Art by Karl Heinz Schweitzer, alias Mjölnir.

In mid–August 1934, London's *Daily Telegraph* reported that Chaplin even wanted to have Hitler legally interdicted from wearing a moustache like Charlie's because of the Kamera's closing.[20]

On April 14, 1936, the head of the Film-Prüfstelle Berlin announced that the revision of old films under the "Sechste Verordnung zur Durchführung des Lichtspielgesetzes" had been completed and that in the future, only films whose approval dated from the time after Hitler's takeover would be screened in cinemas.[21] No more applications for the re-approval of Chaplin films were submitted by any distributor. What happened to the newsreel-style short film *Bei Chaplin in Hollywood*, which had been approved on March 4, 1933, and to which the regulations of the "Sechste Verordnung zur Durchführung des Lichtspielgesetzes" did not apply, is not known.

Modern Times *in Production*

Until autumn 1934, the *Rheinisch-Westfälische Filmzeitung*, the *Lichtbildbühne* and the *Film-Kurier* speculated whether Chaplin's next film would be a talkie. But most of the news from July 1934 to June 1935 concerned the title of this film, and in between there was other news about the progress of production.

This coverage began in January 1934 with a *Rheinisch-Westfälische Filmzeitung* news item that Chaplin had worked "successfully with some well-known language teachers" as early as 1933 and could therefore "dare" to speak and sing in the film together with his leading lady Paulette Goddard.[22] Rumors had been circulating in the U.S. since the fall of 1932 that Chaplin and Goddard were married,[23] but in Germany the marriage was not reported until July 1934,[24] and the couple would not confirm it until the U.S. premiere of *The Great Dictator* in October 1940.

In July 1934, *Der Film* and *Der neue Film* commented on Chaplin's voice: "It is said that his voice is so sympathetic and pleasant that one can now understand his refusal to produce himself in talking films, for 'such a classical organ' really does not suit the roles he plays."[25] At the turn of 1935-36, however, the *Film-Kurier* wrote that Chaplin did not want Tramp Charlie to speak, since "talking would localize him."[26] Chaplin was concerned that his film character would lose its internationality as a result.

In July 1934, "Cosmopolitan" appeared as the title of the expected film in the *Film-Kurier*.[27] In October, it was followed by "Herrenloses Gut," apparently the translation of the title "Street Waif," which was circulating in the English-speaking world. The *Film-Kurier* linked this one to the "Napoleon" film that was supposedly still planned.[28] In November 1934, however, the *Lichtbildbühne* provided the working title "Production No. 5," the only provisional title that can be traced from Chaplin's surviving production notes on *Modern Times*.[29]

In October 1934, the *Rheinisch-Westfälische Filmzeitung* had been the only German film trade journal to offer an overview of the production progress of Chaplin's forthcoming film, relying on a well-founded French source in a reasonably detailed and thoroughly friendly manner:

> Charly [*sic*] Chaplin's studios have come back to life as of September: all preparations for the film have been made and—the script is also ready! This time, Chaplin wants to work through

it point by point. A lot of scenes of his previous films were created by chance or from momentary ideas. Given Chaplin's imaginativeness, you still have to be ready for surprises![30]

When production of the film was further delayed, the *Film-Kurier* reported sharply in March 1935 that Chaplin, according to alleged reports from his entourage, only had excuses to offer: "He is ill, he is not in the mood, he fears the hot season (already now)."[31] This contradicted the journal's report of the same month that United Artists intended to release as many as two new Chaplin films,[32] which, according to the *Lichtbildbühne*, would be at the head of the British United Artists distribution schedule beginning in September 1935.[33] In early May 1935, the *Film-Kurier* stated that Chaplin had meanwhile "begun [the] editing and dubbing [of this] film" and was already "preparing the book and direction for the next Paulette Goddard film." This was to be completed more quickly than its predecessors and would have music throughout, which the *Film-Kurier* had pointed out somewhat earlier.[34] According to the chronology of Chaplin's filmmaking, this would have concerned *The Great Dictator*, which, however, was only conceived years later.

Because Chaplin had drawn his conclusions from the last economic crisis and mass unemployment, he was said to have decided to set his upcoming film "Strandgut der Straße" (Flotsam of the Street), probably another translation of *Street Waif*, in the factory and commercial district of a big city. Goddard was to play the role of a gamine from the street. By May 1935, a little more was known about *Modern Times*' plot. And therefore Heinz Pol predicted in *Die neue Weltbühne* that the film would not be released in Germany because of "[Communist] demonstrations, the strikes, and the struggles in the factories."[35] This is probably why the title "The Masses" came into play in the *Rheinisch-Westfälische Filmzeitung* in June 1935.[36] Chaplin had mentioned the title when he gave interviews to U.S. newspapers in the spring of 1935.[37] Because of its linguistic proximity to *New Masses*, the title of the organ of the U.S. Communist Party, the title "The Masses" is said to have raised concerns in the U.S.[38] Therefore, the *Film-Kurier* wondered in June whether "Production No. 5" would have difficulties being distributed regularly because of an "emphasized political meaning." Since Chaplin had reportedly invested nearly $1 million of his own money in the production,[39] he would already be considering releasing the film on his own, renting large theaters in several U.S. metropolitan areas.[40] Allegedly, Chaplin had even invested his entire fortune of $14 million in the film,[41] which was already supposed to have gobbled up an unusually large amount of money.[42] Concerns about *Modern Times*' political content seemed to be confirmed in September 1935 when the Communist magazine *New Masses* went into some detail about Chaplin's "satire against capitalism," such as the conveyor belt on which Charlie works.[43]

The political direction of the film was also taken up by the July 1935 report of the German exile magazine *Die neue Weltbühne* "No. 54632," whose headline was another title speculation of the composer Hans Eisler, who had returned from the U.S. According to his account, this title had fallen "in the Hollywood circle of friends" and described "the American worker in crisis [...] as a human number" on the conveyor belt, of which Chaplin was one. Chaplin had thus taken a stance on the "sense and nonsense of capitalist rationalization" and on capitalism in general. In its commentary on this portrayal, *Die neue Weltbühne* did not conceal the fact that Chaplin had denied pursuing political ambitions with his film, since he was not concerned with politics, and certainly not with Communism.[44]

In mid–August 1935, the *Lichtbildbühne* announced that "Production No. 5" would henceforth bear the title *Modern Times*.[45]

Projects

From July 1934 to August 1935, there was also speculation about other Chaplin projects. As early as 1933, it had been suggested that Chaplin was planning a remake of *A Woman of Paris* as a successor to *Modern Times*. In April 1934 as well as in January 1935, the *Lichtbildbühne* and the *Film-Kurier*, respectively, substantiated this. The remake was to be titled "Personal Reasons," also starring Goddard. After that, Chaplin allegedly wanted to devote himself to his long-cherished "Napoleon" project.[46]

At the end of September 1934, the *Lichtbildbühne*, referring to the Swiss newspaper *Tribune de Genève*, had carried an astonishing report, which the German journal did not quite seem to trust. Chaplin was supposed to have made two sound films "in secret" in the manner of *City Lights*, but not to have brought them to the market. It claimed that one of these two films was the romantic drama "Der ewige Gatte" (The Eternal Husband), in which Chaplin played "the tyrannized husband of a monster of a wife" alongside his brother Syd. He had screened this film personally and only once to tramps in a tiny Mexican cinema, and they laughed heartily at his jokes.[47] In recent decades, intensive research has been devoted to Chaplin films, including Chaplin's private archive at his Swiss residence Manoir de Ban in Vevey. So far, this has yielded no clues about the two ominous films. But was Josef von Sternberg's 1926 dramatic film *The Seagull*, starring Edna Purviance, one of the two films shrouded in mystery? Chaplin had produced the film, but held it back and finally destroyed it in 1933 for tax reasons.[48]

In mid–April 1935, the *Lichtbildbühne* wrote that Chaplin was slated to direct a U.S. adaptation of Jaroslav Hašek's "The Good Soldier Švejk" starring Peter Lorre.[49] In August of that year, the journal reported that Chaplin had teamed with Mary Pickford to jointly produce no less than six films for United Artists in the coming years, four of them with Goddard playing the female lead.[50]

Every new Chaplin film triggered questions about the next one. It was no different with *Modern Times*. At the end of July 1936, the *Lichtbildbühne* reported that the U.S. writer Sinclair Lewis would pen the screenplay for "Chaplin Production No. X," but without making any reference to *Modern Times*, which by then had had its fate sealed in Germany (see below).[51] Only much later would it become apparent that this follow-up film was to be *The Great Dictator*.

Other Chaplin Reports

In addition, the German trade journals wrote about other Chaplin topics, and sometimes this had an unfriendly character. However, apparently no cause for an outright diatribe had been found by 1936.

In February 1934, the *Film-Kurier* considered the unusually large nose of the American-Italian comedian Jimmy Durante, nicknamed "Schnozzola," "not funny, but sad, like […] Chaplin's big feet."[52] But the polemic, which possibly mistook the non–Jew Durante for a Jew because of his physiognomy, had ignored the fact that Durante's nose was real, but Charlie's big feet were not. The shoes were too big because the Tramp had not found others.

Then, in July 1934, on the occasion of the German premiere of Monty Banks' 1933 British musical comedy *Scherben bringen Glück* (*You Made Me Love You*), starring Thelma Todd and Stanley Lupino, the *Rheinisch-Westfälische Filmzeitung* advocated that "the talkies have long since put an end to [the] old grotesque films of the Chaplins, Keatons and Lloyds"[53]—which seemed odd, given that Keaton and Lloyd had long since gone into talkies. The *Film Journal*, in turn, picked up that same month on U.S. reports of church boycotts of allegedly immoral films and filmmakers aimed at forcing, among others, Chaplin out of business.[54]

Surprisingly, at the end of August 1934, in a compilation of film news from the German press in the *Lichtbildbühne*, it could be read that the *Berliner Morgenpost* had carried the article "Chaplin 13 m groß" (Chaplin 13 m tall) about the design of German cinema facades on August 13, 1934.[55] However, the *Berliner Morgenpost* was only published from Tuesday to Sunday, and August 13, 1934, was a Monday. "Chaplin 13 m groß" has not been found in any other issue of this newspaper either.[56] If the article did appear in an unknown place, without knowing the content it is impossible to determine whether it was about advertising in the Weimar Republic or even in the Third Reich.

In September 1934, the *Lichtbildbühne* wrote nebulously about Chaplin's autobiography, which he supposedly had completed after *City Lights'* world premiere.[57] This neutral news item probably referred to Chaplin's five-part 1933-34 travelogue "A Comedian Sees the World" in the U.S. magazine *Woman's Home Companion*.

In early November 1934, the *Lichtbildbühne* attacked Chaplin politically. The social-critical writer Upton Sinclair had lost the election for California governor against Republican candidate Frank Merriam. Sinclair's election program also concerned the film industry, which he wanted to put under Chaplin's control.[58] Now the *Lichtbildbühne* claimed that people in Hollywood were breathing a sigh of relief that Sinclair had failed to "entrust Charlie Chaplin, of all people, with the purge of the film industry" and thus make him a "film dictator."[59]

In February 1935, the *Film-Kurier* reported on the attraction of big-name film actors and directors. Using the example of *A Woman of Paris*, which he considered one of Chaplin's "best and most interesting" films, a Parisian distributor felt that the actors were the box office draws. The *Film-Kurier* responded that this film's success had only materialized in the French capital because Chaplin had not starred in it.[60]

It was different in mid–November 1935 with the *Film-Ateliers'* news "Chaplin borrows foreign pants, shoes, hat and coat," behind which another attack on Chaplin's originality could have been suspected. However, it was a coherent depiction of the beginning of Chaplin's film career. Apparently, in 1914, he had made a virtue of necessity and, looking for a film costume, borrowed some clothes from Ford Sterling (pants), Mack Swain (shoes), Mack Sennett (hat) and a cane from a stranger, from which he assembled the famous "Tramp costume."[61] According to Robinson's Chaplin biography, rotund Roscoe "Fatty" Arbuckle contributed the much-too-wide pants, the stocky Charles Avery the skimpy jacket, Ford Sterling the oversized well-worn shoes, and Arbuckle's father-in-law the little bowler hat. Mack Swain had been the model for the little toothbrush moustache.[62] Chaplin himself claimed in his 1964 autobiography that the idea for the costume came to him on the way to Keystone's prop room, and that he had been careful to ensure that the individual components contradicted each other.[63]

At the end of October 1936, *Lichtbildbühne* presented a lengthy reflection on "the grotesque in film" and "knockabout comedy," noting that "the joy of the grotesque [...] is deeply innate in human beings." Film comedy had succeeded in making the transition to talkies, and comedians such as Pat and Patachon, Laurel and Hardy (in Germany called Dick and Dof/Doof), Harold Lloyd and Buster Keaton had held their own against revue and other dialogue films. Chaplin's name failed to come up, although he would have belonged in first place because of his undeniable importance for cinema in general and the grotesque film in particular.[64]

Modern Times *Comes to the Cinemas*

Reports about the time and place of the upcoming world premiere of *Modern Times* were contradictory and sometimes vague. Dates ranged from mid–July to the end of September, October 11 to mid–December 1935, and Hollywood, New York and London were listed as premiere locations.[65] In October 1935, according to *Lichtbildbühne*, the world premiere was scheduled for December 16 or 19, 1935, at the London Tivoli Theater, while the *Film-Kurier* continued to assume a possible premiere in mid–November 1935.[66] Even at the beginning of January 1936, speculation was not over. For now *Modern Times* was to start "finally on January 15 or 22" in London for 12 weeks,[67] at the time when Chaplin's divorced wife Lita Grey would be performing in London.[68] The February 5, 1936, world premiere of *Modern Times* at New York's Rivoli Theater[69] ended the speculation.

Shortly before, the *Lichtbildbühne* had dealt with Chaplin's possible closeness to Communism, based on a news item in the French evening newspaper *Paris-Soir*. In line with this, a leading Russian film official had attended the French screening of *Modern Times* for potential buyers and was determined to acquire the Soviet screening rights. With the article "'Chaplin film as Soviet propaganda?' the *Lichtbildbühne* therefore put Chaplin in political twilight": [The Russian representative] described the film as "the best Communist propaganda' in the same vein as the Russian films (*Panzerkreuzer*) *Potemkin*, *Generallinie* (*Staroye I novoye*, Grigori Aleksandrov and Sergei M. Eisenstein, 1929), etc. One eagerly awaits Chaplin's statement in Paris on

Premiere brochure of Sid Grauman's Chinese Theater, Hollywood, for *Modern Times*, 1936 (DFF—Deutsches Filminstitut & Filmmuseum, Frankfurt am Main/Chaplin-Archiv, Dauerleihgabe der Adolf und Luisa Haeuser-Stiftung für Kunst und Kulturpflege).

this sensational classification of his work." Boris L. Shumiatsky, president and general representative of the Soviet State Film Distribution, told the Soviet *Pravda*: "Chaplin gave us a preview of his film *Modern Times*. […] The humor of this film is filled with fearful accusation. It shows the starvation of the unemployed, their lodgings; it unmasks capitalistic rationalization. As the result of chats with us, Chaplin decided to remake the ending of his picture."[70] Chaplin then reportedly replaced the film's pessimistic finish with an optimistic ending with a Communist twist.[71] This is probably a rumor: Chaplin himself, at any rate, had his studio manager Alf Reeves vigorously deny any influence by Shumiatsky on *Modern Times*.[72] Shumiatsky had met Chaplin during his stay in Hollywood, and was shown the rough cut version of *Modern Times*. In fact, Chaplin had conceived a pessimistic ending in which Charlie, after his release from prison, meets his formerly fun-loving companion (Goddard) in the convent as a nun accompanied by her Mother Superior, and is thus alone again. Photographs of this also exist[73]; evidence of Shumiatsky's influence on the film's ending does not exist.

Modern Times is neither "the best Communist propaganda" nor does the film end with "optimistic Communist overtones." Chaplin's film is a parable of the modern working world. On the assembly line, piece-rate standards are constantly raised, restroom visits are monitored, and the production process is interrupted as briefly as possible for breaks. The latest achievement is a machine designed to feed the workers on the assembly line. It is tried out on worker Charlie, but goes haywire. Charlie eventually goes crazy at the factory and is taken to a hospital. After his release, he unexpectedly gets mixed up with demonstrating unemployed workers and is put in jail as a supposed ringleader. At lunch, Charlie sits in the dining hall next to a drug dealer who quickly fills his bag of snow into a salt shaker when he realizes that criminal investigators are on his trail. Unknowingly, Charlie helps himself to the salt shaker. Charlie suddenly feels incredibly strong. He even snatches bread from his much stronger cell and table neighbor, who has forced Charlie to kowtow to him. And when Charlie witnesses an escape attempt, he is able to thwart it thanks to the unexpected courage the narcotic has given him.

From then on, Charlie does well in prison. The grateful warden has had his cell comfortably refurnished. Charlie lies comfortably on his padded cot and reads the newspaper. What he reads about the riots outside only makes him shake his head in sorrow. Charlie would have preferred to stay there, but he is discharged for good behavior. Because of a silly mistake, Charlie has to leave the job that the grateful prison warden has arranged for him and finds himself in a time of great unemployment back on the street. There, a young orphan is eking out a living with petty theft. When the hungry girl steals a loaf of bread and is caught, Charlie sees his chance to go back to prison. He tries to take the girl's guilt on himself, and when that fails, bounces the bill in a self-service restaurant with a sumptuous meal and turns himself in to the nearest policeman. Charlie and the girl are taken away in the paddy wagon.

In front of a middle-class cottage belonging to a couple bursting with the happiness of love, they dream of being able to own such a home themselves. He even wants to work for it. In fact, with the help of the prison warden's letter of recommendation, he gets a job as a night watchman in a large department store and sneaks in with the girl after closing time, where they both eat their fill in the gourmet department. On his patrol, Charlie surprises burglars, but they turn out to be unemployed former buddies from the factory, and they keep toasting the reunion with him. To make matters worse, a barrel of rum into which the burglars had shot a hole beforehand has emptied over him—Charlie is totally drunk! The next morning he is found asleep, buried in a rummage sale for fabrics. Again, Charlie goes to jail. But the girl has been waiting for him and in the meantime has conjured up a "little paradise"—a tiny ramshackle shack, but at least it is a start. The factory reopens, Charlie gets work, but unfortunately it is short-lived. The workers go on strike and the factory is closed. Charlie accidentally steps on a board, with which he flings up a stone which hits a policeman. Again Charlie goes to jail. In the meantime, his girlfriend has been hired as a dancer by the owner of a restaurant. After Charlie's release from prison, she takes him on as a waiter, which turns into a fiasco. Things are better with his attempt to entertain the guests as a singer. Since he cannot remember his lines, the girl writes them down on his cuffs. But he loses them during his performance. He rescues the situation by singing nonsense lyrics, telling the song's story in mime. This sends the audience wild and the landlord hires Charlie. Then employees of the Youth Welfare Office appear and want to take the girl to the orphanage. With Charlie's help, she manages to escape, but she is desperate and wants to give up. Charlie is able to infect her with his confidence, and together they walk into a hopeful future.

Press Controllers' Attack

After the massive changes in film law in 1934 and 1935, *Modern Times* became a matter for the Nazi Reichspressekonferenz (Reich Press Conference). Reichspressekonferenzes had also existed during the Weimar Republic, but as public events of the press to which state representatives were invited. However, the Nazi Reichspressekonferenzes, established in May 1933, took place behind closed doors in the Reichsministerium für Volksaufklärung und Propaganda and were directed by spokesmen of the Reichsregierung (Reich Government) to ensure that the press was kept in line. Reichspressechef (Reich Press Chief) Dr. Otto Dietrich, one of Hitler's closest comrades, was the ruling spirit behind the enforced conformity of the press and the organizer of these Reichspressekonferenzes.[74] As head of the NSDAP's Reich Press Office, Dietrich had already founded the NS press conference on August 1, 1931, and after Hitler's takeover, he quickly forced the German press into the role of government mouthpiece for NSDAP and Hitler, with guidelines and language regulations.[75] In September 1935, he called this function of the press "one of the highest and most important national tasks," referring only to "the German press washed and reshaped with National Socialist baptismal water." All other newspapers, such as those of the "Judo-Marxist press [...] which are contrary to the common welfare, are to be banned!,"[76] because "the public opinion of the German people [...] is National Socialism."

Dietrich outlined the task of journalism in the Nazi state as follows: "The highest political wisdom is that of suggesting to the other what is necessary in such clever form that he takes it for his own will."[77] At the 1948-49 Nuremberg Wilhelmstrasse Trial, Dietrich downplayed his prominent role in Hitler's regime, portraying himself as an "ordinary publicist" and "meaningless lecturer" who had merely passed on Hitler's orders as a "mail carrier" and had had "nothing to do with the organization of the press." With the help of so-called Persilscheine (Whitewash Certificates), he also claimed to have saved opposition journalists and Jews from Nazi persecution. Because of his press campaigns during the Third Reich for aiding and abetting Nazi crimes against humanity, he was sentenced in April 1949 to seven years in prison, which he served only in part.[78]

Participation was mandatory for domestic daily newspapers; foreign journalists had no access. Around 150 journalists accredited personally took part on a regular basis. Major newspapers such as *Berliner Tageblatt, Deutsche Allgemeine Zeitung, Frankfurter Zeitung*, the *Münchener Neueste Nachrichten* and the Nazi press organs *Der Angriff* and the *Völkischer Beobachter* sent their own participants, while smaller regional newspapers had themselves represented by a joint conferee. The Reichsregierung spokesmen issued verbal instructions to the participants and provided "confidential information." By the end of World War II, 80,000 to 100,000 individual instructions had accumulated, or an average of about 19 to 25 directives per day.[79]

All participating journalists had to commit themselves in writing to comply with fixed regulations and to forward the daily results, which had to be secured against access by unauthorized persons, to their editors.[80] A record had to be kept about the destruction of directive files, which had to be signed by the editor-in-chief and a witness, and which could be "verified at any time by a representative of the Press Department of the Reich Government." Violations by journalists were consistently punished with reprimands, disciplinary court proceedings, exclusion from the press conferences, disbarment, internment in a concentration camp, and later even the death penalty.[81] Official minutes of the press conferences have not survived, but several extensive collections of transcripts from the Reichspressekonferenzes have been preserved by journalists who did not abide by their obligation to maintain confidentiality.[82]

Since the beginning of 1936, Alfred-Ingemar Berndt, Ministerialdirigent (Head of Ministerial Section) in the Reichsministerium für Volksaufklärung und Propaganda, was chairman of the Reich press conferences. The former editor-in-chief of the *Deutsches Nachrichtenbüro* was a fanatical Nazi who had direct access to Hitler independently of Goebbels. In his SS files, he was characterized a "daredevil with a soldierly appearance." He did not shy away from inventing news. Among the journalists accredited to the Reichspressekonferenz, Berndt was considered the "rudest embodiment of Nazi aggressiveness" and the "worst agitator in the Ministry of Propaganda." His "sledgehammer policy" earned him the nickname "Gräuel-Berndt" (Atrocity-Berndt).[83] Sometimes Berndt's behavior even embarrassed Goebbels.[84]

One day after the British premiere of *Modern Times* on February 12, 1936, at London's Tivoli Theater, Dr. Kurt von Stutterheim, London correspondent for the *Berliner Tageblatt*, cabled his impressions of the event and linked this to a press review of London dailies. According to this, the silent film *Modern Times* was one of the most comical films ever made, proving Chaplin's gift for fantastic detail and splendid scenes despite "certain formal shortcomings" and appearing like a

From left to right, German press controllers Hans Fritzsche, Joseph Goebbels and Alfred-Ingemar Berndt, November 1939.

"liberation from the talkies with the sudden end of a long toothache." The correspondent's report was entirely positive and therefore did not fit in with the Nazi rejection of Chaplin:

> Since the days of *City Lights*, London has not seen a movie night like last night's, when Charlie Chaplin's new film *Modern Times* had its English premiere at the Tivoli Theater. A strong police force was necessary to regulate the traffic, which at times reached automobile chains of 800 to 900 cars. The audience […] was more like the Covent Garden audience than that of a movie theater. London's social as well as film and acting circles were strongly represented […]. *Modern Times*, with which Chaplin upheld the tradition of the silent film, experienced a resounding success, primarily, of course, because of Chaplin's own performance. Audiences laughed until they cried. Chaplin's new film gives a satire of the mechanized age and the machine man. […] The climax of the laughs is Chaplin being fed by a mechanical feeder to save the lunch break. Interwoven with this social satire [as a counterbalance] is a somewhat sentimental love story."[85]

This article was put on the agenda of the Berlin Reich Press Conference that same day, held at noon in the Pompeian Hall of the Ministry.[86] Berndt considered any positive statement about Chaplin as commercial publicity for him and ordered the journalists present: "Publicity for Charlie Chaplin, in any form whatsoever, is absolutely unwanted." For the Berlin editorial office of the *Frankfurter Zeitung*, journalist Fritz Sänger stenographed Berndt's instruction as follows: "The propaganda publicity which the *Berliner Tageblatt* ran for the new Charlie Chaplin film today in its report from London was felt to be inappropriate. The Ministry does not share this vision of Chaplin's achievements so that his film should not be covered in the German press in that way."[87] Other participating journalists reported Berndt's instruction by telephone to their newspapers. The *Film-Kurier* reacted immediately with a short, low-key report about the "London Chaplin Premiere": "In London, the new Charlie Chaplin film *Modern Times* experienced its English premiere at the Tivoli Theater, before a large selected audience. Chaplin upholds the tradition of the silent film with this work. The *Daily Telegraph* and *Morning Post* call *Modern Times* one of the funniest films of recent years. *The Times* calls attention to a certain lack of form."[88]

British pressbook of *Modern Times*, front cover, 1936.

**Mechanically working store window advertising at London Waterloo underground station for
Modern Times, 1936.**

Something Positive for the Last Time

Despite the obvious dangers, some journalists preserved leeway and their
own thinking. Contrary to Berndt's instruction, *Der Film*'s London editorial staff
reported on February 15, 1936, in a similarly positive and detailed manner as the
Berliner Tageblatt, that *Modern Times* was a "unique" production because Chaplin had "united author, leading actor, composer and director in one person" and was
celebrating a "huge success" with "six showings a day." Among other things, the
trade journal's article read:

> *Modern Times* has high quality. It is a satire on the age of the machine, a work to be taken
> seriously in the last analysis, which with great skill refrains from any political intonation. It
> contains some very good and new situations that are much laughed at. [...]*Modern Times* is
> not on a par with *The Gold Rush*, [... which] was a worldwide success, original and uncon-
> structed in everything. *Modern Times*, on the other hand, undoubtedly shows the veteran
> Chaplin repeating or altering tried situations from his earlier films. The strength of Chap-
> lin's short films was improvisation. It is missing in *Modern Times*. [...] But there is [...] only
> one film clown, and that is Chaplin. Although Chaplin's performance is also great this time,
> he will have to follow the technical progress of film in his next film. *Modern Times*, despite
> great buildings and excellent photography, is still outdated. The sound is missing, the spoken
> word.[89]

This was the last benevolent press article about Chaplin in the Third Reich,
which also knew how to praise him despite some criticism. In passing, it also mentioned the uniqueness of Chaplin's *Goldrausch*, banned just a month ago. The article probably violated Berndt's instruction. What consequences this had for *Der
Film* is unknown. The *Lichtbildbühne* reacted to the Pressekonferenz on February
16, 1936, either cautiously or true to Nazi principles. In its international section, it
commented on the postponed London premiere of *Modern Times* that the film was
scheduled for a "long run."[90]

The *Berliner Tageblatt* and *Der Film* reports on *Modern Times*' London premiere had appeared on the eve of the abolition of the previous "corrosive" art and

film criticism in Germany. It was replaced by Goebbels' "Anordnung des Reichsmin-isters für Volksaufklärung und Propaganda über Kunstkritik of November 27, 1936" (Order on Art Criticism), by the "Kunst- und Filmbetrachtung" (Art and Film Review), whose authors were henceforth called "Kunst- und Filmschriftleiter" (Art and Film Editors). Goebbels demanded of them "not so much evaluation as presen-tation and thus appreciation," because: "In the future, only editors who undertake this task with the sincerity of heart and the National Socialist spirit will be able to review artistic achievements."[91] In short, Goebbels had abolished film criticism.[92]

Ban on Modern Times?

A few days after the Reich Press Conference of February 13, 1936, numerous newspapers from Great Britain, Canada and the U.S. reported that *Modern Times* had been officially banned in Berlin on February 17, 1936.[93] The reasons were:

- Films by Chaplin, a Jew, had already been banned in the Third Reich because they contradicted the spirit of Nazism.[94]
- According to French reports, the film's Communist tendency caused the ban. Moreover, the Nazis could not tolerate poking fun at Hitler.[95]
- Hitler "did not want to be looked at with his moustache from Chaplin films," which is why Chaplin pictures and dolls have now finally been removed from German shop windows.[96] "A few weeks ago" it had been jokingly reported that Chaplin claimed copyright on Hitler's moustache, and German authorities had taken it seriously.[97]
- Because the price for the German screening rights of *Modern Times* will be exorbitant, the German economy must be protected against capital outflow to the USA.[98]

The reports also triggered mocking comments:

- "Did it really take Germany five years to realize that Hitler's heroic [moustache] came from Hollywood?"
- "It's a crazy decision, because everyone knows that Hitler's moustache is like Chaplin's."
- "This should be a case for the barber, not the censor."
- "In truth, Chaplin's [moustache] does not look like Hitler's, but Hitler's [moustache] looks like Chaplin's. If the Germans look at Hitler's funny [moustache] over Chaplin's funny feet, they may even find that Hitler has just such feet."
- "That's about as absurd as suddenly not eating potatoes because they happened to be grown by someone you don't like."
- "Why doesn't Hitler shave off his [moustache] or grow a longer one?"
- "How about […] banning movies featuring Hitler in the US because his [moustache] looks like Charlie Chaplin's?"
- "The ban is almost as funny as the movie itself!"
- "Chaplin is now probably 'Public Enemy Number 1' in Germany."[99]

Of course, this was also an ideal subject for political cartoons[100]:

- On February 14, 1936, David Low's cartoon "The Other Fellow with a Funny Moustache" appeared in the London *Evening Standard*. Hitler, in Charlie's working outfit, performs repair and maintenance work on a machine similar to the one in *Modern Times*. He has set in motion the dangerous gears of international armaments, with the great cog of the German armament industry driving the gears of British, French and Russian arms production.[101] This cartoon is said to have given Chaplin the idea to film *The Great Dictator*.

- Immediately after the news of the ban, the British *The Journal* printed George Middleton's cartoon series "Saving His Face" with the following caption: "They say Chaplin's new film has been banned in Germany because it was made by a Jew. Behind closed doors, however, they say it's about Hitler's Chaplin [moustache]." In front of a mirror, Hitler desperately brushes, twirls and shapes his moustache to avoid looking like Chaplin. Before he shaves off his moustache, he has a brilliant idea. To the shouts of salvation from his audience, he yells in the final image that *Modern Times* must be banned because Chaplin is a Jew.

- On February 20, 1936, the *Glasgow Daily Record* showed in Carey Orr's "How Much It Is!" Charlie shrugging his shoulders, because Hitler had locked him out precisely because of the similarity of their moustaches. But when Charlie subsequently returns with a large, curly moustache, he is greeted by a cheerful Hitler with the "German salute."

- In Alexander George Gurney's cartoon "Professional Jealousy" for the Australian *The Mail*, Charlie dances in the spotlight on an obviously German stage. While the audience cheers him with the Hitler salute, the dictator stands a little apart in the shadows and looks enviously at Charlie.

- In Low's *Evening Standard* cartoon sequence "International Mustache Crisis," Hitler looks at several proposals to solve the moustache problem. At one point. the moustache is shaved off, then Hitler is said to have an enormous moustache with a long ruffled moustache, and finally, in addition to his moustache, he is seen with very long, drooping sideburns. The commentary: "Telegram from Hollywood to Berlin. Moving Picture Union protests against ban on Chaplin film just because his [moustache] is too similar to Hitler's. Suggestion that since Chaplin had his [moustache] first, Hitler should either shave his off or grow more of a [moustache]. Stop. Hitler banned Mickey Mouse and Piccard's Balloon for being too similar to Goebbels and Goering."

- In the Australian *Referee*'s cartoon "David and Goliath" by an unidentified artist, Tramp Charlie walks on a path laid out like a swastika. It is subtitled "Germany has banned the new Chaplin film."

The German exile newspaper *Pariser Tageblatt* had started as the *Pariser Tageszeitung* and from June 1936 it bore the subtitle "Das Kampfblatt gegen den Hitlerismus, für die Freiheit und die Menschenrechte" (Propaganda Journal Against Hitlerism, for Freedom and Human Rights).[102] Its editor-in-chief was Georg Bernhard. On

February 20, 1936, the *Pariser Tageblatt* also reported, citing news from Berlin the previous day, that *Modern Times* had been banned in Germany because of its "Communist tendencies," despite great successes in New York and London.[103] Two days later, it emerged from the article "Adolf Chaplin" in the same newspaper that the ban was only suspected because the British press had reported on it. In the article of February 20, 1936, Chaplin's alleged plan for an anti–Hitler film from 1933 was taken up once again, and in addition, the Nazi treatment of humor was characterized:

> Charlie Chaplin's new film has been banned as being subversive in Germany. It is said to be Communist, mainly overly social, and Nazism just cannot stand that. English newspapers, however, give another version for the ban: the Chaplin moustache, the main epitome of ridiculousness, resembles too much the Hitler moustache. Therefore, Mr. Goebbels intervened and put his foot down against the last work of the great actor. […] The dictators are truly hostile to humor. Laughter does not fit at all to swollen heroic pomposity. […] It is claimed that Mr. Goering understands so much fun that he always lets himself tell the jokes that are made about him. Nevertheless, […] the prison sentences for insulting the majesty of Luft-Hermann [Goering] are numerous. […] Hitler himself already embodies the sacrosanct in himself. He is taboo. […] There was a rumor some time ago that Charlie was considering playing Adolf Hitler in Hollywood instead of Napoleon. That would be a good idea.[104]

In *Die neue Weltbühne* at the end of February 1936, writer and former revolutionary Ernst Toller assumed that Nazi ideology was incompatible with the socially critical references in the film. For they were directed against "the power of states which are serving the ruling class and against the boundless humiliation of the working people."[105]

The *New York Times*, however, had inquired at Goebbels' ministry and learned on February 17, 1936, that *Modern Times* had not been banned and that no decision was to be expected. Shortly thereafter, U.S. film producer Samuel Goldwyn confirmed to the newspaper that Chaplin's film had not been submitted to the Berlin Film-Prüfstelle.[106] In fact, an official German ban is unknown, and no German distributor had applied to Film-Prüfstelle Berlin for approval of *Modern Times*. Whether a preliminary application was made to the Kontingentstelle at the Reichsministerium für Volksaufklärung und Propaganda cannot be determined, because its files have been burned. Goebbels was also silent about it in his diaries.[107] Right after the first news about the alleged German ban on *Modern Times*, United Artists declared in New York's *The Heights News* that they had not yet shipped a copy of the film to Germany. The newspaper was nonetheless certain that *Modern Times* would also have no chance of being approved in Germany.[108] So why did foreign journalists report on the banning of *Modern Times*? One explanation could be an indiscretion on the part of their German colleagues from the Reichspressekonferenz, who, against their obligation to maintain secrecy, passed on Berndt's press instruction against *Modern Times*, which was then misinterpreted as a ban.

As far as can be seen, Nazi authorities did not collect any press reports on *Modern Times*. By March 1936 at the latest, the Hauptarchiv der NSDAP (NSDAP Main Archive) opened a file on Chaplin, collecting newspaper clippings about him until the end of November 1944. The Hauptarchiv der NSDAP had been founded in January 1934 with Hauptstellenleiter (Head of Central Office) Dr. Erich Uetrecht as its first director. It closely cooperated with the NSDAP Reichspressestelle, which in turn "promoted" and "supported" the work of the party newspapers through Gaupresseämter (District Press Offices),[109] and in June 1939, it was placed under the personal supervision of Hitler's deputy Rudolf Hess. The tasks of the Hauptarchiv der NSDAP included the administration of the foreign press archive, as well as the immediate evaluation of current material and its forwarding to the NSDAP's responsible offices.[110] The Chaplin file contains nothing about *Modern Times*.

Modern Times *in Germany, After All?*

A few days after the British news of the ban, during Shrove tide, the *Lichtbildbühne* printed on February 25, 1936, a "Fastnachsseite" (Mardi Gras Paper) of the "unverantwortliche Schriftleitung" (Irresponsible Editorial Staff). This was not serious and gave the impression that it came about in a merry atmosphere:

> Under the influence of the carnival balls on Saturday and Sunday, our staff and correspondents have sent in a number of telegrams, reports and articles, which we cannot take seriously by any stretch of the imagination. But we do not want to withhold them from our readers. Probably you will be as amazed as we are about it and laugh heartily. Whoever would like to reprint such reports, please make sure to mark them explicitly as "Fastnachtsmeldungen der [*Lichtbildbühne*]" [*Lichtbildbühne*'s Mardi Gras News]. [...] We have learned [from one of these news items] that the Chaplin film *Modern Times* will be released by Hammer-Tonfilm-Verleih.[111]

Hans Hammer Jr., 1936. Did he want to distribute *Modern Times* in Nazi Germany?

Hammer-Tonfilm-Verleih actually existed. Hans Hammer ran the distribution company Union-Filmverleih in Munich. In 1934, he also founded Hammer-Tonfilm-Verleih there and transferred its management to his son Hans Hammer Jr.[112] In the same year, Hammer-Tonfilm-Verleih released, among others, Lau Lauritzen's 1932 Pat and Patachon film *Mit Pauken und Trompeten* (*Med Fuld Musik*). In 1936, the company encountered economic difficulties, which were followed by court settlement proceedings. Hammer Jr. then moved the company headquarters to Berlin. After a meeting of creditors, he resigned at the end of August 1936 while the court proceedings were still in progress.[113]

Hammer-Tonfilm-Verleih did not comment on *Lichtbildbühne*'s "Fastnachtsmeldung," did not advertise

Modern Times at any time, and did not release the film. Nor was the film associated with any other German distributor.[114] The distribution of United Artists films had already been discontinued in the Third Reich during 1935 (see Chapter 7). Since the Nazis were fighting Chaplin, buying the German screening rights to his film would probably have been economically risky. On the other hand, given the strained economic situation of Hammer-Tonfilm-Verleih, it would have been quite plausible that Chaplin's film was nevertheless the last straw in February 1936 and that the *Licht-bildbühne*'s "Fastnachnachricht" thus had a realistic background after all.

In any case, it is surprising that *Modern Times*, according to Leni Riefenstahl's 1987 *Memoiren*, was officially shown in the cinemas of the lively German capital during the Berlin Olympic Games, which took place from August 1 to 16, 1936:

> In the meantime, Olympic fever had broken out in Berlin. The city was decorated with thousands of flags, and hundreds of thousands of visitors flocked through the city. More than 80 theaters were playing, the nightclubs were packed, and the movie theaters were showing films like *Traumulus* with Emil Jannings, *Modern Times* by Charlie Chaplin, and the unforgettable *Broadway Melodie* [1936 by Roy del Ruth].[115]

Riefenstahl was one of the most enigmatic personalities in film history. She met Hitler before his takeover. He made her his protégé and secured her an untouchable position within the Nazi circle of power during the Third Reich. Riefenstahl made her films *Fest der Völker* and *Fest der Schönheit*, which premiered in 1938, about the Berlin Olympics. Prior to that, her 1935 Nuremberg Rally film *Triumph des Willens* glorified Nazism and its exponents. Nevertheless, after World War II, she claimed to have had nothing to do with Nazism. One is well advised to question Riefenstahl's claims in *Memoiren*.

This also applies to her claim that *Modern Times* was shown in Berlin cinemas. Riefenstahl did not provide any evidence for this. Since a German ban on the film had been reported in February of that year, especially in English-speaking countries, the public Berlin screening of the film would have been a downright sensation, at least for foreign journalists attending the Olympic Games. They would most likely have reported on this as well. Moreover, the public screening of the Chaplin film without the approval of the Film-Prüfstelle Berlin would have constituted a criminal offense, even more so under the applicable version of the 1934 "Lichtspielgesetz,"[116] which must have attracted the attention of state authorities. Domestic and foreign news about *Modern Times* in Berlin, however, could not be tracked down. Even the avid moviegoer Victor Klemperer mentions nothing of this in his extensive diary entries. In them, he takes a closer look at the Olympic Games, which he found "repugnant as an insane overestimation of sport [and as] a political enterprise."[117]

Nevertheless, there is no mistaking the fact that the Hitler dictatorship endeavored to present itself as cosmopolitan on the occasion of the Olympic Games and to conceal the real persecution of Jews in Germany. For example, the display cases for Streicher's smear journal *Der Stürmer* were taken down for the occasion. For the nature of the Nazi "Doppelstaat," it would have been no contradiction at all to disregard its own rules and show the latest film by the world-famous Chaplin to guests from all over the world, even in Germany.

Chaplin was obviously important to Riefenstahl. In her *Memoiren*, she claimed

German *Stürmer*-Kasten (*Der Stürmer* display case), mid–1930s.

to have received a congratulatory telegram from him on the 1932 fairy-tale feature film *Das blaue Licht*, in which she starred: "Every day the mailman delivered me enthusiastic mail, including even telegraphic congratulations from Charlie Chaplin and Douglas Fairbanks, who had already seen a print of it in Hollywood."[118] In April 1932, the *Film-Kurier* reported on Chaplin's appreciation of Riefenstahl: "During his last stay in Switzerland [Chaplin] recognized [...] especially Leni Riefenstahl's extraordinary [...] qualities and showered her with praise."[119] It is already unclear whether she claims to have received the telegram after the German premiere on March 24, 1932, or after the U.S. release on May 8, 1934. After the U.S. start of *Das blaue Licht*, the *Film-Kurier* reported in February 1935 in connection with the U.S. reactions only one person who had praised the film as "divinely beautiful": Ethel Barrymore.[120] Had Chaplin himself been the source of the *Film-Kurier* in 1932, or had Riefenstahl launched the report? This could not be clarified.

It should not go unmentioned that Riefenstahl manipulated the original credits of *Das blaue Licht* in the Third Reich. According to the March 1932 censorship report of the Film-Prüfstelle Berlin, the film was a "teamwork of Leni Riefenstahl, Béla Balázs and Hans Schneeberger," produced by Riefenstahl's former fiancé Harry Sokal, who was of Jewish origin.[121] In October 1931, Riefenstahl had commented on her collaboration with the Hungarian-Jewish film theorist Balázs to the *Film-Kurier*: "I worked happily under Bela Balaczs [sic] guidance. In general, the collaboration with [him ...] was very prolific."[122] Nevertheless, she failed to pay him for his participation in the film. When he demanded the payment, in December 1933 Riefenstahl authorized *Der Stürmer* editor and Franconian Gauleiter Julius Streicher, to reject claims against her by "the Jew" Balázs.[123] In *Memoiren*, she claimed to have known Streicher personally almost not at all and to have found his Stürmer "abominable."[124] However, Streicher's letters to Riefenstahl, which were safeguarded in May 1945 shortly after Streicher's escape at his Pleickershof estate near Nuremberg, revealed that they had been close friends, if not lovers, until at least 1941. At the end of May 1941, he had also advised her to undergo treatment for her drug addiction at a Bad Wörishofen sanatorium.[125] When *Das blaue Licht* was re-released in 1938 on the occasion of Riefenstahl's *Olympia* films, the new credits no longer mentioned a teamwork with Balázs and Schneeberger, and Sokal's name was also eliminated.[126] After World War II, she corrected the manipulated cred-

Screen shot of Junta (Leni Riefenstahl) in *Das blaue Licht*, 1932 (© Friedrich-Wilhelm-Murnau-Stiftung).

its only to a modest extent: Riefenstahl merely conceded Balázs' collaboration on the screenplay. The 1932 credits have not been restored since.[127]

In addition, Chaplin is said to have based the role of his partner Paulette Goddard in *Modern Times* on Riefenstahl's portrayal of Junta "as an homage to *Das blaue Licht*."[128] In any case, Goddard—particularly in her first scene of *Modern Times*—does bear a considerable resemblance to Riefenstahl in her early mountain films.

Was it perhaps for this reason that Riefenstahl unceremoniously gave the Chaplin film a fictitious German premiere after what had leaked out about him in Germany in 1936? Or did her memory, when she wrote her *Memoiren* at the age of over 80, merely play a trick on her? Other apparent deliberate manipulations in her *Memoiren* suggest intent. However, this can no longer be conclusively clarified.

Screen shot of the Gamin (Paulette Goddard) in *Modern Times*, 1936 (*Modern Times* © Roy Export S.A.S.).

Riefenstahl's private archive, in which Chaplin's and Fairbanks' congratulatory telegrams might be assumed and also a note about *Modern Times*, was not accessible when the German version of the present book was written. According to information provided by her secretary Gisela Jahn in June 2010, "a substantial part of the Riefenstahl archive should be in the U.S., where the documents are scanned and archived with the latest available procedures" in order to catalogue them and to make the digital version accessible for scholarship and research.[129] Documents had indeed been sent to the U.S. and returned when the project failed. In 2016, Riefenstahl's husband and heir Horst Kettner passed away and named Jahn as his sole heir. Jahn, in turn, donated part of Riefenstahl's estate to the Berlin Stiftung Preußischer Kulturbesitz in early 2018: some 700 moving boxes of photographs, scripts and drafts, film reels, letters and personal documents. As of January 2021, Chaplin's and Fairbanks' congratulatory telegrams and any documents about the screening of *Modern Times* in Berlin have not been found in them.[130]

Modern Times *in Europe—a Flop in Paris?*

Lichtbildbühne's "Fastnacht" news meant it was impossible to show *Modern Times* in Germany. Nevertheless, the film remained present in the *Lichtbildbühne* columns about foreign premieres until May 1936, mostly without the journal's comment. Readers could not fail to notice the international response to the film, which was apparently gradually becoming a success. Most recently, it was reported that the film had opened at Prague's Bio Alfa cinema under the title *Die neue Zeit* and was scheduled for a seven-week run.[131] The *Film-Kurier* reported similarly on the screening of current films in European capitals and metropolises in its column "Europa spielt" (Europe Screens). From February to September 1936, *Modern Times* was regularly mentioned; it ran for up to 24 weeks (Stockholm).[132] The journal did not report anything like this for other films during the period, including successful films that the *Film-Kurier* was apparently taken with: René Clair's *The Ghost Goes West* (1935) and William Cameron Menzies' *Things to Come* (1936), based on an original by H.G. Wells. *Things to Come* even had its own column devoted to it.[133] After a reporting break of about three months, the paper printed a note according to which *Modern Times* had again been brought to a Swiss cinema in December 1936.[134]

In addition to the brief notes about *Modern Times*, the *Film-Kurier* announced on March 21, 1936, in the column "Dies und das" (This and That) the Chaplin film's French premiere at the Marigny Stage Theater in Paris on March 13, 1936—the only substantive news about the numerous European screenings. Surprisingly, it said that *Modern Times* had been a flop:

> The new Chaplin film, now being released in Paris, is experiencing a major gala flop. It was to be shown as part of a charity event; the ticket prices had been set at 150 francs per seat, and everyone of distinction in Paris had been invited. But the crème de Paris made themselves scarce, very scarce indeed, so that at five o'clock some people still had to be alerted by telephone in order to avoid the worst, an empty house. The film actually started, but—in front of a barely crowded parquet.[135]

Whether *Les temps modernes*, as the French title read, was really poorly attended on March 13, 1936, does not necessarily reflect playing schedules elsewhere. Yet, the apparently disparaging article of March 21, 1936, gained significance because the *Film-Kurier* did not report screenings of *Les temps modernes* in France in its column "Europa spielt." The German trade journal probably intended to portray Chaplin's film as a failure throughout France, without stating the facts.

About *Modern Times*' London premiere, the *Pariser Tageblatt* had published an excellent review that once again emphasized Chaplin's genius.[136] Shortly before the Paris premiere, it wrote that *Les temps modernes* was "eagerly awaited."[137] The paper printed two advertisements, from which it could be inferred that the film would be

French pressbook *Les temps modernes* (*Modern Times*), front cover, 1936 (DFF—Deutsches Filminstitut & Filmmuseum, Frankfurt am Main/Chaplin-Archiv, Dauerleihgabe der Adolf und Luisa Haeuser-Stiftung für Kunst und Kulturpflege).

shown at the Marigny in Paris in any case beyond April 17, 1936.[138] These contents of the *Pariser Tageblatt* must have been known in the Reichsministerium für Volksaufklärung und Propaganda and also in the German film trade journals. In mid–July 1936, the *Film-Kurier* referred to the newspaper as a "well-known emigrant rabble-rouser,"[139] and occasionally quoted from the Parisian exile press (see Chapter 11). In any case, the Berlin Reichssicherheitshauptamt (Reich Security Main Office) was apparently well-informed about the German exile press, for in March 1937, it devoted a *Leitheft* (Guideline) to "Emigrantenpresse und Schrifttum" (Emigrant Press and Literature), which was declared "secret" and covered a very large number of newspapers and magazines in exile as well as their editors and authors, including the *Pariser Tageblatt* and *Die Neue Weltbühne*. It stated: "For all their common features, each emigrant newspaper has its own face."[140] For the German trade journals, the Communist German exile press still was taboo, but known to the Sicherheitshauptamt. This included the literary monthly *Das Wort*, edited in Moscow by Bertolt Brecht, Lion Feuchtwanger and Willi Bredel, which contained the committed review "The *Modern Times*" in its first issue of July 1936.[141]

Nevertheless, the reporting of the renowned weekly French trade journal *La*

Cinématographie Française virtually unmasked the *Film-Kurier* report of March 21, 1936, as deliberate manipulation and a method that was also to be used about five years later on *The Great Dictator*. In their regular column "A Paris cette semaine" (This Week in Paris), it was reported that *Les temps modernes* had played at the Marigny from mid–March to the end of June 1936—17 weeks![142] In May 1936, the British press reported record screenings of *Modern Times* not only from New York, Barcelona, Madrid, Zurich and Copenhagen, but also from Paris.[143]

So *Les temps modernes* was obviously anything but a flop in Paris! This Chaplin film thus became a harbinger of the Nazi propaganda method of attributing economic failures to rejected films, such as *The Great Dictator* years later, contrary to the truth.

La Cinématographie Française wrote on March 21, 1936, the day of the *Film-Kurier*'s fake news, that it would take several columns to do justice to a film so richly blessed with new gags, humanity and comedy, and which also shone with Chaplin as an expressive actor.[144] The Paris–based German exile journal *Sozialistische Warte* had commented similarly on March 15: It found the film "artistically ravishing."[145] In early April 1936, Lucie Derain summarized in *La Cinématographie Française* the 23 French film premieres of March 1936, including 14 foreign films, among which *Les temps modernes* ranked high. The French trade journal wrote of the film that Chaplin's comedy had revolutionized cinema in terms of ingenuity. He had virtually reinvented himself and embraced the viewer with love and compassion. Derain concluded, "This film is rich in extraordinary and new things. It is the most important film of this season."[146] This must not have escaped the *Film-Kurier* either, because it quoted again and again from *La Cinématographie Française*.

German trade journals maintained their selective-distorting reporting. In the statistics of the *Lichtbildbühne* of January 1, 1937, for the spring of 1936, *Modern Times* was missing because the film had not been officially released in Germany.[147] A few days later, however, the trade journal reproduced the list of the U.S. National Board of Review of the ten best U.S. films of 1936. *Modern Times* was in ninth place.[148] About three weeks later, the *Film-Kurier* commented in its article "Two juries—two value judgments. America chose the best films" another U.S. list of films that had premiered in the U.S. from September 1, 1935, to August 31, 1936.[149] *Modern Times* was not in it, although the U.S. premiere had taken place on February 5, 1936. While the *Film-Kurier* usually named its sources, this time the journal was silent about it. It is hard to believe that *Modern Times* had been accidentally overlooked.

At the end of April 1937, the *Pariser Tageszeitung* reported that *Modern Times* had been judged by Italian critics to be "flawed, incorrect, superficial, and devoted only to ends in themselves." Despite disparaging fascist propaganda, Chaplin's film had initially opened in the major theaters of Italian cities. When it was scheduled to come to suburban theaters, it was banned by the state film censors.[150] Shortly after the *Pariser Tageszeitung* reported the news, the *Lichtbildbühne* also reported that *Modern Times* had been banned in Italy and its colonies, withholding from its readers the run-up to the ban.[151]

Modern Times *in Austria and in the Reichsfilmarchiv*

In Austria, *Modern Times* opened on March 31, 1936, under the title *Die neue Zeit* at the Viennese Apollo[152] and was reviewed in the Austrian *Paimann's Filmlisten*. Again, it was considered a shortcoming that Chaplin's film again lacked sync dialogue, although moviegoers had been accustomed to talkies for years. About the composition of the film and the reaction of the audience, the review read:

> Without a real plot, situations are strung together and cemented together by tableaux intertexts. Some new and many well-tried gags are presented in the directorial manner of former times: Silent movie facial expressions, no dialogue. The human voice is heard only through loudspeakers and a talking machine. Only once Chaplin sings a song and not badly at all. So no need for further muteness! Well-rhythmed background music, satisfactory technique. [...] It should be reported that the majority of the [premiere] audience felt excellently entertained."[153] At the beginning of April 1936, the *Lichtbildbühne* referred sweepingly to a "generally" favorable Viennese press.[154]

Goebbels had inaugurated the Berlin Reichsfilmarchiv at the beginning of 1935 with the words, "It is time to unleash German national ambition on film."[155] There, a complete copy of *Modern Times* with German subtitles was archived as *Die neue Zeit*. The catalogue of the Reichsfilmarchiv included a synopsis of the film. Furthermore, it was characterized on its main index card in a heavily edited résumé as a "grotesque satire on the methods of over-engineering and the machinery of the police apparatus." The latter's draft had possibly understood the film all too clearly: "Intended on the whole as a grotesque satire on the man-exhausting technology and automatic machinery of the police apparatus, from which the little man in particular never escapes." Under "style," it says meaningfully, "Charlie Chaplin," and in the "remarks," some "very grotesquely funny" scenes were mentioned: "the feeding machine that is supposed to save the factory owner time," "the repair of the big machine," the "roller skating scene in the department store," "the shared home in the dilapidated wooden shack" and "the juggling skills with the full tray as a waiter."[156]

Invitation card for the Austrian premiere of *Die neue Zeit* (*Modern Times*), March 30, 1936.

It cannot be determined with certainty when the copy of *Die neue Zeit* was transferred to the Reichsfilmarchiv, because documents such as inventory journals, files on acquisitions and lending card indexes have not survived. Several dates may be considered: soon after the Vienna premiere, after the "Anschluss" of Austria to the German Reich on March 13, 1938, after the annexation of the Sudetenland in October 1938 and after the occupation of the rest of Czechoslovakia in March 1939. Nor is there any evidence of whether Goebbels and/or Hitler or members of the Nazi leadership had the film shown to them. The surviving lists of Hitler's film consumption do not provide any information about this, and Goebbels does not mention the Chaplin film in his diaries.

This leaves only an attempt at a chronological approximation. Laurel and Hardy's 1936 feature film *The Bohemian Girl* (James W. Horne, Charles Rogers), which had been finally banned in Germany in mid–June 1936,[157] was archived under archive number 454. The Reichsfilmarchiv owned three more Laurel and Hardy films produced in 1937 and 1938, which Hitler had screened at Obersalzberg in Berchtesgaden between the end of June and the end of November 1938 and which he liked: *Ritter ohne Furcht und Tadel* (*Way Out West*), *Swiss Miss* and *Block-Heads*.[158] The film copies were archived under archive Nos. 4,975, 4,988 and 5,794, respectively[159]; they have not survived. Since *Die neue Zeit* bears archive number 2,857, there is some evidence to suggest that the film was included in the Reichsfilmarchiv's holdings prior to March 13, 1938, assuming that the archive numbers reflect the order in which movies entered the archive.[160] The numerical gap between Nos. 454 and 2,857 is considerable. If the 1937 copy of Laurel and Hardy's *Ritter ohne Furcht und Tadel* entered the Reichsfilmarchiv soon after the German premiere on October 21, 1937,[161] then *Die neue Zeit* would have been part of the Reichsfilmarchiv's holdings for some time before that.[162] In that case, the copy would probably not have come from holdings commandeered in Austria or Czechoslovakia.

In Germany, people had to wait a long time for *Modern Times*. As *Moderne Zeiten*, it was not released in Federal German cinemas until March 1956, more than 20 years after its world premiere.[163] In the GDR, Chaplin fans had to wait even longer. The film premiered on the TV program of DDR2 on December 3, 1980.[164]

9

"Jew" Chaplin "Steals Intellectual Property," 1937

In 1936, Nazi agitation found a new opportunity to attack Chaplin as a plagiarist, and perfidiously expanded on this in 1937. In addition, other news items placed Chaplin in a bad light. Then in November of that year, he became a prominent target of anti–Jewish agitation in the infamous exhibition "The Eternal Jew." At the end of the year, he was even at the center of a film-political "reckoning" with the "Jewish" film of the Weimar Republic.

This chapter explores the following issues:

- the triggers of plagiarism allegations against Chaplin
- the extended agitation with further allegations and their validity
- other Chaplin reports in the German film press
- the exhibition "Der ewige Jude" and the accompanying brochure
- the book *Film-"Kunst," Film-Kohn, Film-Korruption*
- the Nazi film functionary Curt Belling

Films Sonores Tobis vs. Chaplin

The French company Films Sonores Tobis had produced René Clair's successful 1931 film *Es lebe die Freiheit* (*À nous la liberté*). Shortly after *Modern Times'* French premiere on March 13, 1936, it accused Chaplin of copying parts of Clair's film for *Modern Times*. In particular, his factory conveyor-belt scene was claimed to be a copy of Clair's scene in which convicts assemble wooden toy horses on a conveyor belt–like workstation. Because of this, Films Sonores Tobis demanded that Chaplin and United Artists compensate it for a portion of the revenues from *Modern Times* and withdraw all copies of the film from the market. In mid–October 1936, Clair hinted in *Paris-Soir* that he was distancing himself from the legal controversy: "Chaplin is far too important a man, and I admire him far too much, to justify dragging this creative genius into court. Personally, I owe him a great deal. And by the way, should he have borrowed some ideas from me, he would have done me a great honor."[1]

The *Film-Kurier* reacted to this immediately on October 15, 1936, with its article "Plagiarism Charges Against Chaplin":

Chaplin [is said to have] kept a copy of the René Clair film with him for six months during the time he was working on his film in Hollywood. René Clair himself, according to […] reports, [has] refused to be involved in any such plagiarism allegation. The two companies are said to have reached an out-of-court settlement in the meantime, as *Paris-Soir* now reports.[2]

If the alleged plagiarism was supposedly so blatant, why had the German trade journal not called attention to it after the London and Paris premieres of *Modern Times* in the spring of 1936? In the fall of the year, there was no talk of an out-of-court settlement either. However, the *Film-Kurier* did not necessarily have to be aware of this, and possibly *Paris-Soir* reported erroneously that an out-of-court settlement had been reached. In any case, at the end of November 1936, Clair clarified to the German exile newspaper *Pariser Tageszeitung* that he did not want to participate in a Tobis lawsuit "under any circumstances, since he would never stand up against Chaplin as a plaintiff."[3]

"A Brash Clown Steals Intellectual Property"

As the legal controversy could not be settled out of court, Films Sonores Tobis filed suit against Chaplin, the Charles Chaplin Film Corporation and United Artists Corporation in the U.S. Supreme Court New York County on April 23, 1937.[4] At the end of April, Clair reaffirmed his point of view to *Ce Soir* and declared that he had had no contact with Chaplin during the production of *Modern Times*. Moreover, he could not fully understand Tobis' charge.[5] In mid–May, *Der Film* now used the filing of the lawsuit as an opportunity to portray Chaplin as a filmmaker who regularly helped himself to the intellectual property of others. Therefore, the trade journal retrieved irrelevant or outdated plagiarism accusations against Chaplin from 1928 and 1930 and stated: "Chaplin—a Plagiarist. A 'Genius' Took the Easy Way Out." The article stated:

[The Tobis] trial is keeping the French public very concerned. René Clair himself has stated that he has nothing to do with the trial, as Tobis is the sole owner of the authors' rights. Chaplin, for his part, has declared that he has not seen Clair's film. The French public initially saw the lawsuit as a purely commercial move by Tobis. This changed when the *Agence d'information Ciné-graphique* published a report by its Belgian correspondent Carl Vincent about an experience in 1928. On the trip from Naples to Genoa on board the liner *Roma*, he saw in its on-board cinema, together with the Italian director Mario Almirante, a film that the Roman Pittaluga had purchased with a package of very old American films. In this movie, which had undoubtedly been produced [long before Chaplin's *Goldrausch*], […] was the entire cabin scene from *The Gold Rush* from the first gag to the last. In 1930, Jean Sarment took legal action against Chaplin for *Lichter der Großstadt*. […] An unknown against *Goldrausch*, Jean Sarment against *Lichter der Großstadt*, and now Tobis against *Modern Times*. […] We should not be surprised if it gradually becomes apparent how unabashedly a "schnoddriger Clown des international verwaschenen Films" [brash clown of internationally washed-out film] stole the intellectual property of others in order to use it for objectionable business.[6]

So far he had been held in great esteem there and was affectionately called "Charlot." But, in fact, in France, the mood had meanwhile swung against Chaplin. Thus, at the end of May 1937, *La Cinématographie Française* endorsed the accusations of the Films Sonores Tobis in its article "A propos d'un procès. Charlie Chaplin–René Clair" (On a Word: A Trial Charlie Chaplin—René Clair) and commented on them in a satirical way:

Charlie Chaplin likes to pass off other people's ideas as his own. He never had his own ideas, but used what had long since made its way through all the film studios. Charlot stole a sequence of pictures here, a scene there, and an entire theme there. Even cineastic newcomers will easily be able to prove to you that the reputation of the famous mime consists only of praises and has been established much more by clever advertising than by the real affection of the moviegoers. Yes, poor Charlot never had any luck with women and even less with cineastes. The only thing missing from his fame was to be dragged to court. And there, hopefully, they will have a go at him and forbid him from continuing to make films. The poor martyr Charlot is scourged by René Clair. Quite a modern film to cash in on, since the tailwind of French artists can be relied on. For those who do not know (but is there really anyone left who does not have a clue?): Charlot saw *À nous la liberté* with his own eyes, owned a copy of the film and examined it at the editing table as if under [...] an electron microscope, kept studiously quiet about all this and let America have a good laugh at his new film. This is intolerable and must be expiated. But there are still judges in New York.

The following correspondence would be greatly appreciated:

My dear Charlot,

like all cinéasts of the world, I owe you a great deal. You taught me the first steps. No one is closer to you than I am; no one has more respect for you than I do. That is why I sincerely thank you for having so highly appreciated my film *À nous la liberté* and for having continued it with your *Temps modernes*. You alone could dare let our contemporaries devour your sequel to my film. I envy you all the more because you also had financial success with it. But I, my dear Charlot, have the consolation of having been recognized by Hollywood.

Best regards, my dear Charlot, René

To this, our good Charlot might have replied:

My dear René,

thank you for your kind letter. You alone could be so witty. Please believe me that I only unconsciously processed my memories of your film for mine, just as you remembered mine when you made your films. I admit it openly. But I already know that you are too witty to hold a grudge against me for my memories.

Best regards, my dear René, Charlot"[7]

Surprisingly, German trade journals did not react to this.

As the proceedings in the U.S. dragged on, Films Sonores Tobis also sued the defendants in France in 1939.[8] Both lawsuits were settled out of court years later without Chaplin ever admitting to plagiarism.[9] Therefore, it is not true that the action of April 23, 1937, was dismissed on November 19, 1939, as Timothy Lyons has asserted.[10] That judgment concerned the action of Michael L. Kustoff, attorney at law, which he had filed on December 7, 1937, against Chaplin, his production company and United Artists,[11] and which was reported by *The New York Times* the same day the judgment was pronounced.[12] Kustoff had self-published his book *Against Gray Walls* in 1934 about his involuntary commitment to a psychiatric hospital, parts of which Chaplin was alleged to have used for *Modern Times*.

A *Gold Rush Case?*

The following allegations of plagiarism that appeared in the *Lichtbildbühne* in early May 1937 sounded like fabricated propaganda. But French journals had reported about them earlier. The German trade journal did not question any of this and instead made tendentious conclusions.

Even if the article in the French trade journal *Agence d'information Ciné-graphique*, which has been handed down only fragmentarily, could not be found,[13] it is probably authentic. Jean-Paul Coutisson was editor-in-chief of the French trade journal and Carl Vincent, a well-known Belgian film journalist, its correspondent. In 1939, Vincent's new book *Histoire de l'Art Cinématographique* (History of the Art of Cinematography) included a long, appreciative chapter on Chaplin. He highlighted *The Gold Rush*'s impressive cabin-scene complex in which Big Jim and Charlie rescue themselves from the mountain cabin blown half over the abyss and find the gold mine again. In a footnote assigned to this, Vincent described his 1928 on-board cinema screening and shared his inquiry with the Roma shipping company. This had led him to the Turin film company Pittaluga, which had told him no more than that it had bought the short subject in question en bloc with other silent films. That was all he found out about the provenance of the film.[14] However, a film of another production from the time before the release of *The Gold Rush* with exactly these scene elements is not known.

On May 21, 1937, the *Lichtbildbühne* revealed more astonishing details with "3 lawsuits over plagiarism allegations against Chaplin":

> The Paris Tobis has filed a lawsuit over plagiarism allegations against Charlie Chaplin, since various scenes of his last film *Modern Times* are said to have been modeled on the René Clair film *Es lebe die Freiheit!* At the same time, a lawsuit against Chaplin had been submitted by the heirs of a certain Morrisson. Morrisson is said to have made a comedy long before *The Gold Rush*, in which Chaplin's cabin scene was included from the first to the last meter. In addition, the French writer Jean Sarment sued Chaplin for having filmed *Lichter der Großstadt* based on his novella.[15]

But lawsuits about plagiarism committed by Chaplin with *The Gold Rush* are unknown, just as Morrisson and his heirs cannot be identified. If the alleged spelling "Morrisson" is not taken too closely, probably only two persons can be found in the American comedy film: Ernie Morrison, Sr., who appeared in silent films beginning in 1918, and his son Ernie Morrison Jr., born in late 1912, who appeared in numerous children's comedies under the name Sunshine Sammy from the late 1910s to 1926. Evidence that father and son, who incidentally did not die until decades after the *Lichtbildbühne* report in 1971 and 1989, respectively, produced comedies on their own as producers and/or directors long before Chaplin's *The Gold Rush* has also not been found. Nothing else is known and has been published about "Morrisson" and his unnamed heirs. In his book, Vincent confines himself to informing the reader that the *Lichtbildbühne* brought "Morrisson" onto the scene as the creator of the short subject in question. Finally, a report by the Italian director Almirante about the *Roma* screening is not known. He would have had every reason for it if the content of the said short subject had been that spectacular.

All this is doubtful because Chaplin's *The Gold Rush* was an unprecedented success internationally. Most likely, one of the countless moviegoers or critics would have noticed if the ingeniously conceived cabin scene sequence "leading to the happy ending of *The Gold Rush*" had been known before Chaplin's film. Apart from

Vincent, however, no one had related anything about this. It is true that he did not provide his written account until two years after his oral report to the *Agence d'information Cinégraphique*. But this was done in a matter-of-fact tone, which speaks against a deliberately slanderous intention. Apart from that, all details such as title, content, actors, director, production company and country, time of making, copyright and premiere are missing. Might Almirante and Vincent have seen a montage of crowd-pleasing scenes from different films in 1928 and not realized that the cabin scene, or what had been used of it, was from Chaplin's *The Gold Rush* after all? In later years, there were frequently compilations of various Chaplin films that feigned a continuous plot.

Jean Sarment's City Lights *Case*

Unlike the cloak-and-dagger Morrisson heirs, Jean Sarment had actually demanded that Chaplin compensate him over *City Lights*. But nothing more applied in the articles in *Der Film* and the *Lichtbildbühne* of May 15 and 21, 1937, respectively. Sarment had never filed suit against Chaplin, and certainly not in 1930, because Sarment could not have known *City Lights*, the world premiere of which did not take place until 1931. The German film trade journals also concealed from their readers, against their better knowledge, that the German film trade press had already reported on the matter in 1931, which already at that time had come to nothing. It is therefore astonishing that Michael Hanisch, without sources and contrary to the facts, still claimed as late as 1974 that Sarment had sued Chaplin, and that Chaplin's lawyers had argued at trial that *City Lights* bore resemblance only to a work by Charles Dickens.[16]

The following had happened: After the French premiere of *Les lumières de la ville* (*City Lights*) on April 1, 1931, Sarment claimed in his May 2, 1931, letter to Chaplin that the latter had taken parts from his 1920s comedy *Les plus beaux yeux du monde* (The Most Beautiful Eyes in the World) for *City Lights*; in 1925, the play had been performed in the U.S. Before legal steps were taken, Chaplin should explain how he intended to compensate Sarment.[17] Chaplin did not reply. Thereupon Sarment approached both the French Writers' Union and the editor-in-chief of *Comoedia Illustré, journal parisien théâtral, artistique et littéraire*, stating that he had already retained legal counsel. On May 23, 1931, *Comoedia Illustré* speculated whether Chaplin would be prepared to risk a sensational trial.

The *Comoedia Illustré* also referred to an article that another French author had published the day before in the magazine *Nouvelles Littéraires*. The latter had indignantly criticized Chaplin for his behavior during his April 1931 stay in Paris: although intellectual circles had made him known in France, he had not honored any of the well-known French writers with an invitation. Instead, he had dined with Minister Aristide Briand, who decorated him with the medal of the French Legion of Honor on April 27, 1931. Moreover, Chaplin had not responded to the invitation of the French Artists' Association to its annual charity gala, preferring to travel to the Côte d'Azur. Therefore, French artistic circles would rumor that Chaplin had bad manners in private and played the fine fellow only in his films.[18] In late May 1931, Pierre Lazareff defended Chaplin in *Paris-Midi* against Sarment's "ridiculous" accusations. *City Lights*, moreover, bore more resemblance to Charles Dickens' *The Cricket on the Hearth*. In addition, Lazareff gleefully teased, based on the not entirely serious letter of another journalist, that Chaplin's alleged sources for *City Lights* had already taken on inflationary proportions. Searching for any alleged similarities, it would be possible to find them in Victor Hugo's *L'homme qui rit* (The Man Who Laughs), in *Le voile du bonheur* (The Veil of Bliss) by M. Georges Clemenceau or in an old Spanish film influenced by a Vicente Blasco Ibañez novella. It had also been claimed in Czechoslovakia that Chaplin's music for *City Lights* was essentially the work of a young local composer.[19] In fact, the main musical theme of the film revolved around the Spanish composition "La Violetera" by José Padilla. The only thing missing was the accusation that Chaplin's model was everyday life.

In May 1931, the German trade journals reacted immediately after Sarment's accusation became known. The *Film-Kurier* reported that Sarment had taken legal action against Chaplin's film because of "striking likeness" to his play.[20] According to the *Kinematograph*, "Sarment's complaint does not have much chance of success. Chaplin can justifiably plead that the material of *City Lights* was already anticipated by Dickens [...]. Apart from that, Chaplin's film is grounded on a true story that Chaplin had learned about from the American newspapers."[21] The *Lichtbildbühne* had briefly reported that Sarment had asked the French authors' association to file a suit against Chaplin.[22] After Lazareff's *Paris-Midi* article, the *Film-Kurier* had summarized the hullabaloo of plagiarism allegations: "Whom did Chaplin plagiarize now? One must admit that complicating the case makes it significantly easier. By broadening the debate—if it should come to that at all—Sarment's accusation at least becomes less important."[23]

Shortly thereafter, the *Reichsfilmblatt* finally had taken all the wind out of Sarment's sails with Clair's skillful Chaplin defense "Author Chaplin," and, to a certain extent, ruled out the plagiarism affair in the German trade press. Clair had emphasized that Chaplin could not be admired enough and that his genius as a writer was overlooked because of his acting abilities:

There is nothing more that can be said about Chaplin that is not already banal, and yet everything that has been said about him is insufficient. People still do not know that Chaplin is the greatest dramatic writer, the greatest creative innovator of our time. His acting talent has shadowed his poetic genius. Most critics and writers see him as the "genial mime," the "divine clown"—ill-chosen flattery that only belittles his worth. Chaplin is more than just an actor, even more than one of the best actors. There are great actors who are his equal. As a writer, he is unique, and no film writer can compare with him. Chaplin, the actor, is the most famous man in the world. Chaplin, the author, is unrecognized. The audience—that is, the entire world except a few insiders—knows nothing about how a film is made, and the term "author" remains meaningless to the crowd. If Chaplin did not appear personally in his films, hardly one in a hundred of his present-day admirers would know his name! [...] Chaplin fills us with confidence, awakens our passion for cinema. He proves to us that the spirit can master this industry, this technique, these dollar balances! He makes us forget the mechanism of his craft, its puppets, its financiers, its laws and its fronts. We will never be able to express loudly enough our smallness towards this work and our gratitude.[24]

After all, Sarment's attempt had only been a tempest in a teapot, and of course the German film trade journals were aware of their own coverage of May 1931, according to which Clair had praised Chaplin as a unique film pioneer. By remaining silent, the Nazi trade journals imputed an allegedly established copyright infringement to Chaplin.

Another Plagiarism Allegation

On July 10, 1937, *Der Film* poured more fuel into the copyright fire with its front page story "Plagiarist Chaplin Remains True to Himself" and added "and Continues to Steal" in the headline of this article. The journal's Paris editors combined the rumor about Chaplin's next film project with an attack against him:

> In his next film, after Napoleon's death on St. Helena, his double will appear in Europe. [...]. Léon Treich points out in his article "An idea of Charlie Chaplin?" that already in 1923 the French writer Paul Vimereu [in his novel] *Caesar on the Island of Pan* (*César dans l'île de Pan*) [treated the] idea of the Napoleonic double. [...] Chaplin thus remains true to himself and his [dishonest] methods. We have already reported in a previous issue how this "genius" took the easy way out. Where there cannot be anything of one's own, one helps oneself generously from others.[25]

Chaplin's Napoleon plans were long obsolete, however, and the article contains hardly any traceable details. Indeed, the French journalist and author Léon Treich contributed to various newspapers and magazines. But where to start the search, if all references are missing, where and when he is supposed to have commented on an alleged Napoleon plan of Chaplin? Therefore, there is some reason to assume that *Der Film*'s innuendos were solely intended to reinforce Chaplin's reputation as a plagiarist. But then it is almost surprising that the trade journals did not also revive Hans Buchner and Max Jungnickel's allegations of plagiarism from 1927 and early 1931, respectively (see Chapter 3).

Chaplin and the Spanish Civil War

A month before the latest accusations of the German film trade journals, the Swiss *National-Zeitung* had reported on "Hollywood and Spain" on April 26, 1937. The article, which the Hauptarchiv der NSDAP took to its Chaplin file, reproduced a report from Spain by the U.S. trade journal *Hollywood Reporter* that the Catalan government had sent Chaplin a thank-you telegram "for his declaration of sympathy for Spain's republican cause." Nationalist Spain, on the other hand, would have banned the importation of U.S. films by Chaplin, James Cagney, Paul Muni, the Marx Brothers, Wallace Beery and Douglas Fairbanks. Chaplin's secretary denied ever receiving such a telegram.[26] Moreover, according to the Spanish director Luis Buñuel, Chaplin had refused to "sign an appeal in support of the Spanish Republic."[27]

Marlene Dietrich also came into play in connection with sympathy rallies for Spanish Republicans. In the U.S., the former Ufa actress had become an internationally celebrated star and remained popular in the Third Reich as well. In 1936, Dietrich's U.S. comedy *Sehnsucht (Desire)*, directed by Frank Borzage, had enjoyed a successful run in Germany. Because Goebbels tried to persuade Dietrich to return to Germany, at the end of 1936, the press had been instructed to refrain from attacks on certain German actors living abroad, "since they might also perform in Germany again someday."[28] But when it was reported in 1937 that Dietrich was campaigning for the Spanish Republicans in the Spanish Civil War, demanding "aid for the Red troops" and sharply criticizing Franco's dictatorship, the actress gradually attracted the Nazis' hostility. In June 1937, the *Völkischer Beobachter* commented in "Who has a *Sehnsucht* for Marlene?" Dietrich's undesirable political involvement and took a side blow at Chaplin who, according to the Basel *National-Zeitung*, was also supposed to have supported "red" Spanish troops against the dictatorship of the Spanish Generalissimo Francisco Franco: "In her anger [Marlene] published sharp statements against Franco's government and sent enthusiastic greetings to the 'Republican heroes.' Her partners on this homage address were the Jewish Clown Charlie Chaplin, Douglas Fairbanks and Wallace Beery. [...] Nevertheless, last month her film *Sehnsucht* was re-released [...]. But under the present circumstances, who still has *Sehnsucht* for Marlene?"[29]

Chaplin denied it. But this was no longer an issue for the Nazi press, so that his assumed engagement persisted. Dietrich, on the other hand, received different treatment. On November 9, 1937, the German press was instructed not to report on her until further notice.[30] Apparently, both *Der Film* and *Film-Kurier* were then permitted to write something about Dietrich after all, because this seemed opportune to Nazi propaganda. For ten days after the press instruction, the two trade journals related that the Marlene Dietrich rumors were unfounded. These were about her intention to apply for U.S. citizenship and of having "declared herself in favor of Red Spain" through appeals and monetary donations.[31] Dietrich finally became the Nazis' persona non grata when she obtained U.S. citizenship on June 9, 1939.

The Exhibition "Der ewige Jude"

The NSDAP had planned to fight its main enemies with bold, crude propaganda in a cycle of three large-scale "Wander-Schandausstellungen" (Touring Exhibitions of Shame). "Weltfeind Nr. 1—Der Bolschewismus" (International Enemy No. 1—Bolshevism) aka "The Great Anti-Bolshevik Show" and "Entartete Kunst" (Degenerate Art) were followed by the infamous exhibition "Der ewige Jude" (The Eternal Jew) in the halls of the library building of the Munich Deutsches Museum. Announced in February of that year, it was intended to serve "educational purposes" and to prove the necessity of the Nuremberg Race Laws, with documents and pictures from the collection of Germany's "Anti-Semite No. 1" Julius Streicher.[32] Streicher had been preparing the ground for years with his diatribe *Der Stürmer* and his Stürmer-Verlag, in which Elvira Bauer's "picture book for young and old" *Trau keinem Fuchs auf grüner Heid und keinem Jud bei seinem Eid* (Do Not Trust a Fox on Green Heath or a Jew in His Oath) was published in 1936 with the poem "Das ist der Streicher" (That Is Streicher), in which the hatemonger and his anti–Judaism were glorified.[33] In 1938 and 1940, the publishing house produced Ernst Hiemer's infamous children's books *Der Giftpilz* (The Poisonous Mushroom), with numerous color illustrations by Fips (Philipp Rupprecht), and *Der Pudelmopsdackelpinscher und andere besinnliche Erzählungen* (The Poodle-Pug-Dachshund-Pinscher and Other Contemplative Tales), which were intended to swear "Pimpfe und Jungmädel" and the "Deutsches Jungvolk" (boys and girls of the Hitler Youth's junior section, 10 up to 14 years old and 14 up to 18 years old, respectively) to anti–Semitism.

The outrageous exhibition stirred up fear and envy among the visitors in order to turn them into hatred, which was supposed to suppress compassion for the harassed Jews. Chaplin, the supposed Jew, was specifically singled out and attacked. In 1940, a feature-length "documentary" full of anti–Semitic propaganda was released under the same title, again targeting Chaplin (see Chapter 13). The outdoor advertising for the exhibition, the preparation of which was helped by the Nazi ideologist Alfred Rosenberg, was designed in a particularly aggressive manner in Munich, as could be gleaned from the *Deutschlandberichte der Sozialdemokratischen Partei Deutschlands* published in exile in Prague: "Large yellow posters scream in the streets, and everywhere the face of the eternal Jew can be seen. The huge distorted image of the Jew on the roof of the German Museum is illuminated at night with spotlights."[34]

The exhibition was opened on the afternoon of November 8, 1937, in the museum's crowded Congress Hall by Goebbels and by Streicher, who "deliver[ed] a comprehensive speech in which he let the Jew himself have his say about his claims to world domination."[35] Especially for "Der ewige Jude," Walter Böttcher, director of the Gaufilmstelle (Gau Film Organization) München-Oberbayern, had produced the 20-minute film *Juden spielen sich selbst* (Jews Playing Themselves) about the "whole pernicious effect of Jewish film contamination" for the exhibition. Initially, this film was

Hans Diebow, "Der ewige Jude," front cover of exhibition brochure with poster motif, 1937, art by Horst Schlüter (Hans Stalüter).

screened every half hour, but against Goebbels' ban; he qualified it as a "bad propaganda film."[36] It was therefore replaced with the 36-minute film *Juden ohne Maske*, which Walter Böttcher and Leo von der Schmiede had produced on behalf of the Reichspropagandaleitung (Main Film Office of the Reich Propaganda Directorate) of the NSDAP, Amtsleitung Film, as a "profile of Jewish filmmaking of the system era […] from 17 of the best-known silent and sound films […] with a preface" to show "the devastating role of the Jews in the earlier filmmaking of Germany."[37] According to a report by the *Lichtbildbühne*, the film, which was also shown at events of the NSDAP Gaufilmstellen,[38] drew "the strongest attendance."[39] In addition, Kurt Mühlhardt gave a photo lecture based on film examples from the categories of "morally corrupting enlightenment genre," "criminal film," "class incitement," "military mockery," as well as "stupid and jaded tasteless so-called entertainment."[40] Chaplin does not seem to have been featured in either the film or the photo lecture.

The exhibition included an overview of "the racial composition of the Jewish people," a film about "the process of slaughtering a cow with its unparalleled cruelty and disgusting brutality," and "information" about the film industry. According to the figures prepared by the doyen of German film statistics, Alexander Jason, it had been "more than 90% in Jewish hands" in the Weimar Republic and had thus "poisoned the [German] national soul." Among the exhibits in the very first room was a photograph of Chaplin, enlarged to two meters, in which he can be seen as a smiling private man with folded arms in front of a background that has been retouched away. In the lower left area of the photograph is emblazoned the question "An Englishman?" and to the right of it, in a circle, the answer "No, a Jew." Thus, Chaplin was the poster boy of Jewish prototypes. The "immense photograph" of Chaplin also attracted particular attention in the foreign press.[41]

Chaplin poster from the exhibition "Der ewige Jude," 1937: "Ein Engländer? Nein, ein Jude" (An Englishman? No, a Jew).

The physical contrast between Jews and the supposedly always tall, wiry, blond and belligerent Aryans as "Herrenmenschen" was not matched by some top members of the Nazi leadership itself. In February 1936, a cartoon from *The Labor Front* aptly summed this up in allusion to Hitler's Nuremberg Rally speech of September 14, 1935, in which he had outlined the characteristics of the Hitler Youth as follows: "Flink wie Windhunde, zäh wie Leder und hart wie Kruppstahl" [Swift as greyhounds, tough as leather, and hard as Krupp steel]. Hitler, in professorial regalia, gave lessons from his book *Mein Kampf* to German soldiers along the lines of "The Fuehrer is Germany's greatest Teacher" and presented a diagram. On it, the Aryans are "tall like Goebbels," "well-trained like Göring," "blond like Hess" and "heroic like himself." But the diminutive Goebbels appears like a chimpanzee with arms hanging down long and mouth wide open, while the feisty Goering is about to burst out of his over-decorated uniform, Hess catches the eye with a shock of black hair, and last but not least, Hitler does not remotely resemble a hero.[42] In 1942, anti-fascist Jewish-Austrian Walter Trier from Prague[43] took this up for the British pamphlet *Nazi-German in 22 Lessons* in Lesson 17, "The Aryan Type," which was limited to Hitler, Goering and Goebbels.[44] The same year, Trier's cartoon "Das ist der Weg" (The Right Formula) in the London exile magazine *Die Zeitung* presented how Nazi (and other) war criminals might be brought to justice.[45]

LESSON 17

ARYAN TYPE

(Der arische Typus)

Blond like Hitler ; slim like Göring ; tall like Goebbels.

Lesson 17 Aryan Type: "Blonde like Hitler; slim like Göring; tall like Goebbels," cartoon by Walter Trier, 1942.

"Das ist der Weg" (The Right Formula), cartoon by Walter Trier, in *Die Zeitung* (London) 281, July 24, 1942, 3.

By the end of 1937, the exhibition had had 320,000 visitors.[46] It was prolonged until the end of January 1938, and visitor numbers climbed to over 410,000.[47] After the annexation of Austria, "The Eternal Jew" was also shown in Vienna and even made its way into the Berlin German Reichstag in November 1938,[48] which *Der Angriff* proudly reported.[49] The heavy rush of visitors, however, was controlled by the Nazis, as the *Deutschlandberichte der Sozialdemokratischen Partei Deutschlands* pointed out in 1938: visiting the repulsively designed, perfidious exhibition with its suggestive effect was apparently not only voluntary:

> The entrance fee is 50 [Pfennigs], for members of the DAF [German Labor Front] 35 [Pfennigs]. The tickets were placed in the pay envelopes of the major Munich employers. The ticket price was deducted from the wages. All state and municipal employers enforced ticket sales in the same way. […] The exhibition itself is arranged with the greatest sophistication and does not remain without impression on the visitors. In the first room one sees, among other things, large models of body parts, for example, the Jewish eye, almond-shaped with a piercing look, the Jewish nose, the Jewish mouth, the lips, etc., then the most diverse racial types. There are […]two-meter photographs of Chaplin, etc., everything in the most repulsive form. […] In addition to pictures, film posters, etc., one sees […] probably the most effective piece of agitation in the exhibition. A film that no one can defend and that, in its kitschiness, has never been recognized by serious people. It runs here as proof of Jewish depravity. At the end of the film, Rosenberg appears on the screen. He says: "You are appalled by this film. Yes, it is particularly bad, but this is the one we wanted to show you […]." […] Truth and lie are coupled in such a sophisticated way that the lie must seem like truth. My companion, who had never dealt with politics before, asked me what I objected to and whether all this was not really convincing. I did not know how to explain the hoax to her, where to tackle the lie. You get the feeling that all the people running into the exhibition cannot form an opinion of their own. You can feel the lie eating its way into their hearts as the truth, because they do not know the truth and therefore cannot recognize the lie. […] In any case, I could not explain the truth to my companion either. I was too weak for it.[50]

The exile Ukraine magazine *Jüdische Revue* described the exhibition as a "screeching […] show of hatred" that "prostitutes itself to helpless rage and at best comes up with the destruction of life and existence."[51]

The Brochure Der ewige Jude

The brochure *Der ewige Jude* with many illustrations was sold at the price of one reichsmark. Its author was art historian Dr. Hans Diebow (1896–1975), a NSDAP member since May 1, 1933, who had been editor of the *Illustrierte Zeitung* and then the *Völkischer Beobachter* since the 1920s. As early as 1924, he had published *Die Rassenfrage, Rassenkunde, Vererbungslehre und Rassenhygiene* (The Race Question, Racial Science, Heredity and Racial Hygiene). This was followed in 1930 by biographies of Gregor Strasser, Hitler and Mussolini.[52] The 1932 booklet *Deutscher! So sehen Deine Führer aus* portrayed politicians fought by the Nazis in a similarly disparaging manner as the Goebbels diatribes *Das Buch Isidor* und *Knorke!* from 1928 and 1929, respectively.[53]

Diebow's brochure is one of the most evil Nazi diatribes. The cover featured a depiction of an Orthodox Jew in a caftan with coins in his right hand, a whip in his left, and the Bolshevik Soviet Union under his left arm. This suggested Jewish influence, oppression, expansion and greed for money at the expense of others. Like von Leers in *Juden sehen Dich an*, Diebow strings together many particularly hated Jews as examples of "depravity and nefariousness," calling Justizrat Dr. Werthauer a "fraud from the East," Albert Einstein one of "the three agitators of satanic Germanophobia," and Goebbels' particular enemy Dr. Bernhard Weiß "Isidor."[54] And, as with von Leers, there were also Jews who are not Jews. At the end of his brochure, Diebow paid homage to the Nazi anti–Semitic laws as a historical boon, since "Germany […] was the first country in the world to legislate on the Jewish issue" and to ensure that a "clean separation of the Jewish foreign people was carried out" so that the Jews in Germany remained culturally amongst themselves.[55]

Chaplin was presented twice in the brochure: with the exhibition photo, but here with a background and no caption, and in a scene from *The Kid* with Jackie Coogan. Both images featured Diebow's smear comments about Chaplin being a Jew and Coogan being a "Jew boy," the latter with the birth name "Cohen" from Bessarabia. In fact, Coogan was born in Los Angeles. About Chaplin, Diebow reproduced an excerpt from the last part of Jim Tully's series of articles about Chaplin in the *Prager Tagblatt* of May 11, 1927.[56] Diebow's inflammatory diatribe reads:

Charlie Chaplin emigrated to America (his mother was *née* Thonstein) and in his wake the film child Jackie Coogan (Jacob Cohen). Both came from Eastern Europe. With their maudlin comedy, they pulled at the heartstrings of the simple natured and at the same time ridiculed poverty. The waddling gaits of the flat-footed, clumsy, miserably poor and yet infinitely selfless, noble man with the laughably large shoes was a sensation to gentile eyes. Flat-footed but noble—that is the formula with which Charlie Chaplin can be summed up.

Exhibition catalog *Der ewige Jude*, p. 67: Chaplin and Jackie Coogan in a scene from *The Kid* (1923) (author's collection).

The allegations that Chaplin's mother was *née* Thonstein had emerged in the Viennese Jewish weekly *Die neue Welt* in October 1928, and Goebbels had brought up Coogan's alleged birth name of Cohn as early as the fall of 1924 (see Chapters 1 and 4). Commenting on the photograph of Chaplin as a private citizen, Diebow quoted Rosenberg's June 1927 *Weltkampf* article "Chaplin in Gethsemane":

> The "great philosopher" Charlie Chaplin, the laughing Bajazzo, to whom crying is closer, a clown, yet actually a world-wiser—that was the daily hymn of praise, translated from Jewish into all the newspaper languages of the world. "The mystery of a high intelligence, combined with wildness, fascinated him"—"Like other geniuses, Charlie cannot write orthographically correctly, but he has a large, beautiful vocabulary and has an excellent command of the English language. He rarely mispronounces anything." "I disagreed with Charlie's style of storytelling, though I must say he succeeds at it. His stories are inherently vulgar, only his genius for facial expression and understanding of life elevate them to a higher level."[57]

Chaplin and Jackie Coogan section of the exhibition catalogue *Der ewige Jude*, p. 68.

Diebow's brochure quickly received a circulation of over 100,000 copies and was thus widely distributed. However, the circulation was modest compared to the books by Rosenberg and especially Hitler. They were distributed on a large scale by state control in the Third Reich and were examples of profiteering and enrichment of Nazi bigwigs, among whom Goebbels and Goering were especially grasping. Rosenberg's *Der Mythus des 20. Jahrhunderts* had sold 3000 copies in 1930, the year it was first published; by August 1933, 17,000 copies had been sold, and by 1944, it had totaled some 1.3 million units in 200 individual editions.[58] Hitler's "Book of the Germans" eclipsed Rosenberg's book by far. According to the Honorarbuch (Royalty Book) of the Eher publishing house, only 3015 copies of *Mein Kampf*, published in two parts in

1925 and 1926, had been sold by 1928.[59] In October 1932, a publisher's advertisement stated that sales of the complete one-volume edition had climbed to 200,000. At that time, *Der Angriff* had demanded: "[It] must be joined by millions!," so that each of the "14 million National Socialists" called it his own.[60] This rapid increase in circulation, however, could only be implemented by dictatorial means after Hitler's takeover, and that alone made Hitler a multi-millionaire, who, for example, had the residence on the Obersalzberg built for himself at state expense, not to mention the lavish new Alte Reichskanzlei. By January 1933, a good 241,000 copies of the popular edition of *Mein Kampf* had been sold; by January 1933, the seventeenth edition had been produced. In December 1934, the *Pariser Tageblatt* had already described Hitler as a millionaire.[61] The number of copies sold had jumped to three million in 1937[62] and reached almost seven and a half million with the 621st-625th edition of 1941. With the 1027th-1031st edition of 1944, the last documented one, the number of copies sold of the Volksausgabe had increased to 12.45 million. In addition, there were gift and field editions as well as special editions for bridal couples as a "gift from the Fuehrer" for their marriages, which the German city councils had to purchase for their registry offices, but received only small purchases discount from Eher-Verlag in return.[63] From these sales, Hitler is said to have earned a fee of 15 million reichsmark, of which he had had about 8.5 million reichsmark paid out.[64]

Film-"Kunst," Film-Kohn, Film-Korruption

Christmas 1937 saw the publication of the infamous book *Film-"Kunst," Film-Kohn, Film-Korruption. Ein Streifzug durch vier Filmjahrzehnte* (A Foray Through Four Decades of Film) which followed on seamlessly from the exhibition

Carl Neumann, co-author of *Film-"Kunst," Film-Kohn, Film-Korruption*, 1937.

Curt Belling, co-author of *Film-"Kunst," Film-Kohn, Film-Korruption*, 1937.

"Der ewige Jude"[65] and was, among others, promoted at the box office.[66] "Film-Kohn" is the Nazi collective term for Jews from the film industry that was employed for name polemics, because "Kohn" was the Jewish surname "with the strongest anti–Semitic charge."[67]

It was written by Hans-Walther Betz, then co–chief editor of the trade journal *Der Film*, and the Nazi film functionaries Carl Neumann and Curt Belling. Since 1933, Neumann had headed the Reichsamtsleitung Film, which was affiliated within the Munich Reichsleitung as a party department in the Reichspropagandaleitung der NSDAP and was officially independent of the Reichsministerium für Volksaufklärung und Propaganda.[68] Belling was the Hauptstellenleiter (Head of Central Office) of the Reichsamtsleitung Film. Both disseminated the Nazi film policy into the film press. In 1936, Belling had proudly referred to the Reichsamtsleitung Film as a "command bridge for the ideological education of the German people through film." With the Reichsvereinigung Deutscher Lichtspielstellen e.V., founded in early November 1933, it operated 32 Gaufilmstellen, 771 district and more than 22,000 local groups.[69] Twenty-five thousand employees maintained a virtually party-owned network of traveling cinemas with 350 NSDAP sound film trucks, bringing films to even the most remote parts of Germany. The aim was the Nazi indoctrination of the population, as the tasks of the Gaufilmstellen were described in 1937: "[They] have, first and foremost, to carry out educational propaganda. They were created for this purpose. We take into account the need for entertainment in our events only to the extent that it is expedient and necessary to lighten up an otherwise perhaps too matter-of-fact and instructive subject."[70] By mid–1937, Belling triumphantly reported: "Over 100 million Germans at party film events."[71] At the end of November 1938, *Der neue Film* ran the headline: "Non-stop screenings even in the smallest village."[72]

Film-"Kunst," Film-Kohn, Film-Korruption, **front cover of the hardback edition, 1937.**

Tonfilmwagen der Gaufilmstelle (sound movie vehicles of the Gau movie bodies), February 1937.

Gaufilmstelle barn screening, February 1937.

In general, *Film-"Kunst," Film-Kohn, Film-Korruption* is notable for its martial language, which runs from beginning to end. Already the introduction of the "book of experiences in the struggle for good German film" is a telling example, with catchwords such as "harshness of practical confrontation," "decisive attack on lack of culture and mismanagement" and "reckoning with the Jewish marauders of a [frightening] film past." It is dedicated "to the unknown soldier of true cinematography who, yesterday as today, quietly and joyfully does his duty."[73] According to the *Lichtbildbühne*, the book contrasted the "misery of the Jewish economy" with an "unshakable confidence in victory" and the "commitment of the pioneers."[74] Thus Neumann also reported on his "personal experiences in the struggle for German film."[75] For their reckoning in the Nazi sense, the authors rolled up the film era of the Weimar Republic and defamed numerous artists and intellectuals, such as non–Jewish Chaplin admirer Hans Siemsen, who had already fled Germany in 1933. They also considered him a Jew,[76] as Rudolf Jordan had done in 1926 in *Der Weltkampf*.

The cover picture evoked a sultry, lascivious atmosphere of wickedness with dubious-looking people, bare-breasted ladies and the obese actor Kurt Ehrlich on the phone with a big cigar in his mouth. This image was regarded by the authors as a symbol of parasitic film bosses and general managers, who were supposed to have quickly made money and influence by dubious means and at the expense of others. That is why "Mr. Kohn" was to be "unmasked" in the first main section of the book as a "der Mann mit der Zigarre" (man with a cigar) and "Seelenfänger des 20 Jahrhunderts" (soul catcher of the 20th century) who worked only with "bluff, nothing but bluff." For this purpose, the book was advertised with a picture plate of men smoking big cigars.[77] Chaplin was also depicted on this plate. His picture was certainly taken out of context: It showed him not as a rich film boss, but as Charlie the Tramp from *City Lights*, when he was partying at night with the drunken millionaire in a dance hall and had been dressed in an elegant evening suit by his host for that reason.[78] The authors combined this visual attack with a smear comment: "The 'Ideendieb' and 'maßlos überschätzter' (thief of intellectual property and vastly overrated) clown Charlie Chaplin was the cinematic incarnation of the 'persecuted, threatened and helpless Jewish innocence' who knew how to save himself so wittily from the deserved beating with tricks and shiftiness. What this jokester later performed in a trickier and more cleverly conceived way was the comedy of the man who fell off the ladder."[79] Given the adoring Chaplin contributions of Belling and Betz in the Weimar Republic, this was a 180-degree turn (see Chapters 3 and 4). In the section "And this is what Their Films Looked like," Chaplin was also specifically accused of money-grubbing, because he had sold his film *City Lights* in Germany "for an incredibly high sum."[80] The authors called the former Südfilm AG boss Goldschmid the "Jewish bankrupt par excellence," who was preparing for insolvency "systematically."[81]

Nazi reviews praised *Film-"Kunst," Film-Kohn. Film-Korruption* as a "sensational book" that every "film enthusiast [...] will reach for again and again."[82] *Lichtbildbühne's* editor-in-chief lauded the "courageous way [that the convincing and captivating book] approaches things," while the *Film-Kurier* predicted that it would "open the eyes of broad circles to what it once looked like in German film, and thus effectively fulfill its purpose of cultural-political enlightenment."[83] For *Der Film*, it was "a gripping lesson in cultural-political visual instruction" that would develop into the "Christmas book of film in general" through its "uncompromising openness."[84]

In the wake of the jubilant reviews, the Reichsstelle zur Förderung des deutschen Schrifttums (Reich Office for the Promotion of German Literature) presented its "Gutachten für Verleger" (Expert Opinion for Publishers) on Film-"Kunst," Film-Kohn. Film-Korruption in late January 1938. The expert opinion, which was also published for promotional purposes, may have called for even more decisive action than the authors and concluded as follows:

Der Mann mit der Zigarre

Ernst Lubitsch

Fritz Kortner-Kohn

Otto Wallburg-Wasserzug

E. A. Dupont

Kurt Ehrlich

Charlie Chaplin

The book must be made available to all filmmakers and, moreover, to all Volksgenossen [National Comrades]. Even the last of those who somehow found pleasure in Jewish art and Jewish "artists" must be taught that this kind of art has nothing in common with

"Der Mann mit der Zigarre" (The Man with the Cigar), bookplate from *Film-"Kunst," Film-Kohn, Film-Korruption*, 1937.

German film. It was absolutely necessary to demonstrate the decline of film during the system era with all clarity. We should not always be content with merely bowing to the past. The constructive strengths and paths for the future shaping of German film should also be highlighted at times.[85]

Digression on Curt Belling

The extent to which German moviegoers longed for the cinematic art from the period of the alleged "decline of film during the system era" and wanted to "bow to this past" free from the shackles of Nazi film policy became apparent after the end of World War II. Chaplin regained in all four occupation zones, and subsequently in both German states, the artistic recognition that had been widely paid to him during the Weimar Republic. Thus, among the numerous reactions to the re-screening of

Lichter der Großstadt in early February 1951 at Berlin's Marmorhaus was an enthusiastic review in the film trade journal *Filmblätter*:

> Charlie Chaplin, the genius among the fun makers of the cinema, shows himself here in per-
> haps his finest work. [...] Chaplin's performance is as ravishing as his sense of style as direc-
> tor, with which he cast his film. [...] It is truly amazing how much comedy, jokes, humanity,
> spirit and truth have been crammed into an hour and a half of film! Incredible indeed! Every-
> one should see this splendid film, for we all need such cheerful, contemplative lessons.

An anonymous postscript to this review read: "The pantomime Chaplin plays one
'classic' grotesque scene after another. But in between he gives his philosophi-
cal visual lessons. [A film that] encourages us: [...] There are films that are so ingeniously and so vitally constructed that they never fail to fascinate, every day and
every year anew."[86]

Actually, among the many other enthusiastic 1951 reviews of *Lichter der
Großstadt*, the *Filmblätter* review did not need to be singled out. Yet, it is notewor-
thy that it dates from a time when Abel, a "journalist and specialist writer" living
in Bonn, was the German correspondent of the *Filmblätter*. Abel was the pseudonym of Belling, who had still been agitating against Chaplin until April 1939 (see
Chapter 10).[87] The *Lichter der Großstadt* review, signed HDW, cannot be attributed to
him with certainty. His activity in the German film press, however, is both notewor-
thy and significant. A diehard Nazi of Belling's ilk apparently had no trouble finding a home at a trade journal that welcomed what the former Nazi film officer had
relentlessly and disparagingly fought against. After the beginning of World War II,
he had been Sonderführer (Special Leader) for the soldiers "in occupied enemy territory, in the air bases and in the war harbors." In this function, he had organized
film screenings to the remotest corners until the fall of 1940 according to the motto
"The sound film trucks of the propaganda units accompany the troops."[88] Belling's
metamorphosis from Saul to Paul may have been little more than adapting to the
new political conditions—as so many other Nazis had done in postwar Germany.
Nevertheless, *Filmblätter* editor-in-chief Robert G. Scheuer knew in late summer
1951 who Abel was. Fritz Podehl, head of the Freiwillige Selbstkontrolle der Filmwirtschaft (Voluntary Self-Regulation Body of the Film Industry), known as FSK,
had informed Scheuer at the end of August 1951: "This 'guardian of the Holy Grail' of
democracy [Abel ...] is none other than the former Hauptstellenleiter of the NSDAP
Reichspropagandaleitung, Film Department, whose inflammatory and anti–Semitic
books and writings are still vividly remembered by all people in the film business."[89]
Scheuer did not part company with Belling after the receipt of Podehl's letter. The
cooperation with Belling lasted at least until June 1952.[90]

10

The Run-up
to *The Great Dictator*,
1938–39

After the slanderous attacks on Chaplin in 1937, the plan for his upcoming Hitler satire caused uproar.

Even in the planning stage, beginning in the spring of 1938, there was a great response to this explosive project. In its context, Chaplin was compared to Hitler. This was followed in 1939 by another Nazi diatribe, which also targeted Chaplin. The narrow-minded Nazis did not have a sense of humor, and they were not open to criticism. Thus, they attacked alleged Germanophobe films from abroad, like Chaplin's *The Great Dictator*. This was not limited to agitation in the German film press against the "Film-Jew" with his "true" name Tonstein, who was temporarily regarded abroad as a "Savior." If German diplomats had tried to prevent the screening of *Shoulder Arms* in the 1920s, they now undertook to prevent Chaplin's project from the outset. At this time, the inhuman Nazi campaign against German Jews escalated, and the successes of Hitler's expansionist policies diminished the marketing chances for Chaplin's upcoming film in Europe. Then, in 1939, another Nazi diatribe appeared, attacking Chaplin again.

This chapter therefore deals with:

- the Nazi fight against German Jews in the context of the pogroms in November 1938
- Chaplin's film plan and its coming to the public's attention
- Chaplin's allegedly true Jewish name in the Third Reich and in the U.S.
- journalistic comparisons of Chaplin and Hitler
- the Nazi fight against Germanophobe agitation films
- the Nazi sense of humor
- the Nazi fight against Chaplin's planned film in the press and through diplomatic channels
- the fight against the film project in the U.S. and Great Britain
- Chaplin's reaction to the hostility and changing sales opportunities
- Diebow's diatribe *Die Juden in USA*

Forced Fight Against the German Jews

In 1938, in the charged anti–Jewish atmosphere, Hitler's regime continued to deprive the Jews of their rights with a plethora of laws and decrees. The subject index of the 1938 *Reichsgesetzblatt* included 44 new positions under the keyword "Jews," which also applied to annexed Austria and occupied territories such as the Sudetenland. Similarly extensive were the positions in the *Reichsgesetzblatt* in 1939 and 1940.[1] Thus, from July to October 1938, the licenses of doctors, lawyers and notaries of Jewish origin were revoked. Young academics of Jewish origin were no longer entitled to be educated for these professions.[2]

The assault by the Polish-Jewish Herschel Grynszpan on November 7, 1938, in the German Embassy in Paris on the Legation Secretary Ernst Eduard vom Rath was used by the Nazi regime as a pretext for pogroms against the Jewish population in the night from November 9 to 10, 1938. Throughout Germany, SA henchmen destroyed synagogues, Jewish stores, institutions and homes. As Beauftragter für den Vierjahresplan (Officer for the Four-Year Plan), Göring imposed the economic damage caused by the SA hordes onto the victims of the state terror through the "Verordnung über eine Sühneleistung der Juden deutscher Staatsangehörigkeit" (Decree on Reparation Payment by the Jews of German Nationality) of November 12, 1938: one billion reichsmark, to be paid to the German Reich, because the pogroms were concealed as a "spontaneous discharge of righteous popular anger against the Jews."[3] The order was the beginning of a series of various "atonement payments." Owners of Jewish stores and apartments also had to immediately repair the damage to the streetscape caused during the November pogroms at their own expense.[4]

During the course of the year, cinema operators had already denied access to Jewish citizens on several occasions.[5] On November 12, 1938, the Präsident der Reichskulturkammer (President of the Reich Chamber of Culture) ordered an official ban on cinema attendance for Jews.[6] Through his order of December 3, 1938, Reichsführer SS and Chef der Deutschen Polizei (Commander of the German Police) Heinrich Himmler banned them from driving motor vehicles of any kind, because they did not "to belong to the National Socialist traffic community."[7] From the beginning of 1939, Jews were then prohibited from operating retail and mail order businesses and from running independent craft businesses.[8] In March 1939, Jews were deleted from specialized address books altogether and recorded in residents' address books only in a separate section.[9]

In addition to this, the film *Juden ohne Maske*, which was constantly shown at the exhibition "Der ewige Jude," was used during "a new wave of rallies."[10] In 1939 came the publication of an expanded new edition of Hermann Esser's 1927 book *Die jüdische Weltpest*, which also dealt coarsely with the persecution of Jews. When the U.S. tried to influence South American states to facilitate immigration of Jews from Germany because of increased immigration numbers, at the end of November 1938, the Roman fascist newspaper *Giornale d'Italia* cynically suggested that "the great democracies [should] themselves open their doors and repopulate their depopulated territories with Hebrews." For *Der Angriff*, this came just in time, and it headlined:

"No one wants the Jews. Why does not the ever so compassionate America take them itself?"[11] The U.S. and other countries should prove the truth of this cynical statement. A prominent example is the odyssey of the passenger liner *St. Louis* of the German shipping company HAPAG in late spring–early summer 1939 with over 900 German-Jewish refugees. They had paid for their passage from Hamburg to Havana and were nevertheless not permitted to disembark there by the Cuban authorities, despite having been granted entry visas. Although ordered by his shipping company to return to Germany, the captain tried in vain to let the refugees go ashore in Miami and Canada, one after the other. Only at literally the last second, Belgium, France, Great Britain and the Netherlands each agreed to grant political asylum to a share of the passengers.[12]

Chaplin Plans

Since the early 1936 premiere of *Modern Times*, Chaplin had had difficulty finding material for his next film.[13] He seemed to have overcome them when the *Daily Variety* announced his first dialogue film on April 27, 1938, for the 1938–39 season: "New sound equipment was recently installed by RCA at the Chaplin studio. [...] Konrad Bercovici has been with Chaplin on several trips to Carmel and likely the writers' original story, based on the life of a musician, will be the comedian's choice for his dramatic talker."[14] Nothing more was heard until mid–October. But then Chaplin himself approached the press with a surprise that contained political dynamite. His next film, in which he himself would speak, would not be about a musician, but would be a satire on Hitler![15] Bercovici's involvement in this led to a controversy with Chaplin that resulted in a copyright lawsuit in 1941 (see Chapter 13).

Chaplin had been concerned with Hitler for some time before this announcement, possibly as early as 1932, if one follows Chaplin's statements in the Bercovici lawsuit, or in 1933, when the *Film-Kurier* reacted furiously to the rumor that Chaplin was planning an anti–Hitler film. Around that time, Cornelius Vanderbilt had sent him a series of postcards featuring Hitler in various arranged and melodramatic orator poses, which had been distributed for propaganda purposes since August 1927 and had still "frequently aroused amusement" in the Weimar Republic.[16] Chaplin wrote about this in his autobiography:

> [Hitler's] face was obscenely comic—a bad imitation of me, with its absurd moustache, unruly, stringy hair and disgusting, thin, little mouth. I could not take Hitler seriously. Each postcard showed a different posture of him: one with his hands claw-like haranguing the crowds, another with one arm up and the other down, like a cricketer about to bowl, and another with hands clenched in front of him as though lifting an imaginary dumb-bell. The salute with the hand thrown back over the shoulder, the palm upwards, made me want to put a tray of dirty dishes on it. "This is a nut!" I thought. But when Einstein and Thomas Mann were forced to leave Germany, this face of Hitler's was no longer comic, but sinister.[17]

As reported by Chaplin's screenplay co-writer Dan James, the catalyst for *The Great Dictator* was David Low's cartoon "The Other Fellow with a Funny

Moustache," published in the London *Evening Standard* on February 14, 1936.[18] In 2009, Liliane Weissberg claimed that the catalyst was Diebow's brochure *Der ewige Jude* in 1937.[19] But she confused it with von Leers' diatribe *Juden sehen Dich an.* Robinson dated Chaplin's receipt of this one to 1937 and supposed that it "further spurred" existing plans for a film about Hitler.[20] Earlier, Ivor Montagu had expressed a similar view in his 1968 autobiographical book *With Eisenstein in Hollywood.* As stated by him, he had sent Chaplin a copy of *Juden sehen Dich an* sometime in the 1930s. In one of the three letters Chaplin wrote to Montagu during their 30-year friendship, he responded to the diatribe. Montagu concluded that it had somehow set in motion Chaplin's plans for *The Great Dictator.*[21] Montagu repeated his assumption in his interview for Kevin Brownlow and David Gill's 1983 documentary *Unknown Chaplin,* which was also incorporated into the 2002 documentary Brownlow and Michael Kloft produced, *The Tramp and the Dictator.*

Charlie Chaplin Jr. named another catalyst:

> [The idea] came to him by way of a curious little item which someone clipped from a newspaper and mailed him. The clip concerned an edict by Adolf Hitler banning Chaplin films from Germany because Dad looked so much like him. Something clicked in my father's mind when he read it. In the Little Tramp getup, with the silly mustache, he plainly did resemble Hitler. And the more he thought about it, the more he found parallels between himself and the German dictator. [...] The more Dad thought of the dictator's ban against his pictures and his own resemblance to Hitler, the more intrigued he became by the idea as a whole. He began casting in his mind for a plot and incidents with which to fill it out.[22]

Of the resemblance to Hitler, Chaplin's early biographer Theodore Huff wrote: "It was only natural that Chaplin should capitalize on his screen resemblance to Hitler (or was it vice versa?)."[23]

Chaplin Jr.'s recollections provide few clues to identify the newspaper article. To be sure, there was no Hitler order banning Chaplin films. But the article was probably about the revocation of the approval of *Goldrausch,* which was frequently reported in the English-language press, and the final "end" for Chaplin's films in Germany by the "Sechste Verordnung zur Durchführung des Lichtspielgesetzes, July 3, 1935" (see Chapter 8). Possibly the article reacted to this. Then it would have been published in the second half of 1935.

In 1993, Hermand presented another version: Chaplin had only decided to produce *The Great Dictator* in 1939 after lengthy discussions with Alexander Korda and Montagu. The film plans were leaked "despite great secrecy."[24] Hermand did not provide any sources for this either. On the contrary, the coverage of Chaplin's Hitler film project that began in October 1938 even contradicts Hermand's version.

In his autobiography, Chaplin dated the origin of his idea for *The Great Dictator* to 1937:

> I was trying to write a story for Paulette. [... But h]ow could I throw myself into feminine whimsy or think of romance or the problems of love when madness was being stirred up by a hideous, grotesque Adolf Hitler? Alexander Korda in 1937 had suggested that I should do a Hitler story based on mistaken identity, Hitler having the same moustache as the tramp: I could play both characters, he said. I did not think too much about the idea then, but now

it was topical, and I was desperate to get working again. [...] As Hitler I could harangue the crowds in jargon and talk all I wanted to. And as the Tramp I could remain more or less silent. A Hitler story was an opportunity for burlesque and pantomime. So with this enthusiasm I went hurrying back to Hollywood and set to work writing a script. The story took two years to develop.[25]

Chaplin Jr. reported on his father's then-evolving film plan:

Hitler, [Dad's] double, was spreading monstrous tentacles beyond the bounds of Germany, and within Germany there were terrible persecutions of the Jews. Suddenly, Dad saw a purpose for his comedy beyond the mere art of making people laugh. It could also, through the medium of satire, waken people to the horror of dictatorship. It became his mission to hold up the mirror of ridicule to his alter ego, the mad Hitler, and show him for what he was—an evil buffoon. Dad put aside the script he had worked on so laboriously for the past six months and once more flung himself into the Hitler idea, which he was calling *The Dictator*.[26]

One thing cannot be established in the thicket of allegations: that *The Great Dictator* was Chaplin's vengeance for the banning of his films in Germany. He was looking for a spectacular subject for Goddard, who demanded a starring role in his next film. This may have overlapped with Chaplin's fascination with Hitler and simultaneous disgust for him. Apart from this, the "Peace-Monger"[27] Chaplin was always a critic of inhumanity. Whatever may be true: the truth rests under concrete with Chaplin's body in Corsier sur Vevey.

The Third Reich Intervenes

At the end of January 1938, Albert Schneider picked up in passing in the *Lichtbildbühne* that Paris moviegoers at the re-release of *The Gold Rush* had achieved with shouts "da capo" that the dance of the rolls was repeated. This had also been demanded by the audience at the Berlin Capitol in 1926, which Schneider had reported about enthusiastically in his review at the time (see Chapter 2). Barely 12 years later, his enthusiasm had faded in the Third Reich.[28] But the three remaining German film trade papers did not respond to the *Daily Variety* report of April 27, 1938. On October 14, 1938, however, the *Film-Kurier* picked up Chaplin's alleged name Thonstein, and a month later the film officer Curt Belling even turned it into "Karl Tonstein" in *Der Angriff* (see Chapter 1).[29]

U.S. coverage beginning on October 17, 1938, of Chaplin's upcoming anti–Hitler film and its motivations was updated with the reflection, "Is the Moustache the Idea-Giver?"[30]; as early as 1936, British cartoonist David Low had proclaimed an "international moustache crisis." This obviously put the Nazis on edge, for on October 31, 1938, the German Consul Dr. Georg Gyssling in Los Angeles officially protested in writing against Chaplin's plans to Joseph Breen in Hollywood as head of the Hays Office or Production Code Administration (PCA) within Motion Picture Producers, Inc. The Hays Office supervised the compliance with the Hays Code, which provided guidelines for U.S. film production on the acceptable portrayal of sensitive subjects such as crime and sexual content. Gyssling's protest read:

> I see from a newspaper article under the caption of "Charlie Chaplin will burlesque Hitler" that Mr. Chaplin will play in this film "a defenseless little Jew, who is mistaken for a powerful dictator, while in the other role you will see him as the dictator himself." The article further states that, "while naturally Hitler is not mentioned, it doesn't take any Solomon or Sherlock Holmes to see it is the Fuehrer, whom Chaplin is burlesquing." As this, if it proves true, will naturally lead to serious troubles and complications, I beg you to give this matter your consideration [...].

Breen replied on November 2, 1938, that he knew nothing about the project, but that he wanted to send Chaplin's manager a copy of Gyssling's letter the same day.[31] Breen received no response from there.

The British *Daily Mail*'s article "Chaplin (and Moustache) to Satirize Dictators" (November 22, 1938) was apparently understood by the Nazis as a further provocation. It summarized previous U.S. reports on the subject and linked them to the political situation of the Jews in Germany:

> Recent Nazi reprisals against German Jewry and the effect they have had upon American public opinion have solved Charlie Chaplin's greatest dilemma. He will now definitely make his next film a satire on dictatorship, and he will play a double role. The scenario, now nearing completion, is likely to become a final one, although a week or two ago Chaplin considered rewriting the story in order to avoid a ban of the film by countries maintaining friendly relations with the Reich. Chaplin admits a personal resemblance to Herr Hitler, but insists that this depends mainly on the characteristic moustache, "and I certainly had mine long before we heard of Herr Hitler," he added. Chaplin plans to play a timid Jewish refugee in a German concentration camp who, while cleaning military uniforms as his daily chore, dons one and is mistaken for a dictator he resembles. Unable to explain himself, he is followed by growing crowds, finally finding himself the central subject of a great public demonstration which restores his self-confidence, resuscitates his drooping ego, and makes a new man of him. Whether or not to show him ultimately usurping the power and the position of the real dictator is as yet undecided, as is also the question whether Charlie Chaplin, as the mistaken public idol, should speak or maintain his customary silence. Filming will definitely start in January or February, according to a personal promise Chaplin has given to United Artists.[32]

Three days later, the *Film-Kurier* replied harshly with "Charlie Chaplin wird unverschämt" (Charlie Chaplin Becomes impertinent):

> When Charlie Chaplin, alias Tonstein, produces salon Communist propaganda with sentimentalities or cynicism, the Americans and others may deal with it. [... W]hen he now, as the *Daily Mail* reports, announces a "dictator satire" dealing with the person of our Fuehrer, which [...] will surely amount to a mockery, we must protest against it most sharply. He wants to play a poor Jew who has to brush out uniforms in a concentration camp, puts one on once and is immediately [...] taken for an important personality and receives ovations. [...] The Jewish minority in the USA is thus allowed to mock the Fuehrer without any hindrance.[33]

"Germanophobe Agitation" and Nazi Humor

"Germanophobe smear films" from the U.S. were a perennial Nazi theme that eventually led to U.S. films being banned from the Third Reich. In April 1934, the *Film-Kurier* had lambasted Michael Mindlin's documentary *Hitler's Reign of Terror* as arrogance and rejoiced when it was banned for New York.[34] With German participation, the international film critics' and film journalists' association Fipresci had passed an anti-hate film resolution in 1935[35] and continued to fight so-called smear films in 1938.[36] Another thorn in the Nazi side had therefore been the Anti-Nazi League for the Defense of American Democracy, which filmmakers in the U.S., among them Fritz Lang, had founded in the spring of 1936 as an official Hollywood organization to fight Nazism. In the fall of 1936, the Anti-Nazi League had placed full-page calls for "mass meetings" against "The Menace of Hitlerism in America" in U.S. film trade publications such as *Daily Variety*. These events with politicians and artists had drawn large audiences.[37]

In late October 1938, *Der Film* was pleased to report on the distribution of flyers in the U.S. Midwest attacking the Anti-Nazi League. In them, a Christian audience at least close to the Nazis protested against the "Communist Hollywood Jews," called for a boycott of their films and to buy only from Aryans and to vote only for such. The flyers called Hollywood "the Sodom and Gomorrah where international Jewry controls vice, drug dealing and gambling, and where young Aryan girls are raped with impunity by Jewish producers, directors and casting directors. The Hollywood Jewish Anti-Nazi League promotes Communism in the film industry." Due to such practices, Hollywood stars had suffered economic losses, as the German trade journal wrote, and consequently began to turn their backs on the California film capital.[38] This was followed in November 1938 by the trade journal's own "settling the score with the agitators."[39] *Der Angriff* clamored that Hollywood was "making a haul with agitation." Belling pilloried German-Jewish film emigrants in the propaganda journal who supposedly yearned for their homeland, but nevertheless attacked Germany. For this purpose, they would "make in an Anti-Nazi League,"[40] which remained very active until 1939.

The Nazis did not tolerate criticism of Hitler as an untouchable, ever-heroic Fuehrer, whom the blessings of destiny had supposedly sent to the German people, nor of the Third Reich. Satire of either was therefore considered incitement. In general, humor was not a characteristic of the Nazis. Albert A. Sander's humorless *Film-Kurier* article "A Dog Barking at the Moon/Un petit chien hurle à la lune" had already proven a few months after Hitler's takeover how sensitively the regime reacted to rumors alone that Chaplin wanted to mock Hitler in a film. Even harmless jokes about the Nazi dictatorship were neither forgotten nor went unpunished. Hans Siemsen had already written almost visionary about Chaplin in 1922, only to become a Nazi target himself in 1927:

THE MENACE OF

HITLERISM in AMERICA

•

MASS MEETING

under the auspices of

HOLLYWOOD ANTI-NAZI LEAGUE FOR THE DEFENSE OF AMERICAN DEMOCRACY

SHRINE AUDITORIUM

TUESDAY, OCTOBER 20th, 8:30 p.m.

Mass meeting announcement against "Hitlerism in America" on October 28, 1936.

As harmless as all these Chaplinades look: in reality they are nothing else than a continued undermining of everything that enjoys reputation, office and dignity today— they are one single fight against the social order of today. [...] Chaplin teaches that one should take nothing seriously, nothing but the very simplest human things. And that one should not be afraid of anything, not of big bank buildings, not of generals and non-commissioned officers, not of dignity, not of power and not even of the terrible fat man! He teaches perfect, radical disrespect. God bless him! He is a revolutionary.[41]

Hitler had seen a danger in ridiculing and relied on demonizing enemies.[42] Therefore, Ernst Hanfstaengel's book *Hitler in der Karikatur der Welt. Vom Führer genehmigt!* about the dictator, who was supposedly receptive to humor, was no more than a cover-up. Therefore, Chaplin's film plan in the fall of 1938 was an affront to the Nazis, and the

Anti-Semite U.S. flyer "Boycott the Movies!," ca. 1937-38.

SUICIDE
OF THE
HOLLYWOOD MOTION PICTURE INDUSTRY

UNEMPLOYMENT in the Motion Picture Industry is reaching TREMENDOUS PROPORTIONS. Not more than 50% of the capacity personnel is working today. Thousands of cinema technicians, actors, and extras, are wondering

Why They Are Out Of Jobs

These American workers are DEMANDING TO KNOW the true reasons for this *ALARMING CONDITION* whereby their families are kept on the verge of *STARVATION*, while the JEWISH MONOPOLY of the Motion Picture Industry, BRAZENLY DISCHARGES NON-JEWISH MEN AND WOMEN, and replaces them with refugee JEWS from Europe.
FOR ADDITIONAL REASONS,
          ASK the Jew Motion Picture Producers,
          ASK the Jew-controlled publicity staffs of the Studios,
          ASK the Jew Motion Picture publications,
          ASK the Jew writers of ANTI-American propaganda pictures,
          ASK the Jew actors themselves,
          ASK the Jew-controlled Hollywood Anti-Nazi League,
WHY THEY ARE ENGAGED, day and night, in spreading VICIOUS, UN-AMERICAN propaganda of insult and hate, in order to satisfy JEWS who have been thrown out of Europe; and to antagonize FRIENDLY, ANTI-JEWISH Governments in stirring up INTERNATIONAL WAR for

Jewish Vengeance and Profit

The Hollywood Reporter of April 6, states that Motion Picture business to the amount of 37 millions of dollars has been lost. This probably does not concern the Jew producers who STILL receive their royal salaries and their MILLION DOLLAR BONUSES. They STILL get their 100%, even though only 50% of the capacity personnel is needed. BUT . . . . this great loss DOES CONCERN that great army of UNEMPLOYED MOTION PICTURE actors, technicians, and extras, whose talents and abilities are MAINLY responsible for whatever success has been achieved by the Industry.

Anti-Semite U.S. flyer "Suicide of the Hollywood Motion Picture Industry," ca. 1937-38.

Film-Kurier article "Charlie Chaplin becomes impudent" a typical contribution to the smear film issue.

On December 31, 1938, *Der Angriff* mocked Chaplin, among others, with "Jews: Spies for Germany." The left-leaning populist London Sunday newspaper *The People* had reported that German authorities had promised emigrated Jews their return to Germany and the restitution of part of their property if, in return, they agreed to spy for Germany abroad for five years. *Der Angriff* offered cartoons with a squad of to-be spies recruited from the group of people it had repeatedly railed against. Among them was Chaplin as Tramp Charlie, depicted with an emphatically Jewish physiognomy; Soviet dictator Josef Stalin, with a huge pistol sticking out of his pocket, greets him with a handshake in Moscow in front of Charlie lookalikes. Directed at Chaplin's film plans, the propaganda journal wrote: "The Jewish film actor Charlie Chaplin had been persuaded with unknown promises to come to Stalin's court in Moscow. Because he looked Jewish, he did not attract attention there, as he later confessed. [...] Chaplin later made a film that was released in Hollywood in 1939. It is said to surpass all previous comedies in the world."[43] A few weeks later, *Der Angriff* returned to the scenario. At the suggestion of the Soviet film organization, Chaplin was not only to be awarded the Order of the Red Banner, but also to have a Chaplin Week dedicated to him on his 50th birthday. His next film was also to be released in the Soviet Union, supposedly as "one of the sharpest instruments in the fight against fascism."[44] Yet, *The Great Dictator* was never screened there.

A serious contest held by *Der Angriff* in February 1939 on the topic "Do we still have a sense of humor?" resembled real-life comedy. Goebbels himself had answered the question with "yes" in a jiffy and commented:

There is still enough and more than enough humor in Germany. It is the kind of humor that has been cultivated forever among the broad masses of the people, a humor that is good-natured, decent, and clean but, if necessary, can also be coarse and grasping. But the German people act in line with a clear principle borrowed from the Prussian army, according to which only those who are marching have the right to mock, to grumble or even to scold, and that those who stand by the road and at most once rouse themselves to a modest wave have no other right than to keep their mouths shut about the army.[45]

Der Angriff, **December 31, 1938: "Juden. Spione für Deutschland" (Jews. Spies for Germany), cartoon by Stenberg.**

Goebbels' gag order had a specific reason. The Nazis had always been suspicious of German cabaret artist Werner Finck,[46] and now they had expelled him from the Reichskulturkammer, which meant his professional ban. Finck did not utter satirical punch lines in his stage performances, and thus implied criticism all the more. One example: He entered the stage with just two pigs, a sow and a boar. He introduced the sow to the audience as "Frau Mann" (Mrs. Mann). That was all Finck had to say. The boar's name was, of course, "Herr Mann" (Mr. Mann), and that sounded just like "Hermann," the first name of the adipose Gen-eralfeldmarschall Göring, who stopped at nothing. Finck had thus called him a pig, both physically and in terms of character. Goebbels commented on Finck's exclu-sion that such persons "have no idea of the duties and concerns of a Blockwart [Block leader], but fool about it in front of a disgusting kind of social rabble." He also made unmistakably clear that he was not prepared to allow free thinking to oth-ers: "Political joke-cracking is a liberal remnant. [...] We have no desire to continue to have our party, our state, and our public institutions made fun of by intellectual incompetents."[47]

Chaplin Giving Up?

By mid–November 1938, the dust that the announcement of Chaplin's Hit-ler satire had stirred up seemed to have settled for the Nazis. For on November 19, 1938, the *Pariser Tageszeitung* reported that Chaplin had abandoned his project.[48] This was grist to the mill of *Der Angriff*, which, with a low, stereotypical argumen-tation, followed up propagandistically and totally humorless in Sander's style of 1933:

> Up to now we have frankly considered the news about a Hitler film of Chaplin as an extremely inferior Jewish joke. With the most recent message, only one thing cheers us up: the Jews are slowly beginning to realize that they cannot fool with the Fuehrer and National Socialism after all. We [...] are honestly amazed that [Chaplin-Tonstein] resorted to such means in the urge of his underworld feelings. [...] If Jud Chaplin's Hitler film is in itself an incomprehensi-ble impertinence, [...] he admits his own tastelessness by abandoning the project. An inferior Jew cannot even outwardly compete with true luminaries.[49]

Der Angriff, however, had dropped the following remark of the *Pariser Tageszei-tung*: "Another version, of course, is that Germany had protested against Chaplin's intended film." Obviously, the intervention of the German consul Gysslings of Octo-ber 31, 1938, against Chaplin's film plan should be concealed. The *Film-Kurier*, which reprinted the *Der Angriff* article in its entirety and without comment at the begin-ning of December 1938, followed this example.[50]

Neither the report of the *Pariser Tageszeitung* nor Breen's November 2, 1938, reply to Gyssling satisfied the Nazis. Gyssling therefore sent an official protest to the U.S. Department of the Interior in December 1938. He emphasized that an anti–Hit-ler film would severely strain relations between Germany and the U.S.; therefore, Chaplin's production had to be prevented.

On December 22, the *Hamburger Fremdenblatt* made Chaplin's film project a political issue that endangered peace between Germany and the U.S.[51] Allegedly, Chaplin and U.S. Secretary of the Interior Harold LeClair Ickes, who was supposed to have addressed Zionists in Cleveland with an insulting speech against German politicians,[52] conspired together against Germany.[53] On December 29, the *Pariser Tageszeitung* came to Chaplin's defense against these accusations, referring to the *Paris-Soir*. In it, Chaplin had called it "ridiculous" that he had been instigated by Ickes to make a Hitler film. This was accompanied by a cartoon of Tramp Charlie in Gestapo uniform with his cane and shoes much too large, delivering the Hitler salute.[54]

Gyssling's official protest was also on the December 21 agenda of the Berlin Reichspressekonferenz, which had been chaired since the beginning of the month by Hans Fritzsche. In contrast to his predecessor Berndt, Fritzsche maintained a friendly tone.[55] The surviving transcript of this conference is the only verifiable reaction of the Nazi press control to Chaplin's film plan. In 1936, Berndt had still instructed the attending journalists not to report about Chaplin. Now, however, the Reichsministerium für Volksaufklärung und Propaganda wanted the German press to take a stand against Chaplin. Fritzsche prescribed the following type of presentation for the conference participants: "[It] may be pointed out that Chaplin is making a film called *Nazispionage* against German protest, in which Hitler and pretty much all the Third Reich personalities are portrayed in a hateful manner."[56]

The following day, the *Film-Kurier* informed its readers that Gyssling's protest had been successful: "The Hays organization in New York [the other of two headquarters], which includes all American distribution and production concerns as members, has expressed its disapproval of the Germanophobe hate film planned by the Jew Karl Thonstein (Chaplin), which is to culminate in a tasteless caricature of the German head of state."[57] This was no propagandistic invention. In late January 1939, the Australian tabloid *Smith's Weekly* published the long article "Hollywood Can't Make These Films! Subjects Too Dangerous for Filming," in which it wrote about Chaplin:

> Although [his] pictures are not allowed to be shown in Germany, Hollywood's big noises advised him not to caricature Hitler in his new film. So powerful is this unofficial censorship that Chaplin has had the story re-written and placed it in a mythical kingdom, but the hero could not be mistaken for anyone but the Nazi leader. [...] A recommendation [...] from the Hays Office was responsible for the radical reworking of Chaplin's script for his new film, set in Germany with the humorously ambiguous leading character Hitler.[58]

According to the abovementioned *Pariser Tageszeitung* report, difficulties had also arisen for Chaplin in the rump of Czechoslovakia. They were thinking of withdrawing all Chaplin films from circulation as a result of his Hitler film. But Chaplin did not care: "As the *Paris-Soir* reports, Chaplin objects to the idea that the film he is currently preparing is directed against a living person or existing form of government. Just as with *Modern Times*, he does not intend a political satire. [...] He was not interested in the German protests: his films are banned in the dictatorship states anyway."[59]

Chaplin's "political explanation" apparently did not convince the Nazis. On the six-year anniversary of his takeover, Hitler announced in a radio address that he would answer Germanophobe foreign films with German anti–Semitic films.[60] On

February 1, 1939, the *Film-Kurier*'s article "Will the Fuehrer's Warning Be Heeded?" suspiciously scrutinized the Hollywood Anti-Nazi League as a "center of political agitation against the Fascist idea," turning to Chaplin: "After all, [Hollywood] actually already worked on a film in which Charlie Chaplin wanted to caricature the Fuehrer and thus ridicule him."[61] Hitler's "warning" was swiftly implemented in mid–July 1939 with Hans H. Zerlett's anti–Semitic film *Robert und Bertram*, disguised as a comedy.[62]

In June 1939 the Warner Brothers[63] feature film *Confessions of a Nazi Spy* was banned in Argentina and later that year Sherman Scott's latest movie *Hitler—Beast of Berlin* was banned in New York State. The Nazi trade press reacted with glee. Belling, for example, took this as an opportunity to "inform" the readers of the *Lichtbildbühne* about "The Agitators in American Film," in which he included Chaplin.[64] According to *Film-Kurier* and the magazine *Filmwelt*, "inflammatory films from the USA" served the "encircling agitation" of the U.S. "Jewish fight against 'Nazi films'" and were thus the straight evidence of the "scandalous" Jewish influence.[65] Carey Orr's cartoon "Charlie the Giant Killer" countered this in the *Newcastle Evening Chronicle*, summarizing that Chaplin had begun work on his dictator film despite diplomatic pressure and threats from Germany and Italy: Tramp Charlie puts a stop to the fearful looking dictators Hitler and Mussolini with the cane as weapon of ridicule.[66]

Unbeknown to the Nazis, the self-appointed film censor Walter McKenna was fighting alongside them in the U.S. against the Chaplin project. Writing on February 27, 1939, to U.S. Senator Robert Reynolds as a member of the Senate Foreign Relations Committee, McKenna argued that Chaplin, a foreigner, should not be allowed to abuse the U.S. film industry for his poorly concealed "private grievance" against a foreign government, which would entail international entanglements. Therefore, in order not to "antagonize certain [...] governments," he suggested that the U.S. government take a closer look at Chaplin's motivation. For McKenna, Chaplin's purpose was clearly "to stir up further strife between Germany and the US." Reynolds forwarded the letter to Hays Office head Breen.[67] While Paramount did not want to produce anti–Nazi films and wrote to Breen on December 10, 1938, that such meant danger for the Jews in Germany, Warner Brothers chief Jack Warner in his March 23, 1939, letter to Chaplin encouraged him to stick with his film project.[68]

In his autobiography, Chaplin reported on the Hays Office's attempts to pressure him and United Artists:

> Half-way through making *The Great Dictator* I began receiving alarming messages from United Artists. They had been advised by the Hays Office that I would run into censorship trouble. [...] But I was determined to go ahead, for Hitler must be laughed at. Had I known of the actual horrors of the German concentration camps, I could not have made *The Great Dictator*; I could not have made fun of the homicidal insanity of the Nazis. However, I was determined to ridicule their mystic bilge about a pure-blooded race. As though such a thing ever existed outside the Australian Aborigines![69]

Such attempts by the Hays Office were not new. According to Budd Schulberg in *The Tramp and the Dictator*, Gyssling not only protested, but also threatened a boycott of U.S. films in Germany. Most of the U.S. film production companies bowed to Nazi threats. For example, at Gyssling's request, MGM head Louis B. Mayer removed scenes from a new MGM film that did not suit the Nazi diplomat. Something similar had happened in 1927 with the U.S. film *Mare Nostrum*. Chaired by Will Hays, the Motion Picture Producers and Distributors of America had held 12 conferences with Gyssling's predecessor in office to edit a new version agreeable to the German market.[70] Another example was the 1939 MGM Marx Brothers film *At the Circus*, in which Groucho Marx sings the comic song "Lydia, the Tattooed Lady," written by Yip Harburg and Harold Arlen. A line about Hitler was omitted from the version performed in the film: "When she stands, the world grows littler/When she sits, she sits on Hitler." Groucho reinstated it when singing the song for servicemen and on radio after America's entry into the war.[71] In *The Tramp and the Dictator*, writer Ray Bradbury lamented the immorality of the U.S. film bosses during the Third Reich: When it came to money, they did not take a position, but accepted intolerable conditions or went along with unacceptable requests.

On March 20 and 21, 1939, Chaplin commented on his film project to British and U.S. trade journals and in the *News from Charlie Chaplin*, United Artists' newsletter:

> Owing to erroneous reports in the press that I have abandoned my production concerning dictators, I wish to state that I have never wavered from my original determination to produce this picture. Any report, past, present, or future, to the effect that I have given up the idea, is deliberately false. I am not worried about intimidation, censorship, or anything else. I am making a comedy picture on the lives of dictators, which I hope will create much healthy laughter throughout the world.[72]

This was reported in Great Britain and the U.S. until the beginning of April 1939,[73] and would hardly have escaped the attention of Nazi propaganda. The German film press was silent on the subject. In late April, Chaplin reacted even more unmistakably to the emerging attempt to prevent the screening of his film in the States: "If for some reason they won't let me screen *The Dictator*, I'll have tents set up all over the country and charge 10 cents admission."[74]

The *New York Times* news item "Chaplin Film to Aid Emigration" (June 15, 1939) was not covered in Germany. It was provocative from the Nazi point of view because, according to this, Chaplin had instructed his distributor to donate revenues from the screening of his film in continental Europe to the Aid Committee of the Vienna Jewish Community in order to support German Jews in their emigration.[75] By the end of the month, it was reported that $8 million had been deposited with the Milan Jewish Relief Committee for this purpose; some of it had been raised by Chaplin and other celebrities.[76] The U.S. *Buffalo Jew Review* and the Bombay-based *The Jewish Advocate* reported on Chaplin's struggle "for his people" on June 30, 1939.[77] Jewish associations bestowed the title "Moses of the 20th Century" on Chaplin in late July 1939, following the Old Testament example, and the title was spread across the United States.[78]

In August, the Seattle-based *Jewish Transcript* claimed to have learned that Chaplin had donated a substantial amount of his private fortune to the emigration aid as an advance on his future proceeds from *The Great Dictator*. His example would show that it would need "only a few Chaplins" to overcome the problem of German Jewish refugees.[79] However, no funds were sent to Milan or Vienna. Nor was it reported at any time whether, how, and to what extent the respective aid committees actually supported German Jews willing to emigrate. Other evidence of Chaplin's support campaign, which would certainly have struck a chord, is unknown. No wonder the Vienna Committee is said to have disbanded due to lack of funds.[80] Moreover, doubts about the generosity attributed to Chaplin are appropriate. It is well known that he was particularly economical. At the time of the reports, he had not even begun filming and therefore could not have known the ultimate cost volume. Furthermore, after the beginning of World War II, it soon became obvious that *The Great Dictator* could probably only be sold in continental Europe to neutral Switzerland. Had the reports possibly sought to morally persuade Chaplin to donate money to support Jewish refugees?

Two 50th Birthdays

Chaplin and Hitler's 50th birthdays followed each other shortly on April 16 and 20, 1939, respectively. On this occasion, the foreign press compared the physical similarities of the two and their biographies. According to the article "Charlie Chaplin a 50 ans…" (Charlie Chaplin turns 50…) in the Parisian newspaper *L'Œuvre*, which the main archives of the NSDAP added to its Chaplin file, Chaplin and Hitler had experienced a childhood of abject poverty and had to struggle to make ends meet before becoming idols of the masses.[81] This is true of Chaplin, but Hitler's poverty as a young man up to his allegedly unwanted descent into the Viennese shelter for the homeless is a legend spread by Hitler himself. In 1939, it had not yet been disproved, because documents showing his actually good situation were not accessible.[82] The appeal of both jubilarians, on the other hand, was reflected in books and countless newspaper articles. What the two birthday boys had given their contemporaries could not have been more different. Chaplin's Tramp mastered the struggle for survival full of empathy with endless laughter, irony and optimism. In contrast, Hitler stood for ruthless single-mindedness, hunger for power, contempt for humanity, will to destroy and pride of victory. According to Chaplin Jr., his father was aware of this and therefore vacillated between "disgust" and "fascination" when he thought of Hitler: "If you imagine it, […] he's the madman, and I'm the comedian. But it could just as easily have been the other way around."[83] In its April 21, 1939, issue, the British magazine *The Spectator* concluded "that people should love Chaplin and hate Hitler":

> [Chaplin] still allows [people] to laugh at their universal predicament[. …] For this hope and laughter millions of men and women—white, yellow and black—unite in the tributes and admiration that have greeted him from every quarter of the globe. Hitler's genius, the genius of destruction, is the antithesis of Chaplin's. Germany will pay him honor, part obligatory, part sincere. In the world outside, many are the millions who bless Chaplin, and bless him rightly, for the wholesome gift of laughter, more millions still, and with even greater justice,

execrate the name of the man whose ungoverned ambitions, prostituting right to might, and who has cast over their lives the chill shadow of fear and impoverishment and bitterness and hate. Even Herr Hitler's power has its limits. It has failed to poison the minds of millions of decent Germans who loathe persecution and hate war as much as any lover of Chaplin's films. But in robbing these of their freedom, he has robbed them of their power to veto a policy [...] whose inevitable end is war.[84]

Chaplin's collaborator Dan James contributed an interesting facet some 45 years after *The Great Dictator* was made: "Of course [Chaplin] had in himself some of the qualities that Hitler had. He dominated his world. He created his world. And Chaplin's world was not a democracy, either. Charlie was the dictator of all those things."[85] Against this background, an article headline of the *Film-Kurier* from that year almost seemed like a bizarre coincidence: "The director has to be a dictator!"[86]

A cartoon of Tramp Charlie and Hitler in uniform comparing their moustaches appeared in an as yet unidentified French newspaper to mark their birthdays. Charlie, looking at Hitler, points uncertainly at his moustache: "When I Think That I Invented That to Make the World Laugh."[87] Meanwhile, in Germany, on the birthday of "the Reich's blacksmith," Belling exhibited blind obedience: "Adolf Hitler, command—we follow!"[88]

Goebbels staged Hitler's milestone birthday more pompously than ever before.[89] The newsreel *Ufatonwoche No. 451* was devoted solely to this event,[90] for which an unprecedented amount of preparation was exerted with flagging of streets, arrival of guests of honor from all over the world, collection of gift shipments in the Reichskanzlei, and the dedication of the new Berlin boulevard de grandeur, known as the "East-West Axis." Twelve camera crews exposed some 10,000 meters of film of the four-hour parade of troops of all branches of the armed forces on the birthday itself. At the same time, it was a demonstration of power to foreign countries, from which the second half of the 545-meter-long newsreel edition was compiled.[91] About the prospect of Chaplin's upcoming film, Britain's *Liverpool Evening Explorer* had sighed hopefully in early April 1939: "Thank Heaven. We Can Still Raise a Laugh!"[92] In "Fifty Years of Chaplin," Chaplin admirer Siemsen took a close look from his Paris exile in *Die Zukunft* at how low humor had fallen in Germany:

> Chaplin knows a lot about comic effects. [... His] anxious little man wants so much to be taken seriously for once! Therefore, he wears a moustache. [...]. The other one [Hitler] has no idea of comedy. [...] Oh, who [except Chaplin] can [...] say of himself, when he turns 50, that millions of people of all classes and all languages remember him with love, and with nothing but happy, friendly thoughts?! Only in Germany [...even] his comedies and fairy tales are not allowed to be shown. It was like that before. From 1915 [...] to 1922, when the whole world around was already so happy to recover from its terrible sorrows in Chaplin's films and to learn to laugh again, he was unknown in Germany. Today it is like that again. Chaplin is banned in Germany. Germany is again as isolated as it was back then. The "other one" is at work there.[93]

British Influence

The *Film-Kurier* had concluded its article "Charlie Chaplin becomes impudent" as follows: "In France, a few days ago, an order was issued forbidding the ridiculing of foreign heads of state. When will America summon up this most natural duty of decency of intercourse between nations to prevent such impertinence as the Jew Charlie Chaplin is up to?"[94] In France, it was indeed forbidden to disparage heads of state of allied countries, and the same was true in Great Britain. In 1916, extensive rules had been established there for film censorship, which prohibited, among other things, disparaging the country's allies.[95] By the end of 1938, Germany and Italy were allies of both France and Great Britain, which pursued a policy of appeasement and toleration toward the two fascist regimes. This was reflected in the Munich Agreement of the four states of September 30, 1938, which ceded the Sudetenland to the Third Reich effective October 1.

After Gyssling's intervention in the U.S., opposition to Chaplin's anti–Hitler film arose in Great Britain. First, the British Union of Fascists (BUF), founded in 1932 by Sir Oswald Mosley, mobilized, as the *Film-Kurier* reported in "Die Film-Hetze in USA" at the end of February 1939. In their party journal *Action*, the BUF had urged the BBFC to prevent the screening of the film with a danger alert. It was "the most dangerous piece of celluloid [...] that could ever find its way to England. Jewish film finance should not be allowed to flood the cinemas with Jewish propaganda. Since this would jeopardize relations between England and Germany, Chaplin's film could set all of Europe on fire."[96]

Unlike the British fascists, who were as humorless as the Nazis, the press of India, which did not achieve independence from Britain until 1947, had a sense of satire. Probably in mid–January 1939, the major English-language daily *The Hindu* printed photographs of two boys in shorts. One wears a Chaplin mask, the other a Hitler mask. The boys stage "a war over their funny moustaches," the winner of which gets to shave off the loser's moustache. Since the boy with the Chaplin mask loses out, the boy with the Hitler mask shaves him, and the headline reads, "Confidential: Hitler Triumphs Again."[97] In February 1939, Thomas Arthur Challen's (TAC) cartoon "Goebbels Has a Nightmare" in the British newspaper *Sunday Pictorial* may have been closer to reality. Goebbels starts up from his bed at night and pulls his comforter protectively to his head. With his mouth and his eyes wide open in horror, he stares at his specter: Tramp Charlie and Hitler have exchanged roles. Hitler, in Tramp costume, lifts his bowler hat in salute, while Charlie in Hitler's uniform with swastika armband greets Goebbels with the "German salute." For Chaplin's "idea [...] is to make people laugh [which] has an opposite effect on the Nazi authorities, who are furious at what they consider an insult," as the newspaper commented on the scene.[98] David Low remarked on his recent cartoon "International Moustache Crisis" in the London *Evening Standard* that same month: "Trouble arises concerning the reported new film in which Chaplin is to appear as a dictator. Herr Hitler alleges plagiarism and threatens to produce a film himself and to appear in it as Chaplin. Chaplin holds that he had the moustache first, claims copyright and demands royalties from all sales of *Mein Kampf....*"[99] Months later, David Louis Ghilchik presented a "Moustache Change" in *London Opinion*. Hitler is annoyed by the poster of the Chaplin film with Charlie and his moustache: "Himmel! An insult to the Fuehrer! This cannot be tolerated!" Therefore, a uniformed Nazi has to leave his wide-swept moustache to Hitler: "Consider it sacrificed to the honor of the Fatherland!" Now the Fuehrer is satisfied again: "So the great German Reich answers the challenge of the Western Democracies."[100]

However, the British MP Edward Herbert Keeling was not in the mood for satire. In him, the British fascists had an ally. On February 22, 1939, he sent a concerned letter to Undersecretary Richard Austin Butler at the British Foreign Office about the planned Chaplin film, urging compliance with British censorship regulations and national toleration policies:

> I feel that I must write to you about a film now in course of production in Hollywood which is to be called *The Dictator* and in which Charles Chaplin is to portray Herr Hitler satirically. It is obviously most undesirable that such a film should be exhibited in this country and I venture to think that the Government should make it known immediately to the persons financially interested in its production and distribution that its exhibition in Great Britain will be forbidden, the necessary instructions being issued at the same time to the [British Board of Film Censors, in short: BBFC]."[101]

Butler approached Joseph Brooke-Wilkinson, head of the BBFC, who then sent a cablegram to the U.S. censor Breen on March 2, 1939, in which he asked for assistance: "Chaplin has in mind the production of a film under title *The Dictator*. […] Is it possible for you to outline the story and treatment for our information having regard to the delicate situation that might arise in this country if personal attacks were made on any living European statesman […?]" Breen contacted Chaplin, who only replied on request that he had nothing in writing. Afterwards, Breen informed his British colleague of this on March 13: "I find that the whole thing is rather nebulous. Chaplin has no script, and he has no fixed story in his mind. However, he has before him your cablegram and I think [he] clearly understands what the situation is." Brooke-Wilkinson replied on March 15: "If [Chaplin] decides to continue with the project, I do hope he will be prevailed upon to let us have an outline of the story beforehand."[102]

The British activities apparently came to the attention of United Artists. Chaplin detailed in his autobiography: "[T]he English office was very concerned about an anti–Hitler picture and doubted whether it could be shown in Britain."[103] In early April 1939, the British government officially expressed its disapproval of Chaplin's film plans,[104] because it publicly sought to downplay anti–Nazi movements in Britain. According to the *Daily Variety* of late April 1939, United Artists now also openly was afraid of the loss of the British market.[105] Undersecretary Butler had called in the Intelligence Department of the British Foreign Office, which on April 28, 1939, asked the British Consulate in Los Angeles to shed light on the matter. In a May 17 letter, the consulate regretted that it could do nothing about the Chaplin film. A conversation with Chaplin had also had no effect:

> We have had some personal conversation with [Chaplin] on the subject, and find that he is entering into the production of *The Dictator* with fanatical enthusiasm. His racial and social sympathies are with classes and groups which have suffered most in the dictatorship countries, and he informed us that he was determined to secure distribution of the film, even though it should be necessary for him to invest more of his considerable private fortune in the effort. He already contemplates the expenditure of a million dollars upon the production of the film. [… The] directness of his attack would seem to be, to him, the picture's only motive and reason.

[...] Mr. Chaplin recognizes quite frankly that possibly only in the United States will he be able to show his film, and that even here representations will probably be made which will limit the field of distribution to him. He thinks it possible that the Hays Office will refuse to pass the film, but as we have already mentioned, he is determined to distribute it, if necessary, without recourse to the distribution organization with which he is associated or any other.[106]

In February 1939, the *Film-Kurier* chalked it up as a success that Albert T. Mannon's 1936 anti–Nazi U.S. film *I Was a Captive of Nazi Germany* had been cancelled in two Chicago theaters due to complaints from the public, so Warner Brothers considered dropping their plan to produce *Confessions of a Nazi Spy*.[107] Behind the latter film plan was allegedly the "heavily Jewed American film industry" with the "Jewish Anti-Nazi League" as its spearhead, which put "all dissenters" in Hollywood "under economic pressure."[108] The *Lichtbildbühne* even claimed to have learned that the U.S. production company RKO was "churning out Germanophobe films."[109] And once again, in April 1939, Belling attacked "the Jews in Hollywood" and Chaplin in the trade journal; it was here that he called Chaplin "Tonstein" for the last time.[110]

In late May 1939, the *Film-Kurier* reproduced in "America fears for its smear films" a report from the British trade journal *Kinematograph Weekly* of May 18, 1939, according to which the BBFC had recently banned *I Was a Captive of Nazi Germany* because of its "decidedly anti–National Socialist character." However, the German trade journal had cut the conclusion of the British news item and omitted the brief discussion of Hitler's early days. *Kinematograph Weekly* had written that Chaplin had based his film on the popular British music hall sketch "The Paperhanger" and used it as a parable of Hitler's modest career start.[111] In any case, the British trade journal had nurtured the Nazi hope that the "new Chaplin film *The Dictator* [...] would give rise to official [British] criticism, at least in its present form."[112]

Kinematograph Weekly's assessment proved to be correct. To avoid foreign policy entanglements, the British Foreign Office contacted Brooke-Wilkinson on June 16, 1939, and summarized the letter from the British Consulate in Los Angeles dated May 17, 1939: "We wish to draw your attention to this news so that you may be prepared in any event. If the film is submitted to you with a request to approve it for domestic release, it should be examined most thoroughly." Brooke-Wilkinson then forwarded to the Foreign Office on June 21 the text of his March 2 cablegram to Breen, as well as Breen's response of March 13. He also enclosed the text of the *Hollywood Reporter*'s March 20 report that Chaplin persisted in his film plans, which the British Consulate in Los Angeles had already ascertained. Brooke-Wilkinson concluded his letter to the State Department: "You will agree that we have made it unmistakably clear in our cablegram what we will accept and what we will not. Should [Chaplin] go ahead with his project, he will have himself to blame if his film cannot be approved in this country."[113]

The foreign policy entanglements that the British Foreign Office had been worried about became meaningless by the time Great Britain declared war on Germany on September 3, 1939. France followed a few hours later. This also put an end to the French interdiction of disparaging heads of state of allied countries. Since the Third Reich occupied the country after the campaign against France had begun on April

22, 1940, *The Great Dictator* was not screened until years later, after the country had been liberated.

Marketing Prospects and in Search of a Title

So far it had become known that Chaplin would play a double role and that the film would be about Tramp Charlie as a prisoner of a Nazi concentration camp. In addition, Chaplin wanted to target Mussolini as Gasolini. This increased sales troubles outside the U.S. In Germany and Italy, Chaplin films were already mostly banned. After its German occupation, the Sudetenland had also lost its importance as a lucrative market for Hollywood films. France and Chaplin's native Britain were not even included in the financial planning. In the U.S., the NSDAP was supported by the Nazi-minded German-American Bund (see Chapter 1). Its members and supporters had to assure in writing in the "Application for Membership" and "Sympathizer's Registration," respectively, their "Aryan descent, free from Jewish or colored blood." German and U.S. comrades-in-arms had

German-American Bund, "Application for Membership," ca. mid–1930s: "I am of Aryan descent, free from Jewish or colored blood."

German American Bund

ADDRESS: GERMAN AMERICAN BUND, P. O. BOX 1, STATION "K", NEW YORK, N. Y.

DISTRICT: ....
SECTION: ....
UNIT: ....
ADDRESS: ....
....

Sympathizer's Registration

*) Payable when registering

Registration Fee $1.00
Monthly Contribution $0.75
Voluntary Donation $0.50 up

I hereby register as a Sympathizer of the "German American Bund". The Aims and Purposes of the Bund are known to me and I obligate myself to support them to the best of my ability. I am of Aryan descent, free from Jewish or Colored Blood.

Name: ....

Address: ....

(The address need not be given. A Pseudonym may be used.)

Date: ....

Paid
Initiation Fee .... $: ....
Monthly Contribution . $: ....
Vol. Donation .... $: ....

....
Applicant's Personal Signature
....
Unit Leader

Please do not use this space

No. ....

German-American Bund, "Sympathizer's Registration," ca. mid–1930s.

Members of German-American Bund and NSDAP with *Der Stürmer* display case, New York, 1937.

themselves photographed with their national swastika flags in New York, where *Der Stürmer* was openly sold on the streets.[114] In the Hollywood film studios, the German-American Bund fought so-called Germanophobe smear films and distributed flyers urging filmmakers to refuse to work on these productions.[115] This resembled boycott calls of October 1938 against films of "Jewish-Communist" production. After the Third Reich exerted its influence in Japan,[116] that country also banned all anti–Nazi films.[117]

In February 1939, United Artists boss Murray Silverstone confirmed the planned film title "The Dictators." However, Paramount had already secured this title for a film of their own, which was never realized. Paramount also showed no interest in releasing the title in exchange for cash. Thereupon, in June, Chaplin successfully applied to copyright the title *The Great Dictator* and, just in case, the substitute titles "The Two Dictators," "Dictamania" and "Dictator of Ptomania."[118]

Diebow's Die Juden in USA

After his brochure *Der ewige Jude*, Hans Diebow followed up in 1939 with the

equally distasteful sequel *Die Juden in USA*. Because of the Nazi race laws, the issue of racial defilement took on a broader scope and was exemplified by the film industry "morally infiltrated by Jews."[119] Again in pictures and words, he attacked Chaplin, whose relationship with Paulette Goddard he called "movie stars' racial defilement"—that Goddard *née* Pauline Levy had a Jewish father was something that apparently neither Diebow nor other Nazis were aware of. One of the pictures was captioned "Charlie Chaplin, the "plattfüßiger" (Flat-Footed) Ghetto Clown." On another, he was seen in riding clothes as a guest of the Duke of Westminister's hunt. Diebow elaborated on Chaplin's three wives, Mildred Harris, Lita Grey and Goddard: Today, Harris lived "miserably

Hans Diebow, *Die Juden in USA*, front cover, 1939.

in a New York brothel," while her enterprising successor Grey, "trained his sons to be dollar-earning movie kids," something Chaplin had tried to prevent legally.[120] To this Diebow added a slightly altered rehash of his Chaplin slur from *Der ewige Jude*, drawn broadly from Alfred Rosenberg's mid–1927 *Weltkampf* article "Chaplin in Gethsemane." Using a 1935 press photograph taken as a reminiscence

Filmstars Rassenschande

Paulette Goddard, bekannt aus vielen Filmen, ist längst Frau Charlie Chaplin Nummer drei geworden. Der „große Philosoph", der zwar nicht richtig schreiben und auch nicht korrekt Englisch sprechen kann — der für alles Pathologische brennend interessierte und sich (nach jüdischem Eingeständnis) an ordinären Zoten begeisternde Ghetto-Clown wird von seinen Rassegenossen maßlos gefeiert.

Frau Charlie Chaplin Nummer eins

Das ist Mildred Harris, vormals Film-Schauspielerin, heute lebt sie im Elend eines Neuvorker Freudenhauses.

(A. Ey im „Angriff".)

Frau Charlie Chaplin Nummer zwei

Die frühere Filmschauspielerin Lita Grey mit ihren Chaplin-Kindern, die sie in großer Geschäftstüchtigkeit zu dollarbringenden Filmkindern dressiert. Ein Prozeß des Vaters versuchte das zu verhindern.

Chaplin will sich aus Ärger über den Ausfall der Tantiemen aus Deutschland „politisch betätigen". Nur weiter so! Je mehr ihr euch rührt, desto mehr fallt ihr eurem Wirtsvolk auf die Nerven. Wenn das aber erwacht . . . !

Chaplin section of *Die Juden in USA*, p. 46.

of their roles in *The Kid*,[121] Diebow degraded Chaplin and Jackie Coogan into run-down movie actors: "Outgrown his partner. The most lucrative business that the two "Ghetto-Figuren mit sentimentaler Lächerlichkeit" (Ghetto characters made with sentimental ridicule) is gone for both of them." Coogan, whom Diebow also called "Jakob Cohn," had wrongly demanded that his mother pay out his fortune of $4.5

Charlie Chaplin, der platt-
füßige Ghetto - Clown

Carl Laemmle, der jüdische
Filmgroßunternehmer (Uni-
versal - Film - Corporation), der
erst kürzlich wieder durch
seine bekannte Deutschenhetze
übel von sich reden machte.

Keine Rolle, sondern Wirklich-
keit: Chaplin als Jagdgast des
Herzogs von Westminster.

Chaplin section of *Die Juden in USA*, **p. 47.**

million, which he had earned as a child star.[122] However, Diebow did not mention that the mother, together with Jackie's stepfather, had embezzled her son's money. Finally, Diebow insinuated that Chaplin was seeking revenge against the Nazis because the business prospects for his upcoming film had collapsed: "Chaplin wants to become 'politically active' out of anger over the loss of royalties from Germany. Keep it up! The more you stir up, the more you will annoy your host people. But when they awaken...!"[123]

11

Preparations, 1939–40

Neither the Nazis nor their political comrades-in-arms in Great Britain and the U.S., nor official British and U.S. authorities, nor the threat of limited marketing chances had been able to dissuade Chaplin from his film project. The Nazi campaign against *The Great Dictator* and other "Germanophobe smear films" continued nevertheless, and were met with mockery by the English-language press. This included curious news items which emphasized the special interest in the upcoming film. Early in his career, Chaplin had begun meticulously constructing and shooting his films. *The Great Dictator* was no exception. This time, however, the challenge proved greater than ever, for the political references of the Hitler satire demanded special preparations in order to aptly caricature dictatorship and its exponents. And unlike previous films, Chaplin received threats in the final stages of production and after its completion.

This chapter examines:

- Chaplin and dictators
- Chaplin's analysis of dictatorial language
- influences on the making of *The Great Dictator*, especially Leni Riefenstahl's *Triumph des Willens*
- Nazi reactions to "Germanophobe smear films" up to the shutdown of U.S. distribution branches in the Third Reich
- the continuation of the Chaplin agitation in the German film press
- satirical reactions in the English-language press to Chaplin's forthcoming film
- rumors about the German distribution of *The Great Dictator* and a U.S. interview with Hitler
- threats addressed to Chaplin
- whether *The Great Dictator* is a "Germanophobe smear film"

Chaplin Studies Dictators

Chaplin had already dealt with the dark side of for his finally abandoned "Napoleon" project. Now he prepared himself thoroughly for his dictator film on the person of the Fuehrer. These included, for example, Heinrich Hoffmann's series of postcards from the fall of 1927 with Hitler in orator poses, mentioned by Chaplin in his autobiography. The photos were taken shortly after Hitler's December 20, 1924, release from the Landsberg fortress prison.[1] From the time around 1925–26 came at least one other photograph, which was also used as a postcard subject for propaganda purposes: Hitler as a robust nature boy with brown shirt and swastika armband in short leather pants, rough knee socks and sturdy half shoes; several other photographs of Hitler in a similar guise are known, but their publication as postcard subjects was rejected internally.[2] It cannot be determined whether Chaplin also had this postcard. Film dictator Adenoid Hynkel, however, goes duck hunting in similar Tyrolean outfit with folkloric hat, traditional janker, lederhosen and matching shoes to feign his accidental presence in the borderland of Osterlich.

Chaplin's source was mainly newsreel films with Hitler, which provided him with a vivid impression, as Chaplin Jr. recalled:

> Along with his work on the screenplay, my father began to study his subject. He got together all the newsreels of Hitler he could lay his hands on and looked at them by the hour, either in his home theater or in a projection room at his studio. There were scenes with Hitler talking to children, cuddling babies, visiting the sick in the hospitals, displaying his oratory gift on all possible occasions. Dad studied the dictator's every pose, picked up his mannerisms, and was enthralled by the overall picture. "The guy's a great actor," he used to say admiringly.[3]

Actor Tim Durant, a friend of Chaplin's, recalled that Chaplin repeatedly watched the newsreel footage of Hitler's June 22, 1940, arrival by rail at Compiègne. There, on November 11, 1918, the German Empire, France and Great Britain had ended the fighting of World War I. Now the armistice agreement between the Third Reich and France was signed, which amounted to the French surrender. Chaplin is said to have regarded Hitler's stepping out of the railroad carriage as a little dance and to have commented on it as follows: "Oh, you bastard, you son of a bitch, you swine. I know what's in your mind. [...] This guy is one of the greatest actors I've ever

Hitler orator pose, photo by Heinrich Hoffmann.

seen."[4] The inspiration from the news-reel dance may have been incorporated into *The Great Dictator*.

Chaplin had rightly considered Hitler as an actor. During the Weimar Republic, Hitler had already "read everything attainable" about how a speaker can increase his impact on the audience.[5] On the advice of his ENT physician Dr. Friedrich Karl Dermietzel, he had also taken acting lessons from early April to early November 1932.[6] During the hot phase of the NSDAP's struggle for power in Germany, the opera tenor Paul Devrient had taught him in strict secrecy at all possible venues.[7] The lessons were so successful that Hitler was able to manipulate his audience even better. In 1934, he had the series of postcards with his orator poses from early 1925 withdrawn from circulation because they no longer adequately portrayed him as an

Hitler orator pose, photo by Heinrich Hoffmann.

orator.[8] Hitler's manipulative abilities are probably one of the reasons that Chaplin has Hynkel in *The Great Dictator* wear two boldly drawn crosses, one above the other, as his party emblem, symbolizing the English term "to double-cross."

Chaplin probably also put the Italian dictator Benito Mussolini under the microscope. In *The Great Dictator*, Benzino Napaloni, who was originally to be called Gasolini,[9] rules over Bacteria with the capital Aroma and wears an emblem with two dice, each showing a one and a six, as a sign of his random politics. Hitler and Mussolini shared two pompous public appearances, which were also propagandistically disseminated on German and Italian newsreels. From September 25 to 29, 1937, Mussolini paid a state visit to Germany. Hitler welcomed him each time on train platforms to Kiefersfelden on the German-Austrian border and later in Lalendorf in Mecklenburg for a troop maneuver, which was reported on in *Ufaton-Woche* and *Deuligtonwoche*, respectively. At Kiefersfelden, Mussolini waves from the open train window like Chaplin's Napaloni, and at Lalendorf, the train and red carpet for the Italian state guest are similar to those seen in *The Great Dictator*.[10] Footage exists of Hitler's May 1938 return visit to Italy of the two dictators riding together in an open car through streets lined with people. This bears a striking resemblance to Hynkel and Napaloni's ride through the Tomanian capital.[11]

By the end of March 1940, the shooting of *The Great Dictator* was essentially completed. But Chaplin subsequently shot additional footage, fine-tuned the film, and worked on the post-synchronization.

Newsreel screen shot: Hitler welcomes Mussolini in Kiefersfelden, September 25, 1937.

Hitler and Mussolini in Rome in Italian staff car, May 1938.

Leni Riefenstahl's Triumph des Willens

Riefenstahl's 1935 film about the Nuremberg Rally in early September 1934 is exemplary for the propagandistic, pompous staging of Nazism and its functionaries. With the captivating power of its images, the director covered up the repulsive political content of this major Nazi event. Hitler classified *Triumph des Willens* as a "unique and incomparable glorification of the power and beauty of our movement."[12] In September 1933, Rumpelstilzchen wrote about Riefenstahl: "Among [German film-makers] the most German is Leni Riefenstahl, [... who] formerly could only prevail over the Mischpoke [note: German-Jewish filmmakers] with an almost tremendous physical, mental, artistic effort. [...] Now [... she] has been tasked by the government to agglomerate the Reichsparteitag des deutschen Volkes (Nuremberg Rally of the

Screen shot from *The Great Dictator*, 1940: Hynkel (Chaplin) and Napaloni (Jack Oakie) in Tomanian staff car (*The Great Dictator* © Roy Export S.A.S.).

German People) into a lasting work of art on sound film [...]."[13]

During Hitler's ride in an open automobile from the Nuremberg airfield to the hotel in the city center, in *Triumph des Willens* a little girl in her mother's arms presents him with flowers. There are also newsreel shots that depict him as a friend of children. Chaplin portrays Hynkel similarly after the latter's great speech. There is also a striking resemblance between Hannah's folk costume, which she wears during the rendezvous with the Jewish barber, and that of a young woman seen in the Riefenstahl film before the opening of the Nuremberg Rally.

Screen shot from *Triumph des Willens*, 1935: girl in garb like Hannah (© Friedrich-Wilhelm-Murnau-Stiftung).

In *The Great Dictator*, Hynkel gives his big speech on a huge rostrum, with his party comrades lined up in the background. Crowds of people have paraded in front of it, cheering his speech with mechanical arm-lifting and shouting "Heil." *Triumph des Willens* contains comparable scenes from the opening of the Nuremberg Rally in the great hall and on the second day of the event in the open air, as countless members of the Organization Todt march up with spades shouldered like rifles, followed by the German youth. After dark, Hitler delivers his speech from the rostrum at the Nuremberg Rally grounds, with a squad of NSDAP officials seated behind him, including Reichspressechef Otto Dietrich, Hitler's Deputy Rudolf Hess, Head of the Deutsche Arbeitsfront Robert Ley, Chief Ideologue Alfred Rosenberg, *Der Stürmer* agitator Julius Streicher—plus Propaganda Minister Goebbels as well as Reichskommissar and future Reichsmarschall Göring, who are both caricatured in *The Great Dictator* as Garbitsch and Herring, respectively.

Riefenstahl's projection of the Nazi leadership as well as the mass scenes were certainly most suitable for Chaplin's orientation and as a basis for his work. But did he know *Triumph des Willens* when he worked on *The Great Dictator*? In her 1987 *Memoiren*, Riefenstahl proudly quoted from an undated *New York Times* article with the headline "Riefenstahl's Film Was Too Good," without providing any specific dates:

> The leftist Spanish film director Luis Buñuel was to edit Leni Riefenstahl's documentary about the Nazi party congress in Nuremberg. The idea was to use it as an anti–Nazi propaganda film. Buñuel showed the result to René Clair and Charlie Chaplin in New York. Chaplin bent over with laughter. But Clair had misgivings: Riefenstahl's pictures were so damn

Screen shot from *Triumph des Willens*, 1935: Nazi march (© Friedrich-Wilhelm-Murnau-Stiftung).

Screen shot from *The Great Dictator*, 1940: Tomanian troops march (*The Great Dictator* © Roy Export S.A.S.).

good and impressive, no matter how much they were trimmed. [...] The film [was] quietly relegated to the archives.[14]

This article has not been found in *The New York Times* or in any other U.S. newspaper, and it is not in Riefenstahl's private archives (see Chapter 8).

In his memoir from the early 1980s, *Mein letzter Seufzer*, Buñuel reported on his editing of *Triumph des Willens* and Chaplin's reaction:

> For two or three weeks I worked on [two different German films] in the editing room. The films were ideologically horrible, but fantastically made, impressive. [...] The edited films were shown [...] to all kinds of people, for example in consulates and also to senators. René Clair and Charlie Chaplin watched them together and reacted in completely diametrically opposite ways. Clair was horrified by the impact of the films and said to me, "Don't show this to anyone, or we'll be lost!" Chaplin, on the other hand, laughed like a maniac. He even fell off his chair laughing. Why? Was it because of *The Great Dictator*? I still cannot understand it today.[15]

The 1975 German Hanser book *Luis Buñuel* recounted that Iris Barry in 1939 had hired Buñuel, whom she knew from Europe, to give Riefenstahl's *Triumph des Willens* and another German propaganda film an opposing ideological direction. The wife of the vice-director of New York's Museum of Modern Art and the museum's first film curator, Barry had also founded its Film Library.[16] Buñuel's edited versions have not yet been published.[17]

Did Chaplin bend over laughing at Buñuel's adaptation of *Triumph des Willens* in 1939 or 1940 while working on *The Great Dictator*? Neither Chaplin, his son, nor David Robinson have said anything about it. In his memoirs, Buñuel wrote that he had met Chaplin in the U.S. in 1930 and 1939. In 1939, he had tried in vain to sell Chaplin gags in order to make ends meet financially. After moving to New York, he met Barry after a period of unemployment. Shortly after the beginning of World War II, she recruited him to work in the propaganda Office of Coordination of Inter-American Affairs, founded by Nelson Rockefeller. The Office wanted to convince the relevant authorities of the U.S. government of the effectiveness of political film propaganda. For this purpose, Barry asked Buñuel to edit two German propaganda films, but to remain silent about this task, which she explained as follows:

> An Erster Sekretär (First Secretary) of the German embassy secretly sent us two propaganda films, *Triumph des Willens* and a second one showing the conquest of Poland by the Nazi army. [...] Take the two German films, [...] they are too long, edit them down by half, to ten or twelve reels, and we will show them to the people who should see this, so they will realize the effect.

In 1940, the Museum of Modern Art hired Buñuel as chief editor.[18]

Even though it is doubtful whether Riefenstahl's quote is authentic, some details match Buñuel's account. This, however, also raises questions. Why did a German embassy official secretly leak the film copies to the Office, and how had he gotten hold of them? Did no one notice that the copies were missing? Which "U.S. government circles" did not believe in the effectiveness of cinematic propaganda? And how would such an attitude fit with the fact that propaganda films had already been produced in the U.S. during World War I? Had the propagandistic benefit of these films been researched at that time? These questions can no longer be answered.

The film about the "conquest of Poland by the Nazi army" was probably Fritz Hippler's *Feldzug in Polen*, which premiered in February 1940[19]; Hippler may have used footage of the "Sonderfilmtrupp Riefenstahl" from the ground offensive in Poland.[20] If Barry had also handed over Riefenstahl's *Triumph des Willens* to Buñuel for editing soon after the German premiere of *Feldzug in Polen*, Chaplin could have seen Buñuel's edited version before the main shooting for *The Great Dictator* was completed. Or had Chaplin himself obtained a copy of *Triumph des Willens*, which, according to the unsubstantiated assertions of Robert Cole, Jürgen Trimborn and Stephen Weissman, he watched "again and again" to study Hitler's poses and habits? Trimborn even speculated that Chaplin had only finally decided to make *The Great Dictator* after seeing Buñuel's edit, which, according to Weissman, Chaplin "studied meticulously."[21] However, Chaplin had already officially declared in March 1939, i.e., before Buñuel's employment at the Museum of Modern Art, that he was working on a film comedy about the lives of dictators.

Since Chaplin extensively viewed newsreel footage, he would not necessarily have depended on *Triumph des Willens* as his sole cinematic source for dealing with Hitler and with the staging of large-scale Nazi events. Newsreels also contained Nazi crowd scenes. For example, Hitler looked down from the speaker's rostrum at an NSDAP event in Dortmund in 1933 at formations of SA people lined up in a large square.[22] The *British Movietone* newsreel captured something similar from the 1937 Nuremberg Rally.

Whatever may be true in the context of *Triumph des Willens*, Chaplin brilliantly recreated Nazi-style crowd scenes in his studio. This may be the reason for the groundless rumor that he claimed his film contained scenes shot in Nazi Germany.[23]

Hynkel's Language

As early as late February 1916, Chaplin's collaborator Fred Goodwins had reported that Chaplin had entertained his staff with a parodic character-sketch following the daily shooting, speaking fluently "in an absurd mixture of French, Italian, and German."[24] Chaplin also satirized Hitler's oratorical style, manner of expression and language, which can be heard in *The Great Dictator* on various occasions: on the rostrum in front of crowds, over the radio, and when he is angry. About this, Chaplin Jr. wrote: "All this study paid off for my father. His portrayal of Hitler was a perfect imitation, so perfect that Germans watching the picture said you had to listen closely to realize he wasn't speaking their language with a Hitler accent, but just gibberish."[25]

In fact, Chaplin's linguistic imitation achieved precisely this striking effect. Although not a single complete German sentence is heard in the original film, it is never doubted that *The Great Dictator* is set in the German-speaking world. At the same time, Chaplin managed to capture the fascination that Hitler exerted on Germans of varying education at Nazi mass rallies. This may not have had the same effect on people of other nationalities, because the vast majority of them did not feel affected.[26] Sometimes in the film, Hynkel's tone of voice and gestures alone are sufficient to understand the content of passages of his speech, which is now and then summarized by a radio commentary. When Hynkel urges his audience to tighten their belts because of the difficult circumstances, the fat Herring takes it literally. Applauding, he jumps up from his seat and tightens his uniform belt with difficulty. But when the field marshal sits back down, the belt immediately pops open because it cannot hold the tension!

According to Dan James, Chaplin initially improvised Hynkel's German-sounding gibberish of sibilants and gutturals which starts the rally without a script on location in San Fernando Valley. Most of the scene was reshot in the studio, and most of that studio footage was used in the finished film.[27] Hynkel's onomatopoeic pseudo–German is often a mixture of elements of German and English. His dictatorial credo on democracy, freedom and free speech also sounds like this: "Demokrazi—schtoonk! Liberty—schtoonk! Free spreken—schtoonk!" Hynkel's language uses German words such as "sauerkraut," "delicatessen," "Wiener Schnitzel" and "sprechen," or words phonetically similar to them. Examples are "Dschuten" (Jews), "schtoonken" (stank), "lager beerden" (lager beer) and "bloot" (blood). In addition, there are German-sounding onomatopoeia ("ach," "uch," "acht," "icht"), which are occasionally probably deliberate distortions of German words ("zackt," "trutzt," "grotzter").[28] The term "Blitzkrieg," which stands for unexpectedly quick military victories and has long since become a common international term, can also be heard. Its inventor, however, was not Chaplin. Rather, its origins date back to 1935, were associated primarily with the German invasion of Poland in September 1939, and were increasingly used in the press from then on.[29] *The Great Dictator*, however, may have been the first feature film to use the term.

The tense living conditions in Hynkel's state are reflected in the country's name Tomania. This derived from the English "Ptomaine" (corpse poison) and is a now somewhat archaic term for food poisoning caused by decaying organic matter. But the name may also contain "mania." This also makes sense, because it would describe the psycho-pathological politics of the dictatorship. With Hynkel's first name Adenoid, Chaplin has onomatopoeically and partly in content transmogrified Hitler's name. It could be the contraction of Adolf and paranoid, but more especially the medical term for pharyngeal tonsils. The first option would fit with Hynkel's irrational behavior, the second with his sometimes nasal way of speaking. The names of Officer Schultz and ghetto residents Jaeckel and Mann reveal German and German-Jewish origins, respectively. Hynkel's political henchmen are named Dr. Garbitsch and Field Marshal Herring. Garbitsch goes back to the English words "garbage" and Herring stands for the fish of the same name, which is why Hynkel also calls the Field Marshal Bismarck-Herring. For Hynkel's great speech, Chaplin constructed a word play from Garbitsch and Herring with predominantly English parts: "Herring shouldn't smelten fine from Garbitsch and Garbitsch shouldn't smelten fine from Herring."

Other personal names and geographical designations sound German and have predominantly a veiled meaning:

- Professor Kibitzen: after the Yiddish word "kibitz," which means giving unsolicited advice and thus characterizes the inventor who wants to sell useless inventions
- the Italian Ambassador Spook: in German "Spuk"
- Bacteria: Italy
- Aroma: Rome
- Osterlich: Austria
- Pretzelberg: after the German components "Bretzel" (pretzel) and "Berg" (mountain). The border town of Osterlich, for whose name perhaps the Austrian Salzburg is the godfather.

The signages in the ghetto are frequently borrowed from the artificial language Esperanto, then again composed of various European language elements. For example, the first line of the sign on the Jewish barber's store reads "Razn Barber Harlavado" and is composed of the German "rasieren" (shave), the English "barber" and the German Spanish combination "haarlavado" from "Haar" (hair) and "lavado" (washed). So in the salon you can get a shave, a haircut and your hair washed. The second line "Harü Tondadoz" does not name the Jewish barber; throughout the film he remains nameless. It rather means "haircut": "Harü" is borrowed from the German "Haar," while "Tondadoz" goes back to the French noun "tondeur," which means "shearer." On the left side of the salon's window, a sign "Lipharoj Tondadoz." "Lipharoj" is the Esperanto term for "moustache." So the Jewish barber also trims beards. Appendix 7 offers explanations for all the ghetto signs.

According to Albert Speer's *Spandauer Tagebücher* (Spandau Diaries), Hitler parodied the Italian dictator in the Neue Reichskanzlei (New Reich Chancellery) during Mussolini's state visit in late September 1937, although he was initially impressed by his appearance. But following Mussolini's leaving after a banquet, the Italian dictator "seemed rather operetta-like" to Hitler. Therefore, Hitler imitated him in the presence of Goebbels and Speer, only slowed down by Goebbels, with "individual outré gestures" such as "the jutting chin, the characteristic right hand on the hip, the straddled stance," and shouted Italian or Italian-sounding words such as Giovinezza, Patria, Victoria, Macaroni, Belleza, Belcanto and Basta" (Youth, Fatherland, Victory, Macaroni, Bel Canto, Beauty and Basta). "It was very funny," Speer wrote of Hitler's performance at Mussolini's expense.[30] British Hitler admirer Unity Mitford has reported something similar, claiming that Hitler also parodied Göring, Goebbels and Himmler.[31]

Speer's account, however, will have to be taken with a grain of salt. After the breakdown of the Third Reich, the Nazi careerist and power politician had managed to style himself as a "good Nazi," a minor figure in Nazi crimes, and a basically apolitical contemporary. This is represented by his following career moves:

- March 1931 NSDAP member and SA man
- 1932 switch to the SS and member of other party organizations
- staging of the Nazi mass event on May 1, 1933
- as a result, Amtsleiter für künstlerische Gestaltung von Großkundgebungen in der Reichspropagandaleitung (Head of the Office for Artistic Design of large-scale Rallies in the Reich Propaganda Directorate) with his trademark of long rows of swastika flags as well as
- Hitler's minion and architect
- 1937 Generalbauinspektor für die Reichshauptstadt (General Building Inspector for the Reich Capital)[32]
- from 1942, Reichsrüstungsminister (Reich Armaments Minister) responsible for unusually efficient armaments, the expansion of concentration camps, the use of millions of forced laborers and concentration camp prisoners, and the prolongation of warfare

With his strategy, the major war criminal Speer avoided being sentenced to death at the Nuremberg War Crimes Tribunal in 1946. After serving his 20-year prison term, he deceived the public primarily with his autobiographical books *Erinnerungen* and *Spandauer Tagebücher*, millions of copies of which were sold.[33] Most readers followed him blindly. Germans in particular felt that Speer morally exonerated them from the horrors of Nazism.

Other Influences

Chaplin wrote in his autobiography that he wanted to start his film "with a battle scene of World War I, showing [the artillery piece] Big Bertha, with its shooting range of seventy-five miles, with which the Germans intended to awe the Allies. It is supposed to destroy Rheims Cathedral—instead, it misses its mark and destroys an outside water-closet."[34] The model was Big Bertha, a 42-centimeter mortar of German manufacture and one of the most famous German weapons of the Great War. Its penetrating power, however, found its master in reinforced concrete fortifications.

The Nazis' cultural activities also invited satire. Pithy monumental sculptures of animals and humans, for example, symbolized strength, determination, superiority and heroic stance of system-loyal master race men at the 1940 Munich Große deutsche Kunstausstellung (Great German Art Exhibition) and, like Arno Breker's "Der Künder" (The Herald), looked out over the viewers into infinity.[35] Chaplin admittedly did not recreate such sculptures that were the product of Nazi ideology. Instead, he alienated well-known works of fine art in such a way that their political rape in the service of the Tomanian Fuehrer cult is immediately recognizable. After his great speech, Hynkel rides with Garbitsch in the state carriage past the ancient Greek "Venus de Milo" and Auguste Rodin's "The Thinker." Sculptors have placed right arms stretched upward for them to give Hynkel the "Tomanian salute." After the *Great Dictator* premiere, the British *Daily Express* mocked: "Even Venus de Milo Heils Charlie." The article ended up in the Chaplin file of the Hauptarchiv der NSDAP.[36]

During the November pogroms of the Third Reich, shop windows were daubed with "JUDE" (among other things), and the international press had reported on it in words and vision. This was most likely Chaplin's model for the shop window of the barber's salon daubed with "JUDE." He may also have received ideas from Hitler's monstrous construction projects. These are documented by newsreel and propaganda footage of later Nazi Party rallies on the Nuremberg Zeppelinfeld with its huge buildings, which Hitler had commissioned from Speer. In 1934, there was already a huge eagle there with a metal frame and a wingspan of 30 meters; it can also be seen in *Triumph des Willens*. It was a harbinger of large-scale projects that Speer called "built megalomania" in his *Erinnerungen*.[37] Speer was to transform Berlin into the future world capital "Germania" in the Nazi sense, which was to be completed in 1950.[38] Hitler's 420-meter–long Neue Reichskanzlei (New Reich Chancellery) in Berlin's Voss-Strasse, with a 370-square-meter-large and lavishly furnished study, which was inaugurated in January 1939, was one of the few elaborately planned monstrous monumental buildings[39] that were completed. Money apparently did not play any role. Hitler even assigned Riefenstahl to shoot a (never realized) film about it, which was to be financed with about 700,000 reichsmark from the enormous "Kulturfonds des Führers" (Fuehrer's Cultural Fund).[40]

Parts of Hynkel's government palace bear a resemblance to Hitler's vastly larger Neue Reichskanzlei. In his giant study, the German dictator received visitors seated at his imposing desk to demonstrate his power to them, as Speer echoed Hitler's intent: "When the diplomats see this, sitting before me at this table, they will be taught to fear me."[41] In *The Great Dictator*, Garbitsch advises Hynkel to intimidate Napaloni by having the Bacterian dictator sit on a very low chair with extremely short legs so Hynkel can look down on him from his desk. Chaplin personally, by the way, had had a similar experience. During his trip to Europe in the spring of 1931, he had to sit on a much lower seat during his reception in audience with Belgium's King Albert, who was throned high above everything.[42]

Hitler's study in the Neue Reichskanzlei boasted an enormous globe that escaped the bombing of Berlin. On a much smaller globe in the living hall of Hitler's Berghof on the Obersalzberg near Berchtesgaden, as Speer related, the dictator had drawn a pencil line on the Ural Mountains as a sign of how far he wanted to

Screen shot from *The Tramp and the Dictator*, 2002: Red Army officers in Hitler's destroyed new Reich Chancellery, May 1945 (© Photoplay Productions Ltd. & Spiegel TV).

expand the "German living space in the East."[43] Whether Chaplin was aware of the two globes in Hitler's headquarters is doubtful. For Chaplin probably conceived the essence of Hynkel's entranced dance with the globe to the spherical sounds of the prelude to the opera *Lohengrin* more than ten years earlier. In 1929, Douglas Fairbanks shot a silent home movie with Chaplin in an ancient Greek costume, playing similarly to Hynkel with a small globe. At the end, Chaplin puts a German Pickelhaube on it—and puffs the spiked helmet off.[44]

The scene in the Jewish barber's salon, in which he carefully prepares a customer for shaving to Johannes Brahms' "Hungarian Dance No. 5" and then shaves him with a delicate pattern, can also be traced back to Chaplin himself, at least for the most part. In 1919, he shot a *Sunnyside* scene in which Charlie tries to do a man's hair on a completely rundown barber's chair. The unfortunate customer fares worse than the customer in *The Great Dictator*, because his feet touch a red-hot stove and, for good measure, Charlie shaves a slash into the shock of hair at the back of his head. The scene remained unknown for a long time because Chaplin did not use it for his theatrical release of *Sunnyside*. Decades later, in their documentary *Unknown Chaplin*, Kevin Brownlow and David Gill unearthed Fairbanks' home movies and the cut *Sunnyside* footage.

The model for Chaplin's deleted scene is said to have been Nick Cogley's lost 1915 film *Giddy, Gay, and Ticklish* with Syd Chaplin and Edgar Kennedy. Charlie Chaplin is said to have played the barber in it and also to have been behind the camera,[45] but he had left Keystone by the time Syd's starring comedies really commenced. Perhaps, however, *The Great Dictator*'s shaving scene resembles the one in Syd's 1921 film *King, Queen, Joker*, the theatrical print of which is thought to be lost.

Screen shot from Douglas Fairbanks home movie, 1929: Chaplin in ancient Greek costume toying with small globe (*Unknown Chaplin*, episode 3: "Hidden Treasures," 1983; © Thames Television Ltd.).

Chaplin's personal film stock contained alternate takes of each scene, which have not yet been made generally available. According to descriptions of *King, Queen, Joker*, Syd played a dual role, similar to *The Great Dictator*. The kingdom of Coronia is on the verge of revolution because the king has so far denied his subjects free trade. The chief plotter kidnaps the king and substitutes him with an exact double, a barber's assistant. But the double has no idea of court behavior and in high spirits he gets up to all kinds of nonsense. When the real king at last effects the needed reforms, he is allowed to return to his throne and sentences his double to death. However, the queen helps him to escape.[46]

The historical blueprint for the Tomanian invasion of neighboring Osterlich is the annexation of Austria in March 1938 by the Third Reich. For *Great Dictator*, Chaplin changed the historical background. Mussolini saw himself as the guarantor of Austrian independence. After preliminary negotiations with Hitler, however, he took no action against the Nazi annexation. In *Great Dictator*, instead, Napaloni himself is planning the invasion of Osterlich by Bacterian troops. During his state visit to Tomania, he argues with Hynkel about their plans, which are mutually exclusive, culminating in the threat of war between Tomania and Bacteria.

As early as the fall of 1923 and 1925, a Chaplin film titled "The Suicide Club," based on Robert Louis Stevenson, had been announced and was being talked about shortly before the German premiere of *City Lights* as a follow-up.[47] As stated by Joyce Milton, Stevenson's 1878-82 short story cycle *The Suicide Club* is said to have "indirectly influenced" Chaplin's drawing of the candidate for the suicide mission.[48] Milton did not specify details, but may be referring to the "Story of the Young Man with the Cream Tarts," with which Stevenson's cycle begins. In a bar, a prince and his confidant witness a young man offering other guests cream tarts in vain. Thereupon, the young man introduces both witnesses to the Suicide Club with its bizarre ritual. To relieve club members of the burden of committing suicide, a card game is held every evening to select the next aspirant for death and who will send him to kingdom come.[49] Admittedly, there are no similarities to Chaplin's drawing of lots for the suicide mission. Unlike Stevenson, nothing is distributed openly in *The Great Dictator*, nor is any relationship established between an aspirant of suicide and his future aide. Instead, a "volunteer" is to be drawn by a coin, which has been baked into one of several small cakes. However, sensible Hannah has carried the lottery procedure *ad absurdum* and baked a coin into each cake. Therefore, all participants in the draw find a coin. But everyone conceals his find in a tragically burlesque way by slipping the coin unnoticed onto his neighbor's plate—until all the coins end up with the barber, who has swallowed them for fear of the suicide mission.

The existence of Nazi concentration camps was known long before Chaplin's decision to shoot *The Great Dictator*. At least since the Reichspogromnacht (Reich Pogrom Night) in November 1938, there could be no doubt about the state terror of the Hitler regime against the Jews. At the end of April 1940, while Chaplin's filming was not yet completed, on the orders of Heinrich Himmler the first and largest German extermination camp was constructed in Auschwitz, which was not made public at the time. After the

1921 ads for Syd Chaplin's *King, Queen, Joker.*

Wannsee Conference of January 20, 1942, the inconceivable factory-like state mass murder was planned and carried out by SS-Obergruppenführer (Senior Group Leader SS) Reinhard Heydrich. This Holocaust is without precedent in human history and cost the lives of up to 1.6 million people in Auschwitz and the neighboring Birkenau camp alone. So the horrors of the death camps were neither known nor imagined by Chaplin until the filming of *The Great Dictator* was completed. The storm troopers that Hynkel sends out over the radio to attack the ghetto therefore only provide a rudimentary glimpse of the true horror of marauding Nazi terror troops. They are supposed to "clean up the ghetto in medieval manner," but they do not destroy it, and Schultz can still stop them from lynching the Jewish barber.

The Tomanian concentration camp to which he and Schultz are sent also does not represent the horrors of Nazi inhumanity: it is more like a prison there. When Tomanian soldiers arrest the disguised Hynkel shortly before the invasion of Osterlich, they threaten him that he will be made to talk in the concentration camp. There, certainly, no constitutional interrogation methods are to be expected, but the true horror of the concentration camps also does not emerge in this scene. But after the occupation of Osterlich, Garbitsch, in his speech at the mass meeting, clearly summarizes the Nazi racial policy and illustrates the organization of blind obedience in the Third Reich, in which there are no longer any fundamental rights:

Corona veniet delectis. Victory shall come to the worthy. Today, democracy, liberty and freedom are words to fool the people. No nation can progress with such ideas. Therefore, we think to abolish them. In the future, each man will serve the interest of the state with absolute obedience. Let him who refuses beware! The rights of citizenship will be taken away from all Jews and of all non–Aryans. They are inferior and therefore enemies of the state. It is the duty of all true Aryans to hate and despise them. Henceforth, this nation is annexed to the Tomanian Empire and the people will obey the laws bestowed on us by our great leader, the Dictator of Tomania, the conqueror of Osterlich, the future emperor of the World!

Mockery

Chaplin's filming of "Production No. 6" (*The Great Dictator*'s working title) began two days after the Third Reich's invasion of Poland on September 1, 1939. By spring 1940, the German Wehrmacht had occupied Denmark, Norway and France. Chaplin's reaction to this was described by his son as follows:

Dad was planning to do what others were afraid of doing—hold the little monster of Europe up to public ridicule. He was far ahead of his day in this, as he had been when he made *Modern Times*, which was an outcry against the standardization of man. The only reason events caught up with him in the case of *The Great Dictator* was that Dad progressed slowly, while his counterpart in Europe, encouraged by appeasement, was moving with incredible speed.[50]

Around the beginning of 1940, it was rumored that Syd Chaplin would not only assist his brother as a director, but also occasionally double him in the film. Sixty years later, it became known that Syd had privately documented part of the shooting on 16mm film. This color footage, included in Brownlow and Kloft's documentary *The Tramp and the Dictator*, revealed the care his brother Charlie took with the color scheme of the costumes, even though *The Great Dictator* was conceived as a black-and-white picture. By early 1940, press reports were making reference to Chaplin's "frantic guttural speech" of the film dictator, and there was speculation whether Chaplin would also ridicule Hitler's "German salute."[51]

Satirical reactions to Hitler's "Blitzkrieg" against Poland followed, and at the same time they established a connection between Chaplin and Hitler. For example, comedian Tommy Handley performed in a BBC radio program the song "Who Is This Man? (Who Looks like Charlie Chaplin)" by John Watt and Max Kester. The song went on sale as a record with a cover featuring the

Sheet Music *Who Is This Man?*, front cover, 1940.

newcomer general Hitler in Charlie's tramp outfit with bowler hat in the shape of a pickelhaube and an armband, both bearing swastika emblems.[52] Similarly, a boy had been dressed as Hitler in a spiked helmet for an October 1939 Halloween photo in the *Glasgow Sunday Post*.[53]

Even without such satirical pinpricks from abroad, the German film press was constantly in an uproar about "war and smear films" on the English-language market. In January and February 1940, the *Lichtbildbühne* mobilized with two propaganda articles[54] and also published thoughts on how to counter these undesirable films. Reichspressechef Dietrich spoke at a workshop of "magazine Hauptschriftleiter" about the tasks of the "magazine in wartime." In this context, he "issued paroles," including that "the German press must operate as the intellectual Wehrmacht of the nation."[55] Abroad, however, no one was deterred from poking fun at Hitler.

Berlin Premiere?

In late January-early February 1940, the *Detroit News* and the *Miami News* reported concerns that peace would return to Europe before the film was completed. For this could make it doubtful whether the film would be able to earn the funds already invested in its production.[56] On March 26 and 27, a small flood of mostly identical U.S. articles followed, which probably would not have pleased the Nazi propagandists: Chaplin wanted *The Great Dictator*'s world premiere to take place with a private screening in Berlin for Hitler alone![57] Very quickly, the newspapers backpedaled. Now, allegedly, only "friends of Chaplin" insisted on the plan for a Berlin premiere: Chaplin refused to comment.[58]

Probably the sensational news about the planned Berlin premiere was a fabricated Hitler spoof. Napaloni actor Jack Oakie might have rightly doubted that Hitler would understand the humor of Chaplin's film and draw political conclusions from it: "If Hitler has even an ounce of humor, he'll take one look at the film and wonder what all the fuss is about. If he then understands Charlie's concern, he will immediately end his war and retire to his mountain [Obersalzberg] to laugh."[59]

Yet another news item, also scarcely meant to be taken seriously, imputed this "bit of humor" to Hitler. Henry F. Pringle claimed in the July 1940 issue of the U.S. magazine *Ladies' Home Journal* that in the preceding winter, a German distributor had surprised Chaplin with an offer to pay $250,000 for the German distribution rights to *The Great Dictator*. This meant the equivalent of about one million reichsmark, a larger sum than Südfilm AG had paid for the German screening rights to *City Lights* in 1931. Chaplin's incredulous inquiry is said to have been answered by the distributor as follows: "[The amount] is what the film would bring in if there were a revolution in Germany and Hitler lost his power. That's a good bet, isn't it?"[60] Chaplin's doubts would have been all too justified: By the turn of 1939-40, the nationalization of the entire German film industry had been pushed so far that it could be completed by mid–1941.[61] Moreover, Hitler was still able to bask in the glory of his military successes until the winter of 1942-43.

Chaplin Steadfast

In May 1940, Goebbels' Ministerialrat Fritz Hippler complained, "[I]n America the production level of Germanophobe films [had] reached a record this year." He particularly lamented Sam Newfield's 1939 propaganda feature film *Hitler—Beast of Berlin*, which "probably represents the most tasteless agitation that has ever been conceived." In the same breath, he mentioned Chaplin's forthcoming film.[62] In the U.S., after the beginning of World War II, there were still frequent demonstrations of sympathy for the Third Reich, because many apparently admired Hitler's successful campaigns of conquest. But this was also met with strong counter-demonstrations, as Luis Buñuel recalled. The Nazi-friendly climate ended when the Third Reich declared war on the U.S. on December 11, 1941,[63] but it had had the effect that United Artists had been warned not to promote the production of *The Great Dictator*, and Chaplin himself had received anonymous threats. About this, he wrote in his memoirs: "During the making of *The Dictator* I began receiving crank letters, and now that it was finished they started to increase. Some threatened to throw stink bombs in the theaters and shoot up the screen wherever it would be shown, others threatening to create riots."[64] This is reminiscent of Nazi threats during the Weimar Republic against films which were a thorn in their side. For Chaplin, the threats probably did not work because he did not want to lose his investment in the production (there was talk of at least $1 million). In any case, at the end of May 1940 he denied rumors that he wanted to give up the project: "The report that I have withdrawn my film is entirely without foundation. I am cutting it now, and as soon as it is synchronized, it will be released. At a time like this, laughter is a safety valve for our sanity."[65] In response, United Artists announced that *The Great Dictator* would be released as part of their upcoming distribution schedule.

In June 1940, the German weekly *Das Reich* and the *Lichtbildbühne* reacted with the caustic articles "Hate in Film" and "Hate Outbursts of a Sinking World," using Chaplin's anti–Hitler film as an example. Defiantly, it was claimed that the wind had been taken out of the foreign agitation long ago by "our great documentary films, which are now running all over the world, [... such as] *Feldzug in Polen*."[66] However, this was wishful thinking, and it was no different with the news of *Der Film* "Nazis in uniform" from July 1940 about filming in Hollywood. Once again, Hollywood producers were flatly predicting a "huge failure" with anti–Nazi films, because supposedly soon "no country in the world" would want to show them.[67] This already contradicted Hippler's report on the production record of "Germanophobe" U.S. films. From 1939 to 1945, about 150 such films of this genre were produced and released.[68]

The Reichsministerium für Volksaufklärung und Propaganda drew film policy consequences as a result of the U.S. "smear film production" and arranged for the shutdown of the three U.S. distribution branches of 20th Century Fox, MGM and Paramount that were still active in Germany. Fox and MGM had already produced or announced "Germanophobe" feature films. Paramount had released newsreels in the U.S. that the Reichsfilmkammer considered "Germanophobe." In early July 1940, Reichsministerium für Volksaufklärung und Propaganda informed Fox's German office that its films would have to be completely removed from German theaters over the course of the next few days. At the end of the month, the German Wehrmacht was sent out to stop Fox's activities in German-occupied Western European countries.[69] Officially, the *Film-Kurier* announced on July 27, 1940, "Fox [...] has been banned from the German film market because of its Germanophobe activities."[70] In its issues of August 10 and September 5, the journal published the official announcements of the Reichsfilmkammer about the Germany-wide ban on MGM and Paramount films, which had to be "completely removed from circulation by September 12, 1940, at the latest."[71] The fact that Walt Disney's *Mickey Mouse cartoons* were still being shown in Hamburg's Waterloo Theater and Urania-Filmbühne in early 1941[72] does not contradict this: In Germany, only German distributors had distributed numerous Mickey Mouse and Silly Symphonies cartoons.[73]

Financial Flop and an Interview with Hitler?

In July 1940, the *Film-Kurier* article "Chaplin as Dictator" also predicted a "flop" for Chaplin's film. This was a Nazi stereotype that had already been invoked for *City Lights* and *Modern Times* and for other "Germanophobe smear films." Henceforth, it was regularly prayed over like a mantra. This time, the hook was Chaplin's lawsuit against the U.S. magazine *Life* and the publisher Time, Inc:

> A special case is Charlie Chaplin's dictator film. He has been busy with it for years, and it was said last summer that he had abandoned it because it was uncertain whether the voluntarily acting film censors would agree with the opus. The outbreak of war seems to have given the author new courage, although he has even been told in the press that his enterprise really has quite little prospect, though now for reasons other than censorship. Chaplin has just made a big scene in public because a New York picture magazine, *Life*, had carried a picture of him in the dictator's guise. Chaplin demanded huge compensation, and the lawsuit is pending. The magazine replaced the disputed image with a photograph of Henry Ford, busy at his plane. Chaplin's film is likely to be America's first "epic" war film. It has so far cost its author $1 million to $2 million. [...] It's a lottery [...] for Charlie Chaplin. It is going to be a flop.[74]

Life, which had a circulation of millions, had printed in its June 17, 1940, issue a picture of Chaplin in a Hynkel costume with a double cross emblem and signed "The Dictator with the Double Cross." By this time, Chaplin had essentially completed the shooting of *The Great Dictator*, except for reshoots and the final speech. When the *Life* report appeared, he had not yet permitted the reprinting of images from his unreleased movie. With his summary legal action against Time Inc., he could be sure of the undivided attention of the press. It was spectacular, because Chaplin claimed that the publication of pictures before the premiere would reduce the expected box office takings of $5 million and make it impossible for him to cover the production costs raised from his own funds. Therefore, shortly before the magazine was published, Chaplin demanded that the sale of this issue be prohibited and that the publisher be obliged to remove the objectionable picture from the print run. At the same time, he demanded $1 million in damages for his investment. So far, Time had shipped 1.6 million copies of the issue to distributors, with another 1.2 million still in stock. In its preliminary injunction, the court only prohibited the delivery of the 1.2 million copies still at the publishing house.[75] Chaplin and Time continued to litigate over the damages.[76]

In the final stages of production and until immediately before the premiere of *The Great Dictator*, scheduled for October 1940, Chaplin again received threats. This time he suspected Nazis behind it and tried to ensure that the premiere went off without a hitch:

> At first I thought of going to the police, but such publicity might keep the public away from the theater. A friend of mine suggested having a talk with Harry Bridges, head of the longshoremen's union. So I invited him to the house for dinner. I told him frankly my reason for wanting to see him. I knew Bridges was anti–Nazi, so I explained that I was making an anti–Nazi comedy and that I had been receiving threatening letters. I said, "If I could invite, say, twenty or thirty of your longshoremen to my opening, and have them scattered amongst the audience, then if any of these pro–Nazis fellows started a rumpus, your folks might gently stamp on their toes before anything got seriously going." Bridges laughed. "I don't think it will come to that, Charlie. You'll have enough defenders with your own public to take care of any cranks. And if these letters are from Nazis, they'll be afraid to show up in the daylight anyway."[77]

Henry F. Pringle's *Ladies' Home Journal* pictorial feature "The Story of Two Mustaches" (July 1940) also had to do without pictures from *The Great Dictator*. On the subjects of "leader," "diplomat," "protector," "spellbinder" and "sportsman,"

Hitler poses and images from old Chaplin films were juxtaposed as caricatures, and there were also images of each greeting the other with an outstretched arm. However, Pringle seemed to have a big surprise in store for his unverified article: A respected, but unnamed U.S. reporter had tried to interview Hitler about *The Great Dictator*. Although Hitler did not receive journalists, a high Nazi official was said to have given the reporter hopes in this case: "Ah! If you can really give Der Fuehrer information about the Chaplin film, I am confident that he will see you. He is much interested and very disturbed." But then the reporter was supposedly suddenly ordered back to the U.S., so the Hitler interview ended in smoke.[78] If the unknown journalist had already gotten that close to Hitler, a front-page sensation would have beckoned to him and his publisher. It is hard to imagine that a reporter would then also have been recalled so close to such a scoop, and for unknown reasons too— unless the story was made up anyway, which seems more likely.

In late August 1940, Chaplin met with the well-known gossip reporter Louella Parsons in Hollywood to show her some *Great Dictator* scenes and to talk about the film. He called it timeless, despite its topical political references, and was convinced that "the only way we can survive is to laugh at our troubles."[79] Afterwards, sneak previews of the film were said to have taken place in September 1940, possibly on the East Coast of the U.S., with unsatisfactory results and leading to some changes in Chaplin's cut.[80] Around the time of his conversation with Parsons, Chaplin also no longer objected to a pictorial report on *The Great Dictator*. Therefore, the British newspaper *Sunday Chronicle* was able to print a picture of Hynkel, Garbitsch and Herring for its article "Charlie is the latest Fuehrer" and to refer to the double cross emblem of Hynkel's party in the caption.[81]

Chaplin's *Great Dictator* was by far the most eagerly awaited film of the 1940-41 season, as could be seen from the lively coverage. Hitler thus remained in particular the target of satire, as in early September 1940 in Carl Rose's series of six cartoons in the U.S. magazine *P.M.* First, Hitler earns applause from his own ranks for a speech, and he bows in thanks like an actor. In classic Hamlet pose, he holds several skulls in front of him, each symbolizing one of the countries occupied by the German Wehrmacht. As the Nibelungen hero Siegfried with a swastika shield, the dictator has then slain the "dragon of racial defilement" with his sword, while in the next image he swings as Tarzan in the jungle from the branch of the anti–Comintern pact to the branch of the Communist-Nazi pact. As Salome, Hitler dances the veil dance of the seven secret weapons and finally slips into Chaplin's role of *The Great Dictator*. Arms stretched upward protrude from the globe, arranged like a large wheel, greeting him with the "German salute."[82]

And then there was no longer need to limit satire on Hitler to cartoons: At last, people could also laugh at *The Great Dictator*.

Synopsis

World War, 1918: One of the Tomanian soldiers is a decidedly clumsy but willing private (Chaplin). He brings a totally exhausted flight officer, who has to deliver a war-decisive message to the general through the enemy lines, to his plane. Because the officer is no longer able to fly the plane, the private has to take over despite his inexperience. They escape their pursuers, and thus the private has saved the officer's life. The flight ends in a crash landing, but both escape with their lives. The private is hospitalized. The urgent dispatch had become worthless in the meantime, because Tomania lost the war.

The private, actually a Jewish barber, spends many years in the hospital. Physically, he has recovered, but he has lost his memory. He thinks he has only been there a few weeks and wants to return to his hairdressing salon. In the meantime, Adenoid Hynkel (also played by Chaplin) has seized power in Tomania. A brutal dictator, Hynkel wants to make the country a great power again, demands sacrifices for this, and declares war on the Jews. During his first appearance, he leaves no doubt that under his regime, democracy, freedom and free speech have been abolished.

In the ghetto, storm troopers harass the Jews. When the barber leaves the hospital on his own account, no one stops him; there is nothing more they can do for him. Soon he learns the cruel reality the hard way, when he tries to prevent a storm trooper from scribbling "Jude!" on his shop window. More and more uniformed men approach, the situation escalates, they want to hang the barber on a lamppost. Then a staff car drives up. A high-ranking officer inquires about the incident. It is flight officer Schultz, whose life the barber had saved in the war. Schultz recognizes his rescuer, and gradually it dawns on the barber, whose memory is thus restored. The officer orders the storm troopers to leave the barber and his friends alone in the future, because it is the right of every human being to defend himself against humiliation.

Meanwhile, the dark-haired Hynkel dreams of being the dictator of a blond Aryan world. The beginning of his conquests should be the neighboring country Osterlich, but Benzino Napaloni, the dictator of Bacteria, has his eye on it. Hynkel desperately needs money to forestall him. No bank wants to finance Hynkel's plans, but perhaps the Jewish banker Epstein would be willing. To create a good climate for negotiations, Hynkel orders quiet in the ghetto. Epstein, however, refuses to give a loan to a "medieval madman." Enraged, Hynkel summons Schultz, whom he orders to "clean up the ghetto in medieval manner." Schultz tells Hynkel to his face that the decision is wrong and that the system of inhumanity is doomed to failure. For this, the high-handed Hynkel sends Schultz to a concentration camp as a traitor with the words "You need a vacation. Fresh air and calisthenics." Conditions in the ghetto become worse than ever.

Since Hynkel now has no credit, he must negotiate with Napaloni. Hynkel wants him to withdraw his troops from the border with Osterlich so that the Tomanian troops can march in unhindered. Napaloni is only willing to withdraw if Hynkel signs that he does not intend to invade Osterlich. During Napaloni's state visit, there are heated arguments over this issue, which even lead to assaults. When everything seems to be ending in a fiasco, slick Interior Minister Garbitsch secretly suggests to Hynkel that he sign after all. After all, it is only paper—and if Napaloni withdraws, Hynkel can annex Osterlich without any problems.

In the meantime, Schultz has escaped from the concentration camp and gone into hiding in the ghetto with the barber's neighbor. He plans an assassination attempt on Hynkel, but one of the Jews is to carry it out. However, the storm troopers track Schultz down and arrest him together with the barber. Both end up in a concentration camp, from which they escape in officers' uniforms.

In secrecy, the Tomanian invasion of Osterlich is being prepared. In order not to arouse suspicion, Hynkel, disguised in his Tyrolean outfit, goes duck hunting near the border. At the right time, he is supposed to be picked up by a car and then to march into Osterlich with the army. But Hynkel falls into the water while shooting a duck. He is watched by Tomanian soldiers as he gets out of the water in his sodden outfit. They would never think of meeting the dictator alone duck hunting, so must assume it is the escaped barber. All protest of the "false barber" is of no use. He is knocked down and taken away.

The barber's neighbors had fled to Osterlich to relatives after the conditions in the ghetto had become unbearable. There they had become accustomed to a pleasant life in the countryside. But now the storm troopers appear and smash everything to pieces. Schultz and the barber cross the border to Osterlich on the country road. A soldier recognizes Schultz and thinks that the dictator is walking next to him. A staff car is quickly brought to chauffeur Schultz and "Hynkel" to the rostrum. In front of this, a huge crowd is to attend the speeches, which are also broadcast over the radio. First Garbitsch announces that now, as in Tomania, all freedom will be abolished and Jews and all other non–Aryans will lose their rights. Then the dictator, who is supposed to speak, seems strangely changed to Garbitsch, and he and Herring are surprised that Schultz is back at Hynkel's side, but they do not suspect anything. The barber is afraid—he feels unable to step up to the microphone. But Schultz urges him: "You must, it's our only hope!" The barber pulls himself together, at first hesitantly, then more and more passionately his call for humanity grows, and he asks the soldiers to fight against dictators for a better world. This message goes over the airwaves and also reaches the barber's neighbors, who now look to the future with renewed hope. But after the applause of the masses has flared up, the barber addresses his private message to Hannah, who is lying on the ground: "Don't despair … look up, Hannah." Hannah receives the message as if in a thought transmission, without a radio. And with the motif from *Lohengrin*, the film fades out.

"Germanophobe Smear Film"?

Did *The Great Dictator* become the "Germanophobe smear film" as the Nazi film press, which admittedly equated "Germanophobe" with "anti–Nazi," had constantly claimed? Chaplin depicted Hitler's regime of terror and its representatives with the means of a comedy. In this respect, *The Great Dictator* is an anti–Nazi film that is not propaganda against Germany per se. That the majority of the German population cheered Hitler and his entourage was a fact, not agitation: the Nazis themselves frequently exploited this for propaganda purposes. The way Chaplin caricatures Hitler's dictatorship and fascism and thus unmasks it is also not agitation but satire. Dictatorships do not like to be ridiculed, and so they react allergically.

Is satire allowed to caricature the powerful, and how far can it go? The answer to this question was given by Kurt Tucholsky as early as 1919 in the *Berliner Tageblatt* in his clear-sighted article "Was darf Satire?" (What Is Satire Allowed to Do?), which seems to be tailored to Chaplin:

> If someone makes a good political joke in our country, half of Germany sits on the sofa and resents it. Satire seems to be a thoroughly negative thing. It says, "No!" [...] The satirist is an offended idealist: He wants the world to be good, it is bad, and now he is running against the bad. [...] Does satire exaggerate? Satire must exaggerate and is unjust in its deepest essence. It inflates the truth so that it becomes clearer, and it cannot work at all differently than after the Bible word: The just suffer with the unjust. [...] Genuine satire purifies the blood, and he who has healthy blood also has a pure complexion. What is satire allowed to do? Everything![83]

Chaplin shines in his dual role as Jewish barber and dictator with great comedy and as usual his fine sense of detail. Even when Schultz saves the barber from lynching, he finds room for humor. In response to Schultz's remark that he thought the barber was an Aryan, the guileless barber, who knows nothing about the term, declares, "I'm a vegetarian!" And when Schultz apologizes for the storm troopers, the barber says with an authoritative smile, "Don't mention it."

But Chaplin does not only play comedy. He also holds up a mirror to Nazi Germany by making the atmosphere of the dictatorship palpable. *The Great Dictator*'s introductory panel characterizes the political situation in Tomania between the two world wars as one in which "madness is out of control," "freedom has taken a nosedive to the ground" and "humanity has been played havoc with." The insecure dictator Hynkel seems like a psychopath when he loses his temper. Roaring in rage, he bends the microphone stand during his big speech due to his massive volume and makes even the microphone rotate. And to cool off in between, Hynkel pours water down the front of his uniform pants—is this his way to suppress sexual arousal? Just as animalistically, Hynkel grunts menacingly and grabs the secretary who has been called to take dictation, but drops her like a hot potato when the phone rings. At the same time, Hynkel is so obsessed with power that he plays ecstatically with the globe all alone in his huge study after his diabolical minister Garbitsch has persuaded him that he will be the future ruler of the world.

The Bacterian dictator Napolini is just as irresponsible a statesman as he is a pompous, self-important bogeyman who, apart from the annexation of Osterlich, has no political vision worth mentioning. And what can one expect from a general of Herring's caliber, who cannot even symbolically tighten the belt in front of his cowardly belly, and from whose uniform Hynkel tears his medals during a fit of rage, so that the clown-like striped shirt worn under the uniform jacket is revealed? Garbitsch, on the other hand, as an image of Goebbels devoid of any morals. He's Hynkel's slick, sinister idea-maker, who finally also announces in Osterlich that the end of freedom has come.

For all his satire of the Tomanian dictatorship and its officials, Chaplin balances the film and avoids the danger of black-and-white painting. The Jewish ghetto inhabitants, including the barber, are not the untouchable, squeaky-clean good guys; neither is dissident turned Tomanian officer Schultz. *The Great Dictator* paints a multi-layered picture of the Jews. Neither does he caricature or whitewash them, nor does he describe them as particularly heroic. Almost all the film's Jews are average people with their weaknesses, faults and hopes. Thus, Chaplin portrays human life in general.

In World War I, the barber is the opposite of a heroic front-line soldier who accumulates medals and decorations with a steely gaze. The good-willed klutz does what he is ordered to do. He cannot handle an anti-aircraft gun and is more likely to put his own men in danger. A live hand grenade accidentally slips into his uniform jacket, and while advancing against the enemy he suddenly marches into the middle of the enemy line, from which he is able to escape just in time. Schultz's rescue by plane is no heroic feat either, since the completely clueless barber develops no initiative of his own, but bungles whatever orders Schultz issues.

After the barber returns to his salon and fights off the storm troopers, the young orphan Hannah, who lives with his neighbor, admires him for his courage. She laments that the other ghetto dwellers are not as plucky as he is. But she fails to realize that the barber did not consciously rebel against the persecution of the Jews like a resistance fighter. After all, he was still suffering from his partial memory loss. That is why he mistook the storm troopers for policemen and could not know that these rowdies were responsible for the graffiti "Jude!" on his salon and that they would be the least likely to help him.

Chaplin also unabashedly shows the timidity of the Jewish ghetto population, which prevents them from defending themselves against the terror of Hynkel's dictatorship. Conditions were similar in Nazi Germany. Although there was Jewish resistance, its possibilities for action were very limited under the conditions of the World War II period. Moreover, possibilities for emigration were already limited. Many Jews lost their lives because quite a few believed that the German state and German culture would put an end to the excesses of the Nazis' anti–Semitism, which is why "it's not going to be that bad." Moreover, before the beginning of World War II, hardly anyone considered genocide as a "final solution" imaginable. In the film, the Jews can be reassured simply by the fact that Hynkel temporarily suspended the terror of his storm troopers in the ghetto because he hoped for the loan from the Jewish banker Epstein.

Hannah is equally not a heroic exception, even though she courageously uses her frying pan against the storm troopers to protect the barber. For when the former marauders suddenly meet her in a friendly and helpful manner, she gains hope for better times and wants to stay in Tomania despite the mistreatment she has suffered. And the very next moment she is promenading with the barber in the streets in her best clothes. On top of that, during this phase of deceptive calm, Hynkel badges are offered for sale. Hannah and the barber would almost have been persuaded to buy a badge, if it had not been for Hynkel's most recent speech, which boomed through the loudspeakers in the ghetto, in which he again incited against the Jews after the failure of the negotiations with Epstein. (The banker called Hynkel a "medieval lunatic.") The only skeptic was Jaeckel, the barber's neighbor. He deemed it too good to last and nevertheless emigrated to his brother in Osterlich only when Hynkel ordered the ghetto to be cleaned up in the "medieval manner."

The characteristics of the Jewish ghetto inhabitants include human weaknesses such as dishonesty and cowardice. In Jaeckel's basement, the nocturnal draw of the Hynkel assassin by a baked-in coin is anything but regular and sincere. Unbeknownst to the men present, Hannah has baked a coin into each piece of pastry, so the draw must pass pointlessly. Since the men think that there is only one coin, each of them secretly slips his coin onto his neighbor's plate, to avoid having to undertake the suicide mission. All the coins end up on the barber's plate. To hide them, he swallows the coins. When the draw is called off, all men are deeply relieved. That way, they again had nothing to do with the decision to rebel against Hynkel and did not have to interfere. Even Schultz, who had stood up to Hynkel and wants to organize the assassination attempt, quickly has an excuse ready, why there is no way he can carry it out.

After all, the speech that the barber in Hynkel's uniform delivers did not spring from his will to resist. Schultz put him in the situation. After escaping from the concentration camp, the barber wanted to hide in the bushes rather than go straight across the border into Osterlich on the street and in plain sight of Hynkel's soldiers at Schultz's side. Schultz's invitation to step up to the microphone because he, the barber, was not just their only hope, but also the hope of the whole world, then makes him deliver his blazing speech.

Unionist Bridges had not reassured Chaplin without reason, and likewise the hope-giving United Artists announcement "Soon the world will laugh again!" proved right. For Chaplin's film was not a crude anti–Hitler movie, but a timeless analytical satire of dictators in general with insights into the shallows of human life, which became a great success at the time and is still relevant today.

12

The Great Dictator
Takes to the Stage—1940–41

Hardly any film has ever caused diplomatic interventions and such worldwide attention even before shooting began as *The Great Dictator*. Thus, its premiere was awaited with even greater excitement than any Chaplin film before. Despite prophecies of doom, it was not a failure. *The Great Dictator* was hailed as a masterpiece by most of the critics. Only Chaplin's final speech caused a clash of opinions. The film made Hitler all the more the target of scorn in the English-language press. In Germany, therefore, the Nazi press control ordered the German film press to spread fake news about *The Great Dictator*. Behind the scenes, German diplomats were active on many channels to create a mood against the film. Following the example of their colleagues in the Weimar Republic, in association with Italian foreign missions in South and Central America, they tried to prevent the screening of *The Great Dictator*. In late November 1940, Chaplin was even attacked in a notorious Nazi smear film.

This chapter features:

- the press screening and U.S. premiere of *The Great Dictator*
- the audience response and box office results
- U.S. reviews
- Nazi fake news
- more cartoons about Chaplin and Hitler from the English-speaking countries
- the struggle of German diplomats against *The Great Dictator*
- riots during South American screenings of *The Great Dictator*
- the "documentary" *Der ewige Jude* and its "creator"

The Great Dictator *Starts Up*

Finally, the time had come: the world premiere of *The Great Dictator* was to take place in New York on October 15, 1940. Advance booking for the famous Broadway Astor Cinema began as early as October 7. Because moviegoers stood in line, obstructing traffic, the opening of the box office was accelerated at the request of the police. Soon after, the opening screening was sold out. Since tickets could also

be purchased for the sub-
sequent four weeks of the
season, the cinema's box
office was thus kept busy for
the next few days.[1] Chaplin traveled to New York on
October 13 and was inter-
viewed about his film.[2] The
next day, the first press
screening was held on the
West Coast at the Los Angeles Carthay Circle Theater.[3]
In the *New York Daily News*,
Ed Sullivan suggested that
Chaplin's foreign business
with his film would be very
limited, if the war had not
already ruined it.[4]

The first reactions
before the official pre-
miere were not encourag-
ing. *Daily Variety* felt *The
Great Dictator* did not feature a consistently high
level of comedy. After
nearly five years of waiting since the *Modern Times*
premiere, one had hoped
for more.[5] In New York,
Chaplin attended the East
Coast press screening at the
Astor with Paulette God-
dard and Harry Hopkins,
chief advisor to U.S. President Franklin Delano Roo-
sevelt. Afterwards, Hopkins
drew a gloomy picture:
"It is a great picture, […] a
very worth-while thing to
do, but it has not a chance.
It will lose money."[6] Those
were bitter words after two
years of work and about
$2.2 million in invested
equity.[7]

United Artists promotional sheet for *The Great Dictator*,
1940: "The World Will Soon Be Laughing Again," Hynkel
with globe.

Charles Chaplin

Announces the

PRESS PREVIEW

of

"THE GREAT DICTATOR"

to be held at

CARTHAY CIRCLE THEATRE

October 14, 1940

8:30 P.M.

Released by United Artists Corporation

Ticket admits two

Invitation card for the press preview of *The Great Dictator*
(Archives de Montreux, PP-75 Fonds Charles Chaplin, Roy
Export Co. Ltd.).

Afterwards, Chaplin and Goddard attended the *Great Dictator* screening at the New York Capitol.[8] In front of the cinemas, such crowds had flocked that traffic in the area came to a halt for two hours. Chaplin and Goddard could only break their way to the screening with the help of assistants. There, the "glamorous audience" was "elated and enthused"[9] and did not share Hopkins' pessimistic prognosis. In this situation, Chaplin and Goddard ended years of speculation and revealed they were married to each other.[10]

That night, *The Great Dictator* began its triumphant run and became the most successful film of Chaplin's career.[11] Throughout the U.S., audiences flocked to theaters. The Capitol took in $17,000 on opening day alone and a total of $106,000 in the first week of play. The smaller Astor Cinema showed a revenue of $20,000 during the same period. In New York, Chaplin's film had thus eclipsed the opening success of Victor Fleming's recent spectacular *Gone with the Wind*. That Civil War drama had grossed "only" $71,000 in its first week at the Capitol.

In the second week of *Great Dictator* screenings, the Astor and Capitol box office reports still showed a combined $107,000. In the third week, the film grossed $60,200 at the Capitol, and in the fourth, $48,600. By then, 750,000 people had attended screenings at this movie theater, so its management was still calculating box offices of a good $38,000 for each of the planned additional two weeks. At the Astor, the financial development was comparably favorable. It collected $18,150 for the third week and $15,600 in the fourth. In all, the film remained in these two theaters alone for at least six weeks in parallel. Thus, Chaplin's film at the Capitol had surpassed the record, previously held by a Greta Garbo film. At the Astor, ticket sales were excellent for even longer: in early March 1941, the film was in its 20th week there.[12] After its second week at the Astor

THE
WORLD WILL SOON BE
LAUGHING AGAIN!

Charlie Chaplin

THE *Great* **DICTATOR**
PRODUCED, WRITTEN AND DIRECTED BY CHARLES CHAPLIN
with **PAULETTE GODDARD**
JACK OAKIE · HENRY DANIELL · REGINALD GARDINER · BILLY GILBERT · MAURICE MOSCOVICH
Released thru UNITED ARTISTS

United Artists promotional sheet for *The Great Dictator*, 1940: "The World Will Soon Be Laughing Again," Hynkel saluting.

and Capitol, the New York theaters Loew's State and Orpheum joined in. At least at Loew's State, *The Great Dictator* was prolonged for at least one week.[13]

Chaplin's film was a box office hit elsewhere in the U.S. as well.[14] In the first four Washington days, the daily box office takings set a new record of $22,000, and at the Philadelphia Aldine, the excellent results brought the film into its fourth week. The box office situation in Cleveland was 357 percent above average. In Jersey City, the film was prolongated.[15] At the Los Angeles Carthay Circle Theater, where the film's first West Coast press screening had taken place, it eclipsed everything that had come before. A special screening was held for prisoners at California's Folsom State Prison.[16]

From March 1, 1941, United Artists distributed *The Great Dictator* all over the United States, but due to the excellent revenues so far, only at increased rental fees for the theaters until the summer of the year. It remained a hit throughout the coun-

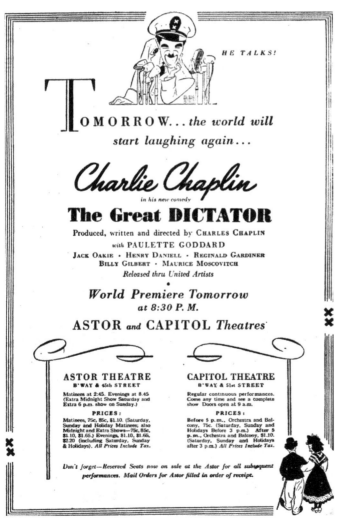

try until at least late April 1941. The reports summed up that *The Great Dictator* "attracted the masses" and "broke box office records everywhere."[17] Its "landslide" success was also known as the "Blitzkrieg." In Desmond Kelem's cartoon "The Pie Blitzkrieg" in the Nebraska *Omaha World-Herald* of late October 1940, Tramp Charlie throws cake from a still well-filled plate at Hitler. The world, which is depicted as a laughing globe, is delighted.[18]

There had been doubts whether Chaplin would master the talkies. But soon it was generally agreed that he had cleared this hurdle by storm. For example, in March 1941, the *Milford News* reported *The Great Dictator*'s "Blitzkrieg on Skeptics."[19] More of a side note, therefore, was the news that the Chicago City Council had suspended *Great Dictator*

United Artists announcement of *The Great Dictator*'s New York world premiere on October 15, 1940.

THE WORLD WILL LAUGH *with Chaplin!*

Charlie Chaplin HE TALKS!

in his new comedy

Collage from *The Great Dictator* pressbook.

screenings because of the city's "strong ethnic-German population," whom they did not want to offend.[20] In neighboring Canada, Chaplin's film was as successful as in the U.S. By mid–November 1940, *The Great Dictator* had played for a total of 111 weeks in Canada, exceeding the usual revenues by 400 percent.[21] Foreign successes were reported from Java, Singapore and other places.[22] On December 16, 1940, *The Great Dictator* opened in several London cinemas simultaneously and subsequently played throughout the United Kingdom, enjoying great success, as reported by U.S. trade journals such as *Daily Variety*, *The Film Daily*, *Motion Picture Daily* and *Motion Picture Herald*.[23] In its first nine weeks, the film had grossed 400,000 British pounds sterling, which, however, remained frozen in Great Britain until further notice due to wartime foreign exchange control regulations.[24]

Critical Voices

The numerous press reports after the premiere had their share in the extraordinary success of the film. In the past, critics had by no means found only words of praise for Chaplin's new films, and *The Great Dictator* was no different. The reviews ranged from "disappointing" to "inspiring."[25] E.D. Ward, also known as "Broadway's gift to Joseph Goebbels," was not sympathetic to Chaplin, caustically commenting on *The Great Dictator*: "Some Chaplin films have been notably dull. But it is the first time I have heard that they're deadly."[26] A controversy unfolded around Chaplin's closing speech. Some saw it as one of the most moving moments in film history; others considered it out of place. But in the end, Chaplin's movie received widespread support from the press.[27]

Bosley Crowther found a few aspects in his detailed and largely exuberant *New York Times* review (October 16, 1940). Crowther was particularly ambivalent about the neuralgic final speech:

> [It ...] is completely out of joint with what which has gone before. [Chaplin] steps out of character and addresses his heart to the audience. The effect is bewildering, and what should be the climax becomes flat and seemingly maudlin. But the sincerity with which Chaplin voices his appeal and the expression of tragedy which is clear in his face are strangely overpowering. Suddenly one perceives with relief the things which make *The Great Dictator* great—the courage and faith and surpassing love for mankind which are in the heart of Charlie Chaplin.[28]

The same day, the trade journal *Variety* wrote of a "shock" at the "complete transformation of the barber" when he delivers the speech. Chaplin had thus set "a peculiar and somewhat disappointing climax" instead of letting his great film satire end with a comical note.[29]

Chaplin promptly answered his critics in the *New York Times*, which was also reported by the New York German exile newspaper *Aufbau*[30]:

> To me, it is a logical ending to the story. To me, it is the speech that the little barber would have made—even had to make. [...] The picture is two hours and seven minutes in length. If two hours and three minutes of it is comedy, may I not be excused on a note that reflects, honestly and realistically, the world in which we live, and may I not be excused in pleading for a better world? Mind you, it is addressed to the soldiers, the very victims of a dictatorship. [...] It would have been much easier to have the barber and Hannah disappear over the horizon, off to the Promised Land against the glowing sunset. But there is no promised land for the oppressed people of the world. There is no place over the horizon to which they can go for sanctuary. They must stand, and we must stand.[31]

The German-Jewish film critic and analyst Rudolf Arnheim, who had emigrated to the U.S. via detours at an early stage after Hitler's takeover, also took a close look at *The Great Dictator*. Despite all the merits that Chaplin and his film deserved, Arnheim thought that more could have been made of it. Above all, he missed that Hynkel was not also shown as a common soldier during World War I before becoming a dictator and that Chaplin had devoted himself to satirizing Hitler instead of tearing the mask off fascism and Nazism itself:

> Chaplin used wonderful raw material without getting its full meaning from it. In the World War sequence, Chaplin makes the little Jewish barber a hero. In fact, the whole sequence has little inner connection to the film it introduces [...]. The World War I sequence could have been a very significant introduction if the future dictator had been the leading character. [...] Just imagine the Chaplinesque Donquichottery of the fanatical little private in the trenches, his strategic fantasies and daredevil ventures, his violent speeches of heroism to his

skeptically smiling, tired comrades. It would have been possible to show where the man came from and how life formed him. [...] Chaplin is the only artist to possess the secret weapon of deadly laughter [...,] because he has discovered [...] the mental weakness, stupidity and falsehood of his opponent. Chaplin could have opened the eyes of a world enraptured by the magic of power and material success. But instead of exposing the common enemy, fascism, Chaplin exposed a single man, *The Great Dictator*.[32]

It can be countered that Chaplin succeeded in showing the inhuman face of the fascist dictatorship precisely with his satire of Hitler as the Nazi leader and exponent of Nazism. This did not require a fundamental reckoning with Nazism. If Chaplin had followed Arnheim's suggestion and, for example, the barber and Hynkel had met in the trenches during World War I, the critics would probably not have been wrong to criticize an "incredible coincidence."

Be that as it may, New York film critics wanted to honor Chaplin as the best actor of 1940 for his dual role in *The Great Dictator* on January 5, 1941. Chaplin was the first actor so far to decline the honor, explaining in his telegram to Crowther that he did not want to compete with other actors. It was rumored that he had been annoyed by comments that considered his film to be "Communist propaganda."[33] But it was also alleged that Chaplin had suspected he would not be the first choice of the critics, who by no means considered him the best actor.[34] None of the assumptions, however, has been confirmed.

"A Normal Decent Human Being"

The Hauptarchiv der NSDAP collected articles on *The Great Dictator*. The first was "His Film Made 'for Freedom'" from London's *Daily Mail* of October 19, 1940. Unlike almost all other newspaper clippings in the Chaplin file, it was translated in excerpts in German, and passages from it were underlined. Apparently, it seemed particularly significant. After *The Great Dictator*'s U.S. premiere, BBC radio had conducted a telephone interview with Chaplin. According to the *Daily Mail's* article, Chaplin had "just done magnificent service for his country and humanity by this brave and sensational" film, which "was hailed as the greatest propaganda for the British cause since the war began." In the interview, Chaplin, in a voice stifled by tears, praised "the splendid courage of the British people" as "the greatest inspiration in the world": Even after the continuing German air raids on London since September 7, 1940, they were "still able to raise a smile" while standing "amid the smoking ruins of their houses." He also predicted a very limited existence of Hitler's "Tausendjähriges Reich," i.e., Nazi Germany:

> I merely tried to use what skill I have in an endeavor to help defeat these horrible totalitarian States. It was because of my strong anti–Nazi feeling that I made the picture. I wanted to do something for freedom and liberty. But the final speech I wrote after the war began. In fact, I only added it just as I was about to complete the film. I wanted that speech to appeal to all the English-speaking world. Many people have different ideas about it—but it is a purely humanitarian aspect. [...] In this speech I am entirely a humanitarian speaking to the military, barbaric people. [...] Totalitarianism cannot last whatever happens. In Europe it is a passing phase.[35]

When Chaplin took part in a dinner with about 50 guests shortly after *Great Dictator*'s New York premiere, the conversation turned to his film, politics and Judaism. One of the guests said: "One must not take your point of view [in your film] seriously, of course." Chaplin responded: "Well, it is a comedy, after all." And he added that he had been decidedly too polite in caricaturing the German dictatorship, considering the "bestial murders and ordeals […] in the Nazi Concentration Camps" which became known to him only in retrospect. When asked why he disapproved of the Nazis, Chaplin replied that he opposed the Nazis because they were anti-human. This prompted the guest to remark: "Of course, you're a Jew, aren't you," which Chaplin acknowledged as follows: "One does not have to be a Jew to be anti–Nazi. All one has to be is a normal decent human being."[36]

Chaplin's attitude and his film were followed by satirical pictorial articles in the English-language press. With his cartoon "No Patched-Up Peace," Kimon Evan Marengo (Kem) caricatured Hitler, Mussolini and Hirohito in the magazine *John Bull* of October 19, 1940, referring to the World War II alliance between Germany, Italy and Japan. These rulers rallied together with their weapons. Horrified by the impact of *The Great Dictator*, they stare at a poster of the film with Chaplin's likeness to Hynkel, and Hitler implores his cronies: "We mustn't let this Upstart Muscle-in on Our Racket…."[37]

In early November 1940, the British magazine *Picture Post* mocked Hitler and Mussolini with a pictorial series entitled "How Chaplin Parodies the Dictators' Pomp and Arrogance" by juxtaposing annotated images of the two dictators with photos from *The Great Dictator*, similar to "The Story of Two Mustaches" in *Ladies' Home Journal* of July of that year. In the first two photos, Hitler and Mussolini, and Chaplin as Hynkel with Jack Oakie as Napaloni, ride through the streets in triumph: "Hitler Has a Triumphal Ride" and "Chaplin Has a Triumphal Ride." Then you see Hitler and Chaplin accompanied by people, and they also take parades: "Hitler Has a Bodyguard" and "Chaplin Hitler Has a Bodyguard" as well as "Hitler Takes the Salute" and "Chaplin Takes the Salute." Both want to instruct diplomats: "Hitler Sends for a Diplomat" and "Chaplin Sends for a Diplomat." And each "has a girl," Hitler Eva Braun and Chaplin Hannah, "and each has a Junior Partner": Hitler pompous Mussolini and Hynkel pompous Napaloni.[38]

In May 1941, Herbert Block's (Herblock) cartoon "What Next?" for the U.S. newspaper *Huntington Herald-Press* alluded to the secret flight of Hitler's deputy Rudolf Hess to Great Britain. In an imaginary sequel to this undertaking, Block sent two more Nazis to the British Isles. Hitler and Göring crash-landed there with a German plane and were captured by the British Army. Both have apparently already seen Chaplin's film and therefore pretend to be Hynkel and Herring, respectively. A British soldier reports to his perplexed officer: "The fat one gives his name as 'Herring' and the other one calls himself, 'Chaplin'."[39]

Chaplin and Hitler's moustaches were also addressed again. In 1936, supposedly, Chaplin had claimed the copyright for his Tramp's moustache against Hitler. Now Jim Russell turned the tables in the Australian tabloid *Smith's Weekly*. In his cartoon "High Spots from the Shows: *The Great Dictator*, with Charles Chaplin," probably published in the fall of 1941, Hitler, Goering and Mussolini showed up accompanied by a bailiff to serve Chaplin with a copyright infringement action in his studio for poking fun at them in *The Great Dictator* without their permission.[40]

Nazi Press Controllers and Alleged Turkeys

Of course, the Nazis fought *The Great Dictator* in the German film press. In addition to the Reichspressekonferenzes, the "Zeitschriften und Kulturpresse" (Magazine and Cultural Press) department of the Reichsministerium für Volksaufklärung und Propaganda had established the Reichszeitschriftenkonferenz (Reich Magazine Conference) in June 1937. This was accompanied by the official press service *Zeitschriften-Information*, from which the weekly *Zeitschriften-Dienst* emanated in May 1939; it existed until mid–April 1945. Until further notice, its editor was Wilfried Bade, who had built up the Reichsarbeitsgemeinschaft nationalsozialistischer Journalisten (Reich Association of National Socialist Journalists) on behalf of Reichspressechef Dietrich. He operated the *Zeitschriften-Dienst* in line with Dietrich's instructions.[41] In 1940, Bade was replaced by the Hauptstellenleiter Max Stampe from the Reichspropagandaleitung of the NSDAP.[42]

The editors-in-chief of journals and magazines had to commit themselves in a "Verpflichtungsschein" (Commitment Bill) "to absolute secrecy of the *Zeitschriften-Dienst* towards everyone" and additionally confirm in writing that violations of this obligation could be prosecuted under criminal law as high treason. The "recommendations, wishes and suggestions of the *Zeitschriften-Dienst*" were "obligatory and [to] be followed unconditionally," while each editor-in-chief had to "pass on his instructions […], as if they originated from his personal wishes."[43] In the event of "violations or lack of cooperation," all recipients of the instructions were threatened with "the most severe measures, especially in the present situation."[44] The loss of an issue of the *Zeitschriften-Dienst* had to be reported to the editorial office by registered mail or express messenger. Editors-in-chief had to communicate their vacations and business trips in advance and to vouch for their absentee representatives, who had to commit themselves separately to secrecy about the content of the *Zeitschriften-Dienst*.[45] The editorial staff regularly reminded the editors-in-chief of these regulations. In order to control the secret procedures and the content of the printed matter, the Hauptreferat Zeitschriften (Main Department for Magazines) in the Reichsministerium für Volksaufklärung und Propaganda had to be presented with "compulsory reference pieces" of all magazines, which were subjected to thorough proofreading.[46] Like the Reichspressekonferenz, the *Zeitschriften-Dienst* issued myriad "recommendations, wishes and suggestions," which totaled nearly 11,200 instructions by mid–April 1945. The resulting control task could only be tamed with detailed, regularly updated registers.[47]

On November 1, 1940, the *Zeitschriften-Dienst* issued the following instruction to the editors-in-chief of journals and magazines: "We ask not to publish anything about […] Charlie Chaplin's *The Dictator*, not even polemics."[48] But this was too late for the *Film-Kurier*, which had already run the news item "Charlie Chaplins Hetzfilm fiel in Amerika durch" (Charlie Chaplin's Smear Film Flops in America) on the same day:

Charlie Chaplin had prostituted his puny character for a Germanophobe smear film. A part of the US press had been busy promoting the project, and now they were waiting for the big "success." But it was a huge miscalculation. As reported from New York, the film has been running for several days in half-empty houses. Empty chairs were gaping at Chaplin's shenanigans. The [...] box office remained empty. A number of film companies in Hollywood have therefore decided [...] to abandon the production of Germanophobe films. As soon as no deal can be cut, even the Jew stops agitating.[49]

This "news" meant an immediate contradiction to the success reports in the foreign press and the German New York exile newspaper *Aufbau*.[50] Significantly, the *Film-Kurier* did not reveal its source.

The *Zeitschriften-Dienst* appreciatively adopted the *Film-Kurier*'s approach and responded to this on November 8, 1940: "The news that Chaplin's smear film *The Great Dictator* was a commercial failure [...] provides an opportunity to write about this film after all. It should not be mentioned, however, that Chaplin [...] portrays the Fuehrer. It shall only be written that it is an anti–Germanophobe smear film by this "berüchtigter Filmjude" (notorious film-Jew).[51] With this instruction, the *Zeitschriften-Dienst* ensured that such fake news remained the standard in the German film press until June 1943—true to the motto attributed to Goebbels, "You only have to repeat a lie often enough until it will be finally believed." Only international locations would be substituted. *Der Film* was the first trade journal to implement the new instruction with its "report" of November 16, 1940, rolling out the content of the *Film-Kurier* article somewhat more negatively:

Mr. Charlie Chaplin is known in Hollywood for his unreliability and sloth. His films were never finished. Now he has finally released his latest work. His Germanophobe smear film was launched with great fanfare in New York. Despite the most zealous recommendations of a kindred press, it became a first-rate failure. According to reports from New York, the Jewish jokester's sorry effort is screened to empty houses.[52]

In mid–January 1941, the *Film-Kurier* again stoked the fire with its teaser "Minus-Geschäft für Chaplin" (Money-Losing Business for Chaplin), allegedly based on a report by the U.S. news agency United Press,[53] and repeated this on May 2, 1941, somewhat modified with "An Expensive Smear Film." This time the "fourth issue" of the Spanish film magazine *Primer Plano* was claimed to be the source, based on the following article in the *New York Telegram*: "By parodying the most powerful man in history, Charlie Chaplin's comedy becomes a tragedy." The news would have suited a film journal from then-fascist Spain, because *The Great Dictator* had no chance there either. Under the Spanish title *El gran dictador*, it was not released there until May 1, 1976, after the November 20, 1975, death of the dictator Generalissimo Francisco Franco. *Primer Plano* had been launched on October 20, 1940, in a weekly schedule. Number four was dated November 3, 1940, but neither this nor the April 1941 issues that immediately preceded "An Expensive Smear Film" contained the supposed article.[54] The *New York Telegram* news could not be found either. On top of that, the *Film-Kurier* added: "The film cost $5 million and five years of work. The countries that might buy it can be counted on the fingers of one hand. Chaplin therefore will lose more than $2.6 million with his political film adventure."[55] This was not true either, since the filming required less time and also cost considerably less. The *Film-Kurier* thus wanted to dramatize Chaplin's alleged flop. The example of "Ein teurer Hetzfilm" therefore demonstrates how necessary it is to question source references of Nazi propaganda.

Four months later, the *Film-Kurier* again invoked Chaplin's financial failure with *The Great Dictator* when it complained that 45 Germanophobe U.S. smear films were in preparation by now.[56] This contradicted the film journal's own assertion that U.S. production of smear films should be discontinued.

Torpedoes and Bombs?

On November 22, 1940, the *Film-Kurier* followed up with "Chaplin's Hetzfilm kam nicht zum Ziel" (Chaplin's Smear Film Did Not Achieve Its Goal):

> The [*Frankfurter Zeitung*] reports that the London premiere of the Germanophobe smear film *The Great Dictator* had to be cancelled, according to a report in *Svenska Dagbladet*. The steamer with the negative of the film destined for England was sunk on its way from America to England. [...] Since further losses of ships in the Atlantic were expected [...], several negatives were now underway on various steamers. [The "hetzender" [agitating] clown] Chaplin thus does not have much pleasure in his sorry effort. [...]. In New York, as we reported recently, the film played to half-empty houses, and on its way across the sea it has now also encountered adverse fate: in a double sense, Mr. Chaplin did not meet his destination.[57]

The London editorial office of the Swedish daily *Svenska Dagbladet* had indeed reported the Chaplin film as "lost in the Atlantic" on November 19, 1940,[58] reproducing U.S. news about the film loss on the same day and United Artists' subsequent shipment of two replacement copies.[59] The day before, for example, *The New York Times* had reported that the copy shipped in mid–October had not yet arrived in London, but that the British premiere of *Dictator* would not have to be postponed because of the replacement shipment.[60] The U.S. newspaper *The Demin Headlight* mockingly remarked in late November 1940 that it would have been best if the real great dictator Hitler had been lost at sea.[61] After the Third Reich had commenced its air and submarine warfare against Britain in the summer of 1940, a British ship presumably had been sunk. The *Frankfurter Zeitung* had reported several times on British ships that had been torpedoed by German submarines,[62] and such reports were also constantly circulating in the international press.[63] However, there was not even a single word that one of the torpedoed ships had had a copy of *The Great Dictator* on board. Since the *Svenska Dagbladet* had also not mentioned any further details about the cause of the film copy's loss, it only could be speculated how a film negative could be lost on the high seas. The *Film-Kurier*'s deliberately nebulous report could thus suggest that the ship had been torpedoed just for the film. This, in turn, added to the fake news about *The Great Dictator*.

At the beginning of 1941, the *Film-Kurier* injected some more fake news with "Chaplin's Dictator Pursued by Bombs." According to unnamed Swiss newspapers, based on the *Nya Dagligt Allehanda*, a London premiere cinema had also supposedly been destroyed in a German air raid. The film journal commented: "So these copies are no different from the famous Ten Little Indians. And then there was only…"[64] Between November 18, 1940, and January 20, 1941, the *Nya Dagligt Alle-handa* had actually printed three articles about *Great Dictator* screenings in Argentina and Chile, but nothing about the bombing of a London theater. Nothing about this could be found in the *Neue Zürcher Zeitung* either. Yet, the two newspapers, like many other international newspapers, also frequently reported on bombardments and torpedoing during this phase of World War II. In general, nothing could be found in the international press about the bombardment of the London premiere theater, which would certainly have been worth reporting. The simultaneous British premiere of *The Great Dictator* on December 16, 1940, in several London cinemas, for example, had been reported on by U.S. trade journals and their British counterpart *Kinematograph Weekly*—journals about which the Nazi propaganda was always excellently informed. It seems difficult to comprehend that this should have escaped the *Film-Kurier*'s attention in the case of a film, of all things, that had been the focus of Nazi propaganda since the fall of 1938. Apparently, the *Film-Kurier* pretended that *The Great Dictator* had no chance in Great Britain either and had not been released in Europe at the beginning of 1941.

Diplomats Move Out

On October 31, 1940, the German Auswärtiges Amt instructed the German Embassies, Legations, and Consulates General, as well as the German representatives in the occupied territories, in a circular on smear films, to "work with the responsible authorities in the host countries or occupied territories to ensure that [foreign] agitation films will no longer be approved by the censors." Attached to the circular was a "compilation of the agitations films produced by American, English and French companies" with 77 film titles, including *The Great Dictator*.[65]

Several months later, on April 24, 1941, the Auswärtiges Amt issued another circular to the German embassies with further instructions and enclosing two more lists: a "List of Actors and Directors Participating in American Smear Films" with 168 names and a "List of Jewish Actors and Directors Participating in American Films" with 250 names, including Chaplin. The instructions read: "It is requested that reports be made on the release of films in which actors or directors who are on either of the two lists appear. Furthermore, […] attempts shall be exerted underhand to ensure that films with actors and directors who have taken part in such agitation films are given a hard time by the boards of film censors."[66]

Central and South America were highly important markets for U.S. films. After the waves of European emigration in the nineteenth and twentieth centuries, many people of German descent lived there. They did not only preserve German traditions and the memory of their former homeland, but they also sympathized with political trends in Germany. Not infrequently they admired from afar the warlike Third Reich, which rushed from one victory to another, seemingly unstoppable. In Argentina, Chile, Paraguay and Uruguay, for example, the Auswärtiges Amt was able to rely on a pro–German attitude in political circles and to make promising attempts to thwart anti–Nazi activities.[67] Likewise, there was a large share of population of

Italian origin, especially in South America, so that the Italian foreign missions could proceed in the same way as the German ones.

Therefore, German and Italian ambassadors campaigned somewhat openly against Chaplin's satire on Hitler and Mussolini. From November 1940 onward, this was reported frequently in the U.S. press. It was not always clear from this whether German or Italian diplomats had had a hand in film bans.[68]

Ban and Time Bomb in Argentina

In Argentina, German diplomats were sometimes successful. On their initiative, for example, the Film Committee of the capital Buenos Aires banned the U.S. film *Confessions of a Nazi Spy*.[69] *The Great Dictator*, on the other hand, was initially approved by it. Italian Ambassador Raffaele Boscarelli saw the film as an attack on the Italian government and downplayed his official protest against the screening of *The Great Dictator* as a "friendly inquiry" to Argentine Foreign Minister Julio Argentino Roca. Less diplomatically, the pro–Nazi Argentine newspaper *El Pampero* took issue with the Chaplin film in a three-column headline, arguing that "Clown mit nur unterdurchschnittlichem Talent" had ridiculed heads of state of countries friendly to Argentina with his film of "particularly inferior quality": "In our country, a Yankee film should not be allowed to comment on political conditions or the meaning of ideals that are being decided on European battlefields."[70] In Argentina, there were pro–Nazi sympathies that made it possible to display Streicher's smear journal *Der Stürmer* in its notorious showcases.[71] Due to the interventions, Buenos Aires Mayor Carlos Alberto Puyerredon banned the screening of *The Great Dictator* in the metropolis.[72] Immediately before the celebrations for his third inauguration

Der Stürmer display case in Argentine, 1937.

as U.S. president, Roosevelt let Chaplin know in a private conversation on January 19, 1941: "Your picture is giving us a lot of trouble in the Argentine."[73] What the U.S. undertook to resolve such troubles in Argentina has not been reported.

Since the individual Argentine provinces had their own censorship authority independent of the central government, the banning of *The Great Dictator* in Buenos Aires did not result in a nationwide ban. For example, the film played in the province Paraná. German Ambassador Edmund Freiherr von Thermann protested this to the Argentine Minister of the Interior Miguel Culaciatti. The latter considered banning the film throughout Argentina, in order not to hurt the feelings of the population of Italian descent and not to strain diplomatic relations with Italy.[74] Argentine President Ramón Castillo regarded *The Great Dictator* as an insult to the Italians living in Argentina. However, it was also an option to screen the film only in an edited version. Then, in early February 1941, the Belgian occupation newspaper *Brüsseler Zeitung* reported that the film had been banned throughout Argentina because it had caused riots.[75] For example, before the first scheduled screening in Gualeguaychú, the third-largest city in Argentina (Entre Ríos province), a time bomb was discovered in a cinema that was screening *The Great Dictator*. In fact, however, the decision on a nationwide ban dragged on. The Buenos Aires City Council even lifted the ban on June 14, 1941.[76] But the German and Italian ambassadors did not let up and succeeded: at the end of June 1941, *The Great Dictator* was banned nationwide to avoid hurting German and Italian feelings.[77]

"Heil" Shouts and Tear Gas in Uruguay

In late December 1940, cinemas in neighboring Uruguay benefited from the Argentine back-and-forth over *The Great Dictator*. For this country, the owner of the large cinema Trocadero, recently built in Montevideo, had acquired the Uruguayan screening rights. Among others, the film also played in the cities of Colonia del Sacramento, Paysandú, Rivera and Salto. Because of the ban in Buenos Aires, Argentines, lured by Uruguayan advertising, traveled in droves to the neighboring country[78]—just as years ago, German moviegoers went to neighboring countries because of *Im Westen nichts Neues* (see Chapter 5). Argentine moviegoers ensured excellent box office in Uruguayan cinemas and prolonged playing times. Italian ambassador Belardo Ricci intervened against *The Great Dictator*. Chaplin's film continued to be shown, but tear gas bombs were thrown during a screening in Montevideo. Six Nazi sympathizers shouted "Down with democracy" and raised their arms in a "Heil" salute as they were hauled away.[79]

Tear Gas and Riots in Chile

In Chile, German and Italian diplomats approached the Chilean Foreign Office about *The Great Dictator*. The German Erste Botschaftsrat (First Councilor of the Embassy), Wilhelm von Pochhammer, veiled his protest as a suggestion that Germans living in Chile might be offended by the film.[80] The Chilean board of film censors did not ban it, but only approved an abridged version. For this, the "major scenes considered offensive by the totalitarian powers" and that could offend the sensibilities of the country's German and Italian minorities were removed. Afterwards, a special screening was held for the Chilean Minister of the Interior, Arturo Olavarria. He saw nothing objectionable in the edited version, especially since *The Great Dictator* was essentially a comedy.[81] It is not known in detail which scenes were cut.

On January 7, 1941, the edited version was released in the four largest cinemas in the capital Santiago de Chile. During the screening at the Teatro Santa Lucia, a group of men threw tear gas bombs into the auditorium and shouted "Viva Hitler," i.e., "Heil Hitler." Two representatives of the Italian Embassy were injured in the riots. Only a police operation could restore calm in the cinema. Before the screening continued, the Chilean national anthem was played. Outside, however, a pro–Nazi-fascist crowd had surrounded the cinema. (German Nazis, who wanted to prevent the screening of the film *Cyankali* in March 1931, had demonstrated something like this in Pforzheim.) When police cars arrived to put an end to this attack, the disruptors shouted, "Viva Hitler! Viva Mussolini! Death to the Jews!" The disruptors who did not leave voluntarily were turned away by the police. After that, further *Great Dictator* screenings in Santiago de Chile seemed to continue undisturbed. But in February 1941, there were once again tumults in cinemas in Valparaiso and Viña del Mar.[82]

Der Angriff turned the politically motivated Santiago disruption into a general reaction of the audience, claiming that it was triggered by the inferiority of the tendentious film: "In Santiago de Chile, the film *Dictator* by Chaplin the Jew was particularly ill-received. The newspapers wrote that the film was not a comedy, but an act of war and artistically a catastrophe."[83] As a matter of course, the propaganda journal omitted the rioters as well as their expulsion by the local police.

Mexican Calm and Record Receipts

In Mexico, the German Ambassador Curt Freiherr Rüdt von Collenberg-Bödingheim had protested single-handedly against the public screening of *The Great Dictator* and had been turned away.[84] The Mexican police, however, did not rule out the possibility of riots. Therefore, in Mexico City, the first *Great Dictator* screening took place on January 1, 1941, in the large cinema Palacio Chino with its more than 3500 seats, under the protection of a police platoon. It proceeded without disruptions. The screenings on the first day were filled to capacity, and the cinema scored a box-office record: On that day alone, as many tickets were sold as otherwise eight out of ten cinemas in the city did in one week.[85]

But news of such success did not stop the *Film-Kurier* from providing its next fake news account on the front page at the beginning of February 1941:

> Chaplin's smear film *The Dictator* suffered the biggest financial fiasco imaginable in Mexico. Theaters had booked the film for four weeks. But the box office receipts were so low that the theater owners had to throw in several thousand pesos of their own money every week to cover the expenses. Therefore, the Mexican agency of United Artists reimbursed

part of the money paid for the screening rights in order to avoid the economic collapse of the cinemas.[86]

A day later, *Der Angriff* followed up with the fictitious article "No Luck in Mexico. Rejection of Chaplin's Smear Film."[87] In this way, the Nazi press spread its film-political fake news to both the professional audience and the general readership. With its daily circulation of 8000 copies, the *Film-Kurier* reached cinema operators as well as professionals from film production and distribution,[88] who spread the news through their professional contacts all the way to cinema fans at the box office. The daily circulation of *Der Angriff*, however, was far higher. In the period 1939 to 1944, it climbed from about 150,000 copies to a good 300,000.[89]

Ban and Theft in Paraguay

Unlike in Chile and Mexico, the mayor of the Paraguayan capital Asunción banned *The Great Dictator* from the outset at the end of January 1941 because residents of German and Italian origin in the city would deem it "unfriendly." Whether German and Italian diplomats had any influence on this is unclear. Due to the ban, United Artists' foreign department did not book any screenings in Paraguay outside Asunción until further notice.[90] When Paraguay broke off diplomatic relations with Germany and Italy in January 1942, the ban on screenings also ended, but not the domestic fight against *The Great Dictator*. Four days before its first screening, scheduled for April 22, 1942, unknown persons tried in vain to steal the film copy. The day before the premiere, however, five masked men broke into the premiere theater. They forced a worker to unlock the film store and escaped with the *Great Dictator* film cans.[91] Since the perpetrators were not identified, it can only be assumed that they belonged to Paraguayan Nazi-fascist circles.

Other Bans and Approvals

The Great Dictator was also banned in Cuba, Brazil and Peru. In Peru, Dr. Willy Noebel, who had fought Chaplin's *Shoulder Arms* in Bulgaria in 1926, was on duty at the time. Whether the German foreign missions in the three countries had their fingers in the pie is not documented. In Havana, the film was at first banned from December 1940 to March 1941. However, after its approval from April, it did well at the box office. The Brazilian Departamento da Impresso e Propaganda (Ministry of Press and Propaganda) banned *Great Dictator* in April 1941 because it violated the principle of political neutrality. When Brazil entered World War II in the spring of 1942, this principle no longer mattered, so Chaplin's film and *Confessions of a Nazi Spy*, which had also been banned, were able to conquer Brazilian audiences. In Peru, *The Great Dictator* was initially approved to play in Lima's most modern and largest cinema, breaking the city's box office records. But then the Peruvian board of film censors banned its further screening nationwide in early March 1941.[92]

In Ecuador and Nicaragua, *The Great Dictator* was approved to be screened publicly without cuts.[93] Nicaraguan President Anastasio Somoza, who was not exactly known as a democrat, declared at the end of January 1941 that his country was a democracy, and if Chaplin's film was propaganda for democracy, it would be shown.[94] Whether German and Italian diplomats had tried to intervene is unknown. The Third Reich did not maintain diplomatic relations with Panama, which was neutral during World War II, but informally had its interests represented by German envoy Otto Reinebeck in Nicaragua. Reinebeck and the Italian envoy tried in vain to prevent the *Great Dictator* screening in Panama.[95] After all, the mayor of Panama City and the state censorship authority approved the film.[96] In Costa Rica, the German Consul Walther Schmidt and his Italian colleague had protested against the approval of *The Great Dictator*. Because state authorities were afraid of Nazi disruptions in the event of public screenings, the film was initially approved to be shown only as part of a closed event at the German Club of San José. But for this alone, "thousands of invitations" were sent.[97] From early March 1941, *The Great Dictator* was finally approved to be shown everywhere in the Central American country.[98]

Outside of Latin America, *The Great Dictator* sometimes did not stand a chance either. Because of the tripartite alliance with Germany and Italy, this was especially true in Japan, of course.[99] Moreover, by the end of January 1941, marketing opportunities in Europe had diminished further. Spain, as already mentioned, had not even imported the film. Politically neutral Ireland banned outdoor advertising for *The Great Dictator* in order to avoid suggesting that a stand was being taken against the Third Reich.[100] At the time, Romania was also still an ally of the Third Reich. The Romanian film magazine *Universul* still reported on U.S. films, and also on *The Great Dictator*. Therefore, in February 1941, the German-language *Bukarester Tagblatt* cautioned against the "insidious effects of Hollywood films" and did not hide its lack of understanding that Chaplin was given any attention at all in Romania: "We Germans are particularly indignant about the fact that […] German film culture is placed side by side with Jewish trash. [… Chaplin's] entire success as an actor rests upon his bodily awkwardness, his flat feet, his overlong arms and his hollow chest. In a wholesome nation, people who resemble Chaplin, are put under lock and key. But in America, such 'Kreaturen' (Creatures) are at large, are ogled, praised, and even honored. And apparently not only in America."[101]

The "Documentary" Der ewige Jude

On November 28, 1940, the anti–Semitic "documentary" *Der ewige Jude* premiered at the Berlin Ufa-Palast am Zoo[102] and received the most prestigious Nazi ratings.[103] Goebbels had scheduled it to follow the 1940 feature films *Die Rothschilds* (Ernst Waschneck) and *Jud Süß* (Veit Harlan)[104] as the final installment of a trio of anti–Semitic films. The intention was to convince moviegoers that it was about time to get the "Jewish menace" under control. However, the "documentary," which was accompanied by dissonant music, only feigned documentary truthfulness and bristled with disinformation. Just as in the 1937-38 exhibition of the same name, "truth and lies […] were coupled in such a sophisticated way that the lie must seem like truth."[105] Real documentary footage about the life of rats combined with manipulative, subsequently shot scenes were designed to portray Jews as dehumanized vermin who had to be fought with pest exterminator's methods. Authentic scenes from feature films were methodically converted into agitation. For example, misleading German intertitles turned the conversation in Alfred L. Werker's U.S. film *The House of Rothschild* (1934), about family cohesion, into a Jewish conspiracy. Film footage from Polish ghettos shot especially for *Der ewige Jude* did show the true poverty of the Jewish population, but according to war newsreel narrator Harry Giese's hate-speaking commentary, they were only camouflaging their wealth with it. As representatives of the "Jewish menace," the film also vilified personalities

German poster art for *Der ewige Jude.*

against whom the Nazis had constantly agitated. Among them was Chaplin, who was shown in a March 1931 newsreel clip of his arrival in Berlin. Giese's commentary portrayed him as an example of the "Jewish corruption" of the German people: "The Jew Chaplin was welcomed by an enthusiastic crowd during his visit to Berlin. It cannot be denied, a part of the German people at that time naively applauded the immigrant Jews, the "Todfeinden" (mortal enemies) of their race. How was that possible?"

The attack against the darling of the audience, Chaplin, seemed particularly repulsive in the overall context of *Der ewige Jude*. Therefore, it is significant who devised this piece of fabricated propaganda. The opening credits stated: "Creator: Fritz Hippler." Hippler was SS-Obersturmbannführer and Ministerialrat in the Reichsministerium für Volksaufklärung und Propaganda, as well as Reichsfilmintendant (Artistic Reich Film Director) until 1943. He had already created the successful propaganda films *Wort und Tat* about the annexation of Austria, *Der Westwall* about the expansion of the 630-kilometer-long so-called Siegfriedstellung and *Feldzug in Polen,* about the Blitzkrieg against Poland.[106] As the Nazis were convinced that "the Jewry of Europe and of a large part of the world" were concentrated in the Polish-Jewish ghettos of Łódź, Warsaw, Kraków and Lublin, Hippler, according to his own statements, was commissioned by Goebbels immediately after the German occupation of Poland to shoot footage there for *Der ewige Jude*. This was meant to capture "the milieu and atmosphere of these Jewish hiding places in all their naturalness" before the German administrative measures would take effect.[107] In the Nazi press, Hippler was enthusiastically hailed as the "spiritual creator" of *Der ewige Jude*.[108] On November 29, 1940, the *Zeitschriften-Dienst* urged the editors-in-chief of "political and entertainment periodicals" to promote it emphatically as a "most effective contribution to the fight against any laissez-faire attitude towards the Jewish issue."[109] In addition, the Hauptamt Film der Reichspropagandaleitung ordered *Der ewige Jude* to be distributed throughout the country by the party-owned traveling venues of the Gaufilmstellen (Gau Film Offices).[110]

Shortly after the end of World War II, Hippler was arrested by the British occupation forces. He was then interned in various camps for suspected war criminals, NSDAP functionaries and state officials, the last of which was Civil Internment Camp No. 5 in Staumühle, Westphalia. On September 28 and 29, 1948, the main trial was held against him before the special court Spruchgericht Hiddesen/Detmold, which represented the German jurisdiction of *denazification*. Hippler's involvement in Nazi crimes and in *Der ewige Jude* were to be investigated. The composer Franz R. Friedl testified as a witness that Hippler had demanded he underscore the film in as dissonant and satirizing a manner as possible with grotesquely distorted Jewish songs and temple chants. In the criminal trial, as the defendant, Hippler was allowed to claim whatever he wanted. He also submitted so-called "Persilscheine" (Whitewash Certificates) to present himself as a functionary who had protected persecuted artists from the Nazis. And for the first time, he suggested that Goebbels was the creator of the "documentary," but that Goebbels had ordered Hippler to be named as such in the opening credits. After the success of his previous films, Hippler had wanted to switch to the lucrative film industry, because he felt his monthly civil servant salary of only a few hundred reichsmark was inadequate. Goebbels turned him down, but put him on the so-called "Führerliste" for artists of merit. Thus, the minister had provided him with annual extra payments of 25,000 reichsmark from 1939 to 1942. The Spruchgericht did not determine that Hippler was the creator of *Der ewige Jude*, but on September 29, 1948, sentenced him to two years in prison and a fine of 5000 marks as an accessory to the crimes of the SS.[111]

Hippler had maintained "good relations over many years" with the publicist Curt Riess,[112] who stated in his 1957 Stern bestseller *Das gabs nur einmal*: "An evil anti–Semitic film, for which Hippler was credited as producer, originated in every detail from Goebbels."[113] According to his 1939 and 1940 diaries, Goebbels had been intensively involved in the production of "our film about Jews." The

Screen shot from the "documentary" *Der ewige Jude*, 1940: credit (Friedrich-Wilhelm-Murnau-Stiftung).

first entry on *Der ewige Jude* reads: "Discussed with Hippler a ghetto film that I am having made in Poland. It must be the most incisive anti–Jewish propaganda imaginable." On September 3, 1940, he noted the following about Hippler: "Now this documentary is quite excellent. A great piece of work. Hippler has done a fine job."[114]

In Hippler's book *Die Verstrickung* (The Entanglement), published in the early 1980s, he expanded on his 1948 account of the criminal proceedings. Now he even wanted to have been a critic of the regime, a risk-taking free spirit and protector of people who think differently.[115] His subsequent book *Korrekturen. Zeitgeschichtliche Spurensuche, einmal anders* (Corrections. A Different Kind of Contemporary Historical Search for Traces) from 1994, however, demonstrated that he was still a diehard Nazi who, for example, denied Germany's guilt for the two world wars and the Holocaust. On this occasion, he modified the previous version of *Der ewige Jude*: After Goebbels got the idea for the film from the footage of the Polish ghettos, he dealt with the project almost daily. He kept Hitler informed about his ideas, and Hitler, according to Goebbels' diaries, was "very interested in the preliminary work on the 'Judenfilm'" (October 17, 1939) and also gave "some suggestions [… about] 'our Judenfilm'" (November 19, 1939) and, according to Hippler, ordered re-cuts and changes of the text.[116] Amazingly, Hippler's memory improved once again after his second book. Before his death (May 22, 2002), in a filmed interview released in 2007 as the DVD *Zeitzeugen berichten: Wunderwaffe Film. Reichsfilmintendant Hippler* (Contemporary Witnesses Report: Silver Bullet Film. Reichsfilmintendant Hippler), he downplayed his role even further and gave the matter another twist: Now he only wanted to have been Goebbels' assistant. Hitler, in turn, supposedly demanded that the "documentary" should be even more inflammatory in order to fuel "anti–Semitism which had not yet been implemented sharply enough" in Germany.[117]

Since the *Der ewige Jude* production documents are long-lost, attributing the responsibility to Goebbels and Hitler was, of course, easy. Both committed suicide shortly before the end of World War II. By 1998, Goebbels' diaries had been made accessible so extensively that, by the time of his interview for the DVD, Hippler could have known all the minister's entries about the "documentary" and about Hitler's involvement. Even today, Hippler's string of allegations may not be refuted with sufficient certainty under the strict standard "in dubio pro reo" in criminal proceedings. His versions, however, breathe the spirit to get himself out of the affair. In particular, his articles on *Der ewige Jude* and his own conduct around the premiere of the film, as well as his receipt of substantial extra payments over a period of years, do make it hard to believe that he was merely Goebbels' puppet. If Hippler was the creator of the "documentary," this would not even have to mean that Goebbels and Hitler had no influence on it. But Hippler would certainly have a motive for historical distortion: Both in *Korrekturen* and in the filmed interview, he declared that because of *Der ewige Jude* "I have suffered for the rest of my life."[118]

13

Bogeymen and *The Great Dictator* in Germany, 1941–45

After the release of *The Great Dictator*, the Nazis aggressively attacked Chaplin and his film on several levels. Such diatribes against him continued into 1942. They focused on two themes: "Germanophobe smear films" and Chaplin in the context of Nazi attacks on U.S. President Roosevelt and his family and on British Prime Minister Winston Churchill. In the U.S., Chaplin was charged with plagiarism because of his film, which led to lawsuits. And then a U.S. Senate Committee accused Chaplin, a pacifist, of being a warmonger. The Nazi propaganda reported on all this only selectively.

At the core of the reception of *The Great Dictator* is the question: Did Hitler see it, how did he react to it, and did he possess enough of a sense of humor to endure that Chaplin made international audiences laugh at him? Hitler could undoubtedly have had *The Great Dictator* screened for him. But where did the copy come from? Supposedly it was lying next to the dictator's corpse after his suicide. Amazingly, *The Great Dictator* was supposed to have been shown in German occupied territory and even have led to a public criminal trial in Berlin.

This chapter examines:

- Chaplin's performance at the third inauguration of U.S. President Roosevelt
- Nazi attacks on Roosevelt, his family, and Chaplin
- Konrad Bercovici's and Charles DeHaven's plagiarism lawsuits against Chaplin
- the U.S. Senate Committee investigating "Hollywood's systematic warmongering," Chaplin's subpoena, and Roosevelt's response
- the U.S. Committee in the Nazi press
- Nazi attacks on Churchill and Chaplin
- Budd Schulberg's claim that Hitler saw *The Great Dictator*
- the German Foreign Office's request to lend *The Great Dictator*
- whether Hitler appreciated Chaplin films
- the provenance of the film copy of *The Great Dictator* in the Berlin Reichsfilmarchiv
- Nicola Radošević's versions of the screening of *The Great Dictator* to German soldiers in occupied Serbia
- the Berlin criminal case over this screening, according to Radošević.

The Great Dictator *and President Roosevelt*

Chaplin was among the artists to perform at the Daughters of the American Revolution's Constitution Hall in Washington, DC, on January 19, 1941, for the third inauguration of U.S. President Roosevelt, which was broadcast live on the radio by CBS.[1] The ceremony was to conclude with Chaplin's final speech from *The Great Dictator*.[2] At the request of the White House, Chaplin had also provided a copy of *The Great Dictator* and met with Roosevelt for about 40 minutes before the broadcast. Apparently the latter received Chaplin in a subdued manner due to the tensions that the film had caused in Argentina, so that one of Chaplin's friends remarked about the course of the personal conversation: "You were received at the White House, but not embraced." Had the White House staff possibly not coordinated Chaplin's invitation with the president?

During his speech, Chaplin was interrupted, as he detailed in his autobiography. Nazis had mingled with the audience to distract him:

> No sooner had I begun my speech than they began to cough. It was too loud to be natural. It made me nervous so that my mouth became dry and my tongue began sticking to the roof of my palate and I could not articulate. The speech was six minutes long. In the middle of it I stopped and said that I could not continue unless I had a drink of water. Of course, there was not a drop in the house; and here I was keeping sixty million listeners waiting. After an interminable two minutes I was handed water in a small paper envelope. Thus I was able to finish the speech.[3]

The disruption was not reported, and the Nazi film press did not drop a word about Chaplin's speech.

In early February 1941, London's *Daily Mail* ran a news story that a British officer had suggested that the Royal Family should knight Chaplin for his merits with *The Great Dictator*. After the Hauptarchiv der NSDAP took this newspaper clipping for its Chaplin file,[4] the *Film-Kurier* attacked him on February 22, 1941: "The 'Hetzjude' [agitating Jew] thus rewarded for his smears with the title of baron [sic]—this would probably be the stuff for a punchy film grotesque on the British cause, which needs to make use of this 'Kämpfer von der traurigen Gestalt' [sad countenance of a 'knight']."[5] Yet Chaplin had not been made a baron. He had only been recommended for a knighthood. It was not until March 4, 1975, that Queen Elizabeth II knighted him.

Around that time, Roosevelt attended a film banquet in Hollywood and praised U.S. films in his introductory speech. These had "carried the hopes and ideals of a free people throughout the world. [...] The dictators who wanted to coerce total government think it is dangerous to let their unhappy peoples learn that in American democracy the heads of government are servants, never masters, of their people." Ministerialrat Hippler, who after World War II claimed to have been a critic of Hitler's regime, reacted to the speech in the *Film-Kurier* on March 5, 1941: He wrote that "capitalist injustice, the corrupt judiciary and the unsustainable gangster system" dominated the U.S. Therefore, the American ideals mentioned by Roosevelt left much to be desired. Most U.S. films would also be rejected abroad as "indisputable," including 18 "particularly mean and tasteless smear films" such as *The Great Dictator*, which, of course, could not be approved to be shown publicly in the Third

Reich. Otherwise, U.S. film producers had done excellent business in Germany, but in return had waged a "smear and trade war" against the German Reich. Since 1933, German film had "eked out its existence only in about 13 small cinemas in North America, which are located in German neighborhoods and which the public could not even reach."[6] To mobilize a broader readership against U.S. films, Hippler's article also appeared on the same day in the *Völkischer Beobachter,*[7] which at the time had a daily circulation of over one million copies.[8]

In the first quarter of 1941, the wife of the U.S. president organized charity events throughout the U.S. to support Great Britain in World War II, and invited Chaplin to attend. The *Film-Kurier,* in early April 1941, attempted to take Roosevelt's claim that Americans were "the tenants and guardians of true democratic culture" *ad absurdum* with "Tingel-Tangel of the Roosevelt Family," using known false allegations. For the culturally mediocre charity events, the president's son and daughter-in-law would have allied themselves with Chaplin:

> The third in the group is none other than the "jüdischer Filmclown" [Jewish film clown], the *Goldrausch*-Chaplin. He qualified for this group by denigrating the Fuehrer in his *Dictator* film in the stupidest and most outrageous way. But he miscalculated. For this sorry effort was rejected and by no means made the dollars expected by the Hollywood film lords. After all: two members of the Roosevelt family tingling, dallying and dancing in company with the Jew Charlie Chaplin—that is one of the strangely "dazzling excrescence" of American "culture."[9]

The Great Dictator—*a Case of Plagiarism?*

For years, Nazi agitation had repeatedly accused Chaplin of lacking his own ideas and of stealing the intellectual property of others. So the U.S. news of April 15, 1941, that Konrad Bercovici was demanding $5 million in damages from Chaplin for the unauthorized use of his draft for *The Great Dictator,* came just in time.[10] This news, in turn, appeared a day later in the French newspaper *L'Œuvre,* which had been Nazi-oriented since the German occupation of France. For its Chaplin file, the Hauptarchiv der NSDAP had the item translated into German.[11] On May 16, 1941, the tendentious article "Chaplin to Pay Damages" was published in the magazine *Filmwelt:* "The Jewish film actor Charlie Chaplin has received a claim for damages of 12 million reichsmark because of his last film. [...] As reported from New York, the Jew has made too much use of the glorified democratic privileges. The American Bercovici wants to prove this to him in court. He accuses Chaplin of having broken contractual agreements and of having 'copied' his draft of the film."[12] *Filmwelt* also enjoyed a considerable weekly circulation of 100,000 copies, a substantial portion of which was sold to German-speaking foreign countries.[13] Its distribution, however, was even larger. During the war, *Filmwelt* regularly appealed to its readers "back home" to pass it on to front-line soldiers either directly or through a Block-leiter (Block Leader): "The front thanks you!"[14]

But that was all that the Nazi film press had to say about the matter. Thereafter, German readers did not learn anything about the progress of Bercovici's trial, nor that it was not solely about *The Great Dictator.*

On April 27, 1938, *Daily Variety* reported that Chaplin might base his upcoming film on an "original story" by Bercovici.[15] Bercovici and Chaplin had known each other for some time and were friends. As early as 1928 and 1930, Bercovici had published the magazine articles "A Day with Charlie Chaplin" and "My Friend Charlie Chaplin."[16] The latter had also been published in Austria.[17] In 1938, Chaplin indeed discussed future film plans with Bercovici, including a Hitler satire. Bercovici sketched several subjects, but none came to fruition. According to Chaplin's son, his father had even abandoned the Hitler theme after the discussions with Bercovici:

> For a while [Bercovici] was a constant visitor at the house. He too commented on Dad's resemblance to Hitler. [...B]efore long Dad and Bercovici were tossing ideas back and forth. Dad often used his friends and acquaintances as sounding boards in this fashion. But long before he began any serious work on the Hitler idea, his enthusiasm for Bercovici had died out. [...] Once [people] are out of sight he forgets them completely, or else he just wearies of them and withdraws himself from their company. So it was with Bercovici. [...] At the same time he also dismissed the whole Hitler thing. Hitler, he decided, was too grim a figure to provide good material for a comedy.[18]

Bercovici later claimed that the idea for *The Great Dictator* came from him. On January 5, 1937, he agreed to develop a script to Chaplin for the film.[19] In April 1938, he sent Chaplin a hastily assembled six-page draft for a Hitler story with a doppelgänger as the dictator's double. He had also suggested three film titles: "The Dictators," "Heil Hitler," and "The Man with the Chaplinesque Mustache." The resulting film partly matched his draft down to Hynkel's gibberish, including the scenes of Hynkel ripping the medals off Herring's uniform and the inventor jumping out the window of Hynkel's government palace with his parachute housed in his hat. Bercovici also claimed that Chaplin had agreed to pay him a 15 percent share of the proceeds from *The Great Dictator* for anything he used from his proposals.[20] Since Chaplin denied all of this, Bercovici sued him and United Artists in New York Federal Court for a revenue share of over $5 million.

In the lawsuit, Chaplin and United Artists claimed that Chaplin had rejected all of Bercovici's drafts and had discontinued working with him on *The Great Dictator*. Moreover, Chaplin had already had the idea for a musical film comedy about Hitler in 1932 and had written song lyrics for it such as "I am Aldoph [*sic*], the great dictator, once I was a waiter." Then he abandoned this film idea. At that time, he had not been able to find a basis for developing it into a feature-length film.[21]

On June 24, 1941, the court dismissed a part of Bercovici's action in the amount of just over $3 million. Thus, Bercovici's claim that he had provided Chaplin with the idea for *The Great Dictator* was refuted.[22] The rest of the case was never ruled on: Bercovici and Chaplin reached a settlement on May 7, 1947. Chaplin paid Bercovici $95,000 on the remaining action, including $5000 for Bercovici's legal expenses. In return, Bercovici renounced rights to *The Great Dictator,* declaring that Chaplin could call himself its sole author. Lastly, Bercovici also assigned Chaplin the world rights to two screenplays he had written, *[In] Old Chicago* and *The Cry of the Wolf.*[23]

The only certain fact is that Bercovici and Chaplin discussed *The Great Dictator* for some time. Whether Bercovici's six-page draft for a Hitler film already existed in April 1938 and Chaplin received it then is unclear. Therefore, it cannot be ruled out that Bercovici penned it later, possibly even after the premiere of *The Great Dictator*.

In April 1941, vaudeville writer Charles DeHaven, no relation to Chaplin collaborator Carter DeHaven, also claimed rights to *The Great Dictator*.[24] Allegedly, Chaplin had borrowed the dance with the globe from the "Comedy Balloon Dance" piece in DeHaven and Fred Nice's 1920 vaudeville play *Mulligan & Mulligan from the West* for the *Follies of 1776* program. DeHaven described the "Comedy Balloon Dance" as an "artistic-comic sequence of steps in which the dancer throws up a balloon in various ways and catches it again." DeHaven sued Chaplin in vain for this,[25] because the "Comedy Balloon Dance" bore no resemblance to how Hynkel danced out his fantasies of world domination with the globe, which then abruptly burst like a bubble. In 1929, Chaplin himself had in any case already pre-sketched the dance, including its political dimension, in Douglas Fairbanks' private film (see Chapter 11). The Nazi film press remained silent on DeHaven's plagiarism claim, despite the suitable smear approach. Otherwise, however, it would have had to be disclosed that Chaplin was caricaturing Hitler and his lust for power by dancing as a dictator in private. According to the *Zeitschriften-Dienst*'s instruction of November 8, 1940, however, it was not allowed to mention that Chaplin portrayed Hitler in *The Great Dictator*.[26]

Finally, many years later, Spanish director Luís Buñuel recounted in his memoirs having dreamt, prior to the completion of Chaplin's film, that a projectile plopped out of a huge cannon—similar to Big Bertha at the beginning of *The Great Dictator*. Unlike Bercovici and DeHaven, Buñuel did not pick a quarrel over this, because: "Chaplin, of course, knew nothing about it."[27]

A Senate Investigation Committee

Indeed, the pro–Nazi mood in the U.S. had changed. Nevertheless, the German Nazis received unexpected support in their fight against anti-fascist Hollywood films, especially those involving non–U.S. citizens. With its resolution of August 1, 1941, the isolationist America First Committee, AFC, accused both the U.S. film industry and the Roosevelt administration of "carrying a campaign of propaganda to get the United States in the war." To put a stop to this, the AFC called for a U.S. Senate investigation committee to be set up. The resolution was co-authored by Senator Gerald P. Nye of North Dakota, who in his speech of the same day painted a grim portrait of the 20 or so 1940 U.S. "smear films with Germanophobe tendencies," including *The Great Dictator*: They were "designed to drug the reason of the American people—to rouse them to a war."[28] This was grist to the *Film-Kurier*'s mill. On August 4, 1941, it quoted Nye, but also put the following words in his mouth: "These smear films suggest to the American that Germany wants to enslave them and to steal their trade, which is why the US must enter the war. [... The] films [are] primarily concocted by foreigners and performed by English actors." In addition, the *Film-Kurier* used the opportunity for its own agitation. Accordingly, "Germanophobe smear films" from Great Britain were "Churchill's film gift to Roosevelt and Stalin" and the 20 U.S. "smear films" were made exclusively by foreigners, "all Jews for whom things had got too hot around in Europe."[29] Soon after, the AFC was also called "Hitler's Front."[30]

The next day, the trade journal ran an even more explicit front page headline about the new U.S. liaison with the Soviet Union: "Moscow and Hollywood hand in hand." The "masterminds behind the whole smear campaign against Germany" were, of course, the Jews. Chaplin was assigned a central role by the *Film-Kurier*: "The Soviet Union's leading all–Jewish film director, Eisenstein, praises his North American Jewish colleague Charlie Chaplin's struggle 'for truth, for human beings, for humanity' with effusive words [...]. This big-capitalist Jewish film clown, of course, is flattered and accepts the Order of the Red Flag awarded to him. [...] The characteristic common feature of American and Soviet 'cultural advertising' is striking: it is controlled by Jews."[31]

Der Stürmer seller in New York, 1937.

The Senate Committee was constituted under the chairmanship of the Democrat Senator D. Worth Clark of Idaho, and Nye was a member. For October 6, 1941, Clark had, among others, the two aliens Chaplin (British) and Anatole Litvak (Ukrainian) subpoenaed for their films *The Great Dictator* and *Confessions of a Nazi Spy*, respectively. Chaplin should explain why he had made his film.[32] It was in the air that he would be officially disapproved for his humanitarian, anti–Nazi commitment. In the fall of that year, Clark and Nye claimed that "the Hollywood film industry was engaged in systematic warmongering" with another 45 war or army films in the pipeline. This did not escape the attention of the *Film-Kurier*, which reported on it on September 2, 1941.[33]

In the U.S. press, the Committee sparked outrage and derision in equal measure. Among the comments: The Committee was a "joke" and the intention was to conduct an "investigation against reality."[34] The *Mount Vernon News* printed a cartoon by Herbert Block on September 20, suggesting that Nazis were behind it. Hitler, in uniform, with a folder of Nazi propaganda under his arm, walks past the Nye Clark Committee, which apparently mistakes him for Chaplin and breaks into a sweat. But then he recognizes Hitler and wipes the sweat from his brow in relief:

"Gee, You Scared Me—I Though' You Were Chaplin!"[35] In a cartoon by an unnamed *Washington Evening Star* cartoonist, Chaplin stands in his Tramp costume and holds his "subpoena before the Senate Committee to Investigate Film Propaganda" in his hand, and comments: "Now what could I possibly tell those past-masters about comedy?"[36] This prompted Roosevelt to ridicule the Committee to reporters as "a scene out of an old slapstick movie" and he recommended that they study the cartoon.[37] On that occasion, he read aloud a mocking telegram that a Connecticut citizen had addressed to a Senator as member of the AFC's investigating subcommittee: "Have just been reading book called the Holy Bible. Written entirely by foreigners, mostly Jews. First part full of warmongering propaganda. Second part condemns isolationism. That fake story about Samaritan dangerous. Should be added to your list and suppressed." Nye's reaction was miffed and defiant: "I'm surprised that the President has not joined earlier in the effort to stop and end the investigation of war propaganda in film. I'm convinced that such efforts will be in vain."[38]

Chaplin's hearing never took place. The committee's activities were put to an end by the Third Reich's December 11, 1941, declaration of war on the U.S. One day later, the *Film-Kurier* called for "brotherhood in arms against the common enemy," against "world Jewry, Roosevelt and consorts."[39] The film magazine *Filmwelt* joined in January 1942 with its long, bilious article "So hetzten sie zum Kriege" (Their Way to Incite to War). It was directed against Roosevelt, Chaplin and others who had fought the Nye Committee.[40] The magazine sharply rejected the idea that Nazis had exerted their influence in the constitution of the Committee. In it, the magazine also rejected that Nazis had lobbied its constitution. Roosevelt had proved with his "infamous 'brain trust' of Jewish minds" that he had become "more and more like the mentally deranged World War I President Wilson." Incidentally, the *Filmwelt* fell over itself with its view of the methodology and scheming of the warmongering U.S. film industry:

> Hate films were made against Germany and Italy: Jews wrote the scripts. Emigrants were hired for the roles. Jews discussed the premieres of these films in psalm-modulating hymns and suggested to the audience that revelations of artistically meaningful interpretations of reality could be found here. Jewish propagandists organized Germanophobe rallies in the cinemas. Expressions of the reasonable will for peace were shouted down or bludgeoned. The USA had to be rushed into the war—although this war was none of their business. As early as 1939, 43 films with warmongering effects were produced in the USA: a proof [...] of the criminal conspiracy between Roosevelt and the film-Jews. In addition, the USA market was flooded with the products of the British hate and propaganda film centers.

The *Filmwelt* also claimed that Chaplin's "deplorable and schizophrenic parody [...] had become a financial fiasco for the producers even in New York." Moreover, *The Great Dictator* had been "banned altogether in numerous South American countries" without the intervention of German diplomats.

"Overestimated Liar Lord" and "Jewish Artiness"

To a certain extent, the *Film-Kurier*'s article "Churchill's Film Gift to Roosevelt and Stalin" had a model in Walter Persich's 1940 book *Winston Churchill ganz "privat." Abenteurer, Lord und Verbrecher.* Persich presented the "true-to-life por-trait of the man who, with a minimum of knowledge and a maximum of hubris, managed to become the most powerful man in England who went from being a lord of lies to become the gravedigger of a world empire." As was to be expected, Persich described the career of the British War Prime Minister in a derogatory tone, insin-uating that he had become jealous of Germany out of boredom and had thus turned into its opponent.[41]

In 1942, an expanded edition was published with the additional chapter "Charly [sic] Chaplin and Winston Churchill—arm in arm." It began with Churchill toast-ing Chaplin at a London press ball in October 1931.[42] Persich put into the mouth of a guest at the event: "The clown of the House of Commons wants to greet his colleague from the film." The chapter was full of the stereotypically recurring Nazi Chaplin agitation *à la* Julius Streicher and Max Jungnickel. It sounded almost reasonably objective that Chaplin, according to a British newspaper article, had risen "from 'Winkelartist' [hack artist] to Hollywood star" and "greatest humorist in the world." But then Persich moved along well-trodden Nazi paths and presented Chaplin as a dubious, parasitic person who had achieved his film fame at the expense of other art-ists. With his Tramp, he had flaunted poverty on the screen, while he himself was indulging in wealth. Persich wrote himself into a downright rage:

> What made Chaplin famous? He portrays the down-and-out man who is in everyone's way. But he muddles through cleverly. He is so cunning, as nobody would expect from such an unimpressive little fellow [...]—and always at the expense of others. His face never reveals the slightest human emotion. Only the eyes seem to live in it, but two forms of expression domi-nate: immense, inwardly blazing hatred and a submissive, almost doglike begging disguised as harmlessness: "Do not hurt me, I am so small...." Charly [sic] Chaplin waddles through all the films with his outward standing toes as the "plattfüßiger Wüstenwanderer" [flat-footed des-ert wanderer] who cannot deny his race. [... He] is [...] the Jew par excellence. In reality, this "humble little man" lives in Hollywood in a fabulous palace. He has a bank account worth mil-lions of dollars, is the owner of a film company and participates in industrial ventures. The for-mer have-not thus leads the life of the Anglo-Saxon American plutocrats who rule the USA."[43]

Did Hitler See The Great Dictator?

This question has repeatedly intrigued Chaplin researchers. In 2002, Kevin Brownlow and Michael Kloft's documentary *The Tramp and the Dictator* about Chaplin, Hitler and *The Great Dictator* was released—in different versions. In the English version, the question is answered in the affirmative. The German version (*Der Tramp und der Diktator*) keeps a low profile in the commentary and does not provide an explicit answer.[44]

The key chief witness in the documentary is the Jewish U.S. screenwriter Sey-mour Wilson "Budd" Schulberg, born in 1914, son of Paramount co-chief Benja-min P. Schulberg. In *The Tramp and the Dictator*, he told Brownlow: "At the end of the war, I was in Berlin. I was in charge of gathering photographic evidence for the war crime trial that was being prepared in Nuremberg. In the course of that, I looked up the files on what films Hitler had ordered to be shown. And this is the true thrill: He ordered *The Great Dictator*, and then he ordered it a day or so after again."

In the German version, the off-screen narrator summarizes that Schulberg drove to the Soviet-occupied Ufa compound in Babelsberg only to clarify whether Hitler had seen Chaplin's film. Schulberg went on in *Der Tramp und der Diktator* in more detail: "I asked there for the catalogue of films that Hitler had ordered from his private cinema. I leafed through it, and to my amazement *The Great Dictator* was listed. The Germans were just very precise. They helped us a lot with that. There was the exact date when the film was sent to Hitler. And whether you believe it or not: a day later, he ordered it again."

At the Babelsberg Ufa compound, Schulberg is unlikely to have been able to find an answer in the files of the state-owned Ufa, since Chaplin produced his film in the U.S. Yet, he could have accessed documents of the Reichsfilmarchiv, which opened in early 1935, in Babelsberg. Some of its office buildings were located in downtown Berlin, for example on Tempelhofer Ufer in the Schöneberg district. However, the main stock warehouse, the so-called "Filmbunker" (Film Bunker), was located about two kilometers from the Babelsberg Ufa compound. There were also special warehouse locations in Harthausen near Munich, Vienna and Prague. After the Reichsfilmarchiv was put under the control of the Reichsministerium für Volksaufklärung und Propaganda at the end of May 1938, the main stock warehouse was also administered from Babelsberg,[45] most likely including stock accounting and records of lending transactions for all storage facilities. Presumably, Schulberg was not familiar with the organization of either the Ufa or the Reichsfilmarchiv and its storage facilities. At the time of the filmed interview, he was about 80 years old. Possibly, Schulberg's memory had faded somewhat over 50 years after his visit to Babelsberg, causing him to confuse the Ufa studio compound with the main stock warehouse of the Reichsfilmarchiv.

In any case, the first place to look for documents on the lending of *The Great Dictator*, including the regular supply of films to Hitler, was the Reichsfilmarchiv's main stock warehouse in Babelsberg. Little is known about the Reichsfilmarchiv so far. Its stock accounts, inventory journals and records of lending transactions have not survived, nor any other documents that Schulberg claimed to have inspected in 1945. In addition, the Reichsfilmarchiv's inventory card index has also been preserved only in very fragmentary form.

Screen shot from *The Tramp and the Dictator*, 2002: Budd Schulberg (© Photoplay Productions Ltd. & Spiegel TV).

However, Schulberg's

report raises the following question: Why did he not secure documents about the lending of *The Great Dictator*, or at least not transcribed them, if that was the only reason he went to Babelsberg? He would then have had in his hands the evidence he was looking for! Unfortunately, this could not be further investigated. Schulberg died in early August 2009, and his memoirs from the early 1980s end with his 20th birthday.[46]

In addition, Schulberg may not even have been able to find the documents he was looking for in Babelsberg. In April 1945, before his trip to Babelsberg, the Reichsministerium für Volksaufklärung und Propaganda had ordered that the Reichsfilmarchiv records be destroyed, probably so that they should not fall into the hands of the Allies. But Reichsfilmarchiv director Richard Quaas did not destroy the archive's files and the storage inventory journal, but transported them to the evacuation storage facility in Munich-Harthausen.[47] The area was occupied by U.S. troops soon after. Nothing is known for certain about the final whereabouts of this material. In February 2008, Wolfgang Klaue, director of the former State Film Archive of the GDR, reported that decades ago, he had the Reichsfilmarchiv's lending book in his hands. It revealed information about lendings of *The Great Dictator*, but Hitler's name did not appear in it. He also no longer remembered the names of other persons.[48] Klaue's report does not contradict the outsourcing of documents from the Reichsfilmarchiv. In fact, in 1954, the Soviet Union had handed over parts of the former Reichsfilmarchiv, which had been stored on the territory of the GDR under the supervision of Soviet troops to the government of the GDR. The lending book could have been among them. As a result of German reunification on October 3, 1990, the Staatliches Filmarchiv der DDR was incorporated into the Bundesarchiv—Filmarchiv. To this day, it has not been found in the archive holdings. Thus, Schulberg's account cannot be completely dismissed for the time being.

Hans Barkhausen was the former Advisor and Head of Division at the Reichsfilmarchiv. According to the Reichsfilmarchiv's business distribution plan of January 11, 1943, he had the following duties: processing of the film material of the Reichspropagandaleitung, processing of domestic and foreign feature films, keeping the sound film index, catalogue processing, user support and the control of incoming films from abroad (transit films).[49] Therefore, Barkhausen had a good insight into the Reichsfilmarchiv. In June 1985, the then 78-year-old reported hearsay reactions to *The Great Dictator*: "We did not see *The Great Dictator* in the Reichsfilmarchiv even once. We only knew that the film was there. But there was a rumor circulating of fits of rage because the film was such an insidious sorry effort. It was the worst thing that could ever have been produced about the Fuehrer of the German Reich. [...] Whether Hitler saw *The Great Dictator*, I do not know." According to Barkhausen, the film was not stored in the Reichsfilmarchiv's Babelsberg main stock warehouse, but on Hitler's orders in a vault at the Reichsministeriums für Volksaufklärung und Propaganda,[50] to which Goebbels would have had access: "I know [...] for sure that it was in a kind of film vault in the Propaganda Ministry, together with a second film that we did not have in the Reichsfilmarchiv, which was [Victor Fleming's 1939] *Vom Winde verweht* (*Gone with the Wind*). [It was] apparently a favorite film of Goebbels, [...] which he showed several times in his relatively large screening room in the ministry to guests. Once I was one of them."[51] So Hitler knew about the existence of a copy of *The Great Dictator* in Goebbels' ministry. Whether Hitler also had the fit of rage Barkhausen mentioned is anyone's guess. Barkhausen suggested in the interview that the former Reichsfilmintendant Fritz Hippler might know whether Hitler had seen the Chaplin film. Hippler did not respond to an interview request. He also would not agree to be interviewed for *The Tramp and the Dictator*. Furthermore, an interview with Quaas, the former director of the Reichsfilmarchiv, could not be arranged before his death in 1989.[52]

Near Hitler

In August 1944, the Auswärtiges Amt requested to the Reichsministerium für Volksaufklärung und Propaganda via the Reichsfilmarchiv for the viewing of the following films by Reichsminister des Äußeren (Minister of Foreign Affairs) Joachim von Ribbentrop and his Personal Staff: *The Great Dictator*, listed in the files as "amerik[anischer] Hetzfilm m[it] Komödiencharakter, 1940" (1940 American smear film with comedy character), *Tales of Manhattan* (Julien Duvivier, 1942) and the 1942 Soviet short *Die Patriotin* (further details unknown). Von Ribbentrop was one of the leading Nazis. His ministry was actively involved in the deportation of Jews and cooperated with Heinrich Himmler's SS in their murder. Von Ribbentrop was sentenced to death as another major war criminal by the Nuremberg War Crimes Tribunal on October 1, 1946, for crimes against humanity.[53]

On August 15, 1944, the director of the Reichsfilmarchiv endorsed the request to the ministry.[54] Whether and when the viewing subsequently took place cannot be concluded from this, nor is it documented elsewhere. However, the group of viewers registered probably included the following persons:

- Reichsminister des Auswärtigen Joachim von Ribbentrop,
- Staatssekretär des Auswärtigen Amts (State Secretary of the Foreign Office) Dr. Adolf Baron Steengracht von Moyland,
- Gesandter I. Klasse (Envoy I. Class) Dr. Franz von Sonnleithner,
- Vortragender Legationsrat (Lecturing Legation Councilor) Rudolf Likius,
- Ständiger Beauftragter des Reichsminister des Auswärtigen für Propagandafragen (Permanent Representative of the Reichsminister des Auswärtigen for Propaganda Affairs) Dr. Karl Megerle,
- SA-Brigadeführer (SA Brigade Leader) Ernst Frenzel,
- Vortragender Legationsrat (Lecturing Legation Councilor) Horst Wagner,
- Legationsrat I. Klasse (Legation Councilor I. Class) Bernd Gottfriedsen[55]

Was this the group of persons Klaue had found in the Reichsfilmarchiv's lending book located in the Staatliches Filmarchiv der DDR? If the screening had taken place, the three films would probably have been shown in the screening room of the Reichsministerium für Volksaufklärung und Propaganda, because *The Great Dictator* was kept under lock and key at the ministry. Whether Goebbels and even Hitler attended remains a matter of speculation. There is no mention of such a screening in Goebbels' extensive diaries with their countless entries on film.

Evidence for the screening of Chaplin's film in Hitler's inner circle does not exist either. Hitler's secretary from 1942, Traudl Junge experienced the last days of the Third Reich in the Berlin "Führerbunker" (Fuehrer's Bunker) under the Alten Reichskanzlei (Old Reich Chancellery). In her memoir, published in 2001 and based on her 1947 notes, she gave a multifaceted description of Hitler as a pleasant, polite boss and fatherly friend. She did not relate anything about film screenings.[56]

Hitler liked to watch movies. He frequently had them screened for him at the Obersalzberg Berghof near Berchtesgaden and at the Berlin Reichskanzlei. German diplomat Reinhard Spitzy belonged to Hitler's inner circle and related in *The Tramp and the Dictator*, "[Hitler] was a film buff. That was his favorite pastime. He especially appreciated [*The Lives of a Bengal Lancer*, Henry Hathaway, USA 1935]. And, of course, he also liked Greta Garbo movies. He would have liked to receive Garbo like a guest of state in Berlin." Hitler's intimate Albert Speer, a frequent guest of the dictator at the mountain fortress, recounted the following in his *Erinnerungen*:

> In the evenings a primitive film apparatus was regularly set up to screen one or two feature films after the newsreel. [...] Hitler discussed the selection of films with Goebbels. In most cases, the films were those that were shown simultaneously in the Berlin movie theaters. Hitler preferred harmless entertainment, love and social films. [...] Night after night [his closest entourage] had to watch trivial operetta films. [...] More often we saw foreign productions, even those that were withheld from the German audience. [...] He maintained the custom of having one or two films shown every evening until the war began.[57]

Rochus Misch was Hitler's bodyguard from 1940 until his (Hitler's) suicide. Unlike Speer, who was only a sporadic guest at Obersalzberg, Misch was constantly near Hitler. He wrote in his memoir about the film screenings:

Great Hall of Hitler's Berghof on Obersalzberg near Berchtesgaden, ca. 1940.

Late in the evening, film screenings began at the Berghof [...]. Hitler was a great movie buff. It was not unusual for him to watch several films in a row. Film projectionist [Erich] Stein had to constantly organize supplies from the Propagandaministerium or the Reichsfilmarchiv. Most of the movies were American productions. Stein was also responsible for the films Hitler watched in the music room of the Reichskanzlei. [...] Since the screenings at the Berghof took place in the large living hall, our escort commando belonged to the audience as a matter of course. [...] I especially remember that we watched *Vom Winde verweht* at least three times. After Hitler was shown this epic for the first time, he immediately summoned Goebbels. With him, he then watched the film again in its entirety. "Something like that," he said to Goebbels afterwards, "our people must be able to do something like that!"[58]

Misch could not contribute anything about *The Great Dictator*: "Unfortunately, I do not remember [...] whether the anti–Hitler satire *The Great Dictator* was screened." Therefore, the following remark by Misch's book collaborators remains pure speculation, which probably goes back to Schulberg's *Tramp and the Dictator* interview: "There are probably documents according to which Hitler had the film requested."[59] Spitzy, too, only speculated in the English version of the documentary: "I was completely convinced that Hitler had the film shown to him and had laughed about it, [for example, about how] Charlie Chaplin [...] sits with Mussolini on two chairs at the barber's and is then cranked up[. ...] After all, Hitler was clever."

Anyway, the recollections of Misch, Speer and Spitzy also do not allow us to determine if and where Hitler saw *The Great Dictator*. The present archive holdings of the Institut für Zeitgeschichte—Dokumentation Obersalzberg do not contribute to this either. On the other hand, it is not impossible that he had *The Great Dictator* shown to him, and it was he who went into a fit of rage over it.

Hitler a Chaplin Fan?

Misch's recollections of the screenings included a certain surprise: "Hitler loved Chaplin films." Hitler is said to have had various Chaplin films screened for him.[60] Chaplin was certainly no stranger to Hitler and his entourage, as Spitzy pointed out in *The Tramp and the Dictator*: "We knew [Chaplin] was Jewish. [... His films] were not what we wanted, of course. We also knew, of course, that he could not and did not love us and that he had great influence. [... But Hitler] was not a killjoy. He could laugh at such things—in the inner circle, but never publicly." Speer, on the other hand, left no doubt in his *Erinnerungen* that Hitler did not like grotesque film comedies at all: "He had [...] no sense for [...] films like the ones I loved at the time, for example with Buster Keaton or even Charlie Chaplin."[61]

Could Hitler have laughed in small circles at *The Great Dictator* and also at himself, as Spitzy stated? In his book *Die Verstrickung*, Hippler made a sweeping claim that in the 1930s, the British Lord Privy Seal Anthony Eden had attested to Hitler's sense of humor.[62] So did his photographer Hoffmann[63] and his admirer Unity Mitford. According to her, Hitler even parodied himself, provoking roars of laughter.[64] Yet, the sharp public attacks of Nazi propaganda against Chaplin and his film suggest that such portrayals seem rather unlikely. They are also contradicted by other sources. In late March 1979, German film critic Friedrich Luft discussed comedians with the German-speaking U.S. talk show host Dick Cavett on German television's *First Program*.[65] Luft reported that the Berlin folk comedian and cabaret artist Erich Carow, operator of the cabaret Lachbühne,[66] had spent evenings with Hitler telling jokes. Carow had not been able to laugh at them, but had let them pass for tactical reasons.

In his *Erinnerungen*, Speer denied Hitler a sense of humor altogether: "He left the joking to others, but laughed loudly and unrestrainedly, could even literally bend over in laughter; sometimes he wiped tears from his eyes during such outbursts of amusement. He liked to laugh, but basically always at the expense of others."[67] Brigitte Hamann, author of a biography about the young Hitler,[68] agreed with this in the German version *Der Tramp und der Diktator*: "Actually, he could not laugh at himself at all. He could only laugh at others. For he was the Fuehrer, and you cannot laugh at a Fuehrer. I am quite sure he would not have laughed at this Chaplin film and would have stopped it immediately."

Nevertheless, Hitler apparently had some form of sense of humor. In December 1937, Goebbels noted in his diary: "I present the Fuehrer with 30 first-class movies of the last 4 years and 18 Mickey Mouse films, including a wonderful art album, for Christmas. He is very pleased and extremely happy for this treasure, which hopefully will be a source of much joy and relaxation for him."[69] Furthermore, the daily logs of the "persönlichen Adjutantur des Führers und Reichskanzlers" document that from the end of June to the end of November 1938, Hitler had the Laurel and Hardy feature films *Ritter ohne Furcht und Tadel* (*Way Out West*), *Swiss Miss* and *Block-Heads* screened for him on the Obersalzberg. They were a lot of fun for him![70]

The Great Dictator *in Goebbels' Vault*

The August 1944 lending request of the Auswärtiges Amt proves that a copy of the original version of *The Great Dictator* was in the Reichsfilmarchiv. In its catalogue, it was recorded as "Hetzfilm mit Komödiencharakter" (Smear Film with a Comedy Character) under No. 15,242, and this categorization appeared on the Auswärtiges Amt's lending request as well. "Hetzfilme" were specially marked in the catalogue. To find them more quickly in its folders, their catalogue cards were printed not on old white and gray paper like the regular cards, but on pink paper. In addition, numbers were stamped in the head of the "Hetzfilm" cards. Presumably, "Hetzfilme" were thus rated politically on a scale of "1" to "6," i.e., from "very good" to "completely objectionable," as the highest Nazi disapproval, similar to German school grades, as a comparison of such catalogue cards suggests. The pink catalogue cards for *The Great Dictator* and, for example, Fritz Lang's *Man Hunt* (1941), which was rated as a "sensation film with a strong Germanophobe diatribe tendency" (No. 14,615), both bear the "6." From the description in the catalogue card of *The Great Dictator*, it is clear that this is the original English version without German subtitles and that the Reichsfilmarchiv archivists knew exactly who the "great dictator" was: Tomania was the "bashful" name of Germany, Osterlich stood for Austria, and Bacteria was the "Mussolini-Italy." Hitler's name was not mentioned, but the conclusion left no doubt: "Smear comedy with the vilest disparagement of the National Socialist regime and especially of the Fuehrer in Chaplin's typical grotesque, almost always more than clumsy manner." Appendix 6 offers the English translation of the catalogue card.

Due to a 1943 decree of the Reichsministeriums für Volksaufklärung und Propaganda from 1943, "Feindfilme" (Enemy Films) classified as Germanophobe had to be preceded by a so-called Geheimhaltungs-Vorspann (Secrecy Opening Credits). Shortly before the Auswärtiges Amt's lending request, the Ministry drew particular attention to maintain that procedure in a circular of July 24, 1944, and requested "a list of the films for which the Geheimhaltungs-Vorspann must be retained. A total of 500 films are concerned. These films are included in

RFA. 15 242   6   Herst.-Jahr: 1940

The Great Dictator

USA
engl. orig.
Länge 3481 m

Art des Films . Hetzfilm mit Komödiencharakter
Herst. u. Verl. . United Artists
Spielleitung . . **CHARLES CHAPLIN**
Manuskript . . Charles Chaplin
Fotografie . . . Karl Struss, Roland Totheroh
Musik . . . . . Meredith Willson
Bauten . . . . . J. Russell Spencer
Darsteller . . . CHARLES CHAPLIN, PAULETTE GOGDARD, JACK OAKIE, Reginald Gardiner, Henry Daniell, Billy Gilbert, Grace Hayle, Carter de Haven, Maurice Moscovich, Emma Dunn, Paul Weigel, Chester Cunklin

Inhalt:

Nach dem Vorwort spielt der Film zwischen zwei Weltkriegen, in einer Zeit, als die Vernunft wenig hoch im Kurs stand ... Westfront 1918 — an einem deutschen Ferngeschütz treibt ein deutscher Soldat, Jude, im zivilen Leben Barbier, grotesken Unfug. Bei einem darauffolgenden Sturmangriff geht der Unsinn weiter. Schließlich hilft er einem deutschen Fliegeroffizier retten, wird dabei verwundet und bewußtlos in ein Lazarett eingeliefert. ... Jahre sind seit dem Waffenstillstand vergangen, in Tomania (wie Deutschland verschämt genannt wird) hat ein Diktator die Macht an sich gerissen, Hynkel, der mit seinen Sturmtruppen ein grausames Regime gegenüber den Juden im Ghetto führt, Hynkel, der Weltmachtsgelüste hat, bereitet gerade die Eroberung des Nachbarstaates Osterlich (Österreich) vor, das den Juden im Ghetto als das gelobte Land erscheint, in das sie zu gerne auswandern möchten. — Um diese Zeit wird der Barbier aus dem Weltkrieg aus einer Anstalt entlassen, in der er bisher gehalten wurde, da er seinerzeit völlig das Gedächtnis verloren hatte. Er kommt jetzt in seinen Laden im Ghetto zurück, den Krieg und die seither verflossenen Jahre hat er vergessen, er glaubt nur wenige Wochen weg gewesen zu sein. Aber Tomania hat sich ja seitdem sehr verändert ... Bald hat sich der arglose Barbier die Wut der Sturmtruppen zugezogen, und er wäre vor seinem Laden aufgeknüpft worden, wäre nicht zufällig Schulz, der Fliegeroffizier aus dem Weltkrieg, der den kleinen Juden sofort wiedererkennt, zu seiner Rettung erschienen. Der Barbier hat jetzt Ruhe vor der Soldateska, und eine zarte Freundschaft bahnt sich zwischen ihm und der im Nebenhaus wohnenden jüdischen Waise Hannah an. Hynkel läßt den Terror gegen die Juden etwas nach, da er für seinen Krieg gegen Osterlich von einem internationalen Geldjuden die Mittel borgen will. Dieser Anleiheplan geht aber schief, wieder beginnt die Verfolgung der Ghettojuden. Schulz warnt den Diktator vor diesen unmenschlichen Methoden und wird von ihm als Verräter ver-

Reichsfilmarchiv catalogue card No. 15,242: *The Great Dictator*, front.

the 'Special Volume of the Reichfilmarchiv,' which is also at the Minister's disposition." The Special Volume has not been identified.[71] It is almost certain that the *Great Dictator* copy in Goebbels' vault also included the secrecy opening credits. Its isolated text is in the holdings of the Bundesarchiv—Filmarchiv and reads as: "Due to a special permission granted to you personally by the Reichsminister für Volksaufklärung und Propaganda, the Reichsfilmarchiv will show you a film of foreign origin that is not approved for public screening in Germany. It is forbidden under all circumstances to inform third parties of a screening and the content of the film."

Goebbels' ministry kept itself constantly informed about "Feindfilme" and enemy propaganda. Hippler's duties as Reichsfilmintendant therefore included the "acquisition of important enemy film material, especially enemy 'Hetzfilme.'" Considerable financial resources were made available for this purpose, demonstrating the high significance that the Nazi state attributed to this task. In 1944 alone, when

Hippler had meanwhile been replaced by Hans Hinkel, 3.75 million reichsmark were allocated to this budget item,[72] even though the German Reich had been bled dry financially by the war effort. According to Barkhausen's recollections, "enemy films" were acquired in various ways: "The films were confiscated in cities like Prague, Warsaw and Paris. But they were also bought in neutral foreign countries (Spain/ Switzerland), or simply copied illegally abroad. In the German embassy in Stockholm, there was a complete film copying facility, with the help of which borrowed films could be copied immediately. Some films also came to the Reichsfilmarchiv from captured ships."[73]

But where did the film copy of *The Great Dictator* in the Reichsfilmarchiv come from? Barkhausen has only "assume[d] that the film came to the Third Reich either via Spain or Sweden."[74]

Greece-Serbia-Berlin?

There is, however, an even more adventurous version of how the copy of *The Great Dictator* could have reached the Third Reich.

For *The Tramp and the Dictator*, the filmmaker-photographer Nicola Radošević (born December 18, 1926, in Belgrade) was interviewed. In the documentary's German version, he claimed that during the German occupation in 1942, "Yugoslav partisans [...] noticed that [Chaplin's *The Great Dictator*, an] explosive stray film lay [in the Belgrade film stock]." Further, Radošević said in the English version in German that as a 17-year-old he had exchanged a German operetta film for the copy of Chaplin's film which came from Greece, in a Belgrade troop cinema for German soldiers:

I belonged to the [resistance organization] Blue Ribbon. We never sabotaged the German occupiers with violence, only culturally. Therefore, we wanted Hitler to know what [...] Chaplin thought about him. At the beginning of the screening, people did not realize right away [that the Chaplin film was playing]. However, [this changed] after 45 minutes. A German SS man shoots at the screen with his shotgun. Everyone quickly dashes out of the cinema. Because the film was directed against Hitler, no one wanted to stay.

During the Balkan campaign in early April 1941, the German Wehrmacht had invaded both Yugoslavia and

Screen shot from *The Tramp and the Dictator*, 2002: Nicola Radošević (© Photoplay Productions Ltd. & Spiegel TV).

Greece. Both countries had subsequently surrendered on April 17 and 23, respectively. Radošević's spectacular film exchange could therefore have taken place in the Belgrade troop cinema, but not in 1942, rather in 1943, if he claims to be about 17 years old at that time. However, his statements are dubious.

During the research for *The Tramp and the Dictator*, Kevin Brownlow came across the decades-old article "How Hitler Saw *The Great Dictator*" by Drogoš Simović in the 1963 English-language Belgrade *Review—Yugoslav Monthly*.[75] At that time, Radošević had presented his story not only somewhat differently, but also more comprehensively than in the documentary. Above all, the trail led right to Hitler! According to Simović's article, Radošević was a Chaplin lover who had surprisingly received an autographed card from him. About the copy of *The Great Dictator* which had been discovered in Serbia in 1942, Radošević had told Simović:

> After the Germans took Belgrade, I got a job at the office that screened films that had been confiscated from all over the occupied Balkans. Those that did not find any pardon with the Nazis were destroyed. Since my friends knew where I worked, they suggested that I steal some Russian and American films from the film storage facility. Once I looked to see what films were available, I was amazed to find Chaplin's *The Great Dictator*. I had read that the film had been made just before the beginning of World War II and had not been shown anywhere in Europe. The Germans had banned it because it made fun of their Fuehrer.

Simović's article went on to state that Radošević had transported the copy of the Chaplin film out of the film warehouse under his coat. Given the length of the film, it must have been about six reels of film, each about 600 meters long, with a total weight of about 30 kilograms—probably a considerable weight even for a 17-year-old and not too easy to carry away secretly under a coat.

Radošević later described this transport differently. According to Petar Volks' 1966 Serbian book on Yugoslav film history, Radošević and his friends did not want to show the film in Serbia's capital, as claimed in *The Tramp and the Dictator*, but in the Central Cinema in the garrison town of Valjevo, located 90 kilometers southwest of Belgrade.[76] Radošević transported Chaplin's film there in a coal wagon. In the Central, German officers and soldiers were anxiously waiting for the film, which was supposed to be about some German victory or something else—not an operetta film, as Radošević said almost 40 years later. At first, the audience still applauded enthusiastically when Chaplin greeted them from the screen with the "German salute." But then they realized that something was wrong: Hitler, Goebbels, Goering and Mussolini were all being caricatured. As a result, several officers immediately fired their guns at the screen.

In 1963, Radošević had also told Simović that the German Wehrmacht had arrested him and some of his friends shortly after the cinematic adventure and had executed one of them. Radošević also had a few more surprises in store. Allegedly, Hitler was personally informed about the unwanted screening of *The Great Dictator*. Therefore, Radošević, together with the film copy, was transported in an armored train to Germany, where he was imprisoned. At the end of 1943, after the bombardment of Berlin, he managed to escape from Germany. Back in his homeland, he went underground. And then Radošević had presented the climax: "After the fall of Berlin [on May 8, 1945], Red Army soldiers reportedly made their way into the 'Wolf's

Lair' under the Reichstag. Not far from Hitler's corpse lay a copy of *The Great Dictator*. Thus, after its 'premiere' in an occupied Yugoslavian city, the film experienced its second European screening in Berlin."

This 1963 account should also be treated with caution. The location described as the "Wolf's Lair" should mean the "Wolfsschanze," but cannot be correct. This was an East Prussian bunker complex near Rastenberg (today: Ketrzyn in Poland), a long way from Berlin. During the final phase of World War II, Hitler had retreated from this bunker to the Berlin "Führerbunker," where he committed suicide on the afternoon of April 30, 1945, together with his newly wedded wife Eva Braun. The "Führerbunker" was not located under the Reichstag building in Berlin either, but on the grounds of the new Alte Reichskanzlei, near Potsdamer Platz and a good half kilometer away from the Berlin Reichstag. Did Simović, in reproducing Radošević's story, confuse the "Wolf's Lair" with the "Führerbunker" and its location in Berlin? In any case, Radošević's account remains mysterious, even if the question of the location is implicitly corrected. How can it be explained that a copy of the Chaplin film, of all things, should have lain next to Hitler's corpse? Radošević, who died on September 11, 2013, can no longer answer that question.

Over the decades, legends have grown up around Hitler's death and his corpse, not least due to deliberate misinformation by the Soviet military after the end of World War II. Some of it has probably not been conclusively clarified to this day.

- Hitler had allegedly escaped from the "Führerbunker." For this claim, Soviet authorities even had a Hitler lookalike appear. Moreover, on May 4, 1945, Soviet soldiers presented their photographers with a virtually intact corpse that resembled Hitler.[77]
- There is also a rumor of four ammunition boxes containing the bodies of Hitler, Eva Braun and Mr. and Mrs. Goebbels being buried somewhere in Berlin. Allegedly, after the capture of Berlin, an unknown unit of Red Army soldiers dug up Hitler's box in the garden of the Reichskanzlei and took it with them. Each time they changed locations within the Soviet Occupation Zone, they would have dug the box in and out. Finally, in 1970, they would have secretly burned Hitler's remains on a riverbank.[78]
- A third version emerges from the transcripts of the interrogations of Hitler's Personal Adjutant Otto Günsche and of Hitler's Personal Orderly Heinz Linge, published in 2005, which had been obtained at least in part under the use of torture during their Soviet captivity from 1946 to 1949. From these, Soviet authorities had compiled an overview of Hitler's activities from January 30, 1933, until his suicide and of the whereabouts of his corpse. According to this, Günsche, Linge, Reichsleiter Martin Bormann and others had burned the bodies of the dictator and Eva Braun on Hitler's orders immediately after the suicides in the garden of the Reichskanzlei near the bunker exit with the help of 200 liters of gasoline, while the area was already under constant shelling by the Red Army.[79] Hitler's bodyguard Misch did not witness the burning of the bodies.[80] The charred remains were buried in the garden of the Reichskanzlei, found a few days later by members of

the Red Army, and exhumed on May 8, 1945, when autopsies were allegedly performed.[81]

So which was Hitler's real corpse? Whatever the truth of the sometimes adventurous versions, there was never any mention of film reels near Hitler's corpse, let alone such spectacular ones as those of *The Great Dictator*. There is good reason to assume that Simović's 1963 article in *Review—Yugoslav Monthly*, containing Radošević's allegations, has added another chapter to the legends that surround Hitler's corpse.

All that can be verified are Hitler's instructions for his body to be burned after his death. From his "politisches Testament" (Political Legacy) of April 29, 1945: "I do not want to fall into the hands of enemies who need a new spectacle arranged by Jews to amuse their enraged masses."[82] Hitler had ordered Günsche and Linge not to let his corpse fall into Russian hands under any circumstances.[83] Possibly Hitler had learned even before his suicide that Italian partisans had summarily shot Mussolini and his lover Clara Petacci the day after their capture on April 28, 1945, and had put the corpses on public display in Milan, hanging by the legs. Hitler's guess as to what threatened to happen to him in case of his capture was not far-fetched. The Soviet Marshal Georgy Konstantinovich Zhukov, who became known as the "victor of the Battle of Berlin," had written in a letter to the then Lieutenant General and later Head of the State and Party Khrushchev: "Soon we will have the slimy beast Hitler locked up in a cage. And when I send it to Moscow, I will send it via Kiev so that you can look at it."[84]

Radošević's claims are all the more dubious because he presented other versions when preparing the filmed interview for *The Tramp and the Dictator*. After Brownlow tracked him down and asked for an interview, around 2001, Radošević sent him his wife's essay "Chaplin Among Hitler's Adherents," to which he had added some comments. According to this, Radošević had wanted to produce a film entitled "Chaplin Visits Hitler and Eva Braun" in 1957 in by-then Communist Yugoslavia, but had been prevented from it by both the Yugoslav board of film censors and the courts. In addition, Radošević wanted to write the screenplay for another film in 2001, which is unlikely to have been produced: "Chaplin on Nazis and Hitler."[85]

According to his wife's essay, Radošević had been taking care of confiscated film stocks for the Serbian Cinema Association in Belgrade from the fall of 1941, and was arrested by the German Wehrmacht in early 1942 after the screening of *The Great Dictator*. The essay described the sequence of events as follows: Radošević exchanged the copy of the Chaplin film confiscated in Greece, which included photos of Chaplin as Hynkel complete with double-cross uniform cap, for that of another American film. He stowed it in a trash can, which he later wheeled out of the camp on a potato and vegetable cart—i.e., neither hidden under his arm in his coat nor carried away in a coal wagon. Radošević told his friends of the Blue Ribbon about his find. Together they decided to show the German occupation soldiers the true face of their Fuehrer by the example of *The Great Dictator*. For safety's sake, this should not be done in Belgrade, but in the more remote Valjevo, where Radošević's grandfather lived and whom he could pretend to visit. The copy of *The Great Dictator* was sent by train in a crate labeled with the title of the 1940 German musical propaganda film

Wunschkonzert (Eduard von Borsody)[86] in order to avoid being discovered. In the Central Cinema, about 700 German soldiers of the Valjevo Kreis-Kommandantur (District Garrison Headquarters) and also members of the Gestapo were anxiously waiting to see the widely announced *Wunschkonzert.* When *The Great Dictator* was shown instead, an SS officer and the Gestapo men fired at the screen. Finally, a panic broke out among the soldiers in the cinema, because they believed that partisans were attacking. Shortly after, Radošević was arrested by soldiers. During his interrogation in a cell of the Kreis-Kommandantur's office, he was beaten because he would not admit having smuggled in the Chaplin film. The Valjevo Kreiskommando reported the incident at the Central to the German Oberkommando (High Command) in Belgrade because word had spread about it quickly. Since it was suspected that German officers might be involved, Berlin was eventually informed. On orders from there, Radošević, guarded by German soldiers, and the copy of *The Great Dictator* were transferred to Germany in an armored train. In Berlin, he was sent to the Alt-Moabit prison. According to Radošević, there were no documents on whether, when and where Hitler saw *The Great Dictator* and how he reacted to it. He assumed that Hitler had seen the film only together with Eva Braun. Probably he excluded Goebbels, Göring and other Third Reich leaders to avoid being ridiculed in their presence.[87]

Even this was still not Radošević's final version. In the unpublished part of his *Tramp and the Dictator* interview, he admitted that he learned about the strange Valjevo film screening from hearsay only: "I was not at the cinema. […]. But people from Vajevo [*sic*] who were in the cinema told [me] that the audience laughed, but only restrained. The Gestapo and the NSDAP men also thought that they were watching an officially released film. […] From the first minute, they were firmly convinced that this film had nothing to do with Yugoslavia, but […] had been made by one of their people." And there was no more talk about one of Radošević's friends being executed after his arrest.[88]

Ufa ad for *Wunschkonzert*, 1940.

A German Criminal Case About The Great Dictator?

Radošević reported about his Berlin imprisonment in the unpublished part of his *Tramp and the Dictator* interview: In Berlin, the SS refused to hand him over to the Gestapo. He was sent to the "German Headquarters," i.e., the Berlin Polizeige-fängnis am Alexanderplatz (Police Prison at Alexanderplatz), not identical with the Berlin Alt-Moabit prison. There, other prisoners congratulated him for the Valjevo film screening and called him a "real friend of Germany," which he did not understand because of his young age. His Alt-Moabit cell neighbors were the Spanish general Munjos Grande (Muñoz Grandes?) and the former chairman of the German Communist Party, Ernst Thelmann [*sic*: Thälmann]. Radošević claimed that, during an interrogation, four of his front teeth were knocked out. He was also interrogated by the Abwehr-Chef (Head of Counterintelligence Corps) General [*sic*: Admiral] Wilhelm Canaris, who treated him well and did not even ask why he had smuggled *The Great Dictator* into the Valjevo cinema. At that time, he did not know that Canaris belonged to the resistance against Hitler. Subsequently, Radošević was sentenced to prison for "unauthorized showing of a film originating from dark channels," not behind closed doors, but in a public main hearing with spectators in a criminal court. Radošević defended himself by claiming that as an ordinary storekeeper, he had nothing to do with the screening of the film. The final speeches of the prosecutor and Radošević's public defender addressed *The Great Dictator*, but they avoided mentioning Hitler. Given the unusual charge originally made against him, Radošević felt he got off comparatively "cheap" with his sentence. This is in line with Radošević's much briefer account in the essay "Chaplin Among Hitler's Adherents."[89] In the unpublished part of his *Tramp and the Dictator* interview, he did not comment on the criminal trial or on his Alt-Moabit cellmates.

Based on Radošević's account, he would have been convicted for the public *Great Dictator* screening, which had not been approved for the Third Reich and the countries occupied by it. This would have been an offense under the 1934 "Lichtspielgesetz."[90] Such an offense fell under the jurisdiction of the so-called "ordentliche Gerichtsbarkeit" (Ordinary Courts), to which the Berlin court belonged, and in whose district Radošević had been taken. However, Radošević's statements about his German imprisonment and his conviction cannot be corroborated—at least not under his name and his date of birth.

The prisoners' file of the Berlin Alt-Moabit men's remand prison for the years 1933 to 1945 has been preserved together with the index of names. Nicola Radošević is not listed, but in 1942 there is a mention of a Serbian projectionist by the name of Nikolaus Radoschew, born on December 19, 1922, in Belgrade; the Serbian spelling is probably Radošev. The similarity of the two names and dates of birth and occupation is striking, only the years of birth are four years apart, as Radošević was born in 1926 according to his data. Were Radošević and Radoschew possibly one and the same person? Had Nicola Radošević provided false information and called himself Nicholas Radoschew, born four years earlier? Or perhaps his personal data was recorded wrongly in the criminal files and has not been corrected since?

According to his account, Radošević was not a resident of Germany, while

Radoschew lived in Berlin. He was in pre-trial imprisonment from July 18 to September 28, 1942, not for "unauthorized showing of a film that came from dark channels" but instead for stealing bread and food stamps. On September 28, 1942, a criminal court judge of the Berlin Amtsgericht (Local Court) sentenced him to two months and one week in prison,[91] which was actually a rather short sentence by the standards of the time. Thus, Radoschew got off easy, just as Radošević considered his sentence light. However, Radoschew was released on the day of his conviction because the sentence imposed on him had been compensated by the preceding pre-trial detention, which means that he did not escape from detention. Radoschew was thus at large when Radošević allegedly escaped from Berlin in 1943 after one of the numerous Allied air raids.

Furthermore, Ernst Thälmann could not have been Radošević's cellmate in Berlin Alt-Moabit. He was in "Schutzhaft" (Protective Custody) there from May 1933 to August 1937 and then served solitary confinement in the Gerichtsgefängnis Hannover (Hanover Court Prison) until August 1943, when he was transferred to the Zuchthaus (Penitentiary) Bautzen and liquidated without trial in August 1944, either in Bautzen or in the Buchenwald Concentration Camp.[92] In contrast, nothing is known about the Spanish general's imprisonment in the Alt-Moabit prison in 1942-43.[93] It also seems doubtful that it was the Spanish General Agustín Muñoz Grandes. The point against it is that he had fought with the Spanish División Española de Voluntarios (Spanish Volunteer Division), or in short División Azul (Blue Division), in World War II on the German side against the Soviet Union, and Hitler decorated him in March 1942 with the Ritterkreuz des Eisernen Kreuzes (Knight's Cross of the Iron Cross). In December 1942, he was awarded the Ritterkreuz des Eisernen Kreuzes mit Eichenlaub (Knight's Cross of the Iron Cross with Oak Leaves). Under these circumstances, it seems unlikely that he was imprisoned in the Berlin remand prison during summer-fall 1942.

However, the striking similarities between Radošević and Radoschew do not ultimately serve as proof that Radoshev was none other than Radošević. Of course, this does not clear up the inconsistencies in his account, which had been changing over the decades. Yet it remains possible that the copy of *The Great Dictator* in Goebbels' vault had been sold to Greece by April 1941, confiscated there by the German Wehrmacht after the country's occupation, and made its way to Germany before the Auswärtiges Amt's lending request of August 1944. Wherever it came from, it had been transported away by the Red Army after the capture of Berlin in May 1945 and stored on the territory of the Soviet Occupation Zone of postwar Germany under the supervision of the Soviet Military Administration. In 1954, it was transferred to the Staatliches Filmarchiv der DDR along with additional film prints and other materials such as the aforementioned Reichsfilmarchiv's storage inventory journal.[94]

14

The Gold Rush and Agitation to the Bitter End, 1942–44

The Great Dictator had stirred up dust everywhere. Its Nazi opponents did much to discredit it in Germany and especially abroad. Chaplin repeatedly declared that, as an apolitical person, he was only interested in humanitarian issues. But ideologues of various shades had never believed him and had insinuated political intentions to him. The Nazi image of Chaplin as an enemy was unintentionally supported by international comparisons of Chaplin to Hitler. It was further fueled when Chaplin advocated expanded Allied warfare against the Third Reich in Europe to aid the Soviet Union. The Nazi propaganda also found moral targets in 1943 from a paternity trial that turned into a nightmare for Chaplin. This provided the Nazi press with news items until 1944, when the downfall of the Hitler regime had long since been sealed and there were more important things to accomplish than to agitate against Chaplin. "We Will Handle the Situation"[1] characterized Nazi propaganda until the last issues of its battle propaganda journals in April 1945. In his 1945 New Year's address, Goebbels feigned confidence in victory to the population with "We have clung to our native soil!" and threatened the Allies: "The German people will only lay down their arms when they hold final victory in their hands, not a second sooner."[2]

The German film industry remained in the service of Nazi propaganda to the end. Although Chaplin films had been banned from public screening in Germany for years and Chaplin supposedly lacked ideas, it was nevertheless opportune to make use of his films. At the end of 1943 and in the late summer of 1944, two such productions were released. Then the "Thousand-Year Reich" lay in ruins, while Chaplin's body of work had survived unscathed.

This chapter discusses:

- Chaplin's advocacy of the Second Front
- final instructions of the Nazi press control concerning Chaplin
- the film *Akrobat Schö-ö-n!*
- the Catalan clown Charlie Rivel
- further satirical comparisons of Hitler with Chaplin
- the Joan Barry scandal: paternity suit and criminal proceedings
- the renewed Chaplin agitation
- the film *Die Frau meiner Träume*

- last newspaper clippings in the Chaplin file of the Hauptarchiv der NSDAP
- Chaplin after the Third Reich

The Second Front

Two more clippings from the Basel *National-Zeitung* of June 13–14, 1942, made their way into the Hauptarchiv der NSDAP Chaplin file. The fact that Chaplin had been found guilty in the divorce case from Paulette Goddard[3] did not arouse the interest of the propagandists. The second article was more significant. It referred to a May 20, 1942, article in the British *News Chronicle* according to which Chaplin had urged that the U.S. actively support the Soviet Union militarily against the Third Reich in Europe.[4]

Since the Soviet Union seemed to be unable to resist the German Wehrmacht, the American Committee for Russian War Relief had organized a major event in San Francisco on May 18, 1942. The Committee thus sought to convince the reluctant Roosevelt administration to open a second front in Europe against the German Wehrmacht. Chaplin stood in at the event for the Soviet Ambassador in the U.S., who had fallen ill. In his impassioned speech, which lasted about an hour, Chaplin called for this Second Front. Because he thought there were many Russians among the approximately 10,000 people present, he addressed them as "comrades," but at the same time made it clear that he was not a Communist sympathizer. He said that he did not believe in any ideology, but that his motives were exclusively humanitarian:

> I am not a Communist, I am a human being, and I think I know the reactions of human beings. The Communists are no different from anyone else; whether they lose an arm or a leg, they suffer as all of us do, and die as all of us die. And the Communist mother is the same as any other mother. When she receives the tragic news that her son will not return, she weeps as any mothers weep. I do not have to be a Communist to know that. And at this moment Russian mothers are doing a lot of weeping and their sons a lot of dying….[5]

Chaplin thus inevitably supported the Soviet dictator Josef Stalin, another murderer of millions in the 20th century, whose inconceivable crimes against his own people became well-known after World War II. On June 22, 1942, another event benefiting the Second Front was held in New York's Madison Square Park, this time hosted by the Union Congress of Industrial Organizations.[6] Chaplin delivered a 14-minute address via radio-telephone from Hollywood to a crowd of about 60,000, stating: "Democracy will live or die on the Russian battlefield. Two million Englishmen are fully equipped and straining to go. What are we waiting for, when the situation of Russia is so desperate?"[7]

Life magazine, in its late August 1942 issue, seemed to claim a third American Committee for Russian War Relief event that month in Hollywood with Chaplin's participation,[8] but no one reported it, and it did not occur. A third major event, however, was scheduled for October 16 at New York's Carnegie Hall by the left-leaning Artists' Front to Win the War, chaired by actor Sam Jaffe, and announced with a press release: "We believe that the immediate opening of a Second Front to be the military expression of the unity of all peoples of the United Nations in their struggle to crush fascism [… and] before Hitler can turn his entire war machine against Great Britain and the United States. [...] We pledge the closest collaboration for Victory with our fellow artists in the United Nations."[9] Chaplin took over the honorary chairmanship, after other renowned artists such as Orson Welles had also agreed to participate, and again focused on his humanitarian concerns: "I am only doing what my conscience and my heart direct me. I have no political ambitions. I belong to a very honorable profession—clowning."[10] A side effect of Chaplin's participation was that about a year and a half later, he was accused of committing a crime under the 1910 Mann Act while in New York (see below).

On October 22, 1942, Chaplin's New York commitment to the Second Front earned him the long lampoon article "Quel pagliaccio di Charlot" (Charlot's Clowning) in the Roman newspaper *Il Regime Fascista*, which was no different in style from Nazi diatribes—and thus fitted well

Promotional photo: Chaplin calls for a Second Front, 1942 (DFF—Deutsches Filminstitut & Filmmuseum, Frankfurt am Main/Chaplin-Archiv, Dauerleihgabe der Adolf und Luisa Haeuser-Stiftung für Kunst und Kulturpflege).

into the Hauptarchiv der NSDAP Chaplin file. Among other things, millionaire Chaplin was reproached on a moral level for abandoning his mother in misery.[11] This fascist newspaper had also employed fake news. In fact, Chaplin had supported his mother financially, brought her to Hollywood in 1921 and rented her a house there until her death at the end of August 1928.[12]

In November 1942, the *Film-Kurier* created its own reality about the Second Front. The trade journal referred to the Croatian weekly *Spremnost*, according to which Chaplin's allegedly Communist-motivated mission turned into a film project of the same name, aimed against Great Britain and the Soviet dictator Stalin was at the bottom of it: "Chaplin's film 'The Second Front' is said to take a dig against England. His Communist sentiments are known. With the film, he wants to protest against

England's attitude, which prevented the Second Front called for by Stalin. [*Spremnost* …] says […] that America is the empire of illusions headed by Roosevelt. He has such illusionary films produced not only for his allies, but also for his people and himself."[13]

Meanwhile, Chaplin's actual film plans for "Shadow and Substance" were ignored by the Nazi film press. The situation was different with the U.S. report that Chaplin had been honored by the Soviet-Russian Consul General Viktor A. Fediushkine on December 3, 1942, at a dinner of the American Committee for Russian War Relief for his support of the Second Front.[14] Not only had the FBI compiled its first secret dossier on Chaplin's alleged Communist activities the next day,[15] but the Nazi press also used it to attack the "Jew" Chaplin as a Bolshevik. On December 6, 1942, the German satirical magazine *Kladderadatsch*, a respectable magazine before Hitler's takeover, reacted to Chaplin's unwelcome engagement. It published a drawing of him as a private citizen and, in addition, an invective poem with a dig at President Roosevelt: "'Plattfuß-Filmstar' [Flat-footed movie star] Chaplin is/now 'Bolschewist nach Geschäftsschluss' [after hours Bolshevik]./He asks for help—and right away—/for the threatened Soviet Empire./The reason for his whining is likely to be,/he wants to outdo the White House clown!"[16]

Daily Paroles and Zeitschriften-Dienst

At the end of January-beginning of February 1943, Reichsfilmintendant Hippler hailed the success of "ten years of film work in the National Socialist Reich" in the *Film-Kurier*.[17] Helmut Sündermann, deputy and confidant of Reichspressechef Dietrich, attested to Hippler's "absolute National Socialist reliability"[18] and spread the morale-boosting slogan "Therefore we will win."[19] The press controllers of the Reichspressekonferenz had no longer been able to effectively ensure the observance of their escalating instructions. Instead, starting in October 1940, Dietrich had "Tagesparolen" (Daily Slogans) issued that summarized everything that was mandatory for the press "in the shortest possible formula."

The Reichspressekonferenz spokesman in November 1942, Erich Fischer,[20] read them out to the attending journalists. On April 7, 1943, one of the "Tagesparolen" requested that the newspapers report on "the formation of a National Council of American-Soviet Friendship with the leading participation of the Jews [Albert] Einstein, [Charlie] Chaplin, and [Leopold] Stokowski."[21] The next day, *Der Angriff* put down briefly: "As to be expected, mainly Jews like Einstein, Chaplin and others are heading the list."[22] The *Völkischer Beobachter*, on the other hand, took the opportunity on the same day to add some of its usual ingredients: "The emigrated Jewish pseudo-philosopher has joined forces with the "widerwärtigster Filmjude" (most disgusting film-Jew) who has so far flourished on the Hollywood swamp. From New York, [Sergei] Eisenstein [… and Ilya] Ehrenburg send their greetings to Chaplin and Einstein."[23] Nothing more appeared about it in the Nazi press. At the end of July 1943, the following Chaplin instruction was issued, which turned out to be the last until the *Zeitschriften-Dienst* (as well as the Reichspressekonferenz) was discontinued in April 1945: "Charlie Chaplin has again appeared in the press. We ask the magazines not to mention him at all. As a rule, we do not deal with American and English film greats."[24]

Akrobat Schö-ö-ö-n!

The Nazis had been unable to erase the memory of Chaplin. In 1943, Wolfgang Staudte directed the Tobis feature film *Akrobat Schö-ö-ö-n!* It starred the Catalan clown Charlie Rivel (Josep Andreu i Lasserre) as a starving grotesque acrobat who becomes world-famous. Even in the first sequence of scenes in his garret dwelling, his clothing reflects almost all the elements of Chaplin's Tramp costume. Moreover, Rivel plays a virtually silent role in Chaplin's air and gestures[25]; except for his spoken trademark "Akrobat schö-ö-ö-n!," he knew no German. Had Rivel donned a derby instead of his flat cap, glued on a Charlie moustache, and had frizzy hair, the impersonation would probably have been perfect. For example, Rivel's pantomimic movements quote the Tramp when he sets the breakfast table. For the trapeze act at Varieté Tabarin, however, Rivel wears almost entirely his own stage makeup, with bald clown face, hair crown, attached rectangular nose, huge clown shoes and a long, tight-fitting shirt-like robe reaching to his ankles. However, he has put on a dark suit jacket and a derby hat, both borrowed from Chaplin's Tramp costume.

Screen shot from *Akrobat Schö-ö-ö-n!*, 1943: Tramp-like Charlie Rivel (© Friedrich-Wilhelm-Murnau-Stiftung).

The February 1943 issue of the film magazine *Filmwoche* printed a pictorial article about the in-production *Akrobat Schö-ö-ö-n!*, together with a lengthy reflection on "grotesque comedy." Supposedly it had been invented particularly for Rivel's film, differed from U.S. "rubber-truncheon comedy," utilized Rivel's "playfulness and pantomimic way to express himself," and with its juxtaposition of comedy and tragedy was timeless. This was Chaplin's trademark, of course, but was hailed as an asset of Rivel's portrayal, which director Staudte, according to the magazine, had aptly staged: "Writer-director Wolfgang Staudte does not just want to skillfully piece together comic situations. He wants to trace a funny man whom we gleefully smile at when a string of misfortunes befalls him. But we also feel his tragedy, because he cannot alter his fate."[26]

In its pictorial article about *Akrobat Schö-ö-ö-n!*, the magazine *Filmwelt* included a comment about Rivel's performance that sounded like what had been said so often about Chaplin in Germany in the past: "In his struggle against the cussedness of the inanimate, he is always the likable underdog. The way Charlie Rivel warm-heartedly, gently and conciliatorily comments human shortcomings, reveals him as the keen observer of the human nature."[27] The *Film-Illustrierte* confined itself to an illustrated synopsis of the film without comment.[28]

Staudte and Rivel never commented on the Chaplin references in *Akrobat Schö-ö-n!* Staudte made his mark after the end of World War II with films against Nazism and the spirit of subservience such as *Die Mörder sind unter uns* (1946), *Der Untertan* (1951) and *Rosen für den Staatsanwalt* (1959). When Staudte was interviewed about his films in the 1970s, he merely described the origins of *Akrobat Schö-ö-n!* Tobis had hired Rivel for a film without having any script. As a result, he, Staudte, drafted an outline for him, wrote the screenplay, and finally also directed the film.[29] The Chaplin reminiscences in Staudte's first directorial work of his career cannot be overlooked and may be due to the fact that he did not let himself be subordinated politically and therefore oriented himself to Chaplin, although the Nazis fought him.

In 1999, Andreas Wöll claimed that Goebbels' "NS propagandists" "wanted to build up Rivel [...] as Charlie Chaplin's counterpart. The Spaniard, who was Franco's partisan, was only too happy to comply with this task."[30] Who "Goebbels' NS propagandists" were and what plans they may have had concerning Rivel have not been disclosed by Wöll, and authentic statements by Goebbels about such a project are unknown.

In 1971, Rivel published his autobiography *Stakkels Klovn* in Denmark. In the 1972 German version *Akrobat Schöön*, there is only one sentence about the film *Akrobat Schö-ö-ö-n!*: "In addition, I was also to play the leading role in the film *Akrobat oh!*, which Wolfgang Staudte wanted to make for Tobis-Film."[31] By contrast, the GDR volume *Das Leben großer Clowns* (The Lives of Great Clowns) from the same year contains Rivel's memoir *Akrobat oh!*, which had been published in Sweden in 1935 and therefore could not have mentioned the film.[32] Yet Chaplin and his films had had a formative influence on the clown since the early days of his career. Around 1910, according to Rivel's account, he saw the clown act "Tingel Tangel/The Drunken Gentleman" performed by the troupe "Billy Reeves and Partners" at the Hippodrome in the Belgian city of Ghent. In it, the clean-shaven Chaplin appeared slickly dressed in tailcoat and top hat. A few years later in Spain, when Chaplin was already an international movie star, Rivel went to the movies before his own circus performance in the evening and laughed himself to tears over Chaplin's Essanay two-reeler *The Champion*. Under the impression of this film, Rivel decided to perform in the circus as Tramp Charlie. He dressed up as Charlie as best he could in his dressing room for his clown act on the trapeze. His fellow artists reacted enthusiastically: "You are pure Chaplin! You look just like him." At first, his father was not at all thrilled with "Chaplin on the Trapeze," but after a year surrendered in order to present his son's Chaplin parody as the attraction of the program. Now Rivel dropped his first name Josep and adopted Charlie for the rest of his life.[33] In the bullfighting arena of Logroño in Spain, Rivel varied his Chaplin parody with his act "Chaplin as Matador." As Tramp Charlie, he staged a grotesque but real bullfight, the bull being killed as usual.[34] It was Rivel's trapeze act as Tramp Charlie that was part of his repertoire for many years. Rivel enjoyed great success with this show in the Berlin vaudeville venues Wintergarten and Scala. In May 1927, after seeing Rivel's show at the Scala, Billy Wilder wrote about the Chaplin parody: "Rivel does his imitation quite consciously. But it emerges from his inner self, and he succeeds so convincingly that it has its own authority. [...] Rivel is a brilliant observer, he knows the genius [Chaplin] like the pocket of his flimsy trousers. He transfers Chaplin discreetly into three dimensions—and surprisingly well."[35]

Around that time, Chaplin and United Artists tried to prohibit Rivel's performances in the Tramp costume as an imitation. After having been informed that Rivel's Chaplin act was a parody that anyone was entitled to do and that he was not attempting to pass himself off as Chaplin, they backed off. In any case, this dispute was welcome publicity for Rivel, who was able to enjoy even greater success with "Chaplin on the Trapeze" and to raise his fee.[36] During the Third Reich, Rivel and his clown troupe remained favorites of German audiences,[37] albeit without the Chaplin parody. Even Goebbels was so taken with Rivel that he attended two of his performances at the Wintergarten in September 1935, at which he laughed heartily.[38] The popularity of Rivel and his family troupe may be judged from the fact that they were guests on the 50th German television program "Wir senden Frohsinn—Wir spenden Freude" (We Broadcast Gaiety—We Are a Source of Joy), broadcast live from the Kuppelsaal of the Reichssportfeld in Berlin in early 1942.[39] German TV broadcasting was launched as early as March 22, 1935, but did not achieve more than a niche existence, because TV sets were too expensive. Broadcasts continued in the Third Reich until well after the beginning of World War II, before they were finally discontinued.

Rivel was not merely one Chaplin impersonator among many. From the combination of his Chaplin parody with his acrobatic skills emerged an artistic achievement of its own. On this, he reported in Fred A. Colman and Walter Trier's 1928 book *Artisten*.[40] The epilogue of the 1972 book *Das Leben großer Clowns* (The Lives of Great Clowns) stated about the distinction between Chaplin and Rivel:

> Not only superficial attributes are being treated, this is a transformation. [... It was] Charlie Rivel's achievement to create the real circus Chaplin. While many circus funsters stumbled around the ring with their derby hats and their Chaplin moustaches, Charlie Rivel adapted the Chaplin type to the world of the circus in a comical acrobatic trapeze act. The cinema Chaplin and the circus Chaplin remained two different people. Their only connection is to play alternately hero and rabbit.[41]

This differentiation is helpful in judging Rivel's performance in *Akro-bat Schö-ö-ö-n!* In the first minutes of the film, Rivel is the impersonator of "Kino-Chaplin." During his acrobatic act in a clown costume, he switches visually, so to speak, to the "circus Chaplin." But ironically, unlike his Chaplin parodies in the circus arena or in vaudeville, he is not parodying Chaplin, but imitating him. About this, nothing can be gleaned from the censorship records for the film, which was approved in early October 1943,[42] if only for ideological reasons.

On December 1, 1943, *Akrobat Schö-ö-ö-n!* premiered at the Berlin Alhambra. The *Film-Kurier* subsequently reviewed the film, for which the *Zeitschriften-Dienst* had allowed preliminary coverage the previous year.[43] Editor Ernst Jerosch had obviously recognized the similarities of Rivel's portrayal to Chaplin's Tramp and endeavored to degrade Chaplin. The review seemed like cynicism, for Rivel was, after all, at least partially imitating Chaplin. By praising Rivel, Jerosch indirectly implied unintentional praise of Chaplin's art: "Charlie Rivel himself plays the little clown with excessively polite humility, without resorting to Chaplin's sleazy gesticulation. The entire misery and felicity of mankind are visible in this little artist. [...] At the same time, one does not feel the need of language, because this character has been very cleverly conceived by the script to the pantomimic gesture."[44] Without Chaplin's name being mentioned, the premiere review of the *Deutsche Allgemeine Zeitung* even elevated Rivel to the rank of philosopher.[45]

Welcome and Unwelcome Birthday Greetings

Bizarrely, Rivel adored both Chaplin and Hitler, whose power-political ambitions he supported. In April 1943, Rivel had put up at the Munich Sonnenhof Hotel. From there, on April 20, he presented the German dictator his congratulations on his birthday via telegram to the "Führerhauptquartier" (Fuehrer's Headquarters): "May the Lord grant you health, strength and vigor also in the future and may he bring ultimate victory and a new happy Europe to the peoples of Europe under your leadership."[46]

These were decidedly different birthday greetings than Oscar Berger's cartoons "Hitler and Chaplin at 54" in the *New York Post* of April 18, 1943, which compared the careers of the two in nine stages.[47] Hitler was "the man who tried to kill laughter" and looked back on the following past: Born as baby Adolf Schickelgruber in Braunau, Austria (his father Alois had assumed the surname Hitler at the age of 39), he cried out at the age of seven: "I want to become an artist!" In 1908, however, the Vienna Art Academy rejected him as untalented, so Adolf made his way through life as a substandard house painter in Munich in 1913. As a failure everywhere, in 1919, he decided to become a politician and, in 1925, he dreamt of world domination in the first volume of *Mein Kampf*. In 1933, as German Reichskanzler, he laid the Reichstag to ashes, burned books and synagogues. In 1939, he invaded Poland. A series of attacks on other states followed, which, contrary to his claims, they had not provoked any more than Poland. Résumé: Hitler, the greatest terrorist in world history.

Chaplin, on the other hand, was "the man who made the world laugh," and his biography was decidedly more philanthropic. Baby Charles Spencer Chaplin was born in London, and at the age of seven he could claim, "I'm an artist!" In 1908, he performed with great success in music halls. In 1913, he went to Hollywood, where he became famous at the age of 23 [*sic*]. By 1919, he had established his own film company, and in 1925 he conquered the world with *The Gold Rush*. He produced *City Lights* and planned the artwork *Modern Times* in 1933. He then declared intellectual war on Hitler and began filming *The Great Dictator* in 1939. Résumé: Chaplin, the greatest fun in movies.

The previous year, the comparison of the two different personalities in Sidney Moon's cartoon "What a Pity They Didn't Get Those Two Babies Mixed Up" in the British *Sunday Dispatch* had not turned out flattering for Hitler either. Moon presented both Hitler and Chaplin as being highly different film directors.[48] Hitler has the extras for his Hollywood Films Inc. stand at military attention, salute with arms raised and march at goose step. He is assisted by the Brown Shirt electricians and the Black Shirt helpers. For the acoustic dubbing of the film scenes, illuminated panels indicate instructions for the extras: "laugh," "clap," "boo," "hiss," "shout Heil," "stomp," "cheer." A woodenly acting couple obviously has absolutely no idea what a love scene is all about, because the precise stage directions on the scoreboard read: "Go to her," "Hold her hand," "Press her to you," "Kiss her" and "Stay like that." Meanwhile, extras who play their roles too passionately are immediately escorted to the overcrowded "concentration camp for the temperamental" to cool off.

In Chaplin's shooting, everything happens cheerfully. There are only bloodless "executions" in which the "condemned" are put up against the wall with the firing squad hurling pies at them. Chaplin's SA men spread just as little fear and terror. Some of them have traded in their brown uniforms for Charlie's derby, cane and oversized shoes, and of course all of them are moustached. And the next moment, one of them is pushing a cake from "Krupp's Cake Factory" into the face of a Nazi. Chaplin, , dressed as Hitler, makes eyes at a German maiden. At the same time, he pulls Goering's legs from under him with his cane, while another participant slips on a banana skin that Chaplin has just thrown away, while Goebbels struggles to throw his uniform cap up like a circus juggler so that it lands on his head. Boys and girls with accessories from Charlie's Tramp outfit stroll for the "Chaplin Youth Movement."

"Run-down Film-Jew" in Paternity Lawsuit

Instead of such cartoons, the Hauptarchiv der NSDAP monitored the Joan Barry scandal, which entangled Chaplin in lengthy, embarrassing lawsuits, and his fourth marriage.

New Yorker Joan Barry had traveled with her mother to California, where Chaplin met the young woman and hired her in mid–1941 for his planned feature film "Shadow and Substance" hoping to train her as an actress. The hope was dashed, and after Barry's escapades, the contractual relationship was mutually annulled a few months later. Chaplin paid her an indemnity, as well as return tickets to New York for her and her mother. He abandoned his film project at the end of 1942.

Chaplin had had an intimate relationship with Barry, which she, unlike him, did not consider to be terminated. Shortly before Christmas 1942, she was back in Hollywood, forced her way into Chaplin's house equipped with a gun and threatened to commit suicide, so he let her spend the night there. The next morning, Barry left voluntarily, but showed up again a week later. This time, she would not leave. Chaplin had Barry removed from his property by the police. She was sent to prison for 90 days for vagrancy and had to leave town. Again, Chaplin paid for her return trip to New York and threw in some extra money. In May 1943, she again appeared with her mother in California, claiming to be pregnant by Chaplin. On June 3, her mother, as legal guardian of the expected child, filed a paternity action against Chaplin in Los Angeles Superior Court. She requested monthly support of $2500 for the child, who was born in October 1943, as well as $10,000 for medical expenses, and finally, Barry's legal expenses of $5000. Chaplin denied paternity and resisted, even though he "knew 95 percent" that the press would be against him due to his support of a Second Front in favor of the Soviet Union.[49] Barry and Chaplin's attorneys, John L. Irwin and Lloyd Wright respectively, agreed to clarify Chaplin's fatherhood by an analysis of blood groups. In case he was then ruled out as the father of the child, Barry's attorney would withdraw the action. Until clarification, Chaplin committed to pay $75 a week in support for Barry's child from birth and also her legal expenses. The trial was then suspended until early 1944.[50]

On June 19, 1943, the Basel *National-Zeitung* wrote: "Last Wednesday Charlie Chaplin married in Los Angeles Oona O'Neill, the 18-year-old daughter of the well-known writer Eugene O'Neill."[51] The Hauptarchiv der NSDAP put this in its Chaplin file. The fourth marriage of the 54-year-old Chaplin with the 36 years younger Oona O'Neill was perfect for propaganda purposes. Also on June 19, the German daily newspaper *12-Uhr-Blatt* concocted its "own" Stockholm report "Krampf um alten Filmjuden" (Tumult About Old Film-Jew) based on an article in the Swedish newspaper *Aftonbladet* of June 17. The result was such a coarse work of slanderous agitation with perfidiously combined stereotypical insinuations and lies that it is reproduced here in full:

> This year, the "glücklicherweise fast vergessene Filmheld von der traurigen Gestalt" (fortunately almost forgotten sad countenance of a film knight) Charlie Chaplin celebrates his resurrection in Swedish cinemas. His soppy Californian film *Goldrausch* ran for months, and other even weaker efforts also vied for Swedish audiences. Now, however, the Stockholmers' interest has waned. His gaiety of a man oppressed by life, which he frantically tries to enforce with lip whiskers, little cane and Jewish gestures, does not work anymore. American audiences are even less interested in his political smear films. In Sweden, they are banned. A publicity expert therefore tries, in true American fashion, to counteract the fading of Chaplin's star in the newspapers of the Swedish capital by sensationalizing his private life and artificially creating a new Chaplin craze.

It goes like this: "Chaplin began his fourth marriage today. The lucky bride this time is 18-year-old Mona O'Neil [sic], who is 36 years younger than her husband," announces Stockholm's *Aftonbladet*. Chaplin, the headline says, was very nervous at the wedding ceremony. "His hand trembled so that he could hardly hold the pen while signing. He looked around incessantly and even forgot to take off his hat." Are these not the sentimentally phony gestures from many a film of the once-celebrated man? The scene is meant to move and irritate at the same time. The man hounded by life finally tied the knot, albeit for the fourth time. His other marriages were divorced because he abused his wives, but this time the newspapers report nothing about it. And here's the juicy bit: last week, Chaplin had to appear in a child support case against him. A New York waitress had sued him. Her Hollywood attorney told the newspapers that the poor woman had fainted when she learned that Chaplin wanted to remarry. The news had leaked out only a few hours ago. Chaplin agreed to all of this in court. He was sentenced to pay $18,500 for childbirth and other hospital expenses.

> And now with the power of a giant at the side of the 18-year-old blonde angel into the future! Mona [*sic*] O'Neill, a daughter of the famous American playwright, studied filming with Chaplin. She was recently able to sign a contract for a role in the film *The Girl from Leningrad*. That might have been the price the "abgetakelte Filmjude" (Run-down Film-Jew) paid for his marriage to the 18 year old. After all, he was able to lure her with a role. What does artis-

tic achievement matter in a Bolshevik propaganda film? Charlie Chaplin of Hollywood recommends himself to an international audience of the sort that will never die out.[52]

None of this matched the facts. The course of the paternity suit was distorted. Chaplin, moreover, was portrayed as a husband who regularly mistreated his wives, which the U.S. press suppressed, and now had also impregnated a New York waitress. To scorn him further, it was blatantly claimed that he had bought O'Neill's wedding vow with her film role in a "Bolshevik propaganda film."

The implied sexually motivated exploitation of professional dependence would probably have earned Chaplin a #MeToo reproach today. In addition, Chaplin's immortal masterpiece *The Gold Rush* had been reduced to a cheap "melodrama," and once again the lie was rehashed that *The Great Dictator* had flopped in the U.S. The *12-Uhr-Blatt* also

United Artists ad for the re-release of *The Gold Rush*'s 1942 sound version (Archives de Montreux, PP-75 Fonds Charles Chaplin, Roy Export Co. Ltd.).

did not reveal to its readers that Chaplin's sound film version of *The Gold Rush* had been released in Sweden and was thus a premiere rather than a re-release.

The *Aftonbladet*, on the other hand, had reported objectively and without the side-blows against Chaplin.[53] About the Barry trial, the Swedish newspaper related the true state of affairs and did not suggest that Chaplin had "bought" his young bride with a film role. *Aftonbladet*'s only inaccuracy was a harmless spelling or printing error: O'Neill's alleged first name, "Mona." Incidentally, the film title *The Girl from Leningrad* did not apply to a Chaplin project, but to Eugene Frenke's 1944 U.S. feature film *Three Russian Girls*, in which neither Chaplin nor his wife were involved. Chaplin had only shot some test footage with her for his planned but eventually abandoned film *Shadow and Substance*.[54]

By mid–February 1944, the analysis of blood groups agreed upon in June 1943 had ruled out Chaplin as the father of Barry's daughter. This was reported by the *Neue Zürcher Zeitung* under the headline "Propaganda Trick About Chaplin?" and indicated that Barry's attorney now probably would withdraw the paternity action. The article was also added to the Chaplin file of the Hauptarchiv der NSDAP.[55] The content of the article meant exactly the opposite of what the *12-Uhr-Blatt* had wanted its readers to believe months earlier. It was not suitable to agitate against Chaplin. The Nazi press therefore did not take up the paternity suit again, despite its further bizarre course.

Despite the results of the analysis of blood groups, Barry refused to withdraw her action against Chaplin. Because her previous lawyer Irwin resigned as a consequence, she hired the eloquent Joseph Scott. He vilified Chaplin[56]—and to good effect to her. Under California procedural law at the time, the analysis of blood groups was not admitted as evidence and thus could not exonerate Chaplin.[57] After the birth of Barry's daughter, the paternity suit was continued in mid–December 1944 and ruled in Chaplin's favor in early February 1945. But it was reopened. After Chaplin had revealed details about Barry's past life and claimed that she had been the mistress of oil billionaire J. Paul Getty, the latter testified as a witness on April 13, 1945: He had invited Barry to Tulsa in November 1942 and January 1943 and had given presents to her, but had not had intercourse with her.[58] Thereafter, on April 17, 1945, Chaplin was sentenced to pay weekly child support of $75 and $5000 in costs for Barry's legal representation based solely on Barry's testimony.[59] Both Chaplin and Barry appealed against the judgment to the State Supreme Court in Los Angeles in early July 1946, but were ultimately dismissed on July 25. Chaplin's case contributed to an amendment to the U.S. Code of Civil Procedure years later, admitting the analysis of blood groups as evidence in U.S. courts. For him, however, this came too late. Barry had successfully foisted her daughter on him, so that he had to pay child support month after month until she was 21![60]

On Trial as a "Sex Offender"

The Joan Barry scandal escalated further. On February 10, 1944, Chaplin was indicted by the Los Angeles Federal grand jury for violation of the Mann Act and on criminal conspiracy charges. The Mann Act aimed to fight prostitution. It was an indictable offense to transport a woman across U.S. state borders with sexual intent. Barry had returned to New York from California on October 5, 1942, and on October 16, 1942, Chaplin attended the Second Front benefit at New York's Carnegie Hall. It was charged that he had arranged both with the intention of having sexual intercourse with Barry in New York. In addition, Chaplin and the Los Angeles police were charged with conspiring against Barry to put her in jail on the false pretense of vagrancy. It caused a considerable stir in the U.S. press.[61]

The Hauptarchiv der NSDAP collected three newspaper clippings from Britain, Belgium and German-occupied Alsace for its Chaplin file on this topic. *The London Times*, on February 12, 1944, had reported succinctly and factually on the charges against Chaplin. The pro–Nazi Belgian newspaper *Le Pays réel* was just as concise with "Charlie Chaplin détourne ... une mineure" (Charlie Chaplin Hijacks ... a Minor).[62] The *Straßburger Neueste Nachrichten* ran the article "Film-Jew Chaplin Seduces Minors" on February 13, 1944:

> The story is offensive even by American standards. It brought the [Jewish] "Filmhanswurst" (Film Tomfool) Chaplin before the Hollywood Supreme Court. He will have to stand trial for kidnapping and seducing minors. The indictment alleges that he took the minor Joan Barry to Neuyork [*sic*] and made her his mistress. Miss Barry claims Chaplin is the father of her illegitimate daughter. If found guilty, Charly [*sic*] Chaplin faces a prison term of up to 23 years and a fine of up to $26,000.[63]

Der Angriff seemed to have been waiting for just such a news item. In its article "Jew Chaplin Indicted. For Seducing Minors," the propaganda journal referred to a wire report from Lisbon and was only interested in the charges under the Mann Act: "Before the Hollywood Supreme Court, the US actor Charlie Chaplin will have to answer for kidnapping and seducing minors. This fits in perfectly with the 'reputation' of this 'jüdischer Interpret schmierigster Hetzfilme gegen Deutschland' [Jewish Performer of Sleazy Germanophobe Smear Films]."[64]

On the same day, the *Völkischer Beobachter* topped *Der Angriff*:

> During the Weimar Republic, the "jüdischer Filmstrolch" (Jewish Movie Rascal) Charlie Chaplin had been hailed as an artist in Germany, too. After 1933, he was busy as one of the wildest, but not witty, "Gräuelhetzer" (Atrocity Agitator). Now he has been indicted by the Hollywood Supreme Court for kidnapping and seducing minors. Of course, it is in doubt whether he will be sentenced. "Großgauner" (Wholesale Crooks) usually go unpunished in the US if they are Jews.[65]

At the beginning of the main hearing on March 21, 1944, Chaplin pleaded not guilty. The *Straßburger Neueste Nachrichten* reacted to this on April 2 with the lurid headline "Sittlichkeitsverbrecher Charlie Chaplin vor Gericht. Der jüdische Wüstling ist wie immer der 'Verführte.' Hollywoods neuester Skandal" (Sex Offender Charlie Chaplin on Trial. Jewish Libertine is the 'Seduced' As Usual. Hollywood's Latest Scandal), which was put to the Chaplin file of the Hauptarchiv der NSDAP. According to "news from Bern" from the previous day, the almost 55-year-old Chaplin had been made five years older and Barry, quasi as an ingénue, about seven years younger:

The only too well-known Jewish Hollywood film actor Charlie Chaplin is at least as famous for his numerous indecent attacks on young girls. He is once again having such an affair: only 18-year-old Joan Barry recently accused the now 60-year-old libertine of a new sexual offense. She claims that Chaplin had raped her and that he is the father of her child. The scandal is already occupying the competent Hollywood courts. Charlie Chaplin displayed all his acting skills during the proceedings in order to present himself as the "innocently persecuted." He even [...] burst into tears (!) in front of the judge.[66]

On the same day, *Der Angriff* presented the matter with its article "Das sind die Götter der Amerikaner. Chaplin als Sittlichkeitsverbrecher vor Gericht" (These Are the Gods of the Americans. Chaplin on Trial as a Sex Offender) as a Chaplin hoax and also "added" to the *Straßburger Neueste Nachrichten* article as follows:

When the judge asked [Chaplin] whether he had ever invited Joan Barry to go to New York to be with him, he firmly denied it. He had [...] met the young lady quite by chance and believed that she had acting talent. He then offered her the chance to play the role of Joan of Arc in a planned film. He had undertaken his trip to New York [...] exclusively for a speech. With this hoax, the Jewish libertine tried to talk his way out in vain. The Barry case is not the first of its kind. It takes all the Jewish impertinence to tell such a pack of lies and to turn the sexual offense into an act of persecution. But people like Chaplin are, after all, the gods of the Americans.[67]

Whether the *Straßburger Neueste Nachrichten* and *Der Angriff* reproduced the unknown "news from Bern" report verbatim or at least adopted it unchanged in terms of content has not been established, but seems doubtful. The agitation of the two journals and the way Nazi propaganda dealt with sources rather suggest just the opposite.

On April 5, 1944, Chaplin, who was defended by celebrity lawyer Jerry Giesler, was acquitted of charges of violating the Mann Act.[68] The criminal trial finally ended with the prosecution also dropping its charges of alleged conspiracy against Chaplin and others on May 15.[69] The Hauptarchiv der NSDAP also kept itself informed about the course of the criminal trial with reports in the *London Times* of April 6 and the Swiss newspaper *Journal de Genève* of May 17-18.[70] Its outcome did not offer any targets for attack, but it also did not cause the Nazi press to rectify anything. Therefore, the Communist German exile magazine *Freies Deutschland* in Mexico had even less chance to be mentioned when it came to Chaplin's defense in April 1944 about this trial.[71]

Parallel to the Barry trials, the FBI also observed Chaplin for the indicted offenses and tried to substantiate them. Barry told the FBI that she had become pregnant by Chaplin several times in the course of her relationship with him. Between June 1941 and January 1942, she had had several abortions, which Chaplin had paid for. A 64-page dossier was compiled on Barry's interrogation,[72] but her claims were never substantiated.

The Gold Rush *and* Die Frau meiner Träume

From June 1941, Chaplin revised his silent film *The Gold Rush* for a sound version. He replaced some scenes from the 1925 theatrical version with outtakes, composed a score, and added narration of his own. Starting in January 1942, this remake was advertised in U.S. film trade journals as "Charlie Chaplin in the World's Great Laughing Picture *The Gold Rush* with Music and Words." It premiered the day after Chaplin's San Francisco speech for the Second Front on May 19, 1942. Again, *The Gold Rush* became an instant box office hit. In Great Britain, moviegoers queued up at movie theaters.[73] As reported by the *Aftonbladet*, the film was also very successful in Sweden. By the time of its Swiss premiere on December 26, 1942,

at the Basel Cinéma Alhambra, Chaplin's film had arrived in the immediate border area with Germany. Its announcement in the Christmas issue of the *National-Zeitung* was also included in the Chaplin file of the Hauptarchiv der NSDAP.[74] However, the new version of *The Gold Rush* could not cross the border into Germany until after the collapse of the Third Reich. Then, in September 1945, it was shown in several cinemas of the devastated Berlin.[75]

Despite *The Gold Rush*'s ban in 1935, Chaplin's "sappy film" was apparently good enough to serve as a model for a scene in the state-run German film production. In 1943, director Georg Jacoby shot the musical comedy *Die Frau meiner Träume* for Ufa with his wife Marika Rökk as the leading lady. At that time, it was obvious that Germany would lose the war. Goebbels therefore fostered the making of escapist, crowd-pleasing non-propaganda films to cheer up the German public.[76]

In *Die Frau meiner Träume,* the successful revue star Julia Köster (Rökk) wants to escape the hype about herself and seeks rest and solitude

United Artists ad for the Swiss release of *The Gold Rush*'s sound version, on December 26, 1942.

in the mountains. There, engineer Peter Groll (Wolfgang Lukschy) and his friend Erwin Forster (Walter Müller) share a mountain cabin during a joint project.

Poster art for *Die Frau meiner Träume*, 1944.

Right now the radio is playing Köster's latest hit song "In der Nacht ist der Mensch nicht gern alleine" (At Night Man Does Not Like to Be Alone)—at that time also a real hit on the German market. Forster is thrilled. After the film has been running for 20 minutes, he reaches for a couple of pens and skewers an eraser with each of them. With this, he performs for about 15 seconds part of Chaplin's dance of the rolls from *The Gold Rush*! When the revue star appears at the friends' cabin, Köster and Groll fall in love, without the engineer being aware of Köster's identity. Before the inevitable happy ending, the star is tracked down by the revue theater's director, who is desperately looking for her to continue her engagement. In no time, he has brought Köster back down to earth and thus almost destroys the lovers' romance.

Location shooting for *Die Frau meiner Träume* had begun in early April 1943. By the end of the month, the studio scenes, including the dance of the erasers, had been shot.[77] On January 16, 1944, Goebbels had the final cut of *Die Frau meiner Träume* screened for him, after which he dictated the following: "Then an Ufa color film with Marika Rökk is screened. Unfortunately, it is a complete failure. It is vulgar and clumsy. It cannot appeal to finer artistic sensibilities."[78] Goebbels' disapproval even went so far as to refuse the audience favorite Rökk the payment of a transitional allowance between *Die Frau meiner Träume* and her next film project.[79] What exactly Goebbels disliked is unknown. Finally, the film could be submitted to the Film-Prüfstelle Berlin, which approved it without objections at the beginning of August 1944.[80] The *Zeitschriften-Dienst* did not issue any instructions for *Die Frau meiner Träume*. At that time, *Der Angriff* and the *Völkischer Beobachter* had already discontinued their film reviews due to the war situation. After the premiere on August 25, 1944, in the Berlin cinemas Marmorhaus and Germania-Palast,

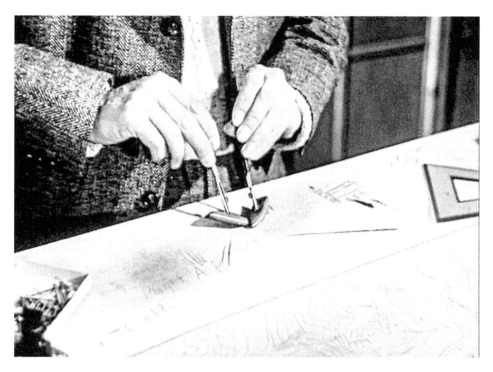

Screen shot from *Die Frau meiner Träume*, 1944: dance of the rolls with erasers (© Friedrich-Wilhelm-Murnau-Stiftung).

Screen shot from *Die Frau meiner Träume*, 1944: another scene imitating part of Chaplin's classic dance of the rolls (© Friedrich Wilhelm-Murnau-Stiftung).

the *Film-Kurier* reported on the strong applause of the visitors. Its reviewer was full of praise: "The film offers the lightest entertainment that does not seek to be taken seriously for a second. This has been precisely designed with great artistic skill. [...] Georg Jacoby's direction sets the proper emphases, for which he is known. He is particularly adept at providing each scene with an eye-catcher."[81] Did the *Film-Kurier* also take notice of the dance of the erasers as the "eye-catcher" that it certainly is?

Clearout

The last three newspaper clippings in the Hauptarchiv der NSDAP Chaplin file dated from June to November 1944 and had no connection with the Joan Barry scandal. In the Nazi press, they remained without resonance, probably not least because of the escalating war situation. In mid–June 1944, the Swiss daily *Die Tat* reported that a Chaplin exhibition had recently opened in Moscow with, among other things, "historical Chaplin films" which had been prolonged by popular demand.[82] Chaplin's frequently invoked closeness to Communism could well have provided cause for an attack.

The Basler *National-Zeitung*'s longer report "Fall Chaplin und seine Lehren" (the Chaplin Case and its Lessons) dated from September 1944. Its author complained that the young generation of moviegoers only attended sound films and knew silent movies only by hearsay. Therefore, "almost without exception, they have no understanding" of Chaplin films. For this reason, he said, the Swiss Film Archive should "put together a film that teaches moviegoers how to read a film," for which, unfortunately, the necessary funds were not available:

> Charlie Chaplin [...] absolutely requires the ability to read pictures. [... In] *City Lights*, a car drove up in front of the blind saleswoman's flower store whenever Chaplin visited her. She was supposed to believe that he came to her in the car. This could have been explained in an intertitle or, in a sound film, by a dialogue. Chaplin, however, wanted to express the necessary moments purely cinematically and without a close-up. Those who do not know how to read pictures are unable to understand such scenes, of which there are many in Chaplin's films.[83]

The concern of the article and its praise of Chaplin were, of course, beyond question for Nazi agitation.

The article "Bomb Explodes at Chaplin Film" from late November 1944 in the Hungarian newspaper *Pester Lloyd* would have been just the thing for Nazi propaganda. Only a few years ago, Italian diplomats had fought *The Great Dictator* abroad. After the liberation of Italy from Mussolini's fascist dictatorship, it could be shown in the Roman cinemas Corso, Moderno and Splendore under the title *Il grande dittatore* on October 24, 1944. Obviously, however, there were still forces at work that did not hesitate to prevent this through violence: "During the screening of the film *The Dictator* by famous Jewish-American film actor Charlie Chaplin, a bomb exploded in a Roman cinema. Two Carabinieries were wounded. Panic broke out among the audience. The assassins could not be identified."[84] This recalls both Nazi bombings against the U.S. film *Im Westen nichts Neues* and fascist violence against *The Great Dictator* in South America (see Chapters 5 and 12).

Chaplin and The Great Dictator Triumphant

Chaplin and his work withstood the countless Nazi hostilities. *The Great Dictator* may be one of the most important film classics. After seeing Christian Herrendoerfer and Joachim C. Fest's *Hitler—Eine Karriere* in 1977, Hitler's minion Albert Speer stated in a letter to Jesse Lasky Jr.:

> My admiration for [Chaplin] dates back to my youth, and, even today, I regard Charlie Chaplin as one of the most important figures, not only in the history of films but—because of his ability to portray that misery can be endured with dignity and humor—also in our general history. [...] I am still convinced that Chaplin's contribution as "The Dictator" has been the best "documentary" about the Hitler period. And it will in all probability remain so.[85]

Whether *The Great Dictator* is the "best 'documentary' about the Hitler period" may be a matter of opinion.[86] But hardly any other feature film branded by the Nazis as a "Germanophobe smear film" is likely to have had a greater political impact. In Europe, it was eagerly awaited. After the September 1944 liberation of Belgium, *The Great Dictator* was released in the Walloon part of the country under the title *Le dictateur*. For this purpose, small, colorful posters were printed with Chaplin as Hynkel in a speaking pose which represent a curiosity of film history. Since there was a shortage of paper in Belgium, the posters were printed on the unused backs of ordnance maps that the German occupiers had left behind. For example, some of these maps, complete with names, showed strategic targets in Leeds and the surrounding area, or around the docks of Hull and Liverpool.[87] War, Hitler and Chaplin simply did not seem to be divisible. Chaplin could not have thought up a better scenario.

On June 17, 1946, according to the *New York*

Belgian poster art for *Le dictateur* printed on the unused back of a German ordnance map, after September 1944 (DFF—Deutsches Filminstitut & Filmmuseum, Frankfurt am Main/Chaplin-Archiv, Dauerleihgabe der Adolf und Luisa Haeuser-Stiftung für Kunst und Kulturpflege).

Times, the U.S. Army newspaper *Stars and Stripes* announced that *The Great Dictator* would not be shown in German theaters.[88] But then, the American Military Government's Information Control Division in the U.S. sector of Berlin scheduled a test screening for August 9. One of the officers in charge was skeptical and did not predict a long run for the film: "Today in Germany the picture misses the point completely. It makes fun of something which isn't funny anymore."[89] In the evening, about 400 German spectators had come to the cinema to see Sam Wood's 1940 love film *Fräulein Kitty* (*Kitty Foyle*). To their surprise, however, Chaplin's film was shown. Reactions were mixed. They laughed the most at Billy Gilbert as Goering and Jack Oakie as Mussolini. After the screening, questionnaires were distributed to be filled out anonymously. The majority of the audience members thought that it was too early to show Chaplin's film in Germany. One statement said: "For us Germans, the 'original fun' has cost far too much to now be able to appreciate the satire of that time. Therefore, the film should be shown in Germany only later—much later."[90] Subsequently, the American Military Government's Information Control Division decided that the Germans were not yet ready for *The Great Dictator*.[91]

Film lovers in the Federal Republic of Germany had to wait until 1958 for the official release of *The Great Dictator*.[92] The Staatliches Filmarchiv der DDR held the copy of the film that had come to the Reichsfilmarchiv via detours. The archive occasionally made it available for screenings in GDR Filmclubs.[93] This was not widely known because GDR authorities did not acquire theatrical rights for *The Great Dictator* from United Artists or Chaplin. Therefore, it was not released by the state-owned film distributor Progress. Thus, the official GDR premiere of *The Great Dictator* did not take place until March 4, 1980, in the program of DDR1.[94]

The Great Dictator marked a turning point for Chaplin in several respects. In his first sound film, Chaplin took a stand against Hitler's inhuman, racist and belligerent dictatorship that would soon industrialize genocide. With Tramp Charlie, Chaplin accomplished an even more profound transition. Until *Modern Times*, Charlie was everywhere and nowhere at home. The Jewish barber, however, went to war for his native Tomania and, after a long stay in the hospital, returned to his barbershop in the Jewish ghetto. He also speaks the local language, which Chaplin cleverly and carefully prepares the audience for in the film. At the beginning, the Jewish barber as a private handles the hand grenade in such a pantomime that the scene is understandable even without sound. In general, the private does not speak much either, and even after returning to the ghetto, he communicates only very cautiously with language.

Nevertheless, the Tramp had become a citizen like you and me, but still without a name. Most of the other ghetto inhabitants are also nameless, and yet they all know each other. Since the barber and the mad dictator Hynkel are the spitting image of each other, Chaplin's Tramp dissolves when the barber unavoidably has to take the part of the dictator. A promotional coloring picture for the U.S. premiere of *The Great Dictator* possibly alluded to the metamorphosis. Chaplin's film character, with moustache, waits in a cape on a barber's chair to be shaved.[95] Will the barber also shave off the moustache? If so, he would also no longer look like Hitler-Hynkel. In his next film, *Monsieur Verdoux* (1947), Chaplin's Bluebeard sported a much slimmer moustache and bore no resemblance to the Tramp. Like Charlie, however, Verdoux was able to outsmart the people around him until he finally lost the desire to live when faced with war and hardship.

After the courageous *Great Dictator* and the controversial *Monsieur Verdoux* about a sophisticated yet still sympathetic killer, Chaplin continued his unprecedented film career with three more feature films: *Limelight* (1952), *A King in New York* (1957) and *A Countess from Hong Kong* (1967). He had remained unafraid to address unpleasant matters about which others would have preferred to keep silent. In 1959, he released *The Chaplin Revue* with *A Dog's Life*, *Shoulder Arms* and *The Pilgrim* in new musically scored versions along with footage from his never-released documentary *How to Make Movies*. And even in his old age, he created new scores for some of his silent films, including *The Kid* and *A Woman of Paris*. Chaplin's films, predominantly infused with humanity and hope, have brought the gift of laughter to generations of moviegoers around the world, beyond political and social boundaries. Moreover, they are thought-provoking. His work, as original as it is valid, has not lost its freshness.

In the same way, it remains valid what Commander Schultz says to Dictator Hynkel's face when he opposes his inhuman order "to stage a little medieval entertainment in the ghetto": "Your cause is doomed to fail, because it's built on stupid, ruthless persecution of innocent people. Your policy is worse than a crime. It's a tragic blunder." He was right in his prophecy that also the Hitler regime was doomed: The "Thousand-Year Reich" collapsed after a little more than 12 years, with the deaths of the dictator and his worst henchmen. "Liberty Schtoonk!" was not and never will be a permanently viable basis for a state, even if dictators and autocrats of the 21st century keep trying with their evil methods.

What has remained of the Nazi attempts to destroy Chaplin? Agitation and lies of the ideologists and their willing helpers turned out to be a miserable failure! Germans who had not appreciated Chaplin's films even before the Nazis remained of the same opinion after 1945. But those who had looked forward to every new Chaplin film in the past and had also enjoyed the films several times, went to the cinema with eager excitement as early as 1945. Despite all the agitation that was still fresh in their minds, they finally wanted to see Chaplin films again: first *The Gold Rush*, and then all the other gems that had previously been banned.

It took almost 77 years after the U.S. premiere of *The Great Dictator* for another satire about one of the world's greatest dictatorships to hit theaters: Armando Iannucci's *The Death of Stalin* (2018). In it, Stalin dies not at all heroically. Immediately after his death, a struggle for his succession begins that has nothing to do with philosophy, ideology, ethics or morality. It is all about greed for power and arbitrariness. Opinions are changed in seconds, if any of the would-be successors even have an opinion of their own. And as with Stalin, murder is carried out without hesitation. Shakespeare's Macbeth would have loved it. When Iannucci's film was to be released in today's Russia, ruled by dictator Vladimir Putin aiming at lifelong leadership, it was accused of attacking the country's honor—while Russia has not yet come to terms with the crimes of Stalinism, which cost millions of people their lives. The film was initially approved, but then very quickly banned by Russian authorities.

Decades ago, the Nazis had also reacted sensitively to *The Great Dictator.* On December 28, 2021, the Russian state even banned the human rights organization NGO Memorial: The crimes of Stalin, who had even more people liquidated than Hitler, should no longer affect Russia's official image as the victor over Nazism—Putin's revisionism *à la* George Orwell. Finally, Putin was breaking international law as he saw fit, and on February 24, 2022, he ordered a long-planned invasion of sovereign Ukraine to restore the former Soviet Union, after lying to transatlantic heads of state and diplomats about his plan until the very end. Shortly thereafter, he barred all free media, threatening punishment, from calling the Russian invasion a war and reporting on the war crimes committed on his behalf. History seems to be repeating itself with Iannucci's film and with Putin!

Appendix 1

The 25-Point Program
of the NSDAP, February 24, 1920

As printed in *Völkischer Beobachter* 57, July 19, 1920.

1. The program of the Nationalsozialistische Deutsche Arbeiterpartei (National Socialist German Workers' Party) is a time-program. The leaders refuse to set up new goals after the goals set forth in the program have been achieved, for the sole purpose of enabling the party to continue to exist by artificially increasing the discontent of the masses.

   We demand the amalgamation of all Germans into a Greater Germany on the basis of the right of self-determination of the peoples.
2. We demand the equality of the German people with other nations, the cancellation of the peace treaties of Versailles and St. Germain.
3. We demand land and soil (colonies) for the nourishment of our people and the settlement of our surplus population.
4. Only those who are national comrades can be citizens. Only those of German blood can be a national comrade, without regard to (Christian) confession. Therefore, no Jew can be a national comrade.
5. Anyone who is not a citizen should be able to live in Germany only as a guest and must be subject to alien legislation.
6. The right to decide on the governance and laws of the state shall be vested only in the citizen. Therefore, we demand that every public office, regardless of its nature, whether in the Reich, local state or municipality, may only be held by citizens of the state. We fight against the corrupting parliamentary economy of appointments only according to party considerations without regard to character and ability.
7. We demand that the state undertake to provide first and foremost for the earning and living possibilities of the citizens of the state. If it is not possible to feed the total population of the state, the members of foreign nations (non-citizens) shall be expelled from the Reich.
8. Any further immigration of non–Germans shall be prevented. We demand that all non–Germans who have immigrated to Germany since August 2, 1914, be forced to leave the Reich immediately.
9. All citizens must be entitled to equal rights and duties.

10. The first duty of every citizen must be to work mentally or physically. The activity of the individual must not be contrary to the interests of the general public, but must be carried out within the framework of the whole and for the benefit of all. Therefore, we demand:

11. elimination of unemployment compensation and effortless income, breaking of the bondage to interest.

12. Regarding the immense sacrifices of property and blood, which every war demands from the people, personal enrichment through war must be called a crime against the people: We therefore demand the complete confiscation of all war profits.

13. We demand the nationalization of all (hitherto) already socialized (trusts) enterprises.

14. We demand profit-sharing in large-scale enterprises.

15. We demand a generous expansion of retirement benefits.

16. We demand the creation of a healthy middle class and its preservation, immediate communalization of large department stores and their leasing at cheap prices to small businessmen, the sharpest consideration of all small businessmen when delivering to the state, provinces or municipalities.

17. We demand a land reform adjusted to our national needs, creation of a law for the expropriation of land for charitable purposes free of charge. Elimination of the rent payable by smallholders to landowners and prevention of all land speculation.

18. We demand the ruthless fight against those who harm the public interest through their activities. Common criminals, profiteers, black marketeers, etc., are to be punished by death, without regard to denomination or race.

19. We demand the replacement of Roman law, which serves the materialistic world order, by a German common law.

20. In order to enable every capable and industrious German to attain higher education and thus to move into a leading position, the state has to provide for a thorough development of our entire system of national education. The curricula of all educational institutions must be adapted to the requirements of practical life. The grasp of the idea of the state must be achieved at the very beginning of its comprehension by the school (civics). We demand that the children of poor parents be educated at the expense of the state, regardless of their status or profession.

21. The state shall provide for the improvement of public health by protecting the mother and the child, by prohibiting youth labor, by bringing about physical training through the legal establishment of compulsory gymnastics and sports, and by supporting to the greatest extent possible all associations engaged in the physical training of youth.

22. We demand the abolition of mercenary troops and the formation of a people's army.

23. We demand the legal battle against deliberate political lies and their dissemination through the press. In order to create a German press, we demand that

   a. all editors and employees of newspapers published in the German language must be national comrades,

   b. non–German newspapers require the explicit permission of the state in order to be published. They may not be printed in German,

   c. any financial participation in German newspapers or their influence by non–Germans shall be prohibited by law, and demand as punishment for transgressions the closure of such newspaper enterprise and the immediate expulsion from the Reich of the non–Germans involved therein.

Newspapers that violate the common welfare are to be banned. We demand the legal battle against an art and literary trend that exerts a corrosive influence on our national life, and the closure of events that violate the above demands.

24. We demand the freedom of all religious confessions in the state, as far as they do not endanger its existence or offend against the morality and moral feeling of the Germanic race.

    The party as such represents the position of a positive Christianity, without binding itself denominationally to a particular (Christian) confession. It fights the Jewish materialistic spirit in and outside of us and is convinced that a lasting recovery of our people can only take place from within on the basis:

    Common welfare before self-interest.

25. In order to implement all this, we demand: The creation of a strong central power of the Reich. Unconditional authority of the central political parliament over the entire Reich and its organizations in general.

    The formation of chambers of guilds and professions to implement the framework laws enacted by the Reich in the individual states.

    The leaders of the party promise to stand up ruthlessly, if necessary at the risk of their own lives, for the implementation of the above points.

Munich, February 24, 1920

Appendix 2

Three Articles

1. The Trigger

8 Uhr-Abendblatt—National-Zeitung 237, October 9, 1925, 8:

"Charlies Geheimnis. Chaplins neuester Film" (Charlie's Secret. Chaplin's latest film), by Walter Hasenclever.

Paris, October

There is a unique artistic event now in Paris, although it has nothing to do with Paris. Chaplin's latest film is being shown on the Boulevard des Italiens. He is installed as a life-size advertisement in cutaway and hat above the entrance to the theater, as he steps into a miserable cabin fleeing the blizzard. His melancholy eye squints into the speeding flight of the automobiles. He stands high like a wooden angel in the storm of the big city, as if he could climb down at any moment, run into the path of a security guard, lift his little hat in front of a lady in a fur coat, and stumble over the outstretched leg of an anonymous gentleman who is consulting his Baedeker.

Chaplin as a gold prospector. In the snowy mountains of Alaska. He swings his little cane above the glaciers. A St. Francis of Broadway, he wanders, lurching, through the eternal ice, with a black bear following him amiably. He is one of the fairy tale characters loved by children and animals. He's already become a myth, a Homeric hero of the 20th century who inhabits the deified sky. Tenderly and smilingly, we weep for his misfortune. As he trolls as a shadow across the screen, he seems to be a poet's invention. Cervantes and Shakespeare gave birth to him. As Don Quixote, he rides against the windmills of our mechanized world; an eternal fool in Christ, he could sing in the steamer's tween deck, while eating noodles, or on the bench in the park: "And it is raining every day…"

Gee, who knows if Jesus and Mohammed visited this oh-so-peaceful earth one more time, they might show up in Charlie's guise at the Pacifist Congress and, beaten down by all the diplomats we imagine like the big, fat gentlemen in his movies, proclaim to the sports-loving crowd, "Love your enemies!"

Chaplin as a gold prospector. Snowstorm. Hunger. He cooks his shoe, serves it, carves it, gnaws off the nails as if they were chicken legs. And then he looks down at his shoeless leg. Balzac would have written a novel around that single glance. The comedy of the implausible, which becomes tragic through its probabilities.

Or he stands in the dance hall, a sinister place of amusement of the Wild West. A scorner scorned in his elegant rags. You can only see his back. He plays with that back for a second of our life that becomes eternity. No woman cares for him, and yet he so badly wants just that. Take care not to let them realize it. Pretend it does not matter. What does he care about women! And in reality, his heart is breaking. You can see his feet stuttering. Slowly and sadly he is pushed aside. Dostoevsky has written such scenes.

Finally, a beautiful girl turns to him on a whim. He dances and loses his belt. The pants slip. Cussedness of the things in gigantic allegory. Not when Mr. [Harry] Piel wins a lightning rod, when Chaplin loses his pants—that is life.

He roams through this life, this puny and mighty one, as a contemporary schlemiel. With Jean Paul, he flies through the electric airs. Not only does he play himself, but with all objects. This is the great secret of his art: he's understood that the settings are alive. The noodles that he enlarges immeasurably, the knife that becomes a universal knife in his hand, the omnipresence of everyday things that are already a part of ourselves, that belong to us like flesh and bone, are with him boosted into the fateful. He's the courage to really perish on a match that doesn't burn. Bankruptcy isn't a reason to commit suicide, but to fulfill a need at the wrong time. The tragic lives in the small things, in the heroic banality. Dramatists of all countries, learn from him!

Three delightful girls have promised to visit him in his miserable Wild West cabin to celebrate New Year's Eve. They've long forgotten about it and are dancing in strangers' arms. It was a joke. But he was dead serious. He's prepared everything nice and carefully, with loving precision: firecrackers, small gifts, a roast, even place cards. The girls don't show up. It's going to be eleven. It's turning twelve. Charlie sneaks out, presses his head against the illuminated panes of the other world, and suddenly he understands everything. Life has passed him by. It doesn't want him. He disappears.

We don't want to bang the drum and shout bravo. Far be Fern Andra from us. Chaplin wrote, acted and directed this film. 10,000 theaters play 10,000 classics every night. This movie features the present.

Every real fame has a deep justification. Chaplin comes from the ghetto. Nowhere does he deny this origin. He carries the symbols with him. He's the eternal Jew. Hence, his immense popularity; he embodies a character we all know, because there's something of him in all of us. The oppressed world traveler and adventurer, comically entangled and tragically resigned, the weaker, always inferior, spiritually triumphant: David before King Saul. Hence, his great successes as an emigrant and now as a prospector; he's the prototype of the modern American who lands without a penny in his pocket in front of the Statue of Liberty, is huffed and puffed through all regions of misfortune, and finally comes to rest as a millionaire in Monte-Carlo. Who succeeds through tenacious and heroic impudence. The reclamation of chance. The high song of the chutzpah. "Toupet" [Audacity], as the French put it.

Thus, in his roles as the last upstart of the scattered people cursed to eternal restlessness, he continues his triumphal procession across the earth. He's conquered the new world and won back the old. A modern Charles V, he can say of his audience, "In my kingdom the sun never sets!"

2. The First Nazi Attack Against Chaplin

Völkischer Beobachter (Bavarian Edition) 68, March 24, 1926, 2 (Section "Below the line"):

"Der mystisch gewordene Charlie Chaplin" (Charlie Chaplin Gone Mystical), by J.St-g (Josef Stolzing-Czerny).

On the occasion of the *Goldrausch* premiere with Charlie Chaplin we read the following hymn in the Jewish press:

"He's one of the fairy tale characters loved by children and animals. He's already become a myth, a Homeric hero of the 20th century who inhabits the deified sky. Tenderly and smilingly we weep for his misfortune. As he trolls shadowy across the screen, he seems to be a poet's invention. Cervantes and Shakespeare gave birth to him. As Don Quixote, he rides against the windmills of our mechanized world.

"Every real fame has a deep justification. Chaplin comes from the ghetto. Nowhere does he deny this origin. He carries the symbols with him. He's the eternal Jew. Hence, his immense popularity; he embodies a type we all know, because there's something of him in all of us. The oppressed world traveler and adventurer, comically entangled and tragically resigned, the weaker, always inferior, spiritually triumphant: David before King Saul. Hence, his great successes as an emigrant and now as a prospector; he's the prototype of the modern American who lands without a penny in his pocket in front of the Statue of Liberty, is huffed and puffed through all regions of misfortune, and finally comes to rest as a millionaire in Monte-Carlo."

Whew! Such adulation takes your breath away, and you cannot help but wonder: Either it was paid for heavily, or the film magic has gone to the author's head to such an extent that he can only view the world from the perspective of the flickering screen.

Charlie Chaplin may have a special ability to act just for the film, which does not surprise us with a Jew, because they are used to waving around with head and limbs so excitedly when they speak that actually the spoken word seems superfluous to us, because we can already understand them by their gestures. And film, as we know, requires vivid facial expressions. But we have enough film actors who mime at least as well as Chaplin, who came from the ghetto, without being hyped up as fairy-tale figures, mythical personalities and Homeric heroes. Not even when they are Jews. Charlie Chaplin, however, seems to have grown especially fond of Jews and Jewish comrades: Probably because of the ghetto atmosphere that mysteriously surrounds him! And Juda needs heroes for the glorification of its world domination, even if it is only such from the flickering box! Whereas the world war has not given us a single Jewish hero.

The author of the hymn of praise of the ghetto scion mentioned at the beginning of this article is Wilhelm [*sic*] Hasenclever. He's made a name for himself by the fact that all the plays he's written so far have gone down like a damp squib. The man has missed his profession: he is a born advertising boss!

3. *The First Major Attack Against Chaplin in the Third Reich by Nazi Film Press*

Film-Kurier 206, September 2, 1933, 8 ("English Section Française"):

"A Dog Barking at the Moon," by Albert A. Sander (his original English version)

About twenty-five years ago, when even in America the motion picture was still an infant in arms, the American industry had already recognized the box office value of actualities. Even if, in those days, there was no production of newsreels in the form as we know them today, the most important events of the day were photographed and screened in the cinemas in the form of shorts. These shorts mostly contained races and other sportive events, in which the American public was especially interested.

In the case of auto or motor races it quite naturally happened that during a minute or two no car passed the track. These empty intervals were, soon after, filled in an original way. On the screen appeared a subtitle reading "A Queer Stranger Pops Up" and now, the following happened: A little man with a bit of a moustache, with enormous baggy pants, impossible shoes of gigantic dimensions, a ridiculous derby hat and a miniature issue of a cane appeared and walked once or twice across the track. The audience roared with laughter. This little man, who was at that time paid five dollars per day, was Charley [*sic*] Chaplin.

This sort of work, however, did not last very long. Soon after, the first slapstick comedies with Chaplin in the main part made their appearance. At that timme [*sic*], Charley's [*sic*] humour was still very crude and primitive. His chief trick was to chew a piece of pie and to spit the contents of his mouth into the face of his partner. And this at a time when Fatty Arbuckle, a decidedly finer actor and better comedian, had given Charley [*sic*] an example of cultivated taste and artistic acting.

Charley [*sic*] Chaplin, a scion of that part of London which is known—and not favourable known—under the name Whitechapel, recognized the inclination of the American public consisting, at that time, of outgrown children, for primitive humour and the result of his instinct was that his success kept growing from year to year, until, finally, he became a member of the United Artists, his own producer and his own director. Charley [*sic*] came to the studio from the vaudeville stage and he knew very well that a vaudeville artist, if he wants to remain in public favour, must never give his audiences all they demand. He must be careful to keep them hungry for more. Having grown wealthy and independent, he decided to restrict himself to one big film per year and this prudent policy helped him making millions of dollars a year.

When the war broke out in 1914, Chaplin was in America and kept filling his pockets, while his fellow-artists and country-men were rotting in the trenches. During this time he was often attacked by the English preß [*sic*] because of his apparent lack of patriotism. Chaplin completely ignored these attacks. Since he did not have a leg to stand on, he was clever enough to refrain from even the faintest attempt of defense. A profound pacifist, he did not change his attitude when America entered the war. Instead of donning the olive drab and to show himself thankful for the millions the American public had bestowed on him, he remained safely in Hollywood and produced "*Choulder* [*sic*] *Arms*," a silly persiflage of the war, in which he captured hords [*sic*] of "Huns" singlehanded.

With the termination of the war, the gigantic expansion of the American film industry came and Charley [*sic*] quickly became a multi-millionaire. After several years, when felt sure that the British public had long forgotten the fact that he had flunked in 1914 as well as in 1917, Chaplin decided to make a trip to Europe. His press agents got busy: the European newspapers were full of Chaplin articles and his many admirers in England, Germany, France etc. were impatiently waiting for their chance to give their idol an enthusiastic reception. At the beginning, everything went well. England received him with open arms and London celebrated the scion of its ghetto like a prince.

Apparently his popularity went to his head. Influential circles in London succeeded in having him invited to a "King's party." In conservative England, the invitations to such an event begin with the words: "His Majesty the King commands your presence..." The Whitechapel multi-millionaire, however, was not satisfied with this invitation, because it did not bear the signature of the King himself.

So he returned the invitation saying that if His Majesty command him to a party, he might as well sign such a command himself. This impudence leaked out and a storm of protest swept through the British press. So Charley [*sic*] decided it wiser, to shake the dust of old England from his boots and to proceed to the Continent. His conduct in France, Germany, etc., was so impossible and his arrogance toward the members of the press was so unbearable, that his European trip made him lose every sympathy in every country he visited. There is no likelihood that he will ever repeat his experiment.

Apparently Chaplin forgets quicker than the public, for, some time ago, there appeared an article in the film section of *Paris Midi*, in which it is stated that the great Charley [*sic*] had decided to shave his moustache in order not be mistaken for—Adolf Hitler. This impossible arrogance is followed by the usual shouting about his next picture. Of course, nothing could be betrayed at this moment about the story of his film, but in order to make the announcement at least a bit attractive to the reader, it is hinted that the picture would be of a political nature. Chaplin, according to *Paris Midi*, intends to make his new picture as "a silent manifestation against the persecution of the German Jews by Hitler." But since Charley [*sic*] was known throughout the world by his little moustache, the Paris paper continues, he has decided to part with it, "in order to avoid disagreeable mistakes."

It is difficult to say whether this announcement is the climax of arrogance or merely a stupefying lack of taste. Just imagine what the American public would say, if, for instance, the famous clown Grock were to announce that his next act would be a protest against the economic dictatorship of President Roosevelt and that had decided to part with his eye-glasses in order to avoid undesirable mistakes. What will be is the moral judgement of a type like Charley [*sic*] Chaplin, who was openly denounced as a slacker by the press of his native country and who has the colossal impudence of announcing a "silent manifestation" against Hitler, who fought on the German front as a common soldier from the beginning of the war to the very end and whose moral, intellectual and spiritual qualities make a man of Chaplin's type look like a dwarf.

Besides, Chaplin is said to intend only a "silent" manifestation. Quite naturally, for Charley [*sic*] is known as a sworn enemy of the talking picture. For some good reasons: Charley [*sic*] Chaplin has no voice. This explains his deadly fear of the microphone. When he announced his arrival in Berlin, the writer of this article went to Hanover to meet him and to arrange a short interview for a German newsreel. Chaplin's answer was: "You can photograph me as much as you want, but as soon as I see a microphone, I shall run away and you will not see me again": "Having heard your voice, I can completely understand your attitude," was the response of the writer.

We have not the least objection against Chaplin's spitting chewed cake in other peoples [*sic*] faces. The creator and leader of the new Germany, the war veteran and staunch friend of the new German film stands much too high to even hear the barking of a dog from London's ghetto.

Appendix 3

NSDAP Main Archive (Hauptarchiv der NSDAP): Chaplin File

In the holdings of the Bundesarchiv Koblenz at ZSg. 117/626.
Places of publication are in parentheses.

Chicago Daily Tribune (Chicago), March 18, 1936: "Charlie Chaplin and Paulette Goddard May Be Wed Today."

Pester Lloyd (Budapest) 233, October 11, 1936, "Theater and Music": "Ein Männchen, das die Welt erobert hat" (A little man who conquered the world), by Karl Sebestyen

National-Zeitung (Basel)189, April 26, 1937: "Hollywood und Spanien" (Hollywood and Spain).

L'Œuvre (Paris), April 16, 1939: "Charlie Chaplin a 50 ans..." (Charlie Chaplin turns 50...).
—Until the invasion of France by the Wehrmacht (July 5, 1940), left-wing daily newspaper

Daily Mail, October 19, 1940: "His Film Made 'For Freedom,'" by Paul Bewsher.

Report 27/1940 of Department IVa of the Hauptarchiv der NSDAP, November 15, 1940, with German translation of the article and text underlining.

Daily Express (London), December 12, 1940: "Even Venus de Milo Heils Charlie," by P.L. Mannock

Brüsseler Zeitung (Brussels) 32, February 1, 1941: "Chaplin-Film endgültig verboten" (Chaplin film finally banned).
—Nazi occupation newspaper

Daily Mail (London), February 8, 1941: "Should Chaplin be 'Sir Charles'?"

New York Times (New York), March 30, 1941, "The Screen": "Bring 'Em in Alive," by Alfred Clark.

L'Œuvre (Paris), April 16, 1941: "Ein jüdischer Schriftsteller fordert von Charlie Chaplin 5 Millionen Dollar" (A Jewish writer demands $5 million from Charlie Chaplin), German translation only.
—After the Wehrmacht invasion of France (July 5, 1940), pro–Nazi newspaper

National-Zeitung (Basel) 267, June 13-14, 1942 (untitled). Short note about Chaplin's divorce from Goddard in Mexico.

National-Zeitung (Basel) 267, June 13-14, 1942: "Charlie Chaplin als Politiker" (Charlie Chaplin as a politician). The article contains a lengthy excerpt from Chaplin's speech at the American Committee for Russian War Relief event in San Francisco in May 1942.

Il Regime fascista (Rome), October 22, 1942: "Quel pagliaccio di Charlot" (Charlot's Clowning), by G.R. Maranzana.
—Fascist newspaper

National-Zeitung (Basel) 599 (Christmas), December 24-25, 1942: Advertisement for the premiere of the sound version of *Goldrausch* at the Cinéma Alhambra (Basel) on December 26, 1942.

National-Zeitung (Basel), June 19, 1943 (untitled). Short note about Chaplin's marriage to Oona O'Neill.

Times (London), February 12, 1944: "Charge Against Mr. Chaplin."

Straßburger Neueste Nachrichten (Strasbourg) 43, February 13, 1944, p. 3: "Der Filmjude Chaplin verführt Minderjährige" (Film Jew Chaplin seduces minor).
—At this time pro–Nazi newspaper

Le Pays réel (Brussels), February 13, 1944: "Charlie Chaplin détourne ... une mineure" (Charlie Chaplin hijacks ... a minor).
—Catholic-Fascist newspaper published by the Belgian Rexist Party

Neue Zürcher Zeitung (Zurich) 273, February 16, 1944, "film": "Propagandatrick um Chaplin?" (Propaganda trick about Chaplin?).

Straßburger Neueste Nachrichten (Strasbourg) 92, April 2, 1944: "Sittlichkeitsverbrecher Charlie Chaplin vor Gericht. Der jüdische Wüstling ist wie immer der 'Verführte.' Hollywoods neuester Skandal" (Sex offender Charlie Chaplin on trial. The Jewish libertine is the "seduced" as usual. Hollywood's latest scandal).

Times (London), April 6, 1944: "Chaplin's Acquittal."

Le Pays réel (Brussels) 10, May 12, 1944: "Cheese-Cakes," by Trissotin

Journal de Genève (Geneva) 117, May 17–18, 1944: "Charlie Chaplin devant les juges de San Francisco" (Charlie Chaplin before the judges of San Francisco).

Die Tat (Zurich) 157, June 18, 1944 (untitled). Chaplin exhibition and screening of numerous Chaplin films in Moscow.

National-Zeitung (Basel) 421, September 10, 1944, supplement "film": "Der Fall Chaplin und seine Lehren" (The Chaplin case and what we can learn from it), by Hanns Sten

Pester Lloyd (Budapest) 270, November 28, 1944: "Bombe beim Chaplin-Film explodiert" (Bomb Explodes at Chaplin Film). On the explosion of a bomb in a Roman Cinema during a *Great Dictator* screening.

Appendix 4

Nazi Authors and Other Authors
Who Wrote About Chaplin
During the Third Reich

Listed in chronological order of their first contribution.
Excluding authors with unidentified author abbreviations.

Agitation Against Chaplin by Nazi Authors

Josef Stolzing-Czerny, March 1926
Rudolf Jordan, May 1926
Julius Streicher, October 1926
Dr. Hans Buchner, 1927
Alfred Rosenberg, June 1927
Joseph Goebbels, March 1928
Max Jungnickel, January 1931
Heinz Henckel, March 1931

Ernst Schwartz, March 1931
Aliquis (pseudonym), April 1931
Dr. Johann von Leers, 1933
Albert A. Sander, September 1933
Dr. Hans Diebow, November 1937
Carl Neumann, December 1937
Dr. Fritz Hippler, November 1940
Walter Persich, 1942

Note: Goebbels praised and rebuked Chaplin's *Zirkus* in his diary entry of March 13, 1928.

Nazi Authors Who Praised Chaplin in the Weimar Republic
and Agitated Against Him in the Third Reich

Hans-Walther Betz, September 1926/December 1937

Curt Belling, August 1927/December 1937

Authors Who Wrote Favorably About Chaplin During
the Third Reich

Dr. Johannes Eckardt, March 1933
Albert Schneider, May 1933
Hermann Ulrich, ca. mid–1933
Walter Timmling, ca. mid–1933

C. Graf Strachwitz, February 1934 (translator
of a French Chaplin article)
Dr. Kurt von Stutterheim, February 1936

Appendix 5

Nazi Chaplin Slurs

In chronological and alphabetical order

1926

October
- Hanswurst (Tomfool),
- Musterjude (Model Jew),

1927

First half of the year
- Bolschewist (Bolshevik),
- Darsteller abgeschauten psychopathischen Kretinismus (Performer of copied psychopathic cretinism),
- Kopist (Thief of intellectual property),

February
- gestürzter König (Overthrown king),
- Kino-Simson (Cinema Simson),

March
- Deutschenfeind (Germanophobe),
- hebräischer und jüdischer Wüstling (Hebrew and Jewish libertine, respectively)
- verhimmelter nigger-groteskhafter Galizier (Glorified nigger-grotesque Galician),

June
- Galizier Chaplin (Galician Chaplin),
- prachtvoller junger Zyniker (Splendid young cynic),
- Zotenerzähler (Teller of obscene jokes),

July
- jüdischer Schweinehund (Jewish bastard),
- Filmjude (Film-Jew),

- großes Riesenschwein (Great filthy swine)

Autumn
- raffinierter Geschäftemacher (Clever wheeler-dealer),

1928

January
- galizisches Heldenideal von heute (Galician ideal of today's hero),

1929

December
- Mauschel (Yiddish-speaking cheater),

1931

January
- gehässigster Deutschenfeind (Most spiteful Germanophobe),
- raffinierter Schwindler (Shrewd crook),

February
- neudeutsches Schönheitsideal: der Idiot (Neo-German ideal of beauty, the idiot),

March
- Filmfratz (Film rascal),
- Filmjüdlein (Little film Jew),
- hergelaufener Jude (Jewish bum),
- jüdischer Filmaugust (Jewish film clown),
- jüdischer Spaßmacher (Jewish jester),

377

- kleiner Schaumschläger (Little windbag),
- kleener Flimmerjüd' (Little flickering Jew),
- kleiner, krummbeiniger, plattfussbehafteter Filmfritze (Little, bow-legged, flat-footed film chap),
- Kriegshetzer Chaplin (War-monger Chaplin),
- obszöner Judäer Charlie (Obscene Judean Charlie),
- Scharlin Schäpplien (Scharlin Schäpplien),
- zerlumpter, sich anschmierender, unsagbar widerlich und lächerlich anmutender Hanswurst (Ragged, brown-nosing, unspeakably disgusting and ridiculous tomfool),

April
- Bajazzo eines minderwertigen Volkes (An inferior people's Bajazzo),

July
- holzgeschnitzte Puppe ohne Seele (Carved wooden doll lacking soul),
- kleines, schmächtiges Filmjüdlein mit einem dummen, nichtssagenden Gesicht, mit starren, seelenlosen Augen, in denen versteckt und verschleiert das Tier, die jüdische Bestie lauert (Small, lanky film Jew with a stupid, featureless face, with staring, soulless eyes, in which hiddden and veiled lurks the beast),
- rassenschänderisches jüdisches Schwein (Racially defiling Jewish pig),

1933

First half of the year
- ebenso hässliche wie alberne Possenfigur (Ugly as well as silly buffoon),
- ebenso langweiliger wie widerwärtiger Zappeljude (Boring as well as disgusting fidgeting Jew),
- Kunstjude (Art Jew),

1937

May
- schnoddriger Clown des international verwaschenen Films (Brash clown of internationally washed-out film),

December
- Ideendieb (Thief of intellectual property),
- der Mann mit der Zigarre (Man with a cigar),
- maßlos überschätzter Clown (Vastly overrated clown),
- Seelenfänger des 20. Jahrhunderts (Soul catcher of the 20th century),

1938

December
- Jud Chaplin (allusion to *Jud Süss*),

1939

- Ghetto-Figur mit sentimentaler Lächerlichkeit (Ghetto character with sentimental ridiculousness),
- plattfüßiger Ghetto-Clown (Flat-footed ghetto clown),

1940

November
- berüchtigter Filmjude (Notorious film-Jew),
- hetzender Clown (Agitating clown),
- Todfeind des deutschen Volkes (Mortal enemy of the German people),

December
- Clown mit nur unterdurchschnittlichem Talent (Clown with only below-average talent),

1941

February
- Hetzjude (Agitating Jew),
- "Kämpfer" von der traurigen Gestalt (Sad countenance of a "knight"),
- Kreatur (creature),

April
- jüdischer Filmclown (Jewish film clown),

1942

- plattfüßiger Wüstenwanderer (Flat-footed desert wanderer),
- Winkelartist (Hack artist),

December
- Bolschewist nach Geschäftsschluss (Bolshevist after hours),
- Plattfuß-Filmstar (Flat-footed movie star),

1943

April
- widerwärtigster Filmjude (Most disgusting film-Jew),

June
- abgetakelter Filmjude (Run-down film-Jew),
- glücklicherweise fast vergessener Filmheld von der traurigen Gestalt (Fortunately almost forgotten sad countenance of a film knight),

1944

February
- Filmhanswurst (Film tomfool),
- Gräuelhetzer (Atrocity agitator),
- Großgauner (Wholesale crook),
- jüdischer Filmstrolch (Jewish movie rascal),
- jüdischer Interpret schmierigster Hetzfilme (Jewish performer of sleazy smear films),

April
- Sittlichkeitsverbrecher (Sex offender)

Appendix 6

Reichsfilmarchiv Catalogue Card No. 15,242:
The Great Dictator

Reichsfilmarchiv Catalogue Card 15,242
Production year: 1940

The Great Dictator USA, engl. orig., length 3,481 m

Type of film: smear film with comedy character
Production and distribution: United Artists
Directed by: Charles Chaplin
Written by: Charles Chaplin
Cinematographers: Karl Struss, Roland Totheroh
Music: Meredith Willson.
Film Set: J. Russell Spencer
Actors: CHARLES CHAPLIN, PAULETTE GODDARD, JACK OAKIE, Reginald Gardiner, Henry Daniell, Billy Gilbert, Grace Hayle, Carter DeHaven, Maurice Moscovich, Emma Dunn, Paul Weigel, Chester Cunklin (sic)

Content:

According to the preface, the film is set between two world wars, in a time when common sense was not at a premium…. Western front 1918—at a German long-distance gun a German soldier, a Jewish barber in civilian life, is constantly getting up to mischief. During a subsequent assault, the nonsense continues. Finally, he helps rescue a German air force officer, is wounded in the process, and is taken unconscious to a military hospital…. Years have passed since the armistice. In Tomania (as Germany is bashfully called) a dictator has seized power, Hynkel, who with his storm troopers is running a tight and cruel ship against the Jews in the ghetto. Hynkel, who is longing for world power, is preparing the conquest of the neighboring state Osterlich (Austria), which appears to the Jews in the ghetto as the promised land, to which they would love to emigrate.—Around this time, the world war barber is released from an asylum where he had been kept until now, having completely lost his memory at that time. He now returns to his local store in the ghetto, he has forgotten the war and the years that have passed since then, he thinks he has been away for only a few weeks. But Tomania has changed a lot since then…. Soon the unsuspecting barber has incurred the wrath of the storm troopers. He would almost have been strung up in front of his store, but by chance, Schultz, the world war air force officer, appears, immediately recognizes the little Jew and rescues him. The barber now finds rest from the marauding soldiery, and a tender friendship begins between him and Hannah, a Jewish orphan living in the house next door. Hynkel eases up a bit on the terror against the Jews, as he wants to borrow the funds for the war against Osterlich from an international money Jew. This borrowing plan goes wrong, however, and again the persecution of the ghetto Jews begins anew. Schultz warns the dictator of these inhumane methods and is arrested by him as a traitor. But Schultz escapes into the ghetto, where he is able to plan an assassination against Hynkel. Schultz and the little barber, however, are arrested by storm troopers and sent to a Concentration Camp. At that time, Hynkel gets into trouble with his rival dictator Napaloni of Bacteria (Mussolini-Italy). Napaloni also concentrates troops on the border of Osterlich. Hynkel invites Napaloni to a state visit, the two almost come to blows, and it is only through a nasty breach of contract that Hynkel tricks Napaloni into withdrawing his troops, thus making the campaign against Osterlich possible again for Hynkel.—Hynkel is about to invade Osterlich, where in the meantime Hannah and some other ghetto Jews have turned up as emigrants, and he heads incognito to the border. In this area is also located the Concentration Camp, from which Schultz and the barber now break out in uniforms. Because of his striking resemblance to Hynkel, the uniformed barber is mistaken for the dictator, who appears for the invasion. At the head of the troops the alleged Hynkel reaches the capital of Osterlich, where he has to deliver a big speech. Up there speaks a completely different Hynkel, an apostle of peace, while the real dictator is mistaken for the escaped Jewish barber and locked up. Hannah, looking hopefully into the future, listens to the speech of the phony dictator, who speaks of the understanding of nations and people and of the peace on earth that he longs for.

Smear comedy with the worst vilification of the National Socialist regime and especially of the Führer in Chaplin's typical grotesque, almost always more crude manner.

Author's Note: Unlike other catalogue cards, this card is printed on differently colored paper. The stamped "6" probably indicates, according to a scale ranging from "1" to "6" as the highest grade, that the Reichsfilmarchiv classified the film as a "particularly nasty" anti–Nazi smear film.

Chaplin's name has been omitted from the music credits.

Appendix 7

Signage in the Ghetto of The Great Dictator

Some words on the signage are Esperanto. Most of them, however, only sound like it. Other words are composed of various European language elements or are entirely in English.

The signage is listed in the order of their appearance in the movie.

1. After a short shot of the sign "Ghetto," we see a merchant pushing his vegetable cart, on it a sign reading "Terpumoj" (Esperanto: "Terpomoj"): potatoes.
2. The barber enters the ghetto. At the front of the street, near his shop, there is a cobbler's shop showing a boot emblem and the following signage:
   (a) On the wall
       "Heinrich" (German first name)
   (b) Sign above shop window
       "Piedvestejok"
       Contains "pied" (French: foot). The sign seems to read "shoe store."
   (c) On the shop window
       "Botisto" (Esperanto): cobbler
3. The barber's shop window
   (a) *Sign*
       "Razn Barber Harlavado"
       Razn (German: rasieren): shaving
       Barber (English)
       Harlavado, composed of "Haare" (German: hair) and the Spanish "lavado," past participle passive of "lavar": to wash

   Therefore, the barber offers "shaving, hairdressing and hair washing."
   (b) On the left
       "Harü Tondadoz"
       Composed of "Haare" (German: hair) and "tondeur" (French: shearer)
       The hairdresser also cuts hair.
   (c) On the right
       "Lipharoj Tondadoz"
       Composed of "Lipharoj" (Esperanto: moustache) and "tondeur" (French: shearer)
       The hairdresser trims beards, too.
4. English-language sign on Jaeckel's plot wall and in the window from which Hannah clubs the storm trooper and the barber
       "Laundry done here. Inquire within"
5. An only partially legible business sign above an awning, opposite Mr. Jaeckel's courtyard door
       "Veset...."
       Possibly from "vestajo" (Esperanto: clothing)

Maybe the sign of a clothing store

6. Store sign to the left of the shoe store, seen as Hannah hides the barber in Mr. Jaeckel's yard
   "...makistz Dank"
   Meaning undeterminable

7. Beverage advertisement on the wall of the barber shop to Mr. Jaeckel's house
   "Drinkum Spizz"
   Probably formed from "drink" (English) and a product name: Drink Spizz.

8. Stores to the left of Mr. Jaeckel's courtyard entrance
   (a) Sign
       "Bierr, Kajejo, Kafu"
       After "biero" (Esperanto: beer), "kaj" (Esperanto: and) and "kafo" (Esperanto: coffee). Hence, a bar where you can get beer and coffee.
   (b) Sign
       "Papervendissen"
       Composed of "paper" and "vendre" or "vender," respectively (French or Spanish, respectively: to sell). The sign indicates a stationery store.
   (c) Window of the stationery shop
       "Paperaj"
       Paperajoj (Esperanto): stationery
   (d) Sign in window display
       "Malnovaj Libroj"
       Esperanto: used books
       Possibly an antiquarian bookshop

9. Stores and signs to the right of Mr. Jaeckel's house, facing the front of Ghetto Street opposite the cobbler's store
   (a) House wall
       "Restoraciz"

Restoracio (Esperanto): restaurant
   (b) Sign
       "Cambroj" (Esperanto): room
       Probably room to rent
   (c) Sign
       "Legomo kaj Fruktü"
       Correctly, "legomo kaj frukto" (Esperanto): fruits and vegetables
       A grocery store
   (d) Small sign
       "Solej Fresaj Legomaj"
       Composed of "solo" (Italian: only), "Fresaj" (Esperanto: strawberries) and "legomo" or "légume" (Esperanto or French: vegetables): fresh vegetables
   (e) Vegetable stand
       "Tomaloy, Rapoj, Bulbojo"
       Tomaloy (borrowed from the English?): tomatoes?
       Rapoj (Esperanto): turnips
       Bulbojo (Esperanto): onion
       Instead of turnips and onions, there seem to be kohlrabi and cauliflower on the cart.
   (f) Sign
       Vestajoj Malnovaj (Esperanto): used outerwear
       A second-hand clothing store

10. Store on the opposite front side of the ghetto street
    (a) Wall
        "Levy Pruvtoj"
        Levy: probably a name
        Pruvtoj (Esperanto): roof overhangs
        Possibly shop awnings or a roofer
    (b) Shield
        "Plumbistz"
        After English "plumber"
        A plumbing business

11. Store on the left next to the plumber's store

(a) Only during the first long
   ghetto scene of the film
   "Cigaroj, Tabakbutiky,
   Cigaredoj"
   Cigaroj (Esperanto): cigars
   Tabakbutiky (Esperanto):
   tobacco products
   Cigaredoj (Esperanto):
   cigarettes
   A tobacco store

(b) Only during the last ghetto
   scene
   Instead of "(tab?)akbutiky
   cigare(...)": "Botisto"
   Botisto (Esperanto): cobbler
   A shoe store or cobbler's
   workshop

Note: The different signs are probably
due to an editing error. It could
have been caused by reshooting in
which opposite ends of the street
were confused with each other.
Chaplin famously worried little about
continuity.

12. Vegetable cart overturned by the
    storm troopers
    "Aveno, Brasikoj"
    Aveno (Esperanto): oats
    Brasikoj (Esperanto): cabbage
    The vegetable cart would belong
    to a greengrocer.

13. Wall at the roof of Mr. Jaeckel's
    house
    "Wartz (...)rickle Factory"
    The second word remains hidden
    during the film.
    Possibly a brickyard called
    Wartz, after the English "brick"
    and "factory"

Chapter Notes

Chapter Notes Abbreviations

Angriff: *Der Angriff*

Autobiography (**book title**): Charlie Chaplin, *My Autobiography*, 1964

(**B**): Bavarian Edition

BArch: Bundesarchiv

BBZ: *Berliner Börsen-Zeitung*

(**Ber**): Berlin Edition

BL: Berlin-Lichterfelde

Bologna, jpg-file No.: in the holdings of the Documents from the Chaplin archives, copyright © Roy Export Co Ltd. Digitization of the Chaplin Archives by Cineteca di Bologna. www.charliechaplinarchive.org

BT: *Berliner Tageblatt und Handels-Zeitung*

B.Z.: *B.Z. am Mittag*

Chaplin file: Chaplin Akte des Hauptarchivs der NSDAP at ZSg. 117/626, in the holdings of the Bundesarchiv Koblenz

David Robinson, *Chaplin: His Life and Art*, 2001

DFZ: *Deutsche Filmzeitung*

DFF—Deutsches Filminstitut & Filmmuseum: in the holdings of the DFF—Deutsches Filminstitut & Filmmuseum, Frankfurt am Main/Chaplin-Archiv, Dauerleihgabe der Adolf und Luisa Haeuser-Stiftung für Kunst und Kulturpflege

(**E**): Evening Edition

8-Uhr: *8 Uhr-Abendblatt*

Film: *Der Film*

Filmuniversität Babelsberg KONRAD WOLF: newspaper clippings in the holdings of the Medienkundliches Pressearchiv

der ehemaligen Landesbildstelle Berlin, Sonderordner Charlie Chaplin nach Jahren, Pressedokumentation der Filmuniversität Babelsberg KONRAD WOLF

FJ: *Film-Journal*

FK: *Film-Kurier*

FOPS: Film-Oberprüfstelle Berlin

FPS: Film-Prüfstelle Berlin

FZ: *Frankfurter Zeitung*

Goebbels-Tagebücher, **volume**: *Die Tagebücher von Joseph Goebbels, Teil 1 "Aufzeichnungen 1923–1941"*

Handbuch: *Handbuch der deutschen Aktiengesellschaften*

HFRT: *Historical Journal of Film, Radio & Television*

Landesarchiv Berlin, folio: Akten des Polizeipräsidiums Berlin, Schutzpolizei Aufsichtsdienstaus besonderen Anlässen," at Pr. Br. Rep. 30 Berlin C, Polizeipräsidium, No. 7512, in the holdings of the Landesarchiv Berlin.

LBB: *Lichtbildbühne*

(**M**): Morning Edition

(**Ma**): Main Edition

Montreux, album volume no.: newspaper clippings from Chaplin's newspaper clipping albums, in the holdings of the Archives de Montreux, PP-75 Fonds Charles Chaplin, Roy Export Co. Ltd.

(**N**): Northern Germany Edition

NS-Presseanweisungen, **volume (book title)**: *NS-Presseanweisungen der Vorkriegszeit*

NYT: *The New York Times*

(**R**): Reich Edition

RFB: *Reichsfilmblatt*

RGBl: *Reichgesetzblatt* Part I

RMVP: Reichsministerium für Volksaufklärung und Propaganda

RWF: *Rheinisch-Westfälische Filmzeitung*

(**S**): Sunday Edition

SFZ: *Süddeutsche Filmzeitung*

Stürmer: *Der Stürmer*

VB: *Völkischer Beobachter*

Vol.: Volume (magazines)

WB: *Westdeutscher Beobachter*

Books listed in the Chapter Notes are cited the first time they are mentioned with the last name of author, editor or adapter, the main title of the work, and the year of publication. First names are used as an exception to distinguish different authors. Full bibliographic data can be found in the Bibliography. It also provides information on the time periods of individual volumes.

Before the date, the title of the periodicals is followed by the number of the issue without the addition of "no." This addition is also omitted for file numbers. Page numbers of references are followed without the addition of the abbreviation "p." In the case of newspapers and periodicals, they indicate either the printed page numbers or page numbers of non-paginated pages, counted from the title page onward.

Chapter 1

1. Robinson, *Chaplin*, 160.

2. Charlie Chaplin (with Bell), *My Trip Abroad*, 1922, 146.

3. *Collier's*, March 14, 1940, quoted after Marcel Martin, "Charles Chaplin" in *Cinéma D'Aujourd'Hui* 43, 1966, 12.

4. von Ulm, *Charlie Chaplin—King of Tragedy*, 1940, 39.

5. Martin in *Cinéma D'Aujourd'Hui* 43, 1966, 12.

6. Huff, *Charlie Chaplin*, 1952, 22.

7. Bessie, *Inquisition in Eden*, 1965, 241.

8. Jost Hermand, "Satire und Aufruf. Zu Chaplins Antifaschismus" in Groenewold, *Charlie Chaplin*, 1993, 32.

9. Montagu, *With Eisenstein in Hollywood*, 1968, 94.

10. For example, Gauteur, "Notes sur l'énigme Chaplin" (Notes on the Chaplin Riddle) in *Image et son. La revue du cinéma* 229, June/July 1969, 38–55. Adolphe Nysenholc, "Charles Chaplin and the Jewish World" in Nysenholc, *Charlie Chaplin. His Reflection in Modern Times*, 1991, 17–24. See also *Limelight* Vol. III-1, Winter 1997, 12, 13: "Was Chaplin a Jew?" by Elliot Levine.

11. According to Joseph Halachmi's essay "è della stirpe dei giudei"/"And He Is of the Seed of the Jews" in *Griffithiana* 73/74, 2002, 164, 165.

12. *Die Weltbühne* 49, December 26, 1923, 564: "*The Kid*" by Peter Panther (Kurt Tucholsky). On Tucholsky, see Benz and Graml, *Biografisches Lexikon zur Weimarer Republik*, 1988, 348, entry by Norbert Frei.

13. General map at Robinson, xix.

14. Charlie Chaplin, *Hallo Europa!*, 1928, 9, 10, 232.

15. *Die Volksbühne* 6, September 1928, 24–28 (25): "Chaplin fängt den deutschen Kaiser" by Erich Gottgetreu.

16. *The Southern Israelite* (Augusta, GA), 1935 article (month and day not given), 14: "Interviewing a Scientist, a Musician, a Comedian" (claiming Chaplin's Jewish origin), *Jewish Post* (Winnipeg, MB), May 4, 1935: "Chaplin not a Jew. But will not Publish a Denial" in Montreux, album 50.

17. *Die Neue Weltbühne* (Prague) 21, May 23, 1935, 664: "Ein Fall Chaplin?" by Hermann Britt (Heinz Pol = Heinz Pollack).

18. *Filmtechnik* 20, October 3, 1931, 13–16 (14): "Chaplins Schuhe" by Hermann Ulrich.

19. *Aufbau* (New York) 43, October 24, 1941, 16: "Charlie Chaplin's Bekenntnis" by Erich Gottgetreu.

20. Hannah Arendt, "Die verborgene jüdische Tradition, 3. Charlie Chaplin: Der Suspekte," reprinted in Wiegand, *Über Chaplin*, 1978, 154, 156, 164, 166. See also Weissberg, *Hannah Arendt, Charlie Chaplin und die verborgene Tradition*, 2009, 17, 18.

21. Arendt, "3. Charlie Chaplin" in Wiegand, 164.

22. Arendt, "4. Franz Kafka" in Wiegand, 168.

23. Sennett as told to Cameron Shipp, *King of Comedy*, 1954, 154.

24. See family tree at Robinson, xxvii, xxviii, and the description starting with 1786 (1–3).

25. Harold Manning and Timothy J. Lyons, "Charlie Chaplin's Early Life: Fact and Fiction" in *HFRT* Vol. 3-1, March 1983, 35–41. Reginald R.

Chaplin, "Charlie Chaplin's Ancestors" in *HFRT* Vol. 5–2, October 1985, 209–212. Robinson, xxviii.

26. Mitchell, *The Chaplin Encyclopedia*, 1997, 26, 27, 44–47 (entries "Birth," "Chaplin, Charles Sr," "Chaplin, Hannah").

27. Riess, *Charlie Chaplin*, 1989, 66.

28. Karasek, *Billy Wilder*, 1992, 292.

29. Herlitz and Kirschner, *Jüdisches Lexikon. Volume 1 (A–C)*, 1927, Column 1,329. Part II: "Die Entstehung des *Jüdischen Lexikons*," VII, stated that the authors of the contributions took "full scientific responsibility."

30. Series of articles by "Landstreicher Jim Tully" (Hobo Jim Tully) in *Prager Tagblatt* 97, April 24, 1927, 3, 4: "Der Landstreicher erzählt Chaplins Lebensgeschichte." *Prager Tagblatt* 100, April 28, 1927, 3: "Chaplin arbeitet." *Prager Tagblatt* 107, May 6, 1927, 3: "Chaplin filmt den *Goldrausch*." *Prager Tagblatt* 111, May 11, 1927, 3: "Chaplin als Privatmensch." After Tully had embarked on a successful career as a writer, he met Chaplin and as Elmer Ellsworth's successor became his secretary: Tully, *A Dozen and One*, 1943, 17.

31. Tully published the new version of his series of articles in *The New Movie Magazine* Vol. II 1 and 2 (July and August 1930) under the title "The Unknown Charlie Chaplin." *A Dozen and One*, which includes a section on Chaplin (11–41), also does not comment on Thonstein. Tully wrote that Chaplin came from the "scum of London" (15).

32. *NYT* 25, 186, January 8, 1927, 19: "Chaplin Files Suit to Halt Life Story." *NYT* 25, 240, March 3, 1927, 25: "Chaplin Loses Suit Here."

33. *Evening Courier* (Camden, NJ) 200, January 22, 1927, 12. *Honolulu Star-Bulletin* 11, October 10, 1927, 5.

34. Such a poem is not included in Ulitz's 1924 collection of poems, *Der Lotse*, nor in his 1926 novel, *Christine Munk*, which mentions Chaplin (259). Rduch, *Unbehaustheit und Heimat*, 2009, 294–309, also does not list it in his comprehensive Ulitz bibliography.

35. *BT* (M) 80, February 17, 1927, 2: "Meute" by Arnold Ulitz. von Ulm, 252, 253, translated the poem into English under the title *Pack of Hounds* and dated it 1929. Lyons, *Charles Chaplin: A Guide to References and Resources*, 1979, 109, has apparently adopted this (377). "Meute," in turn, is not included in Rduch's Ulitz bibliography for 1927, 300.

36. See note 25.

37. Herlitz and Kirschner, *Jüdsiches Lexikon. Volume 2*, 1928, columns 1,727, 1,728.

38. Klatzkin and Elbogen, *Encyclopaedia Judaica*, 1928–1934.

39. *Die neue Welt* (Vienna) 57, October 19, 1928, 8: "Das Judentum Charlie Chaplins. Seine Mutter als Jüdin gestorben."

40. *Hammer* 634, Nebelmonds (November) 15, 1928, 575: "Entlarvt!" by Theodor Fritsch.

41. *Jüdische Presszentrale Zürich* 638, March 13, 1931, 1: "Charlie Chaplin. Zu seinem Besuch in Europa."

42. *Die Stimme* (Vienna) 168, March 9, 1931, 4:

"Chaplin. Randbemerkungen zu seinem Wiener Besuch."

43. *Jüdische Presse* (Vienna and Bratislava) 12, March 20, 1931, 2: "Was aus Ghettojungen werden kann."

44. *Die neue Welt* (Vienna) 185, April 1, 1931, 3: "Geschäft um Chaplin."

45. Schwartz and Kaye, *Who's Who in American Jewry 1926* and *1928*, 1927 and 1928, respectively.

46. Glassman, *Biographical Encyclopedia of American Jews*, 1935, 77.

47. Simons, *Who's Who in American Jewry. Volume 3*, 1938, 161, 162.

48. Simons, vi (preface).

49. *The Palestine Bulletin* (Jerusalem) 1,841, March 11, 1931, 1: "Charlie Chaplin Mistaken For A Jew. Demonstration in Germany."

50. *The Sentinel* (Chicago) 5, October 31, 1940, 12: "From the Watchtower" by Dr. G. George Fox.

51. Joseph Halachmi, "è della stirpe dei giudei"/"And He Is of the Seed of the Jews" in *Griffithiana* 73/74, 2002, 166, 167, 172. Note 14 (173) contains the reference to the 1937 *Encyclopedia Klallit Izre'el* entry, 3,581–3,580 after its 6th edition published by the Tel Aviv Masada Publishing House in 1961.

52. Halachmi in *Griffithiana* 73/74, 172, 173 (note 11).

53. Julius H. Greenstone, "*The Universal Jewish Encyclopedia*" (review), in *The Jewish Quarterly Review* (New Series) Vol. 32–1 (July 1941), 97–102 (97).

54. The quote is from Gilbert Frankau's article "The King of Clowns: How Chaplin Proved his Right to the Throne," which was also printed in *The Pittsburgh Press* (PA) 244, March 1, 1931, 53, 55 ("The Press World of Today," 1, 3).

55. Libby Benedict, "Charlie Chaplin" in Landmann and Rittenberg, *The Universal Jewish Encyclopedia. Volume 3*, 1941, 112, 113.

56. Greenstone in *The Jewish Quarterly Review* Vol. 32–1, 102.

57. *Egyenlöség* (Budapest) 22, March 14, 1931, 3: "Egy nagy zsidó müvész: Chaplin" (A Great Jewish Artist: Chaplin).

58. *Egyenlöség* (Budapest) 23, March 21, 1931, 19: "Hirek" (News).

59. *Uj Kelet* 62, March 17, 1931, 2: "Romániába is ellátogat. A nagy filmkomikus útja a londoni gettótól a világhírig" (Charlie Chaplin also Visits Romania. The Great Film Comedian's Journey from the London Ghetto to World Fame).

60. *FK* 241, October 14, 1938, 3: "Man hört und liest" by Karl F. Franck.

61. David Lobb, "Fascist Apocalypse: William Pelley and Millennial Extremism" in *Journal of Millennial Studies* Vol. 2–2 (Winter 2000), mille.org/publications/winter2000/lobb.PDF. Last visited May 28, 2022, no longer accessible. Bennett, *The Party of Fear*, 1994, 241. Geels, *The German-American Bund*, 1975, 75.

62. *FK* 241, October 14, 1938, 3: "Man hört und liest" by Karl F. Franck.

63. *Angriff* 13, January 15, 1939, 4: "Who's Who in Hollywood. Alles Juden!"

64. Hanisch, *Charlie Chaplin. Über ihn lach(t) en Millionen*, 1974, 118. Michael Hanisch, "Nicht mehr zum Lachen: 'Der Jude Karl Tonstein' und die Nazis" in Radevagen, *Zeitmontage*, 1989, 117.

65. Section 2, paragraph 1 of the "Zweite Verordnung zur Durchführung des Gesetzes über die Änderung von Familiennamen und Vornamen, August 17, 1938" in *RGBI* 130, August 18, 1938, 1,044.

66. Holly A. Pearse, "Charlie Chaplin: Jewish or Goyish?" in *The Jewish Quarterly* Vol. 57-2, 2010, 38–42 (40).

67. Geels, 51–57, 75, 142–149.

68. Pearse, in *The Jewish Quarterly* Vol. 57-2, 39.

69. Libby Benedict, "Charlie Chaplin" in Landmann and Rittenberg, *The Universal Jewish Encyclopedia. Volume 3*, unaltered reprints, 1948 and 1969, 112, 113.

70. *Jew Stars Over Hollywood*, ca. after June 1950, 5.

71. *Red Stars Over Hollywood*, ca. after April 1948, 2, 7.

72. Hermand, "Satire und Aufruf" in Groenewold, 34.

73. *Jew Stars Over Hollywood*, 4, 8, 9, 13.

74. See Bessie, 3–6, 8, 190, 191, 230, 231, 246, 249–253. On the Hollywood Ten, see also Schatz, *Boom and Bust*, 1997, 307–313.

75. FBI files, Charlie Chaplin, dossier, May 4, 1944, comprising 433 pages. The first Chaplin dossier is dated August 14, 1922.

76. Thus, contrary to Weissberg, 47, who claims sweepingly that the FBI "gave Chaplin's file a catchy code word: Israel Thonstein." Her assertion suggests the false conclusion that Chaplin's FBI files were consistently kept under this "code word."

77. FBI files, Charlie Chaplin, report of March 5, 1947, and report with illegible date along with receipt stamp of April 19, 1947 (13: reference to Chaplin's alleged Jewish accent). See on Ulm, 39. Mellen, *Modern Times*, 2006, 73, probably inadvertently gives Chaplin's allegedly Jewish last name as "Thornstein" and claims that part of the tactics of the FBI's fight against Chaplin was to portray him as a Jew.

78. FBI files, Charlie Chaplin, alias names at head of October 31, and November 6, 1952, dossiers. "Israel Thonstein" was not used throughout.

79. See *Charlie Chaplin—Die Schweizer Jahre*, 2002 Swiss TV documentary by Beat Hirt and Felice Zenoni.

80. *B'rith Messenger* (Los Angeles) 43, October 1964, 26: "World Press. Chaplin's Origin."

81. Schoeps, *Neues Lexikon des Judentums*, 1992, 92.

82. McCabe, *Charlie Chaplin*, 1992, 2, 200.

83. Schoeps, *Neues Lexikon des Judentums*, 2000, 97.

84. Jim Hoberman, "Der erste 'jüdische' Superstar" in Stratenwerth and Simon, *Pioniere in Celluloid*, 2004, 121.

85. Pearse in *The Jewish Quarterly* Vol. 57-2, 39.

86. James Jordan, "A Wandering Jew: Writing Jews and Jewishness on British Television" in *European Judaism* Vol. 47-2 (Autumn 2014), 50–58 (57).

87. *Chicago Tribune* (Early Edition, no No.), April 20, 2014 ("Printer's Row"), 10, 11: "Body of Evidence" by Kevin Nance.

88. *VB* 57, July 19, 1922, 1. See on this Fest, *Hitler*, 2006/2007, 207.

89. "Gesetz betreffend die Verfassung des Deutschen Reiches, April 16, 1871" (Law concerning the Constitution of the German Reich), in *RGBI* 16, April 20, 1871, 63 (part II, article 3, 65).

90. Berg, *Antisemiten-Brevier*, 1883. Frey (= Theodor Frtisch), *Antisemiten-Katechismus*, 1887.

91. von Müffling, *Wegbereiter und Vorkämpfer des neuen Deutschlands*, 1933, 37.

92. On Fritsch, see Elisabeth Albains, "Anleitung zum Hass. Theodor Fritschs antisemitisches Geschichtsbild" in Bergmann and Sieg, *Antisemitische Geschichtsbilder*, 2009, 167–191.

93. Stille, *Kampf gegen das Judenthum*, 1891, 233–249, and 8th edition (ca. 1912), 23, 141, 215. For comparisons between Stille's book and the program of the NSDAP, see Döscher, *Kampf gegen das Judenthum: Gustav Stille (1845–1920)*, 2008, 56, 87–114.

94. Hitler, *Mein Kampf*, two volumes in one. Unabridged edition, 355th–359th edition, 1938.

95. For a summary of Hitler's statements, with further references, see Fest, 343, 344.

Chapter 2

1. "Verordnung über das Verbot der Einfuhr entbehrlicher Gegenstände, April 6, 1916" in *RGBI* 31, February 25, 1916, 111. See on this *LBB* 9, March 4, 1916, 9, 10, 12, 15, 18: "Die Filmeinfuhr verboten!"

2. "Bekanntmachung über die Regelung der Einfuhr, January 16, 1917," as well as the official announcement of this decree, in *RGBI* 8, January 16, 1917, 41–44.

3. "Übergangsgesetz, March 4, 1919" in *RGBl* 55, March 7, 1919, 285, 286.

4. "Ausführungsbestimmungen [Implementing Regulations], April 8, 1920" to the "Verordnung über die Außenhandelskontrolle [Decree on Foreign Trade Control], December 20, 1919" in *RGBl* 73, April 14, 1920, 500–504.

5. *FK* 61, March 13, 1931, 3: "Chaplin in Alt-Berlin."

6. Aping, *Charlie Chaplin in Deutschland*, 2014, 20–23.

7. Kevin Brownlow, "Chaplin and World War I," charliechaplin.com.

8. *FK* 202, August 30, 1921, 2: "Chaplin redivivus."

9. *Prager Tagblatt* 169, July 22, 1922, 2: "Der berühmteste Mann der Welt" by Kurt Tucholsky.

10. Aping, *Charlie Chaplin in Deutschland*, 23–28, 31–37, 44, 46–90, 259–261.

11. "Lichtspielgesetz, May 12, 1920" in *RGBI*

107, May 15, 1920, 953–958. "Ausführungsverordnung [Implementing Decree], June 16, 1920" to "Lichtspielgesetz, May 12, 1920" in *RGBl* 136, June 18, 1920, 1,213–1,217.

12. *Der deutsche Film in Wort und Bild* 43, October 28, 1921, 24.

13. *Der deutsche Film in Wort und Bild* 3, January 21, 1922, 4: "Münchener Erstaufführungen. *Chaplin bei der Feuerwehr.*"

14. *SFZ* 5, December 8, 1922, 3: "Kleine Riesen-Geschmacklosigkeiten. Ein Kapitel zur Reklame der Kinos" (Little giant Tastelessness. A Chapter on Cinema Advertising) by Karl Lüthge. According to the report, the comedy was part of the supporting program.

15. Aping, *Charlie Chaplin in Deutschland*, 250–253.

16. For the numerous announcements since 1921, see, for example, *LBB* 17, April 23, 1921, 39: "Was das Ausland meldet." *Kinematograph* 854, July 1, 1923, 11: "Kleines Notizbuch."

17. For the numerous reviews, see, for example, *Film* 47, November 25, 1923, 17, by Th. *Die Weltbühne* 49, December 26, 1923, 564, by Peter Panther (Kurt Tucholsky).

18. *Münchner Neueste Nachrichten* 346, December 21, 1923, 4: "Der neue Film."

19. *VB* 88, October 7, 1920, 5: "Judentum und Bolschewismus sind eins."

20. Hitler, 751.

21. *VB* 89, October 10, 1920, 2: "Auf dem Weg zum jüdischen Filmmonopol."

22. *VB* 215, September 17, 1926, 4: "Filmjuden."

23. *VB* (B) 76, April 2, 1927, 6: "Ufa und jüdisches Finanzkapital."

24. *VB* (B) 139, June 21, 1927, 2: "Die Film-Verjudung."

25. *VB* (B) 173, July 30, 1927, 4: "Jüdische Finanzdiktatur beim Film."

26. *VB* (B) 39, February 15, 1929, 4, Münchener Beobachter: "Jüdische Filmdiktatur in Amerika und England."

27. On this, see Schmitz-Berning, *Vokabular des Nationalsozialismus*, 2007, 598, 599.

28. Köhler, *Kunstanschauung und Kunstkritik in der nationalsozialistischen Presse*, 1937, 25.

29. Köhler, 20.

30. On Brachvogel, see, for example, *RFB* 29, July 23, 1927, 41: "H.U. Brachvogel scheidet aus der Emelka aus." *LBB* 51, March 1, 1932, 1: "Man hört ..."

31. *Der deutsche Film in Wort und Bild* 45, November 11, 1921, 15, 16: "Chaplin-Programm in München aus den drei Kurzfilmen" by Josef Aubinger.

32. *Deutsche Lichtspiel-Zeitung* and *Der deutsche Film in Wort und Bild* did not cover *Shoulder Arms*. The *München-Ausburger Abendzeitung*, which has been examined for the period from July 1921 to April 1922, also did not mention a Chaplin film that was considered Germanophobe.

33. "Stadtanzeiger Augsburg" in *München-Augsburger Abendzeitung* (M) 504, December 1, 1921, 6: "Luitpold-Lichtspiele ad for *Im Rausche der Macht* with *Die Chaplinquelle.*" *München-*

Augsburger Abendzeitung (M) 511, December 6, 1921, 10: "Der Film der Woche. *Im Rausche der Macht.*" *München-Augsburger Abendzeitung* (M) 518, December 10, 1921, 7: Luitpold-Lichtspiele ad for *Sappho* with *Chaplin läuft Rollschuh*. *München-Augsburger Abendzeitung* (M) 521, December 12, 1921, 10: "Der Film der Woche. *Sappho.*"

34. *The Seattle Star* (WA) 207, October 28, 1918, 9: "Balmy Benny—Benny Is Quite an Elaborate Dreamer" by Gene Ahern.

35. *Variety*, October 25, 1918: "Chaplin's *Shoulder Arm*" by Sime. Reprinted in *Variety's Film Reviews*. *Volume 1*, 1983, non-paginated.

36. *NYT* 22, 185, October 21, 1918, 15: "Chaplin as Soldier Drops Old Disguise." *NYT* 23, 550, July 17, 1922, 16: "The Screen."

37. Benz, Mihok, and Bergmann, *Handbuch des Antisemitismus Band 5*, 2012, 191–193 ("Deutschnationale Volkspartei" entry by Werner Bergmann).

38. On Hugenberg and the Ufa, see Kreimeier, *Die Ufa-Story*, 1992, 190–205, 258–267. Spiker, *Film und Kapital*, 1975, 172, 173. On Hugenberg, see also Benz and Graml, 155, 156, entry by Wolfram Selig.

39. Kaiser Theater ad in *Bremer Nachrichten* 317, November 16, 1921, 14 (4th Supplement, 2), and 319, November 18, 1921, 12 (3rd Supplement, 2). Review in *Bremer Nachrichten* 328, November 27, 1921, 11 (3rd Supplement, 3): "Aus den Lichtspieltheatern" by O.

40. *Fridericus* 10, 2nd March issue 1931, 5 (1st Supplement, 1): "Viel Lärm um nichts! 'Chaplin nähert sich Berlin.'"

41. The *Hamburger Warte* has been checked for the period from August 1921 through February 1922.

42. *Bremer Nachrichten* 340, December 9, 1921, 9 (3rd Supplement, 1): "Nationale Würde auch im Film!" by Fritz von Holz.

43. *Bremer Nachrichten* have been checked for the period from mid–August 1921 through the end of March 1922.

44. *BBZ* (M) 583, December 18, 1921, 11: "Chaplins wahres Gesicht."

45. Klee, *Personenlexikon zum Dritten Reich*, 2016, 172.

46. *BBZ* (M) 257, June 1926, 1, 2: "Die Zusammenschließung der Rechtsbewegung" by Valentinus.

47. On German responsibility for the beginning of World War I, see Kautsky, *Wie der Weltkrieg entstand*, 1919, 135. By the same author, *Delbrueck und Wilhelm II*, 1920. See also *Die Weltbühne* 1, January 1, 1920, 1–7: "Wilhelm und Bethmann" by Heinrich Ströbel.

48. Dr. R. (Richard) Jügler, "Die Politik der *BBZ*. 75 im Dienst am Vaterland" in *75 Jahre BBZ*, 1930, 55–64 (63, 64).

49. *LBB* 46, November 12, 1921, 26: "Was das Ausland meldet."

50. *Variety* 11, November 4, 1921, 42: "News of the Films."

51. See Lyons, *Charles Chaplin*, 1979, 27

(October 30 and December 20, 1921, entries in "A Chronological Biography"). *The Film Daily* 38, November 14, 1927, 6: "Chaplin Retrial Opens." According to *The Film Daily*, the jury could not agree on Chaplin's conviction in the first round of the trial.

52. *LBB* 71, June 21, 1924, 21: "Eigener amerikanischer Kabeldienst der L.B.B."

53. Transcripts of hearings held May 4–15, 1927, before Judge William Bondy and jury, Chaplin beginning on 334 in Bologna, no file No. See also report in *Photoplay Magazine* 3, August 1924, 57, 90. Afterward Chaplin made similar comments to his half-brother Syd.

54. *Film-Hölle* 4, April 1922, 9, 10: "Auch Charlie Chaplin hetzt gegen Deutschland?"

55. This newspaper could not be located in Germany, Poland or Russia. Eydtkuhnen is now the Russian city of Chernyshevskoye. In the minor holdings of the Prussian State Archives in Königsberg, which remained in German possession after the end of World War II, the newspaper is not mentioned: Forstreuter, *Das Preußische Staatsarchiv in Königsberg*, 1955.

56. *LBB* 30, July 23, 1921, 48: "Was das Ausland meldet."

57. See Aping, *Charlie Chaplin in Deutschland*, 84–90.

58. *Westdeutsche Film-Zeitung* 16, April 7, 1922, 234: "Charlie Chaplin als Deutschenfresser."

59. On Lydor, see *RFB* 30, July 1928, 25: "'Boykott,' ein neues Filmmanuskript von Waldemar Lydor." *RFB* 38, September 22, 1928, 27: "Aus der Industrie." *Der deutsche Film 1943/44. Kleines Film-Handbuch für die deutsche Presse*, ca. 1943, 249.

60. *FK* 91, April 18, 1925, 18 (4th Supplement, 2): "Mein erster Chaplinfilm."

61. Karney, *Cinema Year By Year 1894–2005*, 2005, 134.

62. Delluc, *Charlot*, 1921. See Timothy J. Lyons, "An Introduction to the Literature on Chaplin" in *Journal of the University Film Association* Vol. 31–1 (Winter 1979), 3–10 (5, 6).

63. Vogel Productions, Inc.: December 1931 overview of worldwide sales of *Shoulder Arms* since 1918. In Bologna, ch15548002.

64. von Ulm, 290. Sabine Hake, "Chaplin Reception in Weimar Germany" in *New German Critique* 51 (Special Issue on Weimar Mass Culture), Fall 1990, 87–111 (89, note 8). Louvish, *Chaplin: The Tramp's Odyssey*, 2009, 208.

65. The FPS approved *Das Gewehr über* on September 25, 1925 (file 11,356) and *Charlie im Schützengraben* on August 21, 1929 (file 23,226). Both are German movies and do not have anything to do with Chaplin.

66. Premiere on September 19, 1957, at the Stuttgart Metropol Cinema: *Filmblätter* 46, November 15, 1957, 1,327, 1,328. Freiwillige Selbstkontrolle der Filmwirtschaft (Voluntary Self-Regulation of the Film Industry) release 14,653, June 25 and August 29, 1957. The program consisted of *The Pilgrim*, *A Day's Pleasure* and *Shoulder Arms*.

67. *ff dabei* 10/1981 (program week March 2–8, 1981), 28, 29.

68. In chronological order of U.S. premieres. Harold Lloyd: *The Freshman* (September 20, 1925). Buster Keaton: *Go West* (November 23, 1925). Larry Semon: *The Perfect Clown* (December 15, 1925). Harry Langdon: *Tramp, Tramp, Tramp* (March 21, 1926).

69. Kerr, *The Silent Clowns*, 1980, 246.

70. For example, *LBB* 74, May 15, 1925, 3: "Der neue Chaplin-Film." *LBB* 94, June 8, 1925, 3: "Der neue Chaplinfilm fertiggestellt." 128, July 17, 1925, 1: "Chaplin kommt—!" *LBB* 156, August 19, 1925, 2: "Chaplin kommt nach Berlin."

71. *RFB* 34, August 22, 1925, 29: "Charlie kommt nach Berlin." *FJ* 35, August 27, 1925, 2: "Ifa and United Artists." *LBB* 166, August 31, 1925, 1, 2: "Der neue Chaplin-Film."

72. *LBB* 124, July 13, 1925, 2: "United Artists verleiht."

73. *LBB* 158, August 21, 1925, 2: "Ifa-United Artists perfekt?" *LBB* 159, August 22, 1925, 11: "United Artists-Ifa. Amerikanisches Geld in einem deutschen Verleih."

74. On Hasenclever, see Benz and Graml, 127, entry by Margit Ketterle.

75. *8-Uhr* 237, October 9, 1925, 8: "Charlies Geheimnis" by Walter Hasenclever.

76. FPS, October 20, 1925, file 11,549 (approved length: 2,423 meters).

77. *FK* 13, January 15, 1926, 2: "Chaplin vor der Zensur." Landsberg-Yorck, *Klatsch, Ruhm und kleine Feuer*, 1963, 21, claims to have translated the intertitles of *The Gold Rush* into German. Tunnat, *Karl Vollmoeller*, 2019, 307.

78. Tunnat, *Karl Vollmoeller*, 307.

79. FPS, October 30, 1925, file 11,646 (reduced length: 2,346 meters). December 22, 1925, file 12,030 (ban).

80. FPS, December 22, 1925, file 12,030.

81. Reasons according to Section 1, paragraph 2, second sentence, and Section 3, paragraph 2, of the "Lichtspielgesetz, May 12, 1920" in *RGBI* 107, May 15, 1920, 953, 954.

82. *LBB* 12, January 15, 1926, 1: "Chaplin vor der Zensur."

83. FOPS, January 9, 1926, file O.948.25 (approved length: 2,324.60 meters).

84. *LBB* 37, February 13, 1926, 3, 6: Ifa-Film/United Artists ad for *Goldrausch*.

85. For the premiere frame, see *LBB* 39, February 16, 1926, 3: "Curt Bois im Capitol" (announcement). *LBB* 42, February 19, 1926, 1, 2: "*Goldrausch*" by Dr. M-l. (Dr. Georg Victor Mendel). German-Jewish actor Curt Bois spoke a prologue to it, written by the later GDR film author Karl Schnog, which was considered "weaker."

86. From the abundance of reactions, see, for example, *Film* 8, February 21, 1926, 19: "*Goldrausch*" by S-r. (Albert Schneider). *FK* 43, February 19, 1926, 2: "*Goldrausch*" by Willy Haas. *FZ*, November 6, 1926: "*Goldrausch*" by Siegfried Kracauer in Kracauer, *Werke Band 6.1*, 2004, 269, 270. *Das Tagebuch* 9, February 27, 1926, 337–339:

"Goldsucher Chaplin" by Alfred Polgar. *Vossische Zeitung* 44, February 20, 1926 (1st Supplement, 1, 2): "Chaplins Schuh" by gol.

87. On Siemsen, see Föster, *Hans Siemsen. Schriften*, 1986, 7–12. Stefan Berkholz, "Mit schluchzendem Herzen lächeln..." in Radevagen, 95–99. Brigitte Bruns, "Der Chronist des Augenblicks" in Aurich, Bruns, and Jacobsen, *Hans Siemsen*, 2012, 11–41.

88. *Die Weltbühne* 10, March 9, 1926, 390–392: "*Goldrausch*" by Hans Siemsen.

89. *Vorwärts* (S) 87, February 21, 1926 (Supplement "Aus der Film-Welt," 1): "Charlie Chaplin in *Goldrausch*" by D.

90. *Die Rote Fahne* 44, February 21, 1926 (3rd Supplement "Feuilleton der *Roten Fahne*," 1): "*Goldrausch*" von Hilde Kr. (Kramer).

91. *Illustrierter FK* 393: *Goldrausch*.

92. *FK* 272, November 19, 1925, 1: "Maximilian Harden über den Film" by H. (Hans Tasiemka). On Harden, see Benz and Graml, 124, 125, entry by Manfred Vasold.

93. *RFB* 48, November 28, 1925, 24: "Max Reinhardt und amerikanische Filme." On Reinhardt, see Benz and Graml, 266, 267, entry by Gerhard Hay.

94. *VB* (B) 194, November 14, 1925, 2: "*Charleys Tante.*"

95. On Rosenberg, see further Weiß, *Personenlexikon 1933–1945*, 2003, 385–387, entry by Froe (Dr. Elke Fröhlich-Broszat).

96. On Stolzing-Czerny, who died in July 1942, see *Film* 31, August 1, 1942, 10: "Zum Tode von Josef Stolzing-Czerny."

97. *SFZ* 34, August 20, 1926, 3: "*Goldrausch*" by Dr. R.P. (Dr. René Prevôt).

98. On this, see Alarich Seidler, introduction to *Der Nichtseßhafte Mensch. Ein Beitrag zur Neugestaltung der Raum- und Menschenordnung im Großdeutschen Reich* (The Non-Sedentary. A contribution to the reorganization Greater German Reich), 1938, 13, with the essays Wilhelm Polligkeit, "Die Haltung der Volksgemeinschaft gegenüber dem nichtseßhaften Mensch," 45, and Robert Ritter, "Zigeuner und Landfahrer," 86.

99. *Die Neue Weltbühne* (Prague) 21, May 23, 1935, 664: "Ein Fall Chaplin?" by Hermann Britt (Heinz Pol = Heinz Pollack).

100. *VB* (B) 68, March 24, 1926, 2 (Section "unter dem Strich" [below the line]): "Der mystisch gewordene Charlie Chaplin" by J.St-g (Josef Stolzing-Czerny).

101. On Jordan, see Weiß, 245, 246, entry by We (Hermann Weiß).

102. *Der Weltkampf*, May 1926, 235–237: "Charlie Chaplins Geheimnis" by Rudolf Jordan.

103. Siemsen, *Charlie Chaplin*, 1924. Essays from *Die Weltbühne*: 11, March 11, 1920, 336–339: "Zwei Postkarten und ein Buch" (Two Postcards and a Book) and the five-part article series in 40, October 5, 1922, 367, 368: "Chaplin I." 41, October 12, 1922, 385–387: "Chaplin II. Der Komödiendichter" (The Comedy Poet). 42, October 19, 1922, 415, 416: "Chaplin III. Der Politiker" (The Politician).

43, October 26, 1922, 447, 448: "Chaplin IV. Der Schauspieler" (The Actor). 44, November 2, 1922, 473, 474: "Chaplin V. Der Regisseur" (The Director).

104. Siemsen, 25.

105. Kraus, *Die Dritte Walpurgisnacht*, 1967.

106. Klemperer, *LTI. Notizbuch eines Philologen*, 2020, 29, 30, 243–245.

107. For example, *Stürmer* 27, July 1927, 3.

108. *Jüdische Revue* (Prague), December 1937, 705, 708: "Der ewige Jude und der Gegengeist" by Observer.

109. Hahn and Wagenlehner*Lieber Stürmer! Leserbriefe an das NS-Kampfblatt 1924 bis 1945*, 1978.

110. On Streicher, see Weiß, 450, 451, entry by We (Hermann Weiß).

111. On Fips and Rupprecht, see Klee, *Das Kulturlexikon zum Dritten Reich*, 2007, 154.

112. *Stürmer* 42, October 1926, 4: "Charlie Chaplin der Musterjude."

113. *Munzinger Internationales Biographisches Archiv*, 05/1950, January 23, 1950, Munzinger-Archiv GmbH, Ravensburg, entry on Hermann Esser. See also Weiß, 113, 114, entry by JR (Dr. Jana Richter).

114. See also Bering, *Der Name als Stigma*, 1992, 289, 290.

115. *VB* (B) 245, October 22, 1926, 2: "Der Idealist."

116. *FK* 174, July 28, 1926, 1: "Chaplin als Christus."

117. Robinson, 395.

118. *BT* (E) 39, January 24, 1927, 2: "Charlie Chaplin."

119. Robinson, 735. *FK* 275, November 21, 1924, 3: "Filmstars als Steuerzahler."

120. *FJ* 8, February 21, 1926, 19: "*Goldrausch*" by S-r. (Albert Schneider). *FJ* 14, April 1, 1926, 3: "Da capo."

121. Full-page ad, for example, in *Film* 13, February 28, 1926, 3.

122. *FJ* 18, April 29, 1926, 6: "Wochenspielplan Groß-Hamburger Lichtspielhäuser." See further in the *FJ* the columns "Die Spielwoche und Wochenspielplan Groß-Hamburger Lichtspielhäuser" in 20, May 14, 1926, 6, 7. *FJ* 21, May 21, 1926, 5, 6. *FJ* 22, May 27, 1926, 6, 7.

123. "Wochenspielplan Groß-Hamburger Lichtspielhäuser" in *FJ* 23, June 3, 1926, 6, 7. *FJ* 24, June 11, 1926, 10.

124. *SFZ* 34, August 20, 1926, 3: "*Goldrausch*" by Dr. R. (Dr. René Prevôt).

125. *FK* 166, July 19, 1926, 2: "Die deutschen Kinos im Hochsommer."

126. Guttmann, *Über die Nachfrage auf dem Filmmarkt in Deutschland*, 1927, 12.

127. Guttmann, 12, 16, 19, 28–30, 32, 38, 39.

128. Guttmann, 7.

129. Guttmann, 42.

130. *FK* 185, August 10, 1926, 2: "*Goldrausch* im Ozean."

131. *FJ* 40, October 4, 1926, 3: "Chaplin kommt nach Berlin."

132. Named after its head Felix Lampe. On

the Committee, see *RFB* 41, October 13, 1928, 22: "Film-Berlin/III. Professor Lampes Bildstelle" by Bernd Neumann.

133. *FK* 143, June 18, 1927, 6: United Artists Filmverleih G.m.b.H. ad for *Goldrausch*.

134. Quoted from a report in the *Hessischer Volksfreund*, in *FK* 51, February 28, 1928, 3: "S.P.D. gegen *Goldrausch*."

135. *FK* 51, February 28, 1928, 3: "S.P.D. gegen *Goldrausch*."

136. *FK* 119, May 21, 1927, 1: "Der Ertrag des *Goldrausch*."

137. Full-page ad, for example, in *DFZ* 26, June 24, 1927, 9. *Film* 12, July 1, 1927, 7.

138. *FJ* 24, June 17, 1927, 4: "Wochenspielplan Groß-Hamburger Lichtspielhäuser." *FJ* 25, June 24, 1927, 4: "Chaplin als Barbier. Schauburg at Millerntor."

139. *Hamburger Echo* 167, June 19, 1927: "Film" and sections "Hamburg. Die Spielwoche und Wochenspielplan Groß-Hamburger Lichtspielhäuser" in *FJ* 31, August 5, 1927, 17, 20. *FJ* 31, July 29, 1928, 9, 10 (2nd Supplement, 1, 2). *FJ* 35, August 26, 1928, 12, 14 (3rd Supplement, 2). *FJ* 24, June 16, 1929, 7, 8. *FJ* 36, September 8, 1929, 7, 8.

140. *FJ* (Ma) 14, April 3, 1932, 5 (1st Supplement, 1): "*Goldrausch*—zum letzten Male?" by -d-.

141. *LBB* 191, August 11, 1931, 2: "Nochmals *Goldrausch* in der Kamera." *FK* 73, March 26, 1932, 5 (2nd Supplement, 1): "*Goldrausch*." *LBB* 71, March 24, 1932, 2: "Abschied von *Goldrausch*. Im Mozartsaal mit Orchester." *LBB* 76, April 1, 1932, 4: "Die Filmbranche erzählt sich …"

142. *LBB* 69, March 21, 1933, 2: "Nachwort zum Chaplin-Zyklus der Degeto."

Chapter 3

1. German premieres at Berlin's Capitol on March 25, 1926, and May 20, 1926, respectively, *FK* 73, March 1926, 2: "*Die Nächte einer schönen Frau*" by Willy Haas, and *FK* 117, May 21, 1926, 2: "*Ein Hundeleben*."

2. *LBB* 38, April 3, 1925, 1: "Chaplins Ehesorgen."

3. *FJ* 3, January 21, 1927, 1: "Der Krach um Chaplin."

4. *FJ* 7, February 18, 1927, 1: "Um Charlie Chaplin."

5. *LBB* 253, October 23, 1926, 28: "Was das Ausland meldet."

6. *Braunschweiger Landeszeitung*, January 9, 1927: "Nervenzusammenbruch Chaplins." In Filmuniversität Babelsberg KONRAD WOLF. *BT* (E) 39, January 24, 1927, 2: "Charlie Chaplin."

7. *FJ* 8, February 25, 1927, 1: "Alle für Chaplin."

8. All movie scandals of that period involved employees of Famous Players-Lasky (Paramount)—Wallace Reid, Mary Miles Minter, etc.

9. Massa, *Rediscovering Roscoe*, 2020, 391–400, 445–481, 563–584.

10. Robinson, 399.

11. *RFB* 32, February 1927, 32: "Amerikanische Theaterbesitzer für Charlie Chaplin." *Kinematograph* 1,044, February 20, 1927, 24: "Die amerikanischen Theaterbesitzer für Chaplin."

12. *Die deutsche Republik* 20, February 17, 1928, 641: "Chaplin und Schinderhannes" by Gong.

13. For example, *Aachener Volksfreund*, February 24, 1927: "Österreichische Juristen an Chaplin." *Neue Leipziger Zeitung*, February 27, 1927: "Ein Aufruf für Charlie Chaplin." *FZ*, March 16, 1927: "Chaplins zweite Ehe und ihr Ende" by Norbert Borg. In Filmuniversität Babelsberg KONRAD WOLF.

14. *RFB* 2, January 15, 1927, 39: "Vor einem Chaplin-Boykott?" by c-c.

15. *FJ* 3, January 21, 1927, 1: "Der Krach um Chaplin." *FJ* 8, February 25, 1927, 1: "Alle für Chaplin."

16. *Charlie Chaplin, der Beklagte*, 1927.

17. *FK* 43, February 19, 1927, 5 (1st Supplement, 1): "Chaplins Kunst bleibt unberührt."

18. *Berliner Illustrierte Zeitung*, July 19, 1927: "'D-5228,' Charlie Chaplins tragischster Film." In Filmuniversität Babelsberg KONRAD WOLF.

19. *VB* (B) 37, February 15, 1927, 2: "Der Eheskandal Charlie Chaplins. Der gestürzte König" by Pix.

20. *VB* (B) 64, March 18, 1927, 2: "Zum Eheskandal Charlie Chaplins."

21. *Der Weltkampf*, March 1927, 135, 136: "Goldgräbereien."

22. *Prager Tagblatt* 111, May 11, 1927, 3: "Chaplin als Privatmensch" by Landstreicher (Hobo) Jim Tully.

23. *Der Weltkampf*, June 1927, 276, 277: "Chaplin in Gethsemane."

24. Rosenberg, *Der Sumpf*, 1930, 213, 214.

25. *Der Weltkampf*, January 1928, 41: "Chaplin, der liebe Jesus." *Hannoverscher Kurier* 209/1927 quoted after Rosenberg.

26. *Stürmer* 27, July 1927, 3: "Charlie Chaplin. Der jüdische Schweinehund."

27. Robinson, 402, 735.

28. Issues from August, 23 1927: *Der Berliner Westen*: "Charlie Chaplin." *Deutsche Zeitung*: "Chaplin ist 'frei.'" *Spandauer Zeitung*: "Charlie Chaplin geschieden." In Filmuniversität Babelsberg KONRAD WOLF.

29. *FK* 292, December 10, 1927, 6 (1st Supplement, 2): "Chaplin will billiger und schneller drehen."

30. *Neue Film Hölle* 6/1929, 15.

31. *Neue Film Hölle* 6/1929, 11.

32. *Deutsche Film-Tribüne* 3, July 1927, 2: "Film-Reklame."

33. *Deutsche Film-Tribüne* 4, August 9, 1927 (Supplement, 2): "Chaplins Gegenklage."

34. Sattig, 45, 46.

35. *Der Deutsche Film* 4, October 1936, 117, 118: "Die Filmarbeit der NSDAP" by Curt Belling.

36. With Strachwitz, *Film in Staat und Partei*, 1936. With Schütze, *Film in der Hitlerjugend*, ca. 1937. As sole author, *Film im Dienste der Partei*, 1937.

37. Neumann, Belling, and Betz, *Film-"Kunst," Film-Kohn, Film-Korruption*, 1937.

38. *LBB* 19, January 21, 1928, 22, 29: "Chaplins Rekorderfolg" and "Was das Ausland meldet." *LBB* 27, January 31, 1928, 2: "Chaplins *Zirkus* in Wien." *LBB* 37, 11 February 1928, 14: "Wiener Groß-Erfolg." *LBB* 67, March 17, 1928, 29: "*Zirkus* in Danzig." *LBB* 67, March 17, 1928, 30: "Was das Ausland meldet."

39. United-Artists-Filmverleih GmbH ad for *Zirkus*, in *LBB* 73, March 24, 1928, 5. *LBB* 85, April 5, 1928, 25. *LBB* 134, June 6, 1929, 2: "Chaplins *Zirkus*." *FK* 34, February 7, 1929, 2: "Armer Chaplin!"

40. *RFB* 6, February 11, 1928, 36: "Filmallerlei."

41. *FK* 40, February 15, 1928, 1: "United-Artists-Filme in Ufa-Theatern." *FK* 61, March 10, 1928, 1: "Chaplins Erfolg in Deutschland. Die Tätigkeit der United Artists—Der individuelle Film setzt sich durch." *FK* 66, March 16, 1928, 2: "*Zirkus* in Danzig." *FK* 67, March 17, 1928, 1: "Charlie Chaplins *Zirkus*-Erfolg in Stuttgart!"

42. *FK* 116/117, May 16, 1928, 1: "Das Ergebnis der Abstimmung."

43. *FK* 92, April 18, 1929, 4 (1st Supplement, 2): "Was Stummfilme brachten."

44. *LBB* 1, January 2, 1929, 1: "Der beste Film des Jahres 1928." *LBB* 37, February 13, 1929, 1: "Die 10 besten Filme." *LBB* 153, July 2, 1932, 4 (Supplement, 2): "Was Stummfilme brachten."

45. *Film* (Special Edition "Kritiken der Woche"), September 10, 1927, 3: masthead.

46. *Film* 26, September 15, 1926, 31: "*Charlie haut sich durchs Leben.*"

47. *Film* (Special Edition "Kritiken der Woche"), February 11, 1928, 1: "*Zirkus* im Capitol" by Betz (Hans-Walther Betz). *FK* 34, February 8, 1928, 2, 3: "Chaplins *Cirkus* [sic]" by Willy Haas.

48. *Moving Picture World* Vol. 85–3, March 19, 1927, 204, 205: "Theaters are cleaning up with *Shoulder Arms*." *Moving Picture World* Vol. 85–8, April 23, 1927, 684: Pathépictures full-page ad for the re-issue of *Shoulder Arms*. *Moving Picture World* Vol. 87–3, July 16, 1927, 142: Pathépictures full-page ad for the re-issue of *Sunnyside*.

49. Other papers of the Hugenberg Group did not comment on *Shoulder Arms*: for example, *Der Montag* (Supplement, "Film-Echo"), special weekly edition of *Berliner Lokal-Anzeiger*, *Der Tag* and the trade journal *Kinematograph*.

50. *Berliner Nachtausgabe* 70, March 24, 1927, 1: "Chaplin als Deutschenfeind! Wieder ein Hetzfilm in Amerika. Ablenkung von seinem Eheskandal?"

51. *B.Z.* 82, March 25, 1927, 16 (*"Film B.Z.,"* 1): "Chaplin als Deutschenfeind. Ein verkannter Kriegsfilm" by K.

52. *Die Weltbühne* 13, March 29, 1927, 522: "Film-Patriot" by Kurt Tucholsky (?).

53. *Hamburger Echo* 92, April 3, 1927, 6, 7 (Supplement, 2, 3): "Film. Chaplin als Deutschenfeind."

54. *BBZ* (M) 143, March 26, 1927, 4: "Wieder ein Hetzfilm in Amerika." For the recut of the film, see Vasey, *The World According to Hollywood, 1918–1939*, 1997, 54.

55. *VB* (B) 70, March 26, 1927, 1: "Wieder ein Hetzfilm in Amerika. Schwacher deutscher Protest."

56. *RFB* 13, April 2, 1927, 36: "*Gewehr über*" by Waldemar Lydor.

57. *LBB* 8, January 11, 1926, 4: "Charlie Chaplin."

58. Letter dated 15 September 1926. In BArch RMI.

59. Letter dated September 18, 1926. In BArch RMI.

60. Vogel Productions, Inc., overview of worldwide sales of *Shoulder Arms* for the period October 11, 1918, to February 16, 1932. In Bologna, ch15548002.

61. Vogel Productions, Inc., overview cited above asserts its investigations are "as accurate as possible." Regarding Holland (Netherlands), it reads "censored." Possibly the film has been banned there. For Germany and Austria-Hungary, the entry is reduced to dotted lines. After that the film has not been screened there. In Bologna, ch15548003. Due to the 1917 Russian Revolution, films from the capitalist United States were not screened in the Soviet Union.

62. *LBB* 81, April 5, 1927, 4: "Deutschfeindlicher Film in Kopenhagen." *LBB* 87, April 12, 1927, 2: "Auch Dänemark zeigt Hetzfilme."

63. *Die Weltbühne* 23, June 7, 1927, 899: "Chaplin in Kopenhagen" by Peter Panther (Kurt Tucholsky).

64. *Literarische Welt* 41, October 14, 1927, 11: "Chaplins Kriegsfilm" by Hans Sochaczewer. Sochaczewer was not raised in the Jewish faith. He later called himself José Orabuena.

65. *Sozialistische Bildung* No. 3, March 1930, 88: "Amerikanische Filme."

66. *La Cinéma d' Alsace et de Lorraine/Elsass-lothringische Filmzeitung* 3, March 1927, 3: Ad for four Chaplin films.

67. *LBB* No. 243, October 11, 1927, 2: "Die französischen Kriegsfilme. Kassensturm im Cinéma Max Linder. *Charlie als Soldat.*"

68. See *Arbeiterbühne und Film* 6, June 1931, 23, 24: "Filmeindrücke in Paris" by Kurt Kersten.

69. *RFB* 2, January 14, 1928, 34: "Chaplin in der Schweiz."

70. *Die Volksbühne* 6, September 1928, 24–28 (28): "Chaplin fängt den deutschen Kaiser" by Erich Gottgetreu.

71. *LBB* 107, May 5, 1927, 1: "Ein neuer Prozess gegen Chaplin."

72. *Goslarsche Zeitung*, May 20, 1927: "'Zeuge' Chaplin spielt im Gerichtssaal Groteske." In Filmuniversität Babelsberg KONRAD WOLF.

73. *LBB* 284, November 28, 1927, 2: "Chaplin gewinnt Plagiats-Prozess."

74. See Lyons, 27 (entries October 30 and December 20, 1921).

75. *LBB* 289, December 3, 1927, 26: "Was das Ausland meldet."

76. *The Film Daily* 40, November 16, 1927, 1, 8: "Burkan Calls Plagiarism Suit Outcome Significant."

77. Buchner, *Im Banne des Film*, 1927, 21–24.

78. *Die Neue Bücherschau* 4, April 1928, 201, 202: "Vor Charlie Chaplin" by Lu Märten. 202–205: "Von Charlie Chaplin bis Wsewold Illarionowitsch Pudowkin" by Hans Georg Brenner.

79. Buchner, 24–26. Buchner quoted from Siemsen, *Charlie Chaplin*, 11–13, 25.

80. Buchner, 107.

81. Buchner, 157.

82. Buchner, 154, 155.

83. Buchner, 81.

84. Buchner, 156, 157.

85. *Berliner Börsen-Courier* (M) 215, May 10, 1927, 6: "Chaplin II. und die andern in der Scala" by Billie (Billy) Wilder.

86. Steve Massa, "Billie Ritchie: The Man from Nowhere" in Scheide, Mehran, and Kamin, *Chaplin: The Dictator and the Tramp*, 2004, 120–122.

87. See Robinson, 225, 705 (note 45).

88. Massa, "Billie Ritchie Filmography" in Scheide, Mehran, and Kamin, *Chaplin*, 126.

89. For example, Langman, *Encyclopedia of American Film Comedy*, 1987, 502 (year of birth: 1877). Miller, *American Silent Film Comedies*, 1995, 209, 210 (year of birth: 1877, place of birth: Glasgow).

90. Asplund, *Chaplin's Films*, 1976, 24, 53.

91. See Mitchell, *The Chaplin Encyclopedia*, 1997, 141 (columns 2, 3). See also Massa, "Billie Ritchie: The Man from Nowhere" in Scheide, Mehran, and Kamin, *Chaplin*.

92. *LBB* 307, 24 December 1927, 38: "Im Banne des Vorurteils. Der Film in völkischer Beleuchtung" by da.

93. *Filmtechnik* 3, February 4, 1928, 49: "Die Literatur des Films" by a. *FJ* 20, May 13, 1928, 3: "Buchbesprechungen. *Im Banne des Films*."

94. *DFZ* 8, February 17, 1928, 3, 4: "Chaplin in *Zirkus* im Phoebus-Palast" by Dr. René Prévôt.

95. *VB* (N) 66, 7 March 1934, 5: "Mjölnir, der Zeichner des Nationalsozialismus" by Gunter d'Alquen.

96. Fröhlich, *Die Tagebücher von Joseph Goebbels, Volume 1/II*, 2005, 339, 340.

97. Charlie Chaplin, *My Trip Abroad*, 121.

98. *VB* (B) 223, September 25, 1928, 2 (section "Unter dem Strich" [Below the line]): "Chaplin über Werthauer."

99. FPS, January 14, 1929, file 21,406 (length: 1,103 meters).

100. *FK* 19, January 21, 1929, 2: "*Carmen*" by Hans Feld. *DFZ* 25, June 21, 1929, 10: "Chaplin's *Carmen* parody at the Phoebus-Palast" by Dr. P. (Dr. René Prévôt).

101. *VB* (B) 134, June 13, 1929, 4 (*Carmen*). *VB* 160, July 13, 1929, 4 (*Abenteuer*), and (B) *VB* 162, July 16, 1929, 4 (*Abenteuer*).

102. David Shepard reconstructed *A Burlesque on Carmen* in Chaplin's sense, among other things, using the trial documents. See booklet of the 2003 German DVD *Charlie Chaplin. The Essanay Comedies Volume 3* (Icestorm, ord. no. 10 5313 9–89049).

103. *Film* (weekly edition "Kritiken der Woche") 4, January 26, 1929, 234: "*Carmen*" by -tz (Hans-Walther Betz).

104. See also *FJ* 17, April 28, 1929, 1: "United Artists schließt mit Terra ab. [...] Bleibt Chaplin bei United?" *FJ* 19, May 12, 1929, 7: "Terra-United Artists." *FJ* 21, May 26, 1929, 3: "Letzte amerikanische Ereignisse."

105. Vogel Productions, Inc., December 1931 overview of worldwide sales of *The Pilgrim* since 1923. In Bologna, ch15548003.

106. FPS, November 19, 1929, file 24,261 (*The Pilgrim*) and December 6, 1929, file 24,416 (*Feine Leute*).

107. Hake, "Chaplin Reception in Weimar Germany" in *New German Critique* 51, 89 (note 8).

108. *FK* 153, June 28, 1928, 1: "Der unbezahlbare Chaplin."

109. *RFB* 49, December 7, 1929, 3: Terra-United Artists full-page ad.

110. *FK* 302, December 20, 1929, 2: "Charlie Chaplin: *Feine Leute/The Pilgrim* im Universum" by Hans Feld.

111. *LBB* No. 303, December 20, 1929, 2: "*The Pilgrim* im Universum" by al.

112. *LBB* 307–309, December 27, 1929, 1: "Glänzendes Weihnachtsgeschäft. In allen Stadtteilen überfüllte Kinos." *LBB* 22, January 25, 1930, 8: Terra-United Artists ad for the two films. *LBB* 23, January 27, 1930, 2: "Großer *Pilgrim*-Erfolg in Berlin." *LBB* 38, February 13, 1930, 2: "*The Pilgrim* und *The New Lords* (*Les nouveaux messieurs*, Jacques Feyder, 1928) in Hamburg."

113. *FJ* 6, February 9, 1930, 5, 6 (1st Supplement, 1, 2): "Die Spielwoche und Wochenspielplan Groß-Hamburger Lichtspielhäuser." *FJ* 7, February 16, 1930, 8: "*The Pilgrim* and *The New Lords* in Hamburg." *FJ* 9, March 2, 1930, 7, 8: "Die Spielwoche und Wochenspielplan Groß-Hamburger Lichtspielhäuser." *FK* 43, February 18, 1930, 7: "Chaplin-Programm überall prolongiert." *FK* 47, February 22, 1930, 1: "Große Abschlüsse für den Terra-Schmeling-Film."

114. *FK* 160, July 9, 1930, 1: "Gegen Chaplins Pilgrim...!"

115. *VB* (B) 301, December 29-30, 1929, 4: "Chaplinfilm."

116. historisches-lexikon-bayerns.de/artikel/artikel_44345.

117. *VB* (Ber) 1–2, January 1-2, 1931 ("Berliner Beobachter," 1): "Chaplin kauft sich Ideen und Ruhm" by Max Jungnickel. *VB* (Ber) first appeared on March 1, 1930, and was discontinued on April 1, 1931. See *Vossische Zeitung* (M) 152, March 31, 1931, 3: "*Völkischer Beobachter* nur noch in München." Thus, contrary to Schilling, *Das zerstörte Erbe*, 2011, 538, who claims that it was first published from 1933 onward.

118. Quoted from Ihering, *Von Reinhardt to Brecht. Volume 3*, 1961, 322, 323. On Ihering, see Benz and Graml, 156, 157, entry by Gesine von Prittwitz.

119. *Der Weltkampf* 53, May 1928, 210–212: "Aufruf!" by Alfred Rosenberg.

120. For example, *WB* 158, July 11, 1931, 4: "Der Vorkämpfer für deutsche Kultur spricht in Bonn."

121. *VB* (B) 14, January 14, 1931, 7: "Von Danzig bis Lindau trommeln unsere Redner."

122. *VB* (B) 148, May 28, 1931, 3 (1st Supplement): "Alfred Rosenberg spricht über 'Blut und Ehre.'"

123. *Angriff* 201, October 4, 1932, 6 ("Roter Adler," 2nd Supplement, 2): "'Was nicht Rasse ist, ist Spreu!' Der 'Kampfbund für deutsche Kultur' an der Arbeit" by B. Orbetomagus.

124. On Koch, see Weiß, 270, 271, entry by We (Hermann Weiß).

125. *Preußische Zeitung* 44, February 20, 1931, 5 ("Umschau in der Heimat"): "Pg. Alfred Rosenberg in der Stadthalle."

126. *VB* (B) 58, February 27, 1931, 7: "Alfred Rosenberg in Königsberg und Danzig."

127. *Leipziger Volkszeitung* 61, March 13, 1931, 12 (3rd Supplement, 2): "Chaplin auf einer nationalsozialistischen Veranstaltung" by Ludwig Hardt.

Chapter 4

1. *B.Z.* 32, February 7, 1931, 4 (1st Supplement, 2): "Chaplin kommt nach Berlin," own radio-telegram from New York.

2. *B.Z.* 49, February 27, 1931, 3 (1st Supplement, 1): "London in Erwartung der Chaplin-Premiere," von mtgls.

3. *LBB* 45, February 21, 1931, 1: "Um den Chaplin-Film." *LBB* 51, February 28, 1931, 2: "Chaplins Europa-Premiere."

4. *LBB* 55, March 5, 1931, 3: "Chaplin triumphans."

5. *FK* 57, March 9, 1931, 2: "Haben Sie gehört?"

6. *Berliner Lokal-Anzeiger* (M) 118, March 11, 1931, 3: "Chaplins zweiter Tag in Berlin."

7. See also *FJ* 28, July 8, 1928, 1, 2: "Charlie Chaplin, der Mensch und Künstler" by Curtis Melnitz.

8. Tunnat, 264, 265, 369.

9. See *Tempo* 58, March 10, 1931, 1, 2: "Erster Bummel mit Charlie Chaplin," by Rut [*sic*] Landsberg. In Landsberg-Yorck, 21, she claims not to remember whether she had been employed by "Ufa, [… Chaplin's] friend Vollmoeller, or Heaven" to work for Chaplin. In *Autobiography*, Chaplin did not mention Vollmoeller.

10. For example, *Breslauer Neueste Nachrichten* 68, March 10, 1931, 3: "Berlin bejubelt Charlie Chaplin." *Buxtehuder Tageblatt* 59, March 11, 1931, 3: "Charlie in Nöten." *Generalanzeiger Dortmund* 69, March 10, 1931, 2: "Charlie Chaplin in Berlin. Der Empfang war stürmisch." *Hamburger Echo* 69, March 10, 1931, 3: "Berlin feiert den größten Humoristen des Films." *Hannoverscher Anzeiger* 59, March 11, 1931, 1st Supplement, 1: "Begeisterter Empfang Chaplins in Berlin. Ungeheure Menschenmengen am Bahnhof und vor dem Hotel Adlon." *Leipziger Volkszeitung* 58, March 10, 1931, 11: "Charlie in Berlin. Die Berliner bereiten Chaplin einen ungemein herzlichen Empfang." *Münchner Neueste Nachrichten* 67, March 10, 1931, 3: "Chaplin-Begeisterung in Berlin." The *Schlesische Zeitung* (Bielitz), the organ of the German Party, acknowledged Chaplin's "ingenious creative power" on this occasion: 71, March 13, 1931, 8: "Charlie Chaplin in Berlin" by F.K.

11. *Rheinisch-Westfälische Zeitung* 110, March 1, 1931, 14: "Chaplins Londoner Premiere."

12. *FK* 141, June 14, 1928, 1: "Chaplin probiert Tonfilm." *FK* 143, June 16, 1928, 12: United Artists advertising for Chaplin's *City Lights*.

13. Section "Letzte amerikanische Ereignisse" in *FJ* 25, June 17, 1928, 5 (1st Supplement, 1). *FJ* 44, October 28, 1928, 3.

14. *FK* 188, August 8, 1928, 1: "Charlie Chaplin kommt nach Berlin." *LBB* 190, August 8, 1928, 1: "Charlie Chaplin kommt nach Berlin. Zur Premiere von *City Lights*?"

15. *FK* 1–2, January 1929, 41 (11th Supplement, 2): "Charlie, wie er verdient."

16. Section "Letzte amerikanische Ereignisse" in *FJ* 8, February 24, 1929, 5 (1st Supplement, 1). *FJ* 43, October 27, 1929, 3. *FJ* 29, July 20, 1930, 3. Also *FJ* 21, May 26, 1929, 5 (1st Supplement, 1): "Vom amerikanischen Tonfilm." *FJ* 36, September 8, 1929, 3: "Das Neueste aus England." *FJ* 29, July 20, 1930, 1: "Melnitz-Schenck-Jolson."

17. *FK* 60, March 10, 1930, 1: "Chaplin gründet Anti-Talkie-Verband." *FK* 188, August 11, 1930, 2: "Haben Sie gehört?"

18. *FJ* 35, August 31, 1930, 2: "*City Lights* im Tauentzien-Palast." *FJ* 41, October 12, 1930, 7: "Das Neueste aus England" and section "Letzte amerikanische Ereignisse" in *FJ* 45, November 9, 1930, 3. *FJ* 49, December 7, 1930, 3. *FJ* 1, January 4, 1931, 11. *FJ* 4, January 25, 1931, 3.

19. *Los Angeles Evening Express* 269, February 3, 1931, 8: "Charlie Sets New Record."

20. *LBB* 28, February 2, 1931, 1: "*City Lights* gestartet!" *FJ* 6, February 8, 1931, 3: "Letzte amerikanische Ereignisse."

21. *LBB* 47, February 24, 1931, 4: "Erinnerungen eines beinahe zu Tode Getrampelten" by Heinrich Fraenkel.

22. *B.Z.* 41, February 18, 1931, 5: caption "Chaplin als Weltboxmeister."

23. *Decatur Herald* (IL, no No.), June 21, 1931, 5: "Chaplin Comedy to Open today in the Alhambra."

24. "Chaplin rechnet mit 32 Millionen" in *LBB* 10, January 12, 1931, 2. *Rheinisch-Westfälische Zeitung* 32, January 15, 1931, 19.

25. *FK* 41, February 18, 1931, 3 (Supplement, 1): "*City Lights* in London."

26. *FK* 47, February 25, 1931, 1: "*City Lights* bei Südfilm."

27. *FK* 50, February 28, 1931, 7: "Chaplin durchs Telefon."

28. *RFB* 9, February 28, 1931, 1: "Charlie Chaplins Berliner Tonfilmstart." *LBB* 52, March 2, 1931, 1: "Chaplin-Film im März." *LBB* 56, March 6, 1931, 1: "Chaplin-Film im Ufa-Palast."

29. *FK* 120, May 21, 1929, 2: "Wird Chaplin in Deutschland verliehen?"

30. *Handbuch*, 1926, 1,329.

31. *Handbuch*, 1930, 4,690, 4,691.

32. *FJ* 18, May 4, 1930, 1: "Gerüchte um die

Terra." *FJ* 23, June 8, 1930, 9 (2nd Supplement, 1): "Terra-G.-V."

33. *B.Z.* 143, June 23, 1931, 4 (1st Supplement, 2): "Terra-Film in Schwierigkeiten."

34. *Handbuch*, 1930, 4,690, 4,691. *FJ* 39, September 28, 1930, 2: "Melnitz gibt Aktienpaket ab."

35. *FK* 306, 30 December 1930, 3: "Neuer starker Terra-Verlust." *Handbuch*, 1931 and 1932, 4,610, 4,611 and 6,307, 6,308, respectively.

36. *B.Z.* 46, February 24, 1931, 4 (1st Supplement, 2): "Wettrennen um den Chaplin-Film."

37. *FK* 47, 25 February 1931, 1: "*City Lights* bei Südfilm."

38. *FK* 47, February 25, 1931, 1: "*City Lights* bei Südfilm," and *FK* 50, February 28, 1931, 2: "Chaplin durchs Telefon." *Kinematograph* 43, February 20, 1931, 3: "Südfilm kauft neuen Chaplin-Film." *LBB* 48, February 25, 1931, 1: "Chaplin bei Südfilm." *LBB* 49, February 26, 1931, 3: full-page ad "*City Lights* für Deutschland bei Südfilm AG." *LBB* 51, February 28, 1931, 2: "Chaplins Europa-Premiere."

39. *LBB* 45, February 21, 1931, 1: "Um den Chaplin-Film."

40. *Vorwärts* (M) 111, March 7, 1931, 6: "Chaplin kommt auch nach Berlin."

41. *8-Uhr* 57, March 9, 1931, 3: "Charlie—heute Berlins Gast! [...] Seine überstürzte Abreise aus London." See also *12 Uhr-Blatt* 57, March 9, 1931: "Heute nachmittag kommt Chaplin. Plötzliche Abreise von London." In Landesarchiv Berlin, folio 260. See also Robinson, 454.

42. *LBB* 50, February 27, 1931, 1: "Schlägst Du meinen Film, schlag' ich Deinen Film!"

43. *Die Welt am Abend* 57, March 9, 1931, 6: "Chaplin in Berlin."

44. *RFB* 9, February 28, 1931, 1: "Charlie Chaplins Berliner Tonfilmstart." *LBB* 52, March 2, 1931, 1: "Chaplin-Film im März." *LBB* 56, March 6, 1931, 1: "Chaplin-Film im Ufa-Palast."

45. On Furtwängler, see Benz and Graml, 98, 99, entry by Reinhard H. Schulz.

46. *B.Z.* 57, March 9, 1931, 1: "Mit Charlie im Expreß über die Grenze." In Landesarchiv Berlin, folio 250: *Berliner Morgenpost* 10, March 9, 1931: "Chaplin in Berlin und sein Programm."

47. *BT* (M) 116, March 9, 1931, supplement, 1: "In Hannover."

48. *FK* 230, October 1, 1936, 1: "Dr. Olimsky Auslandspressechef der R.F.K." *Film* 11, March 12, 1938, 4: "Olimsky in der Fachschule."

49. *Hannoverscher Anzeiger* 58, March 10, 1931, 3: "Charlie Chaplin in Hannover." *8-Uhr* 58, March 10, 1931, 2: "Berlin huldigt 'seinem' Charlie" by Paulus Potter.

50. de Mendelssohn, *Zeitungsstadt Berlin*, 1959, 305–307.

51. *Der Abend* (E of *Vorwärts*) 114, March 9, 1931, 3: "Er kommt. Er kommt. Er kommt."

52. *Tempo* 57, March 9, 1931, 5 (1st Supplement, 1): "Darum Charlie Chaplin" by Heaven.

53. *Vossische Zeitung* (M) 116, March 10, 1931, 5 (1st Supplement, 1): "Gruß an Charlie Chaplin" by Heinz Pol (Heinz Pollak).

54. *B.Z.* 57, March 9, 1931, 5 (1st Supplement, 1):

"An Charlie Chaplin. Charlie, unsere Herzen fliegen dir zu" by Erich Kästner.

55. *Vossische Zeitung* (M) 116, March 10, 1931, 6 (Entertainment section): "*Chaplin*" by Victor Wittner.

56. *Tempo* 58, March 10, 1931, 9 (2nd Supplement, 1): "Lieschen liebt Charlie aus der Ferne" by Lieschen Laßdas (Jane Doe Let it Be).

57. *Die Weltbühne* 11, March 17, 1931, 386: "*Schepplin*" by Theobald Tiger (Kurt Tucholsky).

58. March 9, 1931: "Special Order 23" by Police Captain Juergens and note on Gzresinski's call. In Landesarchiv Berlin, folio 253 (with backside), 254.

59. *Germania* (Ber) 114, March 10, 1931: "Chaplins Ankunft in Berlin." In Landesarchiv Berlin, folio 274.

60. *Tempo* 57, March 9, 1931, 1: "Ordnungsdienst für Chaplins Einzug."

61. *8-Uhrt* 58, March 10, 1931, 2: "'Ich will hier Theater und Gefängnisse besuchen.'"

62. Police notes of March 8 and 9, 1931. In Landesarchiv Berlin, folio 247, 248 (backside), 251–254.

63. *8-Uhr* 58, March 10, 1931, 2: "'Ich will hier Theater und Gefängnisse besuchen.'"

64. Landsberg-Yorck, 21.

65. *Deutsche Allgemeine Zeitung* (Ber, M) 109, March 10, 1931, "Berliner Rundschau," 2: "Chaplin stürmisch begrüßt."

66. For example, newspapers from March 10, 1931: *8-Uhr* 58, 2: "'Ich will hier Theater und Gefängnisse besuchen.'" *Berliner Lokal-Anzeiger* (M) 116, 1: "Menschenmassen auf dem Bahnhof und vor dem Hotel." *BBZ* (M) 115, 5 (Supplement, 1): "Sturmszenen am Bahnhof Friedrichstraße. Sprechchöre vor dem Hotel Adlon" by Oly (Fritz Olimsky).

67. See photographs in Gersch, *Chaplin in Berlin*, 1988, 22, 23, 28–32, 39, 41.

68. For example, *Neues Wiener Journal* (Vienna) 13, 398, March 10, 1931, 5: "Chaplin Berlin. Tens of Thousands Wait for Charlie."

69. Reports of March 10, 1931, in *BBZ* (M) 115, 5 (Supplement, 1): "Sturmszenen auf Bahnhof Friedrichstraße. Sprechchöre vor dem Hotel Adlon" by Oly (Fritz Olimsky). *8-Uhr* 58, 2: "'Ich will hier Theater und Gefängnisse besuchen.'" *FK* 58, 3: "Rekord-Fahrt zum Adlon."

70. Issues of March 9, 1931: *Der Abend* (E of *Vorwärts*) 116, 2: "Chaplin-Empfang als Anlass für politische Demonstrationen." *8-Uhr-Abendblatt* 58, March 10, 1931, 2: "'Ich will hier Theater und Gefängnisse besuchen.'"

71. *B.Z.* 58, March 10, 1931, 1, 2: "Der belagerte Chaplin."

72. *Die Welt am Abend* 58, March 10, 1931, 5 (1st Supplement, 1): "Jagd auf Charlie" by Men.

73. Letter from the Chief of Police dated March 20, 1931, in: "Landesarchiv Berlin," folio 298.

74. *Spandauer Zeitung* 58, March 10, 1931, 5 (1st Supplement, 1): "Tausende am Bahnhof Friedrichstraße und vor dem Hotel Adlon."

75. Adlon, *Hotel Adlon*, 1963, 346, 347.

76. *Spandauer Zeitung* 58, March 10, 1931, 5 (1st

Supplement, 1): "Tausende am Bahnhof Friedrich-straße und vor dem Hotel Adlon."

77. *8-Uhr* 58, March 10, 1931, 2: "Berlin huldigt 'seinem' Charlie" by Paulus Potter.

78. *BT* (E) 117, March 11, 1931, 1st Supplement, 1: "In Charlies Hauptquartier."

79. *The Palestine Bulletin* (Jerusalem) 1,841, March 11, 1931, 1: "Charlie Chaplin Mistaken for a Jew. Demonstration in Germany."

80. *Die Neue Welt* (Vienna) 185, April 1, 1931, 3: "Geschäft um Chaplin."

81. *Die Stimme* (Vienna) 168, March 19, 1931, 4: "Chaplin. Randbemerkungen zu seinem Wiener Besuch."

82. Berlin newspapers from March 10, 1931, for example: *8-Uhr* 58, March 10, 1931, 2: "Berlin huldigt 'seinem' Charlie, wie man früher Könige ehrte." *B.Z.* 58, 1, 2: "Der belagerte Chaplin." *Berliner Lokal-Anzeiger* (M) 116, 1: "Chaplins Ankunft in Berlin. Menschenmassen auf dem Bahnhof und vor dem Hotel." *BBZ* (M) 115, 5 (Supplement, 1): "Sturmszenen auf Bahnhof Friedrich-straße. Sprechchöre vor dem Hotel Adlon." *BT* (M) 116, 4: "Berlin begrüßt Chaplin." *Deutsche Allge-meine Zeitung* (Ber, M) 109, "Berliner Rundschau," 2: "Chaplin stürmisch begrüßt."

83. *Tempo* 58, March 10, 1931, 6: Ufa ad.

84. Only the censorship record for *Deulig-Woche* 12 with Chaplin's arrival as the second of eight segments still exists: FPS, March 11, 1931, file 28,458. *Ufa-Tonwoche* 27 (FPS, file 28,456) and *Emelka-Tonwoche* 25 (FPS, file 28,466) reported on Chaplin's arrival, probably, also *Fox tönende Wochenschau* 11 (FPS, March 12, 1931, file 28,472). See on this *Kinematograph* 62, March 14, 1931, 5: "Die Tonwochen."

85. *FK* 174, July 28, 1926, 1: "Chaplin als Christus."

86. *Tägliche Rundschau* 59, March 11, 1931, 5 (1st Supplement, 1): "Chaplin-Rausch."

87. *Märkische Volks-Zeitung* 69, March 10, 1931, 3: "Sensation um Charlie Chaplin."

88. Chaplin, "A Comedian Sees the World," pt. 2, in *Woman's Home Companion*, October 1933, 16.

89. Chaplin, *My Autobiography*, 386.

90. See Heiber, *Joseph Goebbels*, 1965, 30–39. Weiß, 150–153, entry by Froe (Dr. Elke Fröhlich-Broszat). Klee, *Das Personenlexikon zum Dritten Reich*, 188.

91. *LBB* 33, August 21, 1923, 2: "L.B.B. Tages-dienst." *LBB* 36 September 8, 1923, 10: "Der erste Coogan-Film" by hfr (Heinrich Fraenkel). *FK* 254, November 19, 1923, 1, 2: "My Boy" by M-s.

92. Ruhemann, *Das Jackie Coogan Buch*, 1924.

93. For example, *Film* 43, October 26, 1924, 29: "Jackie in Berlin."

94. *Völkische Freiheit* No. 33, October 1924, 2: "Streiflichter," by Joseph Goebbels. "Jakob Cohn" was adopted a few years later by Hit-ler's propaganda journal. See *VB* (B) 96, April 28, 1927, 4 ("Münchener Beobachter"): "*Jackie, der Außenseiter.*"

95. Cary, *Jackie Coogan*, 2003, 18, 116, 131, 138, 139. Jackie Coogan is not covered in *Who's*

Who in American Jewry (editions 1927 to 1938) and the 1941 *The Universal Jewish Encyclopedia. Volume 3.*

96. See also Bering, *Der Name als Stigma*, 206–211.

97. Goebbels, *Kampf um Berlin*, 1934, 188, 191.

98. *Angriff* 30, July 29, 1929, 2: "Die Juden im Film."

99. FOPS, January 29, 1931, file 27,899 (ban), March 13, 1931, file 28,179 (G-rated approval).

100. Gersch, 44.

101. *Berliner Herold* 11, March 15, 1931, 3, Sup-plement: "Unsere Chaplin-Seite."

102. *Angriff* 55, March 17, 1931, 12: "Münzen-bergs danebengegangene Schnorrerei."

103. Fröhlich, *Die Tagebücher von Joseph Goeb-bels, Volume 2/I*, 359, 360 (entries of March 8 and 9, 1931).

104. Interview with Wolfgang Gersch, March 8, 2008.

105. *Angriff* 49, March 10, 1931, 11: "'Hurra, er ist da!'"

106. *Angriff* 50, March 11, 1931, 11: "Der wid-erliche Rummel um den Kriegshetzer Chaplin." In 1931, there was still no reliable Chaplin filmog-raphy. In his 1929 book *Charlie Chaplin. Bericht seines Lebens*, Erich Burger dates Chaplin's first film to 1912. *Shoulder Arms* follows in 1918 (136, 137).

107. *Thüringer Film-Zeitung* 5, 1st March issue 1931, 5: "'Charlie' in Deutschland."

108. *LBB* 284, December 7, 1937, 1: "'I see almost every film'—says Dr. Goebbels."

109. *Das Tagebuch* 20, May 16, 1931, 783, 784: "Chaplin's Kriegsfilm" by Stefan Großmann.

110. *Die deutsche Republik* 28, April 11, 1931, 888–890 (889): "Chaplins Kriegsfilm" by Paul Ruhstrat.

111. *Die Welt am Abend* 131, June 9, 1931, 5 (1st Supplement, 1): "Chaplins Kriegsfilm."

112. *Der Große Herder. Volume 3*, 1932, columns 178, 179.

113. *Deutsche Nachrichten* (Berlin) 11, March 15, 1931, 2: "Was die Woche brachte." According to Gersch, 110, the *Friedenauer Tageblatt* of March 14, 1931, claimed that Chaplin was born in the "ghetto of Paris." However, the *Berlin-Friedenauer Tageblatt* 59, March 10, 1931, 3: "Charlie Chaplin in Berlin," only once commented on Chaplin's Ber-lin visit. It did not mention the "ghetto of Paris" and did not claim that Chaplin was Jewish.

114. *Der Jungdeutsche* 64, March 17, 1931, 4: "Der große Charlie" by Kurt.

115. Eggebrecht, *Volk ans Gewehr*, 1959, 91.

116. Stein, *Adolf Stein alias Rumpelstilzchen*, 2014, 81, 414.

117. Albrecht, *Die Macht einer Verleumdung-skampagne*, 2002, 175.

118. *Vossische Zeitung* (M) 601, December 21, 1927, 3: "Ein Landsknecht Hugenbergs. Das giftige 'Rumpelstilzchen.'"

119. *Vossische Zeitung* (M) 38, January 23, 1927, 3: "Selbsterkenntnis." Rumpelstilzchen's commen-taries are reported to have appeared, for exam-ple, in the *Göttinger Tageblatt*, the *Niederdeutsche*

Zeitung (Hanover), and the *Schlesische Zeitung* (Breslau). They have not been available for inspection.

120. *Vossische Zeitung* (M) 152, March 31, 1931, 3: "Ein Popanz für den anderen."

121. *Vossische Zeitung* (M) 575, December 1, 1932, 4: "Rumpelstilzchen. Porträt eines Zeitgenossen" by Erich Kästner.

122. Eher-Verlag Nachfolger ad for Rumpelstilzchen's *Piept es?* (1929/1930) in *VB* (Ber) 291, December 7/8, 1930, 2.

123. von Müffling, 25, 39.

124. Rumpelstilzchen, *Das sowieso!*, 1931, commentary 28, March 12, 1931, 216, 217.

125. Rumpelstilzchen, *Das sowieso!*, 1931, 214, 215.

126. *Der Stahlhelm* 25, June 22, 1930, 1: "Stahlhelm und organischer Staat" by Dr. Friedrich Sverling.

127. *VB* (Bay) 152/153, June 1–2, 1931, 2: "Im Zeichen der Kameradschaft zwischen Stahlhelm und NSDAP."

128. Rumpelstilzchen, *Mang uns mang...*, 1933.

129. von Müffling, 37.

130. See on this Schilling, 310, 311.

131. *Fridericus* 10, 2nd March issue 1931, 5 (1st Supplement, 1): "Viel Lärm um nichts! 'Chaplin nähert sich Berlin.'"

132. *Thüringer Film-Zeitung* 6, 2nd March issue 1931, 2: "Gelächter über Berlin."

133. *Hanoverscher Anzeiger* 59, March 11, 1931, 1st Supplement, 1: "Ungeheure Menschenmengen am Bahnhof und vor dem Hotel Adlon."

134. Information provided by the Landesarchiv Berlin on July 30, 2010, and March 1, 2021.

135. *Thüringer Film-Zeitung* 5, 1st March issue 1931, 5: "'Charlie' in Deutschland."

136. *Stürmer* 12, March 1931, 1, 2: "Chaplin Rummel."

137. *Stürmer* 29, July 1931, 3: "Chaplins Bruder."

138. Another major war criminal who was to be tried at Nuremberg after the end of World War II. Ley committed suicide beforehand. On Ley, see further Weiß, 299–301, entry by Den (Monika Deniffel).

139. *WB* 99, April 29, 1931, 8: "*Lichter der Großstadt*" by A-s. (from the Latin "Aliquis": "anyone").

140. *WB* 111, May 13, 1931, 9: "Widerlich! Wie der Clown den Künstler erschlägt."

141. *Der Stahlhelm* 10, March 15, 1931, 4: "*Chaplin*" by Peter Silie (Eduard Petersilie). On Petersilie, see Placke, *Die Chiffren des Utopischen*, 2004, 33.

142. *BBZ* (E) 166, April 10. 1931, 1: "Stahlhelm-Zeitung für 3 Monate verboten!"

143. See on this: Ebinger, *"Blandine...,"* 1985, 107, 108.

144. See Gersch, 90, 91. There is also a photo captioned "Charlie Chaplin in the [Berlin] Pergamon Museum," which opened on October 2, 1930 (*B.Z.* 269, October 3, 1930, 2: "Festakt am Pergamon-Altar"). It shows a man resembling Chaplin in the altar room. But unlike Chaplin, he seems to have a tonsure-like loss of hair. Contemporary newspaper accounts did not mention that Chaplin paid the museum a visit.

145. Goebbels, *Das Buch Isidor*, 1928. Goebbels, *Knorke!*, 1929.

146. *Angriff* 51, March 12, 1931, 11: "'Byzantinismus' der anderen. Noch einmal Chaplin."

147. *VB* (B, Ber) 72, March 13, 1931, 1: "Streiflichter." On Nazi name polemics in general, see Bering, *Kampf um Namen*, 1991, 231–240.

148. Police note of March 13, 1931. In Landesarchiv Berlin, folio 288.

149. Information provided by the Landesarchiv Berlin on July 30, 2010, and March 1, 2021.

150. *Angriff* 52, March 13, 1931, 6: "Wie urteilen Sie über Chaplin?" by Heinz Henkel.

151. *Film* 9, March 1, 1930, 4: "Drei Chaplin-Filme im Atrium" by (Hans-Walther) Betz.

152. *LBB* 55, March 5, 1930, 3: Terra-United Artists ad for *Lohntag, Auf dem Lande* and *Vergnügte Stunden*. See also *FJ* 9, March 2, 1930, 7, 8: "Die Spielwoche und Wochenspielplan Groß-Hamburger Lichtspielhäuser."

153. *Angriff* 52, March 13, 1931, 6: "Wie urteilen Sie über Chaplin?" by Heinz Henkel.

154. *Angriff* 52, March 13, 1931, 11: "Chaplinkult statt Proletkult."

155. *FK* 62, March 14, 1931, 3 (1st Supplement, 1): "Rings um Charlie Chaplin ... Chaplinrausch."

156. *Die Welt am Montag* 11, March 16, 1931, Supplement, 1: "Sums um Charlie" by Dr. Frosch.

157. *Stürmer* 12, March 1931, 1, 2: "Chaplin Rummel." Whether Streicher's information about Chaplin's income is properly researched seems highly doubtful. According to *LBB* 91, April 16, 1927, 34: "Was sie verdienen," Chaplin was third among 26 selected U.S. film actors with an income of $1,125,000, after Harold Lloyd with $2 million. With *The Circus*, Chaplin had taken in $3.8 million: *LBB* 153, July 2, 1932, 4 (Supplement, 2): "Was Stummfilme brachten."

158. *Mitteldeutscher Lichtspieltheaterbesitzer* 4, April 20, 1931, 12: "Chaplin."

159. *Angriff* 55, March 17, 1931, 12: "Münzenbergs danebengegangene Schnorrerei."

160. *Die Rote Fahne* 58, March 10, 1931 (3rd Supplement ["Feuilleton der *Roten Fahne*"], 1): "Lenin hat 'Charlie' sehr geschätzt."

161. *Die Rote Fahne* 59, March 11, 1931, 9 (2nd Supplement, 1): "Besuch bei Charlie Chaplin" by von J.S.

162. *Die Welt am Abend* 59, March 11, 1931, 6 (1st Supplement, 2): "Fährt Charlie nach Sowjetußland?" by Men.

163. *Die Rote Fahne* 60, March 12, 1931 (3rd Supplement, 1): "Hunger—Lohnraub—Faschismus."

164. Quoted from Gersch, 120. Nothing could be located in the "Feuilleton" section of the Friday issue of *Die Rote Fahne* 61, March 1931. Possibly the checked issue is incomplete.

165. *BBZ* (M) 123, March 14, 1931, 1: "'All meine Sympathie für die kommunistische Jugend,' sagt Charlie Chaplin."

166. *Vorwärts* (M) 125, March 15, 1931, 4: "Eine Erklärung Charlie Chaplins. Gegen

kommunistische Fälschungsmethoden." See also *FK* 63, March 16, 1931, 1: "Chaplin gegen die 'junge Garde.' Er bestreitet jedes Interview."

167. *Die Rote Fahne* 63, March 15, 1931, 12: "Chaplin und wir."

168. *Die Rote Fahne* 63, March 15, 1931 (3rd Supplement ["Feuilleton der Roten Fahne"], 1): "*Die Rote Fahne* bei Charlie Chaplin."

169. *Die Welt am Abend* 63, March 16, 1931, 5 (1st Supplement, 1): "Vertreter der Filmkomparsen erhalten das einzige Interview."

170. *BBZ* (M) 125, March 15, 1931, 8: "Chaplinade" by F.O. (Fritz Olimsky).

171. *BBZ* (M) 125, March 15, 1931, 8: "320 englische Kinos verzichten auf Chaplin-Film."

172. Gersch, 126.

173. *BBZ* (E) 128, March 17, 1931, 2: "Charlie" by –oner.

174. *BBZ* (M) 65, February 8, 1931, 14: "Chaplins *Lichter der Großstatdt*. Ein Triumph des stummen Films" by H.B. (Hans Baumann).

175. *Der Jungdeutsche* 64, March 17, 1931, 4: "Der große Charlie" by Kurt.

176. *8-Uhr* 61, March 13, 13 (3rd Supplement, 1): "Chaplin deutschlandmüde?"

177. *Deutsche Allgemeine Zeitung* (Ber, E) 116, March 13, 1931, 3: "Hat Chaplin genug von Berlin?"

178. *FK* 63, March 16, 1931, 1: "Chaplin gegen die 'junge Garde.' Er bestreitet jedes Interview." *FK* 64, March 17, 1931, 3 (Supplement, 1): "Charlie Chaplin in Wien." *LBB* 64, March 16, 1931, 3: "Abschied von Chaplin."

179. From the abundance of newspaper reports, for example, *Neue Freie Presse* (Vienna) 23, 889, March 17, 1931, 3, 4: "Besuch bei Charlie Chaplin. Gespräch mit dem Filmkönig."

180. *8-Uhr* 65, March 18, 1931, 11: "Charlie hat nirgends Ruhe ... Er flüchtet aus Wien!"

181. Chaplin, *My Autobiography*, 387.

182. *Angriff* 55, March 17, 1931, 12: "Münzenbergs danebengegangene Schnorrerei." On Münzenberg, who published *Die Rote Fahne*, see Babette Gross, *Willi Münzenberg*, 1991.

183. *Thüringer Film-Zeitung* 6, 2nd March issue 1931, 2: "Gelächter über Berlin."

184. Rumpelstilzchen, *Das sowieso!*, 1931, commentary 28, March 12, 1931, 217, 218.

185. *Angriff* 57, March 19, 1931, 12: "Werthauer und Chaplin."

186. On this, see Sammons, *Die Protokolle der Weisen von Zion*, Göttingen, 2001.

187. *VB* (Ber) 78/79, March 19 and 20, 1931, 5 ("Berliner Beobachter," 1): "Charlie Chaplin beim Justizrat Dr. Werthauer."

188. *VB* (B) 223, September 25, 1928, 2: "Chaplin über Werthauer."

189. *Die Linkskurve*, April 1931, 3, 4: "Blausäuregas und Lachgas" (Hydrogen Cyanide and Laughing Gas) by Otto Biha.

190. *VB* (Ber) 80, March 21, 1931, 5 ("Berliner Beobachter," 1): "Chaplinade," by -zd-. On Einstein, see Benz and Graml, 72, 73, entry by Lothar Wieland.

191. *Arbeiterbühne und Film* 4, April 1931, 28: "Charlie Chaplin" by Béla Balázs (?).

192. *WB* 99, April 29, 1931, 8: "*Lichter der Großstadt*" by A-s. (Aliquis).

193. *WB* 111, May 13, 1931, 9: "Widerlich! Wie der Clown den Künstler erschlägt."

194. *Stürmer* 29, July 1931, 3: "Chaplins Bruder."

195. *Jüdische Presszentrale Zürich* 638, March 13, 1931, 1, 2: "Charlie Chaplin. Zu seinem Besuch in Europa."

196. *VB* (Ber) 81/82, March 22/23, 1931, 5 ("Berliner Beobachter," 1): "Politische Grotesken."

197. *VB* (Ber) 83, March 24, 1931, 6 ("Berliner Beobachter," 2): "Theo begrüßt Chaplin" by Ernst Schwartz.

198. *VB* (B) 90, March 31, 1931, 3: "Das jüdische Problem."

199. *FK* 73, March 27, 1931, 2: "*Lichter der Großstadt* im Ufa-Palast am Zoo" von Hans Feld.

200. *B.Z.* 46, February 24, 1931, 4 (1st Supplement, 2): "Wettrennen um den Chaplin-Film."

201. *B.Z.* 64, March 17, 1931, 5: start of the advance sale announced. *B.Z.* 65, March 18, 1931, 4: Ufa-Palast am Zoo ad "Die Festvorstellungen vom 26. März 1931 sind bereits ausverkauft." *FK* 65, March 18, 1931, 2: "Haben Sie gehört?"

202. *Film* 13, March 28, 1931, 3: "*Lichter der Großstadt*" by (Hans-Walther) Betz.

203. *LBB* 73, March 26, 1931, 2: "Kommt Chaplin zur Berliner *City Lights*-Premiere?"

204. *Deutsche Allgemeine Zeitung* (Ber, M) 139, March 27, 1931, 1: "*Lichter der Großstadt*."

205. *LBB* 74, March 27, 1931, 2: "*Lichter der Großstadt*," Kritik von W-g. (Dr. Hans Wollenberg).

206. *Rheinisch-Westfälische Zeitung* (E) 161, March 28, 1931, 1: "Der neue Chaplin-Film 'Stadtlichter'" by Cubert.

207. *FK* 73, March 27, 1931, 1: "Großartiger Premierenverlauf."

208. *FK* 73, March 27, 1931, 1, 3: "*Lichter der Großstadt*."

209. *Thüringer Film-Zeitung* 6, 2nd March issue 1931, 2: "Gelächter über Berlin."

210. *Sozialistische Bildung* 4, April 1931, 118, 119: "Amerikanische Filme."

211. FPS, March 24, 1931, file 28,553. The last two German intertitles before the intertitle "End" read: "[The girl] You?—[Charlie] You can see now?—[The girl] Yes, I can see now."

212. *Tempo* 73, March 27, 1931, 9 (2nd Supplement, 1): "Der neue Chaplin-Film" by Manfred Georg. Similarly, *B.Z.* 73, March 27, 1931, 3 (1st Supplement, 1): "Der neue Chaplin-Film" by Kurt Mühsam.

213. *8-Uhr* 73, March 27, 1931, 7: "Chaplins *Lichter der Großstadt*" by Kurt Pinthus.

214. *Film* 13, March 28, 1931, 3: "*Lichter der Großstadt*" by (Hans-Walther) Betz.

215. *Die Rote Fahne* 74, March 28, 1931 (2nd Supplement, 2): "Der neue Chaplin-Film *Lichter der Großstadt*. Landstreicher, obdachlos, arbeitslos."

216. *Die Welt am Abend* 73, March 27, 1931, 6 (1st Supplement, 2): "*Lichter der Großstadt*" by K. Kn.

217. *Düsseldorfer Nachtrichten* (M) 172, April 4, 1931, 7 (Entertainment Supplement): "*Lichter der Großstadt*" by M. Nr. 196 (A), April 18, 1931, 8 (Entertainment Supplement): "In Paris läuft ein deutschfeindlicher Chaplin-Film."

218. *Deutsche Zeitung* 73, March 27, 1931, 3: "Chaplins ausgebrannte Lichter" by apr.

219. *Der Jungdeutsche* 75, March 29, 9: "Chaplin hat den Weg verloren" by –ert.

220. *Rheinisch-Westfälische Zeitung* (E) 166, March 31, 1931, 1: "Zur Essener Aufführung der *City Lights*" by Cremers.

221. For example, *Angriff* 63, March 26, 1931, 3.

222. *FK* 71, March 25, 1931, 2: "Chaplin in Paris."

223. *Angriff* 65, March 28, 1931, 2: "Klamauk um Charlie."

224. *Das Tagebuch* 14, April 4, 1931, 554, 555: "Entlarvt" by Kurt Reinhold.

225. *VB* (B) 99, April 9, 1931, 7 ("Münchener Beobachter," 3): "*Lichter der Großstadt*" by stb.

226. Rumpelstilzchen, *Das sowieso!*, 1931, commentary 31, April 1, 1931, 243, 244.

227. *Fridericus* 15, 3rd April issue, 1931, 5 (1st Supplement, 1): "Zweimal Chaplin."

228. *WB* 99, April 29, 1931, 8: "Bonner Filmschau: Modernes Theater. *Lichter der Großstadt*" by A-s (Aliquis).

229. *FK* 77, April 1, 1931, 3: "Haben Sie gehört?"

230. *B.Z.* 119, May 26, 1931, 4 (1st Supplement, 1): "Chaplin und die Mizzi aus Marienbad."

231. *Nürnberger Zeitung—NZ am Mittag* 141, June 1931, 4: "Sid Chaplin flieht aus Portugal."

232. *WB* 189, August 26, 1931, 6: "Das wahre Gesicht des Films" by Aliquis.

233. *Angriff* 170, September 1, 1931 (2nd Supplement, 1): "Vom Film."

Chapter 5

1. *Reichs Kino Adressbuch 1931*, 1931, 117. *1934*, 1934, 143.

2. Krakauer, *Lichter im Dunkel*, 1947, 8, 9.

3. See Maser, *Der Sturm auf die Republik*, 1973, 272, 295, 303, and 305-309 (goon squads).

4. Hermand, "Satire und Aufruf" in Groenewold, 32.

5. Fröhlich, *Die Tagebücher von Joseph Goebbels*, Volume 1/II, 339, 340. Fröhlich, *Die Tagebücher von Joseph Goebbels*, Volume 2/I, Volume 2/II, 339, 340. Fröhlich, *Die Tagebücher von Joseph Goebbels Volume 2/III*, 2005.

6. Klemperer, *Leben sammeln, nicht fragen wozu und warum*, 1996.

7. Klemperer, *Licht und Schatten*, 2020, 38, 39.

8. Velten and Klein, *Chaplin und Hitler*, 40. Gersch, 163. Hake, "Chaplin Reception in Weimar Germany" in *New German Critique* 51, 103.

9. *FK* 60, March 11, 1926, 2: "Musste es soweit kommen?" *FK* 237, October 5, 1929, 4 (1st Supplement, 1): "Wiedergeburt der Claque!" by Cormo.

10. *FK* 259, November 4, 1931, 2: "Tod einer Kinounsitte."

11. *Der Lichtspieltheater-Besitzer* 7, February 17, 1923, 11: "Radauszenen in einem Kino" by Artur Rannow.

12. See, for example, *FK* 243, October 15, 1925, 3: "Eifersuchtsexzesse im Dorfkino" by C.W. *FK* 1, January 1, 1927, 34 (8th Supplement, 2): "Ein Mord im Kino." *FK* 263, November 7, 1927, 2: "Eifersuchtsdrama im Kino." *RFB* 16, April 21, 1928, 27: "Mordversuch im Lichtspielhaus" by st.

13. Examples from the period 1919 to 1928: *FK* 38, July 19, 1919, 1, 2: "*Die Frau im Käfig*" by Eg. *FK* 74, August 31, 1919, 2: "*Die Maske* im Tauentzien-Palast" by Frank. *FK* 288, December 6, 1924, 1: "Filmgegner und Kinofeinde... " by Ejott (Ernst Jäger). *FK* 79, March 31, 1928, 7: "Mord wie im Film." *FK* special issue of July 2, 1927, 19: "Es gibt noch Kino-Feinde! An die Kinogegner" by Dr. Fritz R Lachmann and "Ratschläge für den Kino-Nörgler" by Georg Herzberg. *FK* 136, June 8, 1928, 2: "Filmhetze in Düsseldorf."

14. *FJ* 33, August 19, 1927, 13: "Unhöfliche Theaterbesucher." *FJ* 17, April 22, 1928, 3: "Wer pfeift im Kino." *FJ* 85, April 12, 1926, 1: "Pfiffe am Kurfürstendamm. Zischen im Kino" by F. *FJ* 89, April 16, 1926, 2: "Pfeifen erwünscht." *FJ* 83, April 6, 1928, 5: "Skandalpremieren in Berlin" by Ej. (Ernst Jäger). *FJ* 215, September 8, 1928, 2: "Pfeifen im Kino." *FJ* 236, October 4, 1929, 3: "Wer pfeift?" *FJ* 23, June 8, 1930, 2: "Werden Premierentheater zu Sammelplätzen für Radaumacher?"

15. See on this *BT* (M) 245, May 29, 1919, 2: "Gegen die antisemitischen Hetzblätter." *BT* (M) 378, August 14, 1919, 4: "Der antisemitische Skandal. [...] Vorbereitete Skandalszenen." *BT* (M) 378, August 15, 1919, 2: "Die antisemitische Propaganda in der Reichswehr." *BT* (M) 378, August 15, 1919, 5, 6 (1st Supplement, 1, 2): "Die antisemitischen Ausschreitungen am Kurfürstendamm."

16. *LBB* 39, September 27, 1919, 15, 16: "Professor Brunner als Wanderprediger" by Hb. *LBB* 45, November 8, 1919, 22: "Brunner in Friedenau." See also *Erste internationale Filmzeitung* 40, October 11, 1919, 39, 40: "Moderne Bilderstürmer."

17. *Film* 44, November 2, 1919, 27, 28: "Antisemitische Radauversammlungen als Kampfmittel [...]?" by Carl Boese. On one occasion, a Brunner event also escalated into a brawl: *Film* 45, November 9, 1919, 23: "Herr Brunner und seine Methode."

18. *LBB* 20, May 17, 1919, 97: Richard-Oswald-Film-GmbH ad for *Anders als die andern*. *BT* (M) 246, May 30, 1919, 4: Premiere ad for the film. *FK* 1, May 31, 1919, 2: *Anders als die anderen. Der neue Aufklärungsfilm*," by B.E. Lüthge (Bobby E. Lüthge = Robert Erwin Lüthge). Helga Belach and Wolfgang Jacobson, "*Anders als die andern* (1919). Dokumente zu einer Kontroverse" in Belach and Jacobson, *Richard Oswald*, 1990, 25, 26.

19. Magnus Hirschfeld, "Das Filmwerk *Anders als die andern* (§ 175). Eine Zusammenstellung" in Hirschfeld, *Jahrbuch für sexuelle Zwischenstufen*, ca. 1919, 17.

20. *Deutsche Zeitung* 318, July 11, 1919, 3: "Ein Skandal!" by K.

21. *LBB* 29, July 19, 1919, 110: Richard-Oswald-Film ad. *FK* 39, July 20, 1919, 2: "Ist der Film *Anders als die andern* unsittlich?" by Dr. J.B. (Dr. Johannes Brandt).

22. *Film* 31, August 2, 1919, 34, 25: "Organisierte Kinohetze?"

23. *Film* 33, August 16, 1919, 22, 23: "Zu den Filmskandalen in Westdeutschland." *LBB* 33, August 16, 1919, 22: "*Das Gelübde der Keuschheit*" by F.-m.

24. *FK* 168, August 7, 1922, 8: Martin Dentler Film AG ad.

25. *FK* 187, August 29, 1922, 2: "Kommunistischer Angriff auf ein Braunschweiger Kino."

26. *SFZ* 15, April 8, 1927, 4: "*Potemkin*-Skandal in München."

27. *LBB* 9, March 3, 1923, 23, 24: "Antisemitische Pöbeleien—Herr Hitler, *Nathan* und der *Völkische Beobachter*."

28. Fest, 229.

29. *VB* 18, February 16, 1923, 3: "*Nathan der Weise*" by H.E. (Hermann Esser).

30. *SFZ* 9, March 2, 1923, 3, 4: "*Nathan der Weise*" by Dr. Gr. (Dr. Gruber).

31. The FOPS approved the film on April 10, 1926, file O.349. *FK* 106, May 7, 1926, 2: "*Potemkin* als Spaltenfüller."

32. *BBZ* (E) 208, May 6, 1926, 1, 2: "Der *Potemkin*-Skandal" by Dr. (Richard) Jügler. *FK* 106, May 7, 1926, 2: "*Potemkin* als Spaltenfüller."

33. *SFZ* 15, April 8, 1927, 4: "*Potemkin*-Skandal in München."

34. *FK* 101, April 30, 1926, 2: "*Panzerkreuzer Potemkin*" by Willy Haas.

35. *BBZ* (E) 200, April 30, 1926, 3: "*Panzerkreuzer Potemkin*" by F.O. (Fritz Olimsky).

36. *VB* 107, May 11, 1926, 1, 2: "Ungehemmte bolschewistische Maipropaganda durch den Film."

37. *VB* 130, June 10, 1926, 2 ("Münchener Beobachter"): "Bolschewistische Filme."

38. *Stürmer* 30, July 1926, 3: "*Panzerkreuzer Potemkin.*"

39. *FK* 137, June 15, 1926, 1: "*Potemkin* in Stuttgart verboten." *RFB* 26, June 26, 1926, 26: "Der ruhelose Fürst *Potemkin*" by F. H. (Felix Henseleit). See also *FJ* 26, June 25, 1926, 2: "In Stuttgart ist es was anderes." *FK* 179, August 3, 1926, 6 (Supplement, "Jeden Tag *Potemkin!*" *FK* 175, July 29, 1926, 1: "Kinderfilm *Potemkin.*"

40. *FK* 260, November 5, 1926, 1: "Reichswehr gegen Reichszensur."

41. *FK* 23, January 27, 1927, 1: "Auch in Swinemünde ein Kino für die Marine verboten!"

42. FPS, July 28, 1926, file 13,346: cut from 1,617 meters to 1,421 meters.

43. *VB* 190, August 19, 1926, 6 ("Münchener Beobachter"): "*Panzerkreuzer Potemkin.*"

44. *VB* (B) 77, April 3/4, 1927, 3 ("Münchener Beobachter"): "Die Regierung machtlos vor dem bolschewistischen Film."

45. *FZ* (E) 251, April 4, 1927, 1: "Bestellte

Ruhestörungen—wie vorauszusehen." *SFZ* 15, April 8, 1927, 4: "*Potemkin*-Skandal in München."

46. On the whole: *FK* 80, April 4, 1927, 2: "*Potemkin*-Krawall in München. [...] Stinkbomben und Radauszenen." *LBB* 80, April 4, 1927, 1: "Provokateure stören die Vorführung des Films." *SFZ* 15, April 8, 1927, 4: "*Potemkin*-Skandal in München."

47. *FK* 81, April 5, 1927, 3: "*Potemkin* wird in München weitergespielt."

48. *LBB* 257, October 27, 1927, 1: "*Potemkin*-Skandal vor Gericht."

49. *FK* 162, July 9, 1928, 3: "Reichswehrposten überwachten den Titania-Palast." *FK* 165, July 12, 1928, 2: "Die Berliner Theaterbesitzer beabsichtigen einen Schritt beim Reichswehrminsterium."

50. *FK* 254, October 24, 1928, 1: "Krakeeler im *Potemkin*-Film." *LBB* 257, October 25, 1928, 1: "*Potemkin* in Württemberg."

51. *LBB* 30, July 22, 1922, 50: "Ein angeblicher Hetzfilm."

52. *RFB* 25, June 23, 1923, 22: "Französische Hetzfilme." The original French title is unknown.

53. For example, *SFZ* 15, April 8, 1927, 2: "Das Maß ist voll!"

54. *LBB* 72, March 26, 1926, 4: "Boykott gegen Hetzfilm-Hersteller."

55. *LBB* 51, December 16, 1922, 13: "Die Hetzfilm-Seuche. [...] Diplomatische Schritte der Reichsregierung."

56. *VB* 250, October 28, 1926, 2 ("Münchener Beobachter"): "Nochmals die Hetzfilme."

57. *SFZ* 41, October 8, 1926, 1: "Gegen den amerikanischen Hetzfilm," by J.A. (Josef Aubinger). 41, October 8, 1926, 2, 3: "Amerika lässt es darauf ankommen" by Dr. R. (Robert) *SFZ* 47, November 19, 1926, 2: "Gegen den Hetzfilm *Die vier apokalyptischen Reiter*" by Dr. R. (Robert) *SFZ* 47, November 19, 1926, 3, 4: "Kommerzienrat Scheer" by Dr. H. (Hans) Spielhofer. See also *Film* 9, March 1, 1930, 1: "Antideutscher Hetzfilm in Rom."

58. *LBB* 55, March 6, 1926, 12, 13: "Metro-Goldwyn-Film *Mare Nostrum*." *FK* 136, June 14, 1926, 2: "Die Schuld an *Mare Nostrum*."

59. *FK* 56, March 7, 1927, 1: "Französische Kritik über *Mare Nostrum*." *FK* 101, April 30, 1927, 1: "Der *Vorwärts* gegen die deutschfeindlichen Hetzfilme der Metro." *Vorwärts* (S) 98, April 24, 1927, 19 (Supplement, "Aus der Film-Welt"): "Der Weltkrieg im Ufa-Palast am Zoo" by D.

60. *RFB* 10, March 12, 1927, 21: "Gegen die Hetzfilme." *LBB* 77, March 31, 1927, 2: "Gegen den Hetzfilm."

61. *RFB* 28, July 16, 1927, 40. *FK* 303, December 23, 1927, 1: "Alle *Mare Nostrum*-Kopien sollen vernichtet werden." *LBB* 306, December 1927, 1: "Friede auf Erden." *Film* 24/1927 (New Year issue, 1928), 24: "Keine Hetzfilme mehr."

62. FPS, August 10, 1926, file 13,423.

63. On the vote, for example, *Die Weltbühne* 25, June 21, 1927, 1,001, 1,002: "*Die große Parade*" by Wolf Zucker.

64. *VB* (B) 139, June 21, 1927, 2: "Der Hetzfilm *Die große Parade* wird in Berlin gezeigt."

65. FPS, October 20, 1926, file 16,991.

66. *FK* 250, October 22, 1927, 3: "*Die große Parade*" by Willy Haas.

67. *Film* (Special Edition "Kritiken der Woche"), October 22, 1927, 6: "*Die große Parade* im Ufa-Theater Kurfürstendamm" by Hans-Walter Betz.

68. Fröhlich, *Die Tagebücher von Joseph Goebbels, Volume I/II*, 283.

69. *Angriff* 18, October 31, 1927, 5: "Film."

70. *Angriff* 40, October 3, 1929, 5 (Supplement, 2): "Deutsche Kunst. Nationalsozialistischer Film."

71. *Angriff* 57, December 1, 1929, 7: "Alljüdischer Propagandafilm am Kurfürstendamm."

72. *FK* 286, December 2, 1929, 2: "Nationalsozialistisches Ultimatum an die Ufa."

73. *Angriff* 58, December 5, 1929, 5: "Die Ufa erklärt."

74. *Film* 49, December 7, 1929, 1: "Herr Jolson hat sich missliebig gemacht—aber nur bei den Nationalsozialisten [...]."

75. *LBB* 293, December 8, 1930, 2: "Nationalsozialisten gegen *Blauen Engel.*"

76. *Angriff* 27, April 3, 1930, 5: "Krach um den *Blauen Engel*" by Bar Kochba.

77. The present account goes beyond the previous literature on the Nazi campaigning against *Im Westen nichts Neues*. See Schrader, *Der Fall Remarque. Im Westen nichts Neues*, 1992 (concludes with December 1930). Odenwald, *Der nazistische Kampf gegen des "Undeutsche" in Theater und Film 1945–1945*, 2006, 108–114.

78. *VB* (B) 40, February 16, 1929 ("Der Deutsche Frontsoldat," 1): "Neudeutsche Kriegsliteratur" by Erich Limpach.

79. Official document reprinted in Bayer, *Carl Laemmle und die Universal*, 2016, 124.

80. *Film-Hölle* 8, August 1921, 10: "Der antideutsche Hetzfilm-Hauptdarsteller kommt!" by Der Filmteufel (Egon Jacobsohn).

81. *Deutsche Lichtspiel-Zeitung* 34, August 20, 1921, 6: "Offener Brief an Herrn Carl Laemmle," von Ludwig Seel. Among other things, Seel attacked Laemmle's film *The Geezer of Berlin*, Arthur Hotaling's 1918 short burlesque film on *The Kaiser, the Beast of Berlin*.

82. *München-Augsburger Abendzeitung* 347, August 21, 1921, 6: "Filmzeitung. An den Pranger!"

83. *Allgemeine Kino-Börse* 35, September 3, 1921, 671, 672: "Offener Brief an Herr Carl Laemmle" by Ludwig Seel.

84. *Film-Hölle* 9, September 1921, 13–15: "Der Höllenbraten. Präsident Laemmle, der Ehrenbürger von Laupheim!" by Der Filmteufel (Egon Jacobsohn).

85. *Der deutsche Film in Wort und Bild* 4, January 27, 1922, 1, 2: "Deutsche Würdiglosigkeit—ausländische Regisseure."

86. Examples: *Film Hölle* 9, September 1921, 1–15: "Der Höllenbraten. Präsident Laemmle, der Ehrenbürger von Laupheim!" by Der Filmteufel (Egon Jacobsohn). *Film* 37, September 13, 1925, 38,
"Deutschland und Amerika," and *Film* 7, February 15, 1930, 6: "Onkel Carl tut viel für den deutschen Film." *LBB* 41, October 8, 1922, 58: "Ein Kronzeuge für Karl Laemmle." *DFZ* 9, February 27, 1931, 2: "Carl Laemmle." Even shortly after Hitler's takeover, *Film* reported positively about him: *DFZ* 9, February 25, 1933, 2: "Carl Laemmle 27 Jahre in der Filmbranche."

87. *FJ* 11, March 18, 1927, 9 (2nd Supplement, 2): "Eine Stiftung Carl Laemmles." *RFB* 37, September 17, 1927, 19: "Zum Laemmle-Preis." According to *LBB* 57, March 8, 1927, 2: "Der Carl-Laemmle-Preis," the prize money was said to be only $2,500.

88. *VB* (B) 272, November 25, 1927, 6 ("Münchener Beobachter," 4): "Film."

89. *LBB* 164, July 11, 1929, 4: Deutsche Universal ad for *Im Westen nichts Neues*.

90. *VB* (B) 209, September 10, 1929, 1: "Der jüdische Deutschenhetzer dreht den deutschen 'Kriegsfilm.'"

91. *VB* (B) 43, April 1, 1930, 1: "Der Jude Lämmle [*sic*] macht aus Remarques *Im Westen nichts Neues* einen gemeinen Hetzfilm gegen die deutsche Armee."

92. Neumann, Belling, and Betz, 73: "III. Laemmle erwarb sich besondere Hetzfilm-'Verdienste.'"

93. *LBB* 191, August 11, 1930, 4: "Carl Laemmle Nobelpreisträger?"

94. *FK* 84, April 7, 1930, 1: "Deutscher Konsul besichtigt Remarque-Film." *LBB* 191, August 11, 1930, 4: "Carl Laemmle Nobelpreisträger?"

95. *FK* 283, December 1, 1930, 1: "Auswärtiges Amt und Remarquefilm. Keinerlei Beanstandungen."

96. FPS, November 21, 1930, file 26,579 (approved length: 2,884 meters).

97. Advocating examples: *Film* 49, December 6, 1930 Supplement, "Kritiken der Woche," 1: "*Im Westen nichts Neues* im Mozartsaal." *FJ* 49, December 7, 1930, 7 (2nd Supplement, 1): "*Im Westen nichts Neues* im Mozartsaal" by A. Schn. (Albert Schneider). *Vorwärts* (M) 571, December 6, 1930, 1st Supplement, 1: "Goebbels leitet Theaterkrach. Stinkbomben und Mäuse gegen den Film *Im Westen nichts Neues*." *Die Welt am Montag* 49, December 8, 1930, 8: "Vom Film." Reserved to rejecting examples: *Deutsche Allgemeine Zeitung* (Ber, M), 573, December 9, 1930, 1, 2: "Offener Brief an Erich Maria Remarque" by Dr. Curt Emmrich. *Kinematograph* 284, December 5, 1930, 4. *Der Tag* 294, December 10, 1930, 1: "Schluss mit dem Filmskandal!"

98. *FK* 284, December 2, 1930, 3: "Reichswehrministerium und *Im Westen nichts Neues*."

99. On the premiere: *FK* 287, December 5, 1930, 2: "*Im Westen nichts Neues*. Mozartsaal." *LBB* 285, November 28, 1930, 3: "Nachtvorstellung." *LBB* 290, December 4, 1930, 2: "Heute *Im Westen nichts Neues*. Prominente bei Remarque." *LBB* 291, December 5, 1930, 1: "Laemmles Remarque-Film."

100. *Film* 49, December 6, 1930, 1: "Stinkbomben gegen Remarque. Mozartsaal von Schupo zwangsweise geräumt. Goebbels in der Loge."

FK 288, December 6, 1930, 6 (1st Supplement, 2): "Der Kampf um den Remarque-Film. Vorführung gewaltsam verhindert!"

101. On Münchmeyer, see Udo Beer in *Biographisches Lexikon für Ostfriesland*, ostfriesischel-andschaft.de.

102. *Vorwärts* (M) 571, December 6, 1930, 1st Supplement, 1: "Goebbels leitet Theaterkrach. Stinkbomben und Mäuse gegen den Film *Im Westen nichts Neues*."

103. *Film* 49, December 6, 1930, 1: "Stink-bomben gegen Remarque." *FK* 288, December 6, 1930, 1, 6 (1st Supplement, 2): "Der Kampf um den Remarque-Film." *LBB* 292, December 6, 1930, 1: "Zensur durch Terror?"

104. *RWF* 50, December 13, 1930, 1, 2: "Im Reichsverband nichts Neues."

105. *LBB* 292, December 6, 1930, 1: "Der Remarque-Film läuft heute weiter!"

106. *Kinematograph* 287, December 9, 1930, 3: "Tumult am Nollendorfplatz." *Kine-matograph* 289, December 11, 1930, 1, 2: "Zirkus Nollendorfplatz."

107. Several examples of this are given in the book by Gimbel, *So kämpften wir!*, 1941, 36–38 (1926), 118, 119 (1931).

108. *Angriff* 112, December 6, 1930, 1: "Pro-teststurm im Mozartsaal. Gegen die Remarque-Sudelei" and *Angriff* 6: "Deutsche Frontsoldaten gegen perverse Juden."

109. *Der Abend* (E of *Vorwärts*) 574, December 8, 1930, 2: "Wieder Nazi-Klamauk."

110. *VB* (B and Ber) 291, December 7/8, 1930, 1: "Proteststurm gegen die gemeine Beschimpfung des deutschen Soldaten und unserer Gefallenen."

111. *Der Führer* 69, December 13, 1930, 2: "Pro-teststurm gegen die gemeine Beschimpfung des deutschen Soldaten und unserer Gefallenen."

112. On Wagner, see Weiß, 474, 475, entry by Ri (Eva Rimmele).

113. *Angriff* 114, December 9, 1930, 1: "Her-aus zum Massenprotest!" and *Angriff* 7: "Der Riesenaufmarsch des deutschbewußten Berlins im Westen. [...] Schupo schlägt Kriegsbeschädigte blutig—Sturmlauf gegen den jüdischen Schand-film." *VB* (B) 293, December 10, 1930, 1: "Straßen-kundgebungen in Berlin gegen den Hetzfilm *Im Westen nichts Neues*."

114. *VB* (Ber) 294, December 11, 1930 ("Ber-liner Beobachter," 1) and *VB* (B) 295, December 12, 1930, 1: "[...] Grzesinski schützt den jüdischen Schandfilm. Die anständigen Deutschen dürfen nicht einmal mehr protestieren!"

115. *WB* 120, December 10, 1930, 1, 2: "Weg mit dem jüdischen Schandfilm! [...] Die besudelte Leinwand."

116. *Stürmer* 52, mid–December 1930, 3: "Uner-hörte Provokation eines amerikanischen Filmju-den. Regierung schützt das Verbrechen am Volke" by Albert Forster.

117. *Der Stahlhelm* 50, December 14, 1930, 1, 2: "Unerhörte Beschimpfung der deutschen Frontsol-daten" by Wilhelm Kleinau.

118. *Angriff* 115, December 10, 1930, 7: "Will man die Massen führerlos machen?—Eine gutge-meinte Warnung."

119. *VB* (B and Ber) 294, December 11, 1930, 1: "Neue Riesenkundgebung gegen die Deserteur-Moral. 60.000 marschieren auf."

120. Neumann, Belling and Betz, 74: "III. Laemmle erwarb sich besondere Hetzfilm- 'Verdienste.'"

121. FOPS, December 18, 1930, file O 1,329. The FPS had barred the film on December 12, 1930, file 27,626.

122. FOPS, December 11, 1930, file O 1,254.

123. *LBB* 297, December 12, 1930, 1: "Universal zog den Film zurück."

124. *Angriff* 117, December 12, 1930, 1, 2: "Grz-esinski geschlagen! Unser der Sieg!" and "In die Knie gezwungen" by Dr. Joseph Goebbels.

125. *WB* 122, December 12, 1930, 1, 2: "Goeb-bels bleibt Sieger: Der Schandfilm zur Strecke gebracht!"

126. *B.Z.* 341, December 16, 1930, 2: "Massen-protest gegen das Remarque-Verbot. Die Kundge-bungen des Reichsbanners."

127. *Sozialistische Bildung* 12, December 1930, 378, 379: "Deutsche Filme." *Sozialistische Bildung* 1, January 1931, 25: "Filmschau."

128. *FJ* 50, December 14, 1930, 1, 2: "Diskussion über die Filmzensur."

129. Fröhlich, *Die Tagebücher von Joseph Goeb-bels*, Volume 2/I, 297–303.

130. *Film* 51, December 20, 1930, 1: "Unruhen im Ufa-Palast beim *Flötenkonzert von Sanssouci*." *LBB* 304, December 20, 1930, 1: "Schlachtfeld: Das deutsche Lichtspielhaus. Radauszenen um Ufa-Palast."

131. *Angriff* 124, December 20, 1930, 7: "Der unparteiische Nazigegner. Pfiffe beim *Flötenkonzert*."

132. For example, *FK* 145, June 24, 1931, 1: "Gefängnis für Kinotumulte. Breslauer Schöffengericht verurteilt Jungarbeiter zu 10 Tagen Gefängnis." *FJ* (Ma) 26, June 28, 1931, 2: "Neues aus Breslau."

133. *FK* 16, January 20, 1931, 4 (Supplement, 2): "Prof. Einstein über den Remarque-Film."

134. *FK* 28, February 3, 1931, 3: "Remarque-Film-Kundgebung der Liga für Menschenrechte."

135. German and English-language reports on train trips from Germany to neighboring coun-tries, including The Netherland's Venlo, for exam-ple, in *FK* 6, January 8, 1931, 3 (Supplement, 1): "Im Westen doch was Neues." *FK* 8, January 10, 1931, 15: "Something Doing on the Western Front" (English-language article). *FK* 29, February 4, 1931, 1: "*Im Westen nichts Neues* im Grenzgebiet." *RWF* 6, February 7, 1931, 7 (Supplement, 3): "*Im Westen nichts Neues* im Grenzgebiet." *FK* 7, Febru-ary 14, 1931, 2: "Westdeutsche Kinobesucher wan-dern aus!" *FK* 9, February 28, 1931, 2, 3: "Neues über *Im Westen nichts Neues*."

136. On Terboven, see Weiß, 458, entry by Ri (Eva Rimmele).

137. *National-Zeitung* (Essen) 18, January 22, 1931, 2: "Zensierter Remarque-Film in Straßburg"

by H.-N. See also *VB* (B) 17, January 17, 1931, 5: "Marxistische Schamlosigkeit. Sonderzüge zum Remarque-Film." *LBB* 23, January 27, 1931, 4: "Remarque-Film für die Saarländer." *LBB* 29, February 3, 1931, 3: "Im Westen etwas Neues. Kleinkrieg um den Remarque-Film."

138. *National-Zeitung* (Essen) 41, February 18, 1931, 3: "Die Arbeit der NSDAP in Sachsen. *Im Westen nichts Neues* aus den Schulen entfernt." On special trains to the Netherlands, see *LBB* 30, February 4, 1931, 2: "*Im Westen nichts Neues* im Saargebiet."

139. *Der Stahlhelm* 9, March 8, 1931, 6 (2nd Supplement): "Aachen und der Hetzfilm" by Dr. Hellmann.

140. *WB* 62, March 14, 1931, 9: "*Im Westen nichts Neues.*"

141. *National-Zeitung* (Essen) 42, February 19, 1931, 3: "*Im Westen nichts Neues* verbrannt."

142. *RWF* 10, March 5, 1931, 3: "*Im Westen nichts Neues* und die Abrüstungskonferenz."

143. "Lichtspielgesetz, March 31, 1931" in *RGBl* 14, March 31, 1931, 953.

144. For example, *LBB* 211, September 3, 1931, 1, 2: "Warum das Remarque-Verbot fiel" by Dr. Hans Wollenberg.

145. FPS, June 8, 1931, file 29,102 (approved length: 2,785 meters). See *LBB* 211, September 3, 1931, 1, 2: "Warum das Remarque-Verbot fiel'" by Dr. Hans Wollenberg.

146. *LBB* 147, June 20, 1931, 1: "Remarque-Film künstlerisch."

147. FPS, September 2, 1931, file 29,656. For this purpose, the Universal cut the film from 2,785 meters to 2,773 meters.

148. *LBB* 148, June 22, 1931, 1: "Die Nazis drohen! Die Polizei hat die Remarque-Film-Vorführungen zu sichern."

149. For example, *LBB* 159, July 4, 1931, 6 (1st Supplement, 2): Deutsche Universal AG full-page ad for *Im Westen nichts Neues*. *RWF* 26, June 27, 1931, 1: "*Im Westen nichts Neues* angelaufen."

150. *VB* (B) 152–153, June 1–2, 1931, 6 ("Münchner Beobachter," 2): "Weg mit den Auslandsfilmen."

151. *FK* 128, June 4, 1931, 1: "Hitlers Bedingungen für wohlwollende Behandlung der Kinos."

152. *FZ* (M) 494, July 6, 1931, 2: "Die Nationalsozialisten machen wieder Krach." *FZ* (1st M) 505, July 10, 1931, 2: "Der nationalsozialistische Tränengasangriff." *LBB* 163, July 9, 1931, 3: "Scharfes polizeiliches Vorgehen gegen Nazi-Krawalle."

153. *FZ* (M) 494, July 6, 1931, 2: "Die Nationalsozialisten machen wieder Krach." *FZ* (1st M) 505, July 10, 1931, 2: "Der nationalsozialistische Tränengasangriff." *LBB* 163, July 9, 1931, 3: "Scharfes polizeiliches Vorgehen gegen Nazi-Krawalle."

154. *WB* 157, July 10, 1931, 3: "Gegen den Schandfilm! Proteste der Bevölkerung."

155. *WB* 158, July 11, 1931, 3: "*Im Westen nichts Neues* unter Gummiknüppeldeckung."

156. *WB* 161, July 15, 1931, 3: "Kölsch Klaaf."

157. *RWF* 29, July 18, 1931, 2: "*Im Westen nichts Neues* läuft ohne Störungen-" by -g. Generalanzeiger Dortmund 189, July 12, 1931, 24: "Remarque-Film in Köln" by Martin Dey.

158. *Generalanzeiger Dortmund* 190, July 13, 1931, 14: "Düsseldorfer Nazi-Pleite. Nazisturm auf den Remarque-Film."

159. *FZ* (1st M) 511, July 12, 1931, 2: "Demonstrationen gegen *Im Westen nichts Neues.*"

160. *FZ* (E) 517, July 14, 1931, 3: "Dauernde Störungsversuche in Stuttgart."

161. *LBB* 166, July 13, 1931, 2: "Störungsversuche werden durch Polizei verhindert."

162. *LBB* 96, April 24, 1932, 3: "Bomben-Anschlag gegen Frankfurter Roxy geklärt." *FZ* (M) 513, July 13, 1931, 2: "Demonstrationen gegen den Film *Im Westen nichts Neues.*"

163. *LBB* 166, July 13, 1931, 2: "Eine Eierhandgranate im Frankfurter Roxy-Palast!" *FZ* (M) 513, July 13, 1931, 2: "Demonstrationen gegen den Film *Im Westen nichts Neues.*"

164. *FZ* (2nd M) 303, April 23, 1932, 2: "SA-Adjutanten als Sprengstoffattentäter. Vier Verhaftungen in Frankfurt."

165. *LBB* 247, October 20, 1932, 3: "Der Kino-Bombenprozess." *LBB* 252, October 26, 1932, 3: "Zuchthaus für Bomben-Attentäter. Anschlag auf Roxy-Palast gesühnt."

166. Gimbel and Hepp, 112.

167. *FK* 177, July 31, 1931, 1: "Ausschreitungen beim Remarque-Film."

168. *FJ* (Ma) 32, August 9, 1931, 4: "Westdeutschland."

169. *LBB* 238, October 5, 1931, 1: "Neue Störungen des Remarque-Films in München."

170. *LBB* 19, January 21, 1933, 3 (Supplement, 1): "Neue Remarque-Film-Krache."

171. *FK* 300, December 20, 1930, 15: "Studenten-Proteste in Dresden." *LBB* 304, December 20, 1930, 1: "Auch in Dresden studentische Störungen." *LBB* 305, December 22, 1930, 2: "Vom Kriegsschauplatz."

172. *FK* 232, September 30, 1930, 2: "*O Alte Burschenherrlichkeit,*" by -n-.

173. *FK* 231, September 30, 1930, 2: "Der Autor erzählt."

174. *FK* 295, December 14, 1930, 3: "Die neuen Kampfmittel gegen Kino und Varieté." *LBB* 299, December 15, 1930, 1: "Wer übt in Deutschland Filmzensur? In Erlangen: Studenten."

175. *VB* (B) 298, December 16, 1930, 5 ("Münchener Beobachter," 3): "Erlangens Studenten gegen die Verhöhnung der studentischen Sitten."

176. *LBB* 301, December 17, 1930, 4: "Kriegsschauplatz Erlangen."

177. *LBB* 299, December 15, 1930, 1: "Wer übt in Deutschland Filmzensur? In Erlangen: Studenten."

178. *Stürmer* 51, December 1930, 3: "Studenten protestieren gegen einen Schundfilm—Ein Rektor, der den Mut besitzt deutsch zu sein."

179. *VB* (B) 298, December 16, 1930, 5 ("Münchener Beobachter," 3): "Erlangens Studenten gegen die Verhöhnung der studentischen

Sitten. Massendemonstration gegen einen amerikanischen Kitschfilm." *VB* (Ber) 299, December 17, 1930, 2: "*O Alte Burschenherrlichkeit* von amerikanischen Filmjuden verkitscht. Erfolgreiche Studentendemonstration in Erlangen."

180. Schmidt, *Albert Speer*, 1982, 39, with reference to Speer's letter to his friend Dr. Rudolf Wolters of August 10, 1946. Speer, *Spandauer Tagebücher*, 1975.

181. *FK* 232, September 30, 1930, 3: "Der Autorenstreit um *Die Dreigroschenoper*." *FK* 300, December 20, 1930, 1: "Brecht-Vergleich im *Die Dreigroschenoper*-Prozess." *LBB* 44, February 20, 1931, 2: "Die Dreigroschenoper."

182. *FK* 49, February 27, 1931, 3 (Supplement, 1): "Nationalsozialisten stören *Die Dreigroschenoper*."

183. *Film* 9, February 28, 1931, 4: "*Dreigroschenoper*-Tumult in Nürnberg."

184. *Stürmer* 10, März 1931, 3: "Polizeiskandal im Phoebuspalast."

185. *DFZ* 11, March 13, 1931, 3: "Der Theaterbesitzer an seine Störer," letter by A. Fr. Kurth, director of the Schwäbische Urania.

186. *LBB* 50, February 27, 1931, 1: "Schlägst Du meinen Film, schlag' ich Deinen Film!"

187. *VB* (B) 70, March 11, 1931, 2 ("Münchener Beobachter"): "*Die 3-Groschenoper*."

188. On Frick, see Weiß, 133, 134, entry by KAL (Dr. Klaus A. Lankheit).

189. *FK* 53, March 4, 1931, 2: "Der Frick-Terror. [...]. War der Nürnberger 'Protest' bestellte Arbeit?" *LBB* 54, March 4, 1931, 1: "Thüringischer Widerruf und Polizei-Ukas *gegen Dreigroschenoper*."

190. *FK* 65, March 18, 1931, 1: "Auch Baden fordert *Dreigroschenoper*-Verbot." *Der Führer* 59, March 11, 1931, 1: "Ein jüdisches Schmutzstück wird in der badischen Landeshauptstadt aufgeführt."

191. *Der Führer* 82, April 9, 1931, 4: "*Dreigroschenoper*-Schweinerei gelassen."

192. FPS, April 2, 1930, file 25,516. April 11, 1930, file 25,592. May 19, 1930, file 25,969.

193. For example, *Film* 21, May 24, 1930, 3: "*Cyankali*" by Dr. K.L. (Dr. Kurt London).

194. FOPS, August 29, 1930, file O 25,969. December 12, 1930, file O 26,831.

195. For example, *FK* 209, September 4, 1930, 3, 4 (Supplement, 1, 2): "Warum man *Cyankali* verbot."

196. *B.Z.* 58, March 10, 1931, 1: "§ 218-Untersuchung greift auf Berlin über."

197. Thus, among others, in March and April 1931 section "Öffentliche Anklage § 218" of *Die Welt am Abend*, for example, 57, March 9, 1931, 10, together with the report "Friedrich Wolf vor den Berliner Arbeitern Arbeitern." *Die Welt am Abend* 72, March 26, 1931, 9 (2nd Supplement, 1): "Der Massensturm gegen § 218." *Die Welt am Abend* 88, April 16, 1931, 9 (2nd Supplement, 1): "Fr. Kienle and F. Wolf sprechen im Sportpalast."

198. *B.Z.* 44, February 21, 1931, 1, 2: "Der Dichter Dr. Friedrich Wolf in Stuttgart verhaftet." *Die Welt am Abend* 44, February 21, 1931, 1: "Dichter

von Cyankali wegen § 218 in Haft." *Die Welt am Abend* 50, February 28, 1931, 2: "Friedrich Wolf freigelassen."

199. *FK* 180, August 1, 1930, 1: "Kulturkampf mit Stinkbomben. Unwürdiger Protestrummel jetzt auch in Danzig." *LBB* 188, August 7, 1930, 2: "Danziger Kesseltreiben *gegen Cyankali*." *LBB* 189, August 8, 1930, 3: "*Cyankali* in Danzig. Der Kampf geht weiter."]

200. *Der Führer* 67, March 20, 1931, 4: "Cyankali."

201. *FJ* (Ma) 15, April 12, 1930, 2: "*Cyankali* in Pforzheim."

202. *FK* 75, March 30, 1931, 1: "Die Straße setzt sich durch."

203. *Der Führer* 78, April 2, 1931, 5: "*Cyankali* polizeilich geschützt."

204. *FK* 75, March 30, 1931, 1: "*Cyankali* in Pforzheim verboten."

205. *Der Führer* 78, April 2, 1931, 5: "*Cyankali* polizeilich geschützt."

206. *FK* 80, April 7, 1931, 1: "Pforzheim gibt *Cyankali* frei."

207. *FK* 87, April 15, 1931, 1: "Für *Cyankali* gibt's keine Straßenbahn, sagt Pforzheims Magistrat."

208. *DFZ* 15, April 10, 1931, 5: "Kampf um *Cyankali*."

209. *Der Führer* 86, April 14, 1931, 5, 7: "Der *Cyankali*-Film in Pforzheim." *Der Führer* 118, June 2, 1931, 2: "Wolf macht einen § 218-Film." *FJ* (Ma) 15, April 12, 1930, 2: "*Cyankali* in Pforzheim."

210. *FK* 155, July 6, 1931, 1: "Bestrafte Rowdies."

211. Köhler, 22.

212. *FK* 128, June 4, 1931, 1: "Hitlers Bedingungen für wohlwollende Behandlung der Kinos." See also *VB* (B) 152–153, June 1–2, 1931, 6 ("Münchner Beobachter," 2): "Weg mit den Auslandsfilmen."

213. FPS, February 24, 1934, file 35,800.

214. Hull, *Film in the Third Reich*, 1969, 45.

215. *NYT* 27, 803, March 9, 1934, 4: "Nazis Tame a Mob at Showing of Film." Spieker, *Hollywood unterm Hakenkreuz*, 1999, 80, with sources.

216. *Kinematograph* 49, March 10, 1934, 3: "Lebhafter Protest gegen *Katharina die Große*."

217. *LBB* 58, March 9, 1934, 1, 3: "Protest gegen *Katharina die Große*" and "*Katharina die Große* im Capitol" by H.U. (Heinz Umbehr). *Film* 10, March 10, 1934, 1: "Bergner-Film abgesetzt."

218. *NYT* 27, 805, March 11, 1934, 26: "Rosenberg Defends Ban of British Film." *VB* (Ber) 69, March 10, 1934, 1, 2: "Warnende Zeichen" by Alfred Rosenberg. "Der Film *Katharina die Große* abgesetzt."

219. *NYT* 27, 816, March 22, 1934, 10: "Film Man's Auto Bombed in Berlin."

220. See, on this, Hett, *Der Reichstagsbrand*, 2016, 94.

221. *FK* 47, February 25, 1931, 6: Ad "Zum Charlie-Chaplin-Besuch spielt jeder Original Chaplin-Grotesken." *FK* 62, March 14, 1931, 11.

222. *Leipziger Volkszeitung* 90, April 18, 1931, 3 (1st Supplement, 1): "Nazi-Beobachter."

223. *Mitteldeutscher Lichtspieltheaterbesitzer* 12, December 15, 1930, 1, 2: "Um Remarque."

Mitteldeutscher Lichtspieltheaterbesitzer 1, January 1, 1931, 16: "Auch Leipzig protestiert gegen Remarque-Film-Verbot."

Chapter 6

1. *Film* 17, April 23, 1922, 48: "Die neue Südfilm-A.G." *RFB* 5, February 1, 1930, 1: "15 Jahre Südfilm." *LBB* 120, May 25, 1932, 3: "Wie die Südfilm wurde."
2. *FK* 25, November 28, 1928, 7: "Direktor Emil Fieg."
3. Spiker, 34, 39, 40.
4. *Handbuch*, 1928, 1,930, 7,248. *FK* 254, October 24, 1928, 3: "Die Bilanz der Südfilm A.G."
5. *RFB* 51, December 24, 1927, 34: "Loslösung der Südfilm von der Emelka." *FK* 30, February 3, 1928, 1: "Südfilmtheater und *Emelkawoche* bei Emelka." 31, February 4, 1928, 1: "Deutsch-englische Zusammenarbeit."
6. *Handbuch*, 1928 1,930. *Handbuch* 1929, 1,117, 1,118, 1,930. *FK* 31, February 4, 1928, 4 (1st Supplement, 2): "John Maxwell." *FK* 53, March 1, 1928, 1: "Aufsichtsratssitzung der Südfilm." *SFZ* 52, December 23, 1927, 2, 3: "Loslösung der Südfilm von der Emelka," by S (Dr. Hans Spielhofer).
7. *LBB* 230, September 30, 1932, 1: "Momentaufnahmen von einer Gläubiger-Versammlung." See also *Handbuch*, 1928, 1,930.
8. *LBB* 3, January 14, 1922, 32: "Monopolverletzungen und deren Abstellung" by Director I. Goldschmid. *LBB* 110, September 20, 1924, 40: Goldschmid's advertising letter from Vienna on his own behalf. *RFB* 16, April 21, 1928, 28: "British International und Pathé." Neumann, Belling, and Betz, 84, 85: "III. Wie Isidor Goldschmidt [*sic*] wurde."
9. *FK* 53, March 3, 1928, 1: "6 Prozent Dividende." *FK* 56, March 5, 1928, 1: "Fieg und Goldschmid im Vorstand der Südfilm." *FK* 61, March 10, 1928, 1: "Die Generalversammlung der Südfilm." *FK* 81, March 3, 1928, 1: "Die Generalversammlung der Südfilm." *FK* 81, March 3, 1928, 1: "Generalversammlung der Süd-Film A.G." *FK* 84, 7 April 1928, 3 (1st Supplement, 1): "Osterüberraschung der Südfilm A.G." *FK* 87, 12 April 1928, 1: "Südfilm hat mit der Vermietung begonnen." *FK* 89, April 14, 1928, 2: "Neues aus dem Südfilm-Programm." *FK* 95, April 21, 1928, 1: "Südfilm-Produktion bereits überall stark gebucht." *FK* 101, April 28, 1928, 1: "Südfilm bei der Arbeit." *FK* 131, June 2, 1928, 3 (1st Supplement, 1): "Das Neueste vom Programm der Südfilm." *FK* 160, July 6, 1928, 1: "Südfilm erzielt im Titania-Palast gute Kassen."
10. *FK* 233, September 29, 1928, 2: "Aufsichtsratssitzung der Süd-Film A.G."
11. *BT* (E) 486, October 13, 1928, 9 (2nd Supplement, 3): "Produktionsbeschränkungen bei der Südfilm A.G.?" *FK* 246, October 15, 1928, 3: "Keine Produktionsbeschränkung der B.I.P.!"
12. *FK* 252, October 22, 1928, 2: "Generalversammlung der Südfilm."

13. *FK* 254, October 24, 1928, 3: "Die Bilanz der Südfilm A.G." *RFB* 43, October 27, 1928, 28: "Die Südfilm-G.-V."
14. *FK* 15, January 16, 1929, 1: "Günstige Aussichten der Südfilm."
15. *FK* 30, February 2, 1929, 3 (1st Supplement, 1): "Emil Fieg verlässt Süd-Film." *FK* 44, February 19, 1929, 1: "Ernst Haller im Vorstand der Südfilm." See also *Handbuch*, 1929, 1,117, 1,118.
16. *FK* 88, April 13, 1929, 2: "Südfilm in der neuen Saison." *FK* 99, April 16, 1929, 1: "Deutscher 100 %-Sprechtonfilm für Südfilm begonnen." *FK* 137, June 11, 1929, 1: "Maxwell in Berlin." *FK* 145, June 20, 1929, 1: "Gesteigerte Aktivität der Südfilm." *FK* 281, November 26, 1929, 3: "Dir. Goldschmid über Elstree."
17. *Film* 37 (weekly edition "Kritiken der Woche"), September 14, 1929, 405, 406: *Blackmail (Erpressung)*" by Dr. Kurt London.
18. *FJ* 15, April 14, 1929, 1: "Wo bleibt die Kapitalerhöhung der Südfilm?" *FJ* 16, April 21, 1929, 1: "Der Vorstand schweigt noch immer."
19. *FK* 282, November 27, 1929, 1: "Günstige Tage der Südfilm." *FK* 284, November 28, 1929, 2, 5: "Von Erfolg zu Erfolg."
20. For example, *FK* 146, June 21, 1929, 1: "Angespannte Tonfilmarbeit!" *FK* 158, July 5, 1929, 1: "Erfolgreicher Saison-Auftakt der Südfilm." *FK* 163, July 11, 1929, 1: "Staaken im Zeichen der Südfilm." *FK* 234, October 2, 1929, 3 (Supplement, 1): "Sechs Südfilm-Premieren im Oktober." *FK* 253, October 24, 1929, 1: "Maxwell in Berlin. [...] Montag Duponts *Atlantic*."
21. *FK* 243, October 12, 1929, 1: "Deutsche Gruppe erwirbt Südfilm." *FK* 253, October 24, 1929, 1: "Maxwell in Berlin. [...] Montag Duponts *Atlantic*." *FK* 256, October 28, 1929, 1: "Die *Atlantic* Premiere. Maxwell in Berlin." *RFB* 42, October 19, 1929, 18: "Südfilm wieder deutsch." *RFB* 46, November 16, 1929, 20: "Die Verteilung der Südfilm-Aktien."
22. *FK* 279, November 23, 1929, 5 (2nd Supplement, 1): "Charlies neuester Filmgag."
23. *BT* (M) 20, January 12, 1930, 38 (5th Supplement, 2).
24. *Handbuch*, 1930, 1,030.
25. *RFB* 3, January 18, 1930, 6: "Geld zum Vertrieb von Chaplin-Filmen gesucht."
26. *FJ* (Ma) 22, 29. May1932, 1, 2: "Der Fall Goldschmid" by Albert Schneider.
27. *FK* 28, January 31, 1930, 1: "[G]estern ein zufriedener Aufsichtsrat."
28. *FK* 193/194, August 18, 1930, 1: "Große Südfilm-Premiere." *FK* 221, September 18, 1930, 1: "*Der Greifer—ein Treffer*." *FK* 227, September 25, 1930, 1: "Bedeutsamer Ausbau des Südfilm-Programms."
29. *FK* 50, February 26, 1930, 1: "Optimistische Auffassung der Entwicklung." *FK* 2: "Die Südfilm-Bilanz."
30. For the origins of Emelka's financial troubles, see Spiker, 46.
31. *FK* 234, October 3, 1930, 1: "Verleiherdebatte geht weiter." *FK* 268, November 12,

1930, 1, 5 (Supplement, 1): "Goldschmid zur Tonfilmdebatte."

32. *FK* 271, November 15, 1930, 3: "Südfilm zahlt 15 % Dividende." *FK* 276, November 22, 1930, 10: "Südfilm zahlt 15 %." *Handbuch*, 1931, 6,279.

33. *FK* 303, December 24, 1930, 1, 2, 6 (1st Supplement, 2): "Erfreulicher Produktions-Optimismus bei der Südfilm."

34. *LBB* 295, December 10, 1930, 1: "Die erfolgreiche Südfilm."

35. *LBB* 307, December 24, 1930, 9, 10 (2nd Supplement, 1, 2): "Südfilm in weiterem Aufstieg."

36. Jason, *Handbuch der Filmwirtschaft*, 47.

37. *FK* 299, December 19, 1930, 2: "Haben Sie gehört?"

38. *B.Z.* 22, January 27, 1931, 3 (1st Supplement, 1): "Chaplins neuer stummer Film" by P.J. Wbg.

39. *BBZ* (M) 65, February 8, 1931, 14: "Chaplins *Lichter der Großstadt*. Ein Triumph des stummen Films," von H.B. (Hans Baumann).

40. *FK* 26, January 31, 1931, 8 (2nd Supplement, 2): "Kampf um den Chaplin-Film. Angebote steigen." *RFB* 9, February 28, 1931, 1: "Charlie Chaplins Berliner Tonfilmstart."

41. *LBB* 45, February 21, 1931, 1: "Um den Chaplin-Film." *FK* 110, May 12, 1931, 2: "Haben Sie gehört?"

42. Aping, *Charlie Chaplin in Deutschland*, 211–214. *LBB* 48, December 1, 1923, 10, 13: "Die Edellizenz" by Heinz Udo Brachvogel.

43. *FK* 47, February 25, 1931, 1: "*City Lights* bei Südfilm."

44. Shortly after Hitler's takeover, Bermann lost his means of existence in Germany and returned to Austria. From there he emigrated via London to the United States in 1938, where he died in 1939. See Britta Eckert, "Richard A. Bermann im Ständestaat und im Exil" in Bermann, *Die Fahrt auf dem Katarakt*, 1998, pp. 325.

45. Bermann, *Die Fahrt auf dem Katarakt*, 287, 288. In his report, Bermann refers to "Mr. G."

46. Hoellriegel, *Lichter der Großstadt*, 1931. On the Austrian premiere, see *Neue Freie Presse* (Vienna, M) 23.907, April 4, 1931, 7: "Sascha Palace ad for *Lichter der Großstadt*."

47. *FJ* (Ma) 10, March 8, 1931, 1: "Südfilm hat *Lichter der Großstadt* für ihre sämtlichen Theater erworben."

48. *FK* 50, 28 February 1931, 2: "Londoner Festpremiere von *City Lights*."

49. *FK* 47, February 25, 1931, 1: "*City Lights* bei Südfilm." *FK* 50, February 28, 1931, 2: "Chaplin durchs Telefon." *Kinematograph* 43, February 20, 1931, 3: "Südfilm kauft neuen Chaplin-Film." *Lichtbildbühne* 48, February 25, 1931, 1: "Chaplin bei Südfilm." *Lichtbildbühne* 49, February 26, 1931, 3: full-page ad "*City Lights* für Deutschland bei Südfilm AG." *Lichtbildbühne* 51, February 28, 1931, 2: "Chaplins Europa-Premiere." *FJ* (Ma) 22, May 29, 1932, 1, 2: "Der Fall Goldschmid," von Albert Schneider.

50. Carlyle T. Robinson, *La Vérité sur Charlie Chaplin*, 234.

51. *LBB* 45, February 21, 1931, 1: "Um den Chaplin-Film." *FK* 110, May 12, 1931, 2: "Haben Sie gehört?"

52. *B.Z.* 73, March 27, 1931, 3 (1st Supplement, 1): "Der neue Chaplin-Film" by Kurt Mühsam.

53. See *B.Z.* 46, February 24, 1931, 4 (1st Supplement, 2): "Wettrennen um Chaplin-Film." According to this, there was talk of a "financial syndicate."

54. Krakauer, 8.

55. *FK* 54, March 5, 1931, 2: "Haben Sie gehört?"

56. *B.Z.* 31, February 6, 1931, 4 (1st Supplement, 2): "Tonfilm ruiniert Filmgeschäft" by K. M. (Kurt Mühsam).

57. According to Jason, *Handbuch der Filmwirtschaf*, 61, 63, 276, 278, 284, 285, 296, 306, 314, 315.

58. *LBB* 153, July 2, 1932, 4 (Supplement, 2): "Was Stummfilme brachten."

59. Paschke, *Der deutsche Tonfilmmarkt*, 39, 40.

60. Wolffsohn, *Jahrbuch der Filmindustrie*, 422.

61. Jason, *Handbuch der Filmwirtschaf* 69, 70. Wolffsohn, 424-435.

62. Paschke, *Der deutsche Tonfilmmarkt*. Wolffsohn, *Jahrbuch der Filmindustrie*, 424.

63. *LBB* 283, November 26, 1930, 1: "3,5 Millionen Erwerbslose. Filmbesuch und Erwerbstätigkeit." See also Spiker, 55, 56.

64. Hagen Schulze, "Vom Scheitern der Republik," in: Bracher/Funke/Jacobsen (editors), *Die Weimarer Republik 1918–1933*, 1998, 637.

65. *Berlin am Morgen* 58, March 10, 1931, 1: "Einer der vielen Millionen Chaplins" by Bi.

66. *Südfilm-Magazin* 3, March 1931.

67. *RWF* 13, March 28, 1931, 2: "Charlie Chaplins *Großstadtlichter*."

68. *RFB* 14, April 4, 1931, 5: Südfilm AG ad for *Lichter der Großstadt*.

69. FPS, March 23, 1931, file 28,553.

70. *FK* 77, April 1, 1931, 2: "*City Lights* wurde vom Lampe-Ausschuss als künstlerisch wertvoll erklärt."

71. *FK* 78, April 2, 1932, 11: "Ihr Kronzeuge."

72. *FK* 73, March 27, 1931, 1, 3: "*Lichter der Großstadt*."

73. Section "Wirtschaftsspiegel. Premierenstatistk" in *LBB* 119, May 19, 1931, 4. *LBB* 141, June 13, 1931, 8.

74. *LBB* 204, August 26, 1931, 3: "Chaplin in ganz Berlin."

75. Jason, *Handbuch der Filmwirtschaf*, 170, 172, 175.

76. *RWF* 14, April 4, 1931, 1: "Chaplins Triumph auch im Rheinland."

77. Residenz-Theater ads from April 1 to 16, 1931, in *Düsseldorfer Nachrichten* (M) 167, April 1, 1931, 8, to (M) 191, April 16, 1931, 15. On the cost of screenings, *Düsseldorfer Nachrichten* (M) 171, April 3, 1931.

78. Asta Nielsen Theater ads in *Düsseldorfer Nachrichten* from (M) 273, June 1, 1931, 4, through (M) 284, June 8, 1931, 12.

79. *LBB* 85, April 9, 1931, 2: "Chaplin-Besuchsziffern im Reiche." *FK* 79, April 4, 1931, 11: "Oster-Spielpläne im Reich." *FK* 199, August 26, 1931, 2: "Haben Sie gehört?"

80. Section "Die Spielwoche und Spielplan Groß-Hamburger Kinos" in *FJ* 15, April 12, 1931, 7, 8. *FJ* 16, April 19, 1931, 12. *FJ* 17, April 26, 1931, 8. *FJ* 18, May 3, 1931, 8. *FJ* 19, May 10, 1931, 8.

81. *FJ* 18, May 3, 1931, 8: "Neues aus Schlesien."

82. FPS, March 23, 1931, file 28,553.

83. *FK* 103, May 4, 1931, 1: "Preßburgs Stadtväter gegen die Steuerfreiheit von *City Lights*."

84. *FK* 98, April 28, 1931, 1: "*City Lights* in Ludwigshafen für Schüler verboten."

85. *RWF* 35, August 29, 1931, 4: "Saisonstart der *Lichter der Großstadt*."

86. *FK* 199, August 26, 1931, 2: "Haben Sie gehört?" *RWF* 35, August 29, 1931, 4: "Saisonstart der *Lichter der Großstadt*."

87. *Film* 26, June 27, 1931, 2: "Stand der Südfilm." *FK* 145, June 24, 1931, 1: "Fast eine Million Vorausbuchungen auf 31/32. 9 Millionen Südfilm-Umsatz."

88. *Film* 26, June 27, 1931, 2: "Direktor Goldschmidt ist vom Urlaub zur Südfilm zurückgekehrt." For the reproaches against Goldschmid, see *FJ* (Ma) 22, May 29, 1931, 1, 2: "Der Fall Goldschmid" by Albert Schneider.

89. *Kinematograph* 155, July 9, 1931, 3: "D.L.S. und Südfilm gehen zusammen."

90. Spiker, 53, 60, 62, 64.

91. *FK* 148, June 27, 1931, 3 (1st Supplement, 1): "Südfilm günstig."

92. *FK* 157, July 8, 1931, 1, 3: "Zusammenarbeit D.L.S.-Südfilm. Tobiskonzern auf Produktionsbasis." *RFB* 28, July 11, 1931, 1: "Presse-Kommuniqué: Interessengemeinschaft DLS-Südfilm."

93. *Kinematograph* 11, January 16, 1932, 3: "D.L.S.-Bilanzziffern." See also Spiker, 40.

94. *Kinematograph* 11, January 16, 1932, 3: "D.L.S.-Bilanzziffern." *FK* 254, October 27, 1932, 1: "D.L.S. beantragt Vergleich. Missstände in der Geschäftsführung." *Kinematograph* 11, January 16, 1932, 3: "D.L.S.-Bilanzziffern." *Film* 9, February 25, 1933, 7: "Gerichtliche Vergleiche."

95. *LBB* 15, January 19, 1932, 2.

96. Section "Haben Sie gehört?" in *FK* 18, January 21, 1932, 2, and *FK* 21, January 25, 1932, 2.

97. *Film* 9, February 20, 1932, 8: Südfilm AG ad for *Knall und Fall* and *Schritt und Tritt*. *Film* 22, May 28, 1932, 4: Südfilm AG ad for *Lumpenkavaliere*.

98. *FK* 113, May 14, 1932, 1: "Südfilm aktiv."

99. *FK* 112, May 13, 1932, 1: "Gestern Aufsichtsratssitzung."

100. *FJ* (Ma) 22, May 29, 1932, 1, 2: "Der Fall Goldschmid" by Albert Schneider.

101. *LBB* 124, May 30, 1932, 1: "'Erlogen.'"

102. *FK* 125, May 30, 1932, 1: "Ehrenerklärung der Lieferanten für I. Goldschmid."

103. *Film* 23, June 4, 1932, 1: "Südfilm-Aufsichtsrat tagte stundenlang." *FK* 130, June 4, 1932, 1, 2: "Vertrauensvotum für Goldschmid." *FK* 136, June 11, 1932, 4: "Ausklang."

104. *Film* 24, June 11, 1932, 5: "Das Kriegsbeil ist begraben." *FJ* (Ma) 24, June 12, 1932, 1: "Erklärung."

105. *FK* 140, June 16, 1932, 1, 2: "600.000 Mark Verlust per 30. Juni 1931 ausgewiesen."

106. Spiker, 60.

107. *FK* 140, June 16, 1932, 1, 2: "Ausfälle bei der Kundschaft." For the Supervisory Board of Südfilm AG, see *Handbuch*, 1932, 2,945, 2,946.

108. *FK* 151, June 29, 1932, 2: "Südfilm-Mitarbeiter versammelt."

109. *FK* 78, April 2, 1932, 11: "Ihr Kronzeuge."

110. *FK* 143, June 20, 1932, 1: "Chaplins schwacher Publikumserfolg."

111. *Die Welt am Abend* 228, September 28, 1932 (2nd Supplement, 1): "Das Ende der Südfilm—Gerüchte um Chaplin."

112. *LBB* 10, January 12, 1931, 2: "Chaplin rechnet mit 32 Mill."

113. *LBB* 11, January 13, 1932, 4: "Amerikas größte Erfolge 1931."

114. Carlyle T. Robinson, *La Vérité sur Charlie Chaplin*, 241, 242.

115. *FK* 259, November 4, 1931, 2: "*City Lights* brings 6 Millionen Francs im Marigny." *LBB* 268, November 9, 1931, 3: "Pariser Premieren."

116. *Autobiography*, 395, 410.

117. *FK* 151, June 29, 1932, 2: "Südfilm-Mitarbeiter versammelt." *FK* 187, August 10, 1932, 1: "Südfilm bringt 14 Filme." *FK* 188, August 11, 1932, 1, 3 (Supplement, 1): "Das Südfilmprogramm." *RFB* 34, August 25, 1932, 2: "Südfilm 1932/33." *RWF* 35, August 27, 1932, 2: "Erfolg mit Südfilm."

118. *FK* 227, September 26, 1932, 1: "Südfilm stellt Zahlungen ein."

119. *FK* 140, June 16, 1932, 1: "600 000 Mark Verlust per 30. Juni 1931 ausgewiesen." *FK* 227, September 26, 1932, 1, 2: "Südfilm stellt Zahlungen ein."

120. One Tobis Group's equity in Südfilm AG, see *FK* 140, June 16, 1932, 1: "600 000 Mark Verlust per 30. Juni 1931 ausgewiesen."

121. *FK* 227, September 26, 1932, 1: "Neuzugründende Firma Europa-Film soll den Verleih weiterführen."

122. *LBB* 228, September 27, 1932, 1: "5 Millionen Passiven." *LBB* 229, September 29, 1932, 1: "Die Vorbesprechung der ungesicherten Gläubiger." Karl Wolffsohn, publisher of the *LBB*, was one of the unsecured creditors.

123. *FK* 230, September 29, 1932, 1, 3: "Rechenschaftsbericht des Vorstandes über die vergangenen Jahre. Sehr erregte Debatten."

124. *LBB* 229, September 29, 1932, 1: "Beginn der Gläubiger-Versammlung der Südfilm."

125. *LBB* 230, September 30, 1932, 1: "Momentaufnahmen von einer Gläubiger-Versammlung."

126. *Film* 40, October 1, 1932, 2: "Südfilm-Treuhänder: Gunderloch."

127. *RFB* 21, May 21, 1932, 7 (2nd Supplement, 1): "*Der Prinz von Arkadien*. Südfilm im Atrium."

128. *LBB* 229, September 29, 1932, 1: "Beginn der Gläubiger-Versammlung der Südfilm."

129. *FJ* (Ma) 40, October 2, 1932, 1, 2: "Zusammenbruch der Südfilm."

130. *Handbuch*, 1933, 2,275, 2,276.

131. *FJ* (Ma) 43, October 23, 1932, 1, 2: "Verluste, die vermeidbar waren." *FJ* (Ma) 44, October 30, 1932, 1: "Wann endlich Südfilm-Status?" *FK*

231, September 30, 1932, 1, 2: "Ein Treuhänder bei Südfilm." *FK* 25, November 2, 1932, 1: "Unbegreifliche Verzögerung."

132. *Handbuch*, 1933, 2,275, 2,276. *FK* 18, January 20, 1933, 1: "Die Situation bei Südfilm." *FK* 21, January 24, 1933, 1: "Südfilm in Berlin." *FK* 23, January 26, 1933, 1: "Südfilm-Vergleich bestätigt."

133. *FK* 300, December 21, 1932, 1: "Der Südfilm-Vergleich." *RWF* 38, September 16, 1933, 10: "Zur Liquidation der Südfilm." *LBB* 64, March 15, 1935, 2: "Vergleich Südfilm-AG." *FK* 63, March 15, 1935, 1: "Gläubiger erhielten bisher 10 Proz[ent]."

134. *FJ* (Ma) 41, October 9, 1932, 1: "Europa Filmverleih AG gegründet." *FK* 237, October 7, 1932, 1, 2: "Die Gründung der Europa."

135. *FJ* (Ma) 45, November 6, 1932, 1: "Ein neuer Großverleih: Europa."

136. *RWF* 30, July 22, 1933, 7: "Europa marschiert."

137. *Handbuch*, 1934, 2,404. 1937, 8,499.

138. *FK* 277, November 24, 1932, 2: "Haben Sie gehört?" *LBB* 284, December 3, 1932, 1: "Man hört." *FK* 85, April 8, 1933 (2nd Supplement, 1): "Isidor Goldschmid hat Deutschland verlassen."

139. Neumann, Belling and Betz, 84, 85: "III. Wie Isidor Goldschmidt [sic] wurde."

Chapter 7

1. Assertion in *The Kellogg News* (ID), October 16, 1942: "Strange as It Seems" by John Hix IN "Montreux," album 64.

2. *Statistisches Jahrbuch für das Deutsche Reich*, 1932, 547.

3. Thus stated without providing sources by Hanisch, *Über ihn lach(t)en Millionen*, 108, 109. Michael Hanisch, "Nicht mehr zum Lachen: 'Der Jude Karl Tonstein' und die Nazis" in Radevagen, 115. Hanisch: "The Chaplin Reception in Germany" in Nysenholc, 17–30. Velten and Klein 64, 73.

4. Walk, *Das Sonderrecht der Juden im NS-Staat*, V.

5. *VB* (N) 45, February 14, 1933, 1: "Minister Göring räumt in der Verwaltung auf."

6. *Ministerialblatt für die preußische innere Verwaltung* Part 1, 1933, 169.

7. *Berliner Morgenpost* 48, February 25, 1933, 1: "Hilfspolizei in Preußen," with wording of Göring's Decree. See also von Engelbrechten, *Eine braune Armee entsteht*, 265. Friedrich, *Die missbrauchte Hauptstadt*, 431.

8. See Mommsen, *Beamtentum im Dritten Reich*, 1966, 34–38. Brechtken, *Albert Speer*, 2017, 10, 11.

9. Hitler, 652, 653.

10. *Angriff* 20, January 24, 1931 (2nd Supplement, 1): "Filmkunst."

11. *FK* 146, June 23, 1932, 2: "Haben Sie gehört?" 149, June 27, 1932, 2: "Jetzt auch in Preußen ein Rassen-Theater-Gesetz."

12. *Angriff* 51, March 1, 1933 (1st Supplement, 1, 2): "Verjudung und Geschäftemacherei im 'deutschen' Film." *FK* 193, August 18, 1933, 4: "Dr. Rainer Schlösser—Reichsfilmdramaturg."

13. "Erlass über die Errichtung des RMVP, March 13, 1933" in *RGBl* 21, March 17, 1933, 104. "Verordnung über die Aufgaben des RMVP, June 30, 1933" in *RGBl* 75, July 5, 1933, 449.

14. Letter and list, see at BayHStA (Bayerisches Hauptstaatsarchiv) Minn 72.695, in deutsches-filminstitut.de/zengut/SGNSDAPx.pdf. See also *LBB* 6, March 16, 1933, 3: "Die geplanten Filmverbote. Kommunistische, pazifistische Tendenz-Filme und Sexual-Filme."

15. *FJ* (Ma) 21, May 21, 1933, 3: "Schwarze Liste für Autoren." Quickly the list was vastly expanded: *FJ* (Ma) 22, May 28, 1933, 4: "Schwarze Liste nur vorläufig." *LBB* 66, March 17, 1933, 1: "Man hört." *LBB* 43, February 18, 1933, 1: "Wiesbadener Regierung verbietet Remarque-Film." *FK* 46, February 22, 1933, 3 (Supplement, 1): "Im Taunus: *Im Westen nichts Neues* verboten—Kopie beschlagnahmt."

16. FOPS, August 10, 193, file 6,861.

17. *RGBl* 17, February 28, 1933, 83.

18. Fraenkel, *The Dual State*, 1941, 3.

19. Hett, 339, 340, 512–528.

20. Fraenkel, 3–6, 9–11, 65–69.

21. Weiß, 294, entry by Ri (Eva Rimmele).

22. von Leers, *Juden sehen Dich an*, 1933, 4–6. The term "Judenkallen" contains the Yiddish "kalla" which means "bride, mistress, or whore."

23. von Leers, 62 (text), 71 (full-page photo).

24. von Leers, 7 (Weiß), 8 (Marx), 22 (Grzesinski), 30 (Werthauer), 32-34 (Einstein), 43 (Wolff), 56 (Hirschfeld).

25. Grau, *Lexikon zur Homosexuellenverfolgung 1933–1945*, 2011, 160.

26. Albrecht, *Film im Dritten Reich*, 1979, 17, 18. On the use of the name Grzesinsky, see *VB* (B) 77, April 3-4, 1927, 2: "Nationalsozialistische Abrechnung mit Grzesinsky." See also Bering, *Der Name als Stigma*, 206–209.

27. von Leers, 27 (Adenauer), 61 (Piscator). On Adenauer and Piscator, see Benz and Graml, 9, 17, 18 (entry by Walter Först) and 252, 253 (entry by Gerhard Hay), respectively.

28. The 1936 6th edition is an unaltered reprint of the 5th edition. Piscator appears there on 61 (text), 68 (picture).

29. *Kinematograph* 39, February 24, 1933, 1: "Opposition auf dem Kriegspfad."

30. Examples: *Film* 12, March 18, 1933, 1, 2: "'Die neue Zeit braucht neue Männer.'" *Film* 1, April 1, 1933, 1: "Adolf Engl hat das Steuer auf 2 Jahre in die Hand genommen." *DFZ* 13, March 31, 1933, 2: "Engl Reichsverbandspräsident."

31. Mastheads: *SFZ* 28, July 8, 1927, 12. *DFZ* 3, January 16, 1931, 8.

32. *FK* 83, April 6, 1933, 1: "An alle deutschen Lichtspieltheaterbesitzer!" 87, April 12, 1935, 1: "Dr. Luitpold Nusser +." *Nationalsozialistische Parteikorrespondenz* 316, February 7, 1933, 3. For Nusser's curriculum vitae prior to Hitler's

takeover, see also *Reichshandbuch der deutschen Gesellschaft*, 1931, 1,343.

33. Film-Prüfstelle München, October 19, 1932, file 4,256 (2.170 meters).

34. "Dr. Nusser +" in *DFZ* 16, April 21, 1935, 4, by E.K. (Ernst Kammerer). *LBB* 89, April 13, 1935, 3. *FK* 87, April 12, 1935, 1.

35. *FK* 105, May 5, 1933, 3: "Tagesschau. Berlin, 5. Mai. Der Ehren-Doktor."

36. *DFZ* 13, March 31, 1933, 1, 2: "Gesinnung und Können [Attitude and Ability]." *DFZ* 16, April 21, 1933, 1, 2: "Auslese. Der neue Geschmack (Selection. The new Style)." *DFZ* 20, May 17, 1933, 2: "Reinlichkeit! [Cleanliness!]."

37. Mastheads: *Film* 8, February 19, 1922, 1. *Film* 26, June 25, 1922, 1. *SFZ* 33/34, August 12, 1927, 40. See also *Nationalsozialistische Parteikorrespondenz* 541, November 9, 1933, 6: "Filme von deutscher Art." *FK* 224, September 25, 1937, 3, 4: "Ein Berufs-Kamerad: Dr. Robert Volz 50 Jahre."

38. *DFZ* 38, September 22, 1933. *DFZ* 39, September 29, 1933, 1: "Zum Geleit."

39. *FK* 80, April 3, 1933, 1: "Dr. Luitpold Nusser. Hauptschriftleiter des *FK*." *FK* 82, April 5, 1933, 4: masthead. *FK* 83, April 6, 1933, 3 masthead. *FK* 85, April 8, 1933, 5: "Jottings from Germany/Chronique de la semaine." *Kinematograph* 68, April 6, 1933, 3: "Der neue Hauptschriftleiter des *FK*."

40. *FK* 85, April 8, 1933, 1: "Der Aufbau beginnt—Die Richtlinien der N.S.K.-SPIO." *FK* 86, April 9, 1933, 1. *FK* 90, April 15, 1933, 4 (1st Supplement, 2): "*FK* Official Organ of New Film Institute." *FK* 134, June 10, 1933, is the last issue as press organ of the NS Kommission-SPIO.

41. Eisner and Grohmann, *Ich hatte einst ein schönes Vaterland*, 1984, 169. *film-echo/Filmwoche vereinigt mit filmblätter* 17, March 25, 1972, 36–43 (41): "Die 25 Jahre zuvor" by Georg Herzberg.

42. Masthead: *FK* 214, September 10, 1932, 11. *FK* 81, April 8, 1942, 4. *FK* 155, July 6, 1942, 4.

43. Masthead: *FK* 80, April 12, 1943, 4. *FK* 78, September 29, 1944, is the final issue.

44. See Aurich and Jacobsen, *Ernst Jäger*, 2006, 40.

45. *La Cinéma d'Alsace et de Lorraine/Elsass-Lorraine Filmzeitung* 4, April 1933, 3, 6, 7, 10: "Im Lande der 'Gleichschaltung'" by Georges Epstein.

46. *FK* 94, April 21, 1933, 1, 2: "Merkwürdiger Artikel im Straßburger Cinéma." *FK* 98, April 26, 1933, 1: "Auffällige Hetze in Rumänien gegen den deutschen Film."

47. *LBB* 107, May 6, 1933, 1: "Jubiläum—Wendepunkt."

48. Masthead: *Filmspiegel* 1, January 1927, 13. *Filmspiegel* 3, March 1933, 8. *Filmspiegel* 4/5, April/May 1933, 8.

49. *LBB* 78, March 31, 1933, 4.

50. *FJ* 78, March 31, 1933, 4.

51. *FJ* 43, October 27, 1935, 1: "Das *FJ* nimmt Abschied."

52. *Kinematograph* 77, April 21, 1933, 1, 2: "Säuberung von außen."

53. *Kinematograph* 64, March 31, 1933.

54. Masthead: *Film* 4, March 1, 1927, 34. *Film* 9, May 15, 1927, 30. *Film* 5, January 28, 1933, 5.

55. Masthead: *Film* 6, February 4, 1933, 6. *Film* 12, March 18, 1933, 8. *Film* 13, March 25, 1933, 2. *Film* 6, February 10, 1934, 4. *Film* 7, February 17, 1934, 4. *Der neue Film* 46/1930 (mid–November), 1. *Der neue Film* 18/1933 (mid–April), 1. *Der neue Film* 10/1934 (mid–February), 1.

56. *Film* 16, April 15, 1933, 1: "*Film* gleichgeschaltet: Neuer Verlag sorgt für neuen Kurs."

57. *Film* 21, May 20, 1933, 1, 2: "Deutschland verbrennt seinen Geist" by Heinz Udo Brachvogel. Similarly, Brachvogel bloviated in *Film* 23, June 3, 1933, 1, 2: "Niemals ...!"

58. Masthead: *Film* 13, March 30, 1935, 4. *Film* 14, April 6, 1935, 3. Also: *Film* 23, June 4, 1938, 1: "Neuer Hauptschriftleiter des *Film*." Masthead: *Der neue Film* 38/1938 (mid–October), 1.

59. *Film* 28, July 15, 1939, 3: "Die Überleitung des *Kino-Journal* in die Wochenschrift *Film*."

60. *Film* 16/17, April 24, 1943, 1: "Zusammenlegung *Film* und *FK*."

61. Sattig, 37, 80.

62. *FJ* 3, September 3, 1926, 1: "Das *FJ* in Berlin."

63. *FJ* (Ma) 19, May 7, 1933, 1: "Jeder hat die Pflicht, Arbeit zu schaffen!" by (Albert) Schneider.

64. *FJ* (Ma) 20, May 14, 1933, 1: "Ruhe für Arbeit und Wirtschaft" by (Albert) Schneider.

65. *FJ* 43, October 27, 1935, 1: "Das *FJ* nimmt Abschied."

66. Masthead: *RWF* 11, March 11, 1933, 6. *RWF* 12, March 18, 1933, 6. *RWF* 16, April 15, 1933, 6.

67. *FJ* (Ma) 1, January 3, 1932, 3: "Die Aussprache am Dienstag" by H.W. Kr.

68. *LBB* 155, July 4, 1933, 4: "Tino Schmidt Filmwart für den Gau Düsseldorf."

69. *RWF* 24, June 10, 1933, 5.

70. *RWF* 19, May 7, 1938, 1.

71. Masthead: *Film* 1, January 4, 1936, 8.

72. *Mitteldeutscher Lichtspieltheaterbesitzer* 12, December 5, 1927, 6: "Weg mit der Politik!" 4, April 20, 1931, 12: "Chaplin."

73. *Mitteldeutscher Lichtspieltheaterbesitzer* 2/3, March 23, 1933, 11: "Große Leipziger Kundgebung für neuen Reichsverband." *Mitteldeutscher Lichtspieltheaterbesitzer* 2/3, March 23, 1933, 9: "Dresdner Theaterbesitzer für Einheit des Reichsverbandes!" *Mitteldeutscher Lichtspieltheaterbesitzer* 4/5, June 9, 1933, 4: "Dresden bekennt sich zum neuen Kurs!" 6-8, September 28, 1933, 1: "Neue Film-Aera brach an!" *Mitteldeutscher Lichtspieltheaterbesitzer* 1, January 4, 1934, 2, 3: "Das neue Gesicht des deutschen Films, by Walter Steinhauer.

74. Ickes was editor-in-chief from *Die Filmwoche* 3, January 13, 1926, 64.

75. "Zu sagen wäre" by Paul Ickes in *Die Filmwoche* 14, April 5, 1933, 43. *Die Filmwoche* 24, June 14, 1933, 754. See also *Die Filmwoche* 17, April 26, 1933, 521, 522: "Unser Kampf für den guten deutschen Film."

76. Masthead: *Filmwelt* 14, March 31, 1933, 31. *Filmwelt* 15, April 9, 1933, 31.

77. "Verordnung über die Aufgaben des RMVP, 30. Juni 1933," *RGBl* 75, July 5, 1933, 449.

According to Bohrmann and Toepser-Ziegert, *NS-Presseanweisungen. Volume 1*, 1984, "Dokumentationsteil," 1, the first surviving instruction is dated May 19, 1933.

78. Quoted from Sänger, *Politik der Täuschungen*, 1975, 35. Statement almost identically repeated on December 4, 1935, in Heiber, *Goebbels Reden. Volume 1*, 1971, 272.

79. Klee, *"Die SA Jesu Christi,"* 25–31.

80. *Variety* 1, March 14, 1933, 3: "Nazi Victim Is Proprietor of Theatre in Rochester."

81. For example, *FK* 74, March 27, 1933, 1, 2: "Der Kampf gegen die Lüge." *Film-Atelier* 6, March 31, 1933, 1: "Schluss mit der Greuelpropaganda" by the editors of *Film-Atelier*. *FJ* (Ma) 14, April 2, 1933, 1: "Schluss mit der Greuelpropaganda." *DFZ* 13, March 31, 1933, 3, 4: "Ein deutsches Wort zur ausländischen Greuelpropaganda" by Munich production manager Lothar Mayring. *RFB* 14, April 1, 1933, 4 (1st Supplement, 2): "Universal gegen Greuel-Hetze" by Titschau. *LBB* 79, April 1, 1933, 1: "Neuer Protest gegen die Greuel-Hetze."

82. Werner Skrentny, "Bestellen Sie bitte Herrn Friedland einen Glückwunsch!" in Bock, Jacobsen, Schöning and Wottrich, *Deutsche Universal*, 2001, 95.

83. *LBB* 80, April 3, 1933, 1: "Der Boykott-Sonnabend."

84. *FK* 79, April 1, 1933, 1: "Umbildung in den Filmfirmen." *FK* 80, April 3, 1933, 4: "Der Boykott-Tag bei Film und Kino."

85. Krings, *Hitlers Pressechef*, 2010, 203, 204.

86. Laws, April 7, 1933: "Gesetz zur Wiederherstellung des Berufsbeamtentums" (Restoration of the Professional Civil Service) and "Gesetz über die Zulassung zur Rechtsanwaltschaft" (Admission to the Bar), in *RGBI* 34, April 7, 1933, 175-177, 188.

87. *LBB* 151, June 29, 1933, 1: "Gegen die Miesmacher."

88. *Einziges parteiamtliches Aufklärungs- und Redner-Informationsmaterial der Reichspropagandaleitung der NSDAP*, installment 6 (June 1934) "Staatsfeinde," folio 1 (backside), 2.

89. Hippen, *Satire gegen Hitler*, 1986, table of contents, 6.

90. Hippen, *Sich fügen heißt lügen*, 1981, 68. Full text of the chanson in Hippen, *Satire gegen Hitler*, 26, 27.

91. See Skrentny in Bock, Jacobsen, Schöning and Wottrich, 95.

92. "Gesetz über die Vorführung ausländischer Bildstreifen, June 2, 1933" in *RGBI* 69, June 27, 1933, 393.

93. "Vierte Verordnung über die Vorführung ausländischer Bildstreifen, June 28, 1933" in *Deutscher Reichsanzeiger und Preußischer Staatsanzeiger* 150, June 30, 1933, 1.

94. *Film-Atelier* 14, July 31, 1933, 4: "Wer darf deutscher Staatsbürger sein?" *Film-Atelier* 16, August 31, 1933, 2: "Arier-Paragraph als Denunziantenwaffe." *FJ* (Ma) 32, August 6, 1933, 1: "Der Arier-Paragraph."

95. Para 3 Section (1) and (3) of the "Gesetz über die Errichtung einer vorläufigen Filmkammer, July 14, 1933" in *RGBl* 82, July 17, 1933, 483, 484. Para 3, Section d and 6 of the "Verordnung über die Errichtung einer vorläufigen Filmkammer, July 22, 1933" in *RGBl* 86, July 25, 1933, 531, 532.

96. Rumpelstilzchen, *Mang uns mang …*, commentary 2, September 15, 1932, 17, and commentary 21, February 2, 1933, 157.

97. Rumpelstilzchen, *Sie wer'n lachen*, 1935, commentary 2, September 14, 1933, 18.

98. For example, *DFZ* 37, September 15, 1933, 2: "Juden im Film."

99. "Schriftleitergesetz, October 4, 1933" in *RGBl* 111, October 7, 1933, 707–713. *FK* 235, October 6, 1933, 1, 2: "Das modernste Gesetz der Welt."

100. *FK* 240, October 12, 1933, 2: "Der erste jüdische Tonfilm in hebräischer Sprache."

101. FPS, March 4, 1933, file 33,364.

102. FPS, April 28, 1931, file 28,880.

103. FPS, April 28, 1931, file 28,861.

104. FPS, 20.843, November 15, 1928.

105. Aurich, *Die Degeto und der Staat*, 2018, 57.

106. *FK* 44, February 20, 1933: "Chaplin-Zyklus der Degeto."

107. *LBB* 44, February 20, 1933, 1: "Man hört …"

108. *LBB* 50, February 27, 1933, 1: "Man hört …"

109. Section "Man hört …" in *LBB* 56, March 6, 1933, 1, and *LBB* 62, March 13, 1933, 2.

110. *LBB* 69, March 21, 1933, 2: "Nachwort zum Chaplin-Zyklus der Degeto." *FJ* 21, May 21, 1933, 4: "Reprisen" by A.S. (Albert Schneider).

111. *FK* 86, April 10, 1933, 2: "Degeto-Matinee im Capitol."

112. *FJ* 21, May 21, 1933, 4: "Reprisen" by A.S. (Albert Schneider).

113. Aurich, *Degeto*, 58-63.

114. Ulrich and Timmling, *Film. Kitsch. Kunst. Propaganda*, 1933, 1. The *LBB* included this brochure in its library at the end of July 1933: 177, July 29, 1933, 8: "Film im Schrifttum. Büchereingang."

115. Ulrich and Timmling, 50 ("Nachwort eines Sachsen"), 60 (on Chaplin and Ozep).

116. See Noa, *Walter Timmling*, 2000, 4.

117. *B.Z.* 102, May 4, 1931, 4 (1st Supplement, 2): "Chaplin hat neun neue Filmprojekte" by H.J.

118. *LBB* 54, March 3, 1933, 1: "Man hört …" *LBB* 62, March 13, 1933, 3: "Chaplin bereitet vor."

119. *Variety* 3, March 28, 1933, 1: "Napoleonic Chaplin." *LBB* 85, April 8, 1933, 3 (Supplement, 1): "Chaplin will Napoleon spielen."

120. *FK* 151, July 1, 1926, 2: "Raquel Meller und Chaplin." *FK* 155, July 6, 1926, 2: "Chaplins Vertrag mit Raquel Meller."

121. *FK* 12, January 13, 1933, 3: "Weiter Rätselraten um Charlie." *LBB* 33, February 7, 1933, 4: "Charlie bleibt stumm." *LBB* 114, May 16, 1933, 2: "Kurze Meldungen." On "The Jester," *LBB* 110, May 12, 1932, 1: "Man hört …"

122. *FK* 12, January 13, 1933, 3: "Weiter Rätselraten um Charlie." *LBB* 33, February 7, 1933, 4: "Uraufführung im September?" See also *LBB* 157, July 7, 1932, 1: "Man hört …"

123. *LBB* 192, August 17, 1932, 1: "Man hört …"

124. *LBB* 62, March 13, 1933, 3: "Chaplin bereitet vor."

125. *FK* 183, August 7, 1933, 2: "Hollywood."

126. *LBB* 212, September 8, 1933, 3: "Außergewöhnlicher Hollywood-Film im Werden."

127. *FK* 210, September 7, 1933, 3: "Chaplin bleibt in Hollywood."

128. *LBB* 94, April 23, 1934, 3: "Chaplins Pläne."

129. *Filmwelt* 19, May 7, 1933, 2: "Charlie Chaplin."

130. *FK* 135, June 12, 1933, 1: "Neuer Chaplin-Film." Information on Goddard's year of birth varies between 1905 and 1914.

131. *FK* 195, August 21, 1933, 2: "Kurze Meldungen."

132. *LBB* 212, September 8, 1933, 3: "Außergewöhnlicher Hollywood-Film im Werden." *LBB* 232, October 2, 1933, 1: "Man hört …"

133. *LBB* 259, November 2, 1933, 2: "Von den Auslandsproduktionen. USA."

134. *LBB* 222, September 20, 1933, 2: "Keine United-Artists-Filme in Deutschland."

135. *FK* 58, March 8, 1934, 1, 2: " United-Artists-Filme in Deutschland. Abkommen mit deutschen Firmen." *FK* 82, April 7, 1934, 1: "25 Filme der Bavaria. Eindeutschung der United Artists Film."

136. FPS, June 15, 1935, file 39,491. *FK* 143, June 22, 1935, 2: "*Der Graf von Monte Christo*" by Georg Herzberg. Thus contrary to Urwand, *Der Pakt*, 2017, 217, who claims United Artists films to have been completely banned in the Third Reich as early as 1933.

137. *LBB* 175, July 27, 1933, 3: "Mordmärchen um Charlie Chaplin."

138. *8-Uhr* 172, July 26, 1933, 1: "Mordplan an Chaplin als Kriegsgrund!" *LBB* 175, July 27, 1933, 3: "Mordmärchen um Charlie Chaplin."

139. For example, *New York Telegraph*, July 16, 1933: "Chaplin Death Plot." *Wheeling News* (West Virginia), July 25, 1933: "Plot to Assassinate Charlie Chaplin is Revealed in Japan." *New York Sun*, July 25, 1933: "Japanese Planned to Kill Chaplin." *Dunkirk Observer* (New York), July 25, 1933: "Sought to Start War by Killing Charley Chaplin." *Toronto Telegram* (Ontario), July 25, 1933: "Japanese Tried to Start War by Bombing Charlie Chaplin." On the Japanese criminal trial, *Leicester Evening Mail*, September 11, 1933: "Death Sentence Demands in Trial of Subalterns." *Belfast Newsletter*, September 11, 1933: "Japanese Assassins and Chaplin." *Morning Post* (no city given), September 12, 1933: "Plot to Murder Mr. Chaplin." *Glasgow Evening Times*, September 11, 1933: "Intend to Kill Charlie Chaplin." In Montreux, albums 42, 45.

140. On Chaplin's Japan stay, see "Tour Itineray" in Stein Haven, *Charlie Chaplin: A Comedian Sees the World*, 2014, 150.

141. *FK* 210, September 7, 1933, 3: "Chaplin bleibt in Hollywood."

142. *FK* 261, November 6, 1933, 3: "Das Neueste."

143. On Ludwig, see Benz and Graml, 213, 214, entry by Margit Ketterle.

144. *FK* 258, November 2, 1933, 3: "Hollywooder Spitzen-Einnahmen, die Präsident Roosevelt herabsetzen will" by Cha (Ernst Chaparral).

145. *FK* 294, December 15, 1933, 3: "Kurze Meldungen."

146. *BBZ* 234 (E), May 20, 1933, 6: "*Buster hat nichts zu lachen*," by -y (Fritz Olimsky).

147. *FJ* (Ma) 34, August 20, 1933, 7: "Gibt es einen internationalen Humor im Film?"

148. *Filmwelt* 37, 10. September 1933, 2: "Die größten Filmerfolge."

149. *Die Filmwoche* 28, July 12, 892. *Die Filmwoche* 29, July 19, 1933, 926.

150. Section "Die Fiwo-Tante antwortet." Inquiries about Gitta Alpar in *Die Filmwoche* 25, June 21, 1933, 795. *Die Filmwoche* 26, June 28, 1933, 827. *Die Filmwoche* 27, July 5, 1933, 859. *Die Filmwoche* 29, July 19, 1933, 924. Inquiry about Szöke Szakall, *Die Filmwoche* 27, July 5, 1933, 857. Books offered in *Die Filmwoche* 16, April 19, 1933, 510 (last offer for the *RFB-Almanach 1933*). *Die Filmwoche* 19, May 10, 1933, 608 (last offer for Richard Tauber's biography).

151. Ross card 7914/1 of the Ross Verlag's fall collection, 1933. The content of this collection was first printed in: *Die Filmwoche* 35, August 30, 1933, 1,112. On Chaplin's stay in St. Moritz, see "Tour Itinerary" in Stein Haven, 149.

152. Thus claimed without reference by Hiroyuki, *Chaplin to Hitler*, 2015, 43.

153. *Die Filmwoche* 15, April 12, 1933, 480. *Die Filmwoche* 31, July 31, 1935, 1,008. Lorant, *Wir vom Film*, 1929, 13–17.

154. *Die Filmwoche* 13, March 29, 1933, 464. *Die Filmwoche* 38, September 27, 1933, 1,216.

155. Section "Fragen, die uns erreichten" in *Filmwelt* 12, March 19, 1933, 29, left column, middle section. "Die Fiwo-Tante antwortet" in *Die Filmwoche* 11, March 19, 1935, 365, left column, upper third. *Die Filmwoche* 49, December 4, 1935, 1,581, left column, middle section.

156. "Die Fiwo-Tante antwortet" in *Die Filmwoche* 45, November 1935, 1,517, left column, upper third.

157. Thus claimed by Hiroyuki, 43, unattributed.

158. *New York World*, October 8, 1923: "Bavarian Facisti, by Clare Sheridan (report from September 25, 1923). In Montreux, album 22.

159. *BT* (E) 17, January 11, 1932, 2: "Chaplin als Erzieher."

160. *Die Weltbühne* 11, March 15, 1932, 411: "Kleine Nachrichten" by Kaspar Hauser (Kurt Tucholsky).

161. *Die Weltbühne* 20, May 17, 1932, 751: "Hitler und Goethe. Ein Schulaufsatz" by Kaspar Hauser (Kurt Tucholsky).

162. *Adolf Hitler in Bilddokumenten seiner Zeit. Band 1*, 1979, 3, 153.

163. Hoffmann, *Jugend um Hitler*, 1935. *Hitler abseits vom Alltag*, 1937. *Mit Hitler im Westen*, 1940.

164. Ley, Dauer and Kiel, *Deutschland ist schöner geworden*, 1936. See also *Angriff* 6, January 8, 1936, 9: "Ein neues Buch Dr. Leys" by mnr.

165. See Reichel, *Der schöne Schein des Dritten Reiches*, 1993. Eberle, *Briefe an Hitler*, 2007, 9–19.

166. *The Bystander* (London), March 22, 1933, 511. In Montreux, album 36 B (1933).

167. *Montes Register* (IA), May 14, 1933. *Baltimore Evening Sun* (MD), May 30, 1933: "Comparing Hitler to Charles Chaplin is Called an Injustice to the Comedian" by Arthur V. In Montreux, albums 36 A, 45.

168. *Paris-Midi* 2,699, August 22, 1933, 2: "Charlie Chaplin jouera dans son prochain film sans sa légendaire petite moustache ... Pour ne pas ressembler à Hitler."

169. The *Prager Montagsblatt* was only available for inspection from November 13, 1933, on.

170. *FK* 179, August 2, 1933, 1: "RKO dementiert. Kein Anti-Hitler-Film."

171. *Film-Atelier* 16, August 31, 1933, 3: "Amerika dreht keinen Anti-Hitler-Film."

172. *FK* 206, September 2, 1933, 8: "'A Dog Barking at the Moon'" by Albert A. Sander.

173. *Variety* 4, April 4, 1933, 17: "Hitler Costs Ufa British Film Biz." *FK* 101, April 29, 1933, 4 (Supplement, 2): "Germany's new Film Production and the World's Markets" by Sa. (Albert A. Sander).

174. *FK* 230, October 1, 1936, 1: "Dr. Olimsky Auslandspressechef der R.F.K." *Film* 11, March 12, 1938, 4: "Olimsky in der Fachschule."

175. Robinson, 454.

176. *Comoedia Illustré, journal parisien theatral, artistique et littéraire,* May 23, 1931, English translation "Has Mr. Chaplin been guilty of Plagiarism in *City Lights*?" In Bologna, ch03252001-07.

177. *FK* 116, May 20, 1931, 1, 2: "'Europa hat mich nicht verstanden.'" See also: *Die Welt am Abend* 117, May 22, 1931, 6 (1st Supplement, 2): "Chaplin über Europa."

178. *Hannoverscher Anzeiger* 58, March 10, 1931, 3: "Charlie Chaplin in Hannover."

179. *Die Filmwoche* 12, March 18, 1931, 365, 366: "Bei und über Charlie Chaplin" by Erwin Ebner.

180. *Los Angeles Times* (no No.), October 23, 1933, 16: "Charles Chaplin on Air Tonight" by Caroll Nye. *The Brooklyn Daily Eagle* (NY) 300, October 29, 1933, 12: "Out of a Blue Sky" by Jo Ranson. See also *Toledo Times* (OH), November 6, 1933: "Chaplin Voice Proves pleasing." In Montreux, album 42.

181. Thus, contrary to Velten and Klein, 59-64, 73.

182. *Kinematograph Weekly* (London) 1.377, September 7, 1933, 5: "Nazis Annoyed with Chaplin. Moustache Offends Hitlerites."

183. *New York World-Telegram,* September 7, 1933: "Schrecklichkeit in Hollywood" by Rolin Kirby. In Bologna, no file No.

184. Original drawing. In DFF—Deutsches Filminstitut & Filmmuseum. According to unconfirmed information from the seller of the cartoon, a French artist created it in 1940. The Karikaturmuseum Krems has not been able to identify him or to date the cartoon.

185. *Motion Picture Herald* (NY) 12, September 16, 1933, 8: "By a Whisker."

186. *Minneapolis Tribune* (MN), October 22, 1933: "Chaplin's Mustache Stirs foreign Press." In Montreux, album 42.

187. *Paris-Midi* 2,716, September 8, 1933, 6: "La moustache de Charlot!" by Gaston Thierry.

188. *Paris-Midi* 2,717, September 9, 1933, 5: "D'un film a l'autre."

189. *FK* 218, September 16, 1933, 8: "A Chaplin Denial."

190. *Paris-Midi* 2,730, September 22, 1933, 6: "Polémique. La moustache de Charlot (Suite et fin)."

191. *Daily Express* (London), June 14, 1933: "Chaplin to Appear minus His Moustache. Because it Makes Him like Hitler." In Montreux, album 42.

192. *Daily Express* (London), May 13, 1933, cartoon by Sidney Strube. The cartoon also appeared in *NYT* 27, 518, May 28, 1933, 43.

193. *Daily Express* (London), August 15, 1933: "Tail-Piece." In Montreux, album 45.

194. *Edinburgh Evening,* August 14, 1933: "Famous Moustache. Charlie Chaplin to Shave it off. Because He Looks like Hitler." *Liverpool Echo,* August 14, 1933: "Chaplin minus Moustache." *Glasgow Daily Report,* August 15, 1933: "Chaplin's Moustache." *Performer,* August 16, 1933: "What next?" In Montreux, album 45.

195. *FK* 232, October 3, 1933, 1: "Chaplin Denies Anti-Hitler Gesture."

196. *FK* 236, October 7, 1933, 4 (Supplement, 2): "Deux démentis." *FK* 242, October 14, 1933, 8: "Two Denials."

197. For example, *Evening Sun* (Vancouver, BC), September 21, 1933: "Berlin hot at Chaplin! 'Nazi' Moustache Gone?" *Express & Star* (Wolverhampton), October 4, 1933: "A Tale of two Moustaches." *Minneapolis Tribune* (MN), October 22, 1933: "Chaplin's Mustache Stirs foreign Press." In Montreux, album 42.

198. *FK* 234, October 5, 1933, 2: "Wieder ein Anti-Hitler-'Werk' geplant."

199. *LBB* 256, October 30, 1933, 1: "Man hört."

200. *Rockford Register Star* (IL), October 22, 1933: "Two Trick Mustaches." In Montreux, album 42.

201. See Aping, *Chaplin in Deutschland,* 23-28. In Austria, Chaplin's name was first mentioned in 1916, when the one-reeler *Die elektrische Puppe* was mistakenly attributed to him, which was actually Max Asher's 1915 short subject *The Mechanical Man.* See *Paimann's Filmlisten* 21/1916, 3.

202. *Die Welt,* October 14, 2010, Section "Kultur": "Berühmtes Hitler-Foto möglicherweise gefälscht" by Sven Felix Kellerhoff. Accessible at welt.de/kultur/article10284920/Beruehmtes-Hitler-Foto-moeglicherweise-gefaelscht.html. For more detail, see Sösemann and Lange, *Propaganda,* 2011, 877–884.

203. Hoffmann, *Hitler wie ihn keiner kennt,* 1932, 7. Hoffmann, *Hitler wie ich ihn sah,* 1974, 24.

204. *Die Zukunft* (Paris), April 14, 1939: "Fünfzig Jahre Chaplin-" by Hans Siemsen. Reprint in Föster, 249.

205. Schnog, *Charlie Chaplin,* 1960, 46.

Chapter 8

1. *FK* 1, January 1, 1934, 1: "Sieg Heil 1934!"

2. *VB* (N) 19, January 19, 1934, 2: "Berechtigung zu Filmvorführungen nur noch für Mitglieder der Reichsfilmkammer."

3. "Lichtspielgesetz, February 16, 1934" in *RGBI* 17, February 19, 1934, 95–98. "Erste Verordnung zur Durchführung des Lichtspielgesetzes [February 16, 1934], February 20, 1934" in *Reichsministerialblatt* 8, January 23, 1934, 83. "Zweite Verordnung zur Durchführung des Lichtspielgesetzes [February 16, 1934], March 8, 1934" in *Deutscher Reichsanzeiger und Preußischer Staatsanzeiger* 58, March 9, 1934, 1, 2, and *Reichsministerialblatt* 11, March 16, 1934, 116–118. "Fünfte Verordnung zur Durchführung des Lichtspielgesetzes, November 5, 1934" in *RGBI* 125, November 16, 1934, 1,105, 1,106. See also *LBB* 45, February 22, 1934, 1: "Ende der Münchener Film-Prüfstelle." *FK* 60, March 10, 1934, 1, 3: "Zwei Verordnungen zur Durchführung des 'Lichtspielgesetzes.'"

4. For example, *NYT* 27, 788, February 17, 1934, 3: "Censors Unmade Movies."

5. *VB* (N) 173, June 22, 1934, 1: "Bekanntmachung des RMVP vom 20. Juni 1934 über die Bestellung des *VB* zum Publikationsorgan der Reichskulturkammer." See also *LBB* 143, June 22, 1934, 1: "Der *VB* amtliches Blatt der Kulturkammer."

6. *Reichs Kino Adressbuch 1934*, 1934, 731–744. *1937*, 1937, 455–457.

7. FOPS, April 21, 1934, file 7,578. According to Seeger's letter of January 7, 1935, the final judgement was publicized on the same day in *Deutscher Reichsanzeiger und Preußischer Staatsanzeiger* 5, 3, and in *Deutsches Kriminalpolizeiblatt* 2.047: deutsches-filminstitut.de/zengut/df2tb456z2.pdf.

8. *NYT* 28, 109, January 9, 1935, 21: "Reich Bans Chaplin Film."

9. For example, *Buffalo News* (NY), January 9, 1935: "Chaplin's *Gold Rush* Is Banned in Germany." *News Chronicle* (London), January 9, 1935: "Banned." *Williamsport Sun* (PA), January 10, 1935 (untitled). *Jonesboro Evening* (AR), January 14, 1935: "*Gold Rush* Barred." *Braddock News Herald* (PA), January 17, 1935 (untitled). *New York Telegraph*, February 2, 1935: "'Non-Aryan' Chaplin is Amused by Reich Ban." In Montreux, album 48.

10. FOPS, April 21, 1934, file 7,324. Reasons in *FK* 97, April 25, 1934, 7: "Die Entscheidung über *Männer um eine Frau*." *LBB* 96, April 25, 1934, 3: "Verbot des Max-Baer-Films."

11. FOPS, July 27, 1934, file 7,390. Reasons in *FK* 181, August 4, 1934, 2: "Verbotene *Frühlingsstimmen*."

12. *NYT* 28, 099, December 30, 1934, 2, 14: "What the Typical Nazi Thinks—and Why" by Harold Callender (London).

13. *Die neue Weltbühne* (Prague) 21, May 23, 1935, 664: "Ein Fall Chaplin?" by Hermann Britt (Heinz Pol = Heinz Pollack).

14. The microfilming of the weekly *Selbstwehr* has been searched for the period from January to May 1935. Possibly, not all issues of the originals are complete. Sometimes pages with cutouts have been microfilmed.

15. "Zweites Gesetz zur Änderung des Lichtspielgesetzes, June 28, 1935" in *RGBI* 67, June 29, 1935, 811.

16. "Sechste Verordnung zur Durchführung des Lichtspielgesetzes, July 3, 1935" in *Deutscher Reichsanzeiger und Preußischer Staatsanzeiger* 155, July 6, 1935, 1, and *RGBI* 74, July 10, 1935, 906. Para 2 (1) of the decree states that the approvals of all sound motion pictures ceased to have effect, as follows:

    1. films approved up to December 31, 1929, as of July 31, 1935,

    2. films approved in 1930 as of September 30, 1935,

    3. films approved in 1931 as of November 30, 1935,

    4. films approved in 1932 and up to January 30, 1933, as of December 10, 1935.

17. "Gesetz über die Vorführung ausländischer Filme, July 11, 1936" in *RGBI* 66, July 14, 1936, 551. "Achte Verordnung über die Vorführung ausländischer Filme, July 12, 1936" in *RGBI* 66, July 14, 1936, 552, 553. "Verordnung zur Änderung der Verordnung über die Vorführung ausländischer Filme, June 26, 1937" in *RGBI* 73, June 30, 1937, 665, 666.

18. *LBB* 100, April 29, 1932, 1: "Stummfilme immer noch stark gefragt."

19. *FK* 25, January 29, 1934, 3: "Umbau der Kamera." *FK* 53, March 2, 1934, 2: "Kamera stellt nicht um." *LBB* 34, February 9, 1934, 3: "Die letzten Stummfilm-Vorführungen in Berlin." *LBB* 93, April 21, 1934, 1: "Berliner Kamera geschlossen." *Film-Atelier* 8, April 30, 1934, 1: "Kamera geschlossen."

20. *Daily Telegraph* (London), August 16, 1934: "Charlie Chaplin Reacts." In Montreux, album 43.

21. *LBB* 93, April 21, 1936, 1: "Nachprüfung alter Filme abgeschlossen." *LBB* 96, April 24, 1936, 1: "1 ½ Millionen Filmmeter nachgeprüft."

22. *RWF* 4, January 20, 1934, 6: "Im Zickzack durch die Woche." *LBB* 176, July 31, 1934, 2: "Chaplin-Film mit Dialog." *LBB* 200, August 29, 1934, 2: "Redivius Chaplin." *FK* 265, November 10, 1934, 1: "Chaplin und die Sprachlehrer."

23. Numerous articles on the marriage rumors starting in fall of 1932, for example, in *Morristown Record* (NJ), March 23, 1936: "Charlie Can't Laugh off latest Wedding Rumor." In Montreux, albums 36 A, 42, 46, 47, and 55.

24. *Der neue Film* 27/1934 (beginning of July), 4: "Charlie Chaplin heiratet wieder."

25. "Das klassische Organ von Charlie Chaplin" in *Film* 3, January 20, 1934, 3. *Der neue Film* 6/1934 (mid-February), 4.

26. *FK* 8, January 10, 1936, 3: "Chaplin—stumm."

27. *FK* 159, July 10, 1934, 2: "Schnell noch lesen."

28. *FK* 255, October 30, 1934, 2: "Schnell noch lesen."

29. *LBB* 260, November 7, 1934, 2: "Amerika." For the consecutive numbering of Chaplin's films according to his production records, see Delage and Cenciarelli, *Modern Times—Tempi Moderni*, 2004, 86 (hand-lettered cover) 88, 90 (daily production reports from November 11, 1933, and July 18, 1935).

30. *RWF* 42, October 13, 1934, 4 (Supplement, 2): "Neues von Chaplin," translation from the French by Carlernst Graf Strachwitz, co-author of Belling's book *Der Film in Staat und Partei*, 1936.

31. *FK* 56, March 7, 1935, 4: "Chaplin-Film erst im Herbst."

32. *FK* 55, March 5, 1935, 3: "Produktionssteigerung bei United Artists."

33. *LBB* 132, June 7, 1935, 2: "United Artists ohne 20th Century." *LBB* 176, July 30, 1935, 2: "24 United-Artists-Filme im England-Verleih." *LBB* 189, August 14, 1935, 2: "Amerika." *LBB* 195, August 21, 1935, 1: "18 Millionen Dollar für das United-Artists-Programm."

34. *FK* 103, May 4, 1935, 1: "Chaplin politisch?"

35. *Die neue Weltbühne* (Prague) 21, May 23, 1935, 664: "Ein Fall Chaplin?" by Hermann Britt (Heinz Pol = Heinz Pollack).

36. *RWF* 25, June 15, 1935, 4 (Supplement, 2): "Dies und das." Huff, 231.

37. For example, *The Hartford Courant* (CT, no No.), April 7, 1935, 49 (part V, 1): "Charlie Chaplin Tells Theme of New Picture" by Karl F. Kitchen. *The Commercial Appeal* (Memphis, TN) 83, May 24, 1935, 51: "Charlie Chaplin Creates a Furore as Cog in *Modern Times*" by Harry Martin.

38. See Maland, *The Evolution of a Star Image*, 1989, 145, unattributed.

39. *FK* 103, May 4, 1935, 1: "Chaplin politisch?"

40. *FK* 135, June 13, 1935, 2: "'Production No. 5' aus dem Atelier."

41. *RWF* 25, June 15, 1935, 4 (Supplement, 2): "Dies und das."

42. *LBB* 195, August 21, 1935, 1: "18 Millionen Dollar für das United-Artists-Programm."

43. Quoted after *The Eansville Press* (IN) 91, September 29, 1935, 59: "Chaplin Picture."

44. *Die neue Weltbühne* (Prague) 29, July 18, 1935, 916, 917: "Chaplin: '54632'" by B.F. (Bruno Frei = Benedikt Freistadt).

45. *FK* 103, May 4, 1935, 1: "Chaplin politisch?" *RWF* 25, June 15, 1935, 4 (Supplement, 2): "Dies und das."

46. *LBB* 94, April 23, 1934, 3: "Chaplins Pläne." *FK* 5, January 7, 1935, 4: "Noch ein neuer Chaplin-Film."

47. *LBB* 224. September 26, 1934, 2: "Chaplin-Tonfilme, die nie gezeigt wurden."

48. Wada, *The Sea Gull*, 2008, VI.

49. *LBB* 91, April 16, 1935, 2: "'Schweyk' als amerikanischer Film. Chaplin als Regisseur?"

50. *LBB* 189, August 14, 1935, 2: "Amerika." *LBB* 195, August 21, 1935, 1: "18 Millionen Dollar für das United-Artists-Programm." *FK* 40, February 16, 1935, 1: "Chaplin-Pickford."

51. *LBB* 176, July 30, 1936, 3: "Man hört."

52. *FK* 49, February 26, 1934, 2: "Jimmie [*sic*] Durante."

53. *RWF* 29, July 14, 1934, 5: "*Scherben bringen Glück.*"

54. *FJ* 29, July 22, 1934, 2: "Boykottkampf in Amerika und England."

55. *LBB* 192, August 20, 1934, 4: "Film im Schrifttum."

56. The completely handed down run of the *Berliner Morgenpost* has been searched for the period from the beginning of July to the end of August 1934.

57. *LBB* 224, September 26, 1934, 2: "Chaplin-Tonfilme, die nie gezeigt wurden."

58. *The Era* (London), October 31, 1934 (untitled). *Daily Herald* (Arlington Heights), November 3, 1934: "Charlie Chaplin Named for big political Post." In Montreux, album 43.

59. *LBB* 261 November 8, 1934, 1: "Chaplin sollte Filmdiktator werden."

60. *FK* 36, February 12, 1935, 3: "Vom Marktwert berühmter Namen."

61. *Film-Atelier* 21, November 15, 1935, 3: "Chaplin borgt sich fremde Hosen, Schuhe, Hut und Rock."

62. Robinson, 106, 118.

63. *Autobiography*, 154, 155.

64. *LBB* 256, October 31, 1936, 5 (Supplement, 3): "Das Groteske im Film."

65. *FK* 155, July 6, 1935, 1: "Chaplins Produktion 5." *FK* 179, August 3, 1935, 3 (1st Supplement, 1): "Schnell noch lesen." *FK* 196, August 23, 1935, 2: "*Modern Times*: 11. Oktober."

66. *LBB* 240, October 12, 1935, 2: "England." *FK* 252, October 28, 1935, 1: "Chaplin-Premiere am 19. Dezember." *FK* 270, November 18, 1935, 2: "Chaplin-Premiere ungewiss."

67. *FK* 4, January 6, 1936, 2: "Die Welt in Kurzberichten."

68. *FK* 8, January 10, 1936, 3: "Chaplin—stumm."

69. *LBB* 36, February 12, 1936, 2: "New Yorker Premieren."

70. *NYT* 28, 372, September 29, 1935, 169: "*Modern Times.*"

71. *Daily Telegraph* (London), December 3, 1935: "Soviet Buys Chaplin Film. *Modern Times* as propaganda." *Sudbury Star* (ON), December 27, 1935: "Russians Buy Chaplin Film. *Modern Times* Ending Changed to make it Propaganda." In Montreux, album 44. See also Maland, 145, 146, 392, 393 (note 41), citing, among others, *New Masses*, September 24, 1935, 29, 30: "Charlie Chaplin's new Picture" by Boris Shumiatsky (translated from Russian).

72. See Maland, 146, 147.

73. The final scene with Paulette Goddard as a nun is described in Lynn, *Charlie Chaplin and His Times*, 1998, 368. Stills in Vance, *Chaplin,* 2003, 226, 227. The last still shows Charlie walking alone into the horizon.

74. *FK* 210, September 7, 1933, 2: "Bücher-Kurier. *Mit Hitler an die Macht.* Ein Buch des Reichspressechefs der NSDAP. Dr. Dietrich."

75. Krings, 106–110, 231.

76. *Angriff* 216, September 16, 1935, 4, 7: "Wir

haben eine öffentliche Meinung! Reichspressechef Dr. Dietrich über die Säuberung des Journalismus. Dr. Dietrich über die deutsche Presse."

77. Krings, 244 (with sources) and front blurb.

78. Krings, 446-450, 460, 461, 467 (with sources).

79. Bohrmann and Toepser-Ziegert, *NS-Presseanweisungen. Volume 1*, 22*, 24*, 43*, 44–49*.

80. Bohrmann and Toepser-Ziegert, *NS-Presseanweisungen. Volume 1*, 43*. Sänger, 30.

81. See Boveri, *Wir lügen alle*, 1965, 540, 550. Bohrmann and Toepser-Ziegert, *NS-Presseanweisungen. Volume 1*, 33*. Bohrmann, Toepser-Ziegert, Kohlmann-Viand, and Peter, *NS-Presseanweisungen. Volume 4/I*, 1993, 44*, 49* (Section "Androhung und Durchführung von Sanktionen gegenüber Journalisten"). Wilke, *Presseanweisungen im zwanzigsten Jahrhundert*, 2007, 121.

82. So far, they have only been indexed up to the beginning of World War II. See Bohrmann and Toepser-Ziegert, *NS-Presseanweisungen. Volume 1*, 53*-59*. *NS-Presseanweisungen 3/I*, 1987, 40*-45*.

83. On Berndt, see Boveri, 237, 238, 546, 547. Krings, 335. Wilke, 124, 125.

84. Fröhlich, *Goebbels-Tagebücher. Volume 5*, 2000, 158 (entry from February 16, 1938).

85. *BT* (M) 74, February 13, 1936, 8: "Charlie Chaplins *Modern Times*" by Dr. K. v. St. (Dr. Kurt von Stutterheim).

86. Other topics were cars, the damage of an airplane during a German-Brazilian expedition, an exhibition and the pricing of eggs.

87. Bohrmann, Toepser-Ziegert, Kohlmann-Viand and Peter, *NS-Presseanweisungen. Volume 4/I*, 159: Instruction 166 and transmission notes ("BArch" Koblenz, collection Brammer at ZSg. 101/7/111) und transmission ("BArch" Koblenz, collection Sänger at ZSg. 102/2a/44 -4-). Boveri, 558, 576. Fritz Sänger in Bohrmann and Toepser-Ziegert, *NS-Presseanweisungen. Volume 1*, 13*.

88. *FK* 37, February 13, 1936, 2: "Chaplin-Premiere in London."

89. *Film* 7, February 15, 1936, 5 (2nd Supplement, 1): "Der große Filmbrand—und die Chaplin-Premiere."

90. *LBB* 39, February 16, 1936, 2: "Londoner Premieren."

91. "Anordnung des RMVP über Kunstkritik, November 27, 1936" in *VB*, November 28, 1936. Bohrmann, Toepser-Ziegert, Kohlmann-Viand and Peter, *NS-Presseanweisungen. Volume 4/I*, 27*-29*.

92. See also *NYT* 28, 600, May 14, 1936, 1: "Reich Orders Delayed Dramatic Criticism; New Rule Allows a More Rigid Censorship."

93. For example, *Winston Salem Sentinel* (NC), February 21, 1936: "No funny Stuff for Germany." *Dayton News* (OH), February 21, 1936: "Humorless Hitler." *Dayton Journal* (OH), February 21, 1936: "Dictators never Laugh." *Indianapolis Times* (IN), February 27, 1936: "Actions Speak louder."

Portland Oregonian (OR), February 23, 1936: "Censoring a Mustache." *Jewish Advocate* (Boston, MA), February 21, 1936: "Charles and Adolph." *To-Day's Cinema* No. 3, 239, February 21, 1936: "An open Letter to Herr Adolf Hitler. Attention. Herr Hitler." *Globe Gazette* (Mason City, IA), February 28, 1936: "One tiny Moustache." *The Patriot* (Dartmouth, NS), May 28, 1936: "Thou Shall not Laugh." *Careta* (Brazil), March 14, 1936: "Evitando a concurrencia" (How to eliminate competition). In Montreux, albums 52, 53.

94. *New Orleans Item* (LA), February 21, 1936: "Foreign Film-frowning." In Montreux, album 52.

95. *Waterbury Republican* (CT), February 23, 1936: "Charlie a Red?" In Montreux, album 52.

96. *New Orleans Item* (LA), February 21, 1936: "Foreign Film-frowning." In Montreux, album 52.

97. *News Chronicle* (London), February 18, 1936: "Charlie's Copyright in famous Moustache. Had It long before Hitler Was Known." In Montreux, album 52.

98. *Daily Herald* (Arlington Heights, IL), February 18, 1936: "Charlie's Moustache Annoys Hitler. Why new Film Is likely to be Banned." In Montreux, album 52.

99. *Kewanne Star-Courier* (IL), February 24, 1936: "Vanity of Vanities." *Oakland Tribune* (CA), February 23, 1936 (untitled). *Oakland Post-Enquirer* (CA), February 21, 1936: "Hitler's Mustache. Charlie Chaplin Has prior Rights." *St. Louis Star-Times* (MO), February 22, 1936: "Chaplin Would Ruin Hitler." *Austin American Statesman* (TX), February 23, 1936: "Chaplin's new Film *Modern Times*, Barred by Herr Hitler." *Reading Searchlight* (CA), February 29, 1936 (untitled). *Haverhill Gazette* (MA), February 28, 1936: "Nazi Logic." *Winter Haven Chief* (FL), February 21, 1936: "A sad Case of Moustaches." *Glasgow Evening Citizen*, February 19, 1936: "Hitler and Chaplin." *Des Moines Register* (IA), March 22, 1936: "Beware Charlie Chaplin, the 'red' Ogre, Nazis Warn good Germans." In Montreux, albums 52, 55.

100. *The Journal* (Newcastle upon Tyne), February 19, 1936: "Saving His Face" by George Middleton. *Glasgow Daily Record*, February 20, 1936: "The little More" by Carey Orr. *The Mail* (Adelaide, SA), February 20, 1936: "Professional Jealousy" by Alexander George Gurney. *Evening Standard* (London), February 20, 1936. 7: "Low's topical Budget. International Moustache Crisis" by David Low. *The Referee* (Sydney, NSW), February 23, 1936: "David and Goliath. Germany has Banned the new Charlie Chaplin Film" by Arthur W...y. In Montreux, album 52.

101. *Evening Standard* (London), February 14, 1936: "The other Fellow with a funny Moustache" by David Low. In Montreux, album 52.

102. *Pariser Tageblatt*'s last issue was 913, June 14, 1936.

103. *Pariser Tageblatt* 800, February 20, 1936, 1: "Chaplin-Film in Deutschland verboten."

104. *Pariser Tageblatt* 802, February 22, 1936, 2: "Adolf Chaplin" by Manuel Humbert. Humbert is the author of the 1936 book *Hitler's 'Mein Kampf.'*

105. *Die neue Weltbühne* (Prague) 9, February 27, 1936, 280, 281: "Der neue Chaplin-Film" by Ernst Toller.

106. *NYT* 28, 514, February 18, 1936, 8: "Reich Has yet to Act on new Chaplin Film." *NYT* 28, 516, February 1936, 15: "Denies Film Was Banned."

107. *Angriff* and *VB* (N) have been searched for the period from September 1935 to March 1936 and from late October 1935 to March 1936, respectively.

108. *Hollywood Reporter* (Los Angeles, CA), February 18, 1936: "Report Hitler Bans *Times*, Sight Unseen." *The Heights News* (NYC), February 19, 1936: "Ban and no Ban." In Montreux, album 52.

109. Krings, 238, 239.

110. See various distributions of business of the Hauptarchiv der NSDAP, especially in 1936, according to the 1936 *Organisationsbuch der NSDAP*, 339, 340, as well as order 147/39, July 21, 1939, of the Führer's deputy concerning the NSDAP archives. In BArch BL: bundesarchiv.de.

111. *LBB* 47, February 25, 1936, 4: "Fastnacht. An unsere Leser! Der Chaplin-Film kommt."

112. *LBB* 181, August 6, 1934, 2: "Münchener LBB."

113. On this distributor, see *Deutscher Reichsanzeiger und Preußischer Staatsanzeiger*, August 7, 1934, July 14 and October 14, 1936, July 22, 1939, and May 8, 1941. *LBB* 89, April 13, 1935, 2: "Hans Hammer, jr." *LBB* 135, 12 June 1935, 4: Hammer-Tonfilm-Verleih ad for the Pola Negri film *Um eine Fürstenkrone*, with reference to the Berlin headquarters. *LBB* 203, August 31, 1936, 2: "Gläubiger-Versammlung." *LBB* 204 September 1, 1936, 2: "Man hört ..." *LBB* 250, October 24, 1936, 3: "Hammer-Vergleich angenommen."

114. For example, *Film* published extensive overviews of German movie offerings every two weeks.

115. Riefenstahl, *Memoiren*, 1987, 265.

116. Para 25, Section 1 of "Lichtspielgesetz, February 16, 1934" in *RGBI* 17, February 19, 1934, 98.

117. Klemperer, *Ich will Zeugnis ablegen bis zum Letzten* 1, 2015, 240, 241 (entry from August 13, 1936).

118. Riefenstahl, 150. Riefenstahl does not provide any references allowing the dating of the telegram.

119. *FK* 78, April 2, 1932, 11: "Ihr Kronzeuge."

120. *FK* 42, February 1935, 1: "Das blaue Licht in Amerika."

121. FPS, March 23, 1932, file 31,269. See also *Illustrierter FK* 1,748, 2.

122. *FK* 233, October 5, 1931, 3: "Leni Riefenstahl: Film-Arbeit in den Tiroler Bergen."

123. Authorization, December 11, 1933, in Infield, picture 12 between 76, 77.

124. Riefenstahl, 207, 208.

125. *Pasadena Independent* (CA) 141, November 11, 1945, 12: "Streicher vs. Streicher. A Nazi War Criminal's Care against Himself. Don Juan of Franken Wrote Hot Love Letters to Leni" by Lieutenant Daniel Causin. Causin had reported on his find in the U.S. for the International News Special Service in a 10-part series of articles in the immediate run-up to the Nuremberg trials against the main perpetrators of the war crimes, which began in some U.S. gazettes as early as October 28, 1945 (for example, *Clarion-Ledger* [Jackson, MS; no No.], October 28, 1945, 1).

126. *Illustrierter FK* 2,797, 2.

127. Kinowelt 2005 DVD *Das blaue Licht* (ord. no. 500871).

128. Trimborn, 119.

129. Letters to the author from Riefenstahl's secretary Gisela Jahn, June 17 and 21, 2010.

130. Letter Dr. Ralf Breslau (Handschriftenabteilung, Referat Nachlässe und Autographen, Staatsbibliothek zu Berlin—Preußischer Kulturbesitz), January 11, 2021, to the author and further information of January 29, 2021, referring to bequest 590 (Leni Riefenstahl).

131. See the section "Londoner Premieren" in *LBB* 69, March 21, 1936, 2. *LBB* 81, April 4, 1936, 2. *LBB* 86, April 11, 1936, 2. See also the section "Das Ausland dreht—das Ausland zeigt" in *LBB* 67, March 19, 1936, 2: "Pariser Premieren." *LBB* 85, April 9, 1936, 3: "Niederländische Premieren." *LBB* 88, April 15, 1936, 2: "Niederländische Premieren." *LBB* 99, April 28, 1936, 2: "Niederländische Premieren." *LBB* 110, May 12, 1936, 2: "Prager Premieren."

132. "Europa spielt" in *FK* 34, February 10, 1936, 4, to 221, September 21, 1936, 4.

133. *FK* 43, February 22, 1936, 3 (Supplement, 1): "Londoner Gala-Premiere. *Things to Come.*"

134. *FK* 302, December 28, 1936, 3: "Europa spielt."

135. *FK* 69, March 21, 1936, 3 (Supplement, 1): "Dies und das." Premiere announcement for the evening of March 13, 1936, in: *Pariser Tageblatt* 822, March 13, 1936, 4.

136. *Pariser Tageblatt* 794, February 14, 1936, 4: "Die europäische Premiere des neuen Chaplin-Films" by A.T.

137. *Pariser Tageblatt* 822, March 13, 1936, 4: image from *Modern Times* with caption.

138. Ads in *Pariser Tageblatt* 836, March 27, 1936, 4. *Pariser Tageblatt* 857, April 17, 1936, 4.

139. *FK* 162, July 14, 1936, 3: "Dies und das."

140. Der Reichsführer SS, Der Chef des Sicherheitshauptamtes, *No. 06, "Geheim," Leitheft: Emigrantenpresse und Schrifttum. März 1937*, 31–33. "BArch" RSHA. The 49-page *Leitheft* focuses on the émigré press on 26 pages.

141. *Das Wort* 1, July 1936, 92–95: "The *Modern Times*" by Arthur Koestler.

142. Section "A Paris cette semaine" (This Week in Paris), first and last entry for *Les temps modernes* at Marigny in *La Cinématographie Française* 906, March 14, 1936, 18. *La Cinématographie Française* 921, June 27, 1936, 174.

143. *Birmingham Weekly Post* (Great Britain), May 16, 1936: "Chaplin's Popularity." *Cumberland Evening News* (Carlisle, Great Britain), May 26, 1936: "Charlie the Incomparable." In Montreux, album 53.

144. *La Cinématographie Française* 907, March 21, 1936, 12: "*Les temps modernes*" by -x.

145. *Sozialistische Warte* 8, March 15, 1936, 198, 200: "*Modern Times* und *La vie future*. Und Chaplin?" by Goetz Mayer.

146. *La Cinématographie Française* 909, April 4, 1936, 10: "Les nouveaux films. Les films du mois."

147. *LBB* 1, January 1, 1937, 3, 4 (1st Supplement, 1, 2): "Filmjahr 1936 in der LBB-Statistik" and "Uraufführungen 1936—Amerika."

148. *LBB* 2, January 4, 1937, 3: "Die zehn Besten in USA."

149. *FK* 20, January 25, 1937, 3: "Amerika wählte die besten Filme."

150. *Pariser Tageszeitung* 323, April 30, 1937, 4: "Chaplin-Film in Italien verboten."

151. *LBB* 103, May 5, 1937, 2: "LBB teilt mit."

152. *FK* 302, December 28, 1936, 3: "Europa spielt."

153. *Paimann's Filmlisten* 1,043, April 3, 1936, 28: "*Die neue Zeit.*" The premiere had taken place on March 31, 1936.

154. *LBB* 80, April 3, 1936, 2: "Österreich."

155. For the inauguration of the Reichsfilmarchiv, see, for example, *LBB* 31, February 5, 1935, 1: "Feierliche Eröffnung des Reichsfilmarchivs."

156. *Katalog des Reichsfilmarchivs*, foreign films, 2,857 and corresponding main index card. In BArch, Filmarchiv BL.

157. *Katalog des Reichsfilmarchivs*, foreign films, 454. Ban of *The Bohemian Girl*: FPS, May 8, 1936, file 42,400, confirmed by FOPS on June 13, 1936, file 7,819.

158. See Aping, *Das Dick-und-Doof-Buch*, 2007, 159, 160. In BArch BL, "persönliche Adjutantur des Führers und Reichskanzlers" at NS 10 44.

159. *Katalog des Reichsfilmarchivs*, foreign films. In BArch, Filmarchiv BL.

160. See *Der Archivar* 1, April 1960, 2: "Zur Geschichte des Reichsfilmarchivs" (9, section "Lagerung und Verzeichnung") by Hans Barkhausen.

161. *LBB* 246, October 22, 1937, 3: "*Ritter ohne Furcht und Tadel* im Berliner Marmorhaus" by Albert Schneider.

162. In BArch BL, "persönliche Adjutantur des Führers und Reichskanzlers" NS 10 Volume 44, folios 116, 119, 132, 134, and Volume 45, folio 2.

163. German premiere on March 31, 1956, simultaneously in many cities of the Federal Republic of Germany: *Filmblätter* 17, April 27, 1956, 476: "Evergreen. *Moderne Zeiten.*" Freiwillige Selbstkontrolle der Filmwirtschaft (FSK), November 28, 1955/March 9, 1956, file 11,090.

164. *ff dabei* 49, program week December 1 through 7, 1980, 22.

Chapter 9

1. *Paris-Soir* 291, October 14, 1936, 12: "À nous la liberté s'etait écrié Charlie Chaplin. Oui, mais nous vivons des *Temps modernes*, ont riposté les éditeurs du film de René Clair!" (*À nous la liberté* cried Charlie Chaplin. Yes, but we are living in *Modern Times*, retorted the producers of René Clair's film!) by Georges Cravenne.

2. *FK* 242, October 15, 1936, 3: "Plagiatsvorwürfe gegen Chaplin."

3. *Pariser Tageszeitung* 167, November 25, 1936, 6: "Plagiatklage gegen Charlie Chaplin."

4. *NYT* 28, 944, April 23, 1937, 24: "Chaplin Sued over Film."

5. *Ce Soir*, April 28, 1937: "À nous la liberté contre *Temps modernes*" by J.M. In Bologna, ch03013001.

6. *Film* 20, May 15, 1937, 2: "Charlie Chaplin—ein Plagiator. Ein 'Genie' hat es sich leicht gemacht."

7. *La Cinématographie Française* 969, May 28, 1937 (section "Technique et Matériel," I): "Charlie Chaplin—René Clair."

8. The action dated April 20, 1937, could not be served on Chaplin personally until much later, because he had repeatedly prevented its service. On March 25, 1939, Films Sonores Tobis also filed suit in France on the same charge. Both actions in "Bologna," ch02647001-13 und ch02701006-15 (English translation of the French action).

9. Settlement agreements in English and French. In Bologna, ch03829002-09.

10. Lyons, 30 (entry April 23, 1937, in "A Chronological Biography").

11. Action dated December 7, 1937, District Court, Southern District of California. In Bologna, ch02824001-08.

12. *NYT* 29, 884, November 19, 1939, 41: "Chaplin Wins Film Suit."

13. The Paris Bibliothèque du Film only holds a sketchy run of the *Agence d'information Cinégraphique*.

14. Vincent, *History of Cinematographic Art*, 1939, 89 (note 1 on *La ruée vers l'Or*). Only the text of the note had been available for the German version of this book. It refers to the Chaplin scene outlined in the main text without describing anything. At the time it was unclear which hut scene Vincent meant.

15. *LBB* 115, May 21, 1937, 3: "3 Plagiatsklagen gegen Chaplin."

16. Hanisch, 98.

17. Sarment's letter of May 2, 1931. In Bologna, ch03239001-03.

18. *Comoedia Illustré, journal parisien theatral, artistique et littéraire* of May 23, 1931, translated into English under the title "Has Mr. Chaplin been guilty of plagiarism in *City Lights*?" In Bologna, ch03252001-07.

19. *Paris-Midi*, May 29, 1931: "Où la querelle 'Charlot—Jean Sarment' s'envenime et prend un tour comique" by Pierre Lazareff. English translation under the title "Where the quarrel 'Charlot—Jean Sarment' gets envenomed and turns into comedy." In Bologna, ch03255001-02.

20. *FK* 120, May 26, 1931, 1: "Chaplins Plagiataffäre."

21. *Kinematograph* 119/120, May 27, 1931, 2: "Chaplin des Plagiats angeklagt."

22. *LBB* 127, May 28, 1931, 2: "Die Plagiat-Beschuldigung gegen Chaplin."

23. *FK* 123, May 29, 1931, 1: "Charlies Affäre."

24. *RFB* 22, May 30, 1931, 2: "Autor Chaplin" by René Clair.

25. *Film* 28, July 1937, 1, 2: "Plagiator Chaplin bleibt sich treu—und stiehlt nach wie vor."

26. *National-Zeitung* (Basel) 189, April 26, 1937: "Hollywood und Spanien" in Chaplin file.

27. Buñuel, *Mein letzter Seufzer*, 1987, 168.

28. Press instruction 1,423, December 23, 1936 ("BArch" Koblenz, collection Brammer at ZSg. 101/8/439) in Bohrmann, Toepser-Ziegert, Kohlmann-Viand and Peter, *NS-Presseanweisungen. Volume 4/III*, 1993, 1,605. See also Odenwald, 312–314.

29. *VB* (Munich) 170, June 19, 1937, 3 (Supplement, "Der Film-Beobachter," 1): "Wer hat *Sehnsucht* nach Marlene?" by erba.

30. Press Instruction 2,726, November 9, 1937 ("BArch" Koblenz, collection Brammer at ZSg. 101/10/339/1,428) in Bohrmann, Toepser-Ziegert and Peter, *NS-Presseanweisungen. Volume 5/III*, 1998, 903.

31. *FK* 269, November 19, 1937, 1: "Gegen Gerüchte um Marlene Dietrich." *Film* 47, November 20, 1937, 1: "Marlene-Dietrich-Gerüchte grundlos."

32. *Binghamton Press* (NY) 259, February 13, 1937, 8: "Nazis Plan Exhibit, 'The Eternal Jew.'" *NYT* 29, 123, October 19, 1937, 7: "Plan anti-Jewish Exhibit." *The Manchester Guardian* (London) 28, 422, October 21, 1937, 9: "'The Eternal Jew.' Nazis' 'Educational' Exhibition."

33. Bauer, *Trau keinem Fuchs auf grüner Heid und keinem Jud bei seinem Eid*, 1936, 29, 30.

34. Rinner (Prague), *Deutschlandberichte der Sozialdemokratischen Partei Deutschlands (Sopade)*, reprint 1980, *Volume 2*, February 5, 1938, marginal number A 62–64: "III. Der Terror gegen die Juden. 8. Einzelberichte aus Deutschland. Bayern. 2. Bericht," 195.

35. *LBB* 226, September 29, 1937, 3: "LBB teilt mit …" *LBB* 261, November 9, 1937, 1: "Film auf der Schau "Der ewige Jude." *NYT* 29, 144, November 9, 1937, 15: "Streicher Opens anti-Semitic Fair."

36. Fröhlich, *Goebbels-Tagebücher. Volume 4*, 2000, 393 (entry of November 5, 1937).

37. *FK* 303, December 30, 1937, 2: "Schnell noch lesen." FPS, July 20, 1938, file 48,696.

38. See Benz, *"Der ewige Jude,"* 2010, 135–138.

39. *LBB* 302, December 29, 1937, 3: *"Juden ohne Maske."*

40. *LBB* 261, November 9, 1937, 1: "Film auf der Schau 'Der ewige Jude.'" *LBB* 264, November 12, 1937, 2: "Interessante Zahlen auf der Ausstellung 'Der ewige Jude.'" *FK* 264, November 12, 1937, 2: "Filmprodukte der Verfallszeit." *DFZ* 42, November 14, 1937, 7: "'Der ewige Jude' im Film." *Film* 48, November 27, 1937, 8: "'Der ewige Jude' im Film." See also *Film* 29, July 17, 1937, 11 (3rd Supplement, 1): "Die Filmstellen der NSDAP."

41. *The Manchester Guardian* (London) 28, 438, November 9, 1937, 14: "Few Jews now to Persecute in Germany."

42. Zeman, *Das Dritte Reich in der Karikatur*, 1984, 114 (cartoon 3, by unknown artist).

43. From 1910, Trier (1890–1951) worked as illustrator and cartoonist in Berlin. Soon he published political cartoons, in which he warned against Nazism as early as the 1920s. His illustrations for the magazines *Der heitere Fridolin* and *Uhu* as well as for Erich Kästner's children's books are particularly remembered in Germany. In 1936, Trier artist fled to London and achieved great popularity with covers, which he created from 1937 to 1949 for the magazine *Lilliput*, founded by Stefan Lorant. In August 1947, he moved to Canada and remained successful there as well. See for an overview Neuner-Warthorst, *Walter Trier*, 2006.

44. Trier, *Nazi-German in 22 Lessons*, 1942, 18.

45. *Die Zeitung* 281, July 24, 1942, 3: "Das ist der Weg" by Walter Trier.

46. *LBB* 302, December 29, 1937, 3: *"Juden ohne Maske."*

47. *LBB* 291, December 15, 1937, 3: "LBB teilt mit." Rinner (Prague), *Volume 2*, February 5, 1938, 195. *FK* 30, February 5, 1938, 2: "Schnell noch lesen."

48. *LBB* 262, November 7, 1938, 2: "LBB teilt mit."

49. *Angriff* 272, November 13, 1938, 4: "Isidor ist wieder da," von js.

50. Rinner, *Volume 2*, February 5, 1938, 195, 196.

51. *Jüdische Revue*, December 1937, 705 (708): "Der ewige Jude und der Gegengeist" by Observer.

52. Diebow, *Gregor Straßer und der Nationalsozialismus*, 1930. With Goeltzer, *Hitler und Mussolini*, both 1931. *Das Deutschland Adolf Hitlers*, in *Illustrierte Zeitung* special issue, 1937.

53. *Deutscher! So sehen Deine Führer aus!*, ca. 1932.

54. Diebow, *Der ewige Jude*, 1937, 7 (Werthauer), 76 (Einstein), 106 (Weiß). *Angriff* 272, November 13, 1938, 4: "Isidor ist wieder da" by js.

55. Diebow, *Der ewige Jude*, 126–128.

56. *Prager Tagblatt* 111, May 11, 1927, 3: "Chaplin als Privatmensch" by Jim Tully.

57. Diebow, *Der ewige Jude*, 67, 68.

58. Plöckinger, *Geschichte eines Buches*, 2006, 187.

59. Weinberg, *Hitlers zweites Buch*, 1961, 36.

60. Ads and editor's call in *Angriff* 200, October 3, 1932, 8.

61. *Pariser Tageblatt* 281, December 28, 1934, 1: "Was verdient Adolf Hitler?"

62. *FK* 29, February 4, 1937, 2: *"Mein Kampf.* 2 ½ Millionen Exemplare verkauft." *FK* 149, June 30, 1937, 3: "3-Millionen-Auflage von *Mein Kampf.*"

63. Plöckinger, 187, 188, 429, 432, 443.

64. Plöckinger, 184.

65. *LBB* 276, November 27, 1937, 4. *Film* 48, November 28, 1937, 3.

66. *Der neue Film* 49/1937 (early December), 3: Ad for *Film-"Kunst"*, Film-Kohn, Film-Korruption.

67. See on this Bering, *Der Name als Stigma*, 206–211.

68. *LBB* 267, November 16, 1937, 2: "Reichsamts-leiter Carl Neumann 45 Jahre."

69. Jason, *Handbuch des Films 1935/36*, 1935, 40, 41.

70. *Film* 2, January 8, 1938, 10 (2nd Supplement, 2): "Die Aufgaben der Gaufilmstellen."

71. For example, see, *Der Deutsche Film* 12, June 1937, 354, 365: "Über 100 Millionen Deutsche in den Parteifilmveranstaltungen" by Curt Belling.

72. *Der neue Film* 48/1938 (end November), 1: "Pausenlose Vorführung auch im kleinsten Dorf."

73. Neumann, Belling and Betz, 5: "Zur Einleitung."

74. *Film* 48, November 27, 1937, 1, 2. *LBB* 276, November 27, 1937, 3: "Film-'Kunst', Film-Kohn, Film-Korruption. Eine Abrechnung mit der jüdischen Filmvergangenheit."

75. Neumann, Belling and Betz, 138: "Carl Neumann hat das Wort."

76. Neumann, Belling and Betz, 92: "III. Die jüdischen Herren der Filmpresse."

77. *Film* 50, December 11, 1937, 3: Publisher's ad for *Film-"Kunst"*, *Film-Kohn, Film-Korruption*.

78. Neumann, Belling and Betz, first plate between 16 and 17.

79. Neumann, Belling and Betz, 32: "II. Die Sache mit den hübschen Mädchenwaden."

80. Neumann, Belling and Betz, 77: "III. Und so sahen ihre Filme aus."

81. Neumann, Belling and Betz, 84, 85: "III. Wie Isidor Goldschmidt [*sic*] wurde."

82. *Film* 48, November 27, 1937, 3: Publisher's ad for *Film-"Kunst"*, *Film-Kohn, Film-Korruption*.

83. *FK* 2, January 4, 1938, 2: "*Film-"Kunst"*, *Film-Kohn, Film-Korruption*" by Günther Schwark.

84. *Film* 52, December 24, 1937, 1, 2: "Gedanken zu dem neuen Buch *Film-"Kunst"*, *Film-Kohn, Film-Korruption*" by Hermann Glessgen.

85. *Film* 6, February 5, 1938, 2: "Gutachten für Verleger," January 29, 1938, on *Film-"Kunst"*, *Film-Kohn, Film-Korruption*, Reichsstelle zur Förderung des deutschen Schrifttums.

86. *Filmblätter* 6, February 9, 1951, 121: "*Lichter der Großstadt*" by HDW.

87. Curt Belling letters to Robert G. Scheuer, the editor-in-chief of *Filmblätter*: September 8, 1951, and June 10, 1952. Draft article "Run auf Harlan-Filme," no date. Belling signed the letter of September 8, 1951, with "Belling Abel" and the draft with "Abel." In Schriftgutarchiv Deutsche Kinemathek Berlin, envelope "Curt Belling."

88. *Film* 42, October 19, 1940, 1, 2: "Das Frontkino—im Weltkrieg und heute" by Sonderführer Curt Belling.

89. Letter from Fritz Podehl, head of the Freiwillige Selbstkontrolle der Filmwirtschaft, dated August 21, 1951, to Robert G. Scheuer, in Schriftgutarchiv Deutsche Kinemathek Berlin, envelope "Curt Belling."

90. Curt Belling letter to Scheuer in Schriftgutarchiv Deutsche Kinemathek Berlin, envelope "Curt Belling."

Chapter 10

1. Indexes to the *RGBl* and part II: 1938, 49, 50. 1939, 56, 57. 1940, 53, 54.

2. "Vierte Verordnung zum Reichsbürgergesetz, July 25, 1938" in *RGBl* 122, August 2, 1938, 969, 970 (Physicians). August 1938, 969, 970 (Physicians). "Fünfte Verordnung zum Reichsbürgergesetz, July 25, 1938" in *RGBl* 165, October 14, 1938, 1,403–1,406 (Lawyers). "Sechste Verordnung zum Reichsbürgergesetz, July 25, 1938" in *RGBl* 182, October 31, 1938, 1,545, 1,546 (Patent Attorneys).

3. "Verordnung über eine Sühneleistung der Juden deutscher Staatsangehörigkeit, November 23, 1938" in *RGBl* 189, November 14, 1938, 1,579. In addition, "Verordnung über die Sühneleistung der Juden, November 21, 1938" in *RGBl* 19, November 22, 1938, 1,638–1,640. "Verordnung über den Einsatz jüdischen Vermögens, December 3, 1938" in *RGBl* 206, December 5, 1938, 1,709–1,712.

4. "Verordnung zur Wiederherstellung des Straßenbildes bei jüdischen Gewerbebetrieben, November 12, 1938," *RGBl* 189, November 14, 1938, 1,581.

5. *LBB* 121, May 24, 1938, 2: "Kölner Filmtheater verzichtet auf jüdische Besucher." *FK* 179, August 3, 1938, 3: "Juden dürfen nicht ins Kino."

6. "Anordnung des Präsidenten der Reichskulturkammer über die Teilnahme von Darbietungen der deutschen Kultur vom 12. November 1938" in *VB* (N) 318, November 14, 1938, 2. *FK* 267, November 14, 1938, 1: "Juden dürfen keine Kinos mehr besuchen."

7. "Erlass des Reichsführers SS und Chefs der deutschen Polizei über die Entziehung der Führerscheine und Zulassungspapiere der Juden, December 3, 1938" in *VB* (N) 338, December 4, 1938, 2: "Allgemeines Kraftfahrverbot für die Juden " (General ban for the Jews on car driving). The decree was printed in the only Jewish newspaper still being permitted to be published after the November pogroms: *Jüdisches Nachrichtenblatt* (Ber) 5, December 9, 1938, 2. See also: Walk, 262.

8. "Verordnung zur Ausschaltung der Juden aus dem deutschen Wirtschaftsleben, November 12, 1938" in *RGBl* 189, November 14, 1938, 1,580. "Verordnung zur Ausschaltung der Juden aus dem deutschen Wirtschaftsleben, November 23, 1938" in *RGBl* 192, November 24, 1938, 1,642. "Zweite Verordnung zur Ausschaltung der Juden aus dem deutschen Wirtschaftsleben, December 14, 1938" in *RGBl* 223, December 23, 1938, 1,902.

9. *LBB* 75, March 29, 1939, 3: "LBB teilt mit."

10. *LBB* 278, November 26, 1938, 3: "*Juden ohne Maske.*"

11. *Angriff* 281, November 24, 1938, 3: "Keiner will die Juden haben. Warum nimmt sie das so mitleidsvolle Amerika nicht selbst?"

12. See Schröder, *Heimatlos auf hoher See*, 1949.

13. *Autobiography*, 424. Chaplin Jr., *My Father, Charlie Chaplin*, 1960, 181, 182.

14. *Daily Variety* 7, April 27, 1938, 3: "Chaplin's 1st Talker for UA in 1938–39."

15. For example, *Detroit Times* (MI), October 19, 1938: "Parody on Hitler. Next for Chaplin. Charlie's Role is a Caricature of the Fuehrer" by Louella O. Parsons. *Denver Post* (CO), October 19, 1938: "New Charlie Chaplin Comedy, All Talkie, Satirizes Hitler." *Detroit Times* (MI), October 23, 1938: "Chaplin Wins with Hitler Gag" by Louella O. Parsons. In Montreux, album 58/1.

16. See Fest, pictures 30–33 between 640, 641.

17. *Autobiography*, 324, 325.

18. Frank Scheide, "*The Great Dictator* and Chaplin's Tramp as an awakened 'Rip Van Winkle,'" in Scheide, Mehran and Kamin, 20, 22.

19. Weissberg 44, 45, 62 (note 46).

20. Robinson, 119.

21. Montagu, 94.

22. Chaplin Jr., 179, 180.

23. Huff, 239.

24. Hermand, in Groenewold, 35, 36.

25. *Autobiography*, 424, 425.

26. Chaplin Jr., 192. From the abandoned screenplay a film starring Goddard and Gary Cooper would have been made. Chaplin Jr. probably meant "White Russians of Shanghai" from which Chaplin's last film *A Countess From Hong Kong* (1966) emerged almost three decades later. See also Milton, 367, 512.

27. Term used by Chaplin in his July 1947 open telegram to House Un-American Activities Committee Chairman J. Parnell Thomas: *NYT* 32, 685, July 21, 1947, 12: "Chaplin Accepts House 'Invitation.'"

28. Albert Schneider in *LBB* 24, January 28, 1938, 2: "Meldungen, wie sie nicht sein sollen." *Film* 8, February 21, 1926, 19: "Goldrausch."

29. *FK* 241, October 14, 1938, 3: "Man hört und liest" by Karl F. Franck. *Angriff* 279, November 22, 1938, 4: "Ein Drittel der Hollywood-Stars sind Juden. Sieben Cohns als Produzenten" by Curt Belling.

30. *Cincinnati Enquirer* (OH), October 17, 1938: "Moustache Is Inspiration?" *Detroit Times*, October 18, 1938: "Parody on Hitler. Next for Chaplin. Charlie's Role is a Caricature of the Fuehrer" by Louella O. Parsons. *Denver Post* (CO), October 19, 1938: "New Charlie Chaplin Comedy, All Talkie, Satirizes Hitler." *Detroit Times* (MI), October 23, 1938: "Chaplin Wins with Hitler Gag" by Louella O. Parsons. In Montreux, album 58/1.

31. Letters Gyssling to Breen and Breen to Gyssling, in MPAA/PCA, file *The Great Dictator*, in the holdings of the Margaret Herrick Library.

32. *Daily Mail* (London), November 22, 1938: "Chaplin (and Moustache) to Satirize Dictator" by Walter Wyndham. In Montreux, album 58/1.

33. *FK* 276, November 25, 1938, 3: "Charlie Chaplin wird unverschämt."

34. *FK* 83, April 9, 1934, 1: "Hetzfilm Trials in Neuyork." *FK* 95, April 23, 1934, 1: "New Yorker Zensur verbietet Hetzfilm." *FK* 167, July 19, 1934, 1: "Amerikanischer Hetzfilm vor dem Obersten Gericht." *FK* 173, July 26, 1934, 1: "Hetzfilm-Fabrikant sammelt 'Unruhen.'" On *Hitler's Reign of Terror*, see King Hanson, *The American Film*

Institute Catalog of Motion Pictures. Feature Films: 1931–1940, 1993, 932, 933.

35. *FK* 128, June 4, 1935, 1: "Anti-Hetzfilm-Resolution von Fipresci gebilligt." *LBB* 129, June 4, 1935, 1: "Anti-Hetzfilm-Resolution einstimmig angenommen."

36. *RWF* 11, March 12, 1938, 5: "Fipresci gegen Hetzfilm."

37. Campaign for the meeting at the Los Angeles Shrine Auditorium on October 20, 1936: *Daily Variety* 37, October 20, 1936, 5: "The Menace of Hitlerism in America." Attendance for the events was between 7,500 and 10,000 people: *Los Angeles Times*, October 21, 1936, A 22. *DV* 38, October 21, 1936, 9. See also Maland, 162.

38. *Film* 43, October 22, 1938, 7 (2nd Supplement, 1): "Das amerikanische Publikum empört sich über die Hollywood-Juden."

39. *Film* 48, November 26, 1938, 2: "Abrechnung mit den Hetzern."

40. *Angriff* 294, December 9, 1938, 4: "Hollywood macht Rebbach mit Hetze." *Angriff* 304, December 21, 1938, 4: "Film-Emigranten hetzen gegen ihre 'Heimat'" by Curt Belling.

41. *Die Weltbühne* 42, October 19, 1922, 415, 416: "Chaplin III. Der Politiker" by Hans Siemsen.

42. Hitler, 198, 199.

43. *Angriff* 314, December 31, 1938, after 14: "Wir sind im Bilde [Episode 52, 1–3], Juden: Spione für Deutschland." Cartoon by Stenberg (first name unknown).

44. *Angriff* 37, February 12, 1939, 9: "Es grenzt ja schon an Hellseherei" by kat.

45. *Angriff* 31, February 5, 1939, 2: "Haben wir eigentlich noch Humor? ['Ja,' sagt der Minister]." With reference to this article, the question was asked again in the movie magazine *Filmwoche* a year later and, of course, again answered with "yes": *Filmwoche* 6, February 7, 1940, 125: "Haben wir noch Humor?" by Konradjoachim Schaub.

46. On Finck, see Budzinski and Hippen, *Metzler Kabarett Lexikon*, 1996, 98–100. Budzinski, *Pfeffer ins Getriebe*, 1982, 138–142.

47. *Angriff* 31, February 5, 1939, 3: "Was ist Humor?"

48. *Pariser Tageszeitung* 846, November 19, 1938, 3: "Chaplin spielt nicht Hitler."

49. *Angriff* 290, December 4, 1938, 6: "Chaplin als Hitler!" by j.

50. *FK* 286, December 7, 1938, 5: "Chaplin als Hitler."

51. The December 22, 1938, issue of the *Hamburger Fremdenblatt* could not be located in German libraries.

52. Unidentified newspaper clipping with Berlin report of December 22, 1938: "Nazi Protest Ickes Remarks to Washington." In Montreux, album 58/1.

53. Quoted from and representative of other U.S. reports with the same wording: *New York Telegraph*, December 23, 1938: "Link Chaplin Ickes in Plot. German Paper Says Film, '*Dictator*, Is 'Blow at Nation at Peace with US,'" *Commercial Appeal* (Memphis, TN), December 24, 1938: "Ickes and

Chaplin Conspire on Nazis." In Montreux, album 58.

54. *Pariser Tageszeitung* 879, December 29, 1938, 4: "Chaplins Diktator-Film."

55. Wilke, 124.

56. Appendix to Press Instruction 3,680 in "Glossen-Konferenz" (Instructional Conference) of December 21, 1938 ("BArch" Koblenz, collection Brammer at ZSg. 101/10/241) in Bohrmann, Toepser-Ziegert and Peter, *NS-Presseanweisungen. Volume 6/III*, 1999, 1,214.

57. *FK* 299, December 22, 1938, 1:" Hays-Organisation gegen den Hetzfilm."

58. *Smith's Weekly* (Sydney), January 28, 1939, 19: "Hollywood Can't Make these Films! Subjects too dangerous for Filming" by Lenore Sayers. In Montreux, album 58/1.

59. *Pariser Tageszeitung* 879, December 29, 1938, 4: "Chaplins Diktator-Film."

60. *FK* 26, January 31, 1939, 1: "Die Ankündigung nazistischer Filme kann uns bewegen, in Zukunft antisemitische Filme herstellen zu lassen."

61. *FK* 27, February 1, 1939, 2: "Wird die Warnung des Führers beachtet werden?" by Dr. W.P.

62. *FK* 162, July 15, 1939, 3 (Supplement, 1): "*Robert und Bertram*" by Georg Herzberg.

63. Warner Brothers feature films had been distributed in Germany since 1928 by the German company National-Film-Verleih und Vertrieb. During the Third Reich, no more films of these producers were distributed in Germany.

64. *LBB* 118, May 23, 1939, 1: "Seltsame Filmpläne im Ausland." *LBB* 143, June 23, 1939, 4: "Filmjuden bluffen in Argentinien." *LBB* 279, November 29, 1939, 1: "Wieder ein Hetzfilm." *LBB* 285, December 6, 1939, 1: "Englisch-jüdische Filmhetze 1914–1939" by Curt Belling. *FK* 139, June 19, 1939, 2: "Argentinien verbietet Hetzfilm." *FK* 280, November 30, 1939, 1: "Jüdischer Hetzfilm im Staate New York verboten." *FK* 289, December 11, 1939, 3: "*The Beast of Berlin*." *Filmwelt* 22, June 2, 1939, 31: "Die Hetzer im amerikanischen Film."

65. *LBB* 162, July 15, 1939, 2: "Jüdischer USA-Kampf gegen 'Nazi-Filme.'" *LBB* 175, July 31, 1939, 4 (Supplement, 2): "Weitere Hetzfilme aus den USA." *FK* 184, August 10, 1939, 2: "Hetzfilme dienen der Einkreisungsagitation" by H.H. (Hans Hinkel?).

66. *Newcastle Evening Chronicle* (Newcastle upon Tyne), June 27, 1939: "Charlie the Giant Killer" by Carey Orr. In Montreux, album 58/2.

67. McKenna's letter and its forwarding to Breen quoted from Gardner, *The Censorship Papers*, 1987, 126, 127.

68. Quoted from Urwand, 219.

69. *Autobiography*, 425, 426.

70. Vasey, 54.

71. Mitchell, *The Marx Brothers Encyclopedia*, 1996, 28 (entry "*At the Circus*").

72. Issues of March 20, 1939: *Hollywood Citizen-News*: "This Is Chaplin Speaking." *Hollywood Reporter* (Los Angeles): "*Dictator* Foldup Denied by Chaplin." *Daily Variety* (Hollywood): "Chaplin Ignores Kicks. Goes after *Dictators*." In

Montreux, album 58/1. United Artists newsletter reprinted in full in Chaplin, *My Life in Pictures*, 1974, 268.

73. *Daily Film Renter* (London), April 6, 1939: "Chaplin Denies He Will Abandon *The Dictators*." *Film Curb* (NYC), March 25, 1939: "C. Chaplin Denies Abandoning Film Dealing with *Dictators*." *Variety* (NYC), March 22, 1939: "Chaplin Denies Gag on Anti-Dictator Pic." Other newspapers, for example, *Daily Worker* (New York), March 23, 1939: "Hollywood Extra!" *Duluth Herald* (MN), April 1, 1939: "Chaplin Denies He Will Abandon Film." *Jewish Ledger* (Hartford, CT), March 24, 1939: "Deny Chaplin Abandons Film." *Knoxville News-Sentinel* (TN), April 2, 1939: "Charlie Won't Back down." *Statesman*, April 1, 1939: "*The Dictators*, not Abandoned by Chaplin." In Montreux, album 58/1.

74. *The Hollywood Tribune*, April 28, 1939. Quoted from Velten and Klein, 100, 131.

75. *NYT* 29, 727, June 15, 1939, 11: "Chaplin Film to Aid Emigration."

76. *NYT* 29, 770, June 28, 1939, 6: "Italy Lacks News on Entry of Jews."

77. *Buffalo Jew Review* (Buffalo, NY), June 30, 1939: "Charlie Chaplin Reported Giving *Dictator* Profits to Aid Emigration." *The Jewish Advocate* (Bombay, India) 6, June 30, 1939, 1: "For His People." In Montreux, album 58/2.

78. For example, from the abundance of reports: *Chicago Sunday Tribune* (IL) 31, July 30, 1939, 6: "Charlie Chaplin Plays 'Moses' to Emigrant Jews." *Sunday News* (NYC) 16, July 30, 1939, 356: "Chaplin 'Moses' to Fleeing Jews."

79. *Jewish Transcript* (Seattle, WA), August 7, 1939: "Chaplin Spends for Humanity." In Montreux, album 58/2.

80. Maland, 171, unattributed.

81. *L'Œuvre* (Paris), April 16, 1939: "Charlie Chaplin a 50 ans." In Chaplin file.

82. Maser, *Der Sturm auf die Republik*. In 1908, Hitler received 58 crowns a month from his father's inheritance, as well as an orphan's pension of 25 crowns. In Austria at that time, young academics in the civil service, such as lawyers and teachers, received monthly salaries of between 70 and 66 crowns. For his furnished apartment in Vienna, Hitler paid a monthly rent of 10 kronen and still had 73 crowns to live on. In 1911 he was able, without necessity, to forego his orphan's pension, still due until April 1913, in favor of his sister Paula. His move to the shelter for homeless people apparently did not stem from economic reasons. The daily rent in the shelter was one crown and was more expensive than the monthly rent for his furnished room.

83. Chaplin Jr., 168.

84. Article "Hitler and Chaplin: The Story of two Birthdays" by unknown author, reprinted in Haining, *The Legend of Charlie Chaplin*, 1982, 158, 162. Eric Koch adapted an excerpt from this article for his 2000 novel *The Man Who Knew Charlie Chaplin*, 2000, VII.

85. Robinson, 528.

86. *FK* 281, December 2, 1935, 1, 2: "Der Regisseur soll Diktator sein!"

87. For example, *Edinburgh Evening News*, April 12, 1939: "A Tale of two Birthdays" by Andre de Hevesi. *Lancaster Daily Post* (Lancashire), April 14, 1939: "Adolf Hitler and Charlie Chaplin" by Andre de Hevesi. *Cleveland Press* (OH), April 20, 1939: "One Was Named Charles and the other Adolf 50 Years ago." *Public Opinion* (Cumberland, PA), April 21, 1939, 364: "'Speechless Fame'—Herr Hitler and Charlie Chaplin Celebrate their 50th Birthday." In Montreux, album 58/2. The mentioned caricature was created by the French caricaturist A.R. (André-René) Charlet, who is said to have been pro-Nazi. It is, also without reference to the source. In DFF—Deutsches Filminstitut & Filmmuseum.

88. *Film* 15, April 15, 1939, 7 (2nd Supplement, 1): "Zum 20. April 1939, dem fünfzigsten Geburtstag des Führers" by Curt Belling. *Der neue Film* 16/1939 (mid–April), 2: "Zum fünfzigsten Geburtstag des Führers" by Curt Belling.

89. In detail, for example, in Kershaw, *Hitler. 1889–1936*, 229–236, and *Hitler. 1936–1945*, 2002, 247–250.

90. FPS, April 25, 1939, file 51,322.

91. See on this newsreel in detail, Barkhausen, *Filmpropaganda für Deutschland im Ersten und Zweiten Weltkrieg*, 1982, 208–211.

92. *Liverpool Evening Explorer* (Great Britain), April 4, 1939: "Thank Heaven. We Can still Raise a Laugh!" by Miles Prior. In Montreux, album 58/1.

93. *Die Zukunft* (Paris), April 14, 1939: "Fünfzig Jahre Chaplin" by Hans Siemsen. Reprinted in Föster, *Hans Siemsen. Schriften II*, 1988, 249–251.

94. *FK* 276, November 25, 1938, 3: "Tagesschau. Charlie Chaplin wird unverschämt."

95. According to rule 20 of 43: "History of British Board of Film Censors/Classification 1912–1949" inbbfc.co.uk/education/university-students/bbfc-history/1912-1949.

96. *FK* 44, February 21, 1939, 2: "Mosley-Bewegung gegen Aufführung eines Hetzfilms."

97. Newspaper clippings: *The Hindu* (Chennai, Madras/India), January 15, no year: "Hollywood & Hitler. Studios Are Losing Fear of Him" by John K. Newham. "Confidential: Hitler Triumphs again," without further information. The first clipping is pasted between January 1939 newspaper clippings in "Montreux," Album 58/1, the second between January and February 1940 newspaper clippings in "Montreux," Album 58/2. The two photos were probably taken during the same photo session and match the early 1939 coverage. *The Hindu*'s editorial office did not respond to the author's inquiries for clarification of the publication dates.

98. *Sunday Pictorial* (London), February 12, 1939, 4: "Goebbels Has a Nightmare" by TAC (Thomas Arthur Challen). In Montreux, album 58/1.

99. *Evening Standard* (London), February 11, 1939, 7: "Low's topical Budget. International Moustache Crisis." In Montreux, album 58/1.

100. *London Opinion*, November 1939, 72, 73: "Moustache Change" by David Louis Ghilchik. In Montreux, album 64.

101. Quoted from documents of the Public Record Office, Kew, London, at FO 395/663, transcribed in K.R.M. Short, "Chaplin's The Great Dictator and British Censorship, 1939" in *HFRT* Vol. 5–1, March 1985, 85–108 (87).

102. Letters Brooke-Wilkinson to Breen and Breen to Brooke-Wilkinson in MPAA/PCA, file *The Great Dictator*, in the holdings of the Margaret Herrick Library.

103. *Autobiography*, 425, 426.

104. *Motion Picture Daily* (NYC), April 4, 1939: "London Says *Dictators* Facing British Government Opposition." In Montreux, album 58/1.

105. *Daily Variety* (Hollywood), April 26, 1939: "UA Execs Worry over Chaplin Pic in Britain." In Montreux, album 58/1.

106. Quoted from documents of the Public Record Office, Kew, London, at FO 395/663, transcribed in Short, in *HFRT* Vol. 5–1, March 1985, 85–108 (87, 88).

107. *FK* 35, February 10, 1939, 1, 2: "Man macht sich bereits Sorgen über die Rentabilität einer neuen Greuel-Lüge."

108. *FK* 39, February 15, 1939, 6: "Filmamerika 1938."

109. *LBB* 88, April 15, 1939, 2: "Film-USA und Film-England provozieren weiter."

110. *LBB* 84, April 11, 1939, 1, 2: "Die Juden von Hollywood" by Curt Belling.

111. *Kinematograph Weekly* 1,674, May 18, 1939, 4: "Long Shots."

112. *FK* 117, May 23, 1939, 4: "Man hört und liest. Amerika fürchtet um seine Hetzfilme." See also the similar report in *LBB* 131, June 8, 1939, 3: "England."

113. Quoted from documents of the Public Record Office, Kew, London, at FO 395/663, transcribed in Short, in *HFRT* Vol. 5–1, March 1985, 85–108 (88–90).

114. Photos, in Streicher and Holz, *Des Stürmer's Kampf*, 1937, 48, 50.

115. Flyer of the German-American Bund, in Velten and Klein, 101.

116. *Flint Journal* (MI), October 1938: "Chaplin Reported Considering Tale of Prisoner in Nazi Concentration Camp Doesn't Fear European Ban. Veteran Star's Pictures now Prohibited in Italy, Germany" by Paul Harrison. *Astonia Gazette* (NC), December 17, 1938: "Chaplin, with Moustache as Start May Play Hitler in New York." *Jewish Chronicle* (London), December 31, 1938: "Charlie Chaplin on His new Film. Will England and France Ban It." *Pittsburgh Press* (PA), February 7, 1939: "Charlie Chaplin Will Come back to Screen in Talkie that Will Burlesque Dictators Mussolini and Hitler." *Tarentum News* (PA), February 7, 1939: "Chaplin to Parody Mussolini and Hitler in new Film." *Rock Island Argus* (IL), February 7, 1939: "Chaplin May Play Hitler and Mussolini in Comedy." *Iowan* (Iowa City), February 7, 1939: "Chaplin again. Will Do *The Dictators* just for Fun." *Iowegian* (Centerville, IA), February 7, 1939: "Charlie Chaplin Plans Satire on *The Dictators*." In Montreux, album 58/1.

117. Gardner, 127.

118. Robinson, 527. McCabe, 190, on the other

hand, claims that Paramount demanded a large sum for the release of the title *The Dictator*, which Chaplin angrily rejected with the words "I can't spend $25,000 on two words!" Since Robinson, unlike McCabe, had access to Chaplin's records, his account is likely to be preferred.

119. Diebow, *Die Juden in USA*, 1939, 21 (Einstein), 32–35 ("Filmstars in Rassenschande"), 41 (Ernst Lubitsch).

120. See on this *FK* 209, September 5, 1932, 1: "Chaplin klagt erfolgreich."

121. For example, *New York Post*, March 27, 1935: "Chaplin's *Kid* no longer that." In Montreux, album 50.

122. On Coogan's lawsuit against his mother, see Cary, 167–185.

123. Diebow, *Die Juden in USA*, 43, 45–47.

Chapter 11

1. See Maser, *Mein Schüler Hitler*, 1975, 7.

2. Illustrations in Velten and Klein, 71. Delage, 112. Kershaw, *Hitler. 1889-1936*, 318.

3. Chaplin Jr., 204.

4. Robinson, 528.

5. Maser, *Mein Schüler Hitler*, 39.

6. Maser, *Mein Schüler Hitler*, 8, 9, 27: The inside of Hitler's nose was deformed. As a result, after countless appearances as a speaker, he had "dangerously overstrained" his vocal cords by the beginning of 1932.

7. On Devrient's teaching methods and instructions, see Maser, *Mein Schüler Hitler*, 38–43, 65-67, 89, 90, 128, 129, 146–150, 173–180, 187, 190–194, 260–274, 277, 278.

8. See Maser, *Mein Schüler Hitler*, 7, 105, 106, 281, 282.

9. Chaplin's script. Chaplin Jr., 204: "Gassolini."

10. *Ufaton-Wochen Nos. 368* and *369*, FPS, September 22 and 30, 1937, file 46,270 and 46,334, respectively. *Deuligtonwoche No. 300*, FPS, September 30, 1937, file 46,335. Newsreels in "BArch" Filmarchiv BL. Scenes from the two state visits are included in the 2007 documentary *Hitler & Mussolini. Eine brutale Freundschaft.*

11. According to Delage, 54, the clip comes from an Italian newsreel about Mussolini's visit to Germany in 1937, but it belongs to Hitler's return visit to Italy in 1938: a decorated Italian officer sits in the passenger seat of the car. In the background, next to a few civilians, are exclusively Italian uniformed men.

12. First of five censorship runs from 1935 to 1942: FPS, March 26, 1935, file 38,956. Hitler's evaluation of March 7, 1935. In BArch PAFR, Volume 44, folio 40.

13. Rumpelstilzchen, *Sie wer'n lachen*, commentary 2, September 14, 1933, 18, 19.

14. Riefenstahl, 713, 714.

15. Buñuel, 170, 171.

16. Hans Helmut Prinzler, "Daten. Biografie" in

Jansen and Schütte, *Luis Buñuel*, 1975, 155, unattributed on this topic.

17. During World War II, the Movietone company, on behalf of the Ministry of Information, commandeered footage of *Triumph des Willens*. Using optical printing, "Len Lye recut the Nuremberg paraders to the rhythm of a popular English tune that happily deflated the ritual" (Leyda, *Films Beget Films*, 1964, 55) and called his 1940 propaganda film *Swinging the Lambeth Walk*, the film was also known under various titles. I thank Kevin Brownlow for providing me with this information. *Swinging the Lambeth Walk* is unlikely to be identically equal to Leslie Winik's *'Schichlegruber Doing the Lambeth Walk' assisted by the GESTAPO HEP-CATS* presenting Hitler gestures and other Nazi marches.

18. Buñuel, 117–119, 168–170, 171, 185.

19. FPS, October 5, 1939, file 52,369.

20. See on Riefenstahl's film work in Poland, during which she witnessed the Konski massacre: Trimborn, 303, 306–313, and Riefenstahl's own account, which differs substantially from this: Riefenstahl, 349–354.

21. Robert Cole, "Anglo-American Anti-Fascist Film Propaganda in a Time of Neutrality: *The Great Dictator*, 1940" in *HFRT* Vol. 21-2, 2001, 137–152 (147). Trimborn, 229. Weissman, *Chaplin*, 2009, 117.

22. Photo in Delage, 61.

23. King Hanson, 824, "*The Great Dictator*," quoted from correspondence of MPAA/PCA, file *The Great Dictator*, in the holdings of the Margaret Herrick Library.

24. "Charlie's 'Last' Film," February 26, 1916, in Goodwins, *Charlie Chaplin's Red Letter Days*, 2017, 11.

25. Chaplin Jr., 204.

26. See Schmidt, *Albert Speer*, 1982, 42, 43.

27. Robinson, 534.

28. See Hans-Joachim Kann, "Pseudo-Deutsch in Chaplins Film *Der große Diktator*" in *Der Sprachdienst*. Vol. XIX–2 (1975), 22–24.

29. Kann, 23, claimed that the term "Blitzkrieg" was used for the very first time in *The Great Dictator*. In fact, it appeared in the German exile press as early as 1935 and subsequently in 1936 and 1938. See Frieser, *Blitzkrieg Legende*, 1995, 5, referring to the first mention of "Blitzkrieg" in the 1935 military journal *Deutsche Wehr*. *Pariser Tageszeitung* 139, October 28, 1936, 2: "Blitzkrieg im Mittelmeer. Der deutsche Generalangriff gegen Frankreich." *Pariser Tageszeitung* 54, August 4, 1938, 2: "'Blitzkrieg'—These nicht mehr aktuell?" *Pariser Tageszeitung* 780, September 3, 1938, 3: "Der Blitzkrieg—ein Humbug."

30. Speer, *Spandauer Tagebücher*, 1975, 199 (entry from March 3, 1949).

31. Pryce-Jones, *Unity Mitford*, 1976, 198.

32. Speer's certificate of appointment in Speer, *Spandauer Tagebücher*, 374.

33. Schmidt had discussed this in his dissertation on *Albert Speer*. His findings were then downplayed and hushed up by Speer's publishers.

Meanwhile, Speer's deceptions are recognized fact: Brechtken, *Albert Speer*, 2017.

34. *Autobiography*, 425.

35. See articles on fine art during the summer of 1940, for example, *Das Reich* 10, July 28, 1940, 24, 25: "Große Deutsche Kunstausstellung München 1940" by Ulrich Christoffel. See also *VB* (N) 200, July 18, 1940, 3: "Renaissance der deutschen Plastik. Zum 40. Geburtstag Arno Brekers." *VB* 271, September 27, 1940, 5: "Aus der Großen Deutschen Kunstausstellung 1940. Paul Bronisch: Weibliche Monumentalfigur."

36. *Daily Express* (London), December 12, 1940: "Even Venus de Milo Heils Charlie" by P.L. Mannock in Chaplin file.

37. Speer, *Erinnerungen*, 63, 67, 68, 71, 72.

38. Hitler's urban development order, June 25, 1940, in Speer, *Erinnerungen*, illustration 8 after 192.

39. Speer, *Erinnerungen*, 166, 167, 537, as well as plates 1–3, 5, 12 between 160, 161. The model of the large hall is now in the holdings of the Landesarchiv Berlin.

40. Speer requested the first funds for the film project in a letter dated May 11, 1940, addressed to Reichsminister und Chef der Reichskanzlei Hans Heinrich Lammers. In BArch BL, "Reichskanzlei" at R 43 I/389 Page 1, folio 13.

41. Speer, *Erinnerungen*, 116, 127, 128. For a comparison between Hitler's Reichskanzlei and Hynkel's government palace, see also Delage, 57–59.

42. Robinson, 458.

43. Speer, *Erinnerungen*, caption of the upper picture on plate 8 between 128 and 129.

44. This scene opens the final episode *Hidden Treasures* of *Unknown Chaplin*.

45. See Hooman Mehran, "Chaplin on the cutting Edge" in Scheide, Mehran and Kamin, l46.

46. For the description of the contents, see Robinson, 524, 525, and Frank Scheide, "Kevin Brownlow Interviewed: The Making of *The Tramp and the Dictator*" in Scheide, Mehran and Kamin, 54.

47. Examples from the announcements in *LBB* 41, October 13, 1923, 20: "Was das Ausland meldet." *FJ* 9, February 26, 1925, 2: "Ein neuer Chaplin-Film, angeblich 'Der Klub der Selbstmörder.'" *LBB* 136, July 27, 1925, 1: "Chaplins nächster Film." *FK* 241, October 13, 1925, 5 (Supplement, 1): "Der nächste Chaplin-Film." *FK* 259, November 2, 1927, 1: "Chaplin kommt im März nach Deutschland." *FJ* 44, November 6, 1927, 1: "Chaplin kommt nach Berlin." *FK* 68, March 21, 1931, 11. *FK* 191, August 15, 1932, 2: "Haben Sie gehört?"

48. Milton, 384, 385.

49. Stevenson, *Der Selbstmörderklub. Der Diamant des Rajahs*, 1979, 38–43.

50. Chaplin Jr., 203.

51. *Weekly Telegraph* (London), January 20, 1940: "Heil Chaplin!" In Montreux, album 58/2.

52. Sheet music cover reprinted in Gifford, *Chaplin*, 1974, 105. Haining, 159.

53. *Glasgow Sunday Post*, October 29, 1939:

"Adolf Ousts Charlie Chaplin from the Halloween Guisers' favourite Role." In Montreux, album 58/2.

54. *LBB* 11, January 13, 1940, 2: "Hollywood dreht 'Kriegsfilme.'" *LBB* 37, February 13, 1940, 2: "USA und der deutsche Film."

55. *LBB* 21, January 25, 1940, 2: "Die Zeitschrift im Kriege." *LBB* 51, February 29, 1940, 1: "Die deutsche Presse als geistige Wehrmacht der Nation. Dietrich gab Parolen aus."

56. *Detroit News* (MI), January 31, 1940: "Dictator Backers Worry over Peace" by Harold Heffernan. *Miami News* (FL), February 4, 1940: "Producers of Chaplin's Film Worry about European Peace." In Montreux, album 58/2.

57. From the abundance of articles, for example, *Sapula Herald* (OK) 175, March 26, 1940, 6: "Charlie Chaplin Would Send new Show to Hitler." *Daily Times* (Davenport, IA) 86, March 27, 1940, 18: "Charlie Chaplin Wants Hitler to See His Picture," by Fredrick C. Othmann. *St. Joseph News-Press* (MI) 182, March 27, 1940, 1, 2: "Chaplin Wants Hitler to View Premiere of Film." *Wisconsin State Journal* (Madison) 177, March 27, 1940, 1: "Chaplin Wants One-Man Audience Hitler—for World Premiere of His Travesty on Dictators."

58. For example, *Wheeling News-Register* (WV), March 27, 1940: "Charlie Chaplin Would Show Hitler His Dictatorship Take-off Privately." Various newspaper clippings on this theme in "Montreux," album 58/2.

59. *Rocky Mountain News* (Denver, CO), March 28, 1940: "If Hitler Gets Charlie's Point He'll Stop War." *Los Angeles Herald & Express* (CA), March 27, 1940: "Hitler May Get first Look at Self. Chaplin Seeks Berlin Premiere of *Dictator*." *San Francisco Chronicle* (CA), March 28, 1940: "A Berlin Premiere for Mr. Hitler's Benefit?" *Wenatchee World* (WA), March 29, 1940: "Maybe Hitler Can Laugh at Chaplin" by Frederick C. Othman. In Montreux, album 58/2.

60. *Ladies' Home Journal* 7, July 1940, 18, 96–98 (97): "The Story of two Mustaches" by Henry F. Pringle.

61. See Spiker, 168–182.

62. *FK* 109, May 11, 1940, 5 (Supplement, 1): "Amerikanische Hetzfilme." With excerpts from Hippler's latest contribution to the *VB*.

63. Buñuel, 171. See also Maland, 163, 164.

64. *Autobiography*, 430.

65. For example, *Boston Christian Science Monitor* (MA), May 23, 1940: "Chaplin Refutes Report on Withdrawal of Film." *Daily Variety* (Hollywood), May 23, 1940: "Chaplin Denies Pic Withdrawal." *Cincinnati Enquirer* (OH), May 28, 1940: "Chaplin Denies Rumor." In Montreux, album 58/3.

66. *Das Reich* 3, June 9, 1940, 6: "Hass im Film" by Dr. Karl Fries. *LBB* 133, June 10, 1940, 1: "Die Hassausbrüche einer versinkenden Welt. Die Hetzfilme unserer Gegner gestern und heute."

67. *Film* 28, July 13, 1940, 3: "Splitter."

68. Filmography in Goetz, *Hollywood und die Nazis*, 1977, 37–43.

69. Spiker, 308, 309. See also letter RMVP of

July 23, 1940, to the Oberkommando der Wehr-macht (High Command Wehrmacht). In BArch BL, "Oberkommando der Wehrmacht" at RW 4/289.

70. *Film* 26, June 29, 1940, 8: "Verleih-Angebot 1939-40." *FK* 174, July 27, 1940, 3: "Amerikanische Hetzfilme."

71. Section "Verleih-Angebot 1939–40" in *Film* 30, July 27, 1940, 4. *Film* 34, June 24, 1940, 12. *FK* 186, August 10, 1940, 3: "Verbot der amerikanischen Metro-Filme." *FK* 208, September 5, 1940, 3: "Verbot der amerikanischen Paramount-Filme."

72. *Film* 52, December 31, 1940, 23: "Lohnende Sonderaufführungen. [...] Micky Mäuse und Märchenspiele." *Film* 1, January 4, 1941, 13: "Micky-Maus-Märchenfilme zu Neujahr."

73. These were Hegewald AG in 1930, Südfilm AG until 1932, Ufaleih in 1934, and Munich-based Bavaria Film AG/Bavaria Filmkunst GmbH from 1934 onward.

74. *Das Reich* 7, July 7, 1940, 18: "USA Kriegsfilme?" by Paul Scheffer. *FK* 162, July 13, 1940, 5: "Chaplin als Diktator."

75. *Washington Times-Herald* (Washington, D.C.), June 12, 1940: "Chaplin Halts Issue of *Life* Magazine." *Allentown Call* (PA), June 13, 1940: "Chaplin Halts Current Issue of *Time* and *Life.*" *Los Angeles Illustrated Daily News*, June 13, 1940: "Chaplin Gets Curb Order against *Life* Magazine." *Dublin Evening Herald*, June 13, 1940: "Charlie Chaplin Brings Action for £250,000." *Scarborough Evening News* (North Yorkshire), June 13, 1940: "Charlie Chaplin Sues for £250,000." In Montreux, albums 58/3, 58/4. £250,000 was the equivalent of about $1 million at the time.

76. *Trade Union News* (Philadelphia, PA), November 29, 1940: "Charlie Chaplin Sues *Time* and *Life.*" In Montreux, album 58/6.

77. *Autobiography*, 430, 431.

78. *Ladies' Home Journal* 7, July 1940, 18, 96–98 (18): "The Story of Two Mustaches" by Henry F. Pringle.

79. *The Scrantonian* (Scranton, PA) 22, September 1, 1940, 12: "Louella Parsons in Hollywood."

80. *The Bangor Daily News* (ME, no No.), September 26, 1940, 9: "The Voice of Broadway" by Dorothy Kilgallen.

81. *Sunday Chronicle* (Manchester), August 25, 1940: "Charlie is the latest Fuehrer." In Montreux, album 58/4.

82. *P.M.* (NYC), September 9, 1940: cartoon by Carl Rose. In Montreux, album 58/4.

83. *BT* (E) 36, January 27, 1919, 2: "Was darf Satire?" by Ignaz Wrobel (Kurt Tucholsky).

Chapter 12

1. *Richmond Times-Dispatch* (VA) 287, October 13, 1940, 62 (Section IV, 10): "Chaplin-Film a Sell-out."

2. *NYT* 30, 124, October 14, 1940, 27: "Chaplin Discusses His *Dictator* Film."

3. *Los Angeles Times*, October 13, 1940, 51 (Section "Drama and Stars," 3): "Chaplin Test." Invitation card. In Montreux, album 58/4.

4. *Sunday News* (NYC) 26, October 13, 1940, 74: "The Passing Show" by Ed Sullivan.

5. *Daily Variety* (Hollywood), October 15, 1940: "Preview. The Great Dictator." In Montreux, album 58/5.

6. *Autobiography*, 431.

7. *The Brooklyn Daily Eagle* (NYC) 267, September 26, 1940, 7: "*Dictator* to Open at Capitol, Astor." See also *Autobiography*, 431.

8. *The Brooklyn Daily Eagle* (NYC) 286, October 15, 1940, 11: Astor and Capitol ads.

9. *Autobiography*, 432.

10. *P.M.* (NYC), October 16, 1940: "Here in New York, It's The Great Dictator." *Biddeford Daily Journal* (ME), October 31, 1940: "Rough Going for Charlie." *The Film Daily* (NYC), October 16, 1940: "Filmdom's Great Greet *The Great Dictator.*" *Motion Picture Daily* (NYC), October 16, 1940, 7: "Roving Camera at *Dictator* Premiere." In Montreux, album 58/5.

11. Schatz, 119.

12. *Motion Picture Daily* (NYC), October 17, 1940: "See $100,000 Capitol Week for *Dictator*. Takes $17,000 in first Day. Astor Capacity." *Hollywood Reporter* (Los Angeles, CA), October 22, 1940: "*Dictator* Headed for $115,000 Week at N.Y. Capitol." *Variety* (NYC), October 23, 1940: "N.Y. Big, Chaplin's Capitol Record, at $106,000 and $20,000 at Astor." *Daily Worker* (NYC), November 19, 1940: "Chaplin Draws Crowds." In Montreux, album 58/5.

13. *Boston Traveler* (MA), October 30, 1940: "Chaplin still Breaking Records." *Rochester Times-Union* (NY), November 5, 1940: "The Great Dictator Held over at Loew's." In Montreux, album 58/5.

14. *Hollywood Citizen-News* (Los Angeles), November 7, 1940: "Advance Seat Sale Heavy for Chaplin Picture Premiere." *Hollywood Reporter* (Los Angeles), November 12, 1940: "*Dictator* Record Smasher all over." *Box Office* (Kansas City, MO), November 12, 1940: "$64,200 for *Dictator* in 4th Week At Two." *Mirror* (London), November 13, 1940: "*Dictator* in 5th Week," by Lee Mortimer. *Daily Worker* (NYC), November 19, 1940: "Chaplin Draws Crowds." *Los Angeles Herald-Express*, December 10, 1940: "The Great Dictator Shatters Precedents." *Motion Picture Herald* (NYC), December 14, 1940: "More *Dictator* Deals." *Daily Variety* (Hollywood), February 12, 1941: "*Dictator* Sets Record in Singapore." *Daily Variety* (Hollywood), February 6, 1941: "*Dictator* Gets general Release March 1." *New York City Inquirer*, March 3, 1941: "*Great Dictator* in 20th Week." *Reading Eagle* (PA), March 23, 1941: Loew's—(Held over)—The Great Dictator." *Brooklyn Citizen* (NYC), April 2, 1941: "Screen Notes. Held over at Loew's Met." *Variety* (NYC), April 23, 1941: "Chaplin, New or Old, still Strong at B.O." In Montreux, albums 58/5–7.

15. *Hollywood Reporter* (Los Angeles), March 12, 1941: "*Dictator* Shatters Phila. House Record." *Bayonne Times* (NJ), March 28, 1941: "*The Great Dictator* Remain at Loew's." In Montreux, album 58/7.

16. *Hollywood Citizen News*, December 25, 1940: "Folsom Prisoners See Chaplin's *Dictator*." In Montreux, album 58/7.

17. *Variety* (NYC), April 23, 1941: "Chaplin, New or Old, still Strong at B.O." In Montreux, album 58/7.

18. *Omaha World-Herald* (NE), October 20, 1940: "The Pie Blitzkrieg," by Desmond Kelem. In Montreux, album 58/7.

19. *Milford News* (CT), March 21, 1941: "Blitzkrieg on Skeptics." In Montreux, album 58/7.

20. Bowden and Tichy, *rororo Filmlexikon 1. Filme A-J*, 1986, 266 (entry on *The Great Dictator*).

21. *Hollywood Reporter* (Los Angeles), November 12, 1940: "*Dictator* Record Smasher all over." In Montreux, album 58/6.

22. *Motion Picture Daily* (NYC), January 24, 1941: "*Dictator* in Java." *Daily Variety* (Hollywood), February 12, 1941: "*Dictator* Sets Record in Singapore." In Montreux, album 58/7.

23. *Motion Picture Daily* (NYC), November 28, 1940: "*Dictator* Rental 50 % in England. to Have Triple London Premiere." December 13, 1940: "English *Dictator* Runs Simultaneously." *The Film Daily* (NYC), December 12, 1940: "Triple London Premiere for *Dictator* Monday." December 13, 1940: "*Dictator* to Play Odeon, GB Circuits Simultaneously." *Motion Picture Herald* (NYC), December 14, 1940: "*Dictator* in London." *Daily Variety* (Hollywood), December 18, 1940: "*Dictator* Bags $30,000 on 1st London Preem." *San Diego Union* (CA), December 18, 1940: "British Acclaim For *Great Dictator*." *Philadelphia Inquirer-Public Ledger* (PA), December 25, 1940: "*The Great Dictator* a Hit in London." In Montreux, albums 58/6–7.

24. *NYT* 30, 339, February 16, 1941, 39: "*Dictator* popular in England."

25. *Box Office* (Kansas City, MI), October 1940: "Varied Criticism Meets *Dictator*." Press review of ten New York newspapers. In Montreux, album 58/5.

26. *P.M.* (NYC), October 20, 1940: "Goebbels Doesn't Like *The Great Dictator*" by J.A.S. In Montreux, album 58/5.

27. *Motion Picture Daily* (NYC), October 16, 1940: "Critics Appraise *Great Dictator*." *Buffalo News* (NY), November 1, 1940: "Grim Reality Overshadows Chaplin at His Comic Best" by Ardis Smith. *Portland Oregon Journal* (OR), November 9, 1940: "Chaplin Film None Will Forget." In Montreux, album 58/5.

28. *NYT* 30, 216, October 16, 1940, 29: "The Screen in Review" by Bosley Crowther.

29. *Variety* (NYC), October 16, 1940, by Char, in *Variety's Film Reviews. Volume 6*, 1983, non-paginated.

30. *Aufbau* (NYC) 44, November 1, 1940, 11: "Chaplin an seine Kritiker."

31. *NYT* 30, 277, October 27, 1940, 133: "Mr. Chaplin Answers His Critics" by Charlie Chaplin.

32. *Films* (NY) 4, Winter 1940, 30–34: "Anti-Fascist-Satire" by Rudolf Arnheim. Quoted from Arnheim and Diederichs, *Kritiken und Aufsätze zum Film*, 1979, 282–287 (286, 287).

33. *NYT* 30, 296, January 4, 1941, 8: "Film Critic's Honor Ignored by Chaplin." 30,297, January 5, 1941, 3: "Chaplin Declines Award by Critics."

34. *Dunkirk Evening Observer* (NY) 16, January 20, 1941, 6: "Harrison in Hollywood," by Paul Harrison.

35. *Daily Mail* (London), October 19, 1940: "His Film Made 'for Freedom'" by Paul Bewsher. In addition, report 27/1940 of Department IVa of the Hauptarchiv der NSDAP, November 15, 1940, with German translation of the article and text underlining. In Chaplin file./6

36. *Autobiography*, 438, 439.

37. *John Bull* (London), October 19, 1940: "No Patched-up Peace" by Kem (Kimon Evan Marengo). In Montreux, album 59.

38. *Picture Post* (London), November 2, 1940, 10, 13: "How Chaplin Parodies the Dictators' Pomp and Arrogance." In Montreux, album 59.

39. *Huntington Herald-Press* (IN), May 14, 1941: "What next?" by Herblock (Herbert Block). In Montreux, album 58/7.

40. *Smith's Weekly* (Sydney, New South Wales), no date: "High Spots From the Shows" by Jim Russell. In Montreux, album 63. Pasted among clippings from September 1941.

41. Krings, 339.

42. *Zeitschriften-Dienst* 80, November 1, 1940 (instructions 3.430–3.479): masthead.

43. Repeated references in the *Zeitschriften-Dienst*, for example, index of names and index for issues 27–39 as a Supplement, to 41, February 2, 1940 (instructions 1,746–1,786), 1: "Wir erinnern."

44. *Zeitschriften-Dienst* 18 September 1, 1939 (instructions 673–717), 1: "Berufskameraden!" (instruction 673).

45. "Merkblatt über die Behandlung des *Zeitschriften-Dienstes*" (Instruction sheet on the appropriate handling of the *Zeitschriften-Dienst*) together with a "Verpflichtungsschein" (Commitment Bill), dispatched with 1, May 9, 1939 (instructions 1–32). "Verpflichtungsschein für Vertreter bzw. Nachfolger," dispatched with "Sonderbeilage" (Special Supplement) to *Zeitschriften-Dienst* 18, September 1, 1939 (instructions 718–723).

46. Krings, 339.

47. From March 1944 and January 1945, respectively, new numerations with "A" and "B" were introduced. *Zeitschriften-Dienst* 310/179, April 14, 1945 (instructions B 212–217) was the final issue. The final index comprised *Zeitschriften-Dienst* 253–277 (period until August 25, 1944). Wilke had worked with a stock of *Zeitschriften-Dienst* which stopped with 215, June 18, 1943.

48. *Zeitschriften-Dienst* 80, November 1, 1940 (instructions 3,430–3,479), 20: "Film" (instruction 3,446). As a substitute for Dr. Kurt Lothar Tank, Hans-Hubert Gensert was responsible for the Cultural and Defense Policy Resort.

49. *FK* 257, November 1, 1940, 1: "Charlie Chaplins Hetzfilm fiel in Amerika durch."

50. *Aufbau* (NYC) 42, October 18, 1940, 9: "Charlie Chaplin in *The Great Dictator*" and "Chaplin's Speech" by Manfred Georg.

51. *Zeitschriften-Dienst* 81, November 8, 1940 (instructions. 3,480–3,514), 9: "Film" (instruction 3,494). The "index of keywords and names for 53–91," 4, and instruction 3,494 refer to "Chaplin" and "Sprachregelung" (Prescribed terminology), respectively.

52. *Film* 46, November 16, 1940, 6: "Splitter."

53. *FK* 15, January 18, 1941, 3: "Hetzfilm-Dämmerung in Hollywood."

54. I thank Juan B. Heinink for the information about *Primer Plano* and about the Spanish premiere of *The Great Dictator*.

55. *FK* 101, May 2, 1941, 3: "Ein teurer Hetzfilm."

56. *FK* 214, September 12, 1941: "Hollywood hat 45 Hetzfilme in Vorbereitung."

57. *FK* 275, November 22, 1940, 1: "Chaplins Hetzfilm kam nicht ans Ziel."

58. *Svenska Dagbladet* (Stockholm) 317, November 19, 1940, 20: "Chaplins *Diktatoren* förlorad på Atlanten" (Chaplin's *Dictator* lost in the Atlantic).

59. *The Brooklyn Eagle* (NYC), November 18, 1940: "Chaplin's Film Lost en Route to England." *Holyoke Transcript & Telegraph* (MA), November 18, 1940: "The *Dictator* lost." In Montreux, album 58/6.

60. *NYT* 30, 250, November 19, 1940, 29: "Chaplin's *Dictator* Film lost en Route to London."

61. *The Demin Headlight* (NM) 14, November 29, 1940, 3: "Strictly Fresh."

62. *FZ* (R) 528–529, October 16, 1940, 1: "U-Boote, Torpedoboote und Flieger gegen England." 565-566, November 5, 1941, 1, and 567–568, November 6, 1941, 2: "Zwei Hilfskreuzer und ein Handelsschiff versenkt." 569–570, November 7, 1940, 1: "Insgesamt 7,1 Millionen BRT versenkt." 573-574, November 9, 1940: "Ein Geleitzug völlig vernichtet." (M) 577, November 11, 1940, 1: "Die Erfolge eines Stuka-Geschwaders." (The report also mentions a British ship sunk by a German submarine.) 584–585, November 15, 1941, 1: "Wieder große Erfolge im Handelskrieg. Ein Munitionsschiff getroffen und versenkt." Shortly before the *FK* 275, November 22, 1940, 1: "Chaplins Hetzfilm kam nicht ans Ziel," the front page of the *FZ* (R) 593–594, November 20, 1940, stated: "Acht bewaffnete Handelsschiffe versenkt."

63. From the abundance of reports, for example: NYT 30,233, November 2, 1940, 5: "Sinking of Cruiser Claimed by Berlin." *St. Louis Globe-Democrat* (MO) 174, November 9, 1940, 1: "British Admit Heavy Sea Losses."

64. *FK* 7, January 9, 1941, 3: "Chaplins *Diktator* von Bomben verfolgt" by pl.

65. "Runderlass [Circular Decree] of the Auswärtiges Amt, October 31, 1940," at Kult.K 9,798, with film listings to (a) German embassies: Ankara, Madrid, Moscow, Shanghai, Peping

([*sic*] Peking, German equivalent for Beijing), and Tokyo; (b) legations: Athens, Belgrade, Bern, Budapest, Bucharest, Helsinki, Kabul, Lisbon, Sofia, and Stockholm; and (c) consulates general: Barcelona, Istanbul, Kobe, Zurich (via Bern). The "Runderlass" also states: "At the same time, the representatives in the occupied territories, the embassy in Rome, and the legations in Copenhagen and Bratislava have been asked to issue appropriate orders for the films of the above-mentioned companies in their respective areas, or to obtain such orders from the competent authorities." In Politisches Archiv des Auswärtigen Amts, files of the German Embassy in Bern at Kult 12, 4d, 3,368. Latin America, for example, is not mentioned for unknown reasons.

66. "Runderlass of the Auswärtiges Amt, April 24, 1941," at Kult.K F 394/41, with list of artists to (a) German embassies: Ankara, Madrid, Moscow, Beijing, and Tokyo; (b) legations: Bern, Budapest, Bucharest, Helsinki, Hsinking, Kabul, Lisbon, Sofia, Stockholm, Tehran, and Bangkok (via Tokyo); and (c) consulates general: Barcelona, Istanbul, Kobe, Shanghai, and Zurich (via Bern). In the holdings of the Politisches Archiv des Auswärtigen Amts, files of the German Embassy in Bern, at Kult 12, 4d, 3,368.

67. There were numerous German embassies, general consulates, legations and diplomats in Latin America. See Berber, *Jahrbuch für auswärtige Politik*, 1940, 292–442.

68. Data on German diplomats according to the Section "The Countries of the World" in Berber, *Jahrbuch für auswärtige Politik*, 1940 and 1941, respectively.

69. See also *Movie and Radio Guide* (Chicago, IL), November 16, 1940 (untitled). In Montreux, album 58/5. *DFZ* 1, January 5, 1941, 2: "Was geschieht im Ausland?"

70. Quoted from *Baltimore Sun* (MD), December 24, 1940: "Argentina Urged to Ban *Dictator* Film" by Walter Kerr. In Montreux, album 58/7.

71. Photo in Streicher and Holz, 48.

72. *NYT* 30, 289, December 28, 1940, 18: "Chaplin Film Forbidden."

73. *Autobiography*, 439.

74. *Nya Dagligt Allehanda* (Stockholm) 353, December 28, 1940, 3: "Chaplin's *Diktatorn* förbjuden i Argentina" (Chaplin's *Dictator* banned in Argentina). *Nya Dagligt Allehanda* (Stockholm) 355 of December 30, 1940, 12: "Stort rabalder i Buenos Aires om Chaplin film" (Chaplin Film Causes great Uproar in Buenos Aires).

75. *Brüsseler Zeitung* (Brussels) 32, February 1, 1941: "Chaplin-Film endgültig verboten." In Chaplin file.

76. *NYT* 30, 458, June 15, 1941, 17: "Ban on Chaplin Film."

77. For Argentina as a whole, for example, *Baltimore Sun* (MD), December 24, 1940: "Argentina Urged to Ban *Dictator* Film" by Walter Kerr. *The Film Daily* (NYC), December 24, 1940: "Asks Ban of Chaplin's *The Great Dictator*." *Mirror* (NYC), December 28, 1940: "Ban Chaplin Film in Buenos

Aires." *Daily News* (NYC), December 28, 1940: "*Dictator* Banned in Buenos Aires." *P.M.* (NYC), December 29, 1940: "Argentina Expected to Lift Ban on Chaplin Film" by Ray Josephs. *Hollywood Reporter* (Los Angeles), December 30, 1940: "U.S. May Protest *Dictator* Ban." February 3, 1941: "Argentine Preparing Nat. Ban on *Dictator*." *Gettysburg Times* (PA), February 4, 1941: "Argentina. Chaplin's Film Offends One out of Three." In Montreux, album 58/7. German Ambassador von Thermann was inadvertently called "Vontermann" by the article of *Hollywood Reporter*.

78. *NYT* 30, 458, June 15, 1941, 17: "Ban on Chaplin Film."

79. *The Film Daily* (NYC), December 26, 1940: "*Dictator* in Montevideo." January 29, 1941: "Prolonged *Dictator* Run Anticipated in Uruguay." *Pasadena Star-News* (CA), January 6, 1941: "Uruguayans to Cash in on Chaplin's Ban." *Washington News* (Washington, D.C.), January 23, 1941: "Nazi Nix on Chaplin Pix." *Waterville Sentinel* (ME), January 24, 1941 (no title). *Boston Christian Science Monitor* (MA), February 13, 1941: "Rough Going for Chaplin Film." In Montreux, album 58/7.

80. *Nya Dagligt Allehanda* (Stockholm) 6, January 8, 1941, 3: "*Diktatorn* stöter tyskarna i Chile" (German encounter with *Dictator* in Chile).

81. *NYT* 30, 297, January 5, 1941, 34: "Censored *Great Dictator* Will Be Shown in Chile."

82. *Binghamton Sun* (NY), January 4, 1941: "Tear Gas Bombs Hurled into Santiago Theater Showing Chaplin Film." *Bronx Home News* (NYC), January 5, 1941: "Chaplin's *Dictator* to Be Shown in Chile." *Daily News* (NYC), January 8, 1941: "'Viva Hitler' Greets *Dictator* in Chile." *Baltimore Sun* (MD), January 8, 1941: "'Viva Hitler' Shouts Interrupt Chile Debut of Chaplin Film." *Boston Christian Science Monitor* (MA), February 13, 1941: "Rough Going for Chaplin Film." In Montreux, album 58/7.

83. *Angriff* 9, 11 January 1941, 4: "Berlin, 10. Januar."

84. *NYT* 30, 292, December 31, 1940, 18: "Mexico Permits Film."

85. *Motion Picture Daily* (NYC), December 31, 1940: "Mexican Police to Guard *Dictator*." *The Film Daily* (NYC), January 5, 1941: "*Dictator* Breaks all Mexican B.O. Records." *Manila Bulletin* (UT), February 6, 1941: "Chaplin Picture Shown in Mexico over Axis Protests." In Montreux, album 58/7.

86. *FK* 29, February 4, 1941, 1: "Fiasko des Chaplin-Hetzfilms auch in Mexiko."

87. *Angriff* 30, February 5, 1941, 4: "Kein Glück in Mexiko. Ablehnung des Hetzfilms von Chaplin."

88. Sattig, 62.

89. Benz, Graml and Weiß, *Enzyklopädie des Nationalismus*, 2001, 362.

90. *NYT* 30, 320, January 28, 1941, 22: "*Great Dictator* Banned."

91. *New York Telegraph*, April 23, 1942: "Chaplin Film Stolen in SA." In Montreux, album 63.

92. *Cuba*: *Honolulu Advertiser*, December 15, 1940: "*Dictator* Picture Congress Subject." *Variety* (NYC), April 9, 1941: "Havannah Grosses." *Motion*

Picture Daily (NYC), June 27, 1941: "Argentina and Chile Ban *Dictator* and [*Dance*] *Hall*." *Brazil*: *Baltimore Sun* (MD), December 24, 1940: "Argentina Urged to Ban *Dictator* Film" by Walter Kerr. *Daily Variety* (Hollywood), April 8, 1942: "Brazilian Press Chief Lauds American Films." *Peru*: *Kansas City Times* (MO), March 5, 1941: "Peru Bans Chaplin Film." *Hollywood Reporter* (Los Angeles), March 11, 1941: "Costa Rica, Ecuador Okay *Great Dictator*." In Montreux, album 58/7.

93. *Denver Post* (CO), March 5, 1941: "Chaplin *Dictator* Will be Guarded." *Hollywood Reporter* (Los Angeles), March 11, 1941: "Costa Rica, Ecuador Okay *Great Dictator*." *Motion Picture Herald* (NYC), March 15, 1941: "Ecuador, Costa Rica Allow *Dictator*." In Montreux, album 58/7.

94. *NYT* 30, 322, January 30, 1941, 18: "Chaplin Film Is Approved."

95. *NYT* 30, 288, December 21, 1940, 23: "May Bar Chaplin Film."

96. *NYT* 30, 282, December 27, 1940, 22: "Chaplin Film Is Passed." See also *Hollywood Reporter* (Los Angeles), December 27, 1940: "Nazis Unable to Stop *Dictator* in Panama." *Motion Picture Daily* (NYC), December 30, 1940: "*Dictator* Banned in Buenos Aires." In Montreux, album 58/7.

97. *NYT* 30, 235, November 4, 1940, 12: "Nazis Curbed in Costa Rica."

98. *NYT* 30, 361, March 10, 1941, 20: "Latins Pass Chaplin Film."

99. See Gardner, 127.

100. *Variety* (NYC), January 29, 1941: "Ireland, Wary of Nazi Ire, K.O.'s Chaplin Ads." In Montreux, album 58/7. See also *FZ* (R) 573–574, November 3, 1940, 1: "Irlands Neutralitätswille." *FZ* (R) 597–598, November 22, 1940, 2: "Irland bleibt bei seiner Neutralität."

101. *Buffalo News* (NY), February 27, 1941: "Nazis in Rumania. Nazis in Attack U.S. Films. Chaplin Ridiculed." In Montreux, album 58/7.

102. FPS, November 1, 1940, file 54,438 (1,820 meters) and 54,449 (G-rated version of 1,653 meters). *FK* 281, November 29, 1940, 2: "*Der ewige Jude* in Berlin uraufgeführt. Ein Dokumentarfilm, der das unverfälschte Gesicht der jüdischen Rasse zeigt" by Günther Schwark.

103. *Film* 46, November 16, 1940, 8 (1st Supplement, 2): "Ein neuer Film Dr. Fritz Hipplers. Hohe Prädikate für *Der ewige Jude*."

104. FPS, July 10, 1940, file 53,998 (*Die Rothschilds*) and September 6, 1940, file 54,227 (*Jud Süß*).

105. Rinner, 195, 196.

106. FPS approvals: April 1, 1938, file 48,135 (*Wort und Tat. Ein Filmdokument*), August 8, 1939, file 51,935 (*Der Westwall*), and October 5, 1939, file 52,369 (*Feldzug in Polen*).

107. For example, *FK* 279, November 27, 1940, 1, 2: "Wie *Der ewige Jude* in Polen gefilmt wurde. Dr. Hippler über seinen neuen großen Dokumentarfilm."

108. *VB* (N) 335, November 30, 1940, 8: "Uraufführung des Dokumentarfilms *Der ewige Jude*" by Hans Hohenstein. *Filmwelt* 49, December

6, 1940, 4: "Wie *Der ewige Jude* entstand. Dr. Hippler über seinen neuen großen Dokumentarfilm." *Die Filmwoche* 50, December 11, 1940, 1,204: "*Der ewige Jude*" by Ludwig Eylux. Trade journals, for example, *DFZ* 48, December 1, 1940, 3: "*Der ewige Jude*" by Annemarie Schmidt.

109. *Zeitschriften-Dienst* 84, November 29, 1940 (instruction 3,596–3,641), 3: "Film" (instruction 3,607).

110. *Film* 48, November 30, 1940, 8 (1st Supplement, 1): "*Der ewige Jude*" by Ernst Jerosch.

111. Hiddesen Spruchgericht, sentence of September 27, 1948, 2, 7, with the legal force note of June 21, 1949, effective May 27, 1949, file 5 S Ls 233/48 (6-62/48) (42), in the holdings of the Munich Institut für Zeitgeschichte, at Sp 44.

112. Hippler, *Korrekturen*, 1995, 148.

113. Riess, *Das gabs nur einmal*, 1957, 546.

114. Entries on *Der ewige Jude* during the period from October 5, 1939, to October 11, 1940, in Fröhlich, *Goebbels-Tagebücher Volume 7*, 1998, 138, 140, 156, 157, 173, 264, 268. Fröhlich and Richter, *Goebbels-Tagebücher. Volume 8*, 1998, 103, 165, 304, 372.

115. Hippler, *Die Verstrickung*, ca. 1982, 206, 207.

116. Hippler, *Korrekturen*, 140–142.

117. *ZeitReisen Video* (ord. no. ZR 225), undated interview.

118. Hippler, *Korrekturen*, 142.

Chapter 13

1. *Daily News* (NYC) 179, January 20, 1941, 154: "Monday's Radio Features."

2. *Hollywood Reporter* (Los Angeles), January 3, 1941: "Chaplin at FDR Birthday Concert." *Motion Picture Herald* (NYC), January 18, 1941: "Chaplin at Inauguration." In Montreux, album 58/7.

3. *Autobiography*, 439.

4. *Daily Mail* (London), February 8, 1941: "Should Chaplin be 'Sir Charles'?" In Chaplin file.

5. *FK* 45, February 22, 1941, 6: "Chaplin soll geadelt werden."

6. *FK* 54, March 5, 1941, 1, 2: "Wir und der amerikanische Film" by Fritz Hippler.

7. *VB* (N) 64, March 5, 1941, 1, 2.

8. See historisches-lexikon-bayerns.de.

9. *FK* 80, April 4, 1941, 3: "Tingel-Tangel der Familie Roosevelt."

10. Issues April 15, 1941: *Atlantic City World* (NJ): "Sued for $5,000,000." *Daily Variety* (Hollywood): "Bercovici Sues Chaplin." *Hollywood Reporter* (Los Angeles): "Chaplin, U.A. Hit in Bercovici Suit." In Montreux, album 58/7.

11. *L'Œuvre* (Paris), April 16, 1941: "Ein jüdischer Schriftsteller fordert von Charlie Chaplin 5 Millionen Dollar." Marcel Déat was editor-in-chief of the paper from September 1940. German translation in Chaplin file.

12. *Filmwelt* 20, May 16, 1941, 539: "Chaplin soll Schadensersatz zahlen."

13. Sattig, 63.

14. For example, *Filmwelt* 20, May 17, 1940, 2: "Wir freuen uns."

15. *Daily Variety* (Hollywood) 7, April 27, 1938, 3: "Chaplin's 1st Talker for UA in 1938–39."

16. Bercovici's articles in *Harper's Magazine*, December 1928: "A Day with Charlie Chaplin." *The Delineator* Vol. 118-1 (December 1930): "My Friend Charlie Chaplin."

17. *Neues Wiener Tageblatt* (Vienna) 76, March 17, 1931, 6: "Mein Freund Charlie Chaplin" by Konrad Bercovici.

18. Chaplin Jr., 180. He claims that his father did not meet Bercovici until 1938.

19. *NYT* 30, 397, April 15, 1941, 35: "Chaplin Is Defendant in Suit for $5,000,000."

20. *NYT* 32, 591, April 18, 1947, 5: "Suit against Chaplin for $6,450,000." Bercovici's cross-examination of March 5, 1942, transcript, 50. In Bologna," ch783052.

21. See Milton, 368, referring to Chaplin's interrogation at trial.

22. *Motion Picture Daily* (NYC), May 28, 1941: "Seek Dismissal of Bercovici Action." *Hollywood Reporter* (Los Angeles), May 27, 1941: "U.A. Asks Dismissal of Bercovici Charges." *The Film Daily* (NYC), June 25, 1941: "Bercovici's Chaplin Suit Is Dismissed." *Motion Picture Daily* (NYC), June 25, 1941: "Court Partly Voids Suit Against Chaplin." *Variety* (NYC), June 25, 1941: "Chaplin Scores Several Points in Bercovici Suit." In Montreux, album 58/7.

23. *NYT* 32, 604, May 1, 1947, 49: "Chaplin on Stand in Plagiarism Suit." *NYT* 32, 605, May 2, 1947, 23: "Chaplin Suit Ends: Actor Pays $95.000." Settlement of the parties to the proceedings of May 7, 1947, in "Bologna," ch0885001-04. See also, for example, *Der Spiegel* 23, June 7, 1947, 3: "Charlie Chaplin."

24. *Daily Variety* (Hollywood), April 1, 1941: "Writer Sues Chaplin over *Dictator* Dance." *Motion Picture Daily* (NYC), April 1, 1941: "Chaplin Sued over *Dictator* Sequence." *Variety* (NYC), April 2, 1941: "Balloon [not Bubble] Dance Suit vs. Chaplin." In Montreux, album 58/7.

25. De Haven's action (4). In Bologna, ch0884007-17.

26. *Zeitschriften-Dienst* 81, November 8, 1940 (instructions 3,480-3,514), 9: "Film" (instruction 3,494).

27. Buñuel, *Mein letzter Seufzer*, 168, 169.

28. *NYT* 30, 506, August 2, 1941, 16: "Nye Says Films Spread War Wave." *The San Francisco Examiner* 33, August 2, 1941, 5: "Senator Nye Assails Films as Propaganda."

29. *NYT* 30, 533, August 29, 1941, 18: "Hitler Front Laid to 'America First.'"

30. *FK* 180, August 4, 1941, 1, 2: "Senator Ney erklärt: 20 Hetzfilme Amerikas gegen Deutschland. Churchills Filmgeschenk an Roosevelt und Stalin."

31. *FK* 181, August 5, 1941, 1, 2: "Juden als

Drahtzieher der Hetze hier und dort" by Fritz von Bühel.

32. *NYT* 30, 549, September 14, 1941, 41: "Chaplin Is Called for Movie Inquiry."

33. *FK* 214, September 12, 1941, 3: "Hollywood hat 45 Hetzfilme in Vorbereitung."

34. From the abundance of reports, see, for example, *Hollywood Reporter* (Los Angeles) 38, September 10, 1941, 1, 4: "Senate Investigation a Joke" by Jack Moffitt. *Sacramento Bee*, September 10, 1941: "Must Screen be Silent?" *New York Herald Tribune*, September 14, 1941: "Propaganda Inquiry Calls Chaplin on *Great Dictator.*" *New York World Telegram*, September 14, 1941: "Chaplin Called to Movie Inquiry." *Cleveland Plain Dealer* (OH), September 16, 1941: "Inquiry against Reality." In Montreux, album 63.

35. *Mount Vernon News* (OH), September 20, 1941, cartoon by Herblock (Herbert Block). In Montreux, album 63.

36. *Washington Evening Star* (Washington, D.C.), September 16, 1941. In Montreux, album 63.

37. *Atlanta Journal* (GA), September 17, 1941: "F.D.R. Compares Film Probe to Old Slapstick." In Montreux, album 63.

38. *The Kansas City Times* (MO) 223, September 17, 1941, 4: "F.D.R. Scoffs at Probe. Film Inquiry is Ridiculed by the President."

39. *FK* 292, December 12, 1941, 1, 2: "Waffenbrüderschaft gegen den gemeinsamen Feind."

40. *Filmwelt* 3–4, January 21, 1942, 18: "So hetzten sie zum Kriege."

41. Persich, *Winston Churchill ganz "privat,"* 1940, 8, 250–256.

42. See Robinson, 449

43. Persich, new expanded edition 1942, 263–267. The new chapter is inserted between the previous chapters "Ein Mann und eine Mauer" (A Man and a Wall) and "Sarah geht tanzen" (Sarah Goes Dancing).

44. The German version *Der Tramp und der Diktator* was broadcast by Spiegel-TV on German TV-station SAT.1 in two parts on February 18 and 25, 2002. The Italian version *Il vagabondo e il dittatore* was not available.

45. See for Goebbels' "Erlass [Decree], May 25, 1938": *FK* 161, July 13, 1938, 1: "Das Reichsfilmarchiv dem Propagandaministerium unterstellt."

46. Schulberg, *Moving Picture*, 1981.

47. Velten's Barkhausen interview from June 29, 1985, in Volume 2 of his research documentation. In "DFF—Deutsches Filminstitut & Filmmuseum."

48. Author's interview with Wolfgang Klaue, February 15, 2008.

49. Contents of the business distribution plan in Volume 2 of Velten's research documentation, 28. In DFF—Deutsches Filminstitut & Filmmuseum.

50. Barkhausen interview in Volume 2 of Velten's research documentation, 20-22. In DFF—Deutsches Filminstitut & Filmmuseum.

51. Velten, "Chaplin and Hitler" in Velten and Klein, 120.

52. See Volume 2 of Velten's research documentation, 14. In DFF—Deutsches Filminstitut & Filmmuseum.

53. On von Ribbentrop, see Weiß, 374–377, entry by We (Hermann Weiß).

54. Letter of August 15, 1944, from the director of the Reichsfilmarchiv to RMVP, at the request of the Auswärtiges Amt, in "BArch" BL, "RMVP" at R 55/665, folio 193.

55. Von Ribbentrop's Personal Staff in consonance with the business distribution plan of the Auswärtige Amt, April 1, 1944, in Politisches Archiv des Auswärtigen Amts, "Akten zur Deutschen Auswärtigen Politik 1918–1945, Serie E, Volume VII." This could also have been the staffing of the Reichsminister's Personal Staff in August 1944. It is possible that Walther Hewel also belonged to this circle. See Berber, *Jahrbuch für Auswärtige Politik*, 1942, 242.

56. Junge, *Bis zur letzten Stunde*, 2001.

57. Speer, *Erinnerungen*, 47, 48, 120.

58. Misch, *Der letzte Zeuge*, 108, 109.

59. Misch, 109 (note 77), 290.

60. Misch, 108, 109.

61. Speer, *Erinnerungen*.

62. See Hippler, *Die Verstrickung*, 152.

63. Hoffmann, *Hitler wie ich ihn sah*, 24.

64. Pryce-Jones, 198.

65. The program *Dick Cavett und Friedrich Luft* was broadcast on 29 March 1979 from 21:15 to 21:20.

66. On Carow, see Budzinski and Hippen, 60.

67. Speer, *Erinnerungen*, 138–140.

68. Hamann, *Hitlers Wien*, 1996.

69. *Goebbels Tagebücher* 5, 2000, 64.

70. See Aping, *Das Dick-und-Doof-Buch*, 159, 160 in "BArch" BL, "persönliche Adjutantur des Führers und Reichskanzlers" at NS 10 44, folios 119, 132 (*Ritter ohne Furcht und Tadel*), folios 116, 134 (*Swiss Miss*), and 45, folio 2 (*Block-Heads*).

71. Letter of July 24, 1944, from the Reichsfilmindendant to RMVP, in "BArch" BL, "RMVP" at R 55/665, folio 209. The Bundesarchiv only holds a list of 35 "Feindfilme mit politischer Tendenz" (Enemy films with a political slant) from the Soviet Union, the United States and Great Britain. *The Great Dictator* does not belong to it.

72. Letter of August 5, 1944, from the Reichsfilmindendant to the State Secretary in RMVP, in "BArch" BL, "RMVP" at R 55/665, folio 210.

73. Velten in Velten and Klein, 120. Written documents about the making of copies in Stockholm and the confiscation of (U.S.) films have been partially preserved: Letters from the Reichsfilmindendant of February 5 and July 5, 1944, to RMVP, in "BArch" BL, "RMVP" at R 55/665, folios 202, 203.

74. Velten in Velten and Klein, 120.

75. *Review—Yugoslav Monthly* (Belgrade), May–October 1963, 30, 31: "How Hitler Saw *The Great Dictator*" by Drogoš Simović. I thank Kevin Brownlow for providing me with this article.

76. Petar Volk, "The Ballad of Horn and Fogs. In the Journal's Shadow" (Serbian title not given), in

Belan, *Sjaj i bijeda filma* (Splendor and Poverty of Film), 1966, 277. Quoted from 5 of the essay "Chaplin among Hitler's Adherents" by Radošević and his wife as an attachment to his letter to Brownlow, both written in English and undated (ca. 2001). I thank Kevin Brownlow for providing me with the letter and the essay.

77. See also Joachimsthaler, *Hitlers Ende*, 2004, 271. Joachimsthaler has examined a host of sources and uncovered countless contradictions to all circumstances.

78. See, for example, *Der Spiegel* 19, May 5, 1965, 94, 97–99: "Wie ich Hitlers Leiche fand" by Ivan Klimenko, Colonel of the Soviet Army. derstandard.at/story/571818, "Ex-Sowjetsoldat will Hitlers Leiche 1970 verbrannt haben." See also schoah. de, "Die acht Bestattungen Hitlers" (Hitler's eight funerals) by Alisa Argunova, commented by Wolf Oschlies.

79. See Günsche's and Linge's accounts in Eberle and Uhl, *Das Buch Hitler*, 2005, 25, 26 (editor's preface), 442, 444, 445, 449, as well as editor's epilogue 464–466.

80. Misch, 221, 224, 316.

81. On the burning of Hitler's corpse in the garden of the Reichskanzlei, see also Kershaw, *Hitler. 1936–1945*, 1,067–1,069 (chapter 30, note 156) and 1 (epilogue), 1,290–1,293 (epilog, note 1, with reference to Joachimsthaler).

82. Hitler's "Mein politisches Testament," reprinted in Joachimsthaler, 190–192 (190).

83. Eberle and Uhl, 444.

84. Joachimsthaler, 354, quoted from Talbott, *Khrushchev Remembers*, 1971, 191, 192.

85. "Chaplin among Hitler's Adherents," 10.

86. FPS, December 21, 1940, file 54,754. German premiere on December 31, 1940, in the Berlin Ufa-Palast am Zoo: *FK* 1, January 2, 1941, 2: *Wunschkonzert* by Günther Schwark.

87. "Chaplin among Hitler's Adherents," 3–6.

88. Non-paginated transcript of the full Radošević interview, 3. I thank Kevin Brownlow for providing the transcript.

89. "Chaplin among Hitler's Adherents," 6, 7.

90. Offense against para 25 1 of the "Lichtspielgesetz, February 16, 1934" in *RGBI* 17, February 19, 1934. February 1934, 98.

91. Radoschew was remanded in custody in the Berlin Alt-Moabit pretrial detention center based on the arrest warrant issued by the Berlin Local Court, file 708 Gs 1.381/42, prisoner book 1,782/42. The records of his conviction still survive in the Handakten (Reference File) of the General Prosecutor's Office at the Berlin District Court, file 3 Ju Js 728/42, comprising the bill of indictment and the public prosecutor's note concerning the main hearing before the Berlin Local Court on September 28, 1942, file 607 Ds 180/42. Prisoner index card Radoschew and reference file in the holdings of the Landesarchiv Berlin, at A Re 366 (Untersuchungsgefängnis) and A Re 358-2 General Generalstaatsanwaltschaft bei dem Landgericht Berlin, 110,845.

92. On Thälmann's imprisonment since Hitler's takeover, see Börrnert, *Wie Ernst Thälmann treu und kühn!*, 2004, 51. The prisoner files of the Berlin Alt-Moabit men's pretrial detention center with the new prisoners of the year 1933 have not been handed down, so that the exact date of Thälmann's transfer to Hanover cannot be traced with a document of this remand prison.

93. No documents about Munjos Grande or Agustín Muñoz Grandes have been found concerning his imprisonment in the Berlin Alt-Moabit men's remand prison.

94. Author's interview with Wolfgang Klaue from February 15, 2008. Velten's Volume 3 of his of his research documentation, 5, contains the information of the deputy director of the Staatliches Filmarchiv der DDR, Manfred Lichtenstein, dated May 10, 1985. According to this the film copy is said to have been "somewhere in the Soviet Union" until 1954. In DFF—Deutsches Filminstitut & Filmmuseum.

Chapter 14

1. *Angriff* 81, April 2, 1944, 2: "Wir werden die Situation meistern."

2. *Angriff* 1–2, January 2–3, 1945, 2: "Wir haben uns in die Heimaterde festgekrallt!"

3. *National-Zeitung* (Basel) 267, June 13/14, 1942, untitled. In Chaplin file.

4. *National-Zeitung* (Basel) 267, June 13/14, 1942: "Charlie Chaplin als Politiker." In Chaplin file.

5. Robinson, 553, 554.

6. *NYT* 30, 831, June 23, 1942, 12: "Addresses of Litvinoff, Hopkins and Green at Russian War Relief Rally in Madison Sq. Garden."

7. For the event, see *Eastern Evening News* (Norwich, Norfolk), July 23, 1942: "Charlie Chaplin Calls for Second Front. Nazis Warn French." *Sheffield Star* (South Yorkshire), July 23, 1942: "'Invade,' Says Chaplin—by Phone!" *Oxford Mail* (Oxfordshire), July 23, 1942: "Chaplin's Voice across U.S. for Second Front." *Daily Mirror* (London), July 24, 1942: "Demand U.S. Second Front Call." *Birkenhead Advertiser* (Merseyside), July 25, 1942: "Support for Roosevelt. New Yorkers Call for Second Front." In Montreux, album 64.

8. *Life* (Chicago, IL), August 24, 1942 (untitled illustration with caption). In Montreux, album 64.

9. For example, *Birmingham News-Ace-Herald* (AL), September 20, 1942: "*The Great Dictator* on Screen at Galax, Is Chaplin Classic." *Hollywood Reporter* (Los Angeles), October 2, 1942: "Chaplin Speaks, Welles Presides 2nd Front Meet." *Brooklyn Eagle* (NYC), October 3, 1942: "Chaplin, Welles Join 2nd-Front Rally." *Daily Worker* (NY), October 3, 1942: "Chaplin and Welles to Speak for Second Front at Carnegie Hall." In Montreux, album 64.

10. For example, *Mirror* (NYC), October 16, 1942: "Chaplin in Town, Asks 2nd Front." *P.M.* (NYC), October 16, 1942: "Chaplin Makes Appeal tonight. Explains Stand on Second Front," by

Hyman Goldberg. *New York Herald-Tribune*, October 18, 1942: "Chaplin Urges a Second Front at Meeting here." *The Worker* (NY), October 25, 1942, 7: "We've Promised It ... Let's Have It now!" In Montreux, album 64.

11. *Il Regime fascista* (Rome), October 22, 1942: "Quel pagliaccio di Charlot" (Charlot's Clowning) by G.R. Marazana. In Chaplin file.

12. Robinson, 262, 282–285, 420.

13. *FK* 265, November 11, 1942, 3: "Neues aus Kroatien." The quoted *Spremnost* article was not available.

14. *New York Post*, December 4, 1942 (untitled). In Montreux, album 64.

15. FBI files, Charlie Chaplin, dossier of December 4, 1942.

16. *Kladderadatsch* 49, December 6, 1942, 6: "Steckbriefe."

17. *FK* 25, January 30, 1943, 3: "Zehn Jahre Filmarbeit im nationalsozialistischen Reich" by Reichsfilmintendant Dr. Fritz Hippler.

18. Krings, 347.

19. *FK* 30, February 5, 1943, 1: "Deshalb werden wir siegen" by Helmut Sündermann.

20. See Wilke, 124, 228, 229.

21. Sündermann, *Tagesparolen. Deutsche Presseanweisungen 1939–1945*, 1973, 252. The source material used is unknown. The transcripts of Reichspressekonferenzes during World War II collected in the Bundesarchiv Koblenz have not yet been indexed. See Bohrmann/Toepser-Ziegert, *NS-Presseanweisungen. Volume 1*, 53*. On Sündermann, see Klee, *Das Personenlexikon zum Dritten Reich*, 615, 616.

22. *Angriff* 84, April 8, 1943, 1: "Jüdische Herzensangelegenheit."

23. *VB* (Ber) 98, April 8, 1943, 3: "Die jüdische Brücke."

24. *Zeitschriften-Dienst* 221/90, July 30, 1943 (instructions 9,146-9,184), 4: "Charlie Chaplin" (instruction 9,174).

25. See also Heinz Kersten, "Ankläger der Mörder und Untertanen" in Orbanz, *Wolfgang Staudte*, 1977, 10.

26. *Die Filmwoche* 5/6, February 10, 1943, 44, 45: "Groteskkomik" by F.R.

27. *Filmwelt* 7/8, February 17, 1943, 59: "Akrobat Schö-ö-ö-n!"

28. *Film-Illustrierte* 3, February 7, 1943, 8.

29. Kersten in Orbanz, "Interview. Wolfgang Staudte über die Produktionsbedingungen seiner Filme" in Orbanz, 65.

30. Andreas Wöll, "Wolfgang Staudte—'Sicher sind es nicht die Filme, die eigenes Nest beschmutzten'" in Fröhlich and Kohlstruck, *Engagierte Demokraten*, 1999, 75.

31. Rivel, *Akrobat Schöön*, 1972, 189.

32. Charlie Rivel, "Akrobat Schööön" in Bemmann, *Das Leben großer Clowns*, 1972, 339, 494.

33. Rivel in Bemmann, 368, 375–377. Rivel, *Akrobat Schöön*, 80, 96–98.

34. Rivel in Bemmann, 379–384.

35. *Berliner Börsen-Courier* (M) 215, May 10, 1927, 6: "Chaplin II. und die andern in der Scala" by Billie (Billy) Wilder. Blouin, Delage and Stourdze, *Chaplin in Pictures*, 2005, 86, 87, date Rivel's appearance to "ca. 1920" and attribute it to an unknown impersonator.

36. Rivel in Bemmann, 394–398.

37. Rivel, *Akrobat Schöön*, 167–192.

38. Fröhlich and Hermann, *Goebbels-Tagebücher. Volume 3*, 2005, 289, 300 (entries from September 8 and 27, 1935).

39. *Filmwelt* 1, January 7, 1942, 10: "Frohe Stunden beim Fernsehen" by a.m.k.

40. Rivel, "Mein Kollege Chaplin" in Colman and Trier, *Artisten*, 1928, 129–131.

41. Rivel, in Bemmann, 485, 486.

42. FPS, October 1, 1943, file 59,440.

43. *Zeitschriften-Dienst* 188/57, December 11, 1942 (instructions 8,011-8,050), 4: "Instructions" (8,046). The *Zeitschriften-Dienst* did not comment the film after its premiere.

44. *FK* 146, December 7, 1943, 2: "Akrobat Schö-ö-ö-n!" by Ernst Jerosch.

45. *Deutsche Allgemeine Zeitung* 576/577, December 3, 1943: "Akrobat Schö-ö-ö-n!" by Werner Fiedler.

46. Eberle, 333–335.

47. *New York Post*, April 18, 1943: "Hitler and Chaplin at 54" by Oscar Berger. In Montreux, album 64.

48. *Sunday Dispatch* (London), April 19, 1942: "What a Pity They Didn't Get those Two Babies Mixed up" by (Sidney D.) Moon. In Montreux, album 63.

49. *NYT* 31, 856, April 13, 1945, 19: "Chaplin Denies Paternity."

50. *NYT* 31, 277, June 4, 1943, 16: "Names Chaplin as Father." 31,184, June 11, 1943, 23: "Chaplin Pays Miss Berry [*sic*]." *NYT* 31, 299, October 4, 1943, 19: "Chaplin Accuser Has Baby."

51. *National-Zeitung* (Basel), June 19, 1943 (untitled). In Chaplin file.

52. *12-Uhr-Blatt* 146, June 19, 1943, 5 (Supplement, 1): "Krampf um alten Filmjuden."

53. *Aftonbladet* (Stockholm) 161, June 17, 1943, 1, 20: "Nervös Chaplin vigd för 4:e gången. Bruden 18-årig dotter till nobelpristagaren O'Neill" (Nervous Chaplin married for the fourth time. The bride is the 18-year-old daughter of Nobel Prize winner O'Neill) by A.P.

54. Robinson, 560. The screen test can be viewed as "Oona O'Neill Screen Test Hollywood 1942" at eoneill.com/tv/oona/oona.htm. An excerpt of it is also part of Richard Schickel's documentary *Charlie: The Life and Art of Charlie Chaplin* (2003).

55. *Neue Zürcher Zeitung* (Zurich) 273, February 16, 1944: "Propagandatrick um Chaplin?" In Chaplin file.

56. See Lynn, 438.

57. See *Sunday News* (NYC) 2, May 13, 1945, 6, 7: "Blood—in Blood Banks and in the Human Body. Few States Accept Test as Evidence."

58. *The Paladium-Item* (Richmond, VA) 88, April 13, 1945, 4: "Joan Barry's Past Disclosed by Chaplin." *The San Francisco Examiner* (CA) 104,

April 14, 1945, 24: "Millionaire Denies Role in Joan Barry's Life."

59. *NYT* 31, 857, April 14, 1945, 13: "Chaplin Case Nears Jury." 31,861, April 18, 1945, 25: "Chaplin Declared Father of Child."

60. *NYT* 32, 303, July 4,1946, 16: "Chaplin Petitions in Child Case." *The Birmingham News* (AL) 115, July 25, 1946, 4: "Court Rules Chaplin Must Support Child."

61. Robinson, 566.

62. *Times* (London), February 12, 1944: "Charge Against Mr. Chaplin." *Le Pays réel* (Brussels), February 13, 1944: "Charlie Chaplin détourne ... une mineure" (Charlie Chaplin Kidnaps ... a Minor). The editor-in-chief of *Le Pays réel* was the Walloon Léon Degrelle, SS-Obersturmbannführer and Volksführer der Wallonen (Walloon People's Leader) by the end of World War II. In Chaplin file.

63. *Straßburger Neueste Nachrichten* (Strasbourg) 43, February 13, 1944, 3: "Der Filmjude Chaplin verführt Minderjährige." In: Chaplin file.

64. *Angriff* 39, February 13, 1944, 2: "Jud Chaplin unter Anklage."

65. *VB* (Ber) 44, February 13, 1944, 2: "VB-Splitter."

66. *Straßburger Neueste Nachrichten* (Strasbourg) 92, April 2, 1944: "Sittlichkeitsverbrecher Charlie Chaplin vor Gericht. Der jüdische Wüstling ist wie immer der 'Verführte.'" In Chaplin file.

67. *Angriff* 81, April 2, 1944, 2: "Chaplin als Sittlichkeitsverbrecher vor Gericht."

68. *NYT* 31, 483, April 5, 1944, 1, 13: "Chaplin Acquitted in Mann Act Case."

69. *NYT* 31, 524, May 16, 1944, 23: "Government Voids Chaplin Charges." *Daily News* (NYC) 279, Mai 16, 1944, 4: "Chaplin Cleared of U.S. Charge but Must Face Daddy Suit Trial."

70. *Times* (London), April 6, 1944: "Chaplin's Acquittal." *Journal de Genève* (Geneva) 117, May 17–18, 1944: "Charlie Chaplin devant les juges de San Francisco" (Charlie Chaplin before the judges of San Francisco). The article "Cheese-cakes" by the journalist Trissotin in the Brussels newspaper *Le Pays réel* 10, May 12, 1944, is about "Chaplin's wife 3" (i.e., Paulette Goddard) She was said to have frolicked with soldiers on a trip through India, Burma, and China. In Chaplin file.

71. *Freies Deutschland* 6, April 1944, 3, 4: "FD" (Freies Deutschland).

72. FBI files Charlie Chaplin, dossier of February 25, 1944, 5–11.

73. From the wealth of newspaper coverage of Chaplin's sound version of *The Gold Rush*, see, for example, *Variety* (New York City), January 14, 1942, 14: *The Gold Rush* ad. The *Brooklyn Eagle* (NYC), April 9, 1942: "Chaplin's *Gold Rush* Due at Globe April 18." *Pathfinder* (Washington, D.C.), April 18, 1942: "Movie World. *The Gold Rush*." *The Cinema News and Property Gazette* (London), July 29, 1942, 7: Picture report of the mass rush in London cinemas to screenings of *The Gold Rush*. In Montreux, albums 63, 64.

74. *National-Zeitung* (Basel) 599 (Christmas issue), December 24/25, 1942, 13: Cinéma Alhambra ad for the premiere of the sound version of *Goldrausch*. In Chaplin file.

75. *Allgemeine Zeitung* (Berlin, published by the U.S. Army) 16, September 12, 1945, 3: "Chaplin in Berlin" by Friedrich Luft. *Berliner Zeitung* 106, September 15, 1945, 3: "Wiedersehen mit Chaplin" by R-a.

76. For example, Viktor Tourjansky's 1944 *Orient-Express* takes place across the Balkans where there is seemingly no war going on. A jazz band even rehearses on a train, even though jazz music was considered degenerate art by the Nazis. In contrast, Josef von Báky's colorful *Münchhausen* (1943) with Hans Albers was probably not yet an example of Goebbels' strategy of diversion through entertainment.

77. Klaus, *Deutsche Tonfilme* 13, 2002, 40.

78. Fröhlich and Schneider, *Goebbels-Tagebücher*. Volume 11, 1994, 103 (entry from January 16, 1944).

79. Moeller, *Der Filmminister*, 1998, 435, with reference to the letter from Heinrich Jonen to Dr. h.c. Max Winkler, February 29, 1944. In UFA.

80. FPS, August 2, 1944, file 60,462.

81. *FK* 69, August 29, 1944, 2: *"Die Frau meiner Träume."*

82. *Die Tat* (Zurich) 157, June 18, 1944 (untitled). In Chaplin file.

83. *National-Zeitung* (Basel) 421, September 10, 1944 (Supplement "Film"): "Der Fall Chaplin und seine Lehren" by Hanns Sten. In Chaplin file.

84. *Pester Lloyd* (Budapest) 270, November 28, 1944: "Bombe beim Chaplin-Film explodiert." In Chaplin file.

85. Speer's August 27, 1977, letter to Jesse Lasky, Jr., on the occasion of the recent publication in Encounter magazine (London) of an interview by journalist James P. O'Donnell, who had published a series of articles on Chaplin in *The Saturday Evening Post* (Indianapolis, IN) in 1958 and interviewed Speer after his release from Spandau prison. O'Donnell forwarded Speer's letter with a lengthy cover letter to Oona Chaplin. In his *Variety* article "The Tramp and the Dictator" of February 21, 2002, David Stratton had claimed that Speer had directly written to Oona Chaplin under August 27, 1977.

86. See Frank Scheide and Hooman Mehran, *"The Great Dictator* In Historical Context. As Reflected in *The Tramp and the Dictator* Interviews" in Scheide, Mehran and Kamin, 98. In the interview with Kevin Brownlow, Speer's biographer Gitta Sereny could not imagine Speer's statement to Lasky Jr.

87. Several Belgian posters of the same motif with backs from different German general staff cards in "DFF—Deutsches Filminstitut & Filmmuseum."

88. *NYT* 32, 287, June 18, 1946, 30: "Berlin Bars *Dictator*."

89. As an example of the numerous announcements: *Paterson Evening News* (NJ) Vol. 194,

August 9, 1946, 24: "*The Great Dictator* in Berlin tonight."

90. As examples of the numerous reports: *NYT* 32, 340, August 10, 1946, 16: "Chaplin Fans See Chaplin's Satire." *The Birmingham News* (Alabama) 49, August 11, 1946, 24: "Germans not so Amused by Film *The Great Dictator*."

91. *Film Comment* Vol. 5–4, January 1969, 40.

92. Premiere on August 26, 1958, at the Berlin Astor. See *Filmblätter* 35, August 29, 1958, 1,074:

"Blubbert & paradiert. *Der große Diktator*" by R.S. (Robert Scheuer).

93. Becker and Petzold, *Tarkowski trifft King Kong*, 2001, 79 (1957 screening at the Greifswald Film Club).

94. *ff dabei* 10 (program week from March 3 through 9, 1980), 21: Tuesday, March 4, DDR1.

95. Coloring picture reprinted in Scheide, Mehran and Kamin, 48.

Bibliography

Archival Collections

Archives de Montreux

PP-75 Fonds Charles Chaplin, Roy Export Co. Ltd.: Chaplin's newspaper clipping albums by numbers and years, respectively, or special inscription: Album 7 (1918–19)/album 13 (1920–21)/album 22 (1923)/album 36 A (1931–32)/album 36 B (1932–33)/album 42 (1933)/album 43 (1934)/album 45 (1934)/album 46 (1934)/album 47 (1934)/album 48 (1935)/album 50 (1935)/album 52 (1936)/album 53 (1936)/album 55 (1936)/album 58/1–7 (*The Great Dictator*, 1940–41)/album 59 (*The Great Dictator*)/album 63 (1941–42)/album 64 (1942)

Bayerische Staatsbibliothek, Munich

Völkischer Beobachter (1930, 1931 Berlin edition)

Bayerisches Hauptstaatsarchiv

BayHStA Minn 72.695

Bibliothèque du Film, Paris

Agence d'information Cinégraphique

Kevin Brownlow

James P. O'Donnell's undated cover letter to Oona Chaplin submitting Albert Speer's dated August 27, 1977, to Jesse Lasky, Jr.
Nicola Radošević's undated letter and the essay "Chaplin among Hitler's Adherents" (ca. 2001)

Bundesarchiv Berlin-Lichterfelde

NS 10: persönliche Adjutantur des Führers und Reichskanzlers

NS 26: Geschäftsverteilungspläne des Hauptarchivs der NSDAP
R 43 I: Reichskanzlei
R 55: Reichsministerium für Volksaufklärung und Propaganda
R 58: Reichssicherheitshauptamt
R 109: Ufa
R 1501 (neu): Reichsministerium des Inneren
RW 4: Oberkommando Wehrmacht

Bundesarchiv—Filmarchiv, Berlin-Lichterfelde

Film-Prüfstelle Berlin and Munich as well as Film-Oberprüfstelle Berlin: Zensurlisten
Film-Prüfstelle Berlin: Zensurkarten
Film trade journals: paper issues missing from microfilms
Hauptkartei des Reichsfilmarchivs

Bundesarchiv Koblenz

BArch ZSg. 101/7/111, collection Brammer
BArch ZSg. 102/2a/44 -4- collection Sänger
BArch ZSg. 117/626: Akte Chaplin des Hauptarchivs der NSDAP

Cineteca di Bologna

Documents from the Chaplin archives, Copyright © Roy Export Co Ltd. Digitization of the Chaplin Archives by Cineteca di Bologna. www.charliechaplinarchive.org.

Deutsche Kinemathek—Museum für Film und Fernsehen, Bibliothek (Library), Berlin

Film-Hölle
Film trade journals: paper issues missing from microfilms

Deutsche Kinemathek— Museum für Film und Fernsehen, Schriftgutarchiv (Document Archives), Berlin

Harald Bredow Archives
Documents on Curt Belling
Newspaper clipping archives

Deutsche Nationalbibliothek, Leipzig

La Cinéma d'Alsace et de Lorraine/Elsass-lo-thringische Filmzeitung
Der neue Film
Zeitschriften-Dienst

DFF—Deutsches Filminstitut und Filmmuseum, Frankfurt/Main

Film-Oberprüfstelle Berlin
Newspaper clipping archives

DFF—Deutsches Filminstitut & Filmmuseum, Frankfurt am Main/ Chaplin-Archiv, Dauerleihgabe der Adolf und Luisa Haeuser-Stiftung für Kunst und Kulturpflege

Cartoons
Film posters
Newspaper clippings
Volumes 2 and 3 of Michael Velten's research documentation for his 1986 diploma thesis, Fachhochschule für Design, Bielefeld

FBI

Chaplin file

Filmuniversität Babelsberg KONRAD WOLF

Newspaper clipping archives of the "Medienkundliches Pressearchiv der ehemaligen Landesbildstelle Berlin, Sonderordner Charlie Chaplin nach Jahren"

Freiwillige Selbstkontrolle der Filmwirtschaft (FSK), Wiesbaden

Freigabekarten from July 1949 on, Federal Republic of Germany

Institut für Zeitgeschichte, Munich

Sp 44: Spruchgericht proceedings against Dr. Fritz Hippler, Spruchgericht Hiddesen/Detmold, file No. 5 Sp. Ls 233/48 (6–62/48)

Landesarchiv Berlin

A Rep. 358–2: Generalstaatsanwaltschaft bei dem Landgericht Berlin
A Rep. 366: Gefangenen-Karteikarten des Untersuchungsgefängnisses (Männergefängnis) Berlin Alt-Moabit 1935, 1936–1945, mit Namenregistern
Akten des Polizei-Präsidiums zu Berlin. Schutzpolizei. Aufsichtsdienst aus besonderen Anlässen. 1931. Buchst.: C, Nr. 9, Band: 21. Angefangen: 2. 3. 31, Abgeschlossen: 27. 3. 1931. Hierzu Band: 22. Nr. 7512: Chaplins Berlin-Besuch, March 1931

Margaret Herrick Library, Academy of Motion Picture Arts and Sciences, Beverly Hills

Documents of the Motion Picture Association of America (MPAA)/Production Code Administration (PCA), file *The Great Dictator*

Politisches Archiv des Auswärtigen Amts, Berlin

Akten zur Deutschen Auswärtigen Politik 1918-1945, Serie E, Volume VII: Geschäftsverteilungspläne
Kult 12, 4d, Volume 3.368: Akten der Deutschen Gesandtschaft Bern

Staatsbibliothek zu Berlin— Stiftung Preußischer Kulturbesitz, Haus Unter den Linden

Neue Film Hölle
Schriftgut-Nachlass 590 (Leni Riefenstahl)

Stadtarchiv Wuppertal

Völkische Freiheit

Interviews

Hans Barkhausen, June 29, 1985 (Andreas-Michael Velten)
Wolfgang Gersch, March 8, 2008 (Norbert Aping)
Wolfgang Klaue, February 15, 2008 (Norbert Aping)
Nicola Radošević, ca. 2001 (Kevin Brownlow, complete interview transcript)
Budd Schulberg, ca. 2001 (Kevin Brownlow)

Online Resources (starting with http://www.), last visited August 6, 2023, unless otherwise stated

bbfc.co.uk/education/university-students/bbfc-history/1912-1949

charliechaplin.com/en/films/14-Shoulder-Arms/articles/332-Chaplin-and-World-War-I (by Kevin Brownlow, 2014)

derstandard.at/story/571818/ex-sowjetsoldat-will-hitlers-leiche-1970-verbrannt-haben

difarchiv.deutsches-filminstitut.de/dt2tai01.htm"difarchiv.deutsches-filminstitut.de/zengut

historisches-lexikon-bayerns.de/artikel/artikel_44345

mille.org/publications ("Fascist Apocalypse: William Pelley and Millennial Extremism," by David Lobb)—last visited May 28, 2022, no longer accessible

ostfriesischelandschaft.de/fileadmin/user_upload/BIBLIOTHEK/BLO/Muenchmeyer_Ludwig.pdf (by Udo Behr, May 8, 2001)

schoah.de/drittes-reich/adolf-hitler/419.html ("Die acht Bestattungen Hitlers," by Alisa Argunova, commented by Wolf Oschlies)

smithsonianmag.com/history

variety.com/review/VE1117917058?refcatid=31 (by David Stratton, 2002)

welt.de/kultur/article10284920/Beruehmtes-Hitler-Foto-moeglicherweise-gefaelscht.html (by Sven Felix Kellerhoff, 2010)

Periodicals (except titles from Chaplin's newspaper clippings albums only appearing in Chapter Notes)

Until the End of the World War II

Trade Publications

AUSTRIA
Kino-Journal
Paimann's Filmlisten

FRANCE
Agence d'information Actinographies
La Cinéma d'Alsace et de Lorraine/Elsass-lothringische Filmzeitung
La Cinématographie Française

GERMANY
Allgemeine Kino-Börse
Arbeiterbühne und Film

Der Deutsche Film
Der deutsche Film in Wort und Bild
Deutsche Filmzeitung
Deutsche Lichtspiel-Zeitung
Erste internationale Filmzeitung
Der Film
Film-Atelier
Film-Hölle
Film-Journal
Film-Kurier
Film-Nachrichten
Der Filmspiegel
Filmtechnik
Kinematograph
Kinotechnik
Lichtbildbühne
Mitteldeutscher Lichtspieltheaterbesitzer
Der neue Film
Reichsfilmblatt
Rheinisch-Westfälische Filmzeitung
Süddeutsche Filmzeitung
Westdeutsche Film-Zeitung

GREAT BRITAIN
Kinematograph Weekly

ROMANIA
Universul

SPAIN
Primer Plano

UNITED STATES
Daily Variety
Film Daily
Hollywood Reporter
Motion Picture Daily
Motion Picture Herald
Moving Picture World
Variety

German Film Magazines

Film-Illustrierte
Filmwelt
Die Filmwoche
Illustrierter Film-Kurier
Südfilm-Magazin

Other Periodicals

ARGENTINA
El Pampero

AUSTRALIA
The Mail
Referee
Smith's Weekly

AUSTRIA (VIENNA)
Jüdische Presse. Organ für die Interessen des orthodoxen Judentums (also Bratislava)

Neue Freie Presse
Die neue Welt
Neues Wiener Journal
Neues Wiener Tageblatt
Die Stimme
Wiener Tag

BELGIUM (BRUSSELS)

Brüsseler Zeitung
Le Pays réel

CZECHOSLOVAKIA (PRAGUE)

Prager Tagblatt
Selbstwehr

FRANCE (PARIS)

Comoedia Illustré
L'Œuvre
Paris-Midi
Paris-Soir
Straßburger Neueste Nachrichten

GERMANY
Newspapers and Magazines

Arbeiterbühne und Film
Berlin am Morgen
Berliner Börsen-Courier
Berliner Börsen-Zeitung
Berliner Herold
Berliner Tageblatt und Handels-Zeitung
B.Z. [Berliner Zeitung] am Mittag
Berlin-Friedenauer Tageblatt
Bremer Nachrichten
Breslauer neueste Nachrichten
Buxtehuder Tageblatt
Deutsche Allgemeine Zeitung
Deutsche Nachrichten (Berlin)
Die deutsche Republik
Deutsche Zeitung
Düsseldorfer Nachrichten
8 Uhr Abendblatt—National-Zeitung
Frankfurter Zeitung
Fridericus
Generalanzeiger Dortmund
Germania (Berlin)
Goslarsche Zeitung
Hamburger Echo
Hamburger Fremdenblatt
Hamburger Warte
Hammer. Blätter für deutschen Sinn
Hannoverscher Anzeiger
Hannoverscher Kurier
Jüdisches Nachrichtenblatt
Der Jungdeutsche
Leipziger Volkszeitung
Die Linkskurve
Literarische Welt
Märkische Volks-Zeitung
Der Montag
München-Augsburger Abendzeitung
Münchner Neueste Nachrichten
Die Neue Bücherschau
Nürnberger Zeitung—NZ am Mittag

Rheinisch-Westfälische Zeitung
Die Rote Fahne
Schlesische Zeitung (Bielitz)
Schlesische Zeitung (Breslau)
Sozialistische Bildung
Sozialistische Warte
Spandauer Zeitung
Der Stahlhelm
Der Tag
Tägliche Rundschau
Das Tagebuch
Tempo
12-Uhr-Blatt
Die Volksbühne
Vorwärts (with late edition Der Abend)
Vossische Zeitung
Die Welt am Abend
Die Welt am Montag
Die Weltbühne

Law Gazettes

Deutscher Reichsanzeiger und Preußischer
    Staatsanzeiger
Ministerialblatt für die preußische innere Verwaltung
Reichsgesetzblatt
Reichsministerialblatt

German Magazines
and Exile Newspapers

Aufbau (New York City)
Deutschlandberichte der Sozialdemokratischen
    Partei Deutschlands (Prague)
Freies Deutschland (Mexico City)
Jüdische Revue (Ukraine)
Die neue Weltbühne (Prague)
Pariser Tageblatt (Paris)
Pariser Tageszeitung (Paris)
Sozialistische Warte (Paris)
Das Wort (Moscow)
Die Zeitung (London)
Die Zukunft (Paris)

Nazi Press

Der Angriff
Der Führer
Illustrierte Zeitung
Kladderadatsch
Deutsche Film-Tribüne
Nationalsozialistische Pressekorrespondenz
National-Zeitung (Essen)
Neue Film Hölle
Preußische Zeitung
Das Reich
Der Stürmer
Thüringer Film-Zeitung
Völkische Freiheit
Völkischer Beobachter
Der Weltkampf
Westdeutscher Beobachter
Wille und Weg
Zeitschriften-Dienst

Miscellaneous

GERMANY

Deutsches Kriminalpolizeiblatt

GREAT BRITAIN

Action
The Bystander (London)
Daily Express (London)
Daily Mail (London)
Daily Telegraph (London)
Evening Standard (London)
Glasgow Daily Record (Glasgow)
Glasgow Sunday Post (Glasgow)
John Bull (London)
The Journal (Newcastle upon Tyne)
London Opinion
The Manchester Guardian
Morning Post (London)
Sunday Chronicle (London)
Sunday Dispatch (London)
Sunday Pictorial (London)
The Times (London)

HUNGARY (BUDAPEST)

Egyenlöség
Pester Lloyd
Uj Kelet

INDIA

The Hindu (Chennai)
The Jewish Advocate (Bombay)

ITALY

Giornale d'Italia
Il Regime Fascista

MANDATORY TERRITORY OF PALESTINE
(JERUSALEM)

The Palestine Bulletin

SWEDEN (STOCKHOLM)

Aftonbladet
Nya Dagligt Allehanda
Svenska Dagbladet

SWITZERLAND

Jüdische Presszentrale Zürich und illustriertes
 Familienblatt für die Schweiz (Zurich)
Journal de Genève (Geneva)
National-Zeitung (Basel)
Neue Zürcher Zeitung (Zurich)

UNITED STATES

The Bangor Daily News (Maine)
Binghamton Press (New York)
The Birmingham News (Alabama)
The Brooklyn Daily Eagle (New York)
Buffalo Jew Review
Chicago Sunday Tribune
Collier's (New York)

The Commercial Appeal (Tennessee)
Daily News (New York)
Daily Times (Davenport)
The Delineator (New York)
The Demin Headlight (New Mexico)
Detroit News
Dunkirk Evening Observer (New York)
Evening Courier (Camden)
Harper's Magazine (New York)
The Hartford Courant (Connecticut)
Honolulu Star-Bulletin
Huntington Herald-Press
The Jewish Quarterly Review, New Series
 (Pennsylvania)
Jewish Transcript (Seattle)
The Kansas City Times
The Kellogg News (Kellogg)
Ladies' Home Journal (Des Moines)
Liberation. The Silvershirt Weekly (Ashville)
Life (New York City)
Los Angeles Times
Los Angeles Evening Express
Miami News
Minneapolis Tribune
Montes Register
Mount Vernon News
Musical Courier (New York City)
New Masses
The New Movie Magazine (New York)
New York Daily News
New York Post
New York Telegram
The New York Times
New York World
New York World-Telegram
The Paladium-Item (Richmond)
Pasadena Independent
Richmond Times-Dispatch
Rockford Register Star
The San Francisco Examiner
The Seattle Star
St. Joseph News-Press (Missouri)
Sapula Herald (Oklahoma)
The Sentinel (Chicago)
The Scrantonian (Scranton)
The Southern Israelite (Augusta)
Sunday News (New York City)
Washington Evening Star
Washington Post
Woman's Home Companion (Springfield)

USSR

Pravda (Moscow)

After the End of World War II

Germany

Allgemeine Zeitung (Berlin)
Der Archivar
Berliner Zeitung
ff dabei (GDR)
film-echo/Filmwoche vereinigt mit filmblätter

Filmblätter
Der Spiegel
Der Sprachdienst

France (Paris)

Cinéma D'Aujourd'Hui
Image et son. La revue du cinema

Great Britain (London)

Historical Journal of Film, Radio & Television
The Jewish Quarterly

Italy

Griffithiana (Pordenone)

United States

The Birmingham News (Alabama)
B'nai B'rith Messenger (Los Angeles)
Chicago Tribune
European Judaism: A Journal for the New Europe (New York)
Film Comment (New York)
Journal of Millennial Studies (Boston)
Journal of the University Film Association (Illinois)
Limelight (Topanga)
New German Critique (Milwaukee)
The New York Times
Sunday News (New York City)

Yugoslavia

Review—Yugoslav Monthly (Belgrad)

Books

By Charlie Chaplin

Hallo Europa! Leipzig: Paul List, 1928.
My Autobiography. London: The Bodley Head, 1964.
My Life in Pictures. London: The Bodley Head, 1974.
My Trip Abroad. With Monta Bell. New York: Harper & Brothers, 1922.

On Charlie Chaplin

Aping, Norbert. *Charlie Chaplin in Deutschland 1915–1924. Der Tramp kommt ins Kino.* Marburg: Schüren, 2014.
———. *Liberty Shtunk! Die Freiheit wird abgeschafft. Charlie Chaplin und die Nationalsozialisten.* Marburg: Schüren, 2011.
Asplund, Uno. *Chaplin's Films.* New York: A.S. Barnes, 1976.
Blouin, Patrice, Christian Delage, and Sam Stourdze, editors. *Chaplin Pictures.* Paris: NBC Éditions, 2005.
Brownlow, Kevin. *The Search for Charlie Chaplin/Alla ricerca di Charlie Chaplin.* Bologna and Recco-Genova: Cineteca di Bologna and Le Mani, 2005.
Burger, Erich. *Charlie Chaplin. Bericht seines Lebens.* Berlin: Mosse, 1929.
Chaplin, Charlie, Jr. *My Father, Charlie Chaplin.* With N. and M. Rau. New York: Random House, 1960.
Charlie Chaplin, der Beklagte. Die Scheidungsklage im Wortlaut. Der Mensch und Künstler. Vienna: "Mein Film," 1927.
Charlie Chaplin, der Vagabund der Welt. Vienna: "Mein Film," 1931.
Charlie Chaplin's Divorce Case. Complete, Exact and Uncensored Copy of his Wife's now famous and Uncensored Complaint filed in Los Angeles Superior Court. N.P., 1927.
Delage, Christian. *Chaplin. Facing History.* Paris: Place, 2005.
Delage, Christian. *Modern Times—Tempi Moderni.* Edited by Cecilia Cenciarelli. Bologna and Genoa: Cineteca di Bologna, Le Mani and Microart, 2004.
Delluc, Louis. *Charlot.* Paris: de Brunhoff, 1921.
Fiaccarini, Anna, Celia Cenciarelli, and Michela Zenga, editors. *The Great Dictator—Il grande dittatore di Charlie Chaplin.* Bologna and Genoa: Cineteca di Bologna, Le Mani and Microart, 2003.
Fleischman, Sid. *Sir Charlie Chaplin, the Funniest Man in the World.* New York: Greenwillow, 2010.
Gehring, Wes D. *Charlie Chaplin: A Bio-Bibliography.* Westport, CT: Greenwood, 1983.
Gersch, Wolfgang. *Chaplin in Berlin. Illustrierte Miniatur nach Berliner Zeitungen von 1931.* Berlin: Henschel, 1988.
Gifford, Denis. *The Movie Makers. Chaplin.* New York: Doubleday, 1974.
Goodwins, Fred. *Charlie Chaplin's Red Letter Days: At Work with the Comic Genius.* Edited by David James and annotated by Dan Kamin. Lanham, MD: Rowman & Littlefield, 2017.
Grey Chaplin, Lita, and Jeffrey Vance. *Wife of the Life of the Party: A Memoir.* Lanham, MD: Scarecrow Press, 1998.
Groenewold, Sabine, editor. *Charlie Chaplin. Schlussrede aus dem Film Der Große Diktator 1940.* Hamburg: Europäische Verlagsanstalt, 1993.
Haining, Peter, editor. *The Legend of Charlie Chaplin.* Secaucus: Castle, 1982.
Hanisch, Michael. *Charlie Chaplin. Über ihn lach(t)en Millionen.* Berlin: Henschel, 1974.
Heinrich, O.F. *Chaplin auf der Verbrecherjagd.* Stuttgart: Union Deutsche Verlagsgesellschaft, ca. 1932.
Hembus, Joe. *Charlie Chaplin und seine Filme.* Munich: Heyne, 1972.
Hiroyuki, Ono. *Chaplin to Hitler.* Chiyoda: Iwanami, 2015.
Hiroyuki, Ono, David Robinson, and Cecilia

Cenciarelli. *Chaplin and War.* Kyoto: The Chaplin Society of Japan, 2007.

Hoellriegel, Arnold (Richard A. Bermann). *Lichter der Großstadt. Der Film vom Strolch Charlie, dem Millionär und dem blinden Mädchen.* Leipzig: E.P. Tal, 1931.

Huff, Theodore. *Charlie Chaplin.* London: Cassell, 1952.

Louvish, Simon. *Chaplin: The Tramp's Odyssey.* London: Faber & Faber, 2009.

Lynn, Kenneth S. *Charlie Chaplin and His Times.* London: Aurum Press, 1998.

Lyons, Timothy J. *Charles Chaplin: A Guide to References and Resources.* Boston: G.K. Hall, 1979.

Maland, Charles. *Chaplin and American Culture: The Evolution of a Star Image.* Princeton: Princeton University Press, 1989.

McCabe, John. *Charlie Chaplin.* London: Robson, 1992.

McCafferty, Donald, editor. *Focus on Chaplin.* Englewood Cliffs, NJ: Prentice-Hall, 1971.

Mellen, Joan. *Modern Times.* London: BFI, 2006.

Milton, Joyce. *Tramp: The Life of Charlie Chaplin.* New York: HarperCollins, 1996.

Mitchell, Glenn. *The Chaplin Encyclopedia.* London: Batsford, 1997.

Nysenholc, Adolphe, editor. *Charlie Chaplin. His Reflection in Modern Times.* Berlin: Mouton de Gruyter, 1991.

Payne, Robert. *Der große Charlie.* Frankfurt am Main: Europäische Verlagsanstalt, ca. 1952.

Radevagen, Til, editor. *Zeitmontage. Alte Welt. Neue Welt. Charlie Chaplin. Ein Hauch von Anarchie.* Berlin: Elefanten Press, 1989.

Reeves, May, and Claire Goll. *The Intimate Charlie Chaplin.* Jefferson, NC: McFarland, 2001.

Riess, Curt. *Charlie Chaplin. Biografie.* Rastatt: Pabel–Moewig KG, 1989.

Robinson, Carlyle T. *La Vérité sur Charlie Chaplin. Sa vie, ses amours, ses déboires.* Paris: Société Parisienne D'Éditions, 1933.

Robinson, David. *Chaplin: His Life and Art.* London: Penguin, 2001.

Robinson, David. *Chaplin: The Mirror of Opinion.* London: Secker & Warburg, 1983.

Robinson, David. *Chaplin. Sein Leben, seine Kunst.* Zurich: Diogenes, 1989.

Sadoul, Georges. *Das ist Chaplin! Sein Leben—Seine Filme—Seine Zeit.* Vienna: Globus, 1954.

Scheide, Frank, Hooman Mehran, and Dan Kamin, editors. *Chaplin: The Dictator and the Tramp.* London: BFI, 2004.

Schnog, Karl. *Charlie Chaplin. Filmgenie und Menschenfreund.* Berlin: Henschel, 1960.

Siemsen, Hans. *Charlie Chaplin.* Leipzig: Feuer, 1924.

Siemsen, Hans. *Wo hast Du Dich denn herumgetrieben.* Munich: Kurt Wolff, ca. 1920.

Stein Haven, Lisa. *Charlie Chaplin: A Comedian Sees the World.* Columbia: University of Missouri Press, 2014.

Tichy, Wolfram. *Chaplin.* Reinbek bei Hamburg: Rowohlt, 1989.

Tully, Jim. *A Dozen and One.* Hollywood: Murray & Gee, 1943.

Vance, Jeffrey. *Chaplin. Genius of the Cinema.* New York: Harry N. Abrams, 2003.

Velten, Andreas-Michael, and Matthias Klein. *Chaplin und Hitler. Materialien zu einer Ausstellung im Münchner Stadtmuseum vom 14. April bis 18. Juni 1989.* Munich: Stadtmuseum, 1989.

Viazzi, Glauco. *Chaplin e la critica. Antologia di saggi, bibliografia ragionata, iconografia e fimografia.* Rome: Edizione "Espresso," 1955.

von Ulm, Gerith. *Charlie Chaplin: King of Tragedy.* Caldwell, ID: Caxton Printers, 1940.

Wada, Linda. *The Sea Gull. A Woman by the Sea. The Chaplin Studio's Lost Film Starring Edna Purviance.* Bend: Leading Ladies, 2008.

Weissberg, Liliane. *Hannah Arendt, Charlie Chaplin und die verborgene Tradition.* Graz: Leykam, 2009.

Weissman, Stephen. *Chaplin. Eine Biographie.* Berlin: Aufbau, 2009.

Wiegand, Wilfried, editor. *Über Chaplin.* Zurich: Diogenes, 1978.

On Film

Aping, Norbert. *Das Dick-und-Doof-Buch. Die Geschichte von Laurel und Hardy in Deutschland.* Marburg: Schüren, 2nd rev. ed., 2007.

Arnheim, Rudolf. *Kritiken und Aufsätze zum Film.* Edited by Helmut Diederichs. Frankfurt am Main: Fischer, 1979.

Aurich, Rolf. *Die Degeto und der Staat. Kulrurfilm und Fernsehen zwischen Weimar und Bonn.* Munich: text + kritk, 2018.

Aurich, Rolf, Brigitte Bruns, and Wolfgang Jacobsen. *Hans Siemsen. Filmkritiker.* Munich: text + kritk, 2012.

Aurich, Rolf, and Wolfgang Jacobsen, editors. *Ernst Jäger. Filmkritiker.* Munich: text + kritk, 2006.

Becker, Wieland, and Volker Petzold. *Tarkowski trifft King Kong. Geschichte der Filmklubbewegung der DDR.* Berlin: VISTAS, 2001.

Belach, Helga, and Wolfgang Jacobsen, editors. *Richard Oswald: Regisseur und Produzent.* Munich: text + kritk, 1990.

Belan, Branko, editor. *Sjaj i bijeda filma.* Zagreb: Epoha, 1966.

Benayoun, Robert. *Buster Keaton. Der Augenblick des Schweigens.* Munich: Bahia, 1983.

Bessie, Alvah. *Inquisition in Eden.* New York: Macmillan, 1965.

Bock, Hans-Michael, Wolfgang Jacobsen, and Jörg Schöning, editors. *Deutsche Universal. Transatlantische Verleih- und Produktionsstrategien eines Hollywood-Studios in den 20er und 30er Jahren.* With Erika Wottrich, technical editor. Munich: text + kritk, 2001.

Bowden, Liz-Anne, and Wolfram Tichy, editors. *Rororo Filmlexikon 1. Filme A-J.* Reinbek bei Hamburg: Rowohlt, 1986.

Bucher, Edmund, and Albrecht Kindt, editors. *Film-Photos wie noch nie.* Giessen: Kindt & Bucher, 1929.

Buñuel, Luis. *Mein letzter Seufzer. Erinnerungen.* Königstein: Athenäum, 1987.

Der deutsche Film 1943/44. Kleines Film-Handbuch für die deutsche Presse. Berlin: Deutschen Filmvertriebs Gesellschaft, ca. 1943.

Eisner, Lotte H., and Martje Grohmann. *Ich hatte einst ein schönes Vaterland. Memoiren.* Heidelberg: Das Wunderhorn, 1984.

Gardner, Gerald. *The Censorship Papers: Movie Censorship Letters from the Hays Office 1934 to 1968.* New York: Dodd, Mead, 1987.

Henseleit, Felix, editor. *Der Film und seine Welt. Reichsfilmblatt-Almanach 1933.* Berlin: Photokino, 1933.

Ihering, Herbert. *Von Reinhardt bis Brecht. Volume 1: 1909–1923, Volume 3: 1930–1932.* Berlin: Aufbau, 1961.

Infield, Glenn B. *Leni Riefenstahl: The Fallen Film Goddess.* New York: Crowell, 1976.

Jansen, Peter W., and Wolfram Schütte, editors. *Luis Buñuel.* Munich: Hanser, 1975.

Jew Stars Over Hollywood. St. Louis: Patriotic Tract Society, after June 1950.

Karasek, Hellmuth. *Billy Wilder. Eine Nahaufnahme.* Hamburg: Hoffmann und Campe, 1992.

Karney, Robyn, editor. *Cinema Year by Year 1894–2005.* London: Amber Books, 2005.

Katalog des Reichsfilmarchivs, ausländische Filme. Berlin: Reichsfilmarchiv, 1935 onward.

Kerr, Walter. *The Silent Clowns.* New York: Da Capo Press, 1980.

King Hanson, Patricia, editor. *The American Film Institute Catalog of Motion Pictures Produced in the United States. Feature Films, 1931–1940, Film Entries, A-L.* Berkely: University of California Press, 1993.

Klaus, Ulrich J. *Deutsche Tonfilme 3, 1932.* Berlin: Klaus, 1990.

Klaus, Ulrich J. *Deutsche Tonfilme 13, 1944/45.* Berlin: Klaus, 2002.

Klemperer, Victor. *Licht und Schatten, Kinotagebuch 1929–1945.* Berlin: Aufbau, 2020.

Kracauer, Siegfried. *Werke 6.1, Kleine Schriften zum Film 1921 bis 1927.* Frankfurt am Main: Suhrkamp, 2004.

Kreimeier, Klaus. *Die Ufa-Story. Geschichte eines Filmkonzerns.* Munich: Hanser, 1992.

Langman, Larry. *Encyclopedia of American Film Comedy.* New York: Garland, 1987.

Leyda, Jay. *Films Beget Films.* London: George Allen & Unwin, 1964.

Lorant, Stefan. *Wir vom Film. Das Leben, Lieben, Leiden der Filmstars.* Berlin: Böhm & Co., 1929.

Massa, Steve. *Rediscovering Roscoe: The Films of "Fatty" Arbuckle.* Orlando: BearManor Media, 2020.

Miller, Blair. *American Silent Film Comedies: An Illustrated Encyclopedia of Persons, Studios and Terminology.* Jefferson, NC: McFarland, 1995.

Mitchell, Glenn. *The Marx Brothers Encyclopedia.* London: Batsford, 1996.

Montagu, Ivor. *With Eisenstein in Hollywood.* Berlin: Seven Seas, 1968.

Orbanz, Eva, editor. *Wolfgang Staudte.* Berlin: Spiess, 1977.

Quaglietti, Lorenzo. *Ecco i nostri—l'invasione del cinema americano in Italia.* Rome-Turin: Bianco & Nero, 1991.

Red Stars in Hollywood. St. Louis: Patriotic Tract Society, after April 1948.

Riefenstahl, Leni. *Memoiren.* Munich: Knaus, 1987.

Riess, Curt. *Das gabs nur einmal. Das Buch der schönsten Filme unseres Lebens.* Hamburg: Sternbücher, 1957.

Ruhemann, Alfred. *Das Jackie Coogan Buch.* Berlin-Charlottenburg: Welt-Film, 1924.

Saunders, Thomas. *Hollywood in Berlin: American Cinema and Weimar Germany.* Berkeley: University of California Press, 1994.

Schatz, Thomas. *Boom and Bust: The American Cinema in the 1940s. History of the American Cinema, Vol. 6, 1940–1949.* New York: Scribner's Sons, 1997.

Schrader, Bärbel, editor. *Der Fall Remarque. Im Westen nichts Neues. Eine Dokumentation.* Leipzig: Reclam, 1992.

Schulberg, Budd. *Moving Pictures: Memoires of a Hollywood Prince.* New York: Stein and Day, 1981.

Sennett, Mack, as told to Cameron Shipp. *King of Comedy.* New York: Doubleday, 1954.

Serra Cary, Diana. *Jackie Coogan: The World's Boy King. A Biography of Hollywood's Legendary Child Star.* Lanham, MD: Scarecrow Press, 2003.

Spieker, Markus. *Hollywood unterm Hakenkreuz. Der amerikanische Spielfilm im Dritten Reich.* Trier: WVT, 1999.

Tichy, Wolfram. *Buster Keaton.* Reinbek bei Hamburg: Rowohlt, 1983.

Toeplitz, Jerzy. *Geschichte des Films, Volume 3: 1934–1939.* Berlin: Henschel, 1979.

Trimborn, Jürgen. *Riefenstahl. Eine deutsche Karriere.* Berlin: Aufbau, 2003.

Ulrich, Hermann, and Walter Timmling. *Film. Kitsch. Kunst. Propaganda.* Oldenburg in Oldenburg: Schulzesche Verlagsbuchhandlung R. Schwartz, 1933.

Urwand, Ben. *Der Pakt.* Darmstadt: Theiss, 2017.

Variety's Film Reviews. Volume 1 (1907–1920), Volume 6 (1938–1942). New York: Bowker, 1983.

Vasey, Ruth. *The World According to Hollywood, 1918–1939.* Exeter: Exeter University Press, 1997.

Vincent, Carl. *Histoire de l'Art Cinématographique.* Brussels: Éditions du Trident, 1939.

German Film Industry

Guttmann, Irmalotte. *Über die Nachfrage auf dem Filmmarkt in Deutschland.* Cologne: University PhD, 1927.

Jason, Alexander. *Handbuch der Filmwirtschaf. Die erste Tonfilmperiode.* Berlin: Verlag für Presse, Wirtschaft und Politik, 1932.

Jason, Alexander. *Handbuch des Films 1935/36.* Berlin: Hoppenstedt & Co., 1935.

Olimsky, Fritz. *Tendenzen der Filmwirtschaft und deren Auswirkung auf die Filmpresse.* Berlin: Friedrich-Wilhelms-Universität PhD, 1931.

Paschke, Gerhard. *Der deutsche Tonfilmmarkt.* Berlin: Friedrich-Wilhelms-Universität PhD, 1935.

Reichs Kino Adressbuch 1931–1934, 1937. Berlin: Lichtbildbühne, 1931–1934, 1937.

Spiker, Jürgen. *Film und Kapital. Der Weg der deutschen Filmwirtschaft zum nationalsozialistischen Einheitskonzern. Zur politischen Ökonomie des NS-Films 2.* Berlin: Spiess, 1975.

Tackmann, Heinz, editor. *Filmhandbuch.* Berlin: Luchterhand, status: 10th supplemental set, November 27, 1942.

Traub, Hans, and Wilhelm Lavies. *Das deutsche Filmschrifttum. Bibliographie der Bücher und Zeitschriften über das Filmwesen 1896–1939.* Leipzig: Hiersemann, 1940.

Wolffsohn, Karl, editor. *Jahrbuch der Filmindustrie, Volume 5.* Berlin: Lichtbildbühne, 1933.

Nazi Press

Bauer, Elvira. *Trau keinem Fuchs auf grüner Heid und keinem Jud bei seinem Eid.* Nuremberg: Stürmer-Verlag, 1936.

Belling, Curt. *Der Film im Dienste der Partei. Die Bedeutung des Films als publizistischer Faktor.* Berlin: Lichtbildbühne, 1937.

Belling, Curt, and Carlernst Graf Strachwitz. *Der Film in Staat und Partei.* Berlin: "Der Film," 1936.

Belling, Curt, and Alfred Schütze. *Der Film in der Hitlerjugend.* Berlin: Wilhelm Limpert, ca. 1937.

Berber, Fritz, editor. *Jahrbuch für auswärtige Politik, Volumes 6–8.* Berlin-Wilmersdorf: August Gross, 1940–1942.

Berndt, Alfred-Ingemar. *Gebt mir vier Jahre Zeit! Dokumente zum ersten Vierjahresplan des Führers.* Munich: Eher Nachfolger, 1937.

Betz, Hans-Walther. *Weißbuch des deutschen Films.* Berlin: "Der Film," 1936.

Buchner, Hans. *Im Banne des Films. Die Weltherrschaft des Kinos.* Munich: Deutscher Volksverlag Boepple, 1927.

Deutscher! So sehen Deine Führer aus! Charakterköpfe des Reichstags und des Preußischen Landtags. Berlin: Brunnen-Verlag Willi Bischoff, ca. 1932.

Diebow, Hans. *Der ewige Jude. 265 Bilddokumente.* Munich: Eher Nachfolger, 1937.

Diebow, Hans. *Gregor Straßer und der Nationalsozialismus.* Berlin: Kampf-Verlag, 1930.

Diebow, Hans. *Die Juden in USA. Über hundert Bilddokumente.* Munich: Eher Nachfolger, 1939.

Diebow, Hans. *Die Rassenfrage, Rassenkunde, Vererbungslehre und Rassenhygiene.* Aschersleben: Felix, 1924.

Diebow, Hans, and Kurt Goeltzer. *Hitler. Eine Biographie in 134 Bildern.* Berlin: Kolk, 1931.

Diebow, Hans, and Kurt Goeltzer. *Mussolini. Eine Biographie in 110 Bildern.* Berlin: Kolk, 1931.

Dietrich, Otto. *Mit Hitler an die Macht. Persönliche Erlebnisse mit meinem Führer.* Munich: Eher Nachfolger, 1933.

Einziges parteiamtliches Aufklärungs- und Redner-Informationsmaterial der Reichspropagandaleitung der NSDAP. Munich: Eher Nachfolger, from 1934 onward.

von Engelbrechten, Julius Karl. *Eine braune Armee entsteht. Die Geschichte der Berlin-Brandenburger SA.* Munich: Eher Nachfolger, 1937.

Esser, Hans. *Die jüdische Weltpest.* Munich: Eher Nachfolger, 1927.

Gimbel, Adalbert. *So kämpften wir! Schilderungen aus der Kampfzeit der NSDAP im Gau Hessen-Nassau.* Edited by Karl Hepp. Frankfurt am Main: NS-Verlagsgesellschaft, 1941.

Goebbels, Joseph. *Das Buch Isidor. Ein Zeitbild voll Lachen und Hass.* Munich: Eher Nachfolger, 1928.

Goebbels, Joseph. *Das erwachende Berlin.* Munich: Eher Nachfolger, 1933.

Goebbels, Joseph. *Kampf um Berlin. 1. Der Anfang (1926–1927).* Munich: Eher Nachfolger, 4th ed., 1934.

Goebbels, Joseph. *Knorke! Ein neues Buch Isidor für Zeitgenossen.* With Knipperdolling Mjölnir, Jaromir Dax, and Orje. Munich: Eher Nachfolger, 1929.

Hanfstaengl, Ernst. *Hitler in der Karikatur der Welt. Vom Führer genehmigt!* Berlin: Rentsch, 1933.

Hiemer, Ernst. *Der Giftpilz.* Nuremberg: Stürmer-Verlag, 1938.

Hiemer, Ernst. *Der Pudelmopsdackelpinscher und andere besinnliche Erzählungen.* Nuremberg: Stürmer-Verlag, 1940.

Hippler, Fritz. *Betrachtungen zum Filmschaffen.* Hesse, 1942.

Hitler, Adolf. *Mein Kampf.* Zwei Bände in einem. Munich: Eher Nachfolger, 1938, 1941.

Hoffmann, Heinrich. *Hitler abseits vom Alltag.* Berlin: Zeitgeschichte-Verlag, 1937.

Hoffmann, Heinrich. *Hitler wie ihn keiner kennt.* Berlin: Zeitgeschichte-Verlag, 1932.

Hoffmann, Heinrich *Jugend um Hitler.* Berlin: Zeitgeschichte-Verlag, 1935.

Hoffmann, Heinrich. *Mit Hitler im Westen.* Berlin: Zeitgeschichte-Verlag, 1940.

Jungnickel, Max. *Goebbels: Männer und Mächte.* Leipzig: R. Kittler Verlag, 1933.

Köhler, Gerhard. *Kunstanschauung und Kunstkritik in der nationalsozialistischen Presse. Die Kritik im Feuilleton des "Völkischen Beobachters" 1920–1932.* Munich: Eher Nachfolger, 1937.

von Leers, Johann. *Juden sehen Dich an.* Berlin-Schöneberg: NS-Druck und Verlag, 1933; Berlin: Verlag Deutsche Kultur-Wacht, 6th ed., 1936.

Ley, Robert, editor. *Organisationsbuch der NSDAP.* Munich: Eher Nachfolger, 3rd ed., 1937.

Ley, Robert, Hand Dauer, and Walter Kiel, editors. *Deutschland ist schöner geworden.* Berlin: Mehden, 1936.

Lydor, Waldemar. *Der deutsche Film 1943/44. Kleines Film-Handbuch für die deutsche Presse.* Berlin: Deutsche Filmvertriebs Gesellschaft, ca. 1943.

von Müffling, Wilhelm Freiherr. *Wegbereiter und Vorkämpfer für das neue Deutschland.* Munich: Lehmanns, 1933.

Neumann, Carl, Curt Belling, and Hans-Walther

Betz. *Film-"Kunst," Film-Kohn, Film-Korruption. Ein Streifzug durch vier Filmjahrzehnte.* Berlin: Scherping, 1937.

Der nichtseßhafte Mensch. Ein Beitrag zur Neugestaltung der Raum- und Menschenordnung im Großdeutschen Reich. Munich: C.H. Beck, 1938.

Persich, Walter. *Winston Churchill ganz "privat." Abenteurer, Lord und Verbrecher.* Berlin: Schaffer, 1940; 2nd expanded ed., 1942.

Der Reichsführer SS, Der Chef des Sicherheitshauptamtes, editor. *No. 06, "Geheim," Leitheft: Emigrantenpresse und Schrifttum. März 1937.* Berlin: Sicherheitshauptamt, 1937.

Rosenberg, Alfred. *Der Mythus des 20. Jahrhunderts. Eine Wertung der seelisch-geistigen Gestaltenkämpfe unserer Zeit.* Munich: Hoheneichen, 99th–102nd edition, 1936.

Rosenberg, Alfred. *Der Sumpf.* Munich: Eher Nachfolger, 1930.

Rumpelstilzchen (Major Adolf Stein). *Das sowieso!* Berlin: Bischoff, 1931.

Rumpelstilzchen (Major Adolf Stein). *Mang uns mang ...* Berlin: Bischoff, 1933.

Rumpelstilzchen (Major Adolf Stein). *Sie wer'n lachen.* Berlin: Bischoff, 1935.

Sattig, Ewald. *Die deutsche Filmpresse.* PhD diss., Universität Leipzig, 1937.

Streicher, Julius, editor, and Karl Holz, technical editor. *Des Stürmer's Kampf.* Nuremberg: Willmy, 1937.

On Nazism

Adolf Hitler in Bilddokumenten seiner Zeit. Volume 1. Jugend und Hitler. Hitler baut Großdeutschland. Hamburg: Verlag für geschichtliche Dokumentation, 1979.

Albrecht, Gerd. *Film im Dritten Reich. Eine Dokumentation.* Karlsruhe: Schauburg Fricker & Co., 1979.

Barkhausen, Hans. *Filmpropaganda für Deutschland im Ersten und Zweiten Weltkrieg.* Hildesheim: Olms, 1982.

Bennett, David H. *The Party of Fear: The American Far Right from Nativism to the Militia Movement.* New York: Vintage, 1994.

Benz, Wolfgang. *"Der ewige Jude." Metaphern und Methoden nationalsozialistischer Propaganda.* Berlin: Metropol, 2010.

Benz, Wolfgang, Brigitte Mihok, and Werner Bergmann, editors. *Handbuch des Antisemitismus, Volume 5. Organisationen, Institutionen, Bewegungen.* Berlin: de Gruyter Saur, 2012.

Bering, Dietz. *Der Name als Stigma. Antisemitismus im deutschen Alltag 1912–1933.* Stuttgart: Klett-Cotta, 1992.

Bering, Dietz. *Kampf um Namen. Bernhard Weiß gegen Joseph Goebbels.* Stuttgart: Klett, 1991.

Bohrmann, Hans, editor, and Gabriele Toepser-Ziegert, technical editor. *NS-Presseanweisungen der Vorkriegszeit. Edition und Dokumentation Volume 1: 1933.* Munich: K.G. Saur Verlag, 1984.

Bohrmann, Hans, editor, and Gabriele Toepser-Ziegert, technical editor. *NS-Presseanweisungen der Vorkriegszeit. Edition und Dokumentation Volume 3/I: 1935.* Munich: K.G. Saur Verlag, 1987.

Bohrmann, Hans, editor, Gabriele Toepser-Ziegert, Doris Kohlmann-Viand, and Karen Peter, technical editors. *NS-Presseanweisungen der Vorkriegszeit. Edition und Dokumentation Volume 4/I: 1936.* Munich: K.G. Saur Verlag, 1993.

Bohrmann, Hans, editor, Gabriele Toepser-Ziegert, Doris Kohlmann-Viand, and Karen Peter, technical editors. *NS-Presseanweisungen der Vorkriegszeit. Volume 4/III: 1936.* Munich: K.G. Saur Verlag, Munich—New Providence—London—Paris, 1993.

Bohrmann, Hans, editor, Gabriele Toepser-Ziegert, Doris Kohlmann-Viand, and Karen Peter, technical editors. *NS-Presseanweisungen der Vorkriegszeit. Volume 5/III: 1937.* Munich: K.G. Saur Verlag, 1998.

Bohrmann, Hans, editor, Gabriele Toepser-Ziegert, Doris Kohlmann-Viand, and Karen Peter, technical editors. *NS-Presseanweisungen der Vorkriegszeit. Band 6/III: 1938.* Munich: K.G. Saur Verlag, 1999.

Boveri, Margret. *Wir lügen alle. Eine Hauptstadtzeitung unter Hitler.* Olten: Wagner, 1965.

Brechtken, Markus. *Albert Speer. Eine deutsche Karriere.* Munich: Siedler, 2017.

Eberle, Henrik. *Briefe an Hitler. Ein Volk schreibt seinem Führer. Unbekannte Dokumente aus Moskauer Archiven—zum ersten Mal veröffentlicht.* Bergisch Gladbach: Lübbe, 2007.

Eberle, Henrik, and Matthias Uhl, editors. *Das Buch Hitler. Geheimdossier des NKWD für Josef W. Stalin, zusammengestellt aufgrund der Verhörprotokolle des Persönlichen Adjutanten Hitlers, Otto Günsche, und des Kammerdieners Heinz Linge, Moskau 1948/49.* Bergisch Gladbach: Lübbe, 2005.

Eggebrecht, Axel. *Volk ans Gewehr. Chronik eines Berliner Hauses 1930–1934.* Frankfurt am Main: Europäische Verlagsanstalt, 1959.

Fest, Joachim. *Hitler. Eine Biographie.* Hamburg: SPIEGEL-Verlag, 2006/2007.

Fraenkel, Ernst. *The Dual State: A Contribution to the Theory of Dictatorship.* New York: Oxford University Press, 1941.

Friedrich, Thomas. *Die missbrauchte Hauptstadt. Hitler und Berlin.* Berlin: Propyläen, 2007.

Frieser, Karl-Heinz. *Blitzkrieg-Legende. Der Westfeldzug 1940.* Munich: Oldenbourg, 1995.

Fröhlich, Claudia, and Michael Kohlstruck, editors. *Engagierte Demokraten. Vergangenheitspolitik in kritischer Absicht.* Münster: Westfälisches Dampfboot, 1999.

Fröhlich, Elke, editor and technical editor, commissioned by the Institut für Zeitgeschichte and supported by the State Archive Service of Russia. *Die Tagebücher von Joseph Goebbels,* part 1 "Aufzeichnungen 1923–1941," volume 1/II (December 1925–May 1928). Munich: K.G. Saur Verlag, 2005.

Fröhlich, Elke, editor and technical editor, commissioned by the Institut für Zeitgeschichte and supported by the State Archive Service of Russia. *Die Tagebücher von Joseph Goebbels*, part I "Aufzeichnungen 1923–1941," volume 4 (March–November 1937). Munich: K.G. Saur Verlag, 2000.

Fröhlich, Elke, editor and technical editor, commissioned by the Institut für Zeitgeschichte and supported by the State Archive Service of Russia. *Die Tagebücher von Joseph Goebbels*, part I "Aufzeichnungen 1923–1941," volume 5 (December 1937–July 1938). Munich: K.G. Saur Verlag, 2000.

Fröhlich, Elke, editor and technical editor, commissioned by the Institut für Zeitgeschichte and supported by the State Archive Service of Russia. *Die Tagebücher von Joseph Goebbels*, part 1 "Aufzeichnungen 1923–1941," volume 7 (July 1939–March 1940). Munich: K.G. Saur Verlag, 1998.

Fröhlich, Elke, editor, Florian Dierl, Ute Keck, Benjamin Obermüller, Annika Sommersberg and Ulla-Britta Vollhardt, technical editors. Coordinated and brought together by Ulla-Britta Vollhardt, with the assistance of Angela Hermann, commissioned by the Institut für Zeitgeschichte and supported by the State Archive Service of Russia. *Die Tagebücher von Joseph Goebbels*, part III "Register 1923–1945," Sachregister A–G. Munich: K.G. Saur Verlag, 2008.

Fröhlich, Elke, editor, Florian Dierl, Ute Keck, Benjamin Obermüller, Annika Sommersberg and Ulla-Britta Vollhardt, technical editors. Coordinated and brought together by Ulla-Britta Vollhardt, with the assistance of Angela Hermann, commissioned by the Institut für Zeitgeschichte and supported by the State Archive Service of Russia. *Die Tagebücher von Joseph Goebbels*, part III "Register 1923–1945," Sachregister H–Z. Munich: K.G. Saur Verlag, 2008.

Fröhlich, Elke, editor, Angela Hermann, technical editor, commissioned by the Institut für Zeitgeschichte and supported by the State Archive Service of Russia. *Die Tagebücher von Joseph Goebbels*, part 1 "Aufzeichnungen 1923–1941," volume 2/I (December 1929–May 1931). Munich: K.G. Saur Verlag, 2005.

Fröhlich, Elke, editor, Angela Hermann, technical editor, commissioned by the Institut für Zeitgeschichte and supported by the State Archive Service of Russia. *Die Tagebücher von Joseph Goebbels*, part 1 "Aufzeichnungen 1923–1941," volume 2/II (June 1931–September 1932). Munich: K.G. Saur Verlag, 2004.

Fröhlich, Elke, editor, Angela Hermann, technical editor, commissioned by the Institut für Zeitgeschichte and supported by the State Archive Service of Russia. *Die Tagebücher von Joseph Goebbels*, part 1 "Aufzeichnungen 1923–1941," volume 2/III (October 1932–March 1934). Munich: K.G. Saur Verlag, 2005.

Fröhlich, Elke, editor, Angela Hermann, technical editor, commissioned by the Institut für Zeitgeschichte and supported by the State Archive Service of Russia. *Die Tagebücher von Joseph Goebbels*, part 1 "Aufzeichnungen 1923–1941," volume 3 (April 1934–February 1936). Munich: K.G. Saur Verlag, 2005.

Fröhlich, Elke, editor, Angela Hermann, technical editor, commissioned by the Institut für Zeitgeschichte and supported by the State Archive Service of Russia. *Die Tagebücher von Joseph Goebbels*, part III "Register 1923–1945," Geographisches Register, Personenregister. Munich: K.G. Saur Verlag, 2007.

Fröhlich, Elke, editor, Jana Richter, technical editor, commissioned by the Institut für Zeitgeschichte and supported by the State Archive Service of Russia. *Die Tagebücher von Joseph Goebbels*, part I "Aufzeichnungen 1923–1941," volume 3/II (March 1936–February 1937). Munich: K.G. Saur Verlag, 2005.

Fröhlich, Elke, editor, Jana Richter, technical editor, commissioned by the Institut für Zeitgeschichte and supported by the State Archive Service of Russia. *Die Tagebücher von Joseph Goebbels*, part 1 "Aufzeichnungen 1923–1941," volume 8 (April–November 1940). Munich: K.G. Saur Verlag, 1998.

Fröhlich, Elke, editor, Dieter Marc Schneider, technical editor, commissioned by the Institut für Zeitgeschichte and association with the Bundesarchiv. *Die Tagebücher von Joseph Goebbels. Sämtliche Fragmente*, part 2 "Diktate 1941–1945," volume 11 (January–March 1944). Munich: K.G. Saur Verlag, 1994.

Goetz, Alice, editor. *Hollywood und die Nazis. Ein Programm der Arbeitsgemeinschaft Kino*. Hamburg, 1977.

Grau, Günter *Lexikon zur Homosexuellenverfolgung 1933–1945*, Berlin: Lit Verlag, 2011.

Grumke, Thomas, and Bernd Wagner, editors. *Handbuch des Rechtsextremismus. Personen—Organisationen—Netzwerke, vom Neonazismus bis in die Mitte der Gesellschaft*. Opladen: Leske + Budrich, 2002.

Hahn, Fred, and Günther Wagenlehner, editors. *Lieber Stürmer! Leserbriefe an das NS-Kampfblatt 1924 bis 1945*. Stuttgart: Seewald, 1978.

Heiber, Helmut. *Joseph Goebbels*. Munich: Deutscher Taschenbuchverlag, 1965.

Heiber, Helmut, editor. *Goebbels Reden 1932–1945*, 2 volumes. Düsseldorf: Droste, 1971.

Hett, Benjamin Carter. *Der Reichstagsbrand. Wiederaufnahme eines Verfahrens*. Reinbek: Rohwolt, 2016.

Hippler, Fritz. *Die Verstrickung. Auch ein Filmbuch ... Einstellungen und Rückblenden*. Düsseldorf: Mehr Wissen, 2nd ed., ca. 1982.

Hippler, Fritz. *Korrekturen. Zeitgeschichtliche Spurensuche, einmal anders*. Berg: VGB, 1995.

Hoffmann, Heinrich. *Hitler wie ich ihn sah. Aufzeichnungen seiner Leibfotografen*. Munich: Herbig, 1974.

Hull, David Stewart. *Film in the Third Reich: A Study of the German Cinema, 1933–1945*. Berkeley: University of California Press, 1969.

Humbert, Manuel. *Hitlers 'Mein Kampf.' Dichtung und Wahrheit*. Paris: Pariser Tageblatt, 1936.

Joachimsthaler, Anton. *Hitlers Ende. Legenden und Dokumente.* Munich: Herbig, 2nd ed., 2004.

Junge, Traudl, with Melissa Müller. *Bis zur letzten Stunde. Hitlers Sekretärin erzählt ihr Leben.* Munich: Clasen, 2001.

Kellner, Friedrich. *"Vernebelt, verdunkelt sind alle Hirne." Tagebücher 1939–1945.* Göttingen: Wallstein, 2011.

Kershaw, Ian. *Hitler 1889–1936* and *1936–1945.* Munich: Deutscher Taschenbuchverlag, 2002.

Klee, Ernst. *"Die SA Jesu Christi." Die Kirche im Banne Hitlers,* Frankfurt am Main: Fischer, 1990.

Klee, Ernst. *Das Kulturlexikon zum Dritten Reich. Wer war was vor und nach 1945.* Frankfurt am Main: Fischer, 2007.

Klee, Ernst. *Personenlexikon zum Dritten Reich. Wer war was vor und nach 1945.* Hamburg: Nikol, 2016.

Klemperer, Victor. *Ich will Zeugnis ablegen bis zum Letzten. Tagebücher 1933–1945,* 2 volumes. Berlin: Aufbau, 2015.

Klemperer, Victor. *Leben sammeln, nicht fragen wozu und warum. Tagebücher 1918–1932,* 2 vols. Berlin: Aufbau, 1996.

Klemperer, Victor. *LTI. Notizbuch eines Philologen.* Ditzingen: Reclam, 2020.

Krakauer, Max. *Lichter im Dunkel.* Stuttgart: Behrendt, 1947.

Kraus, Karl. *Die Dritte Walpurgisnacht.* Munich: Kösel, 1967.

Krings, Stefan. *Hitlers Pressechef. Otto Dietrich (1892–1952). Eine Biografie.* Göttingen: Wallstein, 2010.

Lochner, Louis P., editor. *Goebbels Tagebücher. Aus den Jahren 1942–43, mit anderen Dokumenten.* Zurich: Atlantis, 1948.

Maser, Werner, editor. *Mein Schüler Hitler. Das Tagebuch seines Lehrers Paul Devrient.* Pfaffenhofen: Ilmgau, 1975.

Maser, Werner, editor. *Der Sturm auf die Republik. Frühgeschichte der NSDAP.* Stuttgart: Deutsche Verlagsanstalt, 1973.

Misch, Rochus, with Sandra Zarrinbal and Burkhard Nachtigall. *Der letzte Zeuge. "Ich war Hitlers Telefonist, Kurier und Leibwächter."* Munich: Pendo, 2008.

Moeller, Felix. *Der Filmminister. Goebbels und der Film im Dritten Reich.* Berlin: Henschel, 1998.

Mommsen, Hans. *Beamtentum im Dritten Reich. Mit ausgewählten Quellen zur nationalsozialistischen Beamtenpolitik.* Stuttgart: Deutsche Verlagsanstalt, 1966.

Mussolini Ciano, Edda, as told to Albert Zarca. *My Truth.* London: Weidenfeld and Nicholson, 1977.

Odenwald, Florian. *Der nazistische Kampf gegen des "Undeutsche" in Theater und Film 1920–1945.* Munich: Utz, 2006.

Plöckinger, Othmar. *Geschichte eines Buches: Adolf Hitlers "Mein Kampf" 1922–1945.* Munich: Oldenbourg, 2011.

Reichel, Peter. *Der schöne Schein des Dritten Reiches. Faszination und Gewalt des Faschismus.* Frankfurt am Main: Fischer, June 1993.

Rinner, Erich, editor. *Deutschlandberichte der Sozialdemokratischen Partei Deutschlands (Sopade). Volume 2.* Salzhausen and Frankfurt am Main: Nettelbeck/Zweitausendeins, July 1980.

Sänger, Fritz. *Politik der Täuschungen. Missbrauch der Presse im Dritten Reich. Weisungen, Informationen, Notizen 1933–1939.* Vienna: Europaverlag, 1975.

Schmidt, Matthias. *Albert Speer. Das Ende eines Mythos. Die Aufdeckung seiner Geschichtsverfälschung. Speers wahre Rolle im Dritten Reich.* Munich: Scherz, 1982.

Schmitz-Berning, Cornelia. *Vokabular des Nationalsozialismus.* Berlin: de Gruyter, 2007.

Schröder, Gustav. *Heimatlos auf hoher See.* Berlin: Beckerdruck, 1949.

Sösemann, Bernd, with Marius Lange. *Propaganda. Medien und Öffentlichkeit in der NS-Diktatur,* two Volumes. Stuttgart: Steiner, 2011.

Speer, Albert. *Erinnerungen.* Berlin: Propyläen, 9th ed., 1971.

Speer, Albert. *Spandauer Tagebücher.* Berlin: Propyläen, 1975.

Sündermann, Helmut. *Tagesparolen. Deutsche Presseanweisungen 1939–1945. Hitlers Propaganda und Kriegsführung.* Edited by Gerd Sudholt. Leoni am Starnberger See: Druffel, 1973.

Talbott, Strobe. *Khrushchev Remembers.* London: Sphere Books, 1971.

Trier, Walter. *Nazi-German in 22 Lessons. Including useful information for Führers, Fifth Columnists, Gauleiters and Quislings.* London: Pamphlet, Ministry for Information, 1942.

Weinberg, Gerhard L., editor. *Hitlers zweites Buch.* Stuttgart: Deutsche Verlagsanstalt, 1961.

Wilke, Jürgen. *Presseanweisungen im zwanzigsten Jahrhundert. Erster Weltkrieg—Drittes Reich—DDR.* Cologne: Böhlau, 2007.

Wilmer, Christoph. *Karl Wolffsohn und die Lichtburg. Die Geschichte einer Arisierung.* Essen: Klartext, 2006.

Zeman, Zbynek. *Das Dritte Reich in der Karikatur.* Munich: Heyne, 1984.

On German Antisemitism

Berg, Wilhelm. *Antisemiten-Brevier.* Berlin, 1883.

Bergmann, Werner, and Ulrich Sieg, editors. *Antisemitische Geschichtsbilder.* Essen: Klartext, 2009.

Döscher, Hans-Jürgen. *Kampf gegen das Judenthum: Gustav Stille (1845–1920). Antisemit im deutschen Kaiserreich.* Berlin: Metropol, 2008.

Frey, Thomas (Theodor Fritsch). *Antisemiten-Katechismus.* Leipzig: Beyer Verlag, 1887.

Geels, James E. "The German-American Bund: Fifth Column or Deutschtum?" MA Thesis, North Texas State University, 1975.

Sammons, Jeffrey L., editor. *Die Protokolle der Weisen von Zion. Die Grundlage des modernen Antisemitismus. Eine Fälschung. Text und Kommentar.* Göttingen: Wallstein, 2001.

Stauff, Philipp. *Semi-Kürschner.* Berlin: author's edition, 1913.

Stille, Gustav. *Kampf gegen das Judenthum.* Leipzig: Germanicus, 1891; Hamburg: Deutschnationale Buchhandlung, 8th ed., ca. 1912.

Stratenwerth, Irene, and Hermann Simon, editors. *Pioniere in Celluloid. Juden in der frühen Filmwelt.* Berlin: Henschel, 2004.

Walk, Joseph, editor. *Das Sonderrecht der Juden im NS-Staat. Eine Sammlung der gesetzlichen Maßnahmen und Richtlinien—Inhalt und Bedeutung.* Heidelberg: C.F. Müller, 2nd ed., 1996.

Encyclopedias

Benz, Wolfgang, and Hermann Graml, editors. *Biografisches Lexikon zur Weimarer Republik.* Munich: C.H. Beck, 1988.

Benz, Wolfgang, and Hermann Weiß, editors. *Enzyklopädie des Nationalismus.* Munich: Deutscher Taschenbuch Verlag, 2001.

Glassman, Leo M., editor. *Biographical Encyclopedia of American Jews.* New York: Jacobs and Glassman, 1935.

Der Große Herder. Nachschlagewerk für Wissen und Leben. Volume 3, "Caillaux bis Eisenhut." Freiburg im Breisgau: Herder & Co., 4th ed., 1932.

Herlitz, Georg, editor, and Bruno Kirschner, founder. *Jüdisches Lexikon. Ein enzyklopädisches Handbuch des jüdischen Wissens in vier Bänden. Volume 1 (A-C), Volume 2 (D-H).* Berlin: Jüdischer Verlag, 1927 and 1928.

Klatzkin, Jakob, and Ismar Elbogen, editors. *Encyclopaedia Judaica. Das Judentum in Geschichte und Gegenwart.* 10 volumes. Berlin: Eschkol, 1928–1934.

Landmann, Isaac, and Louis Rittenberg, editors. *The Universal Jewish Encyclopedia: An Authoritative and Popular Presentation of Jews and Judaism Since the Earliest Times.* Ten Volumes. *Volume 3, Canards to Education.* New York: Universal Jewish Encyclopedia Co. Inc., 1941; unaltered reprint, 1948; Ktav Publishing House, unaltered reprint, 1969.

Munzinger Internationales Biographisches Archiv. Ravensburg: Munzinger-Archiv, from 1913 onward.

Reichshandbuch der deutschen Gesellschaft. Das Handbuch der Persönlichkeiten in Wort und Bild. Berlin: Deutscher Wirtschaftsverlag, 1931.

Schoeps, Julius H., editor. *Neues Lexikon des Judentums.* Gütersloh: Bertelsmann Lexikon Verlag, 1992, and new ed., 2000.

Schwartz, Julius, and Solomon Aaron Kaye, editors. *Who's Who in American Jewry 1926.* New York: The Jewish Biographical Bureau, 1927.

Schwartz, Julius, and Solomon Aaron Kaye, editors. *Who's Who in American Jewry 1928.* New York: The Jewish Biographical Bureau, 1928.

Simons, John, editor. *Who's Who in American Jewry. Volume 3, 1938–39. A Bibliographical Dictionary of Living Jews of the United States of America and Canada.* New York: National News Association Inc., 1938.

Weiß, Hermann, editor. *Personenlexikon 1933–1945.* Vienna: Tosa, 2003.

Miscellaneous

Adlon, Hedda. *Hotel Adlon.* Munich: Lichtenberg, 1963.

Albrecht, Niels H.M. *Die Macht einer Verleumdungskampagne. Antidemokratische Agitationen der Presse und Justiz gegen die Weimarer Republik und ihren ersten Reichspräsidenten Friedrich Ebert vom "Badebild" bis zum Magdeburger Prozess.* Bremen: PhD University Press, 2002.

Albrecht, Thomas. *Für eine wehrhafte Demokratie. Albert Grzesinski und die preußische Politik in der Weimarer Republik.* Bonn: Dietz Nachfolger, 1999.

Bayer, Udo. *Carl Laemmle und die Universal. Eine transatlantische Biografie.* Würzburg: Königshausen & Neumann, 3rd ed., 2016.

Bemmann, Helga, editor. *Das Leben großer Clowns, von ihnen selbst erzählt. Aufzeichnungen und Erinnerungen von sechs Spaßmachern der Manege.* Berlin: Henschel, 1972.

Bermann, Richard A. (Arnold Höllriegel). *Die Fahrt auf dem Katarakt. Eine Autobiographie ohne einen Helden.* Edited by Hans-Harald Müller. Vienna: Picus Verlag, 1998.

Börrnert, René. *Wie Ernst Thälmann treu und kühn!—Das Thälmann-Bild der SED im Erziehungsalltag der DDR.* Bad Heilbrunn: Klinkhardt, 2004.

Bracher, Karl Dietrich, Manfred Funke, and Hans-Adolf Jacobsen, editors. *Die Weimarer Republik 1918–1933. Politik-Wirtschaft-Gesellschaft.* Bonn: Bundeszentrale für politische Bildung, 1998.

Brunner, Karl. *Unsere Jugend—unsere Zukunft.* Berlin: Bermühler, 1916.

Budzinski, Klaus. *Pfeffer ins Getriebe. So ist und wurde das Kabarett.* Munich: Universitas, 1982.

Budzinski, Klaus, and Reinhard Hippen. *Metzler Kabarett Lexikon.* Stuttgart: Metzler, 1996.

Colman, Fred A., and Walter Trier. *Artisten.* Dresden: Paul Aretz Verlag, 1928.

Ebinger, Blandine. *"Blandine..." Von und mit Blandine Ebinger der grossen Diseuse der Zwanziger Jahre, der kongenialen Muse von Friedrich Hollaender.* Zurich: Arche, 1985.

Forstreuter, Kurt. *Das Preußische Staatsarchiv in Königsberg. Ein geschichtlicher Rückblick mit einer Übersicht über seine Bestände.* Göttingen: Vandenhoeck & Ruprecht, 1955.

Föster, Michael, editor. *Hans Siemsen. Schriften. Verbotene Liebe und andere Geschichten*, and *Schriften II. Kritik—Aufsatz—Polemik.* Essen: Torso, 1986 and 1988.

Gross, Babette. *Willi Münzenberg. Eine politische Biografie.* Leipzig: Forum, 1991.

Gzresinski, Albert. *Im Kampf um die deutsche Republik. Erinnerungen eines Sozialdemokraten.* Edited by Eberhard Kolb. Munich: Oldenbourg, 2001.

Hagelweide, Gert. *Deutsche Zeitungsbestände in*

Bibliotheken und Archiven. Düsseldorf: Droste, 1974.

Handbuch der deutschen Aktiengesellschaften. Berlin: Verlag für Börsen- und Finanzliteratur, 31st volume, 33rd volume, 35th volume, 37th volume (1926, 1929, 1930, 1932); Verlag Hoppenstedt & Co., 38th volume, 39th volume, 42nd volume (1933, 1934, 1937).

Hippen, Reinhard. *Satire gegen Hitler—Kabarett im Exil. Kabarettgeschichte-n.* Zurich: pendo, 1986.

Hippen, Reinhard. *Sich fügen heißt lügen. 80 Jahre deutsches Kabarett.* Mainz: Schmidt & Bödige, 1981.

Hirschfeld, Magnus, editor. *Jahrbuch für sexuelle Zwischenstufen. Volume XIX No. 1 and 2.* (Leipzig?), ca. 1919.

Kautsky, Karl. *Delbrueck und Wilhelm II. Ein Nachwort zu meinem Kriegsbuch.* Berlin: Neues Vaterland, 1920.

Kautsky, Karl. *Wie der Weltkrieg entstand. Dargestellt nach dem Aktenmaterial des Deutschen Auswärtigen Amts.* Berlin: Cassirer, 1919.

Klemperer, Viktor. *Leben sammeln und nicht fragen warum. Tagebücher 1918-1932.* Two volumes. Berlin: Aufbau, 1996.

Koch, Eric. *The Man Who Knew Charlie Chaplin. A Novel about the Weimar Republic.* Oakville, ON: Mosaic Press, 2000.

Kustoff, Michael L. *Against Gray Walls or Lawyer's Dramatic Escape.* Los Angeles: author's edition, 1934.

Landsberg-Yorck, Ruth. *Klatsch, Ruhm und kleine Feuer. Biographische Impressionen.* Cologne: Kiepenheuer & Witsch, 1963.

de Mendelssohn, Peter. *Zeitungsstadt Berlin.* Berlin: Ullstein, 1959.

Neuner-Warthorst, Antje. *Walter Trier. Politik-Kunst-Reklame.* Zurich: Atrium, 2006.

Noa, Barry (Bernd Nowack). *Walter Timmling. 1897-1948.* Dessau: author's edition, 2000.

Placke, Heinrich. *Die Chiffren des Utopischen. Zum literarischen Gehalt der politischen 50er-Jahre-Romane Erich Maria Remarques.* Göttingen: V&R Unipress, 2004.

Pryce-Jones, David. *Unity Mitford. A Quest.* London: Weidenfeld and Nicolson, 1976.

Rduch, Robert. *Unbehaustheit und Heimat. Das literarische Werk von Arnold Ulitz (1888-1971).* Frankfurt am Main: Lang, 2009.

Rivel, Charlie. *Akrobat Schöön,* Munich: Ehrenwirth, 1972.

Schilling, Karsten. *Das zerstörte Erbe. Berliner Zeitungen der Weimarer Republik im Portrait.* Norderstedt: Books on Demand, 2011.

75 Jahre Berliner Börsen-Zeitung. Berlin: Berliner Börsen-Zeitung, 1930.

Siemsen, Hans. *Wo hast Du Dich denn herumgetrieben. Erlebnisse von Hans Siemsen.* Munich: Wolff, ca. 1920.

Statistisches Jahrbuch für das Deutsche Reich. Berlin: Hobbing, 51st edition, 1932.

Stein, Gerd. *Adolf Stein alias Rumpelstilzchen. "Hugenbergs Landsknecht"—einer der wirkungsmächtigsten deutschen Journalisten des 20. Jahrhunderts.* Münster: LIT, 2014.

Stevenson, Robert Louis. *Der Selbstmörderklub. Der Diamant des Rajahs.* Zurich: Diogenes, 1979.

Tunnat, Frederik. *Karl Vollmoeller. Dichter und Kulturmanager. Eine Biographie.* N.P.: Edition Vendramin, 4th ed., 2019.

Ulitz, Arnold. *Christine Munk. Roman.* Munich: Langen, 1926.

Ulitz, Arnold. *Der Lotse. Gedichte.* Munich: Langen, 1924.

Index

Numbers in *bold italics* indicate pages with illustrations

451

Printed in the USA
CPSIA information can be obtained
at www.ICGtesting.com
LVHW071737130224
771452LV00078B/677